The Middle East

The Middle East

A Political and Economic Survey

FOURTH EDITION

Edited by

PETER MANSFIELD

LONDON
OXFORD UNIVERSITY PRESS
NEW YORK   TORONTO
1973

Oxford University Press, Ely House, London W.1

GLASGOW   NEW YORK   TORONTO   MELBOURNE   WELLINGTON
CAPE TOWN   IBADAN   NAIROBI   DAR ES SALAAM   LUSAKA   ADDIS ABABA
DELHI   BOMBAY   CALCUTTA   MADRAS   KARACHI   LAHORE   DACCA
KUALA LUMPUR   SINGAPORE   HONG KONG   TOKYO

ISBN 0 19 215933 X

© *Oxford University Press* 1958, 1973

First three editions edited by
SIR READER BULLARD
First published 1950
Second edition 1954
Reprinted (with minor corrections) 1955
Third edition 1958
Fourth edition 1973

Printed in Great Britain by
Richard Clay (The Chaucer Press) Ltd., Bungay, Suffolk

Contents

I

A. INTRODUCTION

The Region Defined 1   *History and Politics* 4   *Faiths, Sects, and Minorities* 32   *Economic and Social* 41

B. THEMATIC STUDIES

II ARABIA

III EGYPT

The Land and the People 213   *History and Politics* 214   *The Revolution and After* 223   *Social Survey* 243   *The Economy* 248

25982

Preface to Fourth Edition

So much has changed in the Middle East since the publication of the Third Edition of this Survey that it was clear from the outset not only that the greater part of the Fourth Edition would have to consist of new material but that much of this would have to be written from a different angle of vision. At the end of World War II Britain could be regarded as the paramount power in the Middle East. By the spring of 1958, when the Third Edition appeared, Britain's political and military role had declined but was still of major importance. Today it has virtually disappeared although Britain retains major economic interests in the area. In contrast the role of the two Super Powers, especially the Soviet Union, has steadily increased. But Great Power involvement in the Middle East is more a consequence of the continuation of the Arab–Israeli dispute than a relic of the Cold War and conflicts with the desire of the states of the area to assert their full independence and their increasing capacity to do so.

The previous editions of this book were published for the Royal Institute of International Affairs by the Oxford University Press. The latter has now taken over entire editorial responsibility for the volume. However, the valuable historical sections of the previous editions have been retained wherever appropriate, and for permission to reproduce these the Editor and publishers are indebted to the RIIA. The Middle East Centre at St. Antony's College, Oxford, has acted in an advisory capacity and the Editor is most grateful for the help of Mr. Albert Hourani, Miss Elizabeth Monroe, and other members of the Centre.

In addition to the authors of the new general chapters the following have contributed new material: Tom Little, E. F. Penrose, Dr. V. D. Segre, Sir John Richmond, Saul Bakhash, Dr. Julian Bharier, Dr. Norman Daniel, Professor Geoffrey Lewis, and the Centre for Middle Eastern and Islamic Studies at the University of Durham. The Editor is most grateful for the help of the staff of *Middle East Economic Digest* and the Economist Intelligence Unit in preparing the statistical tables.

Note on Transliteration

In general the transliteration of the Third Edition has been retained and no attempt has been made to introduce a scientific system. Wherever possible the most familiar Anglo-American spelling of the names of prominent figures has been used, e.g. Nasser, Kassem, etc.

Abbreviations*

AIOC	Anglo-Iranian Oil Co.
Aramco	Arabian American Oil Co.
BP	The British Petroleum Co.
Bapco	Bahrain Petroleum Co.
BPC	Basrah Petroleum Co.
FAO, *Yearbook*	Food and Agriculture Organization, *Yearbook of Food and Agricultural Statistics*, pt. 1 : *Production*.
Hurewitz	J. C. Hurewitz, *Diplomacy in the Near and Middle East: a Documentary Record, 1535–1956*. New York, 1956.
IBRD	International Bank for Reconstruction and Development.
ICA	International Co-operation Administration.
IMF	International Monetary Fund.
IPC	Iraq Petroleum Co.
KOC	Kuwait Oil Co.
NIOC	National Iranian Oil Co.
OPEC	Organization of Petroleum Exporting Countries.
QPC	Qatar Petroleum Co.
Tapline	Trans-Arabian Pipeline Co.
UNEF	U.N. Emergency Force.
UNRWA	U.N. Relief and Works Agency for Palestine Refugees.

* Excluding commonly used abbreviations for U.N. agencies.

Currency Exchange Rates

Mid-March 1972

Bahrain	Bahrain dinar	£ = BD 1·145	$ = BD 0·459
Egypt	Egyptian pound	£ = £E 1·1436	$ = £E 0·436
Iran	Iranian rial	£ = Rs 193·5	$ = Rs 75·7
Iraq	Iraqi dinar	£ = ID 0·859	$ = ID 0·359
Israel	Israeli pound	£ = £I 10·941	$ = £I 4·189
Jordan	Jordanian dinar	£ = JD 0·908	$ = JD 0·357
Kuwait	Kuwaiti dinar	£ = KD 0·857	$ = KD 0·329
Lebanon	Lebanese pound	£ = £Leb 8·03	$ = £Leb 3·14
Oman	Saidi rial	£ = RS 1	$ = RS 0·41
Qatar/Dubai	Qatar/Dubai rial	£ = QDR 11·445	$ = QDR 4·65
Saudi Arabia	Saudi rial	£ = SR 11·58	$ = SR 4·145
Sudan	Sudanese pound*	£ = £S 0·835	$ = £S 0·33
Syria	Syrian pound*	£ = £Syr 10⅞	$ = £Syr 4·37
Turkey	Turkish pound	£ = £T 36·87	$ = £T 14·15
Yemen (Aden)	South Yemen dinar*	£ = SYD 1	$ = SYD 0·4
Yemen (Sanaa)	Yemeni rial	No quotations available	

*No quotations have been made available since the $ crisis was resolved in December 1971. Pre-crisis rates given here for guidance only. The $ rates have been calculated: £1 = $2.49 (London buying/selling rate on 29.11.71).

Land Measures

1 hectare = 2·471 acres.
Egypt & the Sudan: 1 feddan = 1·038 acres.

Note on Statistics

The collection of statistics and their compilation are not of a uniform standard throughout the Middle East. In many fields they are still incomplete or in an experimental stage and the figures in the chapters and appendices are, therefore, often no more than rough approximations.

International sources of information have been used in the appendices in order to achieve comparability within each table; therefore these figures may not always agree with those given in the text of the book, if these were taken from another source.

Conversion factors

1 metric ton = 0·984206 long tons.
1 barrel (petroleum) = 35 Imp. gallons = 1/7th ton approx.

I

A. Introduction

Before the First World War it was customary to distinguish between the Near East, comprising Greece, Bulgaria, Turkey, the Levant, and Egypt; and the Middle East: Arabia, Mesopotamia, the Persian Gulf, Iran, and Afghanistan. It then gradually became the practice to use the term 'Middle East' to cover both those areas, less Greece and Bulgaria on the west and Afghanistan on the east, but adding the Sudan and sometimes Libya, and even other North African states. Libya, with Morocco, Algeria, and Tunisia, is dealt with in another volume.[1] The states and territories dealt with in the present survey are: the Arabian Peninsula (comprising Saudi Arabia, the Yemeni Republic, the People's Democratic Republic of South Yemen, Kuwait, Bahrain, Qatar, the Trucial States, and Oman), Egypt, Iraq, Israel, the Hashimite Kingdom of Jordan, Lebanon, Iran, the Sudan, Syria, and Turkey. Their combined area is about 3,726,000 square miles.

Geography, Climate, and Vegetation[2]

Thus defined, the Middle East consists structurally of (1) a geologically ancient and stable platform underlying north-east Africa and the Arabian Peninsula, rifted to form the Gulf of Aden; (2) a more recent and highly disturbed system of folded mountains extending from the Balkans through Turkey and Iran; (3) an intermediate zone comprising the Jabal Akhdhar of Cyrenaica, Palestine, Lebanon, Syria, Iraq, and the highlands of Oman.

Climatically the whole of the Middle East (except for two small regions, one in the extreme north and the other in the extreme south) has a strongly marked Mediterranean rhythm of summer drought and winter rain. The cause of the latter is the inflow of maritime air from the west, which is excluded during the summer by higher pressures in the western Mediterranean. The regions with the highest winter rainfall are those which combine a length of westward-facing coastline with

---

[1] *A Survey of North-West Africa*, ed. Nevill Barbour (London, 1959, new edition in preparation, ed. W. Knapp).
[2] This section is based on W. B. Fisher, *The Middle East: a Physical, Social, and Regional Geography* (London, 1950), pt. 1, p. 432.

elevated uplands, for example, Lebanon and Palestine, western Asia
Minor, the Jabal Akhdhar of Cyrenaica. Where these features are
absent, as in Egypt and northern Sudan and the greater part of the
Arabian Peninsula, winter rainfall is scanty or completely lacking in
some years, and desert conditions obtain. Asia Minor, Armenia, and
much of Iran are exposed to extremely low winter temperatures owing
to their proximity to the Eurasian land mass; farther south, the seas
have a temperate effect, but severe cold may be experienced in the
Arabian interior. In summer the most intense heat occurs in lower
Iraq and the interior of Arabia, but living conditions are worst on the
coasts of the Persian Gulf and the Red Sea owing to their high degree
of humidity, which also affects the Mediterranean coast. The regions
outside the scope of the Mediterranean climatic rhythm are the Black
Sea coast of Turkey, which receives rain throughout the year; the
southern Sudan and south-west Arabia (the Yemen), where a substantial summer rainfall alternates with a dry winter; and Dhufar, in
Oman, which is affected by the monsoon.

In the wetter parts of the Mediterranean coastland and on the lower
flanks of the neighbouring mountain ranges—in western Asia Minor,
western Syria, Lebanon, Palestine, and Cyprus—there is the characteristic Mediterranean cultivation of cereals, vines, olives, and fruit
trees. Farther east, where the rainfall is less and the seasonal variation
of temperature greater, are steppes where grass is luxuriant in the short
spring but largely disappears during the long dry summer—the home
of pastoral nomadism. Sheep and goats give place to the hardier camel
as the steppe passes into the true desert of Sinai, Egypt, and large parts
of the Arabian Peninsula; but the alluvial lowlands of the great rivers
provide a striking contrast, with their intensive irrigated cultivation
and the groves of date-palms. The slopes of the higher mountains were
covered in prehistoric times with woodland, but have been largely
deforested during the past 5,000 years. The uplands of south-western
Arabia have a vegetation reminiscent of that of the African region on
the opposite side of the Red Sea.

Resources

The Middle East supports 80–100 million people. It is estimated that
out of the total area of some 3,726,000 square miles, only about 5 or 6
per cent is at present under cultivation, although the cultivable area is
capable of considerable expansion. The Middle East consists, in fact,
of considerable expanses of virtually unpopulated land, interspersed
with a few areas of relatively dense—and in one area, Egypt, of
extremely dense—population. The finding of petroleum, of which
immense reserves have been discovered in the region within the last
sixty years, is having an increasing effect on the standard of living;
it has already secured the region a prominent place in world interest.

Other important minerals which are now being extracted in the region include iron, phosphates, and, to a lesser extent, copper manganese, coal, and salt. There are also large areas of the Egyptian, Syrian, and Arabian Deserts which have yet to be intensively surveyed and may well prove to be rich in minerals. Large deposits of titanium, an important structural metal element, were discovered in Egypt's Eastern Desert in 1971.

In the long term much of the region's economic future depends upon the full development of all the agricultural and hydro-electric resources provided by the two great river systems of the Nile and Tigris–Euphrates. For the latter it is partly a question of restoring and surpassing the high productivity of agriculture of classical Mesopotamia. The historical evidence of Yemen's former prosperity is also proof of that country's potential. The extent of underground water resources in the Egyptian and Arabian Deserts has yet to be fully determined but considerable new reclamation in both areas may be possible. (Egypt's New Valley scheme to extend the five main oases of the Western Desert to form a single stretch of cultivated land roughly parallel to the Nile Valley is the most important project of this kind which is being undertaken at present.) Of all Middle Eastern countries Sudan is probably the one with the greatest untapped agricultural resources.

International Importance

From at least the foundation of the Roman Empire the position of the Middle East, lying as it does across the main arteries of transport between Europe and Southern and Eastern Asia, has been of very great significance commercially. Constant efforts have been made by countries both within and without the Middle East to control and thereby to profit by, or to prevent others from profiting by, the commerce which passes through the area.

At the end of the fifteenth century the discovery of the route round the Cape of Good Hope somewhat reduced the importance of the area to commerce. Its position was largely restored, and in some respects enhanced, with the opening of the Suez Canal in 1869.

The discovery of immense reserves of oil in the states around the Persian Gulf in the first half of the twentieth century and their accelerated development in the second half enhanced the commercial importance of the whole area. Despite the discovery of other important sources of oil (e.g. Alaska, Nigeria, and the North Sea) and the development of alternative sources of energy (such as nuclear power) the demand for Middle East oil has steadily increased and pipelines to the Mediterranean coast from the oil fields as well as the Suez Canal have had to be utilized to the limit of their capacity to meet existing demand. This situation seems likely to continue. The reduction in the importance of the Suez Canal as an oil route resulting from the building of supertankers to sail around the Cape of Good Hope will be partly offset by the new Suez–Alexandria pipeline. For the foreseeable future Middle East oil will be the principal source of supply for Western European states and Western Europe will be the principal market for Middle East oil. It will therefore be in the interest of the governments of the states of both areas to see that the flow of oil is maintained although the Middle East states will continue to use their bargaining power to increase their revenues from the oil industry. This applies as much to the oil transit states (Syria, Lebanon, and Egypt) as to the major producing countries.

While the Cold War was at its height in the decade following the Second World War, the Western Powers continued to attach great importance to the Middle East as a site for strategic bases within range of the southern borders of the Soviet Union. This importance was greatly reduced as the Cold War receded and nationalist sentiment in the Middle East states brought about by 1971 the liquidation of all Western military bases in the area except for those in Turkey and Cyprus. With the final withdrawal of the French and British military presence from the area only the United States and the Soviet Union among the Great Powers retained a direct strategic interest which was enhanced by their indirect involvement in the Arab–Israeli struggle in which the United States supported Israel and the Soviet Union the Arabs. The United States was chiefly concerned with the rapidly growing Soviet naval presence in the East Mediterranean (which in the 1950s had been dominated by the US Sixth Fleet) and by the increasing number of Soviet military advisers in Egypt. The closure of the Suez Canal in the 1967 Arab–Israeli War was of some strategic advantage to the United States as it blocked the Soviet fleet from direct access to the Indian Ocean and the Persian Gulf and closed Eastern Europe's principal supply route to North Vietnam, but the scaling down of the Vietnam War from 1969 and pressure from some of the United States' allies who were suffering severe economic loss from the continued closure of the Suez Canal caused the United States to take steps to try to secure the reopening of the waterway.

HISTORY AND POLITICS

The Middle East, which in recent times has appeared as a meeting-ground between the civilizations of the West and the East, was to its inhabitants for many millennia the civilized world itself. Of the surviving world religions three, Judaism, Christianity, and Islam, have their geographical sources in the Middle East. Moreover, the technical and scientific mastery acquired by the West is the outcome of a development initiated in the Middle East some three or four thousand years ago. Mathematics and the sciences as known today have grown directly from the work of Greek thinkers, who themselves drew on Egyptian and Babylonian traditions, and whose work was carried on and transmitted by the Arabs.

The predominant language of the region is Arabic, a Semitic language which has invaded and enriched the widely-spoken Persian and Turkish languages. The predominant religion is Islam, but there are various Christian communities, which now as in the past play a part in the public life of the Middle East out of proportion to their numbers: these are mostly descended from Christians who adopted the faith in the early centuries of Christianity and are not modern converts, unless from one Christian sect to another.[1]

The Arab Conquests

The early history of Islam is that of the Arab conquests. Mohammed, the prophet of Islam, himself united the Hejaz and laid the foundation for the unification of Arabia. After his death, in AD 632, the Arab-speaking Moslems poured in successive waves into the empires of Iran and Byzantium. They swept over Iran into Central Asia and India, over Syria, Egypt, North Africa, and Spain, and finally into France, where in 732 they were defeated by the Franks under Charles Martel, near Poitiers.

On the death of Mohammed a group of his followers elected a successor (*khalifa*, hence Caliph), who ruled from Medina. Factions soon appeared, however, and of the first four Caliphs (632–61) only the first died a natural death: the others, who included Ali, the Prophet's male next of kin, were all murdered. In 661 a member of the Mecca family of Umayya secured the Caliphate and so became the first of the Umayyad dynasty which ruled from Syria till 750. Meanwhile, however, a Shii[2] minority had given their support to Hussein, the son of Ali. Hussein was killed in a rising at Karbala in 680, but sporadic movements of revolt by the Shiis continued.

The Umayyads were overthrown and replaced by a new dynasty, the Abbasids (750–1258), who established themselves in Iraq and in 762 founded Baghdad as their new capital. Under the Abbasids, the most famous of whom was Harun al-Rashid (786–809), the Moslem Empire achieved great prosperity and cultural brilliance, and in that empire the Iranians played an important part. Before 850 however the Abbasid Caliphs had lost their personal power to semi-independent provincial governors, often Turkish mercenaries converted to Islam, and remained no more than titular lords of the Empire. Towards the middle of the eleventh century Iran was overrun by Seljuq Turks, converts to Islam from Central Asia, who entered Baghdad in 1055

---

[1] For an account of the foundation of Islam, and of sects and minorities, see below, pp. 32–5.
[2] See below, p. 34.

and eventually established an empire extending from India to the Aegean. In the tenth century rival caliphates were proclaimed by the Fatimid dynasty, ruling in Egypt and North Africa (and at times Syria), and by the survivors of the Umayyad dynasty, ruling in Spain. It is to be remembered that Moslem rule lasted in parts of Spain until 1492, a period of some 750 years, and for about half that time it extended to the greater part of the Peninsula; and that for a considerable period Moslem Spain was one of the two most highly civilized countries of Europe, the other being Byzantium.

The Turks

Through the Arabic language and the Islamic religion the Arabs gave a homogeneous basis to the vast area of their conquests. It was left to a Central Asiatic people, the Turks, to build a unified political system on this basis. The Turks entered the Islamic world as, successively, slaves, mercenaries, condottieri, and adventurers, and eventually they became its rulers. The Mongol invasion which put an end to the Abbasid Caliphate in Baghdad (1258) broke up the Seljuq Sultanate in Asia Minor; but from its ruins the Turkish dynasty of Osmanli (Ottoman) Turks emerged in north-west Asia Minor and gradually extended its influence into the Balkans. Ottoman expansion was crowned by the capture of Constantinople in 1453, which brought to an end the Roman Empire of the East. By the Ottoman annexation of the Mameluke[1] Sultanate of Egypt, Palestine, and Syria, virtually the whole of Sunni Islam (except India) came to be united against Iran, which had itself been reunited about 1500 under a Shii dynasty, the Safavids. For 200 years the Ottoman and Iranian Empires contended for the possession of Iraq, the population of which was mixed Sunni and Shii, and which finally fell to the Ottoman Empire.

The Crusades

The struggle between Christian Europe and Islam falls naturally into two periods. The first, which lasted 1,000 years, ending with the Turkish defeat by John Sobieski of Poland at Vienna in 1683, was on the whole favourable to Islam. At the end of the period Islam emerged in full control of the eastern Mediterranean, south-eastern Europe, and North Africa, although it was ousted from Sicily in 1090 and from Spain in 1492. In the second period, from 1683 onwards, Islam was gradually forced to retreat, and from 1815 to modern times its countries have been to a greater or lesser extent dominated by the West.

Western Christendom had been menaced by Islam from the time of its first expansion, but with the turning of the tide in Spain and Sicily in the course of the eleventh century and the rise of the Seljuqs in the

[1] *mamluk*, a slave. The 'Mamelukes' of Egypt were a slave corps from which the Sultans themselves came to be elected.

Levant, the West was free to embark upon the first of the Crusades, which were designed to secure an 'open door' to the Holy Land. The attempt failed, in spite of the establishment of Latin principalities in Syria and Palestine, the most important of which was the Kingdom of Jerusalem (1100–87); final defeat came in 1291. Nevertheless the Crusades created new commercial relations between East and West; they also reinforced the knowledge of Islamic arts and sciences (such as it was) already acquired in Christendom through Italy, Sicily, and Spain.

The Ottoman Empire

Ottoman rule was a military-religious autocracy of the Islamic pattern centred on a Sultan-Caliph[1] whose office was hereditary in the house of Osman (Othman). The non-Moslem subjects of the Empire, predominantly Christian, were organized in *millets* or religious minority communities, each of which had internal autonomy under an ecclesiastical functionary with temporal powers in matters of personal status and enjoyed a considerable individual and communal freedom. This however was offset by the periodical levy of Christian youths for service as *janissaries* (*yeny chery*, or new troops), which were for long the shock troops of the Ottoman army. Some of these conscripts manned the Sultan's court, and the most promising were trained to run the administration. During the Ottoman Empire's period of decay it became tyrannical, arbitrary, and inefficient, while the janissaries became increasingly rebellious. The massacre of the janissaries in 1826 by Sultan Mahmud II (1808–39) enabled him to pursue the modernization of the army envisaged by Selim III (1789–1807), and gained a century's respite for the Empire. At its zenith the Ottoman Empire ranked with the greatest of Western Powers. France quickly entered into relations with the Sublime Porte,[2] as the Ottoman Government was called, and in 1535 obtained from the Sultan the first formal Capitulations.[3] In 1553 an English traveller to Aleppo obtained from the Sultan a 'safe-conduct or privilege' granting him the same privileges as those enjoyed by the French and the Venetians. This led to the founding of the Levant Company in 1581. The English merchants were seeking to eliminate the middlemen and to reach the sources of supply of oriental wares. They tried two routes through Russia and a third through Syria and the Persian Gulf, but finally adopted as the cheapest

[1] The title of Caliph began to be used by the Ottoman Sultans in the eighteenth century. It became in the nineteenth century a device for persuading the Powers that the Sultan's spiritual status was analogous to that of Pope or Patriarch, so that he could claim the spiritual allegiance of Moslems outside the Ottoman dominions.

[2] A mistranslation of the Turkish, which means rather 'High Gate' (of administration and justice).

[3] Capitulations were originally unilateral charters modelled on those granted by the Byzantines, Crusaders, and Mamelukes to the Italian city-states.

the long sea route round the Cape. They had first to deal with the Portuguese, who, although officially at peace with England, were trying to establish in the East by force of arms a monopoly of trade such as the Spaniards claimed in the West. The pretended monopoly was destroyed when the newly-founded East India Company, at the request of the Shah of Iran, helped the Iranians to eject the Portuguese from the island of Hormuz, in the Persian Gulf. In the wars with Holland and France the Gulf was frequently the scene of hostilities which in the end resulted in British predominance. The British had also to contend with the Arab pirates, whose power was only broken, by the British and British-Indian navies, in the nineteenth century.

As a trade route, and as a line of defence for India and British communications with the East, the Persian Gulf was long of great importance to Britain. To forestall an attempt by Napoleon to establish himself in the Gulf, at the time when he was in occupation of Egypt, the British in 1798 concluded a treaty with the Ruler of Muscat. From 1820, however, they concluded with other rulers in the Gulf a long series of treaties designed to maintain local security as well as to guard against unfriendly intrusion by any other Power.[1] On the other side of Arabia Aden, near the entrance to the Red Sea, was occupied by a British expedition in 1839.[2]

The occupation of Egypt by the French, in 1798, may be regarded as one phase of the Eastern Question: the problem of filling up the vacuum created by the gradual recession of the Ottoman Empire from the frontiers it reached at the height of its expansion. Pressure by Austria on the Ottoman Empire had begun at the end of the sixteenth century; about a century later began attempts by Russia to increase her influence at the expense of the Porte, either by annexation of territory, or by securing control of the Straits, or by acquiring a right to intervene in the internal affairs of the Empire. This policy was illustrated when the forces of Mohammed Ali, the rebellious Pasha of Egypt, approached Constantinople, and Russia, in exchange for protection by Russian troops, extracted from the Sultan the Treaty of Hunkiar Iskelessi, which not only gave Russia a right to interfere in Turkish affairs, but contained a secret clause giving Russia the right to secure the closing of the Dardanelles if she should ever be at war. This treaty, and a second advance by Mohammed Ali's forces on Constantinople, brought about negotiations between the Powers which left Egypt an autonomous territory, and by this and other signs showed how far the power of the Porte had declined. Greece had already obtained her independence, in 1832, thanks to the destruction of the Turkish and Egyptian fleets by those of Britain, France, and Russia. This process continued, and by 1914 all the Christian territories of the

[1] See below, pp. 197–206.
[2] See below, p. 170.

Balkans, as well as the island of Crete, had been freed from Ottoman sovereignty.

During the greater part of the nineteenth century Britain pursued consistently a policy which had first been propounded by William Pitt in about 1791 : to preserve the Ottoman Empire lest, if it disintegrated, parts should fall into more dangerous, specifically Russian, hands. Hence the British (and French) defence of Turkey against Russia in the Crimean War; hence too British policy at the Congress of Berlin, where with the aid of Bismarck the Tsar was induced to grant to Turkey better terms than those of the Treaty of St. Stefano. British support of the Sultan at this time was illustrated somewhat ambiguously when Britain obtained from the Sultan the right to occupy the island of Cyprus in return for an undertaking to defend Asia Minor against further aggression. Nevertheless, British opposition to Russian pressure in the nineteenth century was the main factor in the preservation of the integrity of Turkey and Iran.

The pendulum of power which had swung from the Middle East over Spain in the eighth century, and later over the Balkans and Hungary and Austria, had now, as Western states became stronger, swung back across the Middle East and over much of Asia, even as far as Japan, where the United States and European Powers secured capitulatory rights for their nationals in the 1850s. In the Ottoman Empire the Capitulations enjoyed by most foreigners, in the courts and in matters of direct taxation, had by now developed to such an extent as to place them in a position much more favourable than that of Ottoman nationals. This was the more burdensome to the Porte in that during the nineteenth century the deteriorating finances of the Empire put it increasingly in debt to foreign interests. The Porte could not increase customs dues without the permission of the Powers, which was given grudgingly after being withheld sometimes for years. The Powers even set up, in 1881, the Ottoman Public Debt Administration, on which Turkey had one member (without a vote), to collect and distribute direct to foreign bondholders the proceeds of taxation on tobacco and certain other articles. In Iran the Capitulations, though less elaborate, were nevertheless onerous. It was in Egypt, however, that they had attained their widest extension, and after the occupation in 1882 the British authorities found them obstructing at every turn the task of restoring the finances and improving the administration. It was during the last half century or so before 1914 that the West established in the Middle East certain great enterprises, e.g. the Baghdad Railway, the Suez Canal, and the oil industry in Iran, for which the East had not the capital, the skill, or the experience. These enterprises, however impressive and useful, were to come to be regarded with suspicion and dislike by the local populations and governments as alleged instruments of foreign economic and even political influence.

Towards the end of the nineteenth century Germany came forward as the Sultan's only friend. The Ottoman Empire had lost the Crimea and parts of the Caucasus to Russia, Cyprus and Egypt to Britain, Algeria and Tunisia to France, and Bosnia and Herzegovina to Austria: only Germany of the great European Powers had acquired no Ottoman territory. Germany now embarked upon the training of the Turkish army, and the construction of the railway eastwards from Constantinople which was afterwards known as the Baghdad Railway. Moreover, when the Armenian massacres of 1894–5 aroused general hostility towards Turkey, the German Emperor went out of his way to declare himself the Sultan's friend. When the German railway company secured an extension of its concession, providing for a branch to the Persian Gulf, the British Government became alive to this threat to its interests in the Gulf. It was the looming peril from Germany which induced Britain to join with Russia, crippled by the war with Japan and by internal revolution, in the 1907 agreement about Iran (and Afghanistan and Tibet), and to ally herself with Russia in the First World War. Nevertheless Britain was not intransigent, and by the time war began in 1914, she had arrived at agreements with Germany on all the main points of dispute in the Middle East, particularly the Baghdad Railway, Tigris navigation, and oil concessions.

At the turn of the century the pendulum of power began to swing back from the Far East. In 1899 Japan established herself as a Great Power, and threw off the Capitulations which had been imposed on her less than half a century before; in 1905 the Japanese inflicted on the Russians a victory which sent a thrill of excitement and hope throughout many parts of Asia, since not for a very long time had a European been defeated by an Asian Power. It is believed with some reason that the example of the resurgence of Japan helped to bring about the Iranian and Turkish revolutions in the period 1905–8.

Arab Nationalism

Although the Turkish Constitution of 1878 remained in force only for two years and was followed by thirty years of severe despotism, it left a ferment in the Empire. The Arabs may have been influenced to some extent by Midhat Pasha, one of the authors of the Constitution, who was for several years Governor-General of Baghdad and was later for a short time Governor-General of Syria. Syria and Lebanon were simmering with political ideas which had grown out of a literary movement encouraged by the American and French missions and their printing presses. In Egypt the Arabi movement of 1882, misunderstood abroad and repugnant to the Khedive and the Sultan, found its chief support in the Egyptian agricultural class; it demanded internal reform but it also attacked the subservience of the Turkish-speaking ruling caste to foreign influence. Mustafa Kamil, who led a movement for constitutional reform in the 1890s, was more fortunate than Arabi. At that time the British-inspired regime in Egypt offered a haven to reformers in the Ottoman Empire, whether Egyptian or refugees from Syria or Turkey. Cromer even encouraged the reformist party, Hizb al-Umma, which was inspired by the Egyptian religious reformer Mohammed Abduh. The almost complete freedom of the Egyptian press provided a field for discussion of which good use was made.

Pan-Islamism and Pan-Arabism

The pan-Islamic policy of Sultan Abdul Hamid (1878–1909) was partly designed to attract the Arab element in the Empire. A rival doctrine, of Islamic revival under Arab leadership and an Arab Caliphate, was preached by a Syrian, Abdul Rahman Kawakibi (1849–1903), whose books, published in Cairo, were secretly circulated among Arab nationalists in Syria. But by studied displays of piety, by using Arabs at court, and particularly by the building of the Hejaz Railway, which was advertised and voluntarily subscribed for as a great act of piety to assist the pilgrim to Mecca—whereby its true military importance was disguised—the Sultan-Caliph won considerable support.

The Revolution of 1908

The Arabs of the Ottoman Empire welcomed the Young Turk revolution with enthusiasm, hoping for a regime in which they would have an equal place with the Turks. It became clear, however, that the Turks were outnumbered by the Arabs and other non-Turkish elements combined, and having created the Empire and been for centuries the ruling race, and moreover having been the authors of the 1908 revolution, the Turks had no intention of allowing themselves to be voted down. Arab requests for decentralization and for some concession to the Arabic language and to Arab sentiment were pared down to a derisory level, and the future seemed dark for Arab national hopes in an Empire inspired on the one hand by pan-Turanianism, which regarded every Turkish-speaking area outside the Empire as *terra irredenta*, and on the other by Ottomanism, looking to 'the fusion of the different races into a single Ottoman democracy with Turkish for its distinctive language'.[1] Early in 1914, therefore, the Amir Abdullah, the second son of the Sharif Hussein of Mecca, approached the British High Commissioner in Cairo to find out what attitude the British would adopt if the Ottoman Arabs revolted against the Sultan. Given the traditional British policy of preserving the Ottoman Empire lest worse should befall, the reply could only be discouraging.

[1] G. Antonius, *The Arab Awakening* (London, 1938), p. 102.

The First World War[1]

When the war in Europe began, on 2 August 1914, Turkey was at first neutral, but a secret alliance with Germany was signed that day. On 29 October Turkish warships bombarded Russian Black Sea ports; Russia declared war on Turkey on 4 November, Britain the following day. By the time the Turks signed the Mudros armistice on 30 October 1918 the Arab provinces of the Empire had been almost completely cleared of Turkish troops by the British forces in Palestine and Mesopotamia (Iraq).

The Arab Revolt

The entry of Turkey into the war on the German side induced the British Government to reopen the talks with the Sharif of Mecca.[2] It had become important for Britain to secure his support, in order to reinforce war operations in the Arab countries and also because the Sultan-Caliph had proclaimed a *jihad* (a holy war) and was trying to induce the Sharif to support it. There ensued an exchange of letters between the Sharif Hussein and the British High Commissioner in Egypt, Sir Henry McMahon. The correspondence ended in January 1916, and on 5 June the Arab revolt began. In November Hussein proclaimed himself King of the Arab Lands: Britain and France, however, recognized him only as King of the Hejaz.

Loyalties in the Arabian Peninsula were divided. The Amir Ibn Rashid of Hail sided with the Turks, as did the Imam of the Yemen. The Ruler of Nejd, Abdul Aziz ibn Saud, threw off the overlordship of the Sultan which he had been compelled to accept in 1914, and in December 1914 he signed a treaty with the British Government which gave Britain a large measure of control over his foreign policy, but acknowledged the independence and territorial integrity of Nejd and granted him a monthly subsidy. Ibn Saud made a contribution towards the Arab cause by keeping Ibn Rashid busy from time to time.[3] He might perhaps have given some assistance in the Hejaz campaign, but for King Hussein's persistence in treating him as an insignificant subordinate.

The Arab revolt immobilized some 30,000 Turkish troops along the railway from Amman to Medina, and included valuable guerrilla operations on the right flank of the British army in Palestine. These operations would not have been possible without the help of the British navy on the Hejaz coast, and the participation of numerous British personnel among whom T. E. Lawrence holds a high place.[4]

[1] C. R. M. F. Cruttwell, *A History of the Great War, 1914–18* (Oxford, 1934).
[2] See above, p. 11.
[3] H. St. J. B. Philby, *Arabian Jubilee* (London, 1952), ch. 4.
[4] Sir Hubert Young, *The Independent Arab* (London, 1933); Eric Lonnroth, *Lawrence of Arabia* (London, 1956).

The Arab forces are sometimes stated by Arab writers to have 'captured' Damascus, but Damascus fell because of the total rout of the Turkish armies, and the first Allied troops to enter the city were a body of Australian cavalry.

Partition and Mandates

At the end of the war the Arabs expected the fulfilment of promises made or understood to have been made to them by Britain. These consisted of various statements and declarations (one of them in conjunction with France) during the war,[1] and of the so-called McMahon correspondence. Unfortunately the correspondence is not perfectly clear as to the area of Arab independence. The Arabs maintained that it included Palestine; the British Government and its principal negotiators, that it did not. There are various indications that Hussein and his son, the Amir Faisal, were aware that the British Government always intended to keep a hold over Palestine, but it would have been difficult to deduce the mandate system from the McMahon correspondence, still more the National Home for the Jewish people. In fact the British themselves did not in 1915 foresee such developments: they were trying to safeguard in a general way the vital interests of Britain, particularly in regard to India, Egypt, and British communications with the East, and also those of their French and Russian allies, who were not parties to the negotiations.

French and Russian interests were dealt with specifically in the 'Sykes–Picot' Agreement (1916)[2] which conflicted with the McMahon correspondence in regard to the area and degree of Arab independence. Under its terms Russia was to have, besides Constantinople and a strip of territory on each side of the Bosphorus, the greater part of the four Turkish provinces adjacent to the Russian frontier. Russia laid no claim to any Arab territory, and recognized the claims of France and Britain in regard to them. As between themselves Britain and France agreed that there should be:

(1) an international zone in Palestine (much smaller than the eventual area of mandated Palestine);
(2) a British zone of Basra and Baghdad;
(3) a French zone of Syria (and Cilicia);
(4) an independent Arab state or federation, between the British and French zones, divided into British and French spheres of influence.

The text of the Balfour Declaration (2 November 1917) reads as follows:

His Majesty's Government view with favour the establishment in Palestine of a National Home for the Jewish people, and will use their best endeavours to

[1] Antonius, *Arab Awakening*, pp. 433–5.
[2] Hurewitz, ii. 18.

facilitate the achievement of this object, it being clearly understood that nothing shall be done which may prejudice the civil and religious rights of existing non-Jewish communities in Palestine, or the rights and political status enjoyed by Jews in any other country.[1]

The motives behind the Balfour Declaration were various: messianic, humanitarian, strategic. Many people in Britain, far more in the United States, believed that to promote a Jewish return to Palestine was to help to fulfil prophecies in the Old Testament. There was widespread sympathy for the Jews, scattered in many countries, often suffering from misgovernment or worse, yet preserving through all a memory of a former home in Palestine. Finally, the policy of the National Home might work in favour of the retention of Palestine by Britain as a point in her defensive system, and might moreover win sympathy for the Allied cause among world Jewry, particularly in Russia, where the influence of the Jews, now that the Tsarist regime had fallen, might help to counteract the drift towards a separate peace with Germany. But however strong these considerations may have appeared in Britain, they were never to have any weight with the Arabs.

After the Turkish defeat in Syria the whole area was occupied by British troops with a small French force on the coast and the army of King Hussein in the interior. In Palestine there was a British military administration, in the coastal region north of Palestine a French provisional government, and in the four cities of Aleppo, Homs, Hama, and Damascus, and east of Jordan, an Arab administration under the Amir Faisal, to whom a number of British and French officers were attached. On 30 January 1919 the Peace Conference decided that the Arab provinces of the Ottoman Empire should be wholly separated from Turkey, and announced the adoption for some of them of the mandate system, a kind of trusteeship, as a bridge to complete independence. Britain and France disagreed over the boundaries of the mandated territories. An investigation into the wishes of the population which was to have been international dwindled, through French opposition, into an inquiry by two Americans, and the 'King–Crane' Report which they presented to the President of the United States was ignored at the time, and was only published, and then unofficially, in December 1922.[2] It was opposed to a French mandate for Syria and questioned the wisdom of the Balfour Declaration.

In September 1919 an agreement was reached between Britain and France whereby British troops were withdrawn from Syria (excluding Palestine) and from Cilicia, and replaced by Arab troops in the interior of Syria and by French troops on the coast and in Cilicia. On 20 March 1920 a congress of Syrian notables at Damascus offered the crown of Syria and Palestine to Faisal, who accepted it. This action

[1] Ibid., p. 26.   [2] Ibid., p. 66.

was repudiated by the British and French Governments, who subsequently, at the conference of San Remo (24 April 1920), received mandates: the French for Syria and Lebanon, the British for Palestine, with Transjordan, with the obligation to carry out the policy of the Balfour Declaration. This award was repudiated by Faisal. Subsequently the French Commander-in-Chief advanced into Syria and occupied Damascus. Faisal departed into exile, but later became King of Iraq.

The mandates for 'Palestine' and 'Syria and Lebanon',[1] were formally approved by the Council of the League of Nations in July 1922 and became effective in September 1923.[2] In 1924 the United States gave its concurrence to the mandates. Article 2 of the mandate for Palestine laid on the Mandatory the responsibility for placing the country under such political, administrative, and economic conditions as would secure the establishment of a Jewish National Home without prejudice to the rights and position of the rest of the population. Transjordan was added to the mandated territory, but the Mandatory was permitted to exclude it, and in fact did exclude it, from the area of Jewish settlement. In 1922 Transjordan was constituted a semi-autonomous Arab principality under the Amir Abdullah, subject under mandate to the British High Commissioner in Jerusalem.[3]

The Arabs of the Middle East recognized neither the Sykes–Picot Agreement nor the Balfour Declaration. The former became known to the world in December 1917,[4] when the Bolsheviks, having discovered it in the Tsarist archives, published it and, in so far as it affected Russia, repudiated it. The agreement was modified in December 1918 by an arrangement between Lloyd George and Clemenceau, in which Mosul and Palestine were included in the British sphere of influence.

With the final disintegration of the Ottoman Empire, Western penetration became Western domination, and Arab nationalism, which had allied itself with Britain against the Turks, became the formula for resistance to Western (in particular British and French) economic and political power. It covered also the realization that the adoption of Western techniques and social innovations was a condition of successful resistance. As the dominant foreign Powers were no longer Moslem but Christian, it was inevitable, too, that the Islamic tendencies in Arab nationalism should assert themselves more strongly; yet it embraced, under the name of Arabs, all those whose mother-tongue was Arabic: Moslem fundamentalists and reformers, Orthodox, Coptic,

[1] *League of Nations Official Journal*, August 1922, pp. 1007–12 and 1013–17.
[2] For the arrangements for Iraq see below, p. 316.
[3] Proclaimed 25 May 1923.
[4] Elie Kedourie argues that the Sharif Hussein must have been aware of the Sykes–Picot negotiations and have had a shrewd idea of Anglo-French intentions towards the Aarb territories (*England and the Middle East* (London, 1956), ch. 2).

and Catholic Christians, free-thinkers, and the illiterate masses of peasants just beginning to be aware of the possibility of social reform.

The End of the Caliphate

On 1 November 1922 a law was passed by the Great National Assembly which marked the overthrow of Ottoman rule by the Turkish nationalists under Mustafa Kemal. This law deprived the Caliph of all secular authority in the new Turkish state. The last Ottoman Sultan-Caliph was deposed and expelled and the dynasty came to an end; a relative was elected Caliph, but he became a rallying point for the opposition to Mustafa Kemal, and on 3 March 1924 the Caliphate itself was abolished by the National Assembly and the Caliph expelled from Turkey. Though these acts were strongly challenged at the time, particularly by Indian Moslems, the Caliphate has not been revived. The assumption by King Hussein of the Hejaz of the title of Caliph was not recognized except in the Hejaz, Transjordan, and Iraq, and lapsed some months later when Hussein abdicated after his kingdom had been attacked by Ibn Saud. In May 1926 a Caliphate Congress, attended by delegates from 13 Moslem countries (not including Turkey) was held in Cairo, but was inconclusive. Since then the Caliphate has scarcely been an issue in Moslem politics.

Regional Relations

The internal relations of the Middle East took some time to recover from the disruption of the war and the dissolution of the Ottoman Empire. Memories of the Arab revolt and of Turkish excesses against Arabs were for long a barrier to Turco-Arab understanding. The first step towards improved relations was taken in 1935, when negotiations begun on the initiative of Iraq resulted in a four-Power pact of *bon voisinage*, signed on 8 July 1937 by Turkey, Iraq, Iran, and Afghanistan. This Middle Eastern or 'Saadabad' Pact had in fact little influence before the Second World War, and has had none since. The pact was preceded by agreements settling boundary disputes between Turkey and Iran (23 January 1937) and Iraq and Iran (4 July 1937). Turkey had previously, on 9 February 1934, signed a Balkan pact with Greece, Rumania, and Yugoslavia.[1]

The Arab world itself was split by the quarrel between the families of Hashim and Saud. Ex-King Hussein died in 1931; the reign of his successor, his son Ali, had come to an end on the capture of Jedda by Ibn Saud in 1925. The Hashimis, however, were still represented by Hussein's sons: Faisal in Iraq and Abdullah in Transjordan. A further source of discord were the towns of Aqaba and Maan, annexed by Britain to Transjordan though claimed by Ibn Saud for the Hejaz. It was Ibn Saud who first tried to improve relations with his neighbours,

[1] For text see RIIA, *Documents on International Affairs, 1934*, p. 298.

by signing a treaty of friendship and *bon voisinage* with Transjordan (27 July 1933); a treaty of Arab brotherhood and alliance with Iraq (2 April 1937); and a treaty of friendship with Egypt (7 May 1936).[1]

Turco-Arab relations were also complicated by the question of the *sanjaq* of Alexandretta (Hatay), which formed part of French mandated territory. It was regarded as Arab by the Arabs, but was claimed by Turkey because of its partly Turkish population and its strategic and economic importance. On 29 May 1937 an agreement was reached at Geneva by which the *sanjaq* was transformed into the autonomous Republic of Hatay jointly guaranteed by France and Turkey.[2] Just before the outbreak of the Second World War, and as a prelude to the Treaty of Mutual Assistance of 19 October 1939 between Britain, France, and Turkey,[3] the territory was incorporated in the Turkish Republic by the Franco-Turkish agreement of 21 June 1939. This transaction over their heads was deeply resented by the Syrians.[4]

Arab Unity

Although from 1920 the reunification of the Arab world under an independent political regime was to be a main objective of Arab nationalism (an idea which was given expression at more than one pan-Arab Congress), nevertheless the separate development of each territory created in time political loyalties which accentuated the tendencies to disunity already present. Egypt, detached from the Ottoman Empire in the nineteenth century, had developed, first under Mohammed Ali and then under British occupation, a national consciousness which tended to conflict with pan-Arabism. This detachment had also put Egypt socially and politically far in advance of the rest of the Arab world. Again, the earlier modernization and relative wealth of Egypt gave her a leading position in Arab affairs, and the superior publishing facilities of Cairo made it the centre of Arab influence through books and newspapers, and, later, films and radio.

Saudi-Hashimite rivalry was a factor in Arab politics, and the greater dependence of the Hashimi family on Britain usually induced the nationalists of Egypt and Syria to side with Saudi Arabia. In external relations, however, dislike and fear of Zionism tended to bind all the Arab states together. The first formal recognition of a community of Arab states was seen in the participation of the Arab Governments in the Palestine Conference in London in 1939.

Great-Power Rivalry between the Wars

The Straits. The interests of the Powers in the Straits were regulated first by the Convention signed at Lausanne, on the same day as the

[1] For the text of these treaties see ibid. *1937*, pp. 517 ff.
[2] Ibid. p. 490.
[3] Hurewitz, ii. 226.
[4] RIIA, *Documents on International Affairs, 1934*, p. 506.

treaty of 24 July 1923, by Turkey, Britain, France, Italy, Japan, Bulgaria, Greece, Rumania, and the Soviet Union,[1] providing for full freedom of passage for commercial vessels of all nations both in peace and in war and, subject to certain conditions, for warships of all Powers in peacetime, as well as in a war in which Turkey was neutral; and for the demilitarization of the European and Asiatic shores of the Bosphorus and Dardanelles and of the islands. This instrument was replaced on 20 July 1936 by the Montreux Convention, to which the Soviet Union and Yugoslavia, but not Italy, were signatories, and which maintained the principle of freedom of navigation for merchant vessels through the Straits but by a protocol abrogated the demilitarization of the Straits and allowed Turkey to refortify them. The Soviet Union was further given the right to send any number of warships of any size through the Straits in time of peace without Turkish permission being obtained, while the non-littoral Powers were limited to sending light surface vessels into the Black Sea. In time of war, if Turkey were neutral, belligerent warships were not to pass except to execute obligations under the League Covenant or under a mutual assistance agreement within its framework; if Turkey were belligerent or threatened, the passage of warships was left to Turkish discretion.

Progress towards Independence. The Capitulations disappeared between the wars. Turkey got rid of them by the Treaty of Lausanne of 1923, Iran in 1926, Egypt in 1937. The Turkish Government used its independence to expropriate, on terms favourable to itself, all foreign railway, mining, and other concerns. The Arab territories placed under mandate were dissatisfied with a political status inferior to that of less advanced countries such as Yemen and Hejaz. Nevertheless, except in Palestine, where there was an exceptional regime under international supervision, all the mandated territories made political progress between the wars, and one of them, Iraq, in 1932 attained independence. Egypt too, which when the First World War ended was a British protectorate, became independent, in 1936.

Britain. Britain emerged from the post-war settlements in a predominant position in the Middle East. Nevertheless in more than one area there were dangerous stresses. The British Declaration about Egypt in 1922 followed several years of acrimonious dispute and serious outbreaks of violence, and the agreement of 1936 would have been less popular but for Mussolini's open designs on Egypt. In Iraq the mandate ended in 1932, but the arrangement by which Britain retained two air bases provided the extreme nationalists with a grievance, and, like other Arabs, the Iraqis, however friendly towards Britain, detested the Zionist policy.

Throughout the inter-war period the Palestine problem caused un-

[1] The Soviet Union, however, signed under protest and subsequently refused to ratify.

ceasing anxiety and conflict.[1] There were outbreaks of violence on the part of the Arabs, from 1920 onwards; there were many inquiries and reports and White Papers. In 1937 a Royal Commission recommended the partition of Palestine between Arabs and Jews; in 1938 a Partition Commission found the proposal to be impracticable. Throughout the period, and especially after Nazi brutality had begun to drive the Jews out of Germany, the Mandatory had difficulty every year about the number of Jewish immigrants to be admitted: the Jews asking for a higher quota, and the Arabs demanding that not merely illegal immigration, which was considerable, but all immigration by Jews should be stopped. Finally there was the British White Paper of 1939, providing for the cessation of Jewish immigration, except with Arab consent, when 75,000 more Jews should have been admitted, for a ten-year scheme of preparation for self-government, and for restrictions on the acquisition of land by Jews. This White Paper was rejected by the Arabs, though they were to look back upon it later as a Magna Carta, while the Jews in Palestine and elsewhere attacked it violently. It had critics in Britain; it failed to secure the approval of the Mandates Commission of the League of Nations; and in the United States the voice of Zionism drowned all other opinions on the Palestine problem.

The Totalitarian States. One consequence of British predominance was a tendency for the Middle East nationalists to look to rival Powers for support. Fascist Italy was active in propaganda and political intrigue in Middle East countries, but was handicapped by Arab memories of the ruthless suppression of the Senussi in Cyrenaica. Another and perhaps fatal setback to Italian aims was a speech by Mussolini on 18 March 1934 in which he referred to Italy's 'historic objectives' in the Middle East. Again, one effect of the conquest of Ethiopia in 1935–6 was to make all parties in Egypt anxious to sign the long-delayed treaty with Britain. A more formidable Power in which the Arabs began to see a counterweight to Britain and France was Nazi Germany. Hitler's anti-Jewish policy enabled Germany to pose as the sole champion of the Arabs against Anglo-Jewish imperialism, but at the same time increased Jewish pressure on Palestine through the enforced emigration of Jews from Germany. By 1939 extensive anti-British activities were being conducted from German and Italian missions and consulates in the Middle East. Italian activities concentrated chiefly on Egypt and the Red Sea coast of Arabia, particularly the Yemen, and they did not entirely cease after the signature of the Anglo-Italian Agreement of 16 April 1938, 'regarding questions of mutual concern' in the Middle East. German activities were directed upon Turkey, Iraq, and Iran.

France. By the end of the First World War French financial and

---

[1] George Kirk, *A Short History of the Middle East* (London, 1955), pp. 146–59; Sir Reader Bullard, *Britain and the Middle East* (London, 1952), pp. 94–107.

cultural interests in the Middle East had long been considerable, and French was the language of polite society in Egypt and in other parts of the Levant. France's traditional political interests were now given concrete form by the mandate over Syria and Lebanon, but this was resisted, except by some of the Christians, from the first. In 1936 the French Government initialed agreements with the two states on something like the lines of the Anglo-Iraqi Treaty of 1930, but political changes in France prevented their ratification.

The United States. Until the First World War the interests of the United States in the Middle East were mainly philanthropical, with commercial interests developing slowly.[1] So remote did the United States feel from Middle East politics, that although she went to war with Germany and her European allies in 1917, she remained at peace with Turkey. When, however, the Ottoman Empire broke up, the United States, in spite of her refusal to accept a mandate over Armenia and her attempt to retire into her traditional isolation, was gradually drawn into Middle East affairs: by the Zionist question; by oil; and finally by the requirements of defence.

When the Balfour Declaration was issued by the British Government in November 1917, neither the President of the United States nor the State Department made any official comment. President Wilson seems to have conveyed his approval beforehand, through Colonel House, and in any case the exigencies of internal politics drew the President into public approval of the Declaration as early as August 1918.[2] Zionist interests in the United States, Protestant as well as Jewish, maintained pressure on the administration, and helped to create general hostility to the British White Paper of 1939.

American oil companies at first had some difficulty in securing participation in the oil resources of the Middle East, owing to the exclusive rights that were held, through treaties and in other ways, by Britain. Indeed, in almost every case governmental negotiations on a high level were needed before a commercial project could be realized. In the name of the 'open door' the United States refused to recognize the written promise of the oil of Baghdad and Mosul which the Grand Vizier had made in writing to the Turkish Petroleum Company (Anglo-German) in 1914, and after prolonged pressure secured for American interests a 23$\frac{3}{4}$ per cent share in what became the Iraq Petroleum Company. Between 1930 and 1934 oil concessions were secured by American companies, in Bahrain, in Kuwait (in equal shares with the AIOC, now British Petroleum), and in Saudi Arabia.

---

[1] The leading American educational institutions today are: Robert College, Istanbul (opened in 1863); the Women's College of Istanbul (1890); the American University of Beirut (1866); and the American University of Cairo (1919).

[2] Frank E. Manuel, *The Realities of American–Palestine Relations* (Washington, D.C., 1949).

The Soviet Union. As a continental Power, Russia's first concern in the Middle East has been with the two neighbouring states of Turkey and Iran. From 1917 to 1921 the Bolsheviks followed a 'liberation' policy in that area and exploited the revolutionary appeal with some success among its down-trodden peoples. Then, after the withdrawal of the Soviet armies, the policy from 1921 onwards became one of non-intervention and support of the national independence of Middle East countries against the 'imperialist penetration' of Britain and the West.

There was a steady growth of Soviet trade with these countries, particularly with Iran. An important factor for Soviet–Middle East relations was the economic and social development of the Soviet national republics to the north and east of the region. The policy of cultural emancipation in the new Soviet republics, with their racial and religious affinities with national minorities in the Middle East States, was also used as an instrument of Soviet foreign policy. It had to contend with the distrust of neighbouring communities for anything Russian, and in particular for the Soviet system, and also with the evidence of the political subjection of the republics to the Soviet State. On the other hand Russia's rapid industrial development might well serve as a magnet to areas beginning to resent their backward condition. Whatever the cause, Communist parties began to form in Arab countries, for example in Egypt as early as 1920, in Syria and Iraq in the 1930s.[1]

Soviet relations with the inner ring of Middle East states remained more vague. The Soviet Union, one of the first Powers to recognize Ibn Saud (16 February 1926), concluded a treaty with the Yemen on 1 November 1928. The Soviet missions in both countries, which were under the Soviet representative in Jedda, were closed in 1938. Neither Egypt nor Iraq would admit the Soviet Union to diplomatic relations, even when, after 1922 and 1932 respectively, they were free to do so, and Lebanon and Syria were limited by the French mandate for the whole of the inter-war period. In regard to Turkey, the Soviet Union refused to ratify the Convention about the Straits which was signed at Lausanne in 1923, and secured much better terms in the Montreux Convention of 1936.[2] In Iran, after the failure of the Soviet republic in Gilan, the Russians behaved on the whole with discretion, though it was found that among the thousands of Iranians who were ejected from the Soviet Union in the 1930s on the ground of refusal to take Soviet citizenship there were a considerable number of Soviet agents. On the whole, until 1939 the Russians were content not to push their interests too hard in the Middle East but to wait upon events.

[1] W. Z. Laqueur, *Communism and Nationalism in the Middle East* (London, 1956).
[2] See above, p. 18.

B

The Second World War

It was with relief that the British learned that no attempt would be made by the Palestine Arabs to embarrass them while they were at war with Germany. They were thus able to build up the organization based on Cairo that was to serve them so well. Internal opposition was dealt with early. German assistance for the abortive *coup d'état* of Rashid Ali in Iraq in May 1941 was small and arrived too late. The Vichy regime in Syria was defeated by British and Free French forces, and replaced in July 1941 by a regime dependent on General de Gaulle. In August 1941 British and Russian forces entered Iran, where strong Axis influence had aroused the deep anxiety of the Allied Governments. This opened the supply line to Russia, which was worked largely by American non-combatant troops operating under the British command in Baghdad. Finally, British pressure on King Farouk in February 1942 brought into power the helpful government of Nahas.

The task of denying the Middle East to the Axis Powers and of creating there a base for a counter-offensive against southern Europe was given high priority in Allied strategy; the actual defence of the area was a British responsibility. After the internal threats to the Allies had been removed, the Middle East for about a year was in danger from German forces which in the summer of 1942 were established in Egypt on the west and in the Caucasus on the north. Until after the victories of el Alamein and Stalingrad there was little to persuade the Middle East that the Allies might win the war.

Even after the ending of Axis resistance in North Africa the Middle East retained much of its importance. Among the war activities centred on Cairo were those of the Middle East Supply Centre established by the British Government in 1941 and made into a joint Anglo-American supply agency in the following year. The task of the Centre was to ensure that the civil population of the Middle East was provided with essential supplies and at the same time to limit their imports in order to economize in sea and land transport and in port space. To this end local food production had to be greatly increased, and many short-term measures—changes in method, encouragement of local industries, introduction of fertilizers and agricultural machinery—were put into operation.[1]

Formation of the Arab League

In a speech delivered in May 1941 Anthony Eden said that the British Government would give full support to any scheme that commanded

---

[1] See 'Economic Problems: The Middle East Supply Centre' by Guy Hunter in G. Kirk, *The Middle East in the War* (RIIA, *Survey of International Affairs, 1939–46*), pp. 169–93.

general approval among Arabs for strengthening the cultural, economic, and political ties between the Arab countries. Syrian and Lebanese independence, promised by the Free French and confirmed by the British on their entry into Syria in June 1941, was formally recognized by the British Government on 27 October (Syria) and 26 December (Lebanon) 1941. In December 1942 Nuri al-Said, Prime Minister of Iraq, brought forward a scheme for the unification of Syria, Lebanon, Palestine, and Transjordan, with 'semi-autonomy' for the Jews in Palestine, as a first step towards Arab unity. This proposal was not pursued, but a general Arab Conference met in Alexandria in September–October 1944 which was attended by representatives of the Governments of Egypt, Iraq, Lebanon, Syria, Transjordan, Saudi Arabia, and Yemen, and by an observer on behalf of the Arabs of Palestine. The proceedings resulted in the foundation of the Arab League, and by the signature on 22 March 1945 of the Pact of the League.[1] The League set up a Council with its seat in Cairo and with provisions for various commissions: economic, cultural, etc. The real bond of unity at that time was opposition to the growing Jewish Home in Palestine and fear of its continued expansion, and the defeat of the Arab States in the Palestine War discredited the League and mutual recriminations weakened it from the inside. The Inter-Arab Joint Defence Alliance, which was concluded in the period 1950–2, led to no practical results at the time, and differences as to its interpretation were to exacerbate subsequent disputes about the Baghdad Pact. Attempts by members of the League to establish closer relations between themselves met with little success. King Abdullah strove to bring about the union of Jordan with Syria, but although many Syrians wished for union, there was no general desire in Syria to come under a monarchy, particularly a monarchy alleged to be under British control. After Abdullah's death Jordan for a time tended towards closer relations with Iraq, chiefly because of her financial difficulties. At one moment Syria made overtures for some form of union with Iraq, but withdrew almost at once. Not only vested and other local interests stood in the way of union: the attitude of third states often constituted an obstacle. Egypt, as pretender to headship of the Arab world, looked with suspicion on any combination in which she had no part, while Saudi Arabia opposed any move that might strengthen the rival Hashimite dynasties in Baghdad and Amman.

The National Home and its Consequences

By the end of the Second World War it had become plain that the *status quo* could not continue in Palestine. During and after the war the eyes of thousands of Jews who had suffered from Nazi persecution were turned towards Palestine, not only as containing the Jewish National

[1] Hurewitz, ii. 245–9.

Home but as their only place of refuge, and their fellow Jews, eager to help them, were in revolt against British restrictions on immigration. Jewish demands enjoyed strong support in the United States, where both candidates for the Presidential election in 1944 supported the Zionist 'Biltmore' Programme, demanding that Palestine should become a Jewish state, and that unlimited Jewish immigration, under the control of the Jewish Agency, should be allowed. Terroristic acts against the mandatory authorities in Palestine, begun on a small scale by the Stern Gang in 1940, by the end of the war had reached serious proportions, while President Truman made repeated requests to the British Government to admit into Palestine forthwith 100,000 of the homeless Jews of Europe. The British Government tried unsuccessfully to reach agreement with the United States Government, with the Arabs, and with the Jews, and in February 1947 it referred the problem to the United Nations, to whom it gave warning on 26 September that if no settlement acceptable to both Jews and Arabs could be found it would plan for the early withdrawal of British forces and British administration from Palestine. A United Nations plan for partition of the territory was approved by the Assembly on 29 November, but the Arab States refused to accept it. On 14 May 1948 the British mandate was abandoned and the last of the British troops withdrew from Palestine. On the same day the State of Israel was proclaimed: it was recognized immediately by the United States, followed closely by the Soviet Union. On 15 May the forces of Egypt, Jordan, and Iraq began to invade Palestine. In spite of the efforts of the United Nations fighting did not finally stop until January 1949, while the signature of armistice arrangements between Israel on the one hand and Egypt, Jordan, Syria, and Lebanon on the other, was not completed until July. No peace treaty has followed. In 1950 a tripartite Declaration was issued by Britain, France, and the United States, expressing readiness to supply the Arab States and Israel with arms for internal security and self-defence and to take action, 'both within and outside the United Nations', to prevent the violation by force of any Middle East frontier or armistice line. In November 1950 the Arab League decided to continue the war-time blockage of Israel, on the ground that an armistice did not constitute a state of peace.

The failure to resolve this conflict has been the root cause of the chronic violence and instability which are regarded as characteristic of the Middle East. It is the principal reason for the growth of anti-Western feeling in the Arab countries as two Western powers—Britain and the United States—were held to be chiefly responsible for the creation of Israel. In particular no solution has been found for the tragic condition of the Palestinian Arab refugees who numbered about 900,000 in 1949. Through natural growth and the addition of new refugees in the 1967 Arab–Israeli War their number now exceeds

1·5 million. A resolution of the Assembly of the United Nations, passed on 11 December 1948, that refugees wishing to return to their former homes in Israel should be allowed to do so, has remained a dead letter, the Israelis arguing that the resolution cannot be considered by itself but in connection with a general settlement. Apart from the refugees, about 400,000 Palestinian Arabs acquired Jordanian citizenship when the West Bank of Jordan was joined to Transjordan to form the Hashimite Kingdom of Jordan following the 1948–9 Arab–Israeli War. Some few thousand more have acquired the citizenship of Lebanon, Kuwait, United States, Canada, Australia, or other countries to which they have emigrated but Palestinian national consciousness has not disappeared. If anything it gained in intensity following the 1967 war.

Middle East Defence and the West

What came to be called the Truman Doctrine was first set forth in Truman's address to Congress on 12 March 1947, in which he asked for authority to furnish aid to Greece and Turkey (which Britain could no longer give) to assist them to maintain their integrity and independence. This policy, in which Iran was soon included, can be explained by reference to the attitude of the Soviet Government as shown by the secret Soviet–German negotiations of 1940 (revealed by captured German documents), when the Soviet Union demanded, as part of the price of adherence to the Axis, bases near the Straits, and recognition of a wedge of territory from the Caucasus towards the Persian Gulf as the centre of Soviet aspirations; by the Soviet demand for bases near Istanbul, addressed to the Allies at Potsdam and then to Turkey; by the support of the 'autonomy' movements in Azarbaijan and Kurdistan; and by the retention of Soviet troops in Iran for more than two months after the treaty date, in order to obtain oil rights from the Iranian Government. These facts remained although the Soviet Union was now operating more discreetly, through her diplomatic missions established in 1943 in Egypt and in 1944 in Iraq, Syria, and Lebanon, and through the Russian Orthodox Church in the Middle East whose properties she had taken over after the Second World War.

The Doctrine provided support for the 'northern tier', but behind that lay the mass of Arab countries thinking of defence as defence against Zionism. Such unity of feeling as there was seemed to be strong only against Israel, whose victory over the Arab States dealt it a severe blow. No Arab state could claim the leadership: Egypt, the strongest and the most advanced, had done particularly badly in the war against Israel. Nevertheless the nationalism which had begun at the turn of the century was growing, fed from inside by the French episodes in Syria in 1943 and 1945 and by problems such as Israeli and

British relations with Egypt, and encouraged from outside by the attainment of independence by India and other former British territories. The demonstrations in Iraq against the abortive Treaty of Portsmouth in January 1948 owed something to local grievances against the Iraqi Government, but much more to nationalism. The time was propitious for fresh advances towards independence, and Britain concluded two agreements with Egypt: on self-government and self-determination for the Sudan (12 February 1953), and on the Suez Canal base (19 October 1954). In the Sudan the momentum was so great that the possibility of union with Egypt was eventually rejected for complete independence.

The Baghdad Pact

In the early 1950s the Western countries had not abandoned hope of including the Middle East in an anti-Soviet defence system. Already in 1951, the Wafd Government had rejected a proposal that Egypt should join with Britain, France, the United States, and Turkey in a Middle East Defence Organization. By 1953 the US Secretary of State J. F. Dulles had decided that such an organization was not immediately feasible, but he believed that he had detected in the northern tier of states a greater awareness of danger. It was therefore with American encouragement that the Turkey–Pakistan agreement of 1954 was concluded, and the United States then entered into two agreements: with Iraq for military assistance (21 April 1954) and with Pakistan for mutual assistance (19 May 1954). Nasser, the new leader of republican Egypt, was strongly opposed to any Arab country joining such a pact because he believed that a Western alliance meant the perpetuation of Western influence. However, his efforts to dissuade Nuri Said, the veteran pro-Western and anti-Communist leader of Iraq from joining were in vain. Iraq signed with Turkey on 24 February 1955 an agreement which came to be called the Baghdad Pact. It received on 5 April the adherence of Britain, happy to be able to exchange the treaty of 1930 with Iraq for an arrangement for the reactivation of bases in time of war similar to that embodied in the 1954 agreement with Egypt. Pakistan joined on 23 November, Iran on 3 November. Through Turkey the Baghdad Pact had a link with NATO, through Pakistan with SEATO.

From then on the Arab states were bitterly divided, but the weight of articulate Arab opinion was on Nasser's side. A conservative minority in Syria and King Hussein of Jordan would have favoured joining the Baghdad Pact but they were prevented by a wave of popular hostility supported by increasingly effective Egyptian propaganda. In Saudi Arabia the royal family was opposed to the Baghdad Pact because it feared any increase in the power of its Hashimite enemies reigning in Iraq and Jordan.

The Growth of Arab Neutralism

The dispute between Nasser and his allies in the Arab world on the one hand and the Baghdad Pact countries and their Western allies on the other rapidly grew more serious. Nasser had strong popular support for his policies but Egypt's military weakness had been exposed, on 28 February 1955, by a sudden and heavy bout of fighting with Israel at Gaza. Nasser was aware that Israel was receiving secret arms supplies from France. He still hoped to obtain new arms from Britain and the United States but having failed he turned to the Soviet Union which proved more responsive, and in September 1955 he announced a large-scale purchase of Soviet arms through Czechoslovakia.

Nasser's neutralism (which for him meant cutting Egypt's former ties with the West) gained a new dimension with the Bandung Conference in April 1955 and was further strengthened by his close relations with Premier Nehru of India and President Tito of Yugoslavia. At the same time his relations with the West rapidly worsened and by July 1956 he had become both the West's *bête noire* and the hero of the Arab masses. The Suez affair of July–October 1956, which followed the West's abrupt withdrawal of aid for the Nile High Dam and Nasser's reaction in nationalizing the Suez Canal Company, increased Nasser's hold on Arab public opinion but temporarily divided the Western Powers as the United States opposed the Anglo-French–Israeli action against Egypt. United States pressure helped to secure an Anglo-French withdrawal from the Suez Canal area and an Israeli withdrawal from Sinai and Gaza.

Britain and France's collusion with Israel in the Suez affair served to destroy much of what remained of these two countries' direct political influence in the Arab world. Nasser's diplomatic triumph added to his popularity with the Arab masses which reached its climax with the declaration of the Syrian–Egyptian union in February 1958. In July 1958 the anti-Western trend swept away Nuri Said and the Iraqi monarchy and destroyed the last possibility of including a major Arab state in the West's defence system.

The United States rapprochement with Egypt over the Suez affair was short-lived as the United States Government became alarmed at growing Soviet influence in the Middle East and the Nasserist threat to conservative pro-Western elements in the Arab world. The United States response took the form of a message to Congress from President Eisenhower on 5 January 1957 embodying what came to be called the Eisenhower Doctrine. After stressing the economic and strategic importance of the Middle East area to the West, the message called for joint action by President and Congress to authorize action in regard to the Middle East designed to assist the development of economic strength for the maintenance of national independence; to undertake upon request programmes of military assistance and co-operation; and to secure and protect the territorial integrity and political independence of such nations requesting such aid against overt aggression from any nation 'controlled by international Communism'.

From 1947 onwards the United States had become increasingly involved in Middle East affairs and this trend continued. In 1957 it gave assistance to King Hussein of Jordan in his struggle with his own left-wing opposition, under the terms of the Eisenhower Doctrine and in July 1958 landed troops in Lebanon during this country's muted civil war when the Iraqi Revolution raised fears that all remaining pro-Western elements in the Middle East might be swept away. But the United States' relations with the Arab countries were generally unsatisfactory. Initially, and especially while Mr. Dulles was the US Secretary of State, this was partly due to United States distaste for Arab neutralism in the Cold War but the primary underlying cause has been the United States' enthusiastic diplomatic support for Israel backed by large-scale military and economic aid. Periods of improved relations between the United States and Egypt, founded on a United States belief, in Nasser's lifetime, that Egypt could be a moderating and anti-Communist influence in the Middle East, always proved to be short-lived. Pro-US Arab regimes (such as Lebanon, Jordan, and Saudi Arabia) found it increasingly difficult and dangerous to show their sympathies. Some Arab governments, such as the Syrian and Iraqi, expressed the view after the 1967 war that there was no possibility of any future compromise with the United States since it would always side with Israel. Others, however, including the Egyptian, still hoped that the United States would adopt a more 'even-handed' policy between Arabs and Israelis and based their policies on the assumption that no Middle East settlement was possible without United States participation.

For similar but opposite reasons the Soviet Union has made immense political gains in the Middle East since 1950. Stalin's successors, having abandoned the idea of trying to work through the weak and divided Arab Communist parties, have based their policy on close co-operation with nationalist and non-aligned Arab governments—especially the Egyptian and Syrian. Apart from the building of the High Dam, it has a large and growing economic stake in the Arab countries through its aid for industrialization and the economic infrastructure and it has become the principal supplier of arms to Egypt, Syria, Iraq, and Sudan. The Soviet Union has unarguably established itself as a Middle East Power (like Russia in the nineteenth century) and no political settlement in the area is conceivable without its involvement. These gains have just as clearly brought disadvantages. The Arab states' failure to inflict a military defeat on Israel has caused a growing Soviet involvement in their defence which carries with it the danger of a military confrontation with the United States. Also the possibility of ideological friction with Arab Moslem states remains wherever Arab Communists are capable of making a bid for power (as in Iraq in 1958–9 or Sudan in 1971). Soviet relations with the northern tier states, especially Iran, have improved considerably since the early 1960s.

Following the collapse of the Baghdad Pact in 1958, Britain's military role in the Middle East was restricted to its membership of the Pact's successor the Central Treaty Organization (CENTO) (which has increasingly concentrated on its non-military aspects of communications and economic co-operation), and the military bases in Aden and the Persian Gulf. With the abandonment of these in 1968 and 1971 respectively, British interests in the area, although considerable, were largely economic and commercial and its political influence was negligible.

With the ending of the Algerian War in 1962, France's bad relations with the Arab countries steadily improved and its former close alliance with Israel simultaneously deteriorated. France remained Israel's principal arms supplier until the 1967 war but President de Gaulle's arms embargo, maintained by his successors, and French criticism of Israel's continued occupation of Arab territory, both improved France's image in the Arab world and jeopardized Franco-Israeli relations. While there has been no question of France recovering its former political influence in the Levant, it has gained clear commercial advantages in the Arab countries and traditional French cultural influence in the area has been intensified.

Arab Disunity

The high hopes of Arab nationalists which were raised by Nasser's early successes and the creation of the Syrian–Egyptian union were soon disappointed. Rivalry between Kassem of Iraq and Nasser, between Baathists and Nasserists, and subsequently between Iraqi and Syrian Baathists meant that even the Arab 'progressive' camp was divided. Egypt's support for the Yemeni republicans against the royalists in 1962–7 sharpened the differences between conservatives and radicals and carried the struggle into the Arabian Peninsula. Nasser's efforts from January 1964 onwards to soften the divisions and create a unified Arab front against Israel's plans to divert the waters of the River Jordan to the Negev were only superficially successful. The Unified Arab Command which the Arab Heads of State set up at their summit meetings in 1964 proved worthless because of political mistrust and the Palestine Liberation Organization they created under the leadership of Ahmad Shukairy was an act of inter-Arab political compromise which cost the Arabs dearly in terms of world opinion. Conservative-radical differences reached their height in 1966 with the efforts of King Faisal of Saudi Arabia to create an informal alliance or Islamic Front against Arab socialism.

The results of the 1967 Arab–Israeli War did something to reduce the inter-Arab conflict. A compromise was reached over Yemen and three Arab monarchies—Saudi Arabia, Kuwait, and Libya—joined to provide aid for Egypt but the creation of a common military strategy, which alone could enable the Arab countries to match Israel's military power, remained unattainable. In particular, Jordan's bad relations with both Syria and Iraq prevented the establishment of a solid northern front against Israel.

The formation of the Syrian–Egyptian–Libyan federation in September 1971 raised few optimistic hopes among Arabs and there were obvious difficulties in creating a sound and permanent federal structure to the union although previous unsuccessful experiments in Arab unity provided the means for avoiding past errors. The Arab League, which remained a loose association of states without any strong central authority, still provided the only framework for comprehensive Arab action. Its subsidiary agencies perform an important function in promoting inter-Arab cultural, technical, and economic co-operation.

The Palestinian Movement

Organized Palestinian Arab guerrilla activity, mainly based in Syria, had existed before 1967 but the June war gave the movement a wholly new impetus. Following the disastrous failure of the Arab armies, the Palestinian Arabs came to the conclusion that they must rely on their own efforts to liberate their lost territory. They received strong emotional sympathy and material support from Arab governments and individuals and they were rapidly successful in promoting and canalizing the Palestinian national consciousness which had remained partially dormant since 1949. The name Palestinian came to be world widely used. The publication of their aims as a 'democratic, secular state in which Moslems, Jews, and Christians could live together with equal status' gained them fresh support in many parts of the world. But their political success was not matched by their military achievements. Although their leadership lacked neither courage nor ability the extreme difficulty of the terrain and the lack of co-operation of the inhabitants of the occupied territories prevented them from posing a serious military threat to Israel. (Israeli casualties on the Suez front with Egypt in the years 1967–70 were considerably higher than in Jordan.) Moreover, the political success of the Palestinian organizations alarmed the governments of Jordan and Lebanon where the guerrillas began to act with unjustified over-confidence as a 'State within a State'. At the same time they failed to overcome their own disunity. The guerrillas were united in their broad aims and in their opposition to the UN Security Council Resolution 242 of 22 November 1967 calling for an Arab–Israeli territorial settlement, but a series of attempts between 1968 and 1970 to adopt a common military strategy and a united attitude towards the Arab regimes for all the various Palestinian organizations were only very partially successful. In particular the Maoist Popular Front for the Liberation of Palestine of Dr. George Habash refused to accept the leadership of the larger and more moderate al-Fatah organization headed by Yasir Arafat.

This disunity had fatal consequences for the guerrillas in the civil war with the Jordanian Army in September 1970, and the subsequent operations ended with the virtual liquidation of the movement in Jordan during the following year. In 1971 the Palestinian movement was in a seriously weakened position. Iraq, which had given them the strongest moral support failed to back it with practical action. Syria maintained its own guerrilla force al-Saiqa under strict military control and guerrilla operations against Israel were confined to the Lebanese border. In the occupied territories active resistance to the Israelis was confined to Gaza as the Arabs of the West Bank appeared to have resigned themselves, with reluctance and bitterness, to an indefinite Israeli occupation. There was little enthusiasm for an autonomous Palestinian State on the West Bank either from Israelis or Arabs, and following the events in Jordan of 1970–1 few Palestinians were anxious for a return to Hashimite rule.

Despite the apparent failure of the Palestinian resistance movement in the military field, it remained abundantly clear that there was no simple solution to the basic problem of the Middle East which left the Palestinians out of account. If there was no prospect of their obtaining all that their leaders demanded, they were in a position to ensure that there could be no lasting peace in the area without at least some satisfaction for the aspirations of the Palestinian Arabs.

The Future of the Gulf

While the Arab–Israeli dispute remained the most serious single cause of instability in the Middle East, Iranian–Arab rivalry in the Gulf area following the British withdrawal in 1971 was another potential source of disturbance. Iran was substantially the strongest political and military power in the area and some Arabs feared Iranian expansionism. The settlement of the status of Bahrain in 1970 removed a major source of friction but Iran's claim to three Arab islands in the Straits of Hormuz remained. There were better prospects for reaching a satisfactory accommodation between Iran and Saudi Arabia, Kuwait, and the smaller Arab shaikhdoms than between Iran and the Iraqi Baathist regime which held strong views on the Arabism of the Gulf. Iraq had its own disputes with Iran over navigation rights in the Shatt al-Arab and Iran's alleged support for dissident movements among Iraqi Kurds and Shiis.

Islam and the Arabs

Islam, an Arabic word originally meaning 'submission' (to the will of God), is used in two senses: first, the religion of those who believe in the mission of Mohammed as the final revelation of God's will to humanity, and in the Koran as the Word of God vouchsafed to mankind through Mohammed; and second, the social, cultural, legal, and political system that has grown up around that religion.

Mohammed, who died in AD 632, was an Arab of the family of Hashim, belonging to Quraish, the tribe which occupied Mecca, then a centre of the caravan trade and also of pilgrimage to the Kaaba, the palladium containing a meteoric black stone, long an object of pagan worship and still revered by Moslems at the present day. According to tradition, Mohammed received his first revelation when he was about forty years of age. The Meccans, fearing the loss of the profitable pagan cult centred on their shrine, opposed the new prophet and persecuted his followers, and in AD 622 Mohammed accepted an invitation from the people of Yathrib, thereafter known as al-Madina, 'the City', to settle among them as arbitrator and leader. The Moslem era is reckoned from the beginning of the Arab lunar year in which this migration (*Hijra*) took place. In Medina the Prophet established the first Moslem state which, under his successors the Caliphs (Arabic *khalifa*, deputy), grew into a vast empire.

The chief sources of Islamic doctrine and law are: (1) the Koran, the collected revelations of God to Mohammed, believed by Moslems to be the literal word of God; (2) the *Sunna*, or practice of the Prophet, who is believed to have been divinely inspired in all his deeds and sayings. These were therefore handed down by oral tradition (*hadith*), and later collected and given an authority second only to that of the Koran. From these two sources, supplemented in the course of time from other sources, by means of 'reasoning by analogy' (*Qiyas*) and Consensus (*Ijma*) a complete rule of life and a complex social and legal system were evolved. The Holy Law (*Sharia*) deals with constitutional, civil, and criminal matters as well as with cult, ritual, and belief, and is in strict Moslem theory the only legally valid code. It has, however, from early times suffered the competition of customary and state-made law, and is today displaced from many fields of jurisdiction by secular codes of European type.

The Islamic faith is a strict monotheism. Moslems recognize the divine origin of the Old and New Testaments, and are bidden to tolerate Jews and Christians, as possessors of a divine revelation, albeit an incomplete one. Both are believed to have falsified their scriptures, which are superseded by the Koran, the final revelation granted to the last and greatest of the prophets. Pagans and polytheists must be given the choice of Islam, slavery, or the sword.

Islam has no priesthood, but the *ulema*[1] are the authorized interpreters of the Koran and of its application to everyday life. The body of *ulema* supply the *muftis*, who are officially charged to give *fatwas*, or rulings on problems of doctrine and law, and the *qadis*,[2] or judges, who administer the *Sharia*. Islam has a body of observances of which the five most important are called 'the pillars of Islam'. These are: the profession of faith, contained in the formula 'There is no god but God and Mohammed is His Prophet'; prayer, consisting chiefly of the five daily ritual prayers which the believer must perform, wherever he finds himself, facing in the direction of Mecca, and prayers in the mosque on Fridays (the Moslem day of public worship)[3] and festivals; alms; fasting, obligatory for all believers during the whole month of Ramadan, from daybreak until sunset, and comprising total abstinence from food, drink, perfumes, tobacco, and conjugal relations (exemptions are provided in case of illness, travel, holy war, etc.); pilgrimage, the ceremonial visit to the holy places of Mecca (where the pre-Islamic shrine of the Kaaba remains the sacred centre of Islam) performed on a certain (*Hijra*) date every year, and expected of all believers who can afford it at least once in their lives. Among the tenets of Islam are circumcision, abstention from alcohol, a ban on certain kinds of meat such as pork, and on gambling and usury. An important part is played in all Moslem countries by the system of *waqfs* (Arabic pl. *awqaf*), or endowments for pious purposes, the administration of which is sometimes in the hands of special ministries.

Sects

The sects of Islam originated in the disputes over the succession to the Prophet after his death. They subsequently acquired a rather greater significance, which however in modern times they appear to be losing in many areas. The main division is between the Sunnis and the Shiis. The Sunnis are the followers of the *Sunna*—the practice of the Prophet, and they recognize the orthodox Caliphs. They form the great majority of Moslems in almost all countries. They are divided into four legal schools, recognized as equally orthodox: Hanafi, Shafii, Hanbali, Maliki. The Shafii school predominates in the Arabic-speaking countries of the Middle East, except for Upper Egypt and the Sudan,

---

[1] Arabic *'ulemā*, plur. of *'ālim*, learned. In Turkey they are called *Hoja*, in Iran and India *mulla* (maula), or master.

[2] The title *qadi* is used differently in Yemen.

[3] It is only in modern times, and under Christian influence, that Friday has become a weekly day of rest

which are Maliki, and Saudi Arabia, which is Hanbali. The Hanafi
school is strongest among the Turks, but also has many followers in
Syria and Iraq.

Within Sunni Islam there are many forms of faith which, though not
condemned as heretical, are aberrant and regarded with suspicion by
the *ulema*. Such are the Sufi fraternities (*tariqa*), professing a more
mystical and intuitive kind of religion, often associated with the worship
of local saints and other local superstitions and customs. At the opposite extreme are the puritanical and fundamentalist Wahhabis, followers of the eighteenth-century Nejdi teacher Mohammed ibn Abdul
Wahhab. Wahhabism is the state religion of Saudi Arabia.

The Shiis take their name from the party of Ali (*Shiat Ali*)—those
who believed that on the death of Mohammed he should have been
succeeded by his son-in-law and cousin Ali. Subdivided into numerous
sub-sects, they have in common a belief that the succession was
reserved to the direct descendants of Mohammed through his daughter
Fatima and her husband Ali. The successor, or Imam, who was also the
infallible interpreter of Islam, was generally nominated by the previous
Imam from among his sons.

The many Shii sects may be broadly divided into two groups,
moderate and extreme. The moderate sects are:

(*a*) The Twelvers (Ithna asharis or Imamis), by far the largest and
most important Shii group, believe that there were twelve Imams—
Ali, Hasan, Hussein, and nine in line of descent from Hussein—of
whom the twelfth, Mohammed, born in 873, disappeared mysteri-
ously. They believe that the Imam is only 'hidden' and will reappear as the Mahdi (the rightly guided) to establish the golden age.
Imamism is today the state religion of Iran. It has a considerable
following in Iraq, and a smaller one in parts of Syria and Lebanon,
where its adherents are known as Matawila.

(*b*) The Zaidis, the most moderate, admit the election of Imams
and take their name from a grandson of Hussein whom they recognized as Imam. Their doctrine differs very little from that of the
Sunnis. Zaidism is the state religion of Yemen.

The extremist sects are:

(*a*) The Ismailis, who take their name from Ismail, a son of the
sixth Imam. The Ismailis are subdivided into several groups and
have their main centres at the present day in India. In the Middle
East they are represented by minorities in the Yemen, in central
Syria, and in eastern and north-eastern Iran. The Iranian and some
of the Syrian Ismailis belong to that branch of the sect that is headed
by the Aga Khan, and known in India as Khojas.

(*b*) The Druzes, another occult sect, are an offshoot of the Ismailis,
from whom they parted company in the early eleventh century,
when they accepted the Fatimid Caliph Hakim as the final in-

carnation of the Deity. They are to be found only in parts of Syria, Lebanon, and Israel.

(c) The Alawis (also called Nusayris) carry the Shii tendency to its ultimate extreme and believe that Ali was an incarnation of God Himself. They are to be found in the coastal highlands of northern Syria, and also in the adjoining Turkish provinces.

(d) The Ahl i-haqq profess similar doctrines and are to be found in western Iran and eastern Turkey.

Two other groups which belong neither to Sunni nor to Shii Islam are:

(a) The Kharijites (khawarij = seceders), in early days an important sect in Islam, surviving today only in the Ibadi communities of Algeria and Zanzibar, and in Oman, where Ibadism is the state religion.

(b) The Yazidis, described by their neighbours as devil-worshippers. Their religion is rather a denial of the existence of evil; it seems to be an amalgam containing pagan, Zoroastrian, Manichaean, Jewish, Christian, Moslem, Sabaean, and Shamanistic elements. They are to be found in north-eastern Syria, in the Jabal Sinjar area of Iraq, and in the Caucasus.

The 'Legacy of Islam'[1]

The first Arab rulers made extensive use of Iranian, Syrian, Christian, and Jewish engineers, technicians, and doctors, and from Abbasid times began consciously to encourage learning and the arts. The Caliph al-Mansur (754–75), who founded Baghdad, employed large numbers of astronomers, engineers, and scholars. A need was soon felt for the translation into Arabic of Greek and other scientific and philosophic works. Many of these translations were made not from the originals but from Syriac versions. A pioneer in this development was the great patron of scholarship and science, the Caliph al-Mamun (813–33), who also founded the Arab university system. The encouragement of science and learning came to be a regular part of the functions of a Caliph, and distinguished scholars were attached to the courts of different Moslem rulers of Africa and Spain as well as in the East. By its union of Hellenic with Iranian and Indian scientific traditions, and by the transmission of Hellenic thought, Islam performed what is often regarded as its most important service to the world, though there are hardly any sciences to which it did not also make important original contributions. During the pre-Renaissance period in Europe it was to Arabic sources that Europeans turned in their attempts to rediscover the scientific heritage of Greece and Rome, and the improvement which the Arabs were able to introduce into

[1] Sir Thomas Arnold, ed., The Legacy of Islam (London, 1931).

mathematics by the use of a simplified system of notation of Indian origin was of critical importance in European intellectual development. Islamic medicine was also of great significance. Some leading names were Hussein ibn Ishaq (809–77), the great Baghdad translator, who was also a physician; al-Khwarizmi (d. *c.* 840), the astronomer and mathematician; al-Razi (Rhazes: *c.* 865–925), an Iranian, 'the greatest physician of the Islamic world and one of the great physicians of all time';[1] Ibn al-Haitham (Alhazen: *c.* 965), the physicist, whose work on optics was of the first importance; al-Kindi (b. *c.* 850) who made contributions to philosophy and a number of sciences; al-Battani (Albategnius: *c.* 900), the astronomer who made most impression on Europe; al-Farabi (d. *c.* 951), the Turkish philosopher, who also wrote a treatise 'On music'; Omar Khayyam (d. 1123), the Iranian mathematician and poet; Ibn Rushd (Averroës; d. 1198), 'among the very greatest of Aristotelian philosophers'; and Moses Maimonides (1135–1204), the Jewish physician and philosopher at the court of Saladin.

Minorities in the Islamic World[2]

The emergence of nationalism in the Islamic world had an adverse effect on the conditions of minorities. The use of minorities by great powers, particularly Russia, as an instrument of policy, and the corresponding tendency of such minorities to seek outside assistance against oppression or their communal enemies at home caused the 'atrocities'[3] which have aroused world opinion from time to time.

The victims of these persecutions sometimes achieved national independence themselves.[4] In other cases they found themselves in one of the new nation-states, no longer persecuted perhaps, but precariously situated, and deprived of the communal autonomy and immunities which the Christians and Jews had enjoyed under the *millet* system. Still worse, they might be split up among different states.

A minority is identified either by language, as in the case of the Kurds, or by religion, as in the case of the Copts and the Druze, or by both together, as in the case of the Armenians. While linguistic minorities have tended to become national in character, religious minorities have on the whole tended to become nationally assimilated to their chief linguistic group. In both cases, however, contrary tendencies have also been at work. The most difficult minorities have been those which had a special language, a special national church, and a past history of greatness, like the Armenians or the Jews. Here the

[1] Ibid.
[2] See A. H. Hourani, *Minorities in the Arab World* (London, 1947).
[3] e.g. the 'Bulgarian atrocities' of 1876 and the 'Armenian atrocities' of 1894 and 1915 in Turkey; or the Assyrian massacre of 1933 in Iraq.
[4] Greece, 1832; Rumania (autonomous principality), 1862; Serbia, 1878; Bulgaria (partial self-government), 1878; Montenegro, 1878.

new nationalism merely stimulated a sense of nationality which was already present.

Armenians

The Armenians are the descendants of a people who have had a continuous national existence in Transcaucasia, between the Black Sea and the Caspian, since the sixth century BC. The language, Armenian, is an independent member of the Indo-European family. Armenia had a long tradition of self-government under its own rulers in different relations of vassalage to Iran or Rome, with periods of independence and even conquest.[1] King Tiridates III established Christianity as the state religion in AD 303. The Armenian Church developed independently of the other Christian Churches. In the fifteenth century the Armenians were given *millet* status by the Ottoman Sultan, under the Armenian Patriarch of Constantinople.[2] In the nineteenth century they became involved in the southward expansion of Russia which by 1828 had absorbed considerable parts of Turkish and Iranian Armenia.

In the second half of the nineteenth century Armenian nationalist groups began to form in Istanbul and elsewhere, some with revolutionary aims, and acts of violence were committed. In 1895 the Turks tried to repress the movement by a series of massacres. The position of the Armenians improved after the 1908 revolution, until the liberation and independence of Armenia were proclaimed as one of the Allied war aims when the Russians invaded eastern Turkey in the First World War. In the months of June and July 1915 the Turkish authorities undertook a systematic massacre and expulsion of the Armenian population of Turkey which remained outside Constantinople. After the Russian revolution the Armenians of Transcaucasia, under the auspices of German military leaders and with Turkish compliance, proclaimed their independence. In the abortive Treaty of Sèvres (August 1920) this independence was recognized by the Powers. But in the meanwhile the Kars and Batum districts had been restored to Turkey by the Bolsheviks in the Treaty of Brest Litovsk, and the Turks and Bolsheviks re-entered Transcaucasia. A Soviet Armenian Government was established at Erivan in December 1920. This is Armenia today, a small territory which has achieved a measure of prosperity and cultural development as a constituent part of the Soviet Union. Outside Soviet Armenia there are communities of varying sizes in a number of Middle East countries. Those of Syria and Lebanon are the largest. Some of them hope for a return to a really independent Armenia. Their views find expression in the Tashnak Society, which was originally founded at Tiflis in 1890. But some Armenians prefer the

[1] Notably under King Tigranes I (*c.* 94–56 BC) who for a while ruled on the Seleucid throne at Antioch.
[2] The Armenian *millet* was laicized by the reforms of 1863.

prospect of autonomy within the Soviet Union, and after 1945 a number of those in the Middle East returned there.

Assyrians

The Assyrians are Nestorian Christians speaking a form of Syriac. At the outbreak of the First World War they were living in three main groups: in the Hakkiari highlands of south-eastern Turkey, the plains to the west of Lake Urmiya in north-west Iran, and the lowlands to the south of the Hakkiari district, now part of Iraq. 'In their mountain-home they lived as shepherds, feudally organized under their *maliks* with their Patriarch, the Mar Shimun, as their temporal as well as spiritual ruler.'[1] During the war the Hakkiari Assyrians revolted under Russian instigation against the Turks. They were expelled and joined the Urmiya Assyrians and the Russians. After the collapse of Russia they fled, and the British military authorities disarmed them and sent them to the refugee camp at Baquba near Baghdad. In 1919 there were 25,000 of them there. The frontier settlement of 1925 assigned almost the whole of the Hakkiari highlands to Turkey, so that it was impossible for the majority of them to return home. A great deal was done to resettle them in Iraq, and many were recruited by the British (during the mandatory period) into the Assyrian Levies to guard aerodromes and police the tribes—tasks which did not increase their popularity. A section of them led by the Mar Shimun were intransigent and petitioned to leave Iraq or to be granted autonomy there. After Iraq had become an independent member of the League and accepted as a member an obligation to protect her minorities, a clash occurred on 4 August 1933 between Iraqi troops and some Assyrians who had crossed the Tigris into Syria and then tried to return under arms. The Assyrians were repulsed and the Iraqi army then organized a massacre of unarmed Assyrians at Simel. About 600 were killed here and in other places, and sixty Assyrian villages were looted. Their spirit broken, about 6,000 Assyrians crossed over into Syria, where they have since been settled, while those who remained in Iraq have not been involved in further incidents.[2]

Kurds

A people with an ancient history, of mountain origin, speaking an Indo-European group of dialects (Kurdish) related to Persian, the Kurds inhabit an arc stretching from Kermanshah in Iran across the north-eastern corners of Iraq and Syria, to Kars and Erzerum in Turkey, just crossing the western frontier of Soviet Armenia, and from there south-west as far as Birjik. Many are now plain-dwellers and

---

[1] Hourani, *Minorities in the Arab World*, p. 99.
[2] RIIA, *Survey of International Affairs, 1934*, pp. 135–74. Large numbers of Assyrians from Syria were again recruited into British levies during the Second World War.

townsmen, which has favoured the growth of nationalism in a group of communities which are still fundamentally tribal and disunited. The Kurds are mostly Sunni Moslems. The 1957 census in Iraq gave the Kurdish population of Iraq as 1·2 million. An estimate of their distribution elsewhere is Turkey, 2·5 million; Iran 1·4 million; Syria 250,000 and Soviet Transcaucasia 60,000 making a total of about 5·5 million.

The Treaty of Sèvres of 1920 between the Allies of the First World War recognized an independent Kurdish state of Kurdistan but this was cancelled by the Treaty of Lausanne of 1923. The Kurdish minorities have been in frequent conflict with the authorities, particularly in Turkey, Iraq, and Iran. During the period of Soviet-sponsored Azarbaijan autonomy in 1945–6, an independent Kurdish Republic was set up at Mahabad of which Zaki Mohammed was elected President on 22 January 1946. After the Iranian reoccupation of Azarbaijan, Zaki Mohammed was arrested, sentenced to death, and hanged on 31 March 1947. In Iraq there were Kurdish uprisings against the Government in 1922–3, 1931–2, 1944–5 and almost continuously throughout the 1960s following the return from exile in the Soviet Union of the Kurdish Democratic Party leader Mustafa Barazani. Fighting ended following the Iraqi Government's agreement with Barazani and his followers in March 1970 but it seemed unlikely that the Kurdish problem in Iraq had been finally settled.

Christian Communities:[1] *A. The Greek Orthodox and Western Churches*

The Orthodox Eastern Church is a group of autocephalous churches using the Byzantine rite. It comprises the four original Eastern Patriarchates, out of which it grew historically, and a number of national branches. Its adherents in the Middle East are nearly all Arab or Greek. The Eastern Patriarchates, which finally broke with the Western Church in AD 1054,[2] are Constantinople, Alexandria, Antioch, and Jerusalem. In addition there are the Church of Cyprus and the Church of Mount Sinai, consisting of little more than the monastery of St. Catherine.

The Oecumenical Patriarch at Constantinople enjoyed in Ottoman times almost the same exalted position as he had under the Byzantine Emperors. Modern Turkey has been persuaded to allow the Patriarchate to continue, though it is of much diminished importance. But it still has jurisdiction over the Greeks who have remained as Turkish subjects in Constantinople. In Greece the Church has been autocephalous since 1850.

The Patriarch of Alexandria, resident in Cairo, has a following of about 100,000 Arabs and Greeks. The Patriarchate of Antioch, with its

[1] Hourani, *Minorities in the Arab World*.
[2] They were excommunicated by Pope Leo IX. There was a brief period of reunion in the fifteenth century.

seat now at Damascus and some 300,000 members, is 'almost wholly Arab'[1] in hierarchy, laity, and liturgy. In the Patriarchate of Jerusalem, with 30,000 members, 'the upper clergy are Greek, the lower clergy and most of the laity Arab'.[2]

Roman Catholics, Anglicans, and Protestants. The Roman Catholics are subdivided into Roman Catholic and Uniate Churches. Roman Catholics of the Latin rite are ordinary members of the Church of Rome. They have a Roman Catholic (Latin) Patriarch in Jerusalem and Apostolic Delegates or Nuncios in Beirut, Cairo, and Baghdad. The Uniate Churches are those which have been allowed to retain their own Oriental rites and customs. They enjoy autonomy under their own elected Patriarchs. Those in the Middle East are:

1. The Greek Catholic Church (ex-Greek Orthodox). Greek liturgy; Patriarch of Alexandria, resident in Cairo.
2. The Syrian Catholic Church (ex-Syrian Orthodox). Syriac liturgy; Patriarch of Antioch, resident in Beirut.
3. The Armenian Catholic Church (ex-Armenian Orthodox). Armenian liturgy; Patriarch of Constantinople, resident near Beirut.
4. The Chaldean Catholic Church (ex-Nestorian). Syriac liturgy; Patriarch of Babylon, resident in Mosul.
5. The Coptic Catholic Church (ex-Coptic Orthodox). Arabic liturgy; it has a Patriarch of Alexandria resident in Cairo.
6. The Maronite Church (ex-Monothelete).[3] Syriac liturgy; Patriarch of Antioch, resident in Lebanon.

The Anglican Church, besides ministering to the British communities distributed throughout the Middle East, has a few thousand non-European baptized members, for whom it maintains colleges and schools.

The Protestants are converts made by English, Scottish, American, and other Protestant missions during the nineteenth and twentieth centuries. Though few in numbers, they have produced some leading intellectuals, notably through the medium of the American University at Beirut.

Christian Communities: B. The Oriental Churches

The Monophysites emphasized the single nature of Christ and rejected the Council of Chalcedon. Monophysite Churches in the Middle East are:

1. The Coptic Church in Egypt (of which the Ethiopian Church is a branch) has its own Patriarch of Alexandria (now resident in Cairo) and has a liturgy in Coptic and Arabic.

[1] Hourani, *Minorities in the Arab World.*
[2] Ibid.
[3] A modification of Monophysitism abandoned by the Maronites in the twelfth century.

2. The Syrian 'Orthodox' Church (Jacobite Church), organized under a Patriarch of Antioch (resident in Homs), which has a Syriac liturgy.

The Armenians, accounted Monophysites, disclaim Monophysitism and should perhaps be listed with the Greek Orthodox. The Armenian Orthodox ('Gregorian') Church, the national Church of the Armenians, dates from the fourth century.

The Nestorians stress Christ's dual nature. The Church grew up in the fifth century in Syria, Mesopotamia, and Iran and sent missions across Asia as far as China. It was largely destroyed by the Mongol invasions of the fourteenth century and today the Assyrians are all that remain.

ECONOMIC AND SOCIAL

Many elements of similarity still run through the economic and social life of the Middle East. Because of the dominance of the desert and the seasonal concentration of water, there has evolved a three-fold agricultural pattern of irrigation, dry farming, and nomadic pastoralism. In Ottoman times most of the region was subjected to the same economic and commercial politics.

Many of these basic similarities remain despite the strong forces of social and economic change which accompanied the political awakening at the end of the nineteenth century. In some parts of the Middle East this awakening was long delayed. Yemen and Oman were isolated and virtually immune to the forces of change until recent years. But when changes have come they have all tended in the same direction. Beirut on the Mediterranean may seem a thousand years apart from Muscat, the Omani capital, on the Indian Ocean but when Oman was opened to the world in 1970 one of the first new buildings to be constructed in Muscat was a Lebanese type of luxury hotel.

Two factors, which are interrelated, have accelerated the changes and established the pattern they have taken. One is the rapid increase in the output and profits of the Middle East oil industry and the other is the strong nationalist tide which has caused the Middle Eastern states to seek to match their political sovereignty with economic power and independence through industrialization and the development of their resources.

The immense increase in oil revenues has enabled some of the Middle Eastern oil-producing states with small populations, such as Kuwait, Qatar, and Abu Dhabi, to transform themselves socially and economically in less than a generation despite their lack of other resources. Through the oil industry Saudi Arabia has achieved power and political influence out of all proportion to its natural capabilities. Much of the oil wealth has spread and is spreading to other parts of the

Middle East through private investment, public investment (through
institutions such as the Kuwait Arab Development Fund) or government subsidies such as those paid to Egypt by Kuwait and Saudi
Arabia since 1967. All the present trends indicate that the growth in
oil revenues will continue and accelerate with the increase in demand
for oil and oil products from the non-oil-producing industrialized and
industrializing nations. With some 60 per cent of the world's crude-oil
reserves, the Middle Eastern countries are in a position to enhance their
economic power and importance until these reserves are exhausted.

Economic nationalism, like political nationalism, in the Middle
East, has usually meant reducing dependence on the West. The
process was first seen most clearly in Egypt in 1956 with the take-over
of the still considerable French and British interests which was followed shortly afterwards by the 'Egyptianization' of the whole
economy. Syria and, more recently, Iraq and Sudan have followed
Egypt's example. In each case the trend has resulted in closer economic
ties with the Soviet Union and Eastern European states. Since the
Soviet Union undertook to help build the Nile High Dam in 1958
(following the withdrawal of the offer of Western aid) it has expanded
its relations with nearly all the Arab states as a trading partner and for
some it has become the major source of financial and technical aid
for their economic development programmes. Iran has also recently
increased its economic ties with the Soviet Union as a result of an
agreement to supply Soviet industry with large quantities of natural gas.

The impulse for Arab political unity has been reflected in the
economic field but is hampered by the lack of complementarity
between the economies of the Arab states. An Economic Unity Agreement was signed in 1962 by Jordan, Egypt, Morocco, Kuwait, and
Syria and later adhered to by Yemen, Iraq, and Sudan. The aims were
similar to those of the EEC: the abolition of internal tariffs and the
complete freedom of movement of labour and capital. Another agreement establishing an Arab Common Market was signed in 1965 by
Egypt, Jordan, Iraq, Kuwait, and Syria. Yemen and Sudan have since
adhered to this agreement but the Kuwait National Assembly voted
against ratification. Considerable progress has been made towards
reducing tariffs between members but freedom of movement of labour
and capital remains a more distant goal.

The members of CENTO have concentrated heavily on strengthening the economic links between them and in 1964 Iran, Turkey, and
Pakistan set up RCD (Regional Co-operation for Development) with
headquarters in Tehran. Its most notable achievement has been the
completion in September 1970 of a 212-mile link between the Turkish
and Iranian rail networks with a ferry across Lake Van. This provides
Mediterranean outlets for Iran and a direct rail link between Western
Europe and Tehran.

Agriculture

Agriculture and pastoralism are the basic economic activities and the major employers of the population in most Middle Eastern countries. The chief exceptions are Kuwait and the other small desert oil-producing states, Israel in which industry is now the major sector and Lebanon whose economy is dominated by trade and services. Nomadic pastoralism is gradually declining with the spread of irrigation and the efforts of governments to settle nomads on the land.

In general, the harsh environment has hindered cultivation, which is restricted to small areas imprisoned by vast stretches of desert and steppe. Outside the mountains annual rainfall totals are low and inconsistent. Moreover, the seasonal concentration of rainfall is restrictive; much falls in one or two months (during winter and early spring in the north), leaving the rest of the year virtually rainless. In Iraq, the rivers flood when additional water is least needed, i.e. in the spring.

Because of these climatic facts, irrigation and flood-control are of capital importance, particularly along the lower Nile and Tigris–Euphrates valleys and in the Gezira district of the Sudan. Modern methods of irrigation offer an escape from the severe droughts which frequently afflict the dry-farming areas and enable a wide range of summer crops to be grown—cotton, rice, vegetables, and others—besides the traditional winter staples of wheat and barley. Two or occasionally three crops a year can be grown on the same land. Silting greatly reduces the need for the long fallow periods characteristic of unirrigated fields. Hence irrigated zones are the most stable and intensive producers in the area.

Middle Eastern farming is still largely for local subsistence. Only in a few places like the lower Nile valley, the Lebanon, and the Shatt district of southern Iraq is there significant regional specialization. Elsewhere the overwhelming emphasis is on cereals—wheat, barley, maize, rice, millets, and others—and to a lesser extent fruit and vegetables, with commercial crops receiving much less attention.

Excluding petroleum, about 90 per cent of the Middle East's exports are agricultural. Turkey, Syria, and Iraq are small and fluctuating exporters of barley and wheat. Of the cash crops, cotton is exported mainly from Egypt, the Sudan, Syria, and Turkey, dates from Iraq and Iran, dried fruit from Turkey and Iran, citrus from Israel, many kinds of fruit from Lebanon, and tobacco from Syria and Turkey. Opium in Turkey, coffee in Yemen, and silk in Lebanon are of local and limited importance. Although the olive is by far the leading fruit tree in the northern half of the region, most of the fruit is consumed locally.

Productivity is very low. Nevertheless, in spite of natural hazards, unsatisfactory land-tenure systems, fragmentation of holdings, rural indebtedness, and other drawbacks, cultivation has improved in the last twenty years.

The two major irrigation schemes in the area are the Nile High Dam in Egypt (completed in 1971) and the Euphrates Dam in Syria (the first stage due for completion in 1974) but Iran, Turkey, Sudan, Iraq, Jordan, Israel, Lebanon, and Saudi Arabia have also extended the irrigated area through the building of dams. The main achievements of desert reclamation have been in Egypt and Israel.

Industry

Although agriculture remains the principal activity in the area, the share of industry is increasing in the economies of nearly all Middle Eastern states. The urge towards industrialization depends heavily on the relation between population and agricultural resources. It is less in Syria, Sudan, and Iraq where there are large areas of potentially cultivable land which are now unproductive than in Egypt where the limits of cultivation have nearly been reached and industrialization is an urgent necessity. The Egyptian manufacturing sector has expanded rapidly over the past decade and now accounts for over 20 per cent of GNP. In Lebanon light manufacturing industry is the fastest growing sector of the economy. The desert oil-producing states, such as Kuwait and Saudi Arabia, with their limited agricultural potential, see in industrialization a means of diversification to reduce their present dependence on crude-oil production but they are handicapped by the lack of a local labour force and their small domestic markets. Israel is a unique exception to all these considerations. For political reasons it is cut off from its natural markets and sources of fuel and raw materials but it receives massive external aid. Over the past ten to fifteen years it has developed a range of technically advanced industries and can no longer be included among the developing countries.

Social Change

The most significant social development in the Middle East since the Second World War has been the increase in size, importance, and political power of the new middle class at the expense of the traditional élite of kings, tribal shaikhs, and bourgeoisie.[1] In the more advanced areas the traditional élite has lost its political power or disappeared entirely as a consequence of agrarian reform, nationalization, and revolutionary changes in the political structure. Egyptian agrarian reform in 1952 was followed by similar measures in Syria and Iraq. In Iran a parallel 'White Revolution' has been conducted from the top. Even in the more backward areas, such as Yemen or Oman, the strength of tribalism has begun to decline.

[1] See Manfred Halpern, *The Politics of Social Change in the Middle East and North Africa*, Part II (Princeton, 1963).

In spite of agrarian reform, industrialization, and the adoption of various radical and socialist measures in Middle Eastern countries, industrial and agricultural workers and peasant farmers have only begun to enter the field of politics. While it is the declared intention of the Arab Socialist Union in Egypt (which is the model for similar organizations in Sudan and Libya) and the Baath Party in Syria and Iraq that these majority elements in society should participate in the political process, none of them has yet made it possible to any significant extent. On the other hand the 'new middle class' has gained steadily in power and influence. This bears little resemblance to the property-owning entrepreneurial Western middle class of the nineteenth century; it consists mainly of salaried administrators and 'technocrats'. Because of the increase in the scope and function of the state in most Middle Eastern countries, the great majority are working directly or indirectly for the Government. It is significant that even in Lebanon, which adheres closer to nineteenth-century economic principles than any other Middle Eastern state and where the traditional élite still largely dominates parliament, a government of young 'technocrats' from outside parliament was formed in 1970. The military is also a key element in this new middle class and army officers or ex-officers are playing a vital political role in the majority of Arab countries.

The secularization of the State and society is proceeding inexorably even in those countries where it can scarcely be seen to have begun. The areas of human activity covered by the Islamic *Sharia* law have already been reduced in most countries and even in the most traditional and conservative societies economic development has enforced the introduction of secular commercial codes. However, no Arab country has yet adopted a deliberate secularization policy comparable to that of Atatürk in the Turkish Republic and in every case, except Lebanon, Islam remains the official religion of the State. The latent strength of Islamic feeling among the masses in both town and countryside can scarcely be exaggerated. In many respects the Egyptian revolutionaries of 1952 were a secularizing force but many Egyptian intellectuals are impatient with the slow pace at which secular reforms have been introduced and the failure of a uniquely powerful regime to hasten the process. If anything, the pace of secularization has slowed down since the late President Nasser's death. The trials of the Moslem Brotherhood in Egypt in 1965 revealed how strong and widespread the movement remained not only among the poor and illiterate masses but among members of the new middle class. Egypt is no exception in this matter for the same phenomenon can be observed in all the Moslem states of the Middle East including Turkey where the secularization process has officially been carried furthest but where the 'Islamic backlash' has consequently been one of the most powerful.

A NOTE ON THE POSITION OF WOMEN IN THE MIDDLE EAST

The position of women in Arabia in pre-Islamic times is a subject of much dispute, Moslem accounts being at variance in some respects with the picture of society as painted in pre-Islamic poetry. It seems best therefore to begin with the provisions of Moslem law, based mainly on the Koran, which permit a Moslem to have four wives at any one time, besides as many other women 'as his right hand possesses', and to divorce a wife without her being able to divorce him. There are parts of the Arab world where these provisions are still held to be inviolable; in other parts, however, the position of women is being gradually improved.

In Turkey there is legal equality between the sexes, although in the remoter country regions social practice may lag behind the law. In Iran too the position of women has been greatly improved both by law and custom, but by a strange exception polygamy has been retained. At the other end of the scale from Turkish modernity is Saudi Arabia, where the status of women has hardly changed despite the spread of girls' education.

In most Arab countries of the Middle East, however, the position of women is improving, thanks partly to legal enactments, partly to social development. Important laws affecting the position of women have been passed, sometimes on the strength of an unusually liberal opinion attributed to one of a number of recognized authorities on religious law, sometimes going beyond even the most liberal of such opinions. All the reforms mentioned below have been introduced in one or more of the Arab countries: Syria, Lebanon, Jordan, Iraq, Egypt, and the Sudan. The provision that if a man divorces his wife by 'triple divorce' he cannot take her back unless in the meantime she has been married to someone else has been limited in its scope: if the divorce is a single pronouncement in the triple form, or even a threefold formula pronounced on one and the same occasion, it is now regarded as single and revocable. A woman may include in the marriage contract a clause, enforceable at law, that if the husband takes a second wife she may obtain a divorce from him. Divorce has been made much easier for the wife, who now has a right to claim a divorce if the husband fails to support her, deserts her or treats her intolerably, or contracts a dangerous disease. Moreover the court may forbid a man to take a second wife unless he can show that he is in a position to support two wives properly. An ingenious method of discouraging child marriages has been found. To forbid such marriages would be difficult because one of the Prophet's wives was very young at the time of her marriage, but this difficulty is circumvented by a law which provides that a marriage cannot be registered unless the bride is at least 16 and the bridegroom 18, and that the courts shall not entertain any suit relating to an unregistered marriage, except in the matter of legitimacy.[1]

Besides the changes brought about by law there are those resulting from the erosion of old customs.

The most important agent of change has been the general acceptance of the principle of Moslem girls' education. In Iran, Turkey, and most Arab countries this has led to the employment of women in factories, offices, and almost all branches of economic activity with a consequent increase in their freedom and independence. Women still wearing the veil are handling textile machinery in the Chinese-built factory in Sanaa, Yemen. It is only in parts of Arabia that the status of women has lagged behind the advance in their education. In Saudi Arabia most girls of the settled population go to school and a substantial number to university either at home or abroad, but a Saudi woman is still not permitted to drive a car. In Kuwait where education has been provided for all girls for nearly a generation the social freedom of women is still highly restricted although change is now coming rapidly. A Women's Liberation Movement in Arabia is still a distant prospect, but it is likely to come sooner than most Moslem males imagine.

B. Thematic Studies

1. THE ORIGINS OF THE PALESTINE PROBLEM

Before the First World War, Palestine was labelled desolate and barren by visitors; it was a neglected Turkish district run as to its southern half as the *sanjaq* of Jerusalem and as to its northern half as part of the *vilayet* of Beirut. There are no vital statistics for this area while under Turkish rule but its pre-war population is thought to have consisted of about 600,000 Arabs and about 80,000 Jews[2] most of whom were long-standing residents in holy cities and lived in the same poor conditions as their Arab neighbours. About 12,000 were different; they lived in agricultural 'colonies' which Western philanthropy and money had wrung out of the Sultan and which worked to establish the Hebrew language, a flourishing agriculture and Jewish culture in the land of the Return. Their pretensions were disliked by the Turks, who caused them to become Ottoman citizens; just before the war, a few

[1] J. N. D. Anderson, 'Law Reform in the Middle East', *International Affairs*, January 1956.
[2] Statistics for 1919 are given in the Peel Report (Cmd. 5479 of 1937) p. 23. The Jewish population had fallen during the war, because some left, as refugees, under American and other auspices (see N. Bentwich, *Palestine*, London, 1934, p. 80).

educated Arabs had begun to take exception to their exclusiveness.[1]

On the outbreak of war between Britain and Turkey, the one Jewish member of Asquith's Government, Herbert Samuel, drew attention in two successive memoranda to Jewish dreams of establishing a State in Palestine, to the drawback constituted by a non-Jewish majority, and to the advantage that Britain might derive from a protectorate over a grateful Jewish community on the east flank of the Suez Canal.[2] He was written off by Asquith as a dreamer. For biblical as well as imperial reasons, his ideas interested Lloyd George.

The imperialist aspect of his suggestion coincided with planning inside the War Office and India Office, both of which had been brought up on Kipling's 'great game' and the concept of eventual war with Russia. Were the Ottoman Empire to collapse, both departments recommended that Britain should seek a strip of British or British-controlled territory that might hold a railway from the Mediterranean to the Persian Gulf.[3] Later, the Admiralty put in a memorandum in the same vein, and the roving mind of its Director of Naval Intelligence, Captain Reginald Hall, added that 'the strong material and very strong political interest of the Jews in Palestine' was worth British consideration.[4]

The Zionists in Britain were unaware of these British calculations. They were an insignificant group by comparison with the phalanx of famous British Jews that formed the Conjoint Committee which had for forty years worked for better treatment of Jews in their countries of residence. Throughout 1915 and 1916 the Zionist leaders—Weizmann and Sokolow—were locked in combat with the Conjoint and seem to have reckoned that their moment would not come until the end of the war.[5]

Anomalously, therefore, it was not they but the Conjoint that the Foreign Office consulted when, in late 1915 and early 1916, it received from two quarters a suggestion that there would be propaganda advantage in a declaration to the Jews about Palestine. The first reached it from America, where well-wishers of Britain were seeking for means of diminishing American distaste for the allies of anti-semitic Russia. The second came from the head of the large Jewish colony in Alexandria. Since the idea dovetailed with British imperial desiderata,

[1] N. Mandel, 'Zionism and the Indigenous Population of Palestine, 1882–1914'. Unpublished thesis, Oxford University, 1965.
[2] The more important of his two memoranda is dated March 1915. Copy in the Samuel Papers, St. Antony's College, Oxford, ref. DR 588.25.
[3] Public Record Office (hereafter PRO) CAB/42/2/8 and 10 of 16 March 1915.
[4] FO 371/2767/938 of 12 February 1916.
[5] For the two best accounts of their thinking and on British aims see L. Stein's *The Balfour Declaration* (London, 1961); M. Verete 'The Balfour Declaration and its Makers', in E. Kedourie (ed.) *Middle Eastern Studies*, vol. 6 (London, 1970).

the Foreign Office talked with Lucien Wolf, a member of the Conjoint and an anti-Zionist; as an outcome of these conversations, Wolf drafted a formula. His draft mentioned the possibility of Jewish settlement in Palestine because he recognized that this was the line of greatest appeal to Jews in the United States. The Asquith Government forwarded this formula to France and Russia in March 1916, but it foundered on French objections; it did not fit in with French claims to Syria.

Towards the end of 1915, impending failure at Gallipoli caused the soldiers to ask for other means of harrying the Turks.[1] An obvious one was to foment an Arab rising, since the Arabs were known to resent the Young Turks' Ottomanization policy. On the basis of plans drafted in Cairo, the High Commissioner there was instructed by London to get into touch with the Sharif of Mecca, whose ambitious aim was Arab independence under himself and over a wide area. His demands did not tally with those of the French for predominance in Syria; therefore McMahon was sent by Grey and Kitchener a basic outline instructing him not to alienate the Arabs but not to create in France the impression 'that we were not only endeavouring to secure Arab interests but to establish our own in Syria at the expense of the French'.[2] (His director of Military Intelligence, Clayton, remarked to a friend that the Foreign Office 'in their usual way left several openings for making a scapegoat in the event of necessity, and there is many a man who would have funked it'.)[3] But McMahon, because a messenger was leaving for Mecca, did not funk it. With Clayton's help he evolved a draft in which he reckoned that he had included in the area of Arab independence only the regions 'wherein Great Britain is free to act without detriment to the interests of her ally France'.[4] Unfortunately, though he specified some of the excluded areas by name, he did not mention Palestine. That he thought he had covered it by his reservation about French interests, and that other Englishmen thought so too, is plain from a communication to him by his colleague Wingate, the Governor-General of the Sudan, who reported that he had discussed 'the frontier question' with his own intermediary with Mecca 'and pointed out the necessity for the reservations we have made in Syria, Palestine and Mesopotamia'.[5] Two days after McMahon's letter went off to Mecca, he

[1] McMahon in Wingate Papers, Durham University, Box 141/4.
[2] PRO FO/371/2486/7882 of 19 October 1915.
[3] Wingate Papers, loc. cit., Box 135/4. The best secondary source on these events is Elie Kedourie 'Cairo, Khartoum and the Arab Question', in *The Chatham House Version and other Middle Eastern Studies* (London, 1970), pp. 13–32. See also Isaiah Friedman, 'The McMahon–Hussein correspondence and the Question of Palestine', in *Journal of Contemporary History*, V, 2, April 1970.
[4] Text of McMahon's letter of 24 October 1915 in Hurewitz, ii, pp. 14–15.
[5] Wingate Papers, loc. cit., Box 135/5.

told Grey that he had left latitude in the matter of French claims because he was unaware of their extent.[1]

The mystery is less what Britain meant to say,[2] than why she behaved for twenty years as if she had something to hide, and refrained from publishing the McMahon letter and the inter-departmental remarks that suggested what he had meant. A possible explanation is that until the Arab Rebellion of 1936–8 Britain tried to insulate her Palestine policy from pressures outside Palestine;[3] this consideration was outdated by the time Britain first published the letters[4] which she did, with some but not all of the supporting evidence, in 1939.

The main stumbling block in the way of British imperial desiderata was this French claim to the whole of Syria. To settle it, negotiation by a Francophile with a knowledge of the area was desirable, and for this task the Government's choice was Sir Mark Sykes, a Kitchener disciple who had a way with him, and who was fresh from a trip to the Middle East during which he had criticized a 'Fashoda spirit' in Cairo. 'It is most important', he told the Cabinet on return, 'that we should have a belt of English-controlled country between the Sherif of Mecca and the French.'[5] Yet when he embarked on his famous negotiations with France's negotiator Picot he came up against unshakeable French determination. The best bargain that he could get was French agreement to a British enclave at Haifa, and to international management in the part of Palestine that was dubbed 'the brown area' because so coloured on their map.

Before Sykes and Picot set out for Petrograd to clear their arrangement with the Russians, the Foreign Office had received the Wolf draft, Hall had mentioned the Jews in his comment on the Sykes–Picot draft, and Samuel had shown Sykes his 1916 memorandum.[6] At the time when the two men reached Petrograd, the proposal about the

[1] Wingate Papers, loc. cit., Box 135/4. Professor Arnold Toynbee, who was working in the Foreign Office on these papers in 1918, and with McMahon personally in 1919 on the proposed Middle Eastern settlement, argues in the *Journal of Contemporary History* (V, 4, 1970) that McMahon's reservation about French claims was contingent on France's claim to Palestine, and so lapsed on 24 April 1920 when the Palestine mandate was allocated to Britain 'and thus France implicitly renounced any interest in Palestine that she may previously have claimed' (p. 192). He rates the McMahon drafting as 'not disingenuous, but hopelessly muddleheaded'.

[2] Though men with access to the papers confused the issue by expressing the opposite view, e.g. Curzon to the Eastern Committee on 5 December 1918 (PRO CAB/27/24) and Kitchener's assistant, Sir Vivien Gabriel in *The Times*, 12 July 1922.

[3] See Gabriel Sheffer 'Policy Making and British Policies towards Palestine'. Unpublished thesis (Oxford University, 1970), pp. 9–14.

[4] Cmd. 5964 of 1939.

[5] PRO CAB/42/6/10 of 16 December 1915, p. 5. Copy in the Sykes Papers, St. Antony's College, Oxford (ref: DR 588).

[6] Samuel Papers, St. Antony's College, Oxford (ref: DR 588.25, letter dated 26 February 1916).

propaganda advantage of doing something for the Jews arrived, and Sykes (who told Picot of it) telegraphed back some excited suggestions for a scheme that would satisfy everybody. But nothing came of the proposal. The only result was the germination of a seed already planted in Sykes's mind.

A turning point in Palestine's story takes place with the accession to power of Lloyd George's Government in December 1916. The Zionists, by now growing as important as the Conjoint and talking among themselves in terms of a State or Commonwealth in Palestine, wanted it to be under the British. They may have known through their best informant, Lloyd George's friend C. P. Scott of the *Manchester Guardian*, that the new Cabinet had a premier whose ideas dovetailed with their own; they knew that two sympathizers with their aims, Balfour and Cecil, were in the Foreign Office; they did not know that the many imperialists working in and for the new Cabinet (notably Milner and Amery) would be easy converts to their cause. The history of Anglo-Zionist relations in 1917 is a history of the slow movement into conjunction of two groups both of which, for different ends, wanted a British Palestine.

First, the Zionists got wind of the agreement with the French, and, in February 1917, with Samuel, met Sykes and taxed him with it.[1] Sykes, who was optimistically confident that conflicting views could be reconciled, said that nothing was settled. Next, the attack at Gaza that was supposed to lead to swift capture of Jerusalem was launched, and Lloyd George and Curzon, when dispatching Sykes to that front as Chief Political Officer, on 3 April instructed him to work for a British Palestine, to give no pledges to the Arabs, and to do nothing to prejudice the Zionist movement. The instructions suited him. He travelled east via Paris and prodded Picot about Zionism on his way through.

The French were still the obstacle, and while Weizmann was the chief charmer of the British, the man who overcame French resistance was Sokolow. The memorandum which for the first time used the phrase a 'Jewish National Home' was chiefly his work, and, encouraged by Sykes, he had with consummate diplomacy by June 1917 wrung from Paris, Rome, and the Pope a declaration of 'sympathy for your cause'.[2] Further delays ensued; one was caused by the possibility of a separate peace with Turkey; another was because at the cabinet meeting of 3 September which considered a draft declaration for which Lord Rothschild had been asked, Lloyd George and Balfour were both absent and the only Jew in the cabinet, the anti-Zionist Edwin Montagu, successfully opposed the step because it suggested that Jews

---

[1] A record taken by one of the Zionists present is among the Samuel Papers at St. Antony's College, Oxford (ref: DS 149).
[2] Cambon to Sokolow, 4 June 1917, quoted in Stein, op. cit., pp. 416–17.

had a double loyalty; he was able to defer the matter. By the end
of October a combination of Lloyd George's inclinations and the
immediate necessity of inducing Russia's Jews to keep Russia fighting
had restored the subject to the Cabinet agenda, and Balfour's famous
letter to Lord Rothschild was dispatched on 2 November 1917.

Also during 1917, the tide began to turn against Turkey on other
fronts. In March the British captured Baghdad; in June the Sharif's
men performed their first feat of value, and captured Aqaba. In
December, Allenby captured Jerusalem. Meantime, the British in
Cairo began to see evidence that fear of the Sharif's pretensions was
exercising the sophisticated Arabs of Syria. They soothed these with
talk of a confederacy of Arab states and promised their spokesmen
'support in their struggle for freedom' in all areas that the Arabs
liberated for themselves.[1] In the following October, they allowed the
Sharifian forces to take pride of place in Damascus. This fact colours
the Palestine scene, for there were no Arab claims that the independence promise included Palestine until after Faisal had been
ejected from Damascus by the French in July 1920.

Two attempts were made to explain to the Sharif British obligations
to the French. The first was by Sykes and Picot in the paralysing heat
of Jedda in May 1917. The second was by Hogarth of the Cairo Arab
Bureau in January 1918—that is, after the Bolsheviks had published
the secret treaties. Hogarth reported that the Sharif said he was 'quite
in sympathy with both international control in Palestine and the
encouragement of Jews to settle there';[2] the same opinion was expressed
by the only British eyewitness of talks between Faisal and Weizmann
at Aqaba in June 1918; this was Colonel Joyce, who thought that
Faisal would 'welcome a Jewish Palestine if it assisted Arab expansion
further North'.[3] Lawrence thought likewise.

But the townsmen 'further north' thought differently. Especially did
they do so after the arrival in Palestine in April 1918 of a Zionist Commission whose manners offended them, as did proprietary articles in
Jewish newspapers saying in so many words that the Jews expected
'predominance'. By the second half of 1918, reports about Palestinian
Arab anxiety were flowing in from Allenby's political officers, and even
Sykes, who visited Palestine shortly before his early death in the flu
epidemic of February 1919, had lost much of his ingrained optimism.

At the time of the Peace Conference, the whole world was ringing
with the word self-determination. Yet the realists among the British
knew that 'it would not be indiscriminately applied to the whole world,

---

[1] Text of this so-called Declaration to the Seven Syrians in Hurewitz, ii, p. 29.
[2] Arab Bulletin, no. 77, p. 22, January 1918. Copy in St. Antony's College, Oxford.
[3] Milner Papers (Palestine folder), New College, Oxford.

and Palestine was a case in point'.[1] The Foreign Office memorandum for the Peace Conference recommended 'a single power mandate which should not be given to France or Italy but either to the USA or Great Britain'.[2] Lloyd George was still all for Britain, and, says Clemenceau, struck a bargain with him to this effect—Palestine and Mosul for a free French hand in Syria. Therefore the British worked for an agreement between Faisal and Weizmann (which they got, but subject to an Arab reservation that later invalidated it) and against an American wish to consult the views of the inhabitants.

A year of delays had increased the apprehensions of the Palestine Arabs. A Syrian Arab congress of March 1920 called in vain for the full independence of Syria within its 'natural boundaries', which included Palestine, and proclaimed Faisal its king. By then, the British troops which had helped him into power had gone from Syria; the French became the mandatory power in April, and by July had fought him and turned him out. In the British Foreign Office in January 1921, he claimed that the McMahon letter had, according to Arab understanding of the text, not excluded Palestine from the area of Arab independence. By then the British had been the mandatory for Palestine for over a year. Faisal's claim was part of an Arab case that they denied—to him there and then, and forever thereafter.[3]

When, in 1937, the Royal Commission chaired by Lord Peel produced by far the most searching and understanding of all the British Blue Books and White Papers on Palestine, they reported that the situation they had found there was not new: 'The present difficulties of the problem of Palestine were all inherent in it from the beginning. Time has not altered, it has only strengthened them.'[4] This home truth, so plain in retrospect, was not apparent to the British for more than a decade.

The military administration that ran the territory until the allocation of the mandate did its best to repair the physical damage caused by war, famine, and deportations. Mental disquiet it could not cure because of Arab and Jewish uncertainty about British intentions. In April 1920, after mutual dislike had exploded into riots in Jerusalem, the military administrator complained to London that the privileges accorded to the Zionist Commission 'has firmly and absolutely convinced the non-Jewish elements of our partiality'[5] while the Jews complained that the administration showed pro-Arab bias. The terms

---

[1] Balfour to Meinertzhagen on the eve of the latter's departure for Palestine, Paris, 30 July 1919. Cited in the latter's *Middle East Diary* (London, 1959), p. 25.
[2] CAB 23/42 of 19 December 1918.
[3] See Friedman, op. cit., p. 120.
[4] Cmd. 5479 of 1937, p. 62.
[5] Quoted in Nevill Barbour, *Nisi Dominus* (London, 1946), p. 97.

C

of the mandate, when published, reinforced the Arab impression because of the ample provision they made for Jewish institutions. When the mandate was accorded to Great Britain, Arab fears were increased by the appointment of the first High Commissioner— Herbert Samuel, a Jew. Samuel, though interested in the future of Palestine had never been an active member of the Zionist movement in Britain. He knew Weizmann from December 1914, but acted on his own when he launched the idea of a Jewish Palestine in 1914 and re-launched it on becoming Home Secretary in 1916.

Samuel, who held office in Palestine from 1920–5, had had mis-givings about a Jew in the job, but being a good liberal and a dutiful Englishman, he took it and endeavoured to be fair. He set up an ad-ministration that employed all three faiths, and for a time worked with an advisory council that did the same, hoping that this pattern would lead to a partly elected legislative council and ultimately to self-government for a joint community. But these hopes were dashed by the Arabs, who boycotted the elections and demanded a national govern-ment. In February 1921, 'disturbances' described by the subsequent commission of inquiry as 'no ordinary riot' caused many casualties not only in Jaffa but in the Jewish colonies around it. By 1922 Samuel was reporting home that the main cause of trouble continued to be un-certainty about British intentions; he therefore secured from Whitehall a statement of policy which defined a British intention to hold the balance between two communities neither of which was to predominate. This satisfied most British critics; Clayton, for instance, told Samuel that it enabled him to take up a job he had hitherto felt unable to accept.[1] The Zionists accepted it as the best they could get; the Arabs rejected it and, citing the McMahon correspondence, called for an immediate national government because they read the White Paper as meaning 'that self-government will be granted as soon as the Jewish people in Palestine are sufficiently able through numbers and powers to benefit to the full by self-government, and not before'.[2]

Samuel tumbled over himself to be fair to the Arabs. At one point he overdid himself in attention to their affairs, for, in order to keep the balance between the feuding first families in Jerusalem, he upset an election to the Muftiship of Jerusalem in 1920, and in 1921 installed as Mufti a young nationalist, Hajj Amin al-Husseini, whose religious qualifications for the job were slighter than those of other candidates, and who thus obtained control of considerable religious endowments— *Waqf* funds. Samuel also attempted to match the Jewish Agency with an Arab Agency, but was turned down. Nevertheless, he was reported

---

[1] Letter of 4 July 1922 in the Samuel Papers, St. Antony's College, Oxford (ref: DS 126).
[2] Cmd. 1700 of 1922 quoted in *Great Britain and Palestine 1915–1945* (Londen, 1946), which reprints many useful documents.

at the time to be thought by the Arabs 'a favourable exception' to the usual run of the Jews that they knew.[1]

His successor was Lord Plumer (1925–8)—a Field-Marshal, dignified, and a martinet, yet endearing because so well aware of the history of both communities. The story that best illustrates Plumer's handling of the job is his retort when the Mufti told him that he could not be responsible for what might happen if a certain Jewish march were to take place. The answer was: 'You are not responsible: I am.'[2] Nevertheless, Plumer was lucky in the events of his term of office. Owing to a slump in Eastern Europe and the collapse of the Polish zloty, Palestine suffered an economic setback, Jewish immigration fell off, and in one year (1927) more Jews left Palestine than entered it. The British doctrine of the day was that mandates must be made to pay their way, and the garrison was reduced to a level that brought a warning about 'the danger of not maintaining adequate local forces' from the Permanent Mandates Commission;[3] but British policy-making was seldom affected by the comments of this dispassionate body. British complacency was such that Plumer's successor felt able to say in 1929 that 'relations between the two communities continue to improve'.[4]

But in fact Plumer's three years were the last in which the British could justifiably look on Palestine as an imperial asset the problems of which could be insulated from those of the Diaspora and the rest of the Arab world. For during the first months of the reign of his successor, Sir John Chancellor (1928–31), several important shifts of emphasis took place. First, the Palestinian Zionists made up long-standing differences with the World Zionist Organization and, with British consent, the two created an enlarged Jewish Agency in which half the members came from outside Palestine; to the Arabs this change increased the material resources behind the Jews. Next, Arab nationalism seemed to be making strides, and Arab independence to be growing closer in neighbouring Arab countries; the British were making new arrangements with Transjordan and Iraq, and the French had set up a constituent assembly in Syria. Third, the slump passed, and Jewish emigration ceased to count. Unnoticed at the time, another outside event affected the scene. The 1929 election in Great Britain returned a minority Government, led by Ramsay MacDonald, to power; Chancellor was not in the same strong position as Plumer had been.

Arab fears first manifested themselves in a scuffle over a Jewish ceremony at the Wailing Wall on the Jewish day of Atonement in September 1928—an incident used by the Mufti to fan Moslem

[1] *Daily Mail*, 20 January 1923, quoted in J. de V. Loder, *The Truth about Mesopotamia, Palestine and Syria* (London, 1923).
[3] Told in Norman and Helen Bentwich, *Mandate Memories* (London, 1965), p. 118.
[3] Permanent Mandates Commission: Minutes of 9th Session, 1926, p. 184.
[4] Ibid., 15th Session, 1929, p. 79.

sentiment. In August 1929, another Jewish demonstration at the Wailing Wall provoked counter-demonstrations, which within a week had become nationwide killings. The scantiness of the garrison was manifest and order was restored only after troops were rushed from Egypt and ships from Malta.

For the first time, the High Commissioner labelled these Arab passions 'nationalism'. If the British were not prepared to enforce protection of the Jews, he said, they must reshape the mandate, remove the clauses that seemed to give the Jews a privileged position, restrict their land purchases and give the Arabs a measure of self-government.[1] His recommendation fluttered Whitehall, which had for ten years lived from hand to mouth over the key questions of immigration and land settlement; it had done nothing firm about the several reports that it had commissioned on a topic rendered difficult by Turkish removal of the Ottoman land registers, by the ready availability of Jewish funds for land purchase, and by the readiness of Arabs, including absentee landlords with no compunction for their tenants, to sell land for cash down.

The upshot of the Shaw report on the 1929 riots was the same as that of 1921, except that a minority report laid special blame on the Mufti. It called for a clear statement of policy especially about immigration, and for this purpose recommended an inquiry into how many people the land would hold. Sir John Hope Simpson of the Indian Civil Service was set the task of estimating this, and his answer was categoric. Either the land must be made to hold more people by means of expensive development projects, or else immigration must be stopped. He thought in terms of £6–8 million, and, in September 1930, with the world economic crisis looming ahead, the Treasury threw up its hands in horror. A White Paper, already approved in draft by the then Colonial Secretary, Lord Passfield, on the basis of Hope Simpson's recommendations, was at the last minute cut about to meet Treasury limitations. In brief, it recommended help to landless Arabs, partial restriction of Jewish immigration, total restriction of land sales to Jews, and, hoping on hoping ever that the Arabs could be pacified, the establishment of a Legislative Council. All idea of a massive development scheme of benefit to both communities had been left out.

Immediately, the Jewish Agency raised a storm. Led by Weizmann, the moderates in its ranks resigned. At home, a Labour Government that lacked a clear majority trembled at the possibility of a Conservative–Liberal alliance on the Palestine issue, especially when two eminent lawyers (Hailsham and Simon) wrote to *The Times* saying that the White Paper infringed the mandate. Helped by many Members

[1] On 17 January 1930; for a detailed account of the events summarized in the next four paragraphs see G. Sheffer, op. cit., Chapter I.

of Parliament, the Jewish Agency bypassed Chancellor and began to
pull all available strings in London.

In fact the Prime Minister, when he went back on the White Paper,
was influenced less by their lobbying than by his Government's
position at home and in foreign affairs. He was apprehensive about his
majority in parliament; about the outcome of an imminent by-election
in Whitechapel where the electorate was 40 per cent Jewish; about the
danger of being taken to the Hague Court over infringement of the
mandate at a moment when Britain was preparing to pull her weight
at the 1932 Disarmament Conference; about the prospect of complications during the Round Table Conference with India; about the
risk that American Jewish pressure on Congress might jeopardize the
London Treaty on naval parity that had just been hammered out with
difficulty. MacDonald therefore gave in to Zionist and pro-Zionist
pressure and wrote a letter to Weizmann which in effect rescinded the
White Paper. It promised that the control of land sales would be only
temporary and that there would be no stoppage of Jewish immigration.
It pleased the Zionists and the Tory imperialists, and Labourites who
liked the socialist characteristics of the National Home. The Arabs
christened it the Black Letter, but did not immediately vent their
dismay in violence partly because they had had a polite reception
during a delegation to London organized for them by Chancellor to
ensure that they too should get a hearing, partly because they were
busy with Moslem affairs, and partly because Palestine, unlike the rest
of the world, in 1931–4, was enjoying a boom; prosperity was brought
about partly by the British devaluation of the pound, and partly by
some excellent citrus harvests. At the time, citrus accounted for about
four fifths of Palestine's exports.

Chancellor, though a good administrator, had not been a success.
He had worked against odds, and had disliked the job by comparison
with the serenity of governing Rhodesia. The Prime Minister, unaware
of the extent to which things had changed since 1925, cast about for
'another Plumer'. His choice fell on Sir Arthur Wauchope, the
Commander-in-Chief in Northern Ireland. Wauchope was a Scot,
cautious but tenacious; he was also a rich bachelor with a known
capacity for making friends. He was to possess one immense advantage
over his predecessor. As a result of the British general election of 1931
he served a majority Government and his minister in it was a powerful
Tory grandee, Philip Cunliffe Lister.

Cunliffe Lister believed that there were economic answers to most
ills; Wauchope soon came to the conclusion that the lion and the
lamb were more likely to lie down together if the communities were
approximately equal in size. Since money for development was not to
be had from the Treasury but was available from the Jews, a British
policy that was in any case pledged to promote Jewish immigration

became a policy largely dependent on Jewish capital and effort. Both men intended that this should benefit the Arabs, for they disapproved of Jewish exclusiveness in matters such as employment, but this trait they were never able to break down.

The rise in Jewish immigration which took place in the first half of the 1930s was chiefly due to their conception of Palestine's future and not, as is so often thought, to British compassion for Jews fleeing from Hitler;[1] this last was exercised chiefly in Britain. Hitler's dates are relevant. Though immediately after his accession to power in 1933 he purged the civil service of Jews, he was thereafter taken up for eighteen months with purging his own party. The Nuremberg Laws which deprived German Jews of citizenship and gave Nazi thugs the freedom of the streets were not passed until September 1935, by which time British limitation of Jewish immigration into Palestine was on the upgrade. The rise which Cunliffe Lister and Wauchope furthered began in 1932 and tailed off in 1935. It diminished partly because the world crisis was over and Palestine had ceased to attract so much investment, and partly because of security difficulties once the Arab rebellion began in 1936. Another relevant piece of evidence is the relatively small proportion of immigrants coming from Germany in the peak years:

	Total population 000s	Total legal Jewish immigration	Jewish immigration in the 'free entering' category bringing in more than £1,000	Percentage coming from Germany
1931	1,036	4,075	233	
1932	1,074	9,553	727	
1933	1,141	30,327	3,250	
1934	1,211	42,359	5,124	16
1935	1,308	61,854	6,309	11
1936	1,367	29,727	2,970	
1937	1,401	10,536	1,275	
1938	1,435	12,868	1,753	
1939	1,501	16,405	1,629	49·8

Sources: G. Sheffer, op. cit., p. 164 and ESCO, vol. II, p. 677, and Mandatory's Annual Report for 1938.

Thus Wauchope was from 1931–5 able to think in optimistic terms of proceeding towards self-government in a bi-national State. Towards this end, he created mixed municipalities, some of which worked, notably that in Haifa. But he was unable to follow through with a Legislative Council which he thought of as a safety valve for Arab fears, but which was now opposed not only by Arabs arguing that their majority status entitled them to a permanent majority but by Jews averse to a body that would emphasize their minority status. His

[1] For the best available analysis of this immigration policy see G. Sheffer, op. cit., pp. 160–93.

complacency was little shaken by an Arab disturbance in 1933—the long-term result of the Black Letter. This was put down without difficulty thanks to the availability of a larger garrison, though Wauchope felt bound to admit that it was inflamed by 'a genuine national feeling', and was anti-British rather than anti-Jewish. He nevertheless flattered himself that he had good friends in both communities, and was making headway.

His illusions, like Chancellor's, were shattered by a series of outside events. A personal blow was the transfer of Cunliffe Lister to the Air Ministry when Baldwin took over the premiership in June 1935; none of the quick succession of three colonial secretaries that followed—Malcolm MacDonald, J. H. Thomas, Ormsby Gore—ever had the same degree of influence in London. But far more fundamental were the effects of other world events—the Ethiopian war and the loss of British prestige that it brought; Italian pretensions in the Mediterranean and the effect of Mussolini's Arabic broadcasts from Bari; the formation of Arab parties each of which canvassed a champion among foreign Arab statesmen—one the Amir Abdullah, another Nuri Pasha of Iraq, the Mufti's King Ibn Saud.

The Arab rebellion of 1936–8 did not at once burst into flame. Its chief cause was the endemic one—fear of Jewish numbers; its immediate cause, the discovery that the Jews were smuggling in arms for self-defence. The whole Jewish community was not at one over this; conservatives felt that it should be content with the locked arms stores that the Government sanctioned for emergency use; younger men and left-wing groups had long run a secret body called the Haganah which reckoned that Jews must fend for themselves. Arab resistance to immigration and to this doctrine became serious when at the end of April 1936 the Arab parties banded together into an Arab Higher Committee, declared a general strike, and preached civil disobedience on the Gandhi model. Attacks on Jews and Jewish colonies took place. But the Jews did not hit back; with the exception of the military organization of the Revisionist party, they decided to practise *Havlagah*, or restraint. Their best hope of succouring German Jewry seemed to be to work with the British, and with this in mind they restored to power Weizmann, whom, in discontent with his policy of partnership with Britain, they had voted out of the presidency of the World Zionist Organization in 1931. To Wauchope's chagrin, the situation soon passed the stage of friendly talks with Arab leaders.

The British struggled against any appearance of concession to violence; they reinforced the garrison, reduced immigration, and proposed the usual palliative—another Royal Commission, which was not to go to Palestine till the Arabs called off violence and the strike. This they did in October 1936, but not until British armed force looked decisive, and the Foreign Office had encouraged the Arab kings to press them to do so—pressure which was applied in high-flown Arabic that enabled them to give in without loss of face.

The 1937 Royal Commission—the Peel Commission—proclaimed aloud a solution that had previously only been mentioned privately. It reported[1] that the gulf between the two communities was unbridgeable, and that the only solution was partition. In the context of Italian and German expansion and the Spanish war they could not suggest that Britain should disappear. Their partition plan provided for a Jewish State in the coastal plain and most of Galilee, an Arab State in the hills and the south, to be joined to Transjordan, and a surviving British mandate that was to consist of Jerusalem, a corridor to it that contained the airport of Lydda, and the port of Haifa with a hinterland that included Nazareth. Christian as well as strategic motives were at work. As Ormsby Gore wrote to the new High Commissioner, Sir Harold MacMichael, in December 1937: 'I believe with the Royal Commission that some form of partition is the only eventual solution. . . . But we must continue to rule in Jerusalem and Bethlehem and Nazareth, and I believe we can never give up our control of Haifa and the Gulf of Akaba to Jews or Arabs or any other power.'[2]

The Cabinet accepted the solution; for the last time, it took a decision based on thoughts of Palestine alone. But it was in a minority. Weizmann too belonged to this minority; there are one or two first hand descriptions of the degree to which he was moved by the offer of a Jewish State, however small.[3] But the size and variety of the opposition to the scheme was impressive. Weizmann could not carry the Zionist Congress with him; by a majority of 142 out of 458 votes it turned down 'Zionism without Zion', and asked for better terms. Lord Samuel, in a great speech in the House of Lords, deplored partition and suggested instead an interim limit to immigration and the formation of a great Arab confederation of states in which the Jews would co-operate. All Arabs except the Amir Abdullah turned partition down; so did the Moslem League in India, and the British House of Lords. The House of Commons and the Permanent Mandates Commission instructed the Mandatory to think again.

The Arabs stepped up their rebellion until parts of the hills were in the hands of their guerrilla bands. Deposing the Mufti, and arresting party leaders yielded no result; many Jews stopped practising restraint, and a young British army intelligence officer, Orde Wingate, got permission to organize them into night squads. A resistance movement that

---

[1] Cmd. 5479 of 1937, published on 7 July. The Commission was in Palestine from 11 November 1936 till 30 January 1937.
[2] Letter of 15 December 1937 in the MacMichael papers, St. Antony's College, Oxford (ref: DS 126.2).
[3] See J. L. Meltzer in *Chaim Weizmann: A Biography by Several Hands* (London, 1962), pp. 240–1.

enjoys the support of the inhabitants is always difficult to stamp out. Only in the context of the war scare that ended at Munich did the British develop that sense of urgency which caused them to import enough troops to stamp rebellion out.

There were two major and constant factors in the Palestine equation. One was Arab fear of Jewish numbers,[1] the other British reluctance to use force to impose a solution. Opposition and rebellion brought home the fact that partition would call for enforcement; so the Cabinet back-pedalled and in March 1938 sent out a further Commission armed with the advice that the best course would be to let things be, and leave an undivided country under British rule. It reported accordingly just after Munich.[2]

The next expedient was a Round Table Conference on the Indian model, but this was a failure. So were the two conferences into which it developed, one with the Jews and the other with the Arabs, including representatives of other Arab States. Every British suggestion was rejected.

Before the British imposed their own solution in May 1939, Mussolini had swallowed Albania and Hitler Prague. Their proposal, though couched in the form of a plan for progress towards an independent State, was in fact a plan for a peaceful Middle East and safe oil supplies in the likely event of a European war. It reflected the fact that if war did break out the Jews had no other course than to help fight Hitler, whereas the Arabs might be attracted by his anti-Semitism, and become awkward neighbours. The British proposal prescribed independence in five years; till then 75,000 Jews were to be admitted, 25,000 at once in recognition of the emergency created by Hitler's excesses, and thereafter 10,000 a year until 1944. The Jews were of course aghast; even the Arabs were not satisfied, thinking to wait and see; the Permanent Mandates Commission said that the arrangement was incompatible with Britain's obligations under the mandate. Thereafter war set in to the accompaniment of Ben-Gurion's much-quoted remark that the Jews would fight the White Paper as if there were no war and the war as if there were no White Paper.

Jewish historians often claim that the White Paper failed to influence the Arabs, but British historians who remember the Middle East in the war reckon that this argument does not hold water until 1943. At Britain's two moments of hopeless weakness, which were when German planes landed in Syria to help Rashid Ali's rebellion in Iraq in 1941, and when there seemed to be no holding Rommel at the gates of

---

[1] See a graph forecasting future population trends on p. 281 of the Peel Commission's report, which shows that Jewish immigration at the rate of 30,000 per annum (the optimum asked for by extremists in 1931) would produce a Jewish majority by 1960.
[2] Cmd. 5893 of 1938.

Alexandria and von Rundstedt in the Caucasus in June–August 1942, more Arabs helped than hindered her, and the older men in power gave active help—the Amir Abdullah, Nuri Pasha, King Ibn Saud. Axis propaganda scarcely affected Palestine: Hitler, though a better propagandist than Mussolini, had to be careful in an area that purported to be Italy's sphere of influence.[1]

From the standpoint of all three parties to the Palestine imbroglio, the Second World War falls into two halves—before and after Rommel's defeat at Alamein. Before it the Jews, though sick with anxiety about the fate of their relations in Europe, had no choice but to help the war effort. Some thought that they could do this by joining the British army; others that they should concentrate their strength in an authorized *Haganah* that would fight in Palestine and not wherever the British wished; yet others reckoned that it mattered little by which means Jews got the military training that would ultimately serve their own purposes. The British, sensing this, were reluctant to use Palestine Jews except in the British army until, in the two years of their own worst straits, they began training special squads for dangerous work in the Balkans and in Vichy Syria; one Jewish detachment that was sent off to blow up Tripoli refinery was wiped out to a man.[2] Yet their bitterness against the British grew; they watched deportation to the Seychelles of such refugees as contrived to reach Palestine; they underrated the peril through which Britain herself was passing, and blamed on Sir Harold MacMichael Britain's failure to arm them (when in fact there were no arms for her own defence), and also blamed him for the fate of every ship that failed to reach Palestine.[3] The Arabs, sick of their rebellion, were ready to recoup the economic losses they had suffered in its course by taking the war jobs that became plentiful; enjoying temporary relief from pressure of Jewish numbers, they worked willingly.

From the summer of Alamein, the scene changed. The Jews began to learn of the dimension of Hitler's mass murders; till then, stories had reached them only in fragments. They were also encouraged in their hopes by the issue in New York in May 1942 of the Biltmore programme that rejected the White Paper and called for a Jewish Commonwealth in the whole of Palestine. They transferred their hopes and pressures from London to the United States. Inside Palestine, they began systematically to steal British arms, and extremists, notably the Stern Gang, perpetrated some symbolic murders. In August 1944 they tried

[1] For the best account of their differences see L. Hirszowicz, *The Third Reich and the Arab East* (London, 1966).
[2] For the Jewish dilemmas of the period see Y. Bauer, *Studies in History* (Hebrew University of Jerusalem, 1961), pp. 220–53.
[3] For the *SS Patria* and *Struma* disasters, see in particular C. Sykes, *Crossroads to Israel* (London, 1965), pp. 268–70 and 271–4.

and failed to kill Sir Harold MacMichael, who was about to retire, and in November successfully murdered the British Minister of State in Cairo, Lord Moyne. Many Jews deplored these tactics; simultaneously, many British became anxious about mounting evidence that some Zionists wanted to alleviate Jewish distress in Europe only if the process swelled the numbers in Palestine.[1]

These Jewish activities revived Arab fears, but the Palestinian Arabs lacked leaders; all their tried ones were in internment or exile. Therefore they relied for protest on other Arab States. To the embarrassment of its British sponsors, the Arab League took up the cudgels on their behalf. Its protocol of 1944 proposed the establishment of a special fund for preventing land sales to Jews, and its pact of 1945 contained provisions about working for Palestine's independence.[2]

The end of the war found the British in a worse position than before. In Palestine, all their familiar difficulties still prevailed, while, additionally Europe was teeming with displaced persons, many of them Jews who did not want to go back to their countries of origin, so making the British look inhumane if they refused access to Palestine. Massive but secret Jewish help for a huge illegal exodus complicated their problems.[3]

The election of a Labour Government to power in 1945 raised Jewish hopes because the Labour Party had opposed the 1939 White Paper, and had at its congress in 1944 passed a resolution suggesting that the Arabs could move out of Palestine as the Jews moved in. But once in power, the Attlee Government found itself obliged, if it was to fulfil other aspirations such as bringing about real independence for Egypt and Iraq, to take all the pre-war considerations into account. As the victor, it looked powerful enough in the Middle East, but it was in fact poor, war weary, and beset with problems in Europe which included the realization—long before the Americans—that Russian policy was engulfing Eastern Europe. Unable to enforce partition, it fell back on the old aim of creating a bi-national state.

The Foreign Secretary, Ernest Bevin, took on the job of reconciling American, Jewish, and Arab opinion to this course. His chief characteristics were an abiding concern for the underdog—whether the British unemployed, the Egyptian peasant, or the inmate of a displaced persons camp—and a conviction born of long experience as a trade union leader that any difference, however profound, could be solved by negotiation. He therefore unwisely told parliament that he would

---

[1] See Morris Ernst, *So Far So Good* (New York, 1948), pp. 170–7, and the proceedings of the Anglo-American Bermuda Conference, April 1943 summarized in C. Sykes op. cit., pp. 288–9.
[2] Text in Hurewitz, ii, p. 248.
[3] For accounts of *Brichah* (flight) see J. and D. Kimche, *The Secret Roads* (London, 1954), and Y. Bauer, *Flight and Rescue* (New York, 1970).

'stake my political future' on solving the Palestine problem. But it defeated him, because in handling it he found himself dealing not with a Jewish underdog but with an American President bent on pleasing his Jewish supporters.

The sorry tale of the end of the mandate need not be told at length here.[1]

The British, with Jewish terrorism, illegal immigration, and treaties with various Arab states on their hands, naturally reckoned that all displaced Jews could not go to Palestine, though when the White Paper quota was exhausted they allowed in a further 1,500 per month; arrivals over and above this number they deported to Cyprus. Bevin, aware that both the State Department and the Pentagon had the measure of Britain's problem, invited the Americans to serve on a joint commission for Palestine; they agreed, and he pledged himself to execute the Commission's findings, if unanimous. He discounted the objection that he was giving the Americans a say in policy without responsibility for carrying it out. The Commission presented in April 1946 a unanimous report consisting of ten interlocking recommendations the most important of which were that it rejected partition and recommended a unitary state; that it recommended the issue of 100,000 immigration certificates, and that the Jewish Agency should forthwith join in suppressing terrorism. For the British, the issue of the certificates was conditional upon this last proviso; to Bevin's fury, President Truman underwrote the 100,000 certificates in isolation.

The condition was not fulfilled and the solution not attempted. Nevertheless, both states made one further half-hearted attempt at a new joint plan; but this, which amounted to indefinite prolongation of British rule, came up against American anti-imperialism and fell through likewise.

By the summer of 1946 Jewish terrorism had reached one of its peaks with the blowing up of British military headquarters in the King David hotel at Jerusalem; at the same time the more moderate Jews were in despair about their chances of statehood. These last made it known that the 100 per cent Biltmore demand for Palestine as a Jewish State was not their last word, and that they would accept a smaller state in 'a viable area of Palestine'. Bevin saw them and took heart. But his hopes were dashed, as those of the Zionists were raised, when Truman again intervened. In a speech timed to catch the voters in a New York election, Truman backed a smaller Jewish state. Bevin's chances of persuading the Arabs to talk in terms of partition sank to zero. In vain he warned them that they might do better at British hands than if the matter were referred to the United Nations. Both they and

[1] It is told in detail in E. Monroe, 'Mr. Bevin's "Arab Policy" ', in *St. Antony's Papers*, no. 2 (London, 1961).

the Jews turned down his final shot at a plan, and Britain turned the problem over to the UN in February 1947.

Thereafter a total shift occurred in British thinking. In one way, the problem was eased: Soviet behaviour in Eastern Europe, and European dependence on Middle Eastern oil for rehabilitation, were such that all Americans began to see the worth of Middle Eastern bases; March 1947 is the date at which the Americans agreed to take over a northern tier from the penurious British, and 'Truman aid' began to Greece and Turkey. So that, in turning to the UN, the British did not at once abandon the mandate: they merely asked for advice as to how it could best be administered. But by the end of the summer several events had made Britain change her mind. A United Nations commission (UNSCOP) recommended partition without provision for its execution; the cost of military operations in Palestine was at its highest, and in August public opinion in Britain turned against the Palestine version of the white man's burden when Jewish terrorists hanged two young British sergeants as a reprisal for death sentences on some of their number. Additionally, Egypt had just spoilt its case at the United Nations against the British base in the Canal Zone by overcalling its hand on the subject of the Sudan; the Canal Zone base therefore remained available. On 26 September 1947 the British announced that they were giving up the mandate in the following May: overnight, the exodus of troops and stores from the Canal Zone went into reverse.

In November the United Nations voted by a narrow majority for the partition plan. The ensuing six months were a period of mounting chaos: as the British moved their troops towards their departure point, Haifa, with instructions that the saving of equipment was their first priority, armed Jewish and Arab bands took over and began to fight one another. The British handed over to whichever community was locally in the ascendant and since Jewish cadres were ready to administer locally whereas Arab cadres were lacking, order was best preserved in Jewish areas. The British, proclaiming unwillingness to enforce a solution unless it was acceptable to both sides, refused to admit UN representatives until a fortnight before the end of the mandate because they were unwilling to be responsible for the safety of UN lives.[1]

The country was so manifestly in the grip of war that the Americans backpedalled. In March 1948 they proposed to the United Nations a temporary trusteeship that would allow time for tempers to cool. But tempers were past this point; while the United Nations were still

[1] The most graphic descriptions of this humiliating period are by the last British mayor of Jerusalem, R. Graves, *Experiment in Anarchy*, and Jon and David Kimche, *Both Sides of the Hill*, Part II (London, 1960). For the British military aspect: R. D. Wilson, *Cordon and Search* (London, 1948) and *Palestine Diary*, vol. II (Palestine Research Center, Beirut, 1970).

discussing the idea, and appointing a mediator to execute their wishes, the mandate expired and the independent State of Israel was declared. On 14 May 1948 Jewish excitement and Arab determination to resist caused such emotion that the hauling down of the British flag was scarcely noticed. The last British High Commissioner sailed from Haifa in May 1948.

ELIZABETH MONROE

2. ARAB POLITICAL MOVEMENTS

The decline and fragmentation of the great Arab Empire created by the conquests of the eighth century AD culminated in the Ottoman occupation of Cairo in 1517. All the Arab lands (except Morocco which remained a separate Sultanate and Nejd which retained a form of independence under its own amirs) were incorporated in the Ottoman Empire. The Arabs ceased to be rulers, Istanbul became their capital and the Ottoman Sultan assumed the title of Caliph.

For three centuries the Arab peoples were politically quiescent. They first stirred in their slumbers when Napoleon Bonaparte landed in Egypt in 1798. But the potential for a political revival remained because, even when politically dismembered, they retained their cultural unity through their language. ' . . . Though Ottoman rule was generally sterile in that it imparted no new cultural values or creative impulses to the Arab world, and though it was often harsh and destructive of the sources of wealth in it, it did not impinge on the Arabism of its people, so that when they began, three and a half centuries later, to awaken to a new life, it was as Arabs that they did so.'[1]

It was in Egypt that the first symptoms of the Arab political renaissance were seen. Through the rough genius of Mohammed Ali and the generalship of his son Ibrahim, Egypt became an important Mediterranean power in its own right and shook the structure of the Ottoman Empire. But Mohammed Ali was neither an Arab nor an Arab nationalist and although Ibrahim toyed with the idea of an Arab Empire based on a national movement it never matured. Egyptians in the nineteenth century who rebelled physically or mentally against Turkish (or, later, British) domination were either pan-Islamists or Egyptian nationalists. Nevertheless the relative intellectual freedom enjoyed by Egypt in the nineteenth century was a powerful element in the Arab political revival. Non-Egyptian Arab writers and intellectuals were able to escape from Ottoman control in Cairo.

[1] Edward Atiyah, *The Arabs* (London, 1955), pp. 47–8.

The Egyptian national movement survived the failure of the Arabi revolt and the British occupation in 1882 and pursued its course until the achievement of full independence with the final British withdrawal in 1956. But its development was parallel to, rather than part of, the Arab national movement. The two did not begin to merge until after the Second World War.

In Central Arabia the Wahhabi movement, which started as a puritanical religious revival in the eighteenth century, developed into a strong politico-military threat to the Ottoman Empire when it allied itself with the House of Saud. Ironically, the Ottoman Sultan defeated the Wahhabis with the help of Mohammed Ali's forces. The Wahhabis were a purely Arab movement based on the heart of Arabism. But they were too extreme and reactionary to form the nucleus of a modern Arab revival.

'The first organized effort in the Arab national movement can be traced back to the year 1875—two years before Abdul Hamid's accession—when five young men who had been educated at the Syrian Protestant College in Beirut formed a secret society.'[1] In his seven years rule of Syria, Ibrahim had allowed American and French mission schools to establish themselves in the country. In 1866 the Americans founded the Syrian Protestant College (now the American University of Beirut) and a few years later French Jesuits also established the University of St. Joseph. The intellectual revival stimulated by these centres of education provided the essential background for an Arab political renaissance.

The originators of the movement were Christians although the leadership later passed into Moslem hands. The society displayed placards in Beirut and other cities demanding the abolition of press censorship, the granting of self-government to Syria and Lebanon, and the use of Arabic as an official language. When the Turkish secret police took action against them, the leaders of the society moved to Egypt which was now under British protection.

For the next thirty years the infant Arab national movement was largely quiescent. Men such as the Moslem Abdul Rahman Kawakibi and the Christian Neguib Azuri published books and articles denouncing Ottoman tyranny in Cairo and Paris but the Turkish hold over the Arab provinces—except Egypt—was not relaxed. In 1908 there was a brief period of optimism following the successful revolt of the Young Turks in Istanbul who declared equality of all races in the Ottoman Empire. But the Young Turks soon reverted to a policy of Turkish racial domination, the short-lived Turco-Arab Brotherhood Society was dissolved and the Arab nationalists turned to organizing themselves as an underground movement. Several secret societies were formed of which the two most important were *al-Fatat* (Young Arab)

[1] George Antonius, *The Arab Awakening* (Beirut, 1955), p. 79.

and *al-Ahd* (Covenant). There was a steadily growing nationalist ferment throughout the eastern Arab world but there was still little possibility of co-ordinated action—not least because of the poor communications between the different provinces.

The First World War provided the opportunity that had been lacking. As soon as Turkey entered the war on the side of the Central Powers the Allies acquired an interest in promoting an Arab revolt against Turkish rule. (But it could only be in the eastern Arab world. In Egypt and North Africa the Ottomans had been replaced by England, Italy, and France who thus became the enemies of any national movement in these countries.)

The leadership of the Arab revolt was undertaken by the Sharif Hussein of Mecca who had been appointed Custodian of the Holy Places of Islam by the Young Turks Committee of Union and Progress in 1908. After a lengthy correspondence with the British High Commissioner in Egypt, Sir Henry McMahon, the Sharif Hussein raised the flag of revolt declaring the independence of the Arab provinces in the belief that the Allies would support this independence after the war.

The nascent pan-Arab movement of the late nineteenth and early twentieth centuries had been effectively stunted by the actions of the Great Powers. But even if there had been no mandate system and Arab independence had been recognized throughout the Fertile Crescent, it is highly improbable that a unified Arab State would have survived. It is almost inconceivable that any centralized administrative system could have held together the area with its varied pattern of local interests and loyalties. The mandate system guaranteed the partition of the eastern Arab world and as its components developed separately the local loyalties became stronger. When political parties emerged, like the Wafd in Egypt or the National Bloc in Syria, they tended to be local coalitions of different social elements seeking independence from the protecting power for their own country rather than for all the Arabs. Where pan-Arab or pan-Islamic movements appeared, they were strongly opposed not only by the mandatory power but also by the local national political groups. For this reason they tended to be revolutionary in their aims and violent in their methods.

Hashimite Pan-Arabism

The Hashimites were exceptions to this general rule. Despite King Hussein's expulsion from the Hejaz his descendants still regarded themselves as the rightful leaders of the pan-Arab movement. But since they were the established authority in Baghdad and Amman they could not and did not pursue revolutionary methods. There was a degree of rivalry between King Abdullah of Transjordan, whose aim was a 'Greater Syria' of Syria, Lebanon, Transjordan, and Palestine and his younger brother King Faisal of Iraq, who did not abandon his claim to the

throne of Syria after his ejection by the French. Abdullah did not for-
give Faisal for accepting the throne of Iraq for which he had been
destined by his father.

To some extent these rival ambitions cancelled each other out. King
Faisal's position was the stronger both because Iraq carried much more
political and economic weight than Transjordan and because in Nuri
al-Said he had the most considerable statesman in the Arab world
during the inter-war years. After Faisal's death in 1933, Iraq's claims
to Arab leadership were in abeyance during the brief reign of his son
Ghazi but were revived by his nephew Abdul Ilah who was Regent for
the young Faisal II until 1953 but remained the effective power behind
the throne until his assassination in 1958. Abdul Ilah also had ambitions
to recover the Hejaz for the Hashimites but his greatest desire was to
become King of Syria.

During the inter-war period the Hashimites continued to embody
Arab nationalist aspirations for many of the Arabs. But although it was
not immediately apparent at the time, they ceased to do so as the
consequence of two events. One was the Hashimite restoration by British arms in Iraq after the briefly successful Rashid Ali al-Gailani revolt
in 1941. The other was the Palestine War of 1948–9 in which King
Abdullah's role caused him to be regarded as a traitor by the majority
of pan-Arab nationalists.

Some pro-Hashimite feeling survived among the older generation in
Syria and there were still loyalists on the East Bank of the Jordan. In
1954, after the downfall of the Syrian dictator Colonel Shishakli, the
concept of a Syrian–Iraqi union under a Hashimite crown seemed to
come alive again. But in fact no such possibility existed, for the
Hashimites had ceased to satisfy the aspirations of the new generation
of Arabs who had already begun to look to President Nasser for leadership. Nuri al-Said remained a formidable figure in the Middle East
arena and the young King Hussein proved himself a natural leader of
men—but it was as an individual not as a Hashimite. When Jordan and
Iraq hastily formed a federation in February in the wake of the Syrian–
Egyptian union it aroused a cynical response in the Arab world, and
with the July revolution in Iraq and the assassination of Nuri al-Said,
Abdul Ilah, and the young king the Hashimite pan-Arab movement
came to an end.

In 1943 Nuri al-Said drafted a proposal, which he presented to the
British Minister of State in Cairo, for the United Nations to declare
that Syria, Lebanon, Palestine, and Transjordan would be reunited and
an Arab League formed of Iraq and this Greater Syria which other
Arab states could join at will. But although Britain felt benevolent
towards Nuri al-Said, it was never prepared to exert itself to further his
Fertile Crescent policies. Moreover, it is more than doubtful whether
any British-sponsored form of Arab union would have succeeded.

The Syrian Social Nationalist Party (al-Hizb al-Suri al-Qawmi or Parti Populaire Syrien)

The SSNP has been described as 'the first organized party in the Arab East to have a definite national doctrine and a well structured ideology'.[1] It was founded in 1932 by Antoun Saadeh, the son of a Lebanese Greek Orthodox emigrant to Latin America, who returned to the Near East in 1929 and worked on a Damascus newspaper. His personality and ideas soon attracted followers so that by 1935 he was arrested and jailed by the French authorities.

The first of his eight principles which he published in his book *Nushu' al-umam* (Beirut, 1938) states that 'Syria is for the Syrians, and the Syrians are a complete nation'. He said he had come to the conclusion after extensive research that the Syrians were a distinct national entity. They were not Arabs but the people whose natural home had been Syria since prehistoric times. The Syrian nation is the ethnic fusion of the 'Canaanites, Akkadians, Chaldeans, Assyrians, Arameans, Hittites, and Metannis'. When the Arabs arrived in the seventh century the Syrian character had already been formed.

In exalting the Syrian nation he preached the absolute need for social unity: 'Through national unity, the conflict of loyalties and negative attitudes will disappear and will be replaced by a single healthy national loyalty which will ensure the revival of the nation.'[2] In his eighth principle he said: 'Syria's interest supersedes and is prior to every other interest.'[3] Thus he identified society with the nation which he placed above everything. This essentially totalitarian doctrine was decked out in his writings with a great deal of dubious philosophical and historical argument which most of his followers neither understood nor appreciated. But, 'What was attractive was the accent on youth, the rigid disciplines, the Fascist conception of the role of the leader as well as the simple thesis that "natural Syria" was a great nation which had played, and would play once more, a great role in history.'[4]

Saadeh also proposed five principles of reform which he regarded as an integral part of his doctrine. They were: (1) separation of Church and State; (2) prevention of the clergy from interfering in political and judicial matters; (3) removal of the barriers between the various sects and confessions; (4) abolition of feudalism, i.e. the organization of the national economy on the basis of production, the protection of the rights of labour, and the interests of the nation and the State; and

[1] Labib Zuwiyya Yamak, *The Syrian Social Nationalist Party: an Ideological Analysis* (Harvard Middle Eastern Monographs), 1966.
[2] *The Principles of the Syrian Social Nationalist Party* (Beirut, 1949), pp. 28–9.
[3] *The Principles*, p. 32.
[4] Patrick Seale, *The Struggle for Syria* (London, 1965), p. 67.

(5) formation of a strong army which will be effective in determining the destiny of the nation and the State.[1]

These were practical ideas which appealed to many Arab intellectuals from the 1930s onwards even if they rejected Saadeh's exaltation of Syrian, as opposed to Arab, nationalism. His anti-sectarianism was especially attractive to the religious and racial minorities—Christians, Druzes, Kurds, and Alawis—who became a majority in the party hierarchy.

Saadeh possessed all the natural qualities of leadership. He had a magnetic and dominant personality and was fluent and eloquent in discussion. In the preamble to the party's constitution, drafted in 1934, it states that the 'SSNP is founded on the basis of a contract between the legislator, who originated the idea of Syrian social nationalism and all those who have accepted it, on condition that the formulator of the principles of the Syrian social nationalist renaissance shall be the leader of the party for life and that all those who believe in its principles and mission shall therefore become members of the party, defend its cause, and give absolute support and allegiance to the leader, his legislations and constitutional administration.' Thus the idea of absolute obedience to a single leader (al-zaim) became enshrined in the party's principles.

Not unnaturally, while the SSNP attracted some enthusiastic and even fanatical adherents it was deeply repugnant to many of the inhabitants of geographical Syria. Lebanese separatists and Arab nationalists rejected it for opposite reasons, the French authorities found it subversive. Others disliked its anti-democratic Fascist tendencies and still others its secularism. The history of the party was troubled and violent.

Initially the party was a secret, tightly-knit organization with branches and cells in Syria and Lebanon, but concentrating mainly in Lebanon. But the organization was uncovered by the French authorities in 1935. Saadeh was arrested, charged with plotting against the State and sentenced to six months imprisonment. Soon after his release he was again arrested with some of his followers and charged with criminal assault against some Lebanese journalists. From then onwards Saadeh and the party were constantly at odds both with the Lebanese and the French authorities. In 1937 the party was allowed freedom of activity in Lebanon after giving assurances that it did not stand for the destruction of the Lebanese entity but only for the unity of the Syrian entity. In 1939 Saadeh was caught by the outbreak of war in South America on a visit to Syrian emigrants and was unable to return to the Middle East until 1947. Meanwhile the French authorities banned the party in October 1939 and arrested many of its leaders who were charged not only with plotting against the internal security of the State

[1] Yamak, p. 9.

but with complicity with the Axis. Despite the Fascist tendencies of the SSNP there was no real evidence of links with the Italian or German governments.

In 1941 the party members who were still in detention were released on the intercession of a group of Lebanese notables and three years later it was licensed as a legitimate political party in Lebanon. In return it changed its name to al-Hizb al-Qawmi (the National Party) and concentrated on domestic Lebanese matters. However, this new orientation was disputed by Saadeh on his return in 1947. He expelled many senior members of the party and re-established his personal authority and centralized leadership.

Friction between Saadeh and the newly independent Lebanese Government was resumed at once. Saadeh went into hiding and Government forces raided party strongholds in the mountains in a vain attempt to find him. Eventually a compromise was reached with Saadeh once again affirming his respect for the political entity of Lebanon. But Saadeh immediately resumed his critical campaign against both Lebanese and Arab nationalists. In particular he claimed that the loss of the Palestine War in 1948 proved the failure and bank-ruptcy of Arabism. Several prominent Lebanese joined the party and although he never secured any mass support from among the Lebanese people his success was enough to arouse the enmity of the traditional political leaders.

In June 1949 there was a serious armed clash in Beirut between the SSNP and members of the right-wing Lebanese nationalist Katayib Party. Whether or not, as the SSNP alleged, the incident was provoked by the Lebanese Government of Riyadh al-Sulh the authorities used it as grounds to suppress the party and arrest more than 2,000 of its members. Saadeh eventually fled to Syria where he was at first warmly received by the leader of Syria's first post-independence military coup, Husni al-Zaim. But Lebanese diplomatic pressure combined with anti-SSNP elements inside Syria persuaded him to agree to Saadeh's ex-tradition to Lebanon where he was tried and sentenced by a secret military tribunal and executed the following day.

Armed resistance by the SSNP militia, which Saadeh had ordered on the strength of Zaim's initial support, ceased after his execution. The party had suffered a catastrophe; it was leaderless and demoralized but it did not collapse completely. It even gained public sympathy from the manner of Saadeh's execution. At first this was most marked in Syria where Zaim was overthrown and executed after a coup in which SSNP officers were prominent. In the November 1949 elections nine SSNP members were elected to the Syrian National Assembly. The party headquarters under the new President, George Abdul Masih, moved to Damascus. However, the party never made real headway against the combined strength of the Syrian traditional forces and rising power of the left—Baath socialists and communists. After the assassination of Colonel Malki in 1954 by a sergeant in the SSNP the party was ruthlessly suppressed in Syria. This led two years later to a split in the party and the expulsion of Abdul Masih by decision of a secret party tribunal.

The party managed to survive this new disaster. In Lebanon its recovery was more lasting than in Syria. In 1951 three members assassinated Riyadh al-Sulh in Jordan and in 1952 the SSNP was an important element in the bloodless coup which overthrew Bishara al-Khoury and brought Camille Chamoun to power.

The party was still officially illegal in Lebanon but it enjoyed Chamoun's protection. It had its own newspapers and a disciplined organization. During the muted civil war in the summer of 1958 it gave Chamoun effective armed support for which it was rewarded by official recognition.

But the SSNP with its rigid dogma was unhappy in the post-1958 Lebanon of President Chehab and his policy of national reconciliation. While the party was detested by the pan-Arab nationalists and the left it was still suspect to its temporary allies the Lebanese nationalists on the right. It had virtually no support in the army which was over-whelmingly loyal to President Chehab. In the 1960 elections it was heavily defeated. Shortly afterwards Dr. Abdullah Saadeh (no relative of the founder) was elected president of the party. Since he was more flexible than his predecessors and aware that if the party was to thrive it must come to terms with both Lebanese and Arab nationalism the SSNP might have improved its prospects. Instead Saadeh allowed himself to be persuaded to endorse an attempt to overthrow the Lebanese Government by force on 31 December 1961. Since it was opposed by every other political group in Lebanon the gesture was hopeless and futile. Mass arrests of party members were followed by long and laborious trials. The eight death sentences were later commuted to life imprisonment.

Since the party has survived more than one apparently final disaster, it cannot now be pronounced extinct. Yet it has few prospects. Because its activities would never be licensed by any conceivable regime in Syria its survival as an organized group depends on the toleration of the Lebanese Government.

The Moslem Brotherhood

The Moslem Brotherhood has been called by one distinguished Arab writer 'the greatest of modern Islamic Movements',[1] although it never succeeded in spreading beyond the frontiers of the eastern Arab states. But it was not confined to Egypt, its country of origin. Branches were formed in other Arab states—notably Syria and Sudan—which helped

[1] Ishak Musa Hussaini, *The Moslem Brethren* (Beirut, 1956).

to preserve the movement from extinction after its suppression in 1954 by the Egyptian military regime.

The Brotherhood was founded in Ismailia in 1928 by a 22-year-old elementary school teacher named Hassan al-Banna, the son of a respected orthodox Islamic scholar. 'At its inception the Brotherhood was in essence a religious revival movement—a "revitalization movement" in the terminology of modern anthropologists. It soon developed into a politico-religious action society, and eventually, as it gained political influence, it became more political than religious.'[1]

Banna was small, vital, eloquent, and intelligent, with outstanding qualities of leadership. Initially his movement was concerned with protecting Islam against the forces of immorality and secularism encouraged by Western influence. In a sense he was a successor to Islamic reformers such as Jamal el-din al-Afghani or Rashid Rida, but Banna simplified their arguments to a simple demand for a return to the laws of the Koran and the Tradition.

In the early years Banna appealed most to the poor and uneducated but in 1934 he moved his headquarters to Cairo and began to attract supporters from all classes including students, teachers, civil servants, and army officers. By 1934 there were fifty branches in Egypt and by 1939 these had increased to five hundred. In 1946 he claimed half a million followers, which may well have been close to the truth. Already in the 1930s Banna had expanded his programme from religious revival to demands that the entire political, legal, and administrative system should be based on the Koran. But despite Banna's vigorous assertion that Islam could provide everything needed for the social order without recourse to alien Western systems such as Communism or Fascism, he had no clearly thought out political programme. The Brotherhood published many books but at this stage they had no consistent theoretical basis. What Banna did concentrate upon was the disciplining and organization of the movement into a formidable political force. He overrode the objections of some of his followers and became increasingly authoritarian. He changed his title from General Guide to Supreme Guide.

The Brotherhood was organized in a network of branches whose activities included social welfare, education, and physical training. There were youth groups which were given paramilitary training. From the start the Brotherhood laid great stress on Islam's call for *jihad* in its literal sense of fighting to spread the faith. In 1936 Banna denounced the Wafdist Government's treaty with Britain and in the following year gave active assistance to the Arab rebellion in Palestine. Successive Egyptian Governments began to seek his support or to reach an understanding with him, although when a strong Prime Minister was in office he skilfully played down his political activities and emphasized

[1] Christina Phelps Harris, *Nationalism and Revolution in Egypt* (London, 1964).

the movement's religious aims. Intervention in Palestine helped the movement to spread outside Egypt. The first branch was founded in Damascus in 1937, followed by others in Lebanon, Palestine, Sudan, and Iraq, although in this last it was hampered by opposition from the Shii population. Congresses were held in various Arab cities.

In the first years of the movement, Banna had frequently called for the freedom and independence of the whole Islamic world in his speeches. He continued to do so, but events in Palestine caused him to concentrate especially on the need for reform in the Arab world. Inevitably, the movement's xenophobia and anti-Westernism turned heavily against Britain, the occupying power, and with the emphasis on *jihad* and military training it was perhaps also inevitable that the Brotherhood should turn to terrorism. On the outbreak of the Second World War Banna was briefly interned for his well-known anti-British sympathies. After his release he reached a temporary understanding with the Wafd and refrained from opposing it while it was in office, 1942-4, but after this he both joined the mounting criticism of the Wafdists' record and attacked the various governments which succeeded them.

In 1948 many of the Brotherhood volunteered to fight with the Arab armies in Palestine where they showed courage and gained valuable guerrilla experience. In Egypt the political atmosphere was sharply deteriorating. The already unpopular regime, beset by scandal and accusations of corruption, was blamed for the disasters of the war. Terrorism and assassination, for which the Moslem Brotherhood bore much of the responsibility, were on the increase. In December 1948 the Prime Minister, Noqrashi Pasha, made use of wartime martial law to strike back by proclaiming the Brotherhood dissolved and closing its branches. On 28 December, Noqrashi was murdered, almost certainly by the Brotherhood, and two months later Banna himself was assassinated—probably by King Farouk's counter-terrorist forces.

After this shattering blow the movement remained largely quiescent until the lifting of martial law in 1950 when it was declared legal provided it refrained from political activity. But on the election in 1951 of a new Supreme Guide, a well-educated ex-magistrate named Hassan al-Hudaybi, the movement began to reorganize and to give itself a more consistent ideological position. Rapidly the Brotherhood recovered its spirits, denouncing the Government for the continued restrictions on its liberty and resuming its paramilitary activities. An opportunity came with the Wafdist Government's denunciation of the Anglo-Egyptian 1936 Treaty in October 1951, which was followed by guerrilla operations against the British in the Canal Zone. As Egypt sank into near-anarchy the Brotherhood saw its opportunity. Although the shares of responsibility for the burning of Cairo on 26 January 1952 have never been allocated, the Moslem Brotherhood undoubtedly played an important role. Much of the destruction was of restaurants and bars which were special objects of the Brotherhood's hatred.

The Brotherhood had reason to hope that when the monarchical regime collapsed it would take a leading role in the new Government if not control it entirely. But the movement was weakened by internal divisions. Al-Hudaybi was never able to establish his authority as al-Banna had done and he had powerful opponents within the movement. In particular he was disliked for his continued good relations with King Farouk.

So it was that when the Free Officers carried out their coup in July 1952 they did not consider handing over power to the Brotherhood. In general they were favourably disposed towards the movement. They admired their courage and a few of the Free Officers, such as Abdul Muneim Abdul Rauf, actually went over to their side. But when the Brotherhood asked the new Revolutionary Command Council to create an Islamic state with an Islamic constitution, it declined.

Nevertheless, the RCC acknowledged the contribution of the Brotherhood to the success of the Revolution and was prepared to make conciliatory gestures. It reopened the investigation into the assassination of Banna and released all Brethren who were held as political prisoners. But the Brotherhood over-estimated its strength and misjudged the Free Officers. After waiting to decide whether to lend its support to the Revolution it rather arrogantly proposed terms which included the right of the Supreme Guide to vet all new legislation. When the RCC refused, the movement silently resolved to go into opposition. It issued its own reform programme and when this was ignored by the RCC (although many of the Brotherhood's social and economic ideas coincided closely with its own) it turned to organizing a subversive movement within the police, armed forces, and labour unions.

The Government was aware of the potential threat of the Brotherhood but still refrained from taking action. Many of the Free Officers still believed that co-operation between the two movements was both possible and desirable. The decree of January 1953 dissolving all political parties was primarily directed against the Wafd, and the RCC accepted the Brotherhood's declaration that it was a non-political organization. But behind the scenes Colonel Nasser, who was only just emerging as the real leader of the Free Officers, began to show his great ability as a political tactician. Making skilful use of divisions within the Brotherhood, he broke up its cells in the police and army. In January 1954 the Brotherhood openly challenged the RCC at a joint meeting with the Communists at Cairo University; Moslem Brotherhood students assaulted members of the Government's Liberation Rally. The RCC dissolved the Brotherhood as a political movement and arrested

several leaders, including the Supreme Guide. The Brotherhood temporarily recovered as a result of the Nasser–Neguib crisis in February
in which Neguib at first came out on top. Neguib had never been a
sympathizer but he was prepared to be used by any potential opponents
of Nasser and the RCC majority.

During this summer Nasser was engaged in prolonged negotiations
with Britain for an agreement on evacuation. In order to show that he
could ensure security in the Canal Zone he arrested and dispersed the
Communists and Brotherhood guerrilla groups in the area. Hudaybi at
once toured the Arab states denouncing Nasser as a 'traitor to the
national cause'. The Brotherhood also attacked the draft Anglo-
Egyptian treaty as a sell-out. Nasser replied by depriving the Egyptian
Brotherhood's leaders in Syria of their nationality.

When on 26 October 1954 a simple-minded member of the Brotherhood tried unsuccessfully to murder Nasser at a rally in Alexandria the
Government was fully prepared. Police and army broke up all the
Brotherhood's cells, confiscated their arms, and arrested more than
4,000 people. The subsequent trials never clearly revealed whether the
Supreme Guide and his close associates were party to the assassination
attempt or whether it was the work of the so-called Secret Organ or
terrorist wing of the Brotherhood acting on its own initiative. The
would-be assassin and three terrorists were executed together with two
members of the Supreme Guidance Council. Hudaybi himself was
sentenced to life imprisonment.

The nature of the association between the Communists and the
Brotherhood has also never been clearly established. That the Communists saw the advantage of co-operating with the Brotherhood at that
stage, and that they succeeded in penetrating many of the movement's
cells is known. Very probably the Brotherhood's leaders believed that
they could make use of the Communists while remaining the senior
partners in the association.

In 1954 the movement seemed to have few prospects. ('Is it worth
our while to write a history of the Moslem Brethren now that the movement has been ended in Egypt and its future is largely ambiguous?')[1] A
strong branch remained in Syria as an outspoken opponent of Nasser's
Egypt. But in the 1950s it was swimming against the powerful current
of triumphant Nasserism which was sweeping the Arab countries. In
Egypt itself Nasser's political control was virtually complete and for
years the Brethren shared political prison camps with Communists.
When Syria was united with Egypt in 1958 the Syrian Brethren had to
go underground also. They had a brief opportunity to reassert themselves after the secession in 1961 but had little sympathy from the
Baathists who took control of Syria in 1963—still less from the neo-
Baathists in 1966.

[1] Ishak Musa Hussaini, *The Moslem Brethren* (Beirut, 1956), p. vi.

President Nasser's announcement in August 1965 that a widespread Moslem Brotherhood conspiracy had been uncovered in Egypt therefore caused some surprise. Some 2,000 people were arrested and about 400 stood trial on charges of planning to assassinate the President and sabotage all major government installations. It seems likely that the seriousness of the physical threat posed by the Brotherhood to the regime in 1965 was exaggerated. No evidence was produced of any widespread infiltration of the police and army by the Brotherhood's organization; on the other hand the fact that prominent members included a number of university lecturers, scientists, and engineers was alarming for the regime. Police investigations were tough and thorough and there was a partial setback in the cautious moves towards liberalization of the previous year (when the remaining Moslem Brotherhood and Communist political prisoners had been released).

Those of the Egyptian Brotherhood who escaped were able to find refuge in the Sudan, where the Moslem Brothers had a flourishing organization in political alliance with the Umma Party, and to Saudi Arabia. But although the Saudi regime was sympathetic and held the suppression of the Brotherhood as proof of Egypt's irreligion, it did not consider it necessary to encourage the growth of a branch of the movement in Saudi Arabia, the home of Wahhabism and Islamic puritanism.

Despite the Brotherhood's recovery from virtual extinction in Egypt, the movement's prospects in the principal Arab states remain doubtful. Its orthodox Sunnism repels Shii Moslems and it is feared and disliked by the politically important Christian minorities in the Arab world. Much of its early success in Egypt depended on Banna's ability to organize effective direct (and often violent) action against the regime in power. It was this, rather than his message, which attracted Egyptian students in the 1930s and 1940s and although a conservative peasantry in any Arab country might still respond to the call of Islamic revival and *jihad* (or Mahdism) it makes little appeal to the rising generation of politically-minded Arabs. Its recrudescence in Egypt, even among some of the intellectual elite, was more than anything the consequence of the frustration of political liberties.

Nasserism

Nasserism cannot be regarded as an organized political movement, still less as a political party. Gamal Abdul Nasser himself denied its existence ('Let them [the imperialists] say what they may. . . . Let them say "Building an Empire", "Nasserism", "Imperialism" . . . But for us, brethren, it is Arab nationalism and Arab unity.')[1] Yet the term is used to describe something which most people can identify. In its time it has

[1] Speech in Damascus, February 1960.

influenced the lives of almost every Arab and for several years it was infinitely more powerful than any political movement in the Middle East. (Perhaps the best parallel is with 'Bonapartism'.)

As the leader of the Egyptian Free Officers, Nasser was essentially a pragmatist with little interest in ideology. His energies were concentrated on the twin problems of ridding Egypt of the British and of purging its corrupt monarchical parliamentary regime. He had read much political and military history and biography but only a little socialist literature which had had small influence on his thinking. The Free Officers had drafted an agrarian reform programme which was implemented soon after they came to power but its purpose was less to solve Egypt's agrarian problems than to break the political power of the big landowners. For similar reasons Nasser opposed the restitution of Egyptian political parties. He was convinced that the parliamentary system had prevented Egypt from obtaining 'independence with dignity' but he had no plan for anything to replace it. He created out of his own mind a single political organization—the Liberation Rally—which was succeeded by the National Union and, in 1962, the Arab Socialist Union.

But it was not the political ideas of the Free Officers which constituted the appeal of Nasserism to the Arab world. Egyptian agrarian reform had some influence as the first measure of its kind in the Middle East but it was not the factor which put Nasser at the head of the Arab nationalist movement in the 1950s.

In the first years after 1952 Nasser was regarded with suspicion in many nationalist quarters. Intellectuals looked on him as a Latin American type of military dictator. Baathists, Communists, and Moslem Brothers felt he was compromising with the West. In 1953 he was widely regarded as pro-American. The change in his standing in the Arab nationalist movement came in 1954 with his determined opposition to the Baghdad Pact, his adoption of non-alignment, and his defiance of the West with his recognition of Communist China and the Czech arms deal. The doubts of more traditional Arab nationalists (Hashimites and Saudis) were outweighed by the immensely popular appeal of these measures. To the Arab man in the street Nasser was a new Saladin who, having shown he could successfully defy Western opinion, would lead the Arabs to unity, independence, and the recovery of Palestine. His photograph appeared in every corner of the Arab world. The Suez War, in which Nasser triumphantly survived a determined Western attempt to overthrow him, swelled the Nasserist tide which reached its crest in 1958-9 with the union of Syria and Egypt and the downfall of the Iraqi Hashimites.

It would be hard to exaggerate Nasser's influence in these years. In every Arab state—but especially Jordan, Lebanon, Syria, and Iraq—there were hundreds of thousands who were prepared to place

complete trust in him. Nasserism was backed by money, numerous
agents, and an increasingly potent propaganda machine. But if it had not
satisfied the emotional aspirations of millions of Arabs it would never
have been so successful. At the same time its weaknesses as a political
movement soon became apparent. Outside Egypt, Arab regimes which
feared the rising tide of radical nationalism were able to appeal to local
pride and interests. Adherents of Nasserism could always be described
as Nasser's agents or stooges. With varying success, President Chamoun
of Lebanon, King Hussein of Jordan, Abdul Karim Kassem of Iraq,
and King Saud of Saudi Arabia were all able to make capital out of the
fact that because Nasserism was Cairo-based its triumph would mean
Egyptian domination. Perhaps inevitably, Nasser could never make
Nasserism synonymous with Arab nationalism or Arab unity, although
for a time he seemed to come close to success.

The first counter-attack came with King Hussein's ousting of the
pro-Nasser Nabulsi Government in 1957. This was followed by
Kassem's adoption of anti-Egyptian policy within a few weeks of the
Iraqi Revolution in 1958 and Syria's secession in 1961. Nasser was
aware that in all three countries a mass of the people—perhaps a
majority—still supported him. But as long as he was not in physical
control of the government of these states—as he had been in Syria
during 1958–61—there was little he could do to help the Nasserists. If
he attempted to organize them as a political movement this would
merely expose them to persecution at the hands of the regime in
power.

In face of this dilemma, the approach he adopted was to declare that
Arab unity must wait until the Arab states had progressive rather than
'reactionary, secessionist' regimes or, as he was to put it in 1961–2,
there must be 'unity of aims' before 'unity of ranks'. At the same time
he claimed that the bonds between him and the Arab people were
stronger than ever. ('The unity linking us is the unity of blood. It was
never the unity of constitutions, the unity of a plebiscite, or the unity
of politicians. It is rather the unity of peoples, and of blood, which
associates us with the Arab nation at large.')[1]

In May 1962 Nasser had presented his National Charter to the
National Congress of Popular Powers which had unanimously approved
it a month later. In the ten years since the Revolution, Nasser had
acquired some interest in political theory. The 30,000-word Charter,
although often repetitive and rhetorical, clearly revealed his development as a political thinker. It showed the influence of Marxism and
Yugoslav revisionism but it also confirmed that Nasser remained first
and foremost an Egyptian nationalist in the tradition of Arabi and
Zaghlul. Starting from the assumption that Egyptian parliamentary
democracy before the Revolution was a sham, the Charter states:

[1] Speech on the tenth anniversary of the Revolution, July 1962.

'Political democracy cannot be separated from social democracy. No citizen can be regarded as free to vote unless he is given the following three guarantees: (*a*) he should be free from exploitation in all its forms; (*b*) he should enjoy an equal opportunity with his fellow citizens to enjoy a fair share of the national wealth; (*c*) his mind should be free from all anxiety likely to undermine his future security.' In other words, true democracy can only be achieved through socialism and the welfare state. The Charter lays down that the entire economic infrastructure (roads, railways, ports, etc.), the majority of heavy, medium, and mining industries, the import trade, banks, and insurance companies should all be in the public sector.

In the Charter and elsewhere, Nasser emphasized where his political and economic ideas differ substantially from Marxism. He rejects the atheistic state, the dictatorship of the proletariat, and the inevitability of the class struggle. He also says that the production of consumer goods should not be neglected through the concentration on heavy industry because 'the masses of our people have been long deprived; to mobilize all of them for the building of heavy industry and overlook their needs as consumers is incompatible with their right to make up for their long deprivation and delays.'

In the first part of the Charter Nasser refers to the Arab Revolution which would reach its objectives of Freedom, Socialism, and Unity through 'consciousness based on scientific conviction arising from enlightened thought and free discussion, unaffected by the forces of fanaticism and terrorism'. Freedom has come to mean 'freedom of the country and of the citizen' and socialism has become both a means and an end 'namely, sufficiency and justice'. He emphasizes that the Arab Revolution is now facing new circumstances demanding appropriate solutions. 'The Arab revolutionary experiment cannot afford to copy what others have achieved.' After listing these new circumstances the Charter says: 'The great part of the responsibility for this pioneering revolutionary action devolves upon the popular revolutionary leadership in the UAR since natural and historical factors have given the UAR the responsibility of being the "nucleus state" in this endeavour to secure freedom, unity, and socialism for the Arab Nation.' From this point onwards, the Charter concentrates upon Egypt's revolutionary struggle and its problems.

In the 1950s when Nasserism was at its apogee in the Arab world, Nasser does not seem to have given much thought to how the Arab states should be governed if they achieved union under his leadership. He regarded the Syrian Baathists' request for immediate union in 1958 as ill-considered and hasty but once he had agreed he insisted on a centralized system of government and the uniform application in both regions of the UAR of all social economic measures with little regard for their different circumstances. When Syria seceded in 1961 his first reaction was to believe that Syrian bourgeois reactionaries, who had succeeded in infiltrating the National Union organization in the Syrian region, had engineered the break to prevent the application of the UAR's socialist measures. Nevertheless, he later admitted (in the 1963 union talks) that one of his mistakes in Syria had been the dissolution of all political parties which had left a vacuum at the heart of the national union. It would have been better to have formed a national front among existing nationalist progressive forces.

The fact that Nasserism, in the sense of Egypt's politico-economic system, was not necessarily applicable to other Arab states became even more apparent with the Egyptian intervention in Yemen in 1962. Before long the Egyptians found themselves virtually administering a medieval tribalized society in which the basic concepts of the National Charter had little meaning.

Although Nasser was sceptical about the outcome of the union talks with Syria and Iraq in 1963, he was in theory prepared to accept a federal system which would have left the Baathists in control of these two countries and potentially given them influence inside Egypt. When the union was still-born he bitterly attacked the Baathists but he could have few illusions that the Nasserists in either Syria or Iraq were capable of ousting them. When the Iraqi Baathists were replaced by a more sympathetic (though not purely Nasserist) regime in November 1963 the Egyptians welcomed the event but remained extremely cautious about proposals for an Iraqi–Egyptian union. An agreement was signed in September 1964 for complete constitutional unity between Iraq and Egypt in two years but it was never implemented. Similarly, an Iraqi Arab Socialist Union formed on Egyptian lines remained moribund.

Nasser had come to believe that political union between the Arab states was still unfeasible. In February 1965 he told an Iraqi delegation 'We have only achieved what we have done here after first ensuring our own national unity.' To President Sallal of Yemen's repeated requests for a union he replied that it was out of the question as long as Egyptian troops were in Yemen. In fact he seems to have concluded that only a common military front against Israel was worth considering. It was for this reason that he called the first Arab Summit meeting in January 1964 which set up the United Arab Command. But even this was bedevilled by political differences. When the June 1967 war came, Egypt had bilateral defence treaties with both Jordan and Syria but the United Arab Command had virtually ceased to exist. Syria and Jordan broke off diplomatic relations the day before the war. Nasser's reaction to renewed Syrian approaches in May 1967 was that Syria should make a common front with Jordan and Iraq.

In 1968 Nasserism could no longer be identified with the modern Arab nationalist movement as it could have been ten years earlier.

Abdul Nasser himself might still be the most outstanding figure in the Arab world but henceforth no non-Egyptian Arabs could believe that he was capable of solving their problems for them. The Saladin image had been destroyed. Yet Nasserism had had a profound effect not only on all the eastern Arab states but further afield in Africa, Asia, and even Latin America. It had proved that a military coup in a developing country could mean much more than a colonel occupying the Presidential Palace. The example of Egypt's social and economic revolution was noted throughout the Third World and in many cases the threat of Nasserism was enough to frighten corrupt and extravagant rulers into making concessions to their people. In one sense the influence of Nasserism has been a negative one; it has dealt heavy blows to the forces of reaction but there has been little attempt in other Middle Eastern countries to imitate Nasser's methods of government which have been personal and peculiar to Egypt. But in the broader sense that Nasserism proved the ability of a small, underdeveloped, and poor country to pursue a dynamic autonomous policy largely independent of the Great Powers, it has been one of the most important political movements since the Second World War.

The Baath

The Arab Baath Socialist Party can claim to be the only Arab political movement that has successfully transcended the frontiers of the Arab states. Although the Moslem Brotherhood and the SSNP spread into more than one Arab country, the one was Islamic more than Arab while the other specifically rejected Arabism. Nasserism, which in its heyday was infinitely more powerful than the Baath has ever been, was never an organized political movement.

The Baath Socialist Party was formed by the union at the end of 1952 of the Baath ('resurrection') party in Syria and Akram Hourani's Socialist Party. The alliance arose out of common opposition to the Shishakli dictatorship and the Syrian right-wing parties. Hourani, with his strong regional base in the Hama area, was a formidable force in Syrian politics. But in many ways he was in the traditional mould of Arab politicians with little interest in the political ideas of the Baath who gave the united party its character and ideology.

The founders of the Baath were two Syrians, Michel Aflaq and Silah Bitar, who met as students in Paris in the early 1930s. Both of them flirted with Communism but became disillusioned as they reached the conclusion that the policies of the Soviet-based Communist movement were unsuited to the special problems of the Arab people. While teaching in a Damascus secondary school they began to hold political meetings and write pamphlets until they abandoned teaching in 1942 to devote themselves to full-time political work. The founding of the Baath Party dates from 1944 although it only emerged as an officially constituted political movement after the departure of the French in 1946.

Aflaq was more the party philosopher and Bitar the organizer. Aflaq, a withdrawn ascetic, has been called the 'Gandhi of Arab nationalism'. His writings, which are romantic and idealistic in tone, are far from lucid. Yet his personality and ideas, which he expounded at private meetings, attracted ardent disciples. These ideas, which owed something to Marxism and to romantic German nineteenth-century nationalism, he gave a specifically Arab character. He summarized the three Arab objectives as 'Freedom, Unity, and Socialism'. (The Baath could claim that these were ultimately adopted by all progressive Arab movements—including Nasserism.) He injected all three terms with his own somewhat mystical idealism summarized in his central slogan 'One Arab nation with an eternal mission.' Freedom meant political, cultural, and religious liberty as well as liberation from colonial rule. Unity meant not only the political unification of the Arab peoples but their regeneration through the release of the 'hidden vitality' which is the true source of nationalism (hence the name Baath). Socialism, which comes last in the Baath trinity, is less a set of socio-economic principles than a rather vague means of national moral improvement. Neither Aflaq nor Bitar ever showed much interest in the adoption of specific socialist measures (whether Marxist or Scandinavian). All they said was that socialism was a means of abolishing poverty, ignorance, and disease, and achieving progress towards an advanced industrial society capable of dealing on equal terms with other nations.

Running through all Aflaq's writings and statements is a belief in the need of revolution in the Arab world, but revolution in the sense of a total and organic change of mind and attitude involved in what he called 'the awakening of the Arab spirit at a decisive stage in human history'. He constantly emphasizes the need for love. 'Nationalism is love before everything else' because the renaissance will not take place until the Arab people show selfless unquestioning love for each other and their nation. In this context, although a Christian himself, he emphasizes the importance of Islam in its close connection with the spirit of the Arab nation.

In the 1940s the Baath and Akram Hourani campaigned for universal suffrage and a secret ballot. Ultimately they were successful, but it was not until 1954 that they reaped their reward. Aflaq and Bitar were imprisoned several times by the civilian and military regimes of those years. Aflaq never succeeded in being elected to the Chamber of Deputies and only once, reluctantly, held office for three months as Minister of Education in 1949.

In the 1949 election the Baath won three seats in Parliament. In 1954, after playing a prominent role in the overthrow of the Shishakli dictatorship, it won 16 out of 140 seats in parliament. It had benefited from its alliance with Hourani and its improved organization but also from the widespread disillusion among the younger generation with the older political parties. These still had a majority in parliament but the Baath, which remained in opposition until 1956, was stronger than it appeared. It was actively gaining support among army officers and it was benefiting from the general anti-Western radical current in the Arab world. In 1956 they entered a Coalition Government with the key posts of Economics and Foreign Affairs.

In Abdul Nasser's first years in power the Baath regarded him with suspicion as a regionalist and compromiser with the West. But with his increasingly successful defiance of the West the party cast away its doubts and called for union with Egypt. The feeling was strengthened by the Suez crisis and its consequences.

The year 1957 was a crest in the Baath party's fortunes. In Jordan the party had been legalized in 1954, although it had been active for several years before and had attracted a substantial youthful following on both East and West Banks. In 1956 a Baathist, Abdullah Rimawi, became Deputy Premier in the Nabulsi Government and although this was overthrown by King Hussein's counter-coup in the following year, the Baathist organization, with Syrian and Egyptian support, survived in Jordan. In Iraq also the regional branch of the Baath was growing in strength and importance to become one of the major forces behind the overthrow of the monarchy in the following year.

However, the left-wing trend in Syria was also benefiting the Communists (one of whom, Colonel Bizri, had become Commander-in-Chief of the army). The Soviet Union had seen the wisdom of supporting Arab nationalism and was making full use of the West's débâcle at Suez. It is not certain how far the Syrian Baathists believed a Communist takeover was possible (or whether they merely wished to avoid being forced into a compromise with the right-wing parties). What is certain is that in leading their unwilling coalition partners into the union with Egypt in 1958 they thought that Nasser would guarantee their control of Syria. More than this they believed that they would be able to propagate their ideas throughout the union and provide Nasser with the philosophy that they thought he lacked.

After pointing out that the union was badly unprepared, Nasser insisted that authority should be centralized in Cairo. The Baath accepted his terms and even officially dissolved their organization along with the other Syrian political parties on his instructions. They believed that they would have the running of the UAR's National Union in the Syrian region. But this was not Nasser's intention (although he seems to have at least partly regretted it later). He appointed Baathists to high office in the UAR Government but allowed them no privileged position within the National Union. The consequence was that the

D

Baathists were heavily defeated in the National Union elections in 1959 by independents and right-wingers.

The Baath's position rapidly deteriorated. In August 1959 there was a split; Rimawi and another prominent Jordanian Baathist who believed that the Baath should merge with the Nasserists, were expelled from the party. In September, Nasser dismissed the Baathist Minister of National Guidance in the Syrian region and in December all remaining Baathists in the UAR central and regional governments, including Hourani and Bitar, resigned.

From then until Syria's secession in September 1961 Nasser ruled Syria through the Baathists' former ally the head of the intelligence service, Colonel Sarraj, and Field-Marshal Amer, whom he sent as his proconsul to Damascus. But the Baathists remained in disgruntled retirement. Only Hourani actively and enthusiastically supported the secession when it came and he and his faction were shortly after expelled from the Party. Bitar signed the secession manifesto with misgivings and later repudiated his signature.

The secession placed the Baath in a cruel dilemma. It was not enough to blame the break on Nasser's authoritarian rule. The act of secession went against everything the Baath had stood for. The Baath organization consisted of a National Command for the whole Arab nation and Regional Commands which theoretically existed in each Arab country. The National Command was now divided. Although communications between the different branches were now very difficult the party structure had survived the dissolution of the organization in Syria and the National Command continued to hold secret meetings in Lebanon. The Syrian regional command said that the secession should be accepted but the majority of the Lebanese, Iraqi, and Jordanian Baathists condemned it and demanded immediate reunion. Eventually the National Command proposed that the Party work for a new union on a federal basis.

In Iraq, as in Jordan, the Baath were now in opposition again as hopes raised by the 1958 Revolution were rapidly disappointed. Fuad Rikabi, the head of the Iraqi Baathists, joined Abdul Karim Kassem's first government but within three months Kassem had turned against the pan-Arabs, Nasserists, and Baath. Rikabi followed the Jordanian Rimawi in advocating the Baath's merger with the Nasserists and for this he too was expelled in 1961.

The Party was in disarray but once again events were moving in its favour. In Iraq, Kassem 'Presided over a strange regime that drifted in a twilight zone between Communism and a shapeless, anarchic radicalism, resting on no visible organized support.'[1] He survived largely because of divisions between his Arab nationalist opponents, but his ultimate overthrow seemed inevitable. In Syria also the Baath could

[1] Malcolm Kerr, *The Arab Cold War 1958–64* (New York, 3rd ed., 1971), p. 17.

feel confident that the series of unpopular and unstable governments, lacking the courage of their right-wing convictions, would ultimately cause their own downfall.

In Iraq the Baath's opportunity came in February 1963 following a widespread students' strike against the Government. Kassem was arrested and executed; the Baath formed the majority of the Government although Abdul Salam Aref, a non-Baathist, became President. A coup in Syria could not be long delayed. Aflaq paid a triumphal visit to Baghdad where he was treated with respect and honour by the young and inexperienced Iraqi Baathists. One month later the Damascus Government had also been toppled. Superficially, the Syrian Baathists were more prepared to share power with others than their Iraqi colleagues. In the new Syrian Government half the twenty ministers were non-Baathist Nasserists or Arab nationalists of various kinds.

The two coups were warmly welcomed by Egypt. The Iraqi and Syrian leaders flew to Cairo and there was a public reconciliation between Nasser and Bitar. The way seemed to be open for a union between three progressive Arab countries subscribing to the slogan 'Freedom, Unity, and Socialism'. Discussions began immediately and continued intermittently until a formal agreement was announced on 17 April 1963. In fact the union was doomed before it came into existence. On the one hand, Nasser, although prepared to deal with the Iraqi Baath as the main instrument of Kassem's overthrow, insisted that the Syrian Baathists share power with other nationalists. The Syrians were equally determined that they would not suffer the same fate as in 1958/9. Much of the union discussions was spent in recrimination and although an agreement was hammered out it glossed over the real difficulties, especially the question of the existence of political parties. With his prestige and experience Nasser could dominate the discussions but he could not control what was happening in Syria.

Nasser was aware that he still had a wide following among the Syrian people. But the Baathists, with the help of a determined strongman, General Hafez, held to the reins of power, suppressed opposition and dismissed all anti-Baathist officers. Friction between Cairo and Damascus sharpened especially when Nasser realized that the Syrian Baathists were receiving strong encouragement from the Iraqi left-wing Baathist leader Ali Saleh Saadi. But all hopes of union visibly collapsed only in July when the visit to Cairo of a Syrian delegation in a last-minute effort to save it coincided with an unsuccessful pro-Nasser revolt in Damascus which was ruthlessly suppressed. Nasser and the Baath declared war on each other.

The two Baathist regimes in Iraq and Syria grew closer together in common defence against Nasser. In September they concluded an economic agreement and when the Iraqis renewed military operations against the Kurds the Syrians sent a battalion of troops. In October the Sixth National Convention of the Baath, the most important in the party's history, was held in Damascus following regional conferences in Iraq and Syria. But the alliance was short-lived. Although the Syrian Baathists were widely regarded as weaker it was the Iraqi Baathists who were first overthrown.

When the party split into a left-wing faction, led by Saadi, and a right-wing led by the Foreign Minister Taleb Shabib and Interior Minister Hazem Jawad, President Aref and senior non-Baathist officers seized the opportunity to oust the Baath entirely.

In its nine months in power in Iraq the Baath had made itself exceedingly unpopular. Ali Saleh Saadi had organized a people's militia of students and peasants who had terrorized the populace. Imprisonment and torture were widely used against all opponents of the Baath—Communist and Nasserist. There was also a strong element of resentment among the Iraqi people that Iraq should be placed in a subordinate position to Syria, the headquarters of the Baathist movement.

The Baath's overthrow left the Syrian regime in a weakened and dispirited state. Its situation worsened when Saadi came to Damascus and began to rally support against the traditional leadership among the younger Baathists attracted by his radicalism and vigorous personality. Aflaq and Bitar rallied their supporters and with some difficulty managed to retain control of the National Command which ultimately expelled Saadi.

The Baathist regime in Syria survived these external and internal troubles because its opponents remained divided and leaderless. It overcame a merchants' strike, backed by religious elements, which started in Hama and spread to the rest of the country. However, the Government was forced to make concessions to the middle classes and to mark time on its socialization measures. In December 1965 the left-wing of the party was ousted and Bitar took office with a programme of moderation and rapprochement with Egypt. In consequence, in February 1966 it too was overthrown by a group of left-wing neo-Baathists (of Saadi's type though without his participation) led by Colonel Salah Jedid, a former chief of staff. The old Baathist leaders were either imprisoned or escaped into exile. Aflaq left the Arab world altogether in disgust.

This seemed like the end of the road for the Baathist movement. It was now in power in only one Arab country and there it had repudiated its own founder (rather as if a Communist Government should denounce Marx and Lenin). In the short time that it had controlled the Governments of Iraq and Syria it had shown its declared faith in freedom and democracy to be theoretical rather than practical; it had as consistently refused to share power as the authoritarian regimes it denounced. In the social and economic fields it had done little more than revive the Nasserist measures which had been partially emasculated by governments of the post-secession period.

In 1966 the Syrian Baathists were at violent odds with Iraq, Jordan, and Egypt. But in November Syria's weakness and isolation *vis-à-vis* Israel forced the regime to swallow its anti-Nasser sentiments and seek a joint defence agreement with Egypt, although its consistent refusal to allow Egyptian bases on Syrian territory made the pact largely ineffective. After the Six Day War of June 1967, in which Syria played an unheroic role, the Government was deeply unpopular at home and throughout the Arab world. Its armed forces had been weakened by drastic Baathist purges. Some even believed that it was in secret collusion with Israel although its actions (including its arrest of some of the leaders of Palestinian commando organizations) could be explained by an absolute determination to remain in power.

Contrary to the expectations of many, the neo-Baathists remained in control of Syria after the 1967 war without relaxing in any way the defiant extremism of their policies. They boycotted the Arab summit at Khartoum in August 1967 and rejected any efforts to reach a political solution with Israel. At home they strengthened State control of the economy; the private sector came virtually to a standstill. At the same time, the State was able to take credit for Syria's becoming an oil exporting country in the summer of 1968 and the first Arab country to develop its oil resources without foreign capital. In the same year work also started on the huge Euphrates Dam with Soviet aid. Although resting on a very narrow base (the Alawite minority being predominant) the regime survived through its own determination and the divisions among its many enemies. But reports of attempts to overthrow it became increasingly frequent.

When President Abdul Rahman Aref of Iraq was ousted in July 1968 and replaced by a regime in which moderate 'orthodox' Baathists were dominant, the Syrian Government did not welcome the event. Obviously it strengthened the hand of moderate Syrian Baathist exiles in Lebanon. However, the Baathist revival in Baghdad did show the survival power of Baathists' ideas despite extreme unpopularity of some of their actions when in power. With the possible exception of the people's militia in Syria, the Baathists could not claim to have originated new policies. In the economic field, land reform and socialization measures were taken over from the United Arab Republic. Syria's Baathists were perhaps more ardent secularizers than President Nasser but it was only a difference of emphasis. Nevertheless, by 1968 the Baath had proved that despite its failures and disappointments and its frequently tyrannical behaviour in power, the kernel of its doctrine of an Arab renaissance survived in the hearts and minds of the Arab people. That it did so even when the party philosopher had been repudiated by the Baath in his country of origin showed that the party's fortunes were not bound to the fate of one man.

PETER MANSFIELD

3. THE UNITED STATES IN THE MIDDLE EAST

For more than fifty years, American policy in the Middle East has been dominated by the problem of Palestine. The Middle East as a whole hardly figured in United States' concern during the First World War; President Wilson supported Lord Balfour's Declaration more to influence Jewish opinion elsewhere than to affect events in the area itself. In the Second World War, Britain had chief responsibility for the Levant in Allied efforts against the Axis. In post-war politics, the Truman Administration gave erratic support to Zionist efforts to form a Jewish State; but in the process, the Administration's eyes were on American domestic politics, not on the future of the Middle East.

America's first efforts to shape policies for Middle East countries other than Palestine began only in 1950, with the tripartite Declaration and the abortive attempt to forge a Middle East Defence Organization, but the first of these steps was in fact designed primarily to promote the future of Israel, and the second to include the Middle East, which had previously been of peripheral concern to Americans, within the concept of a global cold war.

Throughout the 1950s this dual approach was continued but the United States never created a set of policies that focused on the region itself. There was little general American concern for the Middle East behind the fiasco over the Aswan Dam which helped to produce the Suez War and to bring the Soviet Union into the area. Even America's act of principle during the Suez War and its efforts at conciliation afterwards did not amount to a thought-out approach to Middle East problems. The Eisenhower Doctrine which followed was directed against a remote and hypothetical threat from the north and thoroughly misjudged the nationalism of the Arab states.

It was not until the 1960s, during the brief Administration of President Kennedy, that the United States began to recognize the broader problems in the region and to understand the place of Nasser's Egypt in Arab politics. But by the mid-1960s American concern again focused on Israel. The United States began supplying arms directly to Tel Aviv and withdrew its aid to Egypt in a move that recalled the withdrawal from the Aswan Dam project. However, after the Lebanon landings of 1958, the Americans had learned the value of non-intervention, even in support of friendly Arab regimes.

United States' concern with Israel's problems was largely isolated from its rivalry with the Soviet Union in the Middle East. American support for Israel reflects a deep personal commitment on the part of millions of Americans of all faiths—a commitment which is partial atonement for American inactivity during the holocaust suffered by European Jews under the Nazis. The role of Jewish votes and money in American electoral politics also influences policy towards Israel.

In the past another element in the American attitude towards Israel was a relative ignorance of the structure of the Middle East conflict. The Six Day War of 1967, however, changed the dimensions of American concern for the Middle East—perhaps for all time. From the first day of that conflict, when the hot-line connecting Washington and Moscow came into use for the first time, the United States could no longer keep separate its support of Israel and its concern with the role of the Soviet Union in the Middle East. If possible, these two concerns had to be reconciled; if not, they would pose grave difficulties. Most important, the aftermath of the war made Soviet involvement more explicit, especially in Egypt; and the issue of Soviet–American competition began to crystallize into a single insistent question: would there be a confrontation between the super-powers, or could they learn the ways of peaceful co-existence?

This was not an easy question to answer. In addition to Russia's growing role, America's emergence as the sole supplier of Israel's advanced military equipment, and as her single diplomatic champion, threatened to place Russians and Americans rigidly on the opposite sides of a conflict that was of intrinsic importance to neither of them. In the process, it was becoming clear that an American policy of giving unqualified support to Israel could not be pursued without providing new opportunities and gains for the Soviet Union. The dilemma, therefore, was complete.

This dilemma remains, for the United States Government now sees the Middle East conflict from a broader perspective of Soviet–American rivalry in many parts of the world. It will no longer be possible for the United States to treat Israel as a discrete issue, nor to accept Israel's own evidence of its needs, either in terms of military weapons or diplomatic support; and it will no longer be possible to consider the Middle East as a region of minor importance, with United States' interests confined to the oil of the Arab states and the special relationship with Israel.

This change in United States' policy towards the Middle East has already begun to have effect. To begin with the United States has accepted a larger share of responsibility for leading the Arab–Israeli conflict in the direction of some partial settlement. If this effort were to succeed, it could promote Israel's security. Its more basic motive, however, is to narrow the scope for Soviet activity in neighbouring Arab states, and hence to provide opportunities for improving American relations with them.

In part, this American role as peacemaker was the result of a growing recognition in Washington that its support of Israel involved America in a situation over which it had no control. In 1970, for example, it was demonstrated that Israel would stimulate increased Soviet activity in Egypt as a reaction to the use of American-supplied aircraft against targets deep within Egypt, thereby making it apparent that the United States could be led into confrontation with the Soviet Union without itself having determined the circumstances or the points at issue. For a super-power, this was intolerable, and all the more so in view of evidence that the Russians had similar difficulties in restraining Egyptian military ventures.

Despite the United States Government's efforts to bring peace to the Arab–Israeli conflict, however, there are few people in Washington who have any illusions that this endemic struggle can be brought to an end easily. At times, American policy has appeared to be over zealous in looking for a settlement in which all issues could be resolved. But in general, the United States has rightly concentrated on the *process* of settlement, in which outsiders would slowly try to direct Israel and the most important of her Arab neighbours—Jordan and Egypt—away from war and towards less threatening means of pursuing their competing objectives. 'Peace with justice' is the slogan; but it is less important for the United States that anyone reach this goal than that the course be set correctly, that there should be a continuing cease-fire, and that there should be few opportunities for the Soviet Union to exploit its position in the area.

The changed imperatives for United States policy have also altered the American view of the 'balance of power' in the Middle East. The United States Government (at least in the State Department) has long understood that there is no true military 'balance' as between Israel and her Arab neighbours. This fact was amply demonstrated by the Six Day War, and it has not altered substantially since then. Until Israel's deep-penetration air raids against Egypt in 1970 the United States had had indifferent success in resisting Israeli calls for more armaments to offset increasing arms flows from the Soviet Union to Egypt. Since then, the American Government has been more willing to say publicly that Israel retains a superiority of force over her neighbours, despite continuing arms shipments from the Soviet Union. This difference in emphasis derives partly from greater US concern over the possibility of a confrontation with the Soviet Union, and partly from the recognition, as a result of the Suez War, that Israel does not hold all the moral or political arguments in the Arab–Israeli conflict. There has been a growing awareness in the United States of the status of Arab Palestinians, whether in Israel-occupied territories or in refugee camps elsewhere.

The fact that Israel proved unwilling to clarify its policy on the eventual return of Arab lands for many months after the beginning of the cease-fire in August 1970 also helped provoke public debate about United States relations with Israel, the first of its kind for nearly a decade and a half. It is problematic, however, whether such questioning will continue and whether it will permit the United States Government to make its own judgements about arms shipments to Israel.

Most important, the events of 1970 and early 1971 reinforced the American belief that effective arms-control in the Middle East requires the co-operation of the Soviet Union. To achieve this, both super-powers must be able to exercise more control over the actions of their client states. Ironically, it was the Soviet Union that appeared to have done most to operate a policy of 'arms control'. After the Six Day War, it had limited its shipments to weapons that would help deter Israeli attack, but not to increase Egyptian offensive capabilities. American Phantom aircraft supplied to Israel, on the other hand, could be—and were—used in ways that actually stimulated further escalation in the arms race.

It is not easy to define America's interest in the Middle East, especially since its concern with Israel is not based on traditional political or economic factors. But whatever the American interest may be, there remains a fundamental United States commitment to Israel's ultimate security. In the past this fact was often used by Israel to gain United States arms and diplomatic support. In theory such indirect American involvement in Israel's defence would make direct military action unnecessary. But with the increasing risks of a Soviet–American clash resulting from large-scale armed conflict among the local states, the United States has felt compelled to temper its support for Israel's long-term security with more cautious policies in the short term.

The Americans, therefore, have a difficult task. On the one hand, they must continually impress upon the Russians the risks of super-power conflict if Israel is directly threatened; on the other hand, they must not allow Israel so much latitude that a super-power conflict becomes inevitable.

In an era of *détente*, it has proved easier to achieve the first of these objectives. Both super-powers are now acting more cautiously towards one another. In order for the Americans to deter Soviet adventures in the Middle East it is probably only necessary for them to retain the ability to apply force in the area, and such a force is represented by the US Sixth Fleet.

It is more difficult for the United States to limit Israeli activities, even if there were a total embargo on further arms shipments—an act that is not remotely possible, barring a comprehensive United States–Soviet agreement on arms control. Here, too, the United States requires the active co-operation of the Soviet Union in seeking to reduce Arab hostility to Israel likely to provoke rash retaliation. Some co-operation has been forthcoming. For several years the Russians have acknowledged Israel's right to exist, and have been willing to help promote cease-fires and limited steps towards a settlement.

Yet an earlier dilemma remains: how can the United States induce the Soviet Union to be more positive about securing a partial settlement? After all the Soviet position in the Arab world—and especially in Egypt—has rested largely upon the threat of renewed hostilities in the area. The death of Nasser may provide part of an answer. On the one hand, his successors feel less need to continue the conflict with Israel beyond recovering lands that are still occupied. Ironically, efforts begun by Nasser to stabilize the conflict may have more success now that he is dead. More than any other Arab leader, he used hostility to Israel to promote an idea of Arab unity. With Nasser's death, that idea has altered—how much it is too early to tell.

On the other hand, Nasser's successors are as anxious as he was to reduce Soviet influence in Egypt. It is doubtful, however, whether they could exclude the Soviet Union totally from Egypt, whatever the outcome of the Arab–Israeli conflict. Since Nasser's death, Soviet actions in supporting a cease-fire and in moving towards a limited settlement seem to indicate that Moscow no longer needs a low level of continuing conflict in the Middle East to ensure that it will be needed by the Arabs.

As a result, the American dilemma has been somewhat reduced, although it still remains for the United States to accept in positive terms something she has so far accepted only by default—namely, a continuing and active Soviet presence in the Arab Middle East, for the foreseeable future.

Since 1969 the Americans have been diligent in seeking Soviet co-operation in their attempts to secure a partial settlement. There have been direct talks between the super-powers and among the four Great Powers at the United Nations. The United States has also advanced the idea of establishing a peace-keeping force in the Middle East that would have the support of the super-powers if not their troops. In these ways, the United States has helped to make the presence of the Soviet Union in the area more legitimate, while seeking to damp down the risks of war.

Before the Soviet Union will accept an end to hostilities, however, the United States will almost certainly have to grant even more legitimacy to its presence in the Middle East, and especially in Egypt. Some Americans still oppose this idea, primarily on the grounds that the Soviet Union would use a continuing presence in Egypt as a platform for ventures farther afield. These fears may be exaggerated and are based in part upon a dying tradition of 'gun-boat' diplomacy. Even with a reopened Suez Canal, the value of Soviet military and naval forces south and east of the Middle East will not necessarily be decisive in political developments in those areas. Even failing a hypothetical arms-control agreement designed to limit naval forces in the Indian Ocean, the mere presence of United States naval forces there would limit the diplomatic influence to be gained by either super-power through a military show of force.

Moreover, the United States' recognition of the Soviet Union's continuing presence in Egypt could affect the character of that presence. As the United States has found in places like South-east Asia—as an axiom of military life since Clausewitz—the presence of military forces is a strong incentive to find a justification for their use. But a Soviet presence in Egypt that is *seen* to be legitimate by all concerned could develop from one based essentially on military factors into one based primarily on economic involvement—as, for example, during the building of the Aswan Dam.

The attempt to shape the character of the Soviet presence in Egypt may founder on the shoals either of the Russians' ambition or their failure to appreciate the distinction between a military and an economic presence. But for the United States, faced with a Soviet Union that *is* present in Egypt, and which has still not joined wholeheartedly in the search for a settlement of the Arab–Israeli conflict, there is value in trying, over the coming years, to shift Soviet competition with the West from the military to the economic sphere.

It will now be clear that the present analysis is concerned with broader issues than those intrinsic to the Middle East itself. Indeed, this is part of the problem. The Soviet presence in the Middle East means that the United States is no longer merely annoyed at an endemic conflict in an area of peripheral interest, but is acutely aware of its effects on Soviet–American relations in general. Consequently the Middle East is being accorded a value by the United States that it would not warrant on its own.

It is essential, however, that the United States should not see the Middle East as more important than it really is, simply because the Russians happen to be there. The Soviet Union may still be acting on the basis of a nineteenth-century concept of the worth of this nexus of continents and oceans; but this is no reason for the United States to mimic such an outdated view through a failure of imagination. Similarly, the United States Government is still acting on the basis of a cold war belief that all parts of Soviet–American relations are interdependent. Experience throughout the 1960s, however, indicates the opposite, and shows that both super-powers are now able to see each area of their political competition in its own terms, to be resolved or continued according to the matter at issue. Strategic arms-limitation talks continue despite crises in the Middle East and South-east Asia; and

Europe, formerly the bell-wether of United States–Soviet relations, has remained quiet throughout.

As far as the Middle East is concerned the US Government must learn to assess how far a Soviet presence there threatens United States' interests in the area and how far peaceful competition is tolerable. Otherwise the United States will accord the area undue importance and perhaps cause the Russians to do the same.

Basically, the problem the United States faces in the Middle East is: how to share influence in a region that has no history of Soviet–American competition. Farther north, in Turkey and Iran, Great Power competition involving the Soviet Union has a far longer history. There, Moscow and Washington are beginning to share influence without alarming effects. But what happens in the Arab Middle East will remain the great test of American purpose and ingenuity for the foreseeable future: can the United States learn to live with a Soviet presence in the Middle East, limiting it and shaping it where possible, without over-reacting to the point of provoking a deeper Soviet involvement?

The main object of the American pursuit of shared influence is to reduce Soviet mischief-making in the Arab–Israeli conflict. But there is also a matter of American relations with individual Arab states. Clearly it would not do for the United States to offer itself to Arab states as a complete alternative to relations with the Soviet Union, even if this were possible in view of America's concern for Israel's ultimate security. If the Arabs could replace the Soviet Union with American or other Western connections, there would simply be no further progress in Soviet attitudes towards a continuing cease-fire or partial settlement.

Yet the United States does need to cultivate good relations with Arab states, if only to prevent the 'polarization' of states in the area between the two super-powers. Such a development would only prove the very point which the United States is striving to deny, namely that there is a connection between the limitation of Soviet activity in the Middle East and the promotion of Israel as the only 'democratic bastion' in the area. As the Americans have found, it is only by denying this link that they can hope to prevent the Arab–Israeli conflict from becoming a straightforward competition with the Soviet Union.

Fortunately, the United States maintains good relations with at least three of Israel's immediate Arab neighbours—Jordan, Saudia Arabia, and Lebanon. These relations proved of indifferent value during the Six Day War, when Jordan felt compelled to join the common Arab military effort. Yet along with increasing uncertainty about the 'radical' character of other states following the death of Nasser and shifts in Syria and Iraq, they do permit some flexibility in the pattern of super-power relations in the immediate area.

Unfortunately for the United States, however, the stability of at least two of the three regimes in question—in Amman and Riyadh—is in serious doubt. Since 1970 the potential role of the Palestinians in Jordan has been reduced, at least for a time. But in the longer run, there is likely to be a change in government in all of the 'traditional' Arab states. If the United States is caught on the losing side after these changes take place, then the possibilities open to the Soviet Union will be increased.

To guard against this development, the United States must exercise a clear neutrality with regard to Arab politics, and particularly to individual Arab states. Such an attitude would not in itself be likely to gain the United States any friends among those Arab states which place emphasis either on the continuing struggle with Israel or on preventing a resurgence of imperialism. Nor would the Americans stand to gain from hastening the process of change. Yet the character of American actions in the Arab Middle East during the next few years is crucial, and it may determine whether or not a state seeks relations with the Soviet Union as a counterweight to an American presence.

For the United States, the adoption of a neutral attitude towards Arab politics will not be easy. As recently as the autumn of 1970, the American Government revived memories of the Lebanon landings with its over-anxious preparations to intervene in the Jordanian conflict with the Palestinians. Still, the long-term value for the United States of changing its attitudes and practices seems clear; and these changes would be especially beneficial if, to begin with, they took the form of a continuing and positive assertion of the rights of the Palestinian refugees.

This injunction takes on added importance in view of the one great resource in the Middle East that has any value for the West—oil. For the United States, this is a commercial interest, not a strategic one. Americans control about 60 per cent of Middle East production; but the United States itself imports only about 3 per cent of its domestic consumption from there. Any American strategic interest is indirect—occasioned by the dependence of both Western Europe and Japan on Middle East oil supplies (although American direct interest will grow as it is estimated that 30 per cent of its oil needs will come from the Middle East by 1985).

Nevertheless, the Americans remain preoccupied with securing the flow of oil from the Middle East at a reasonable price. And of late this preoccupation has come increasingly to focus on the likelihood of active Soviet involvement in Middle East oil, either through commercial channels or a direct presence in the areas of the Persian Gulf vacated by Great Britain.

In this sphere, too, fears expressed about Soviet designs seem to be exaggerated. On the one hand, Soviet demand for Middle East oil—perhaps 200 million tons by 1980—would be dwarfed by demand from

West Europe and Japan, and although oil producers would welcome an additional market for their product, they would resist stoutly any efforts to replace their existing markets. On the other hand, the oil producers would not look kindly upon anyone who was disposed to play a 'spoiler's' role. Nor will countries, such as Iran, welcome a Great Power presence in the Persian Gulf to replace departing Britain.

The threat to Western oil interests—whether commercial or strategic—comes less from the Soviet Union than from the nature of relations between the oil producing and oil consuming states. Again, the United States has a direct interest in cultivating good relations with Arab states. During 1971, members of the Organization of Petroleum Exporting Countries (OPEC) demonstrated, for the first time, that they could co-operate in opposing Western oil companies over negotiations over price, royalties, and output. Algeria and Libya also took steps to improve their terms of trade with the consuming nations. These do not appear to be isolated ventures, but rather are part of the trend of events throughout the developing world with regard to the supply of raw materials.

In the not-too-distant future, it is probable that these steps will be taken even further, leading to the nationalization (as in Algeria) of all Western holdings in Middle East oil. For the West, what happens then will be of critical importance. It is unlikely, of course, that the producing countries will cut off supplies of oil—although its price will continue to increase, as at present. But oil producing states will be looking for alternative means of marketing and selling their supplies. In short, they will offer management contracts—either favouring existing companies and countries, or favouring new entrants, including Japan and perhaps also the Soviet Union and countries of Eastern Europe. For the United States, therefore, a sizeable commercial interest may be at stake.

There may be little that can be done to reverse this trend but relations between the West and individual states will do much to influence the direction of events when the inevitable process of nationalization begins. Unfortunately, the first round of negotiations did not go well from this point of view, since it included an obvious effort by the West to combine against the Middle East oil producers. Significantly, Japan —which has most to gain from a change in present marketing arrangements—remained aloof from the concerted pressure by consuming states.

A repetition of this practice will only further jeopardize the Western —and hence the American—position in Middle East oil, with consequent commercial penalties.

Moreover the West—and especially the US—will have to take a greater interest in the problem facing all of the countries in the Middle East to a greater or lesser degree: the need for economic development.

Some of these countries already have vast wealth, but lack the technical assistance to make it effective. Still others are thwarted by a lack of both capital and a satisfactory way of sharing what wealth there is.

There is considerable scope for the United States to give support to the development efforts of individual Arab states and political gains to be made from it. The United States, for reasons of its political relations with Israel, cannot perhaps become involved directly in any such scheme. The World Bank could be an acceptable alternative, even though the bulk of financing would come from the United States. But the important point is that a Western-sponsored programme of aiding development in the Middle East is a possible step towards improving US relations with Arab states, in a way that would help to meet Arab needs without jeopardizing those of Israel.

At the same time, such an effort would be a practical step forward in a non-military competition with the Soviet Union. Here, however, it would not be a question of 'buying friends', in the manner of American aid policies during the 1950s. Rather, it would be an effort to prevent someone else doing the buying. Any development effort launched in the name of reducing Russian influence would be rejected out of hand by most Arab states. But a development programme offered without any such argument might be accepted by Arab leaders and produce the same result.

Finally, a development effort supported by the United States might have the salutary effect of providing an answer to the problem of how to reduce the impact of the Arab–Israeli conflict on United States–Soviet relations. It would be foolish to expect the economic development of Arab states to resolve the Arab–Israeli conflict in this generation. Linking development assistance to peace would only bring rejection from every Arab leader. Yet in the very long run—say, over fifty years—the development of the Arab world might help to mitigate the intensity of the conflict with Israel, as the disparities between societies are reduced. Support for the development of Arab countries would therefore represent one of the few constructive steps that are open to the United States in the Middle East.

The United States faces a difficult decade in the Middle East. The Arab–Israeli conflict continues, along with the dilemmas that it poses for United States' relations with Israel and with the Soviet Union. Nor is the United States likely to find that its own responsibilities in this conflict, as arms supplier or peacemaker, can be much reduced. In addition United States relations with Arab states have entered an uncertain period, while at the same time they have become all the more important now that the Soviet Union has an active presence in the Middle East. United States–Arab relations will not be easy to cultivate and maintain, especially if Arab–Israeli antagonism remains intense. And the United States has new concerns about oil resources, though less because of the Russians than because of changes taking place in the terms of trade between oil producing and oil consuming countries, and because of the development of Arab nationalism.

Finally, the United States faces the greatest test of all in coming to terms with the Soviet presence in the Middle East—a presence that will require the Americans to share position and influence, whether they like it or not. This will take more patience, understanding, and forebearance than Americans have exercised in their relations with adversary nations elsewhere in the world.

The United States is finding that there is a break in the historical continuity of its central preoccupation with Palestine—a break that is creating new demands. Not the least of these is a need to keep the Middle East in its proper perspective, without discounting the added significance given to it by the Russian presence, but also without exaggerating its importance simply because of outmoded ideas about unitary, global competition. The possibilities for error in American policy are immense. But so are the rewards which would result from leading the contending parties of the Middle East towards a situation in which their conflicts will no longer threaten to spread to other areas—and which would allow the Middle East states to spend less effort on bitter strife, and more on their own development.

ROBERT HUNTER

4. SOVIET POLICY IN THE MIDDLE EAST.[1]

The Soviet conception of the Middle East (as a political division of the world) is different from that of the West. Although Soviet writers occasionally use the terms Middle or Near East, they more often use the phrase South-west or West Asia in which they include Turkey and Afghanistan but not, of course, Egypt. The Asian part of the Middle East borders immediately on the almost exclusively Moslem southern fringe of the USSR, as it did on the southern fringe of the Tsarist Russian Empire from the end of the nineteenth century. In fact, from the point of view of culture and to a considerable extent of race, the Middle East and the southern Moslem fringe of the USSR, now occupied by the six Moslem Soviet republics, are one; they were both part of the Moslem East of the Caliphates. But the two parts have developed quite differently: South-west Asia now consists of eleven independent states in place of the three states, two independent and one semi-

[1] Written in 1968.

independent, which existed at the time of the Revolution. The Moslem peoples of Russia are in no sense independent and remain firmly within the confines of the USSR; but their proximity to and affinity with the non-Soviet Moslems is still a matter of great concern to the Soviet Government.

Russia's relations with Islamic countries are of much longer standing than, and have been very different from, those of the West. For 250 years Russia was ruled by a Moslem people, the islamized Mongols. In the middle of the sixteenth century the purely Moslem Tatar khanates of Astrakhan and Kazan became integral parts of *Russia* as distinct from the Russian Empire; in the eighteenth century the Crimean khanate followed suit. By the end of the nineteenth century the Russian Empire as a whole not only contained some 15 million Moslems, but its frontiers marched with those of the only two Moslem states which could be regarded as fully sovereign—the Ottoman Empire and Iran. Russia, therefore, had good reason to attach far more importance to the Moslem world than did the West. The Russians have always regarded Islam as hostile to them, and Communism, while recognizing—and even exaggerating—the power of Islam as a counter-revolutionary force, seeks to represent it as artificially maintained by Western imperialist intrigue. But the Soviet Government undoubtedly reckons with the prevalence and staying power of Islamic culture both inside and outside the USSR.

Before the Revolution, Russia's aims in the Middle East could be described as the replacement there of Western by Russian political, economic, and cultural influence, particularly in the eastern Mediterranean. Since the Revolution, there has been a tendency in the West to regard these aims as superseded by that of establishing international Communism in the Middle East as if this were an aim in itself. Of recent years, however, it has become apparent that, while the Soviet Union is prepared to use Communism when and where it seems appropriate as a means to an end, her ultimate objective is now as much concerned with the national security, national economy, and national prestige of the Soviet or Russian State as it was before the Revolution. But these national considerations are often found to be in serious conflict with those affecting the international position of Communism, and the Soviet Government sometimes experiences difficulty in finding ideological justification for its foreign policies.

Early Soviet policy in the Middle East was based on the belief that Communism, or at least Socialism, would prove an instant attraction for peoples who in the past had been dominated or exploited by Turkey, Britain, or Tsarist Russia, and whose countries at the end of the First World War were in a state bordering on anarchy, and partially or wholly under Western occupation. The Soviet Government was aware of the nationalist movements which by 1920 were well under

way in the Arab countries and in Turkey and Iran; but it misunderstood their character and believed that it would be a comparatively
easy matter to gain control of them, at any rate in Turkey and Iran,
and to manipulate them to the Soviet advantage. These hopes proved
illusory: the Turkish nationalists were quite prepared to accept Soviet
arms and money in their struggle against the West, but they had no use
for Communism and continued to regard Russia as their traditional
enemy. In Iran, Soviet tactics included an attempt to create a Soviet
Republic in the northern province of Gilan, the establishment of eight
Soviet consulates and a number of commercial organizations, clubs, and
propaganda agents, the creation of an Iranian Communist party, and
the exploitation, if not the actual instigation, of mutinies in the Iranian
army. The effect of these ill-conceived and badly executed actions was
further to rally the forces of Iranian nationalism which had already
been set in motion by the Anglo-Iranian Agreement of 1919, and, in
the event, Soviet interests and prestige suffered much more heavily than
British. By 1934 all but one of the Soviet consulates and all the trade
agencies and clubs had been closed.

The Soviet Union's plans for the extension of its influence in the Arab
countries of the Middle East were blocked by the continued British
occupation and political control of Egypt and by the mandatory system
which gave Britain and France control of Iraq, Jordan, Syria, and
Lebanon. Small Communist parties were formed in some countries
(Palestine 1922, Egypt 1923, Syria and Lebanon 1924, and Iraq 1934),
but they had to work underground and had little influence. Generally
speaking, it can be said that up to the outbreak of the Second World
War, the Arab world was barely conscious of the existence of the Soviet
Union. But Russia's entry into the war in 1941 made her an ally of the
Western powers. She thus gained a respectable introduction to the new
Middle Eastern states and her diplomatic representation, which had
hitherto been confined to Turkey and Iran, was extended to most of
the Arab countries. The Soviet Government, however, continued to
confine most of its attention to Turkey and Iran, a further advantage
having been gained from the Soviet military occupation of North Iran
by agreement with Britain and the United States. A separatist movement was started in Iranian Azarbaijan and at the same time Turkey
was called on to return to the USSR the provinces of Kars and Ardahan
ceded to her in 1921. These moves were ill-conceived and they resulted
in a period of strained relations with both countries which lasted for
over ten years. This situation was extended to Iraq in 1952 when the
latter broke off diplomatic relations with the USSR. Soviet Middle
Eastern policy was in the doldrums until after Stalin's death in 1953,
and when it came to life again in 1955, it tended to bypass Iran,
Turkey, and Iraq as nuts which were too hard to crack for the present
owing to the establishment there of Western influence.

Lenin had favoured the plan of supporting 'bourgeois nationalism', even if it meant the collapse of local Communist movements. He argued that nationalism would result in the forced retreat of imperialism and thus in the eventual downfall of capitalism. He died before the soundness of his policy could be fully tested, and it was to a large extent reversed by Stalin, who believed that local Communist parties should be the spearhead of Soviet policy, and that as far as the Middle East was concerned, Soviet interests were best served by a programme of subversion and, where it seemed appropriate, by direct action. On Khrushchev's accession to the leadership of the Party in 1953, Soviet Middle Eastern policy seemed to revert to Lenin's theory. It now strove to create a new image of the Soviet Union as a powerful but benevolent moral and material supporter of newly independent nations against the Imperialist West in the apparent belief that they would form a firm alliance with the Communist bloc, and that this alliance would isolate the 'Imperialist bloc' and deprive it of markets and cheap raw materials.

Since 1947, a number of changes had taken place in the situation in the Middle East. In 1948, the Soviet Union had been one of the first countries to recognize the new state of Israel, and it seemed for a time that the Soviet Government saw a better future in friendship with Israel than with the Arab countries, particularly since Britain's relations with Israel had become tense and she had come out in strong support of the Arab League. By the early 1950s, however, there had been considerable Soviet rethinking: Anglo-Israeli relations had greatly improved; anti-Western and neutralist tendencies had increased in the Arab countries, and particularly in Egypt; and the Soviet Union began to take an interest in 'national-liberation movements' and in Arab unity.

The year 1955 saw the foundation of the Baghdad Pact, with what appeared to both the Middle East and the Soviet Union as strong militarist implications; of the Bandung Conference with its affirmation of the five principles of peaceful co-existence; and of great advances by the pan-Arab nationalist ideology of Colonel Nasser. The adjustments of Soviet policy and ideology which were necessary to take advantage of these developments were made during 1955 and received formal confirmation at the 20th Party Congress in February 1956. This Congress disclosed a new Soviet attitude towards the 'bourgeois nationalist' governments of Asia and Africa. Although they were still supposed to be under the economic tutelage of the West, their *political* independence was for the first time recognized, as well as the fact that the 'bourgeois nationalists' were, at any rate for the time being, the *de facto* rulers of their countries. In literature published after the Congress it was emphasized that not only local Communist parties, the peasants, and the industrial proletariat where it existed, but all strata of society, including the big bourgeoisie, the armed forces, and the clergy, were to be regarded as taking part in the struggle for national liberation from the West and as such to be deserving of Soviet support.

Soviet policy now began to concentrate on the Arab states, and further east, on Afghanistan and India. During the 1950s, the new Soviet policy was aided by the trend of Western policy and action. Britain attempted to develop a Middle East Defence Organization, which failed to attract any of the Arab states except Iraq, whose association with the Baghdad Pact of 1955 was to prove only temporary. In 1955, the Eastern bloc began to supply arms to Egypt and Syria, and in 1956 events began to play directly into the hands of the Soviet Union. The West had attempted to rally the military potential of the Middle East against what seemed to the Arab countries to be a purely hypothetical threat of attack from the Soviet Union. When, therefore, in 1956, attack came not from the East but from the West in the shape of the Suez operation, it was not difficult for the Soviet Government to convince the Arab countries that it was they who had saved the Middle East from further Western aggression, and Soviet prestige rose accordingly.

The Soviet Union now came forward as the champion of pan-Arab nationalism against Western, and particularly British, 'imperialism' and 'colonialism'. During 1957, Soviet writers were lyrical in their praise of Arab unity and Arab nationalist aspirations and louder than ever in their condemnation of the reactionary regimes in Iraq and Jordan, regimes kept in place, they claimed, only by British support. Meanwhile, however, Nasser's pan-Arab nationalist ideology was advancing faster than the Soviet Union either expected or wanted. The creation of the United Arab Republic in February 1958 was greeted with only qualified approval. Nasser's subsequent campaign against Communism, the revolution in Iraq in July 1958, and reactions to it in Jordan and the Lebanon, and perhaps most of all renewed Anglo-American co-operation in the Middle East were decisive in modifying the Soviet attitude to Arab nationalism.

The sudden downfall of the Royalist regime in Iraq probably occasioned as much surprise in the Kremlin as it did in Whitehall. Since the Soviet Government had long been expressing its strong disapproval of Iraq as a satellite of Britain, it naturally welcomed the new regime and quickly re-established diplomatic relations. But it soon became clear that the alleged Communist leanings of Abdul Karim Kassem, the muddled activities of the Iraq Communist party, and, finally, the establishment in Baghdad of a heavily staffed Chinese embassy were as alarming to the Soviet Union as they were to the West. The last thing the Soviet Union wanted was a self-styled Communist regime in a Middle Eastern country which bordered not on the Soviet Union but on Turkey and Iran, states which had firmly associated themselves with the West. It was apprehension on this score which impelled the Communist party of the Soviet Union to check the extravagances of the Iraq Communists, and caused the Soviet Government in March 1959 to make an unsuccessful attempt to wean Iran from Western influence by the offer of a new treaty. In the same month, Khrushchev addressed a party of Iraqi journalists in Moscow in terms which strongly suggested that the Soviet Union had become disillusioned with the idea of Arab nationalism as a co-ordinated movement.

The emphasis laid at the 20th Party Congress of 1956 on the participation of all classes in 'national-liberation movements' had indicated that the Soviet Government no longer regarded local Communist parties as the main instrument of its policy towards developing countries. This change was particularly noticeable in the Middle East, where Communism had made far less progress as a movement than had been expected and where local Communist parties were liable to become a serious embarrassment. It is probable that in 1956 when the movement was at its zenith, the total of registered party members in the Arab countries and Turkey did not exceed 50,000, and the decrease since then must have been considerable. Membership of the Iranian Tudeh party started to fall in 1946, and since the party was proscribed in 1949, it has become very low indeed. In none of the Moslem countries of the Middle East does the Communist party enjoy any legal political status; Communist influence is confined to certain sections of the bourgeois intelligentsia, and its contact with the masses to the still very small industrial proletariat. In addition, at almost all levels of society there is some confusion between the attraction of Marxism and sympathy with, or respect for, the Soviet Union as a rich and powerful state, with which it is possible for governments to maintain good relations while openly decrying Communism and even persecuting its adherents. The progress made by Communism in the Middle East, however, has not been entirely insignificant, nor does the prevalence of the religion and philosophy of Islam provide an impregnable bastion against it. Islam and Communism have certain aims in common, notably the continued struggle against the West and Western 'imperialism'. Many Middle Eastern regimes have declared a preference for a socialist system of government, although not as yet for the scientific or Marxist socialism advocated by the Soviet Union. After some early misgiving, this reservation seems now to be accepted by Soviet ideologists. Egypt's Arab Socialist Union, which has absorbed the Egyptian Communist party and was the subject of much hostile comment in 1962, is now favourably described, and the existing political regime is said to be 'underpinned by a wider social base'. But although local Communist parties are no longer regarded as the spearhead of Soviet penetration and are precluded from becoming identified with opposition to national bourgeois governments, local Communists are still expected to perform services useful to the Soviet Government as expert political advisers inside the ruling nationalist-revolutionary parties. This tactic was approved at a meeting of Arab Communist representatives—not of Communist parties—reported by *Pravda* as having been held in an unspecified place in December 1964.

From the beginning of 1959, the Soviet Government concentrated on improving its relations with all the Moslem states of the Middle East irrespective of the ideological attitudes of their leadership. While Soviet propaganda continued to encourage hostility towards the West, this was not regarded as a pre-condition of Soviet friendship. After two years' hesitation, the Soviet Government finally agreed to provide financial and technical aid in the building of the Aswan High Dam. This alone greatly increased Soviet influence and prestige in Egypt. Soviet relations with Iraq, which had been bad after the overthrow of Kassem's regime in February 1963, began to improve at the end of that year, in spite of the reported execution of thousands of Iraqi Communists. Soviet comment on Iraqi policies was generally favourable, an exception being the Kurdish question to which reference will be made presently. Following talks in Moscow in August 1963, the Soviet and Jordanian governments agreed to establish diplomatic relations, and after years of hostile criticism Soviet commentators began in 1964 to take a favourable view of Jordan's economic plans.

Between 1959 and 1964 Soviet policy seemed to be directed towards a general lowering of the political temperature in the Middle East, a trend which was also observable in the Soviet attitude towards the non-Arab states. Relations with Turkey began to improve after the Turkish 'Revolution' of May 1960, and with Iran after the Iranian Government's declaration of September 1962 that foreign rocket bases would not be established in Iranian territory. Even towards Israel the Soviet attitude was much more moderate than the Arab states could have wished: Israel was classed as an aggressor nation, largely because of her association with the United States; but on only one issue—that of the Jordan waters—had the Soviet Union openly supported the Arab case, and she in general avoided taking sides in a dispute which, so she claimed, did not concern her. This was in marked contrast to the Chinese attitude which was one of full support for the Arab states without any qualification.

In the beginning of 1964, however, there were signs of another change. Soviet commentators, who had kept silent on the subject of Arab unity since 1959, came out in favour of the conference of Arab Heads of State held in Cairo in January 1964 as 'the most representative conference of Arab leaders in history'.[1] Commentators now spoke hopefully of the prospects of Arab unity: peace in the Yemen seemed nearer, and Egypt's relations with Saudi Arabia and Jordan were im-

[1] *Pravda*, 14 January 1964.

proving. *Pravda* described the establishment of a joint Arab military command as a 'completely justified step to ensure the security of the Arab peoples and to defend their interests'.[1] In retrospect it seems probable that the initiative in this return to a policy of solidarity with the Arab cause was taken by Khrushchev. His enthusiastic pronouncements during his visit to Cairo in May 1964 and during Ali Sabri's subsequent visit to Moscow may well have caused some head-shakings in the Party, and may even have been one of the reasons for his replacement in October 1964. But as in the case of China, the Soviet Government were soon to come back to Khrushchev's policies. During 1965, doubts were expressed whether the extension of such lavish Soviet aid to the Third World was really worth it. At the same time, however, the Soviet Union seemed to be getting more and more involved in Arab affairs, an important factor in this involvement being the changed political climate in Syria.

Russia's interest in Syria is traditional and dates back to before the Revolution. The Syrian left-wing intelligentsia had always preserved a friendly attitude towards the Soviet Union, even when the other Arab countries had taken an anti-Soviet line. Ideologically, the Baath Party had appeared as a rival to Communism. In 1964, however, the Baath took a marked swing to the left and the coup of February 1966 brought the left-wing element to power with a new Government containing what the Soviet press hopefully described as 'representatives of the progressive forces'.[2] This was the political climate which the Soviet Union had now come to regard as most favourable to its policies: a nationalist government which was not Communist, but which contained Communist or near-Communist elements. But there is no evidence whatever that this situation was reached as a result of Soviet machinations, or that the new Syrian Government was in the pocket of the Russians. The Syrian Government was pursuing a line of its own which happened to be attractive to the Soviet Union to the extent that the latter was ready to offer it substantial economic aid and to associate itself much more openly than before with Syria's stance in the Arab–Israeli dispute, in which Syria had always been the most vociferous protagonist. In April 1966 the Soviet Government agreed to provide three-fifths of the 250-million dollar Euphrates Dam and hydro-electric project and a few weeks later participated in a joint Soviet–Syrian communiqué which stated that 'the two sides affirmed their solidarity with the Palestine Arabs, and support their lawful rights in the just struggle against Zionism, which is used by the Imperialist forces to aggravate tension in the Near and Middle East'.[3] This was much more specific than any previous Soviet pronouncement on the Arab–Israeli

[1] *Pravda*, 28 January 1964.
[2] Farid Seyful'mulynkov, Moscow radio commentary, 2 March 1966.
[3] *Pravda*, 26 May 1966.

conflict. During the ensuing year, the Soviet Government lost no opportunity of condemning Israeli aggressiveness and association with the West, and of applauding any indication of Arab unity. A Soviet statement of May 1966 on the alleged Israeli threat to Syria concluded with a declaration that 'for its part, the Soviet Union cannot and will not remain indifferent to attempts to destroy peace in an area in such close proximity to its borders'.[1] Insubstantial as this affirmation turned out to be, it probably afforded considerable comfort to the Arab leaders.

A careful examination of Soviet statements and writing on the events leading up to the Six Day War of June 1967 does not provide any evidence of the Machiavellian designs attributed to Soviet policy by some Western commentators. So far from deliberately manipulating events so as to achieve a desired outcome, the Soviet Government seems to have made a number of serious miscalculations about the military potentialities of the situation and about Arab and Israeli intentions. These miscalculations led them to discount the possibility of any major military operations of the kind which actually took place. It is possible that they genuinely believed that Israel would attack Syria on a small scale, and they may have advised the Egyptian Government accordingly. But the most probable Soviet appreciation was that there would be no Israeli attack either on Syria or on Egypt and that as in 1956 the Soviet Union would gain credit for having averted a major catastrophe by the issue of grave warnings and by hinting at Soviet intervention.

There can be little doubt that in retrospect the Soviet Government realized that by their renewed support of the Arab cause since 1964 and by exaggerating the prospects of Arab unity and the extent of the Western commitment to Israel they had in fact exacerbated the Arab–Israeli conflict. It would not, however, have been in the Soviet character to withdraw support from the Arab states after the débâcle of June 1967: before the Arab states could begin to ask themselves whether their trust in the Soviet Union had not been misplaced, they resorted to the only means open to them of restoring their prestige—the replenishment of Arab armaments. At the same time, while continuing to fulminate against Israeli aggression, they have urged the Arabs to settle their differences by political means and to avoid extreme action.

The stepping-up of Soviet support for the Arab cause did not have very much effect on Soviet relations with Turkey and Iran. In the case of Turkey, improvement had been very gradual until 1966 when there were exchanges of delegations and a trade agreement was signed. The following year saw the inauguration of several aid projects, including an oil refinery near Izmir and an iron and steel complex. In September 1967 Ankara radio announced that the value of Soviet–Turkish trade had increased from seven million rubles in 1961 to 45 million in 1966. Relations with Iran improved much more rapidly. An agreement

[1] *Pravda*, 28 May 1966.

signed in January 1966 promised Soviet technical aid for a number of projects (iron and steel works, a gas-pipe line, etc.). In February 1966 a $110 million arms agreement was signed and the USSR provided a $100 million credit to be repaid in eight years at $2\frac{1}{2}$ per cent interest. Under a new long-term trade agreement signed in March 1967, Iran and the USSR agreed to exchange $540 million worth of goods during the next five years.

Apart from its concern with the Arab–Israeli conflict, Soviet Middle Eastern policy is also interested in three other general Middle Eastern matters, namely, the Kurdish question, Middle East oil, and the Persian Gulf. Western commentators on Middle East affairs often suppose that the Soviet Union advocates and aims at the creation of an independent Kurdistan embracing the six million Kurds distributed more or less equally in Turkey, Iraq, and Iran. In theory the creation of such a state would be in line with Communist ideology; but even if it were a practicable proposition, it is hard to see what possible advantage it could have for the Soviet Union. On the contrary, the existence of a new state in the shape of a united Kurdistan on the very borders of Transcaucasia, whose national problems are already a source of anxiety to the Soviet Government, would seem to be the very last thing the Russians would want. There is in fact no evidence whatever that they have ever gone beyond advocating the grant of a degree of autonomy to the Kurdish communities within the framework of the countries in which they live. In the words of the principal Soviet expert on Kurdish affairs, Kurdoyev, presumably himself a Kurd, 'the democratic elements among the Kurdish people know well that the only way to the solution of the Kurdish question is by the unity of the Kurdish workers with the progressive forces of the Iranian, Turkish, and Iraqi people and the formation of one front of struggle for freedom and democracy'.[1]

The Soviet Union has always been strongly critical of the exploitation of Middle Eastern oil by Western companies, and has encouraged all moves towards nationalization. Formerly, it was said that, while the Soviet Union aimed at denying oil to the West by organizing labour unrest and promoting nationalization, it was not able to provide alternative markets. Some Western economists now say that this position has changed and that there is now a genuine Soviet need for Middle Eastern oil. But this theory may have been outdated by the recent discoveries of new oil deposits in Western Siberia. Payment for Soviet services in working the South Iraq oil deposits according to the agreement reached in December 1967 are to be made in oil rather than in currency, but the Soviet Union may intend to market this oil for its Eastern European satellites rather than for itself. Given the chance, it is probable that the Soviet Government would still be ready to undertake the exploitation of oil in Iran, but since the Iranian failure to ratify the

[1] 'The Kurds', an article in *Narody Peredney Azii* (Moscow, 1957).

Qavam–Sadchikov agreement of 1945, there is no record of any move having been made in this direction.

Russian interest in the Persian Gulf is of very long standing. At the beginning of this century when the question of dividing Iran into spheres of Russian and British influence was first raised, the Russian Government made a strong claim for a stake in the Persian Gulf and it was only with difficulty, and largely as a result of her defeat in the Russo-Japanese war, that she was induced to abandon it. Apart from a brief and not unprofitable trading venture in the Gulf in the early 1930s, the Soviet Union had manifested little interest in the Gulf until Britain's reappraisal of her commitments there made by the Prime Minister in Parliament in January 1968. A statement made two days later by the American Under-Secretary of State, Mr. Eugene Rostow, to the effect that Iran, Turkey, Pakistan, Saudi Arabia, and Kuwait were interested in assuming responsibility for regional security in the Gulf was seized upon by the Soviet Union as indicating the existence of a British–American plot to establish in the area 'a military bloc' with the object of consolidating the positions of the Western oil companies in the area, and of thwarting national liberation movements. The Tass statement[1] in which this accusation appeared also declared that these plans were aimed at 'poisoning mutual relations' among the Gulf states, 'bringing Iran into opposition with the Arabs' and threatening national sovereignties, which the USSR would, as always, defend. Western plans were also 'directed against the southern frontiers of the Soviet Union'. It is not yet known to what extent the Soviet Union proposes to interfere in Gulf politics. It must be clear to the Soviet Government that the complexities of this issue are far greater than those of the Arab–Israeli conflict, in which Soviet support for the Arab cause could gain the approval of the whole Arab, and indeed of the whole Moslem, world. In the Persian Gulf it is not only the Arab states which are at variance; there is also the major question of whether the Gulf is an Iranian or Arabian sea. Iran is the only Gulf state which borders directly on the Soviet Union, but Soviet support for the Iranian case in, for example, the question of Bahrain, would inevitably have an adverse effect on the Soviet Union's relations with the Arab states, and par-ticularly with both Egypt and Saudi Arabia which are rival champions of the 'Arabism' of the Gulf. It may of course turn out that the Soviet Government simply intends to use the Persian Gulf issue as a useful theme in its anti-Western propaganda campaign.

During the past fifteen years Soviet writing on the East has become progressively more thoughtful and discursive and in consequence much more informative. The changes that have taken place in Soviet policy during this period can be attributed partly to a greater sense of realism, and partly to such other factors as the internal situation of the

[1] *Pravda*, 4 March 1968.

USSR, the progress of Soviet policy in Europe, and the attitude of China. The sense of realism probably originated after the failure in 1945–6 of Soviet plans for Iran and Turkey and assumed a more definite form at the 20th Party Congress of 1956. The practical effect of this change was a new scepticism about the attractions of Communism and about the efficacy of subversion and direct action. Some Western commentators and perhaps some Western governments continue to insist that subversion is still practised by the Soviet Union as an essential instrument of its policy and suspect that the Soviet Government would be ready to resort to direct action at any given moment. The Soviet Government, for its part, continues to see the hand of the West in any Middle Eastern development which seems to run counter to Soviet interests. The fact seems to be, however, that neither the West nor the Soviet Union is now in a position to manipulate Middle Eastern governments to their own satisfaction without the use of force, and that the use of force by one side or the other would have disastrous consequences. The West, by a painful process of trial and error, seems to have realized this. Russia, still in pursuance of her traditional aim of replacing the West as the political, economic, and cultural mentor of the Middle East, is engaged in the same process; but if she has for the present ceased to rely on the use of local Communist parties and of subversion and direct action, she may be under the impression that her aims can be achieved by the more conventional methods of technical and economic aid, political mentorship, provision of arms, military missions, and naval demonstrations, all of which have been used by the West in the past, but with surprisingly little effect.

GEOFFREY WHEELER

5. THE OIL INDUSTRY IN THE MIDDLE EAST

Ever since the end of the Second World War the industrialized and industrializing countries of the world outside North and South America and the Communist countries have come increasingly to rely on the Middle East for their supplies of oil. Although the United States in 1970 was still the largest single oil-producing country in the world, accounting for nearly a quarter of world production, it needed all of the oil it produced and more. The USSR was the next largest producer with 15 per cent of world production, but its exports, together with those of Eastern Europe, came to less than 4 per cent of world exports. These went mostly to Western Europe and met some 7 per cent of the area's requirements. Venezuela was the third largest producing country, with about 8·3 per cent of world output, exporting primarily to North America, while Iran was a very close rival with 8·1 per cent.[1]

Although these three countries together produced much more oil than the Middle East (1,087 million tons in 1970 as against 689 million for the Middle East), and no Middle Eastern country produced as much as any one of these countries, nevertheless, the importance of the Middle East in world trade was much greater, accounting for 50 per cent of total exports, and when combined with North Africa, accounting for over two-thirds. Western Europe, with very little oil of its own, was already taking nearly half of its total imports from the Middle East and over one-third from North Africa; Japan imported over 80 per cent of its needs from the Middle East alone.

With the rapid industrialization of Japan and the recovery of Europe after the Second World War, oil consumption in the eastern hemisphere grew very fast indeed, averaging over 11 per cent per year in the 1950s and 1960s. United States consumption, though in total still somewhat greater than that of Western Europe and Japan combined, grew at a very much smaller rate (around 4 per cent). As time goes on an increasing share of these supplies can, in the normal course of events, be expected to continue to come from the Middle East as well as from North Africa. But conditions in the Middle East in the 1960s and early 1970s were not 'normal' even by the ambiguous norms of that region and a number of events interfered with, or seemed to threaten, the 'security' of the oil supplies on which the consuming nations had come to depend, and also to raise drastically the cost of oil: the Suez Canal was closed, pipelines were cut, output was restricted by government action, threats to cut off supplies accompanied bargaining over taxes, and governments became increasingly unwilling to abide by the terms of their established concession agreements as inflation eroded the real value of revenues and as they saw new possibilities of increasing their oil receipts. All of this intensified the pervasive concern and long-standing unease of the importing countries over their increasing dependence on the Middle East for oil, and intensified efforts to discover alternative sources of oil even at considerably higher cost. As always, one cannot predict the outcome of such efforts or the final results of developments in the North Sea or elsewhere. Nevertheless, world demand has become so great that it is safe to say that very large amounts of oil will continue to come from the Middle East for the foreseeable future regardless of what is discovered elsewhere.

In 1970 the largest producing countries in the Middle East were Iran (138 million metric tons), Saudi Arabia (176 million tons), and Kuwait

[1] All of these figures are from British Petroleum, *Statistical Review of the World Oil Industry, 1970* (London).

(138 million tons). Of these only Iran, where oil had been discovered in 1908, was an important producer before the Second World War, when she ranked fourth in the world. Although oil was discovered in Saudi Arabia and Kuwait just before the war, its development was held up by the war, especially in Kuwait, and exports only became important from the middle 1940s from Saudi Arabia and later in the decade from Kuwait. Iraq, producing 77 million tons in 1970, was the smaller, though older, producer. Commercial oil had been discovered in 1927 but exports did not begin until seven years later, partly because of the need to build a pipeline from land-locked Kirkuk to the sea, partly because of the depression, and partly for other reasons. These four countries accounted for 84 per cent of Middle East oil production, the rest coming from Abu Dhabi (33 million metric tons), the Neutral Zone (26 million), Qatar (18 million), Oman (17 million), Egypt (18 million), Bahrain (4 million), and Syria (4 million). Most of these smaller producers arrived on the scene in the 1960s; only Bahrain, where oil was discovered in 1932, was exporting before the Second World War. Oil was discovered in Qatar in 1939 but development there, as in Saudi Arabia and Kuwait, was hindered by the war and exports did not begin until 1949. In other words, apart from Iran and Iraq, the emergence of the Middle East as the world's greatest exporting region dates only from the middle of the century. Oil from northern Iraq reached the sea through pipelines before the war but Tapline for Saudi oil and additional Iraqi pipelines came into operation only after the war.

The Advent of Profit Sharing

It is not surprising, therefore, that it was during 1950/1 that the first big change occurred in the nature of the concessionary relationships between the governments of the crude-oil producing countries and the great international oil companies which discovered and developed their oil resources. The production and export of oil in the Middle East at mid-century was controlled by eight companies, either directly or through subsidiaries set up as consortia for the purpose of producing crude oil.[1] The same international companies were also the world's largest refiners and marketers of oil products outside North America, and most of the oil they produced in the Middle East went to their own refining subsidiaries; only a small proportion was sold to third parties in free markets.

These companies produced the oil under concessions obtained before the war from the governments. The terms of the concessions varied, but essentially they gave the companies the right to explore, produce,

[1] These companies were Standard Oil Co. (New Jersey); Royal Dutch/Shell; Anglo-Iranian (now British Petroleum); Gulf Oil Co.; Texaco; Standard Oil of California; Socony Mobil (now Mobil Oil Co.); and Compagnie Française des Pétroles.

transport, and sell oil in return for various fees and (except in Iran) a tonnage royalty. Only in Iran was the oil produced by a single international company; in the other countries it was produced by consortia of two or more international companies. The original Iranian concession dated from 1901, and after a series of abortive negotiations was cancelled in 1932/3 and re-negotiated, the new concession to run until 1993. The Iranians were to be paid a royalty and 20 per cent of the dividends distributed by the Anglo-Persian Company. (This provision naturally caused trouble after the war when the British Government, as part of a domestic austerity policy, restricted dividend payments generally, but the problem was quickly resolved.) In 1951, after a bitter dispute, the company's properties were nationalized by the Government of Mussaddiq; Iranian oil was shut down for nearly four years before a new agreement was made, this time with a consortium of foreign companies,[1] accepting the new profit-sharing arrangements that had by then become prevalent in the Middle East as noted below.

The Iraq Petroleum Company, together with its sister companies, Mosul Petroleum and Basra Petroleum Companies (hereafter jointly referred to as the IPC), was a non-profit-making British company owned in equal shares by Anglo-Iranian, Royal Dutch/Shell, Compagnie Française des Pétroles, and the Near East Development Corporation composed of Standard Oil Company (New Jersey) and Mobil Oil Company, with 5 per cent for the C. S. Gulbenkian interests. The Kuwait Oil Company, also British, was owned equally by Anglo-Iranian and Gulf Oil Company. Aramco, whose concession covered most of eastern Saudi Arabia, was an American company owned by Standard Oil (New Jersey), Standard Oil of California, Texaco, (30 per cent each) and Mobil (10 per cent). These eight international companies took all of the oil exported by the three countries, using almost all of it in their own refining operations throughout the world, either directly or as a result of agreements and swaps among them.

After the war demand for oil rose rapidly and although the revenues of the oil producing countries rose as exports increased, the governments wanted a greater share of the profits from their oil. Ibn Saud was most pressing in his demands on Aramco, and at the end of 1950 he obtained a fundamental revision of the financial arrangements with Aramco. Revenues were to be received by Saudi Arabia in the form of an income tax which, including a royalty of $12\frac{1}{2}$ per cent, would equal 50 per cent of the profits attributed to crude oil. (Venezuela already had an income tax which enabled the Government to obtain 50 per cent

---

[1] The consortium was composed of British Petroleum (40 per cent), Royal Dutch/Shell (14 per cent), Mobil Oil (7 per cent), Standard Oil Co. (New Jersey) (7 per cent), Texaco (7 per cent), Gulf Oil (7 per cent), Standard Oil of California (7 per cent), Compagnie Française des Pétroles (6 per cent), Iricon (a group of American Independents) (5 per cent).

of the companies' profits). Under US tax laws Aramco got credit for these income-tax payments to the Saudi Government against its United States tax liability so that, in effect, the US Treasury lost what Saudi Arabia gained within the limits of Aramco's tax liability to the US Government. Naturally, the '50/50' arrangement spread quickly to the other countries and became standard in the Middle East, constituting the first major change in concession arrangements in the area generally.

As a result of the adoption of the income-tax method of paying revenues to the Governments, however, it became necessary for the companies to define what was meant by 'profits' on crude-oil production, since little crude had been sold in international trade before the war and no recognized price for crude had been established. They did this by posting a price in the Middle East at which they were prepared to sell crude to outsiders as well as to transfer it to their own refining subsidiaries, the latter being by far the most important outlets.

Traditionally the price of products had been calculated with reference to a type of basing-point system. After the war, as refineries were established in consuming countries and crude oil entered increasingly into international trade, this method of pricing was extended to crude oil. The 'system' was somewhat unsystematically, loosely, and erratically applied and became increasingly weakened after the war. But when crude-oil prices were for the first time publicly announced in the Middle East in 1950 as the result of the introduction of '50/50', they naturally reflected the previously prevailing levels; valued at these prices, crude-oil production appeared extremely profitable in relation to refining and marketing (although it must be remembered that crude is of little use unless it is refined). This distribution of profits was advantageous to the US companies since under the US tax laws profits attributed to crude-oil production are taxed at a lower rate than profits on refining and marketing. Moreover, the higher the price of crude oil, the higher the revenues of the oil-producing countries and the higher the costs of competing oil companies without access to 'owned' or 'cost' crude.

Posted prices were intended to be, and for a time were, the prices at which Middle East crude oil actually moved to the world's refineries, as well as the prices used to value oil for tax purposes. They were not determined by impersonal 'market forces', nor could they have been, given the nature of the 'market', and were soon seen not to be so determined. In consequence, before the decade was out, the right of the companies to post prices without consultation with their host governments, and thus to determine unilaterally the unit tax revenues of governments was to be strongly challenged by the governments of crude-oil-producing countries.

At the beginning of the 1950s the full development of Middle Eastern oil was in the early stages; in the next ten years production nearly tripled and tripled again in the following ten. One of the chief problems of the companies was to bring this oil into world markets in a way that would not create an abrupt disruption of the world price structure. Since such a large proportion of both refining and marketing was in the hands of the same international companies that controlled the Middle Eastern crude oil, it could be expected that if each of the companies adjusted the production of its own crude to the growth of its own market outlets, the result would be a smooth integration of the new supplies of oil into international markets.

The difficulty was, however, that the companies had a great deal of very cheap oil to dispose of. As a result, during the 1950s effective delivered prices began to reflect the competitive pressures on the companies to find outlets for this oil, at first in a concealed form (e.g. a company might itself absorb some of the freight in order to cut delivered prices) and later overtly in the form of open discounts. Thus developed the so-called 'world oil surplus' that afflicted the industry from the late 1950s until the 1967 war with Israel sharply disrupted the prevailing patterns of supply.

For a while the emerging 'surplus', that is to say the increasing availability of oil at prices below the prices posted by the companies, was masked by various fortuitous circumstances: the conflict between Iran and the AIOC took Iranian oil off the market for almost four years, the Korean war gave an unexpected boost to demand, the closure of the Suez Canal in 1956 and the shutdown of pumps on the Iraqi pipeline through Syria further interrupted supplies. As soon as the effects of the Suez crisis wore off, prices of oil and products in world markets began to fall in earnest. To the companies, it seemed obvious that in such circumstances the prices on which they paid tax—the posted prices— should reflect this development and in consequence the posted prices were reduced in 1959 and again in 1960.

The Formation of OPEC

The producing countries reacted immediately with the formation in 1960 of the Organization of Petroleum Exporting Countries (OPEC) dedicated to the restoration of posted prices. This did not prove to be possible, but OPEC did succeed in preventing any further cuts in posted prices in spite of the fact that market prices continued to fall until after the 1967 war. The freezing of posted prices by OPEC was the beginning of a concerted struggle by the host governments to increase their revenues from oil. The remnants of the allowances for marketing expenses that the companies had been able to claim for tax purposes were abolished; in 1964 an agreement was obtained to treat royalties as an expense rather than as part of the 50 per cent 'income' tax; in 1970, following a settlement with Libya this tax was increased from 50 per cent to 55 per cent; and early in 1971 the oil companies acceded, under the threat of unilateral legislation, to demands, led by Iran, not only that tax-reference prices should be raised substantially but that they should also be increased regularly to take account of inflation in world prices generally.

In the 1971 agreements, the governments of the producing countries agreed, for oil delivered in the Persian Gulf, to a five-year period of 'tax stability', that is a period over which they would not press for further increases in tax prices other than those provided for in the agreement. At this time the Suez Canal was still closed and it was clear that there would have to be a larger than usual difference between the prices of oil in the Gulf and in the Mediterranean. In demanding 'tax stability' for five years, the companies which still had tax prices for oil delivered at Mediterranean terminals to negotiate (with Libya in particular, but also with Iraq and Saudi Arabia) wanted to ensure that if Libya were to obtain a greater increase from them than freight differentials and other objective factors would justify, this would not lead to a further round of general increases, as had the 1970 Libyan settlement. In this they had not been entirely successful at the time of writing since, although agreement had been reached with Libya, Iraq had not yet accepted the terms for its oil available in the Mediterranean and Iran did not seem to be entirely content.

In addition to these financial gains, in the 1960s the OPEC countries insisted on and obtained widespread relinquishment by the companies of the areas held under concession but not exploited. The original concession agreements before the war had covered very much larger areas than the companies were in a position to explore, let alone develop. This was becoming increasingly unacceptable, and most of the new concessions granted after the war contained provisions for progressive relinquishment according to a stated timetable in order to confine each concession after a stated period to the areas actively exploited. The major companies accepted the principle of relinquishment for all their concession areas, which were thereby quickly reduced to a small proportion of their original size. In 1961, however, Iraq unilaterally expropriated some 99·5 per cent of the IPC's concession area, even though the IPC had already expressed its willingness to give up over 90 per cent of its area provided only that it be allowed to choose the parts to be retained. This the Government was not prepared to permit. As a result of relinquishment, all of the governments of the producing countries have acquired, and continue to acquire, large tracts of the potential oil-bearing lands not being exploited, which can then be made available to new concessionaires or developed by the national companies of the countries themselves, alone or in joint ventures with foreign companies.

Two other objectives of the OPEC countries, however, met with little success during the 1960s: the introduction of an effective programme to control supply, and the acceptance of government companies as partners in their major oil concessions. As market prices continued to

E

fall in response to competition in the market place, OPEC's hopes of raising tax prices became fainter and OPEC even began to fear that the existing level of tax prices might at some point be endangered. The obvious answer was to restrict the rate of supply. In 1965 a production programme was drawn up and supply quotas were allocated to member countries, but neither governments nor companies paid much attention to them and the scheme was a failure. Further attempts were to be made, however, and at the Caracas conference of OPEC in December 1970 it was resolved to set up a standing committee to study the problem anew. Essentially OPEC's objective was to establish an effective monopoly over supplies in order to force higher market prices; Libya cut back output unilaterally in 1970 and was successful in raising its tax prices, largely because of the tight supply position in the Mediterranean with both the Suez Canal and Tapline closed, but what OPEC wanted was co-operation among the producing countries to regulate supply.

During the negotiations over taxes in early 1971 the OPEC countries threatened to cut off supplies entirely if their demands were not accepted by the companies without delay; there is no way of knowing whether they would or could have done so, but the companies were not prepared to risk the dislocation that would result from such action, and agreements were hammered out, the US companies receiving a dispensation to act collectively in spite of the anti-trust laws. There is no doubt that a concerted and effective effort to control supply would put the OPEC countries in a position virtually to dictate the price of crude oil until alternative sources of energy could be developed. In the few years after 1967 the producing countries with oil available in the Mediterranean were in the strongest possible position in view of the problems caused by the closure of the Canal and by the insecurity of Tapline. If a surplus of oil re-emerges, however, the difficulties of maintaining a close control over supply may well increase. No predictions as to how far OPEC will be able to carry its cartel power can reasonably be attempted at the time of writing.

Moreover, another objective of the OPEC countries with very different implications for the companies was also being strongly pressed in the 1960s: equity participation. As the development of the countries of the Middle East accelerated after the war and their peoples became better educated, their administrators and technicians more numerous and more skilled, and their knowledge of the oil industry more extensive, they naturally wanted to take a greater part in the exploitation of their own resources. Apart from anything else simple national pride could, in the circumstances, be expected to lead to an insistence on a reduction of the role of foreigners in their economic affairs in the name of economic independence and national sovereignty. Such sentiments frequently led vocal groups in each country to demand nationali-

zation of the foreign companies, but except for the Iranian nationalization of 1950 and the Iraqi expropriation of nearly all of IPC's properties
in 1960, such demands made little impact. Most governments preferred
to continue with the oil companies and to exercise to the full their power
to tax and otherwise regulate the activities of the companies, assisted by
codes developed by OPEC. The more insistent demand was for
'participation'—a share in the ownership of the crude-oil producing
companies. Late in 1971 OPEC formally resolved that member countries should take immediate steps to implement the principle of participation in existing oil concessions and drew up the basis on which
negotiations with the companies should be opened, but the companies
declared their resistance.

The governments of the major oil-exporting countries all established
their own national oil companies, some of which by the end of the
decade had made numerous sales abroad on their own account and
were actively pushing both their domestic and international operations.
Nearly all of the new concession arrangements in the 1950s provided for
joint ventures between the national companies and the foreign companies. Perhaps it was to be expected that the Japanese would be the
pioneers among the foreign companies, followed closely by the Italians.
The agreements in 1957/8 between the Japanese and the governments
of Saudi Arabia and Kuwait for a concession in the Neutral Zone gave
each Government the right to purchase 10 per cent of the company
after the discovery of oil in commercial quantities. The Petroleum Law
of 1957 in Iran gave preference to companies agreeing to take NIOC,
the national company, as a partner, and AGIP, a subsidiary of the
Italian ENI, was the first to sign. Others followed and four of the
numerous Iranian joint ventures were producing a total of 250,000 b/d,
rising to an expected half million by 1970. In the 1960s Saudi Arabia
took the lead in pushing joint ventures with its national company,
Petromin, and in obtaining more and more favourable terms. Iraq has
not made use of partnership arrangements for the development of the
areas taken from the IPC (partly because of difficulties raised for foreign
companies by the doubtful legality of the Iraqi expropriation) but has
gone in for a variety of contractual and service arrangements, notably
with French companies. In both Iran and Iraq new forms of agreement
were pioneered by the French company, ERAP. All of Egypt's oil is
produced under joint ventures, the most important producing area
being the Morgan field in the Gulf of Suez owned jointly by Egypt's
national oil company and Pan-American, a subsidiary of Standard Oil
of Indiana, which began commercial production in 1967.

For a long time the major companies resisted proposals to form joint
ventures with the governments of the producing countries, although
Shell did make such an agreement in 1951/2 for offshore Kuwait, and
some agreed to joint ventures in an abortive agreement with Iraq in

1965. But to grant equity participation in their major producing operations, let alone in their refining and marketing operations in Europe, as requested by the oil minister of Saudi Arabia and urged by OPEC, was completely unacceptable to them. In this respect, the OPEC countries have made no headway whatsoever.

The Positions Reversed

Thus, in the short space of ten years the relative power of companies and governments was almost completely reversed. From being little more than receivers of revenues with token representation in the affairs of their concessionaires and having only the power that the companies' need for stable political relations conferred on them, the governments of the oil-producing countries steadily improved their bargaining power. By the end of the 1960s they were in a position to deal with the companies on terms of equality—indeed in most cases with the effective authority of a sovereign power.

There were many reasons for this change. The advent of dozens of independent oil companies and of new national interests from Europe and Japan brought new proposals and new ideas and reduced the long-standing dependence of the governments on the traditional major companies in spite of the fact that these companies continued to provide their revenues. Consuming countries emerged willing to make direct arrangements with the producing countries. The revolution in Iraq severely reduced the influence of the IPC, and the subsequent acceptance of help in the development of the industry from Russia and Eastern Europe decreased the traditional trade ties with the West. The supply of qualified technicians and others with experience and competence in negotiations increased. The bargaining position of the major companies was weakened, at first by the increased competition in world markets as newcomers at all levels entered the industry with supplies of oil and products, and later, by the newly found ability of the producing countries to combine and hold together in order to take advantage of the dependence of Europe and Japan on Middle East oil in the conditions of tight supply following the 1967 war. Undoubtedly, too, the general spirit of independence and nationalism sweeping Africa and Asia in the post-war years had a profound effect on the climate of opinion in the countries of the Middle East.

Increased competence, increased national contacts, the ferment of new ideas, and the driving forces of independence and nationalism combined to stimulate the development of national oil companies. At the beginning of the 1970s these companies, though for the most part still young, inexperienced, and feeling their way, were vigorous and active. The National Iranian Oil Company the oldest of them, had become a fully fledged oil company, making numerous crude-oil sales abroad, had begun producing and distributing at home and acted as a partner in international refining ventures. Petromin of Saudi Arabia and the Kuwait National Petroleum Company were not established before the 1960s, but both were following the steps of the NIOC in joint ventures, with more emphasis, however, on ancillary activities such as fertilizers and petrochemicals. All of them could obtain royalty oil for foreign sales. The Iraq National Oil Company was chiefly fully occupied with French, Russian, and Czech help in attempting to develop the southern Iraqi fields that had been taken over from the IPC. Progress was not very rapid for a variety of reasons. Although the INOC had taken over already proven fields, exports had not yet begun by 1971.

In addition to these developments, not only had tax rates been raised but the governments had for all practical purposes achieved their long-standing objective of bringing tax reference prices under their own control. OPEC was not responsible for all of these changes, perhaps not even for most of them, but the organization did have an extremely powerful influence, especially in promoting a degree of unity among the producing countries which made their combined bargaining position very effective indeed. The fact that the oil was in the hands of international companies rather than sold by national companies or independent producing companies in the Middle East made it possible for the governments to raise their tax prices and force the companies to raise product prices.

Impact of Oil on the Middle East

The rapid development of this industry has had a pervasive and truly revolutionary effect on the countries of the Middle East, including those that are not major oil exporters. The demand by the industry for labour, and especially skilled labour, though not very great in relation to the value of output, stimulated the development of a skilled labour force, while the payment of wages and salaries and the purchase of local materials and imports through local merchants raised incomes directly.

More important, however, were the direct payments to governments of large amounts of foreign exchange by the oil companies, primarily in the form of royalties and income taxes, but also as signature payments, rents, and fees of a variety of kinds related to the acquisition of concessions. For the Middle Eastern countries, these exceeded $1,000 million by 1956, $2,000 million by 1964, and $4,000 million by 1970. Saudi Arabia and Iran alone received about half of the total, Kuwait about 20 per cent, and Iraq about 10 per cent. As a result of the price settlements in Tehran and Tripoli in 1971, which enormously increased posted prices at both the Gulf and Mediterranean terminals, and of the increased rate of tax, additional revenues exceeded $2,000 million in 1971 and were expected to exceed $4,000 million in 1975 for the Middle Eastern countries.

From the beginning oil revenues were paid directly to governments and rulers. This alone created a difference between the major oil exporting countries and most other non-Communist countries where, by and large, a variety of domestic exporters are engaged in the business and are the recipients of export proceeds. As a result, the rulers of the oil-exporting countries (and before the Second World War a number of them could hardly be classed as modern governments) came into large and unexpected sums of money which nothing in their experience or training equipped them to handle: whether or not they were willing or able to undertake the management of such sums, they had to learn to do so.

Oil revenues did encourage the fabulous personal consumption of local rulers and shaikhs which many Westerners apparently still believe is the chief characteristic of Middle Eastern rulers, especially in the Arab desert countries. But the need to spend the money in ways acceptable to their peoples increasingly influenced by the outside world, and to spread the benefits to others besides members of the royal families and their friends, sooner or later forced not only different attitudes in government but extensive reorganization of the bureaucracy, and even of the State itself, along more modern lines.

In Iraq a large proportion of oil revenues was earmarked from the start for government development expenditures, rising to 70 per cent of the total revenues after the '50/50' agreements until the start of the military regimes in 1958. In Bahrain, Qatar, and Kuwait, the use of oil revenues in the earlier period was much influenced by British guidance and advice; the funds devoted to the personal uses of the ruling families were large, but limited, and as time went on increasing shares went to economic development, especially in Kuwait. Similarly in Saudi Arabia, Ibn Saud and his traditional free-spending attitudes, in which no distinction was made between the Government budget and the privy purse, soon got the country into financial trouble even after oil revenues became really large, and extensive governmental financial organization was required. The old ways and the old rulers had to go and by the 1960s modern budgets and administrative and financial institutions had taken a firm hold. Even in the newer oil-producing shaikhdoms, Abu Dhabi and Oman, a similar process can already be detected. Iran began to work out a co-ordinated development programme in the 1940s, and in 1949 established its Plan Organization; by the middle of the 1960s development was well under way and oil revenues were urgently needed to sustain the momentum.

Oil has thus not only made possible, but has virtually forced modernization on the great oil-exporting countries of the Middle East, and as a result they have helped to bring both governments and people to the point at which they could successfully challenge the oil companies themselves. National oil companies have been created in all the larger exporting countries and in addition to taking over local marketing, they have already successfully sold oil abroad, and have established joint ventures with foreign companies in exploration, production, and even refining. The national companies can be expected to grow and play an increasingly important role even in the international industry.

Two of the newest exporters, Egypt and Syria, are still, and probably will remain, of minor importance relative to Kuwait, Iran, Iraq, Saudi Arabia, and even Abu Dhabi, although one can never be absolutely sure that large oil resources will not be discovered in either country. Each is, and has long been, among the most advanced in the Middle East, with a much more diversified and developed economy than the major exporters, with the exception of Iran. Production and prospects in Egypt, where the industry has been developed almost entirely by joint ventures between American companies and the Egyptian national oil company, are greater than those in Syria, where the industry has been developed with the help of the Russians. For both countries, oil exports provide a welcome addition to their foreign exchange earnings but do not dominate their economies in the way they have in the major exporting countries.

EDITH PENROSE

6. CONTEMPORARY TRENDS IN LITERATURE AND ART IN IRAQ, SYRIA, LEBANON, AND JORDAN

Literature in the Arab world is often closely associated with political movements and social reform. At the turn of the century, and for the first thirty years of this century, a major concern of Arab writers was to revive tradition in a way that would clarify the dimensions of Arab nationhood and revitalize Arabic language to suit the requirements of a modern age. The struggle for independence was another of their concerns as none of the Arab countries (with the exception of Yemen) enjoyed the status of a fully independent State. Centres of learning, such as the American University and St. Joseph's University in Beirut, and, on a smaller scale, the Arab College in Jerusalem, were producing an educated elite that was soon to be responsible for an even greater change to come. After the First World War colleges for specialized studies began to appear one after the other in Baghdad and Damascus. The revival was thus accelerating, and with the spread of education, which was accompanied by the flourishing of journalism and the publication of books, Arabic writing became increasingly important and complex.

It is often the poets among Arab writers who activate change not only in style but in outlook. Poetry is widely read in the Arab world, and it is equally widely discussed and written about, which gives the average Arab poet a position of prominence perhaps unknown to poets in other countries. In the 1930s and 1940s a number of poets in Palestine, Lebanon, Syria, and Iraq left their mark on a society that had begun to regain its mobility, and their work soon proved seminal for the following two or three decades. In the Lebanon there were Bishara al-Khouri (al-Akhtal al-Saghir), Said Akl, Elias Abu Shabakeh, Amin Nakleh (apart from such luminaries as Gibran Khalil Gibran, Iliya Abu Madi, and a host of others who lived in the Americas); in Palestine, Ibrahim Touqan, Abdul Rahim Mahmoud, Abdul Karim al-Karmi; in Syria, Omar Abu Risheh; in Iraq, Jameel Sidqi al-Zahawi, Marouf al-Rasafi, Mohammed Mahdi al-Jawahiri. The prose works of Gibran, Amin Rihani, Mikhail Naimy, Yousef Awad, Said Taqiuddin, all of Lebanon, achieved a distinction between 1925 and 1950 that makes them today the classics of twentieth-century Arabic belles-lettres.

The Palestine disaster of 1948 was the great turning-point in modern Arabic literature. The post-war world was indeed ripe for change, but the traumatic experience of the Palestine tragedy gave the transition a speedy and unexpected course. New names, new talents, suddenly burst forth on the scene. Although many of the earlier good poets and prose-writers continued to write and to be widely read, there was now a departure in style and content that was truly revolutionary. For what happened to Arabic writing after 1948 was cataclysmic. With the shock and the bitterness over the transformation of Palestine into a Zionist State, young people all over the Arab world not only saw things in a new light but had to express them in a new way, more immediate, less form-ridden, taking Western innovations in their stride in a struggle for a freer imagination. The word 'new' was mysterious, seductive. A myth was in the making, or re-making, as the Babylonian myth of Tammuz, like the Arab myth of the phoenix, was 'discovered' and seized upon by many poets as their symbol: a myth of death and resurrection, in which the nation's tragedy and hope could find expression.

Influences from East and West, from Mayakovsky to Eliot, ravished the minds of the young, who freely abandoned themselves to contemporary fads and fashions in an attempt to cope with their experience. They were fascinated by the European art movements of the previous fifty years, especially surrealism and expressionism. Mythology was used as never before—Greek, Arab, Babylonian, Christian, and Moslem alike. Gilgamesh and Icarus and Sinbad, Tammuz and Ishtar and Sisyphus, all became urgent and unavoidable allusions. And in less than twenty years Arabic poetry and fiction acquired a stance that had perhaps been forgotten since the great mystics of the past: a private, individual stance, both critical and analytical. Now that the nation had embarked upon a new phase in its search for identity the writer's stance was one of intense consciousness of self. It was history-conscious, humanity-conscious, and, above all, freedom-conscious.

One of the striking characteristics of the new poetry was a 'prophetic' tone of voice in rejection, denunciation, suffering. The use of an individually invented set of symbols and allusions marks the best poets of this period. Their work, when not in book-form, appeared mostly in three magazines that came out in Beirut: *Al-Adeeb*, *Al-Adab*, and *Shir*. These three magazines, which still flourish, are a microcosm of the new movement in Arabic writing, with all its names, its theories, and its polemics.

The pioneers of this movement appeared first in Baghdad in the late 1940s and early 1950s, led by the late Badre Shaker al-Sayab, although their work came out regularly in the Beirut magazines. (Beirut was gradually becoming a publishing centre as active as Cairo, and as regards avant-garde writing perhaps even more influential than Cairo.) The movement, true to its pan-Arab spirit, had no regional colour. The talents converging on Beirut hailed from all over the Arab world, including Egypt. Among the most notable men and women who set the pace for this revolutionary movement in poetry were: Badre Shaker al-Sayab, Nazik al-Malaika, Buland al-Haidari, Abdul Wahab al-Bayati (from Iraq); Youssef al-Khal, Khalil Hawi, Unsi al-Hajj, (from Lebanon); Adonis (Ali Ahmad Said), Mohammed al-Maghout, Nizar Kabbani (from Syria); Tawfiq Sayigh, Jabra Ibrahim Jabra, Salma al-Jayousi, Youssef al-Khatib (from Palestine).

The new poetry has been generally called 'free verse', *al-shir al-hurr*, a convenient but inaccurate term still hotly contested. The error stemmed from an initial misunderstanding of the Western term by poets in Baghdad who were the first to break away from the old distich form. Most of this new poetry uses a relatively simple metre (as opposed to the highly intricate metres of traditional verse), repeating a *tafila* rather like an iambus or a trochee in English verse, and employs irregular and varied rhymes allowing some of the lines, which are usually of unequal length, to remain unrhymed. Some poets write free verse in the accepted sense of the term, and their work is at the opposite extreme from traditional Arabic poetry: it is spare, terse, concrete. It rejects abstractions and seeks a visual effect.

In fiction too, during the 1930s and 1940s the Iraqis were the first to strike a new note of social realism, as evidenced in the work of Zannoun Ayoub, taken up in Syria and elsewhere soon after. Although concern with social and political affairs remained, the art of fiction developed technically throughout the 1950s and 1960s with the advent of the new writers, many of whom made a careful study of the techniques of the Western novel. They employed the stream-of-consciousness technique, interior monologues, flash-backs, inter-cutting, etc., sometimes betraying the influence of Joyce, Faulkner, Sartre. Their shrewd and sympathetic observation of Arab society in transition with all its inner workings, anxieties, and upheavals gives their work a place of particular significance in contemporary Arabic culture. Among the best are: Abdul Malik Nouri, Fuad Takarly, Ghayeb Toma Farman (Iraqis); Samira Azzam, Jabra Ibrahim Jabra, Ghassan Kanafani (Palestinians); Suhail Idriss, Leila Baalbaki, Halim Barakat, Toma Khouri (Lebanese); Zakariya Tamer, Mutaa Safadi, Ghada Samman, George Salem (Syrians); Amin Shunnar, Tayseer Sabboul (Jordanians). Although some of these authors have written successful full-length novels, it is noticeable that they write mostly short stories, which seem to be an effective medium for their skill.

The academic study of literature is pursued on a large scale at Beirut, Damascus, and Baghdad, where the revivalist tradition continues with unabated vigour. Not so numerous, however, are the critics of contemporary writing who are known to possess a 'modern' vision and a truly analytical method, which may comprise several disciples and fields of knowledge. In the 1920s Mikhail Naimy wrote *Al-Ghurbal* ('The Sieve'), which was a turning-point in literary criticism. Other good Lebanese critics followed, notably the late Maroun Abboud, who during his long literary life never seemed to miss a new book or author of significance until the end of the 1950s. Some of the poets and prose writers already mentioned produced a body of critical work in essay or book form which was remarkable for its penetration and cogency and which often expounded or defended the new techniques employed in poetry and fiction. Other critics with these qualities are: Mohammed Youssef Najm, Ihsan Abbas, Antoine Ghattas Karam, Asad Razzouq, Riad Najib al-Rayyes, all of whom work in Beirut.

Drama in this part of the Arab world, unlike Egypt, has not done so well. It has relied almost entirely on translation and adaptation. Until the 1950s perhaps the only writer who wrote good original drama was Said Taqiuddin. In the Arab capitals interest in the theatre has been growing. Productions are mostly of Shakespeare, in new translations, and of some contemporary European dramatists (particularly Beckett, Ionesco, Brecht, Dürrenmatt), but two or three Arab writers in recent years produced original plays that have caught the public imagination, for example the plays of Issam Mahfouz in Beirut and Youssef al-Ani in Baghdad.

The Arab writers of this generation, whatever their theme or commitment, have been enormously stimulated by the discovery of dynamic form. Convention still holds its sway, but it is now generally admitted that tradition itself will atrophy if sanctified and repeated by rote *ad infinitum*: to keep a heritage significant, it must be constantly enriched by invention. Thus the old idea that art forms are immutable and implicitly sacred is no longer acceptable. Form must reflect the inner workings of the subject-matter, and every work of art must embody its own rules and justification.

In painting and sculpture this is particularly evident. In Iraq there was an explosion of artistic talent which occurred at about the time of the literary revolution of the years after 1948. The new style in the visual arts, even more than in literature, expresses a conscious fusion of ancient local tradition—Sumerian, Assyrian, or Arab—with the latest Western innovations. In Baghdad the late Jewad Selim, a brilliant painter and sculptor who combined a masterly technical skill with an intense historical consciousness, set the tone for the new movement in art. His work, together with that of his colleagues and disciples, proved to be a dynamic search for a style which stressed its own Arab—or Iraqi—qualities without isolating itself from the great modern movements. The results in Iraq has been a remarkable genre of painting in which problems of form and significance find a solution that is traditional and yet relevant to the times. A similar trend is emerging in Lebanon, Syria, and, to a lesser extent, Jordan.

JABRA I. JABRA

7. CULTURAL TRENDS IN MODERN EGYPT

The *leitmotif* of most cultural manifestos in Egypt between the late 1950s and 5 June 1967 was that all cultural values held by any true Egyptian revolutionary ought to emanate from the 'Egyptian reality'. Originally the injunction had been formulated by President Nasser in several of his speeches and was later incorporated into the Charter of 1962, but with socio-political overtones. Since then, this conception, which probably meant little more than political 'realism' and a warning against abstract and imported political doctrines, has been elaborated by literary critics to provide a definition of Egypt's national culture. A cult of national art kept pace with that of national literature. Eventually, when Egypt's national identity was modified by its merger with Syria in the United Arab Republic, the denomination 'Egyptian' was dropped and replaced by 'Arab'. This caused much confusion because the Egyptian reality did not always correspond to the Arab reality. It is worth noting that the word used by Abdul Nasser and the National Charter to mean 'emanating'—*munbathiqa*—is a Christian theological term meaning 'being an efflux' and was originally connected with the historic schism over Consubstantiation, i.e. Transubstantiation in the nature of the Godhead. It was presumably a loan-word from Baathist jargon which was mainly fashioned by Michel Aflaq, the Christian philosopher of the Levantine Arab Baath party. How it crept into Egyptian political vocabulary in the 1950s requires investigation. However, to the Egyptian mind the epithet *munbathiq* means little more than 'stemming from'.

Socially and politically this *inbithaq* or 'emanation' led before the 1967 war to the spirited controversy over the nature and substance of Egyptian socialist doctrine and practice which was enunciated in the Charter and which materialized in agrarian reform and partial nationalization. Reactionaries, would-be Fascists, and some well-meaning under-educated conservatives insisted on a strictly 'Arab Socialism' while the Egyptian left in general preferred to talk of an Egyptian road to, or practice of, socialism on the understanding that socialism *per se* has no particular nationality although it may be adaptable to the local conditions of each individual country. In effect the former group, which believed in the concept of 'Arab Socialism', sought at best to reduce socialist theory and practice in Egypt to a kind of moral rearmament within the framework of Islam or something akin to the Christian Socialism of F. B. Maurice and Charles Kingsley. They denounced the materialism of 'scientific' socialism and the theory of class struggle and the egalitarianism of Marxist theory. Instead they recommended solidarity of all classes of an almost Fascist character and invoked the force of national experience in social justice. They were inspired by a sense of existential identity and of existential destiny integrated in the concept of Arab nationalism. In racially non-Arab countries such as Egypt, Algeria, and North Africa in general, Arab nationalism meant the unity of the Islamic world and the revival of the classical period of the Islamic ideal. Among the Arab Arabs, however, the concept oscillated between racial and racist nationalism aiming at the revival of the Arab Empire of the classical period. The choice was one between the patristic theocracy of the four Rashideen and the far-flung dominion of the Umayyads. The challenge for both schools of thought was how to reconcile Arab nationalism with Arab socialism and how to keep to the idiom of the National Charter which, despite the broad range of political and cultural choices that it offered, had an overall character of secular modernism akin to European radicalism.

When applied to culture in its broadest sense, the theory of *inbithaq* or 'natural emanation' becomes even more complex. It is immediately arrayed against all imported cultural values and value judgements not only in the religious, philosophical sphere but in literary and artistic sensibilities. It presupposes an original source of artistic creation which must not be allowed to be contaminated with alien cultures and which provides an all-embracing and self-sufficient ethos with answers to all the questions. It is complex because there is no standard interpretation of life which is common to all epochs, all cycles of civilization, all classes and intellectual levels—in Egypt or anywhere else. This *Ursprung* which seems so native and pure to the educated middle classes is as puzzling and alien to the *fellahin* as the mini-skirt or supersonic aircraft.

The distinguished Islamic historian Jacques Berque has long been preoccupied with the interplay in various Arab and Arab-speaking societies of two principles, those of *assala* and *tajaddud*, i.e. authenticity and regeneration. Stripped of its philosophical trappings his *authenticité* is, in the last analysis, synonymous with conformism and traditionalism, adherence to some immutable Islamic culture which in his scheme of things is responsible for the preservation of the 'Arab World'. Berque's theory never truly explains what the 'Arab World' is being preserved against and it lumps everything together in a single mass: specific pagan survivals, strictly Islamic concepts, recognizable Arab influences not necessarily commensurate with Islam, and Mameluke-Ottoman customs and practices. These components are often fused or superimposed but still fairly distinguishable in any serious analysis of what is called Moslem culture. In this respect Moslem culture is no less synthetic and stratified than what is commonly called Christian culture. Latin, Germanic, and Slavonic notions of Christianity are sufficiently distinguishable to make the concept of a typical Christian nation as absurd as that of a typical European or Indo-European nation.

The theory of *assala*—or *authenticité*, to hold to Berque's term—involving an irrevocable return to the original spring or springs of national culture, is no new concept to Egypt. It has always represented the alternative, although not necessarily the main, stream of consciousness in the Egyptian national awakening, at least since Bonaparte's expedition. It has been embodied in three distinct 'revivalist' cults: Pharaonism, Islamism, and Arabism. Arabism never truly struck roots in Egypt even at the height of Abdul Nasser's popular appeal except as a political expedient and predominantly among segments of the highly volatile middle class who found Arabism attractive because it meant wider social and economic opportunities for Egyptians and the submergence of the class struggle in a new quasi-national metaphysic and the promise of power and progress without the usual restrictions and responsibilities of a comprehensive philosophical, ethical, or social ideal. Consciously or unconsciously a dream of the past glories of the Pharaoh Ramses II lurks in the hearts of some modern Egyptians. For others Arabism was more likely to evoke the image of Saladin and so provide an attractive version of Islamism. Pan-Arabism, in the secular sense, originally flourished in modern times, i.e. since 1798, as an antidote to Ottoman theocratic hegemony. More recently it was revived as an antidote to Russian Communist hegemony but in both cases it was a brand of nationalism peculiar to the people East of Sinai. Wherever it proved inadequate it was superseded by the broader concept of pan-Islam. The liquidation of classical nationalism in the area was simply due to its inability to cope with the ever-increasing power of Soviet

Russia since the Second World War which enabled nationalist feeling
to be fused with leftist protest.

During the inter-revolution period in Egypt (1919–52) which was
imbued with the ideals of classical nationalism and liberal democracy,
the concept of *assala* meant an evocation of Egypt's Pharaonic past. The
Egyptian parliament had its Pharaonic Hall, Mukhtar sculpted the
'Awakening of Egypt' as an Egyptian *fellah* woman awakening a
sphinx; Saad Zaghlul had his Pharaonic mausoleum and also his
Pharaonic pedestal at the foot of Kasr al-Nil Bridge and Tewfik al-
Hakim, in his splendid novel *The Spirit Revived* (*Audat al-Rouh*) used the
myth of the resurrection of Osiris to symbolize the resurrection of
Egypt. These were the days when a Minister of Public Works could
construct Giza railway station and his own private mansion in the
Pharaonic style.

Politically the contribution of Pharaonism was that it dissolved the
contradictions between Moslems and Copts by returning to a pre-
Islamic and pre-Christian heritage. Even Egyptian Jews could feel
indigenous and share in the national heritage by evoking Ptolemaic and
Roman days when Alexandria had a sizeable Jewish community. It is
interesting to recall that in the 1920s and 1930s the degree of Pharaoh-
philia was such that Moslems vied with Copts in claiming direct lineage
from the Ancient Egyptians, not only in customs and manners but also
in racial purity. They quoted famous anthropologists and Egypto-
logists to disown any Arab ancestry. Professor Tewfik Shousha Pasha
even surprised the Egyptian intelligentsia of the 1930s by publishing
an anthropological study providing evidence that the Moslems of Egypt
were more akin to the Ancient Egyptians than were the Copts.

The Pharaonic authenticity was presumably the surest road to
tajaddud or Regeneration that Egypt has ever had. In the first place it
involved no ancestor worship or revival of the past except in a purely
symbolic sense. Hence it neither impeded nor conflicted with the
building of a modern secular state in Egypt. No one could hope or
pretend to want to revive the paganism of Ancient Egypt. While the
Egyptians drew considerable strength from their ancient glories and
their monumental achievements no one wanted to revive the concept
of divine kingship. On the contrary, it is a paradox of Egyptian history
that its Pharaohphile phases were always associated with an upsurge
of secularism and the democratic spirit while its Pharaohphobe phases
always involved a return to some absolutist ideal and the triumph of
form and ritual. This appears less paradoxical if we remember that the
same principle was operative in European history. In its absolutist eras
it was always the Roman ideal that was invoked while the revival of the
Greek ideal always marked periods of secularism and democratic
struggle.

It was no accident that the birth of the two major absolutist movements in Egypt in the 1930s, the Moslem Brotherhood and the Young Egypt Party, coincided with the opening of the fierce controversy over Egypt's Pharaonic or Arab identity in which the illuminating spirits of the period, Taha Hussein, Abbas al-Aqqad, Hussein Heikal, and Salama Moussa vigorously defended Egypt's Pharaonic identity while the neo-theocrats and quasi-Fascists combined to fight for Arabism. In those distant days the cult of Arabism did not seem to attract the Egyptian intelligentsia but the mere fact that these questions were raised was ominous for Egypt's hitherto integrated identity, its classical nationalism and liberal democracy.

From the mid-1930s until the sudden and momentous decision in 1958 by which Egypt was submerged in the UAR there was no search for any new political or cultural identity among the Egyptians. Even the creation of the League of Arab States in 1944 struck the average Egyptian of the 1940s in much the same way as the creation of the Afro-Asian People's Solidarity Conference affected him in the 1950s; a mere political apparatus to foster goodwill and concerted moral action. The problem of identity was never brought into question. It is highly doubtful whether the ten years from Egypt's union with Syria in 1958 to the débâcle of June 1967 were enough to change the concept of *assala* or authenticity in the Egyptian mind although all the mass media of indoctrination and all school and university curricula were geared to effect the change. The glories of Arabism were too ephemeral and too costly to permit the new concept of an Arab national identity to strike deep roots in Egypt. The dissolution of the union with Syria, the failure of the Lebanese civil war, the fiasco of the Yemen campaign, the fall of Ben Bella, and finally the disaster of 1967 all created confusion and perplexity although the official position has not changed. The final upshot of all this is that wherever Arabism in any sense other than that of a State-sponsored collective security policy is still seriously considered in Egypt its position remains substantially the same as before: among the masses it is the inexpensive expression of Islamism without tears and among the sophisticated simply a bid for *Lebensraum*. It is still the handiest excuse a well-meaning or cynical bourgeois can give with an easy conscience for shirking his responsibilities towards the Egyptian *fellah*.

Since Refaa al-Tahtawy (1801–73), classical nationalism and democracy in Egypt have permitted the Egyptian intelligentsia to accept a renaissance in Egypt along Western European lines without necessarily renouncing Egypt's title to a specific identity. The Khedive Ismail's conception of Egypt as 'part of Europe' was probably the poetic expression of that state of mind. Renaissance along Western European lines meant above all the renunciation of the theocratic ideal and the acceptance of total secularism. Tahtawy's ideas run equally through the rationalism of Osman Galal, Qasim Amin, Lufti al-Sayyed, Taha

Hussein, Hussein Heikal, Ali and Mustafa Abdul Razek, Salama Moussa, Mahmoud Azmy, Tewfik al-Hakim, Kamal Hussein, and Hussein Fawzi as well as through the Romanticism of Abbas al-Aqqad, Sayyed Darwish, Mahmoud Moukhtar, Manfalouty, Ibrahim Naguy, and Mohammed Mamdour. Both trends flowed from the same fountain-head, the great Tahtawy whose complex genius combined reason and revolution, poise and passion. Tahtawy himself owes much to his master and sponsor Shaikh Hassan al-Attar who was Shaikh of al-Azhar University under Mohammed Ali and had been a diligent visitor to the Institut d'Egypte under Bonaparte.

In the arts the same attitude expressed itself as in literature and the history of ideas in terms of acceptance of European forms and media. The enthusiasm of al-Gabarti (*fl.* 1800) for the art of figurative painting brought into Egypt by Bonaparte's Rigo and fellow-artists (quite unexpected in a religious conservative of al-Gabarti's type), flowered more than a century later in the achievements of Mahmoud Moukhtar, Ahmad Sabry, Mohammed Naguy, Mahmoud Said, Ragheb Ayyad, and Youssef Kamal during the inter-revolution period. It was a thorough break with the medieval past in which a rigid monotheism completely proscribed the plastic arts, with the exception of architecture, and left no scope for self-expression in line and colour except in decorative abstract stereotype patterns or arabesque. The decay of sculpture in Coptic Egypt shows that Christianity too was hostile to three-dimensional figuratism, although to a lesser degree since the Ancient Egyptian sculptor survived in the Coptic painter who retained memories of the three-dimensional in the religious and secular paintings of the Coptic era. (It may be recalled that a similar process took place in medieval Europe under the influence of Christianity. It was marked by the triumph of architecture, the decay of sculpture and the development of two-dimensional painting which reached its crowning achievement in Giotto. The Ancient Egyptians, like the Ancient Greeks, had little use for three-dimensional painting since they could say everything they wanted to say through the pagan art of sculpture. Moreover, European Renaissance art, which was based on the revival of sculpture and the rediscovery of three-dimensional painting, was only possible through the revival of paganism, politely called humanism, and the return to the cultural sources of Rome, and especially Greece.)

Similarly, Egyptian humanism in the 1920s and 1930s was only possible through the revival of the Pharaonic ideal as the *idée force* of Egyptian nationalism. The Pharaonic revival gave impetus to figurative, as opposed to abstract, art. An Egyptian Moslem could reconcile Islam with humanism. When in 1924 Saad Zaghlul voted £E5,000 for the first official fine arts student missions to France and Italy one fellow-member of parliament moved to object; Zaghlul curtly silenced him by asking him not to talk of matters he knew nothing about. It was clear that medieval iconoclasm was no more in Egypt. Humanism brought God nearer to man and ennobled him with a spark of divinity.

Between the 1919 and 1952 revolutions there was generally no conflict in the Egyptian mind between the concept of authenticity and that of renovation or modernity, between drawing from the original springs of national culture and discipleship to Europe. There had been a break of two thousand years in the tradition of the plastic arts as a result of which the Egyptian artist, without losing the natural gifts that made him the wonder of the Ancient World, had lost his technical dexterity and sense of form. Discipleship to Europe was necessary to re-acquire his lost technique and even to enrich him with the added experience of lost civilizations. It was therefore a period of learning and imitation which was mainly spent in mastering, or re-mastering, the grammar of painting and sculpture.

As far as the plastic arts are concerned, the 1952 revolution gave no less of an impetus to painting and sculpture than the 1919 revolution through the enlightened patronage of the Ministry of Culture which instituted a system of long-term grants to painters and sculptors. This rescued an entire generation of painters and sculptors who would have been lost as a result of the decline of the old system of patronage with the liquidation of the semi-aristocratic *ancien régime* and the mass exodus of local foreign communities after 1952. Most of the older generation of artists had already been formed in Europe in the 1940s and six years of reluctant but almost uninterrupted State patronage enabled them to preserve their talents and even to mature under the revolution. This was the generation of Ramses Younan, Taheyya Haleem, Gazbeyya Sirry, Fuad Kamel, Seif Wamly, Abdul Hadi al-Gazzar, Adham Wamly, Kanaan, Salah Tahir, Bicaar, Ingy Aflatoun, and Rateb Siddiq. Strictly speaking, they had all been formed under the *ancien régime* and most of them were able to continue to express themselves under the revolution in their own idioms and techniques. Most of them were well-educated and sophisticated. The following generation is that of Adam Henein, Hamad Nada, Sageemy, Salah Abul Karim, Youssef Francis, Kamal Khaleefa, George al-Bahghoury, Hassan Sulaiman, Rifaat Ahmad, Omar al-Nagdy, Mustafa Ahmad, Saleh Reda, and Razzaz. Most members of the group must have been in their early twenties when the 1952 revolution took place and many of them have also had the opportunity of completing their studies in the fine arts in Europe. However, there is a basic difference between this generation and that of the pre-revolutionary period. With very few exceptions there is a clear trend among the post-revolutionary artists away from the purely aesthetic ideal to one of utility and most of them have passed from the field of the fine arts to that of the applied arts. Most of them have used their talents to serve the cinema, stage, press, or architecture. The shift of emphasis from the purely aesthetic ideal has been a conscious one. It was encouraged and subsidized by the state and the battle raged within the corridors of the Ministry of Culture itself and found expression in the alternating leadership of Hamad Said and Abdul Kader Rizk, two senior artist-administrators. Hamad Said sided with the aesthetic ideal, favoured the older generation of artists, and liberally provided government grants for abstract painters, impressionists, expressionists, cubists, and all varieties of self-expression. He was himself a high priest of the defunct liberal ideal in a country where even liberalism needs high priests. Abdul Kader Rizk, on the other hand, sided with the ideal of utility. He invoked the spirit of the revolution to gear art to immediate social uses. An impressive sculptor himself, he wanted sculpture to embody the grand ideas of the revolution and to symbolize its achievements. His approach was a dangerous one because less gifted people soon began to insist that government funds should only go to artist-designers serving the textile industry or improving Egyptian handicrafts. They attacked abstract art, surrealism, impressionism, expressionism, etc., as decadent schools imported from an alien civilization which ought to be extirpated because they were remnants of imperialist influence. In the name of authenticity some of the best artists in the country lost their grants in 1965–6.

The concept of *authenticité*, which in the 1920s produced the grandeur of Moukhtar, was no longer possible under Arabism. The Pharaonic ideal having been discredited, at least since 1958, some new meaning had to be given to 'authenticity' and to the theory of 'emanation'. Since Islamic tradition and Arab culture provided no heritage in the plastic arts outside architecture and the decorative arts, 'authenticity' came to mean drawing from figurative folk themes while still preserving the sophisticated techniques of the European tradition. There have been some limited achievements in this direction. The trend was strengthened by the wider interest in folklore created by the social aspect of the revolution and its concentration on the *fellahin* and workers. Thus the humanism of the plastic artist in Egypt has been able to survive despite the constant appeal to the non-plastic, or even anti-plastic, medieval culture.

Today the Egyptian plastic artist lives in bleak solitude; he is an image-maker in an iconoclastic society, a prophet or clown without a public. Ironically, this very solitude has greatly helped to protect him from the puritans. He is relatively well-protected by the state and relatively well-received by the press but the general public remains completely indifferent to his work. He is left to create in peace, isolated from the conflicting ideologies. The only pressure that the plastic artist has been exposed to under the 1952 revolution has been an abortive attempt by certain deferential or politically-minded administrators to harness him to the theory of engaged art.

The three main problems confronting the artist in Egypt today arise from the following: (*a*) that he belongs to a community which, from the most ancient times and even in the pagan period, has always participated in the artistic experience as a public function and rarely as an intimate individual experience; (*b*) that the natural gift of the Egyptian plastic artist has always tended towards applied, as opposed to pure or fine, art; indeed the great enigma of Ancient Egypt was its genius in elevating the mundane to the stature of the divine and in reaching the universal through the particular; and (*c*) the purely temporary difficulty that the general pride in attaining majority has, in art as in many other departments of life, cut short the period of discipleship to European techniques. This should prove only a temporary difficulty although it could be disastrous for a country of lost skills and dim reminiscences of a glorious past of two thousand years ago.

LOUIS AWAD

II

Arabia

I. SAUDI ARABIA

THE LAND AND THE PEOPLE

The Arab Kingdom of Saudi Arabia is the creation of the late 'Ibn Saud' (King Abdul Aziz ibn Abdul Rahman ibn Faisal al-Saud), although in fact he was reviving ancestral claims. In 1921 he was proclaimed and recognized officially by the British Government as Sultan of Nejd and its dependencies, including the former Sultanate of Hail. On 8 September 1926 he was proclaimed King of the Hejaz at Mecca and six years later King of Saudi Arabia, formed by the union of the Sultanate and Kingdom, with its capital at Riyadh. The new kingdom comprised 90 per cent of the entire Arabian Peninsula, its western coastline stretching from Aqaba in the north, some 1,000 miles southwards down the Red Sea to the frontiers of Yemen. Its southern and south-eastern borders, which are still mostly ill-defined, march with Yemen, Democratic Yemen, Oman, Qatar, and the Trucial States on the Gulf. On the east its coast stretches along the Arab/Persian Gulf through Hasa northwards to the partitioned zones shared with Kuwait. To the north lie Jordan and Iraq. At the time of its creation Saudi Arabia was a primitive and backward state. The population was estimated between one-and-a-half and two million: probably more than a quarter of whom were nomadic, about a half were agricultural and concerned with cultivation in a widely dispersed zone, and the remaining quarter inhabited the relatively numerous market towns and the Holy Cities. Mecca, which was the largest town, probably had a population of 50,000. Administration and organization was essentially tribal, the economy was basically subsistence-orientated except for the small component of pearling in the Gulf and the income derived from services given to the Mecca-bound pilgrims.

Physical characteristics

The physical landscape of the Arabian peninsula owes much to its structural character. Briefly, a geologically ancient and relatively stable platform of crystalline rocks has been tilted so that the western edge is uplifted in the highlands which extend from Hejaz south to Aden. This western uplift was accompanied by extensive fracturing and faulting, which gives the pronounced steep scarp edge overlooking the Red Sea and also extensive volcanicity, including great basaltic flows. The south coast of the Democratic Republic of Yemen is similarly fault defined.

The platform tilts eastwards from the Red Sea to the Gulf and is largely covered by more recent sedimentary rocks which attain great thickness where the old block plunges into the great structural depression of the Gulf. In the extreme east the Oman highlands are part of the fold mountain complex of the Zagros mountains of Iran.

The oil wealth of Saudi Arabia is found along the eastern zone where, in sandstones and limestones laid down in shallow water, organic material has been transformed into petroleum hydro-carbons. Recent exploration has established that these are to be found both at relatively great depth in the Gulf itself and also in the shallower land deposits of ancient marine transgressions well inland as in the Rub al-Khali.

On this basic structure arid and semi-arid erosion processes produced during the wetter phases of the Pleistocene Ice-Ages great wadi systems that are, as in the case of the Wadi Batin, now relics in the present more arid epoch but along the lines of which lie some of the linear patterns of wells of great traditional importance. These ancient wadis generally trend south-west to north-east, cutting through the opposing, structurally controlled series of scarps, one of which, the Jabal Tuwaiq, dominates the surrounding plateaux for hundreds of miles.

In the north, eroded sandstones alternate with sand desert basins in the Great Nafud. In the south far greater sand seas dominate the 400,000 square miles of the Rub al-Khali. Central Nejd is a diversity of hills and basins which, where shallow groundwater permits, support oasis settlement.

Only along a narrow zone in the south-western highlands of Saudi Arabia, the Assarah region, does precipitation permit rainfed and irrigation-assisted agriculture and support regionally extensive communities of sedentary cultivators. Elsewhere sub-surface hydrology is all-important since rainfall is minimal and evaporation extremely high; only in the Esh Sham region south of Palmyra does winter precipitation support even relatively stable pastoralism. The traditional centres of life have therefore been oases and well complexes as at Mecca and Medina in the west, Riyadh in Nejd and al-Hasa in the east. The Saudi Arabian coastlands along the Red Sea are dissected and waterless while those on the Gulf are characterized by lagoons, mangrove swamp, and *sabkha*, the better favoured coastal locations all having been pre-empted by the independent amirates, now sovereign States of Kuwait, Bahrain, and Trucial Oman (United Arab Emirates).

The People

No census has been held and estimates of the total population of Saudi Arabia vary from 3·5 million to 10 million. A Saudi Government estimate of 1963 of 6·6 million is generally thought to be too high. About half the population is thought to be nomadic. Recent estimates of the population of the principal cities are Riyadh (170,000); Mecca (160,000); Jedda (148,000); Medina (72,000). The people are nearly all Sunni Arabs and most of them are Wahhabis. There are no native Christians or Jews but several thousand Christians (US, European, and Arab) are employed in the oil industry. Non-Moslems are forbidden within the sacred areas surrounding Mecca and Medina, and foreign diplomatic missions are located in Jedda rather than Riyadh, the capital. Jews are forbidden entry into Saudi Arabia.

THE RELIGIOUS BACKGROUND

The Holy Places and the Pilgrimage

Until recently the possession by Saudi Arabia of the Holy Places of Islam was the central political fact and the main source of wealth in the kingdom. The custodianship of the Holy Places remains a most important element in the political status of Saudi Arabia and even today spending by pilgrims provides the third largest revenue item in the kingdom's balance of payments. During the month of the hajj in 1971 almost 400,000 foreign pilgrims as well as more than 700,000 Saudis are believed to have visited the Holy Places.

Mecca had been a Holy City before the time of Mohammed, a centre of a religious blend of animism together with ritual worship of the sun, moon, and other deities and part-mythical heroes. The Kaaba, a square building in the courtyard of the main mosque—the Haram—was traditionally reputed to have been built by Adam and rebuilt by Abraham and Ishmael, who inserted into one of its corners the famous Black Stone; a present, the tradition continues, from the Archangel Gabriel. The same tradition names the nearby well of Zam-Zam as the well to which Hagar and Ishmael were guided by God to find water. They both have traditional graves near the Kaaba itself, while Eve's grave was believed to be located at Jedda. (The visiting of such graves is discouraged by the Wahhabis.) The tradition of pilgrimage to Mecca was taken over by the Koran, and is enjoined on Moslems as a sacred duty. The date of the pilgrimage is fixed for the tenth day of the twelfth month of every Moslem year, the climax named the Feast of Sacrifice.

The ritual of the pilgrimage is strict. Once within the sacred area, which starts sixteen miles west of Mecca, all pilgrims must wear the pilgrim's garb—the '*ihram*'. On reaching Mecca the first duty of every pilgrim is prayer at the Kaaba, followed by a procession seven times round the building, after which each kisses the Black Stone. A drink of water is then taken at the well of Zam-Zam. The Feast of Sacrifice itself is celebrated in the plain of Muna, and the following morning each pilgrim stones the three pillars where the Devil is supposed to have been chased away by stones thrown by Abraham, Hagar, and Ishmael. The sacrifice follows. Each family slays its goat or sheep with traditional ritual, and the rest of the day is passed in eating and thanksgiving. Every true believer who accomplishes the pilgrimage is entitled thereafter to call himself 'hajj' and, if he wishes, to wear a green cloth folded round his headdress.

The organization of the reception and handling of the yearly pilgrimage has become a very considerable responsibility in that no longer is it possible or desirable to allow the numbers of pilgrims to find their own transport, food, sleeping accommodation, and transport facilities. On arrival at Jedda, which is still the main point of entry for most foreign pilgrims, the individual pilgrim must produce vaccination certificates or be vaccinated on the spot; any sickness is dealt with in the hospital outside Jedda, a hospital of 3,000 beds built exclusively for the hajj. Transport is now supplied to carry the pilgrims between Jedda and Mecca as a decreasing number do the whole journey on foot, and further transport facilities have to be arranged for the journeys to Medina and once more back to Jedda. Accommodation however spartan must be arranged at Mecca, Medina, and Jedda, in each case capable of holding some 100,000 people; the supply of food and potable water is an equally vast operation. Since the State has been able to rely in the main on oil revenues, the fee which traditionally was paid by pilgrims has been abolished. It is now probable that the organization of the hajj results in costs being incurred by the Saudi Arabian Government which far outweigh the indirect profit made from sales of commodities and services to the pilgrims. There is the further matter that the custodianship involves the State in very considerable expenditure on maintenance and improvement of many of the buildings. It has been estimated that, for example, an extension of the Medina Mosque, completed in 1955, cost more than £5 million. There can also be unexpected responsibilities such as those resulting from the repatriation of pilgrims who either cannot afford to pay for their return journey or who wish not to return.

HISTORY AND POLITICAL ORGANIZATION

History

The present ruler of Saudi Arabia is King Faisal, a direct descendant through his father's lineage of the founder of the house of Saud and through his mother's lineage of the founder of the Wahhabi movement. Ibn Saud died in 1953 and was succeeded by the former Crown Prince Saud. Prince Faisal, his younger brother, who presided over the Council of Ministers, was called on to take over the Government between 1958 and 1960. In 1961 Faisal once more became *de facto* ruler, as King Saud's health deteriorated and his control of affairs became increasingly of concern to the Royal Family and the Ulema. In 1964, following traditional procedure and in response to persuasion, Faisal replaced his brother on the throne.

The royal house of Saudi Arabia has ruled in Nejd since the eighteenth century. The founder of the house of Saud in Nejd, Saud ibn Mohammed ibn Muqrin, died in 1747, and was succeeded by his eldest son, Mohammed ibn Saud, who offered asylum to the religious reformer Mohammed ibn Abdul Wahhab (1703–91) the founder of the Wahhabi movement. The latter had been driven out of his own country by local opposition to his new creed, which preached the purification of Islam. All worship other than of God was false worship; the cult of saints, their invocation in prayer, the veneration of their tombs, and other similar practices implied unbelief in God; and among its precepts for the stricter observance of Islam were obligatory attendance at public prayers and a ban on smoking. Wahhabi mosques are built with the minimum of architectural adornment.

From 1746, except for short intervals of peace, Nejd was at war for the next century and a half. Slowly the Wahhabi rule spread throughout Nejd and later into Hasa province on the Gulf, though its spread was generally resisted. In 1801, to avenge an attack by Iraqi tribesmen on a pilgrim caravan the Wahhabis had agreed to protect, they invaded Iraq, sacked Karbala (the Shii Holy City), massacred its inhabitants, and desecrated the tomb of Hussein. Two years later they captured Taif and Mecca in the Hejaz, destroyed several shrines, and stripped the Kaaba of its ornaments. By 1806, Yanbo, Medina, Mecca, and Jedda were in Wahhabi hands.

These victories and their religious repercussions had an immediate effect in Egypt, where Mohammed Ali had just begun to consolidate his personal supremacy. With the approval of the Ottoman Sultan an Egyptian expeditionary force was organized, and in 1811 it invaded Arabia. The campaign lasted eight years and ended in the complete defeat of the Wahhabis and the fall of Riyadh, the capital of Nejd. This victory restored the Sultan's control over Mecca and Medina, the Holy Cities of Islam, and up to 1840 Turkish and Egyptian influence on the Hejaz and Nejd was unchallenged; the ruler of Nejd was forced to accept Ottoman suzerainty.

Meanwhile, north of Nejd the Rashidi family of Hail had succeeded in establishing itself as a powerful rival of the Saudi family, and for many years fighting was almost unbroken between the two. Fortunes fluctuated, but in 1891 the head of the Saud family, Abdul Rahman was forced to flee the country with his young son Abdul Aziz and took refuge in Kuwait, where they and their followers remained as refugees until 1902, when Abdul Aziz with a few followers recaptured Riyadh by a brilliant surprise attack. Rashidi power in Hail declined and, with the danger of attack from the north thus removed, Abdul Aziz, who was recognized as leader even in the lifetime of his father, was free to contemplate the recovery of the Wahhabi territorial losses of the past hundred years. In 1913, his army suddenly occupied the Turkish province of Hasa, on the Gulf.

During the First World War, on 26 December 1915, Ibn Saud signed a treaty with the British Government and received British recognition of the independence and territorial integrity of Nejd and a subsidy of £5,000 monthly; but the growing power of King Hussein of the Hejaz inevitably brought the two neighbours into conflict, which ended in a disastrous Hejaz defeat at Turaba in 1919. Ibn Saud then advanced against Hail, where the last Rashidi ruler surrendered in November 1921. Following an abortive attack on Transjordan in 1922, he agreed to refrain from aggression against Iraq, Kuwait, and the Hejaz, and to co-operate with Britain in furthering peaceful conditions and economic interests in Arab countries. In 1924, after the subsidy had ceased, a Wahhabi force raided the Hejaz, where King Hussein abdicated in favour of his son Ali. In December 1925 Jedda, Medina, and Yanbo were overrun by the Wahhabi armies and Ali abdicated and withdrew to Iraq, where he died in 1934. Ibn Saud was proclaimed as King of Hejaz at Mecca on 8 January 1926. British recognition followed in the Treaty of Jedda, signed on 20 May 1927.

Meanwhile Asir to the south of the Hejaz, which had been ruled by a branch of the Idrisi family of North Africa, had also come under Ibn Saud's domination. He had acquired the mountain districts in 1920, and in 1925, during a civil war between two Idrisi rivals in which the King of the Yemen had supported one pretender, the other accepted what amounted to a protectorate from Ibn Saud; on his death Asir was annexed to Nejd. In 1934 hostilities broke out between Yemen and Saudi Arabia. Saudi forces were quickly victorious and the settlement which followed led to amicable relations for the next thirty years. On Saudi Arabia's northern borders, suspicion of the Hashimite kingdoms of Transjordan (later Jordan) and Iraq ruled over by the sons of the ill-fated Hussein of Hejaz remained strong. Ibn Saud also remained deeply suspicious of British actions in Palestine but as the prospects of oil revenue appeared during the late 1930s and as the need and opportunities for pursuing remarkably successful policies of internal consolidation became more apparent so also did the Saudi Government's freedom of international manoeuvre grow more limited.

Following the Second World War and the creation of Israel in 1948 Saudi Arabia pursued a more vigorous but yet cautious foreign policy utilizing in particular its growing economic power and status. A founder-member of the Arab League, Saudi Arabia joined with Egypt and Syria in opposing Abdullah of Jordan and Nuri al-Said of Iraq in their Greater Syria ambitions, this policy continuing in Saudi opposition to the Baghdad Pact. The assassination of King Abdullah in 1951

and the overthrow of the Egyptian monarchy in 1952 did not in themselves alter Saudi attitudes except that suspicion of Hashimite intentions decreased and the traditional policy of friendship with Egypt was
not as easy to maintain. Ibn Saud's personal control of government up
to the time of his death in 1953 not only coloured his attitude to his
northern neighbours but also towards those in the south-west bordering
the Buraimi group of oases. The discovery of oil only emphasized the
traditional claims made in this region by the rulers of Abu Dhabi,
Oman, and Saudi Arabia; and the continued British championing of
the cause of the smaller states somewhat strained Ibn Saud's friendship
with Britain. In 1949, after three years of dispute with the British
Government (which by treaty automatically acted for Abu Dhabi and
by invitation also for Oman), Saudi claims to the whole region were put
forward very strongly and Saudi forces occupied one of the oasis
villages. In 1954 the forces withdrew but neutral arbitration proceedings
broke down within a year; the Shaikh of Abu Dhabi and the Sultan of
Muscat and Oman thereupon resumed control of the whole area
approximately up to the lines expressed in a Saudi claim map of 1935.
Since that time the *status quo* has remained in being but the full Saudi
claims remain on record.

The reign of King Saud was a period of greater difficulty for Saudi
Arabia. Oil-derived wealth under Ibn Saud had already led to some
degree of public extravagance and of the personal enrichment of the
Royal Family and Court at variance with strict Wahhabi tradition, but
the personal status and strength of the creator of the kingdom prevented
internal strains and tensions from becoming too great. Similarly with
administration, where only a life-time of exercising authority and the
unchallengeable respect he commanded enabled Ibn Saud to rule a
rapidly changing and modernizing State with little except traditional
tribal machinery. King Saud inherited none of these advantages. He
was faced by an accelerating pace of change at home and increasingly
delicate situations abroad, and, as ultimately was recognized by the
Royal Family and their advisers, he did not possess the ability to meet
the various and heavy demands made on a ruler in such a situation.

Within Saudi Arabia the unity created by Ibn Saud appeared less
strong as divisive forces reappeared. In a theocratic state, the Ulema,
the learned Islamic judiciary which interprets and administers the
sharia, the divine law of Islam, was a body whose strength Ibn Saud
appreciated and utilized. As Riyadh, the centre of government, became
more and more associated not only with personal wealth and laxity but
also with the graft and corruption which accompanied the growth of
disorganized administrative machinery and the inflow of advisers and
administrators many of whom were blatantly self-seeking, so members
of the Ulema were alienated. Regionalism, always a danger to a weak
central Government, grew as the Hejaz began to lose respect for the

once conquering Nejd and also as the Hasawis of the east contrasted the efficiency and prosperity resulting from the activities of Aramco and the provincial Government of al-Hasa, with the increasingly infirm character of the Riyadh Government. All this was doubly dangerous because the results of early investment in education produced a growing number of young people who were beginning to think for themselves, and who provided fertile soil for the concepts of Arab socialism and nationalism propagated by immigrant teachers and administrators. Moreover, the flood of Egyptian radio propaganda, included a strong element of anti-Riyadh sentiment. Prince Faisal, who had conducted foreign affairs for his father, remained President of the Council of Ministers, a nominated body largely drawn from the Royal Family, but King Saud pursued the system of largely personal rule drawing support increasingly from a group of favourites. Dissension was met by increased expenditure on internal security and the taking of more power by the provincial governors.

Externally, circumstances were even more confused and policy equally vacillating. Friendship with Egypt was maintained after Nasser's rise to power even though the new brand of Egyptian Arab Socialism was anathema to Saudi ruling circles. In 1955 Saud joined Egypt and Syria in a joint command system aimed at the Baghdad Pact group; in 1956 he publicly supported Egypt's seizure of the Suez Canal; and after the Suez venture he broke off relations with Britain—these were not restored until 1964.

In January 1957 Saudi Arabia joined with Egypt and Syria in undertaking to pay Jordan for at least ten years £12·5 million annually to replace the British subsidy. But King Saud was already apprehensive about the rapid rise of radical revolutionary Arab nationalism led by Abdul Nasser and about the increasing Soviet influence in the Middle East. In April, during the disturbances in Jordan, he sent troops there, as much to forestall any Syrian attempt to take over the country as to guard against an attack by Israel. He settled his differences with the Hashimites in order to create a common monarchical front against the revolutionary republics. The United States responded by showing its approval of King Saud's anti-Communism and the State Department seems to have considered the possibility of buttressing Saud as a rival to Nasser's leadership of the Arabs.

Saud and his advisers still tried to avoid an open clash with Nasser. He worded his acceptance of the Eisenhower Doctrine so that it should appear as approval without full acceptance. But a crisis was reached in February 1958 when the Syrian Colonel Abdul Hamid Sarraj publicly accused Saud of attempting to have President Nasser assassinated on the eve of the formation of the United Arab Republic of Egypt and Syria. The princes, shaikhs, and Ulema who represented public opinion in Saudi Arabia combined to force the King to hand over full powers in domestic and foreign affairs to his younger brother Prince Faisal who at that time was regarded as relatively pro-Egyptian. Saud's forays in foreign policy and his wild extravagance had made Saudi Arabia something of a laughing-stock in the Arab world.

Faisal initiated a period of economy and restraint to restore Saudi Arabia's chaotic finances. But although Saudi Arabia's image abroad was improved, financial austerity was unpopular at home—especially among the tribesmen who had received regular subsidies from Saud. Saudi 'progressive' intellectuals saw their opportunity and formed an undeclared alliance with Saud on the understanding that if they helped him recover his powers a constitution providing for some form of representative government would be introduced. Saud did recover his authority in December 1960 when Faisal resigned as Prime Minister, but constitutional government did not follow and the small group of progressives went into jail or exile.

Saud's new period of rule was only brief. The republican coup in Yemen in September 1962 was a direct threat to the Saudi monarchy. Saudi Arabia at once began helping the Yemeni royalists but Saud's position was precarious. In October he reshuffled his Government and announced a reform programme which included the abolition of slavery. The loyalty of the regular Saudi forces was far from certain and two of the small band of trained Saudi pilots defected with their planes to Egypt. In failing health, Saud was obliged to return power to Faisal who by the end of 1963 had once again become the effective ruler of Saudi Arabia.

Austere in his private life, astute and experienced in international diplomacy, Faisal was a much more real threat to President Nasser's position than his brother had been. He made no concessions to those Saudis who wanted a more liberal regime but he earned their respect. At the same time he encouraged steady progress in social and economic development. In his previous period of power he had tried to avoid any heavy involvement in Arab politics in order to concentrate on domestic affairs. This time he embarked on a vigorous diplomatic offensive in favour of the conservative Arab monarchies and against the radical republics. He was helped by Egypt's increasing difficulties in Yemen where he was able to continue supplying the Yemeni royalists with money and arms without involving his own forces.

In November 1964 Saud was formally deposed by a majority of the princes and the council of religious leaders and Faisal became king. Saudi–Egyptian relations were generally worsening although there was some brief improvement after August 1965 when President Nasser flew to Jedda to conclude the so-called Jedda agreement for peace in Yemen. But while the abortive Haradh peace conference which arose out of this agreement was in progress, King Faisal paid a state visit to Iran where in a speech to the Iranian Majlis he proposed closer collaboration be-

tween Moslem states against alien and atheist influences. He later
denied that he was proposing any form of political alliance but there is
little doubt that he was attempting to establish a common front of
conservative regimes against Nasser's Egypt. Cairo's press and radio at
once began to denounce what it called Faisal's Islamic Pact.

During 1966 King Faisal made a series of diplomatic visits mainly to
Moslem states such as Turkey, Pakistan, and Sudan. He was advised
in Riyadh by a group of anti-Egyptian Arab emigré politicians. His
public speeches were consistently anti-Communist with the implication
that Egypt, and to a lesser extent Syria too, was responsible for the
growing Soviet power and influence in the Arab world. Saudi Arabia
was diplomatically strong but militarily weak and in 1966 the Government began a major rearmament programme which included a £300
million deal with British firms to provide an air-defence network.
Egyptian Yemeni-based planes had on several occasions bombed with
impunity Saudi border towns which the Egyptians alleged were being
used as bases by the Yemeni royalists.

King Faisal's challenge to President Nasser was genuine and powerful as he was the acknowledged leader of anti-Nasser elements. But his
diplomatic achievements were limited because, except for Iran and
Jordan, the key states in his potential Islamic front—Pakistan, Turkey,
and Sudan—declined to commit themselves to an anti-Egyptian policy
and his proposal for a summit meeting of Moslem Heads of State in
Saudi Arabia came to nothing.

The 1967 Arab–Israeli war transformed the situation. In the short
term it brought several advantages to King Faisal. The Egyptian army
was badly beaten and President Nasser's prestige shaken. At the
Khartoum Arab summit meeting in August he took the lead in proposing that, in return for a general agreement, the pumping of oil supplies to the United Kingdom and United States cut off during the war
should be resumed, and that the three leading Arab oil states, Kuwait,
Libya, and Saudi Arabia, should provide Jordan and Egypt with an
income to compensate for the losses of the war. Egypt was thus placed
in a position of accepting Saudi charity. At the same time, President
Nasser was finally obliged to agree to withdraw all his troops from
Yemen—a cardinal aim of Saudi policy.

The disadvantages to Saudi Arabia of the Arab defeat, though less
obvious, were equally genuine. King Hussein, his foremost ally among
Arab leaders was now in such a weak position that he could not afford
to join Faisal in opposing radical elements in the Arab world. The war
had if anything pushed the Arabs further to the left and although
Britain fairly rapidly mended its bridges with the Arab world the
United States remained deeply unpopular for its continued diplomatic
support for Israel. The Russians, on the other hand, were championing
the Arab cause and King Faisal's extreme anti-Communism aroused

little response. Even in South Arabia events did not develop as King
Faisal might have hoped. The withdrawal of Egyptian troops did not
lead to the expected collapse of the Yemeni republican regime and the
NLF takeover in South Yemen meant that another revolutionary republican regime had been installed on the Arabian Peninsula—something King Faisal had striven to prevent. His efforts to establish a form
of protectorate over the Hadhramaut states failed when the rulers
returning from a visit to Saudi Arabia found their territory in the hands
of the National Liberation Front (NLF).

The June war had exposed the fact that Saudi Arabia was still not
a military power. Saudi troops, which in May were reported to be
concentrating near Maan to help Jordan were never engaged and in
fact never entered Jordanian territory, although some 5,000 were
stationed there after the war.

Following the 1967 war, Saudi foreign diplomacy was very much less
active and the King no longer attempted to take any strong lead in the
Arab world. He refused to agree to the holding of a further Arab summit meeting on the ground that this should await the outcome of the
mission of Dr. Gunnar Jarring, the UN Special Envoy. King Faisal
pursued his efforts to achieve a *rapprochement* between Iran and the
Arab states—a matter which had become more urgent with Britain's
decision to withdraw all its forces from the Gulf by 1971. His relations
with Egypt and other socialist Arab states were correct but cool. He
scored a diplomatic success when a meeting of Islamic Heads of State
was held in Rabat in September 1969, as an alternative to an Arab
summit meeting, following the al-Aqsa Mosque fire in Jerusalem. When
an Arab summit was finally held in Rabat in December 1969, its failure
was due at least partially to Saudi Arabia's refusal to increase its financial support for the Arab nations directly confronting Israel by the
amount these countries desired. The Saudi Government as well as
private individuals continued to give considerable financial assistance
to the Palestine guerrilla organization al-Fatah; King Faisal showed
his preference for al-Fatah rather than its Marxist rivals such as the
Popular Front for the Liberation of Palestine.

The Saudi Government refused to recognize the revolutionary
Government of South Yemen on the ground that it threatened Saudi
Arabia's security. On the other hand, it finally recognized the Government of Yemen in July 1970 following the compromise settlement of
the Yemeni civil war. The Saudi regime was alarmed at the spread of
left-wing influences in the Arabian Peninsula. In June and September
1969 there were attempted coups against the regime by Baathist and
Arab nationalist elements in the armed forces and civil service and
again in March 1970 several prominent civilians were arrested.

The improvement in Saudi–Iranian relations was confirmed by the
visit to Saudi Arabia of the Iranian Foreign Minister in July 1970.

Saudi policy continued to be to encourage the formation of a federation of Arab shaikhdoms in the Gulf although a potential threat to the stability of the area was the renewal during 1970 of the Saudi claim to the Buraimi Oasis.

Constitution and Government

Saudi Arabia has no constitution except the Koran. Its law is the *sharia* supplemented by various decrees. While the last ten years have seen the growth of Cabinet Government and the development of a modern type of ministry, budgeting, etc., the reins of power remain in the hands of the King who is also Prime Minister and Foreign Minister. The King's brother Khalid ibn Abdul Aziz is Crown Prince. The capital is Riyadh but the King and most of the Government reside and work in Taif during the summer months. All foreign embassies are in Jedda, the commercial centre.

The administrative areas are the Hejaz, Nejd, the Eastern Province (al-Hasa), Asir, and Najran. There are General Municipal Councils—each with an Administrative Committee—for the towns of Mecca, Medina, and Jedda. In the rest of the country there are district councils, tribal councils, and village councils.

ECONOMIC AND SOCIAL SURVEY

Saudi oil wealth began to flow in large quantities in the early 1950s and led to heavy spending by a Royal Family about 5,000 strong. By 1956–8, though revenues were rising, the country was plunged into a balance of payments crisis. Devaluation and a monetary stabilization programme devised by the Saudi Arabian Monetary Agency (SAMA), headed by a Pakistani (Anwar Ali), succeeded in remedying the situation; the budget was balanced over successive years, and the Saudi rial is now a hard currency, equivalent to $4·65.

The change of target from luxury expenditure at home and real estate purchases abroad to domestic development projects began when the IBRD was asked to make a survey in May 1960. By 1961 a first attempt at a planning board was in being, advised by technicians from IBRD on two-year contracts. But the key matter of personnel was not solved and by 1963 a different organization was set up directly responsible to the Prime Minister. This Supreme Planning Board embarked on infrastructure projects, and in particular on the building of a road network, but the first planning body which aimed to co-ordinate the efforts of individual ministries and to establish priorities between their needs was King Faisal's Central Planning Bureau set up by the Cabinet in 1969. In 1969 a Five-Year Plan for the period 1970/1 to 1975/6 was announced with the broad aim of maintaining the rate of economic growth, developing and creating fresh opportunities for the country's human resources, and diversifying and broadening the base of the economy.

The Oil Industry

The transformation of Saudi Arabia within three decades has been made possible by the discovery and exploitation of oil on a vast scale.

The first oil concession was granted in 1933 and the first exports took place in 1938. The Second World War resulted in the virtual shutting down of the first oil-fields but from 1946 onwards production soared dramatically. In 1968 revenue from oil totalled $926 million and production reached 1,114·1 million barrels, making Saudi Arabia the largest Middle East producer and the fourth largest producer in the world. The rate of increase slowed down somewhat during 1969 and both Libya (much nearer European markets) and Iran (which put great pressure on producing companies) overhauled Saudi Arabia in tonnage raised. Nevertheless the kingdom possesses the largest national proven oil resources in the world, capable without further exploration of supporting present extraction rates for a further century. In 1971 it was reported that Aramco was planning to increase production three-fold in the next three years. Taking into account price increases this would raise Saudi oil revenues to about $5,000 million by 1975 and increase its share of world production from 7·5 per cent to about 15 per cent. Extending from the Neutral Zone from which oil receipts are shared with Kuwait, offshore as at Safaniya and near Bahrain and onshore as at Abu Hadriya and the giant Ghawar field, a series of oil-fields stretch south into the Rub al-Khali and border the territories of Abu Dhabi and the State of Oman. The extent and wealth of these fields increases with each exploratory survey. Aramco, the consortium of Standard Oil California (30 per cent), Standard Oil New Jersey (30 per cent), Texaco (30 per cent), and Mobil (10 per cent), still produces over 90 per cent of the crude petroleum. The remainder comes from the Getty onshore concession and the AOC Japanese offshore concession in the Neutral Zone. The Saudi oil and mineral corporation Petromin, established in 1962, is now, however, in association with other foreign groups such as the French and Italian State corporations of Auxerap and AGIP, and also Phillips, National Oil, and the Pakistan Government, itself moving from refining and marketing into exploration and exploitation along the Gulf and in the Red Sea.

The crude oil is channelled to market in a variety of ways. The first shipments of oil were made in 1938 from the Dammam field to the Bahrain oil refinery of Standard California and Texaco. Today Bahrain still takes some 10 per cent of Saudi production. In 1950 a pipeline system was completed, running from the Aramco fields to Sidon in Lebanon, a distance of over 1,000 miles. Tapline carries crude oil not only to the Mediterranean tanker terminal but also to the growing industrial complex at Sidon. Ras Tanura, the Gulf tanker terminal, has become the major outlet for crude exports and the site of a major oil refinery from which liquefied petroleum gas is exported in increasing quantities. The offshore field at Safariya together with the main Aramco fields are now linked with Ras Tanura in a vast pipeline complex. At the centre of this great web of operations lies Dammam, the Aramco headquarters and also now a large complex community.

Agriculture

Saudi economic policy has increasingly turned towards the utilization of oil revenues for the diversification of the economy as a whole. Agriculture, the mainstay of the traditional pre-oil period, has been estimated to employ between 50 per cent and 60 per cent of the population but its contribution to the GNP is less than 10 per cent. Cultivation until recently has been dependent on the application of traditional technology in arid and semi-arid environments; for this reason it has been tied either to the relatively pluvious highlands of the western ranges in Asir and parts of Hejaz or to the dispersed zones where groundwater can be easily extracted. Wherever simple irrigation has not been possible nomadic pastoralism is dominant. Considerable investment has been made in hydrological and agricultural potential surveys organized on a national basis in eight regions. These have revealed that the centre and east of the country overlie an aquefer containing a reservoir of sweet fossil water at least 29,000 years old. Estimates of how long these resources will last vary from 30 to 100 years. Development implementation now involves major dam water-storage projects and the setting up of agricultural centres from which equipment, seeds and plants, and advisory services are made available. Increasing food production is regarded as important not only for import-substitution but also as an essential part of rural development plans for the improvement of the socio-economic viability of communities which are unlikely to be directly influenced by industrialization.

Of the total land area of 225·3 million hectares, FAO estimates show 373,000 hectares under arable and perennial crops and 1·7 million hectares classified as forested. The Saudi Ministry of Agriculture statistics enumerate 3,524 agricultural villages with 462,615 hectares of land. The proportion of agricultural owner-occupied holdings ranges between 81·4 per cent in the eastern region to 99·9 per cent in the northern region, a marked contrast to the situation found elsewhere in the Middle East. Over half the holdings are smaller than 0·5 hectares in extent. An FAO dietary study carried out in 1962 estimated that the calorific intake is, on average, low but that the consumption of animal protein is high.

F

A policy of economic diversification and of resource development has led to a vast expansion in agricultural development. In 1971 more than 300 million rials were allocated for the completion of various projects of which the major were: the Faisal Resettlement Project which has involved the establishment of a 4,000 hectare irrigation scheme on virgin land at Haradh—this primarily for settlement of about 5,000 bedouin; a completely new irrigation and drainage system for the ancient irrigated area of southern al-Hasa, this covering some 20,000 hectares and involving almost 100,000 inhabitants, and including a major and successful sand stabilization protection scheme; the Wadi Jizan water storage dam and land reclamation scheme in the southern Tihama on the Red Sea littoral. A large number of other projects ranging from fisheries to plant protection are also in hand.

However, there remain substantial obstacles both to the improvement of output in existing agricultural communities and to the settling of bedouin on the land. For the first it is essential that improved agricultural techniques should be demonstrated to the farmers and at present only Aramco has the personnel to do this. There is a serious danger that the extension of irrigation will lead to soil salination. Planned attempts to settle bedouin have yet to prove successful anywhere in Arabia as the bedouin usually prefer to take the houses offered to them and let the land to established cultivators. The agricultural training centre which is being organized with UN assistance in Riyadh is therefore of the greatest importance for the future.

Other Sectors

Such developments as those based on mineral extraction, urban development, and transport planning, are made possible by the national resource surveys carried out since 1962 and the establishment of air survey and map production organizations.

In terms of the gross domestic product, while the average annual growth rate in agriculture was some 6 per cent between 1963 and 1967, manufacturing industry has grown at 10 per cent per annum and in value now represents a quarter of the agricultural contribution. The other main areas of rapid growth have been construction, mining and quarrying (other than petroleum) and electricity/gas/water, all averaging about 10 per cent per annum. Transportation and wholesale and retail trade have increased at an even faster rate.

The Central Planning Organization together with the Ministry of Commerce and Development, and the Industrial Studies and Development Centre together with other institutions and agencies have moved cautiously forward into the field of diversification and industrialization. Control of inflation, primarily as a result of the activities of the Saudi Monetary Agency, and the encouragement given to private sector investment as well as to foreign participation have allowed progress in recent years to be steady rather than spectacular. Petromin is the main public sector agency for development implementation and as hydrological and geological surveys as well as industrial feasibility studies proceed so new industrial plant is not only being planned but constructed. The Yamama cement plant, the steel mill at Jedda, the urea and ammonia production of the Saudi Arabian Fertilizer Company at Dammam and the planned sulphur production at Abqaiq are all viable and realistic developments in which public and private Saudi and foreign investment are involved. Further growth of this kind depends largely on a continued increase in oil revenue; the planning assumption is that a 9 per cent annual increase will allow a similar rate of growth of the GNP and also permit heavy and increasing capital investment as well as a rise in consumption of goods, utilities, and services, including health, education, and welfare. It is impossible to specify what constraints may be imposed by the need to avoid the social and cultural dislocation consequent on changing economic values and living habits in general and also arising from inevitable regional variations in the speed of change.

In spite of his religious scruples, the Saudi is by temperament an investor, and a company offering a higher rate of interest than can be got by banking Euro-dollars on deposit is sure of selling the shares it offers. But he is not the kind of investor who will wait for years for a return on his money, and the chances that exploitation of promising minerals on remote sites will tempt the private investor are small because of the heavy investment required in infrastructure before there could be any yield. Quick-yielding industries are another matter and the private investor has already earned good returns in fields ancillary to the construction industry, notably cement and electricity companies.

Transport

Communications are the most vital infrastructure requirement in Saudi Arabia; budget allocations for them increased fourfold between 1964 and 1969. The design and supervision of work on the new main road network, begun in 1963, was entrusted to foreign consultants (from Italy, US, UK, West Germany, and Lebanon) usually with Saudi contractors. Where, in 1963, there were only 1,322 miles of surfaced roads, there were 4,232 miles by the end of 1968 with 1,864 miles more under construction. Rural dirt roads are increasing their length by about 25 per cent a year. Maintenance of the new roads is likely to be a heavy charge on future budgets.

Major improvements to the ports of Jedda and of Dammam on the Gulf are under way. Eight new berths, with warehouses and handling facilities, were completed at a total cost of SR140 million in 1970. Until the Dammam improvements, which include a new fertilizer loading pier, are completed much of Saudi imports from the east will continue to come by dhow from Bahrain.

Saudi Arabian Airlines, which has been an independent public corporation since 1963, was admitted to IATA in 1967. Over 50 per cent of the pilots are Saudis trained under TWA supervision. The Dammam–Riyadh railway built in the time of Ibn Saud has now largely been superseded by road traffic.

Education

High expenditure on social services has been a marked feature of Saudi Arabia in recent years. Education is free at all stages, and at the stage of higher studies, particularly in technical studies and for teachers' training, the student is paid to study. The Ministry of Education budget increased from SR114·6 million in 1960 to SR389 million in 1969 and over the same period the number of boys in primary and special education rose from 96,000 to 254,000. The number in intermediate and secondary boys' schools rose from 4,280 to 39,501. There are universities at Riyadh (with science, agriculture, engineering, and pharmaceutical faculties), Medina, and Jedda and a College of Petroleum and Minerals at Dahran. The number of anti-illiteracy schools rose from 66 in 1960 to 598 in 1970. The Ministry of Education runs technical schools called Vocational Training Centres and the Ministry of Labour gives trade courses.

Girls' education started only in 1960, with 16 primary schools, but in deference to the religious authorities these were placed under the direction of the shaikhs. In 1970 there were 406 girls' schools with 115,000 pupils of which five were secondary schools (four of them private) and 26 were teachers' training institutions. Religion is taught by blind shaikhs. Women may take an external degree at Riyadh University but by January 1970 only three had done so. There are about 100 Saudis training as nurses and a few are studying medicine abroad.

Health

Hospitals—both government and private were built as soon as oil revenues became substantial but the emphasis has always been on curative, rather than preventive, medicine except for the quarantine regulations for the Pilgrimage. There are about ten private fee-paying hospitals which are run and staffed by private doctors. Both government and private hospitals are seriously short of nurses, who are mainly recruited abroad, despite the high salaries offered. As a result, the emphasis is now on automation. There is a need for health clinics and prenatal clinics. At present hygiene is not taught on television or through extension courses in government clinics.

Social Services

The Social Security Department of the Ministry of Labour and Social Affairs pays public assistance to certain needy categories such as widows, orphans, invalids, divorced women, and indigent families, but rural poverty is largely confined to foreign workers—Yemenis, Hadhramautis, Omanis, etc., who are the inhabitants of the shanty towns to be seen in most Saudi cities. There is no low-cost housing provided by the State.

Of the greatest importance are the Community Development Centres run by the Ministry of Labour and Social Affairs in collaboration with the Ministries of Education, Health, and Agriculture and working, when well organized, in co-operation with local committees which help with conveying new ideas to uneducated people. But in 1970 there were only 16 of these centres serving a relatively small proportion of the population.

THE FUTURE

Oil revenues, which are likely to grow at an accelerated rate, provide Saudi Arabia with the means for very rapid social and economic transformation. But there are a number of serious obstacles to change and development. One is the very high degree of centralization of the administration. A strong provincial governor may acquire some real authority as long as he retains the trust of the King but all important decisions are taken in Riyadh. Religion is also an immensely important factor and no ruler, governor, or director can afford to ignore the religious authorities who run their own police (the *mutuwwa*) and are much consulted by the King.

One of the most serious problems is that the average Saudi has no inclination for sustained work (especially as a technician or manual labourer) and the growth rate of the Saudi economy has so far depended exclusively on the money available to hire expertise and labour from abroad. The high drop-out rate in the educational system is due to the fact that any Saudi can obtain undemanding and adequately paid work as soon as he has reached the intermediate level. As in other oil-rich countries, an early method of spreading the flow of income downwards was to overstaff the civil service at all levels. This is a trend which is now difficult to reverse.

2. YEMEN

THE LAND AND THE PEOPLE

Yemen lies at the extreme south-western corner of Arabia. It has an estimated size of 74,000 square miles, comprising two well-defined climatic and topographical zones—the highlands inland, and the Tihama (the coastal strip along the Red Sea). Its frontiers march with Saudi Arabia on the north (Asir) and east (Najran). The western boundary is the Red Sea from a point opposite the Farasan Islands to Shaikh Said Peninsula, opposite Perim Island. On the south Yemen is bounded by the People's Democratic Republic of Yemen. The climate of the highlands is considered the best in all Arabia. Summer conditions are temperate and winter temperatures cool, with some frost. The rainfall is usually heavy, varying from 32 inches in the extreme south-west (monsoon region) to 16 inches at Sanaa, but periods of lighter rain and even droughts are not infrequent. On the coast the climate is hot and damp, and there is little rainfall. The population is estimated at 5 million. The people of the highlands, who are Shiis of the Zaidi sect,[1] constitute about 40 per cent of the total; the remaining 60 per cent are nearly all Sunnis of the Shafii sect.[2] They live in the Tihama and along the Aden frontier. A minor group of Ismailis owes allegiance to its own Imam, who is not a Yemeni, and is paid a separate tax, sent to Bombay. Nearly 42,000 Jews emigrated from the Yemen to Israel in 1949–50 and fewer than 6,000 are now believed to remain.

History

No country in the world—except Tibet until 1951—has succeeded in keeping itself so isolated as Yemen. Until quite recently few strangers had ever penetrated its fastnesses.

In classical times Yemen, with the Hadhramaut, formed the south-eastern area of Arabia Felix, which also included southern Hejaz and the remainder of the peninsula south of Arabia Deserta. The best-known of the southern Arabian kingdoms was Saba (or Sheba or Sabu). It had a recorded history from 950 to 115 BC, but no authentic evidence has yet been found of a 'Queen of Sheba'. The Sabaeans earned great profits from the incense trade; but their prosperity slowly dwindled in competition with the Indian trade routes through Iraq and Syria, and with the Roman exploitation of commercial navigation from the Persian Gulf and the East through the Red Sea to Egypt and Europe.

The Sabaean religion of those days was pagan, and monuments of pagan cults are still to be found near Sanaa. In the fourth century Christian missionaries settled in the country. There was also a blend

[1] See above, p. 34.   [2] See above, p. 33.

of Judaism owing, it is believed, to Jewish immigration after the fall of Jerusalem in AD 70. From the sixth to the second century BC Arabia Felix was ruled by the Himyarite dynasty, from whom the modern Imams claim descent. Some of these rulers embraced Judaism, others were Christian. In AD 525 the Christian Ethiopians of Axum invaded and overthrew the Himyarite kingdom. Ethiopian rule in its turn was overthrown in AD 575 by an Iranian invasion; but within another hundred years the country had made a nominal submission to Islam, and although Christianity and Judaism and even paganism still survived, the Sunnis of the Shafii rite had established their power in the Tihama, while the Zaidis, a moderate branch of the Shia, held the highlands.

In the ninth century the Zaidi Imam Yahya al-Hadi ila'l Haqq founded the Rassid dynasty of the Yemen. It survived, with some interruptions of power, until 1962. Its name comes from al-Qasim al-Rassi, who was a direct descendant of Mohammed through Hassan, a son of Fatima and Ali.

In 1517 Yemen was conquered by the Ottoman Sultan Selim I, but for the next two centuries Ottoman authority there and throughout the coastal regions of Arabia was in turn wooed and contested by various European nations seeking, after the discovery of the Cape route to India, for openings for their commercial fleets. The Turks maintained themselves on the coast, however precariously; and the European penetration was sporadic and never established with any permanence inland.

At the opening of the nineteenth century the Yemen was entered, but not subdued or converted, by the Wahhabis. After the Egyptian victory of 1818 Ibrahim Pasha descended on the Tihama, which had been overrun by Wahhabi forces. The Wahhabis were expelled, and the Zaidi Imam restored to nominal authority in return for a subsidy to the Sultan in Constantinople, who placed Egyptian garrisons in Hodeida and Moka, the main ports. The Egyptians withdrew in 1840, but Turkish suzerainty remained. Turkish policy alternated between appeasement and ruthless suppression, until in 1911 a full-scale revolt, headed by the Imam Yahya (1904–48), compelled the Turks to intervene in strength. Sanaa fell, and the campaign ended with a treaty which confirmed Turkish suzerainty and divided administrative control between the Imam in the highlands and the Turks in the Tihama. Meanwhile to the north, during the Italo-Turkish war, the Asiri tribes, under the leadership of Sayyid Mohammed ibn Ali al-Idrisi, had risen against the Turks, and with Italian help succeeded in establishing a degree of independence, which they consolidated during the First World War by overrunning much of the northern Tihama. When war began in 1914 the Turkish army of occupation, numbering some 14,000 men, marched southwards against the British in Aden, while British

war vessels bombarded Yemeni ports in the interests of the Idrisi invaders from Asir. These operations were continued intermittently
during the next four years; but with the Mudros Armistice in October
1918 the Yemen became free of Turkish suzerainty. The Imam lost no
time in asserting his authority over the Shafii-occupied areas of the
south and west which the Turks had kept under their administrative
control.

The Imam Yahya became ruler of an independent and unified
Yemen. As both Imam and King he was the temporal and spiritual
head of his people. He was chosen as Imam, or head of the Zaidis, from
among the Sayyids or descendants of Ali, of whom there are some
thousands in Yemen, all enjoying special privileges.

Yahya was faced with the formidable task of creating a governmental structure for the country. Although he persuaded some of the
former Ottoman officials to remain to assist him, his methods were
highly autocratic. He established a system of extreme personal rule in
which every item of government business depended on his decisions.
His son the Imam Ahmad (1948–62) maintained the system during
his reign.

Yahya and Ahmad both accepted the continuing strength of tribal
loyalties in Yemen. They made little attempt to supersede tribalism with
a regular army loyal to the throne but endeavoured to manipulate
tribal alliances to ensure that the balance of tribal power was on their
side. As Yahya extended his control over all his territory he resorted
increasingly to an ancient Yemeni tradition: the taking of hostages.
One or more of the relations of the heads of important tribes would be
held in a prison school maintained by the Imam. Both Imams were
fairly successful in this policy. Yahya and Ahmad also tried as far as
possible to keep Yemen isolated and insulated from foreign influences
which would undermine their own autocratic power as well as the
Yemenis' traditional religious way of life. Again they were fairly successful but at the cost of keeping Yemen in a state of medieval backwardness which provoked increasing criticism from those Yemenis who
were aware how the outside world was changing and who demanded
reforms.

In accordance with his isolationist policy, Imam Yahya kept his
relations with foreign powers to an absolute minimum. However, he
was concerned to establish his claim to all the territories that had once
been ruled by his ancestors and which could be said to form a 'Greater
Yemen', i.e. in addition to the internationally recognized Yemeni
Kingdom, Asir on the Red Sea (now part of Saudi Arabia) and the
territories which now form the People's Democratic Republic of Yemen.
His claim to Asir brought him into conflict first with Britain and then
Saudi Arabia. In 1919 British troops occupied Hodeida in support of
the Idrisi ruler of Asir who had fought against the Turks in the First

World War. The British troops withdrew and in 1920 Ibn Saud (then Sultan of Nejd) sent his son Faisal to annex the highland areas of northern Asir. On the death of Mohammed al-Idrisi in 1925 a small-scale civil war broke out between two rival Idrisi claimants, with the Saudis and the Imam supporting opposing sides. Yahya seized the opportunity to occupy the Tihama coastal plain including Hodeida but Wahhabi military superiority forced him to accept what amounted to Ibn Saud's protectorate over the rest of Asir. In 1932 the Idrisi ruler rebelled against Ibn Saud and was defeated. Yahya supported his claims and in 1934 war broke out between Saudi Arabia and Yemen. The Yemeni forces were quickly routed and a treaty of peace was signed in Taif on 20 May 1934. The Saudis annexed the disputed Asir and Najran areas but otherwise imposed only minor frontier adjustments. Ibn Saud's moderation, which was due to foreign pressure, made Yahya his friend for life.

Immediately after the First World War Imam Yahya sent his troops to occupy several frontier areas which Britain regarded as part of the Western Aden Protectorate. Attempts at negotiation failed until 1934 when a forty-year Anglo-Yemeni treaty of peace and friendship was signed in Sanaa which accepted for the time being as Yemen's southern boundary a line slightly more favourable to the Yemen than the one agreed between Britain and Turkey in 1914.

To strengthen his hand with Britain, Yahya had turned to Italy which had begun to take an interest in Yemen as early as 1877. After the establishment of the colony of Eritrea in the early 1880s this interest quickened. Between 1897 and 1900 there was considerable recruiting of Yemenis for labour and military service in Eritrea. After the rise of Fascism Italian doctors of Fascist allegiance were established in Sanaa with the Imam's permission. An Italo-Yemeni treaty of amity and commerce was signed on 4 September 1926 and this was followed by a secret agreement signed on 1 June 1927. But the sympathy between the two powers was unreal and disappointing to Italy, which at the time had hopes of a sphere of interest in Southern Arabia and in the 1930s redoubled its efforts in Yemen. This was one of the dangers Britain had in mind in concluding with Italy, on 16 April 1938, an agreement regarding questions of mutual concern in the Middle East.

On 1 November 1928 the Soviet Union concluded with Yemen a treaty of commerce and friendship. A Soviet commercial office was opened in Sanaa under the direction of the Soviet representative in Jedda but was closed in 1938.

Yemen remained neutral in the Second World War but after the defeat of Rommel yielded to British requests to intern Axis nationals in its territory.

It participated rather hesitantly in the talks leading to the creation of the Arab League but soon ratified its covenant.

In February 1948 the Imam Yahya, over eighty and partly paralysed, was assassinated and Abdullah al-Wazir, his personal adviser, was proclaimed Imam. This was the result of increasing discontent, both in the country and among the prosperous Yemeni communities abroad in Indonesia, Singapore, Aden, and elsewhere, at the autocratic rule of the Imam and the system whereby he and his family treated the country's revenues and most of the government and commercial positions as their personal perquisites. Abdullah al-Wazir promised to rule as a constitutional monarch but his rule lasted barely a month. Crown Prince Ahmad,[1] who secured some tribal support, defeated him, and had him and other leaders of the revolt executed.

The Imam Ahmad, a formidable character, tinged with sadism, made no fundamental changes in his father's system of government. He appointed some Shafiis to the administration to reduce Shafii-Zaidi hostility and made some nominal concessions to demands for reform. He was slightly more willing than Yahya to call upon the assistance of foreigners but the circumstances of his accession made him deeply suspicious of his own people. Until his death he never visited Sanaa which had sided with the al-Wazir revolt. The social and economic backwardness of Yemen was even more striking at the end of his reign than at the beginning.

As soon as Imam Ahmad had consolidated his position at home he took up his father's claim to the Aden Protectorate and there was a series of border incidents. Anglo-Yemeni talks in London in 1950 ended in an agreement to establish diplomatic relations (hitherto conducted through the Governor of Aden) and to establish a joint commission to settle the disputed frontier. But the agreement was abortive and the frontier incidents were resumed. Incensed by British plans to form a federation of Protectorate shaikhdoms and sultanates, Imam Ahmad stepped up his campaign of bribery and infiltration among the Protectorate tribes. This anti-British campaign led Imam Ahmad to seek outside support despite his ingrained xenophobia. Yemen sided with Egypt in the controversy over the Baghdad Pact and in April 1956 signed a mutual defence pact, providing for a unified command, with Egypt and Saudi Arabia. Yemen had Arab League support for its claim to the island of Kamaran and to the whole of the Aden Protectorate as part of the ancestral territories of Yemen. In the late 1950s Abdul Nasser had become the most important figure in Arab politics and his star was rising. When Egypt and Syria joined to form the United Arab Republic in February 1958 Imam Ahmad cabled President Nasser asking for Yemen to be allowed to join the new federation. Egypt, Syria, and Yemen then formed a somewhat tenuous and ill-defined union known as the United Arab States.

[1] In 1927 Yahya had established the principle of primogeniture against strong conservative Zaidi opposition.

Imam Ahmad turned also to the Soviet bloc for support. In November 1955 he signed a friendship pact with the Soviet Union and in the summer of 1956 he sent his son Crown Prince Mohammed al-Badr on an extensive tour of East European capitals which resulted in a variety of trade and friendship agreements with the Communist states. In 1956 Yemen recognized Communist China which offered technical and economic aid and later undertook the building of a metalled road from Hodeida to Sanaa.

Anglo-Yemeni negotiations to settle the dispute between the two countries came to nothing and the sporadic border war continued. The Communist states sent some arms and equipment but the Arab League provided little more than moral support for Yemen's anti-British campaign. Imam Ahmad was aware of the danger to his conservative regime of the import of revolutionary socialist ideas. He attempted to balance Soviet influence by developing relations with the USA and in 1959 he allowed a US aid (ICA) mission to be established in the country. He also kept to a minimum the number of Egyptian officials and technicians who were loaned to Yemen under the United Arab States agreement.

As under Imam Yahya, opposition to Imam Ahmad was of two kinds: (*a*) progressive reformers who wanted to bring Yemen into the twentieth century; and (*b*) conservative traditionalists who resented the virtual monopoly of government by the Hamideddin family. In 1955 there was an attempted revolt led by Colonel Ahmad al-Thalaya which the Imam put down with the aid of his son Mohammed al-Badr (whom he made Crown Prince as a reward). Two of the Imam's own brothers who were implicated in the revolt were executed.

In the late 1950s a number of Yemeni exiles in Aden and Cairo formed opposition groups of Free Yemenis. They hoped that their cause would be assisted by Imam Ahmad's introduction of Soviet and Egyptian technicians into Yemen although some feared it might strengthen the Imam's position. In 1959 Imam Ahmad was obliged to go to Italy for medical treatment and in his absence Crown Prince al-Badr took the opportunity to implement some of the reforms that had been promised at the beginning of Ahmad's reign. On his return, however, Ahmad not only cancelled the reforms but attempted to withdraw some of the generous subsidies al-Badr had paid to the powerful northern tribes. The result was severe tribal unrest which required all the aged Imam's skill and ruthlessness to master. In March 1961 he narrowly escaped assassination while visiting the Hodeida Hospital. There was an outbreak of sabotage in the towns.

While Yemen was theoretically federated to the UAR, the Imam's regime was protected from the powerful attacks of Cairo's propaganda machine. But in September 1961 Syria seceded from the UAR and Imam Ahmad who was delighted to see Arab revolutionary socialism in decline condemned Nasserist ideology and policies in a poem which was broadcast on Sanaa Radio. In December 1961 President Nasser declared the United Arab States dissolved and Radio Cairo at once opened a strong campaign against the Imam and his regime.

Throughout the first half of 1962 violent opposition increased but Imam Ahmad succeeded in containing it until his death on 18 September. Mohammed al-Badr succeeded him and announced a general amnesty for political prisoners and other conciliatory measures. But the UAR Government and the Free Yemenis in Cairo remained sceptical in their attitude towards him while Yemeni conservatives, alarmed by al-Badr's liberal tendencies, exerted their influence to make him adopt more traditional attitudes.

Civil War

On 26 September 1962, eight days after Imam Ahmad's death, Brigadier Abdullah al-Sallal, who had al-Badr's confidence and had been made Commander of the Royal Guards on his succession, seized Sanaa and declared a Republic. It is uncertain whether the revolutionaries were provoked by al-Badr's retreat from his liberal position or would have acted anyway. The coup was only partially successful because although the revolutionaries controlled the main towns and roads al-Badr escaped to loyal tribes in the north and raised the flag of royalist counter-revolution.

Sallal at once formed a Revolutionary Command Council and announced the establishment of the Yemeni Arab Republic which was promptly recognized by Egypt, Syria, Iraq, and the Soviet bloc. But al-Badr's uncle Prince Hassan returned from New York where he was Yemeni UN representative, and a concerted movement began, to restore the monarchy with the aid of royalist tribes, Saudi Arabia, and Jordan. Sallal appealed to President Nasser for assistance and within three days of the coup a steady stream of Egyptian troops and equipment was moving up the Red Sea to Hodeida. The promptness of Egypt's action shows that it expected the Yemeni revolt but not necessarily that it inspired and organized it. A revolutionary opposition had proved its existence in Yemen even before Abdul Nasser came to power in Egypt.

King Saud and Prince Faisal of Saudi Arabia believed that only the presence of Egyptian troops prevented the collapse of the republic and the restoration of the monarchy which in their view the majority of Yemenis supported. Yet the mere existence of a republic in Yemen was an obvious threat to the Saudi monarchy and their apprehension increased when President Sallal announced his intention of establishing a 'Republic of the Arabian Peninsula'.

This marked the beginning of royalist–republican civil war which

lasted with varying intensity for over seven years and affected principally the northern and eastern parts of the country. Whenever the
royalists made military gains the Egyptians increased their commitment
until by 1964 they had an estimated 40,000 troops in Yemen. This was
enough to ensure that the principal towns and roads would remain in
republican hands but it increased the natural xenophobia of the Zaidi
tribes some of whom rallied to the royalist cause after initially supporting the republic. In December 1962 the US Government (followed by
fifty nations but not the UK) recognized the Yemeni Republic which
was then seated at the UN. But US hopes that the Republic would be
secure enough for Egypt to withdraw its troops were not fulfilled.
US and UN attempts at mediation between Egypt and Saudi Arabia
were unsuccessful and both countries maintained support for opposing
sides in the civil war. On 30 April 1963 the UN did obtain Saudi agreement in principle to cut off all aid to the royalists and Egypt agreed
to a phased withdrawal of its troops. A 200-man UN observer mission
arrived in Yemen in June to ensure that the terms of the agreement
were implemented. But the mission's task proved impossible and it was
withdrawn in September 1964.

In their first offensive in October 1962 the royalists captured Marib,
Harib, Sarwah, and other key towns. The Egyptians and republicans
counter-attacked in March 1963 and regained Marib and Harib. The
royalists regrouped and succeeded in recovering most of their earlier
gains by the spring of 1964. In the summer of 1964 reinforced Egyptian
and republican forces mounted an offensive in the north-east which
succeeded in clearing the royalists out of several areas but failed in its
aim of capturing al-Badr in his headquarters.

The Egyptians had superior equipment and command of the air but
they were hampered by a lack of experience in guerrilla warfare in
which the Yemeni tribesmen excelled. The lack of roads in most of the
country made it difficult to supply their forward outposts. The royalists,
on the other hand, were assisted by foreign mercenary officers (mostly
British and French) and the Egyptians were unable to prevent the
infiltration of supplies of money and arms from Saudi Arabia and
Beihan State in the Aden Protectorate. Finally, the Egyptians encountered extreme difficulty in building up the regular Yemeni
republican forces from among the unmartial urban Yemenis; generous
subsidies to the fighting tribesmen were not enough to ensure their
continued loyalty to the republic, and the Egyptians could always be
outbid by the superior financial resources of Saudi Arabia.

Political stability consistently eluded the republic. The difficulty was
in forming a government which could reconcile Yemeni national pride
with the reality of the republic's heavy dependence on Egypt. In April
1964 President Nasser paid his first visit to Yemen and on 28 April a
new constitution was announced providing for a president, prime

minister, consultative council, municipal organizations, and judiciary. Sallal remained President, General Hamoud al-Jaify became Prime Minister and Ahmad Naaman, a civilian Shafii political leader, President of the Consultative Council which was to be elected by the various districts of Yemen.

At the end of October, royalist and republican representatives met at Erkhawit in east Sudan in presence of Egyptian and Saudi observers and a ceasefire throughout Yemen was declared on 8 November. However a National Congress of tribal, religious, and military leaders which was to have been held on 23 November never took place because the different factions could not agree on a formula for representation and the ceasefire gradually broke down.

In December 1964 Ahmad Naaman and two Deputy Premiers Mohammed Zubairi and Qadi Abdul Rahman al-Iriani resigned. Naaman's motive was partly resentment at continued Zaidi domination of the republic in which the Shafiis formed at least 60 per cent of the population. But Naaman, Zubairi, and Iriani also constituted a political Third Force opposed to Sallal, who was increasingly unpopular and regarded as an Egyptian puppet, and favoured a compromise solution to the civil war, to be worked out by the Yemenis themselves.

Sallal replaced the Premier al-Jaify with General Hassan al-Amri, regarded as a hard-liner in the civil war. On 1 April 1965 the Third Force leader Mohammed Zubairi was assassinated; whether the responsibility lay with the Egyptians and republicans or royalists is uncertain but the consequence was to increase sympathy for the Third Force within the republic and on 18 April President Sallal appointed Ahmad Naaman as Prime Minister. Naaman held a conference with republican tribal leaders at al-Khamir in northern Yemen when it was decided to form a committee to make peace overtures to the royalist leaders. But Naaman was not supported by President Sallal or the Egyptians and at the end of June he was forced to resign by Sallal who took over the premiership with a group of hard-line army officers. Realizing such a government would have little popular support, Egypt obliged Sallal to reappoint General Amri as Prime Minister and widen the Cabinet to include more moderate elements. Nevertheless, on the next day a group of prominent republicans defected to the pro-royalist state of Beihan. The highly unfavourable political situation in the republic, combined with a new series of royalist military successes in the spring and summer of 1965, were factors which induced President Nasser to go to Saudi Arabia to conclude what became known as the Saudi–Egyptian Jedda agreement on Yemen. This provided for an immediate cease-fire, the formation of a royalist–republican provisional government to be followed one year later by a national plebiscite by which time all Egyptian troops would be withdrawn.

Although President Nasser's move appeared at the time to be an admission of defeat it later became clear that his strategy was to gain a breathing-space in which to withdraw his troops from their exposed positions in the northern half of the country to the safer areas around the main towns where the royalist tribes did not have the advantage in guerrilla warfare. It is unlikely that he intended to allow King Faisal to pour in money and arms to restore the monarchy after the withdrawal of the Egyptian forces. Neither side fully trusted the sincerity of the other in the Jedda agreement.

As part of the agreement a royalist–republican conference was held at Harad in north Yemen in November to decide on the form of the transitional government. This broke down over royalist refusal of republican claims that the Imamate had already been permanently abolished and replaced by the republic. Meanwhile the cold war within the Arab world intensified. While the Harad Conference was still in progress King Faisal launched his idea on a visit to Iran of a grouping of Islamic nations. Egypt regarded this as a plan to form an anti-Nasser front and reacted accordingly. President Nasser's conviction that Britain was supporting the Yemeni royalists was strengthened by a British agreement to supply Saudi Arabia with large quantities of arms including an air-defence system. However, the British Government's announcement in February 1966 that it intended to withdraw all its forces from South Arabia by the time it achieved independence was a powerful boost for Egypt. From Yemen it had been giving active support to the national liberation movement in South Arabia against the ruling shaikhs and sultans who were sustained by Britain. A British withdrawal was certain to weaken the Saudi/royalist cause. But still no progress was made towards establishing a strong and stable republican regime although the Egyptians attempted to assist the process by keeping the unpopular Sallal in Egypt for more than a year. Faced with renewed royalist harassment after the inevitable breakdown of the ceasefire President Nasser and his military advisers decided in the spring of 1966 to withdraw all Egyptian forces from the north and east of the country to the 'triangle' based on Hodeida, Taez, and Sanaa. While this left about half the country in royalist hands it ensured the defence of the main centres of population and greatly reduced the cost of maintaining the Egyptian force in Yemen.

In the summer of 1966 the Egyptians learned that General Amri, formerly an extreme pro-Egyptian in his views, was planning to seize power in Sanaa and demand the withdrawal of Egyptian troops. Hastily the Egyptians sent back Sallal who ousted Amri and took power himself. Amri and some other leading republicans went to Cairo where they were interned at Sallal's request although President Nasser refused to allow them to be extradited to Yemen to be tried for treason.

President Sallal, with the aid of a handful of fairly ruthless lieutenants, succeeded in improving the security situation in the republic but there was still no prospect of the Egyptian troops being able to withdraw.

The situation was transformed by the 1967 Arab–Israeli war. Yemen took no part in the war but one of its consequences was that President Nasser decided to withdraw all his troops from Yemen. At the Khartoum Arab summit conference (29 August–1 September) he reached an agreement with King Faisal, through Sudanese mediation, to withdraw in return for a Saudi undertaking to halt all aid to the royalists. Egyptian troops had all left by the end of the year (at about the time when British troops had all withdrawn from South Arabia).

On 5 November 1967 Sallal was overthrown while he was on a visit to Iraq, in a bloodless high-command coup that brought to power a group of moderate republicans with Qadi Iriani as Chief of State and Mohsim al-Aini as Premier. Hopes that this would make it possible to end the civil war were dashed when the royalists launched an all-out assault on Sanaa which nearly succeeded. But the republicans rallied their forces and with emergency assistance from Syria, Algeria, and the USSR succeeded in lifting the siege, although the main Sanaa–Taez road remained cut by the royalists. In May a serious rift appeared in the royalist ranks with opposition to the ex-Imam led by his cousin Prince Mohammed ibn Hussein. The republicans were also divided between conservatives and young radicals as well as between Zaidis and Shafiis. In August there was serious fighting with heavy casualties between republican forces but General Amri as Commander-in-Chief succeeded in ending the strife and on 15 September formed a new government with seven Shafiis and nine Zaidis.

During 1969 the position improved for the republicans as King Faisal cut off his aid to the royalists although he still refused recognition of the Yemeni Republic on the ground that he was awaiting the establishment of a government freely chosen by the Yemeni people, despite friendly overtures from the Yemenis and attempts at Arab mediation.

In March the Republican Council resigned to make way for a new National Council to elect a president and premier. A new National Assembly was formed with 57 seats of which 12 were left vacant for Democratic Yemen. The republican Government maintained that the two countries were only prevented from uniting by the extremist intransigence of the Government of Democratic Yemen.

In January 1970 there was sharp fighting in the north, and in February the key town of Saada, which had changed hands several times in the previous months, fell once more to pro-royalist forces. But the civil war was drawing to its close. On 5 February a new republican government was formed by Mohsin al-Aini and on 21 March he went to Jedda at the head of a Yemeni delegation to the Saudi-sponsored Islamic foreign ministers' conference. In April fighting ceased in the north and Saudi Arabia once again cut off aid to the royalists. On

23 May a party of prominent royalists headed by Ahmad al-Shami, a former royalist foreign minister, arrived in Sanaa. He was appointed an additional member of the three-man Republican Council. In July al-Aini returned to Saudi Arabia which then recognized the Sanaa regime and was followed by France, Britain, and Iran. The civil war had ended with a compromise although it was the moderate republicans who held the majority of posts in the Government.

GOVERNMENT AND ADMINISTRATION

The functions of Head of State are performed by a Presidential Council whose membership was reduced from five to three in April 1971. There is also a Consultative Council with 159 members. Twenty per cent of its members are appointed by the Presidential Council and the rest are elected by popular vote. Elections were held in the summer of 1971 and are supposed to be held every four years. The Consultative Council has the task of drafting a permanent constitution.

Yemen is divided into six provinces (*liwas*) which are in turn divided into districts and sub-districts. The *liwas* which are named after the chief towns, are: Sanaa, Ibb, Taez, Hodeida, Hajja, and Saada.

ECONOMIC AND SOCIAL SURVEY

Agriculture has always been the mainstay of the Yemeni economy and almost all products are consumed locally. The only exceptions are coffee and hides which form a very small proportion of the total. Although there is enough rainfall in the hills for dry farming—mainly millet and sorghum—most of the cultivated lands are irrigated. Yemen is known to have begun to lose its pastures from the time when the great Marib Dam broke down some time between AD 542 and 570. The great forests which existed in classical times have also largely disappeared.

The traditional crops are millet, sorghum, maize, barley, and oats (mainly along the coast) and of these the first two are much the most important. Green vegetables are also grown—especially around Sanaa and Taez—and because of the climatic conditions a variety of fruits which range from dates, bananas, papayas, and mangoes on the tropical Tihama plain to citrus, apples, pomegranates, grapes, apricots, and others above 200 m. The famous Yemeni 'moka' coffee is the principal export crop; Yemen is the only country in the world where coffee is grown on irrigated land. Coffee exports between 1952 and 1962 ranged from 4,000 to 5,500 tons but in some areas coffee cultivation has given way to the planting of *qat*, a shrub of which the leaves are chewed as a narcotic by most of the population. *Qat* has been a more profitable cash crop than coffee, and efforts to control its export to Aden and South Yemen have never been very successful.

Cotton has long been grown in Yemen in the Tihama but on a very small scale until 1951 when the industry began to expand. From a production of 800 tons from 80 hectares in 1952/3 it rose to 3,200 tons from 2,500 hectares in 1961/2.

Share-cropping is practised in the large properties which form a substantial proportion of the cultivated area. Techniques are primitive and productivity low although there is still abundant evidence of the existence of the fine agricultural system which has steadily declined over the centuries. At present Yemen is largely self-sufficient in food but with the growth in population increasing quantities of food will have to be imported (unless a rapid increase in productivity can be achieved), especially in years of severe drought such as 1970/1. It is estimated that about 15 per cent of Yemen's total area or 3 million hectares is cultivable. About one half of this is cultivated at present.

Currency, Banking, and Trade

At the time of the 1962 revolution there was virtually no government administration of the financial and economic system and no banking facilities. In 1964 a Yemeni Currency Committee was created with the task of issuing a new paper currency (no quotations available, 1972) to replace the old Maria Theresa dollar. Other laws issued in 1963, 1964, and 1967 provided for the registration of all commercial companies in Yemen and for the control and organization of imports and exports. The value of imports rose rapidly after 1962 from 12·5 million rials in 1963 to 23 million rials in 1964, 27·8 million in 1965 and 55·8 million in 1966. In 1964 a law was passed providing guarantees for the investment of foreign capital in Yemen. Deposits in the Yemeni Building and Construction Bank founded after the 1962 revolution rose from 3·99 million rials at the end of 1963 to 14·48 million rials at the end of 1966. An Agricultural Co-operative Bank with a capital of 3 million rials was founded to provide loans to farmers. In 1966 a Development and Construction Organization was established by the Government.

Industry

Since 1962 a few light industries have been founded with the help of Yemeni emigrant, Arab, and foreign capital. They include salt, aluminium furniture, and pharmaceutical factories. The most important is the spinning and weaving factory (with 10,816 spindles and 360 looms in 1967) which was built under an agreement with People's China in Sanaa.

Communications

Lack of roads has probably been the greatest single obstacle to Yemen's economic development. In 1962 the only metalled road in the country (apart from a few miles in Taez) was the Chinese-built Hodeida–

Sanaa road. Since then Taez and Sanaa and Taez and Moka have been linked by dust roads built with US aid funds and the Russians have completed a highway from Taez to Hodeida. In 1971 the Chinese had started work on a road from Sanaa to Saada in the north. The port of Hodeida has been expanded and modernized with Soviet aid.

Education and Health

In 1962 the educational system in Yemen was rudimentary and affected only a small proportion of the population. There were no schools for girls of whom only a few of the privileged learned to read the Koran at home. Accurate statistics are not available but according to secret Education Ministry documents at the end of 1958[1] there were 38,653 boys in 688 primary schools, 468 in 4 intermediary schools, 228 boys in the single secondary school, and 1,766 in the 16 advanced secondary schools. There were about 500 boys studying abroad.

The republican regime had a strong desire to expand education as rapidly as possible but it was handicapped by the prolonged unrest in many parts of the country. The total number of pupils in primary schools rose from 61,325 (including 1,780 girls) in 1963 to 72,107 (including 6,003 girls) in 1970. In Taez, which was relatively undisturbed by the civil war, the number rose from 7,000 to 29,000 during this period. The number of pupils in intermediary and secondary schools rose from 730 in 1963 to 4,057 in 1970.

Since 1962 Egypt, Kuwait, Bulgaria, the USSR, and People's China have all provided aid for the building and equipping of primary, secondary, and technical schools in Yemen. In October 1970 the nucleus of a Yemeni University was established with the opening of faculties of law and education in Sanaa. Kuwait announced a grant of KD100,000 towards the new university.

Despite the healthy climate of the high plateaux on which three quarters of the population live, the almost complete lack of medical facilities, malnutrition, and addiction to *qat* have kept drastically low health standards in Yemen. In 1962 there were three hospitals in the country with a total of about 1,500 beds and twenty doctors. The most common diseases were tuberculosis in the mountain areas and malaria and amoebic dysentery in the Red Sea plain.

During the civil war years 1962–9 the situation was particularly desperate in the royalist-held areas where, apart from some limited Red Cross aid, there were no medical facilities. In Republican Yemen, on the other hand, some real progress was made with assistance from UN organizations, Egypt, Kuwait, Italy, and several East European countries. By 1967 there were 40 hospitals and clinics with a total of 4,470 beds.

[1] See Mohammed Said el-Attar, *Le Sous-développement économique et social du Yemen* (Algiers, 1964), pp. 90–2.

3. PEOPLE'S DEMOCRATIC REPUBLIC OF YEMEN

(Formerly The Aden Colony and The Aden Protectorate)

THE LAND AND THE PEOPLE

The People's Democratic Republic of Yemen (or the People's Republic of Southern Yemen as it was then called) came into existence on 30 November 1967, incorporating the Aden Colony and both the western and eastern administrative regions of the Aden Protectorate. It forms a triangle of territory based on the western half of the Arabian Peninsula's southern coast, reaching from Bab al-Mandeb, at the entrance to the Red Sea, to the frontier of the State of Oman. It is bounded on the north by Saudi Arabia and the west by Yemen and occupies about 112,000 square miles.

The republic also possesses those islands which were protected or governed by the British from Aden. They are: Kamaran Island, one of a group which lies off the Salif peninsula of Yemen about 200 miles north of Bab al-Mandeb; Perim, which is in the Bab al-Mandeb; and Socotra, the largest island in an archipelago lying about 220 miles off Qishn near the eastern end of the republic's Arabian coast. The Kuria Muria islands off the coast of the State of Oman are claimed by the republican Government but were transferred to Oman by the British in the 1967 settlement on the grounds that they were only nominally the responsibility of the Governor of Aden, were in practice administered by the British Resident, Persian Gulf, and formerly belonged to the Sultanate.

The area of the former Colony of Aden is the most notable urban complex. The high, rocky and volcanic structure of the peninsula falls sharply into the sea around the harbour, and the original town, Crater, lies in an extinct volcano of the eastern promontory where the enclosing ridge opens to the Arabian Sea. The modern harbour and town, Steamer Point, are about five miles away and between them and Crater the original village of Maalla has been developed as an industrial and residential area. The eastern promontory is joined to the mainland by the isthmus of Khormaksar on which stands the airport and the former British military town. The town of Shaikh Othman on the mainland has some cultivation and from it a road sweeps south-west round the bay to the western promontory and the oil refinery and township of Little Aden.

The western region of the republic is divided into the littoral belt varying between 4 and 40 miles in depth; the maritime range, between 1,000 and 2,000 feet above sea-level; the intra-montane plains, over 3,000 feet high; and the highland plateau, ranging from 5,000 to

8,000 feet, which falls away steeply into the Rub al-Khali desert plateau at about 2,500 feet. The eastern region (formerly the Wahidi Sultanates of Balhaf and Bir Ali, the Qaiti State of Shihr and Mukalla, the Kathiri State of Saiyun and the Mahra Sultanate of Qishn and Socotra) is notable for the fertile Hadhramaut valley. Its wide upper and middle reaches run almost parallel with the coast about 125 miles inland but at its lower eastern end it turns sharply to the south and becomes a narrow gorge through the hills as it descends to the sea. For the rest, the territory is desert and barren mountains intersected by wadis, some of which are fertile enough for cultivation. There are some comparatively large towns, notably Mukalla and Saiyun.

Climate

The maritime plains are damp and hot in summer and are subject to sandstorms and high winds. From October to March they are cool— sometimes cold—at night and are much less humid. There is little rain in the littoral and maritime hills and cultivation depends mainly on irrigation from seasonal water-courses and channels. The Aden promontories share the climate of the plains modified sometimes by the closely sheltering hills and at others by the surrounding seas; the climate is not unhealthy but the humidity makes it oppressive at times, notably in May, June, and September.

Population

There are no accurate figures for the population of the republic but the Government claims that there are nearly 1,500,000 inhabitants. There are about 850,000 in the western region, of whom more than 200,000 are in the Adens, Maalla, and Shaikh Othman, and nearly 400,000 in the eastern region. Almost the entire population consists of Arabs who are the direct descendants of the pagan peoples who were part of the ancient Minaean, Sabaean, and Himyarite kingdoms which flourished in succession between about 1500 BC to AD 500. Aden is the exception to this general rule, as reflected in the 1955 census which enumerated the population as follows: Aden Arabs, 36,910; Protectorate Arabs, 18,881; British, including military, 3,763; other Europeans, 721; Indians, 15,817; Jews, 831; Somalis, 10,611; Yemeni Arabs, 48,088; others, 2,608.

Since that census there has been a substantial increase of Protectorate Arabs (i.e. from the tribal areas outside Aden) and of Yemenis. During the troubles before independence and since the formation of the republic there has been a decline of British and other European inhabitants, Indians, Somalis, and Jews. The greatest single population change took place after the Palestine war of 1948 when almost the entire indigenous Jewish population, whose ancestors had settled in south-west Arabia about 2,000 years ago, emigrated to Palestine. There were 15,000 in the western region alone, almost all of whom departed; 7,000 emigrated from Aden.

Religion

The population is predominantly Moslem of the orthodox Shafii sect, as are the lowland Arabs of Yemen. The Yemenis in Aden Port, however, include some of the unorthodox Zaidi Moslems who came from the Yemen highlands.

HISTORY

Democratic Yemen was part of the tribal empire of the Minaean people whose origins are lost in antiquity but who are known to have had kings in the fourteenth century BC and to have ruled over an area roughly corresponding to the territories of the Yemen Republic and Democratic Yemen. The wealth of this kingdom derived from frankincense which was found nowhere else in the ancient world and was transported by camel caravan or by ship to the sacrificial fires of Egypt, Babylon, Iran, and Greece. The caravan trains formed in time the Incense Route, perhaps the most famous of its kind in history, which had its starting point at Husn al-Ghurab, a tiny island 200 miles east of Aden.

The Minaeans were succeeded by the Sabaeans and then the Himyarites, all of whom had their royal capitals in the region of Sanaa in Yemen. The decline of Himyarite power began in the first century AD, in the main because the Arab transport monopoly was broken by the development of sea routes through the Persian Gulf and Mesopotamia. At this time Judaism and Christianity penetrated the region and in 356 the first church was built in Aden. The Christian emperor of Abyssinia overthrew the last Himyarite ruler, Dhu Naawas, a Jew, in 525 AD. Fifty years later the kingdom was conquered by the Iranians and within another century South Arabia was conquered by the Islamic Caliphate.

During the later period of Himyarite rule the tribes of South Yemen became more and more independent of the central power and during Abyssinian, Iranian, and Caliphate periods they were to all intents and purposes independent, living in a state of anarchy modified only by tribal custom and a primitive form of religious law. The tidal conflicts of Islam touched it slightly but it almost disappeared from history for a thousand years. Aden had a flourishing trade and magnificent fortifications in Roman times but was in considerable decay when Europe, in the form of the Portuguese fleet, first attacked it in the sixteenth century: and when the British conquered it in 1839 it was no more than a fishing village with 500 inhabitants.

At this time Democratic Yemen was nominally part of the Ottoman Empire. The British annexation in 1839 inaugurated 130 years of British rule in Aden and increasing influence in tribal hinterland, interrupted only briefly by Turkish reoccupation during the First World War.

The Aden Settlement was attached to the Bombay Presidency which had despatched the expedition to conquer it and in 1932 it became a Chief Commissioner's province under the central Government of India. The leaders of the Adeni community, fearing that they might one day be annexed to an independent India, persuaded the British Government in 1937 to make the Settlement a Colony administered from London by the Colonial Office.

Treaties of Protection

In the latter half of the nineteenth century the Turks were actively trying to subdue the Yemen and laying claim to the whole of South Arabia. The tribes surrounding Aden were anxious to prevent their subjection either to the Turks or to the unorthodox Zaidi Imams of Yemen and nine of them therefore accepted British Protection, although without formal treaty, and became known as the Nine Cantons. In 1886 the British Government signed a formal treaty of protection with the Mahra Sultan of Qishn and Socotra and in the following year the Sultan of Lahej accepted protection in return for a monthly stipend. In 1954, when the last was signed, there were 31 treaties of this sort, by which Britain undertook to protect each Ruler and his heirs forever and the Ruler promised not to have dealings with other powers or to cede any of his territory to any country other than Britain.

Meanwhile the British took control of the main islands off South Arabia. The Kuria Muria islands were ceded by the Sultan of Muscat and Oman in 1854 and became part of the Aden Settlement, as did the island of Perim which was occupied in 1857. The island of Socotra came under British protection when the Mahra Sultan signed the treaty of 1876. The British ousted the Turks from Kamaran Island and the Lighthouse Islands in 1915 and made the Governor of Aden responsible for their security and administration.

The land frontiers of the Aden Protectorate were never satisfactorily defined. For years before the First World War the British Government sought to demarcate the frontier with Yemen by agreement with the Turks and in 1914 signed a convention with the Porte establishing what became known as the Violet Line. The Aden Government thereafter based itself on this line but when Yemen became independent after the war, the ruler, Imam Yahya (1903–48), rejected the convention and his forces over-ran substantial protectorate areas between 1920 and 1926. In 1928 the British began to use aircraft to fulfil their promise of protection, on which the Imam had brought discredit, and their success (and the Imam's defeat at the hands of the Saudi bedouin forces of King Abdul Aziz ibn Saud) forced the Imam to accept a new agreement in 1934 which established the Violet Line as the *de facto* frontier without, however, either side renouncing its claims. An uneasy truce was maintained on the basis of this agreement until 1943.

The aggressiveness of Yahya's policy compelled the British to pay more attention to the protectorate areas which they had hitherto been content to leave in their natural state of tribal anarchy. They formed and trained Tribal Guards in each tribal area, created a security force of Government Guards under British and Arab officers and then in 1934 recruited a tribal force called the Aden Protectorate Levies which was the army of the western Protectorate region. Aden became an Air Command in 1928 and the RAF flew to the support of the Guards or Levies whenever necessary and provided for the first time rapid communications between Aden and the tribal centres.

Advisory Treaties

Because British policy was concerned primarily to protect Aden which had acquired great importance as a bunkering port for trade and naval vessels, the Aden Government policy was concerned almost entirely with the protected area surrounding it, neglecting the larger eastern region. There the abiding enmity between Qaiti and Kathiri Sultans and tribal and family feuds had reduced the region to anarchy and even the great Hadhramaut valley was known only to a few intrepid travellers. During 1936 and 1937 Harold Ingrams conducted an ill-defined mission in the eastern protectorate on behalf of the Aden Governor and persuaded the tribes and rulers to sign a truce which became known as Ingrams's Peace.

In 1938 the Qaiti Sultan signed a new treaty with the British Government under which he accepted a Resident Adviser, the first being Ingrams. This was the first of a series of advisory treaties by which Britain was able to establish its influence over the entire eastern area of protection. The Aden Government subsequently extended the system to the western region and by 1954 thirteen advisory treaties had been signed. They were simple in form and in general committed the rulers to accept the advice of the Governor of Aden except in matters of tribal custom and religion. The resident advisers had very limited powers and were directed at all times to strengthen the authority of the rulers and help them to establish workable administrations. These advisory treaties, superimposed on protection, completed the arrangements made by Britain in the two regions. Although they did not constitute direct rule they led Britain more and more to control the ruler, either by removing anyone who disobeyed advice or supporting an obedient ruler against the will of his family.

Federation

In 1948 Imam Yahya of Yemen was assassinated and the reign of his son Ahmad opened with extreme bitterness towards Britain because the plot against his father had been hatched by the Free Yemeni movement in Aden. When the Aden Government granted the British firm, Petroleum Concessions Limited, the right to explore in the disputed border area of Shabwa in the following year, the conflict over the frontier intensified. Although the Aden Governor and Imam Ahmad negotiated an ineffectual *modus vivendi* for demarcating the frontier in 1950, the latter disputed the Sanaa Agreement of 1934 and claimed the right to rule both the Protectorate area and Aden.

This worried western protectorate rulers who assembled in Aden in 1955 to consider a plan of federation drafted by the British. They failed to agree but the Imam decided to forestall further federal plans by mounting an offensive in 1957 against the frontier state of Beihan. He continued to cause trouble at various points and in 1959 he entered into a loose federation with the United Arab Republic just formed by the union of Egypt and Syria and secured Russian and Egyptian instructors to train his forces in the use of automatic weapons. Six of the western protectorate rulers thereupon federated as the Arab Amirates of the south on 11 February 1959, and were joined later by most of the other western rulers.

The colony of Aden was given a Legislative Council without elected members in 1947 and in 1955 this was changed to permit a minority of elected members. There was increasing pressure from the trades unions and embryo political parties for more self-government and in 1959 elections were permitted to give elected Adenis a small majority on the Council. The formation of the Arab Amirates made it obvious that a federation could not exist without Aden and that Aden could not remain a colony and be denied further constitutional advance if it joined. Overcoming strong objections from the Adenis, who feared the feudal power of the tribal rulers, the Aden Government rail-roaded a Council vote in favour of the merger in September 1962 and the Federation of South Arabia came into existence in January 1963.

The Struggle for Independence

A coup d'état in Yemen which overthrew the Imam and established a republic, and the entry of Egyptian troops to support the republic, strengthened resistance to the merger in Aden, led by the People's Socialist Party (PSP), the political wing of the Aden TUC. Behind the scenes the National Liberation Front (NLF) supplied with arms from Yemen was preparing militant resistance. The campaign opened in October 1963 and in December an attempt was made at Aden airport to assassinate the Governor in which one of his senior staff was fatally wounded. A State of Emergency was declared and 57 members of the PSP arrested.

Aden was at this time an important British military base. It was intended that the new federal State would be granted independence in 1968, by which time the retention of the base would be negotiated and the States of the eastern protectorate region brought in, but as good order crumbled the British troops were needed more and more to maintain security in Aden and up-country. On 25 September 1965, the High Commissioner (the former Governor) suspended the Aden constitution and imposed direct rule in the colony because some Adeni ministers would not co-operate in the suppression of terrorism, which was daily increasing.

The federal rulers and the few moderates in Aden who supported the federation did so in the firm conviction that the British base would remain to guarantee security but in February 1966 a new British Defence White Paper stated that the base would be withdrawn by 31 December 1968 and there would be no defence treaty with the South Arabian Federation. This further encouraged the militants who now included the Front for the Liberation of South Yemen (FLOSY), which was led by the PSP; and the NLF and FLOSY competed in violence against the British, and those who collaborated with them, and against each other. A new draft constitution prepared by two British specialists at the request of the federal Government, and the intervention of a UN mission at the request of the British Government, failed to halt disorder.

The British called from retirement a distinguished ambassador, Sir Humphrey Trevelyan, to be High Commissioner and on his arrival in May 1967, he stated that Britain would continue to base itself on the federal Government but invited *all* leaders to help him to broaden it. This invitation to the opposition was repeated by the British Foreign Secretary in the House of Commons in June. He announced that British troops would be withdrawn by 9 January 1968, when South Arabia would be given independence, and that for a limited period afterwards Britain would give the new State naval and air support.

As the British troops withdrew from the tribal areas in June 1968, the NLF progressively took over; in August the federal Government collapsed; and in October the NLF took control of the eastern protectorate States, none of which had joined the federation. The federal army (formed of the former Protectorate Levies and still partly officered by British) remained largely intact and it asked the High Commissioner to negotiate with the NLF and FLOSY, at the same time ordering the two movements to stop fighting in Aden. After negotiating for a month in Cairo they agreed on 1 November to form a joint delegation to negotiate with the British, and it was announced in London that British troops would withdraw by the end of the month. This forthright declaration precipitated the final struggle between FLOSY and the

NLF in Aden which ended in victory for the NLF when the army supported it. It was therefore an NLF delegation which negotiated the take-over from Britain at a conference in Geneva, and the Republic of South Yemen came into existence at midnight on 30 November with Qahtan al-Shaabi, leader of the NLF, as President.

Independence

Apart from the President, who was forty-seven, the government consisted of young men in their thirties whose attitudes covered the political spectrum all the way from Chinese Communism to Nasser-type Arab socialism. The President declared the new Government's policy to be socialism at home, non-alignment abroad, Arab unity, the liberation of Palestine, support for national revolutionary movements and 'the re-unification of the Arab peoples of North and South Yemen'. This 'progressive' policy was in conflict with the penury of the State which required maximum financial support from all quarters, including rich but traditional Arab states, and there quickly developed a dispute between the left-wing ideologists and those pragmatists in the Government who put the economic problem first. This soon manifested itself in the eastern region where pro-Chinese Communist elements of the NLF began to act independently of the central Government. When purges in Aden and the western region threatened the army, the Command intervened in March 1968 to compel President Qahtan to get rid of extremists in his cabinet, notably Ali Salem al-Baidh, the Minister of the Interior, and Abdul Fatah Ismail al-Jaufi, the Minister of National Guidance, both of whom went into exile. Some weeks later the extreme elements staged a revolt in the regions of Zingibar and Jaar, about forty miles from Aden, but this was overcome by the army which then proceeded to restore its authority in Mukalla, in the eastern province. In September a violent dispute within the army led to the exiling to Algeria of twenty-two officers. In June 1969 President Qahtan al-Shaabi was ousted from power in a further move to the left. He was replaced by a five-man Presidential Council headed by Salem Ali Rubayyi. Mohammed Ali Haitham, whom President Qahtan had recently dismissed from the post of Minister of Interior, became Prime Minister in the new Government. In March 1970 the Government claimed to have forestalled a reactionary coup backed by Saudi Arabia and the US and led by a former Governor of the Fifth (eastern) Governorate. A score of prominent army officers and civilians were arrested; eight were charged with treason before a newly established People's Court, and seven were executed. Further arrests then took place including ex-President Qahtan al-Shaabi and former Premier Faisal Abdul Latif who was later declared to have been shot while attempting to escape.

These early troubles were only to be expected. The State was born in poverty and made insecure by the abundance of arms accumulated during the years of militant resistance to the federal Government and the British. Its political, social, and economic problems were, and are, immense.

GOVERNMENT, ADMINISTRATION, AND JUSTICE

The draft constitution approved by the ruling National Liberation Front and published on 2 August 1970 refers to southern Yemen as a 'popular democratic republic' with Islam as its religion. It provides for free and direct elections to a 101-member People's Supreme Council, to be held before November 1971. On 30 November the country was officially named the People's Democratic Republic of Yemen.

Democratic Yemen has been ruled since independence by a President and Council of Ministers chosen by the president from the 40-man General Command of the ruling National Liberation Front. The Command is the interim legislative body but it meets in secret and most of its members are unknown to the people.

The republic is divided into six governorates which, broadly speaking, are arranged numerically from west to east.[1] The governors are appointed by the President and at the outset three of them were army officers.

Before independence Aden Colony had a Supreme Court with unlimited civil and criminal jurisdiction. Appeals from the Supreme Court were heard by Her Majesty's Court of Appeal for East Africa and could be carried to the Privy Council in London. In the States of Lahej, Fadhli, and Qaiti a formal judicial system was being evolved, but in general the judicial system outside the colony was based on *sharia* (religious) and *urf* (tribal) laws, and was administered by the rulers or their deputies, sometimes assisted by family State Councils. The aim of the republic is one system of law for the whole country but this will take time because of the lack of trained personnel and funds and, even more important, the nature of the people who have known only tribal law since time immemorial. The Government's first plan is to codify tribal laws and to open offices in all governorates to standardize the registration of land ownership and to supervise *Waqf* (religious endowment) properties.

The judicial system inside the area of the former Aden Colony still functions except that the right of appeal to the East African Court of Appeal or the Privy Council ceased to exist after independence. The

---

[1] The governorates are: 1st, Aden and the nearby villages of Dar Saad and Imran and the islands of Perim, Kamaran, Socotra, and Kuria Muria; 2nd, Lahej, Subbeyha, Haushabi, Alawi, Radfan, Shaib, Halmain, and Muflahi; 3rd, Upper and Lower Yafa, Fadhli, Audhali, Dathina, and Lower Awlaqi; 4th Beihan, Upper Aulaqi, Wahidi, and the north-western Hadhramaut; 5th, Hadhramaut except the north-western area; 6th, Mahra, bordering Oman.

Appeal Court provided for in the reorganization of the judiciary was not established in the first year of the republic and sentences were executed despite appeals. The Aden Supreme Court functions under an acting Asian judge because the Arab Chief Justice and three other Arab judges were dismissed by the republican Government. Five non-Adeni magistrates preside over the Courts of First Instance and the language of the courts and the laws were changed from English to Arabic in 1971. Costs of litigation have been reduced by lowering and fixing the fees of the nine practising lawyers, most of whom are Indian.

Government Policy

The first statement of policy of President Qahtan (see *History*) established a theoretical position that the Government desired to pursue but the harsh economic facts dictated greater pragmatism. This contributed to Qahtan's fall from power and the development of theoretical 'leftism'.

Qahtan's Nasser-type socialism in which national and private capital are combined under State control was pushed after his fall to a point at which private capital ceased to be a partner in the national enterprise. There was, furthermore, very little national capital accumulation and could be little unless substantial foreign aid were received. Agrarian reform was based on land seized from Sultans, Shaikhs, and former federal ministers and distributed to the people.

The original policy of non-alignment yielded to more overt association with the Soviet bloc and People's China after the political changes of 1969 but the profession of non-alignment remains and relations with Britain have been maintained.

The basic elements of the policies of all Arab states—Arab unity and the liberation of Palestine—are firmly held, and in June of 1970 Democratic Yemen permitted the PFLP to use its island of Perim, in the Straits of Mandeb, for a motor-boat attack on an Israeli ship bound for Eilat.

Democratic Yemen is aligned in effect with Algeria, Egypt, Syria, and Iraq in its support for national revolutionary movements, and this involves support for peoples who seek to overthrow kings and traditional rulers in the Arab world or foreign overlords anywhere. The Popular Front for the Liberation of the Arab Gulf, for example, has its headquarters in Aden and the rebellion in Dhufar, in the State of Oman, is mounted from the Sixth Governorate.

The aim of all radical movements before independence was re-unification of the two Yemens, and it remained the official policy, but the drift apart began as early as 1968 when southern Yemen accused Yemen of harbouring members of FLOSY and other 'reactionary elements'. The deterioration of relations continued through 1969 and 1970, when the Yemeni Republican Government virtually became a client of Saudi Arabia which, according to the Aden Government, was financing and arming dissidents in a border war.

The dominant geo-political factor was the large and wealthy Saudi Arabia to the north and east. It could give Democratic Yemen the economic support the country desperately needs but the Government's revolutionary policies precluded this. Its support for revolutionary forces in the State of Oman equally excluded financial help from that side. Those Arab countries with which Democratic Yemen claimed friendship—Egypt, Syria, Iraq, and Algeria—were not in a position to give the required economic support.

Democratic Yemen is a member of the United Nations and the League of Arab States.

ECONOMIC AND SOCIAL SURVEY

The State is not viable: this is the essential fact. Aden Port achieved relative prosperity as a colony and in the final few years before independence was enriched by income of various sorts totalling about £11 million a year from the British military base, but even in this condition of artificially expanded wealth there was little it could do for the protectorate hinterland where only one per cent of the land is cultivable and yet 75 per cent of the population lives by agriculture.

The civil disorders of 1967 reduced the port trade but the closing of the Suez Canal as a result of the Arab–Israeli war of June that year was a disaster.[1] Whereas in December 1966 533 ships used the port, only 109 called in December 1967 and most of these were small coastal vessels; as a result the bunkering trade was only three per cent of normal. (In the first six months the Port Trust itself lost £1 million from its reserves.)

The BP company keeps the refinery running almost to capacity by refining crude oil intended for elsewhere, but the Aden area itself has little to offer for the time being.

The total withdrawal of British forces in the last half of 1967 greatly accentuated the economic depression by putting 25,000 people out of work. The general reduction in the purchasing power of the people progressively hit the small indigenous consumers, thus increasing the unemployment which was still widespread in 1971.

There would be substantial recovery with the re-opening of the Suez Canal and the restoration of port and bunkering trade but it may take a longer time for confidence to be re-established in the port and indigenous trade to recover. The much greater tribal areas behind Aden have no comparable prospects. The harsh terrain provides too few opportunities for development on a scale that would be economically

[1] The Suez Canal was still closed in autumn 1972 and there were no immediate signs of its reopening. It imposed a loss of about £15 million in the first year.

rewarding. For example, the inadequacy of road communications is due to the fact that the area offers too little in the way of commodities to justify the vast cost of building roads through the difficult and insecure terrain. The British could never visualize a State rich enough to maintain an adequate road network even if the money were available to build it.

The Democratic Yemen Government could not afford this practical, though possibly unhopeful, attitude, because public works of almost any sort were absolutely essential. In 1971 there were 25,000 unemployed in the once thriving Aden. The Government therefore canvassed for aid for road-building even though there seemed little likelihood that it would have, in the foreseeable future, the money to maintain the roads when built. The biggest success in this direction was an undertaking by People's China to provide £18 million to build a 300-mile coastal road from Aden to Mukalla. This was the main item in a bulk offer of £21 million aid.

The British found it difficult to find schemes that would justify the capital expenditure they would require and those schemes they did execute only created small pockets of relative prosperity and could not provide a general rise in the standard of living. Even in those days when the people were content with the barest necessities young men were compelled to emigrate in search of a living, becoming military mercenaries or traders in India, South-east Asia, and Zanzibar, or factory workers and shopkeepers in Britain, or merchant seamen. In latter years many found work in Aden and the Abyan Delta, in the military and paramilitary forces enlisted by the British before independence, and in Saudi Arabia. Numerous families, notably in the eastern region, depend on remittances from their children abroad, but with the growth of independent nationalist States in Asia this source of revenue has greatly declined.

Nor do the prospects of mineral wealth seem promising. Mica, gypsum, and potash are to be found but the deposits are either too small or too far from the coast to be economically workable. The hope that oil would bring wealth to the country has not so far been fulfilled. Explorations in the western region proved abortive. In 1961 the Pan-American (Hadhramaut) Oil Company found oil in a concession covering 5,000 square miles of the eastern region but not in commercial quantities and the company withdrew in 1966 after 'costly and negative' explorations. Despite these unpromising words, a joint Democratic Yemen–Algerian company was formed in 1970 for the exploration and marketing of oil. It seemed insufficiently capitalized for the undertaking.

In these circumstances, the only hope of immediate relief from abject poverty depends on substantial foreign aid. The British Government provided £12 million for the first six months of independence but negotiations for further aid collapsed in May 1968 because the British offered £1·8 million (net £1·25 million after deduction of Democratic Yemen's financial obligations to Britain) whereas the Democratic Yemen Government expected at least £60 million over three years, the amount promised to the former Federal Government. In 1970, the British Government relented enough to pay £430,000 as *ex gratia* payments to former Adeni Government officials and police to cover the period from 30 November 1967, to relieve their hardships. This covered unpaid pensions and Britain was continuing to pay the pensions thereafter. In that year, also, the Libyan Government promised £8 million in aid and loans and the Iraqi Government £3 million for development.

The rich Arab oil states which could have provided substantial aid are most reluctant to do so because of the professed 'revolutionary' policies of the Government, although Kuwait was moderately generous. Saudi Arabia not only withheld recognition in 1968 but also stopped further contributions to the 6·5 million dinars it had pledged in November 1966 for building 365 miles of trunk roads. In the summer of 1968 a determined effort was made to get Arab aid and the President announced financial support from Egypt, Algeria, and Iraq but it proved to be modest. People's China was the chief backer. Soviet Russia showed little desire to help, except in the provision of armaments, despite Democratic Yemen's professed socialist character; nor did the United States, because of it.

Thus in the first years of independence the situation remained bleak and offered little scope for the Government.

Currency

The unit of currency is the South Yemen Dinar, equivalent to the pound sterling, which replaced the East African Shilling (20 shillings to the pound sterling). The Government banned the circulation of the Maria Theresa dollar. There is strong backing for the currency despite the adverse economic situation. The Board which issues the dinar is required by law to maintain 70 per cent cover but in the first year of independence external reserves were equal to 90 per cent of the currency in circulation; as was expected, however, it was necessary in the second year to raid these reserves because adequate foreign aid was not forthcoming. The reserves were nevertheless retained at an adequate level.

Public Finance

The British Government contributed about two-thirds of the budgetary income of the States now comprising the Democratic Republic of Yemen until the financial year 1967/8. By far the largest item of expenditure was for the armed forces, which was more than 50 per cent of the gross income of the former federation and one-third of the income of the overall area. The Ministry of Economy, Commerce, and Planning issued the following figures in 1968:

Years	Total actual expenditure £	Military expenditure £	Actual local revenue £	British Aid £
EX-FEDERATION				
1963/4	8,238,981	3,623,316	3,363,697	4,875,284
1964/5	10,779,376	5,148,597	3,695,743	7,083,633
1965/6	13,730,512	6,147,052	4,133,565	9,596,947
1966/7	17,220,086	8,984,048	4,372,576	12,847,510
1967/8	25,168,117	13,983,458	4,803,700	20,364,417
EX-STATES (Including Aden)				
1963/4	6,550,480		5,006,372	1,964,419
1964/5	7,107,278		5,030,314	1,816,188
1965/6	7,707,840		5,626,275	1,935,973
1966/7	8,632,312		5,713,996	2,327,828
1967/8	7,866,730		4,114,476	2,508,493

The closure of the British military base and virtual cessation of British aid has also reduced taxable income. From 1966/7 and 1967/8 local revenue declined by just over £1 million and the ministry forecast a further serious decline in the following year. Commenting on these facts the ministry stated:

From the general budgetary analysis, it is quite clear that the People's Republic of Southern Yemen is in a financial predicament. The general economic situation and its previous dependence on the British presence make sufficient remedial action by the Government almost impossible in the immediate future. This is especially so since the Government finance itself was based on British aid, and the problem is greater when the military takes a big share of Government expenditure, while the rest is not sufficient for the simple administrative machinery and the rudimentary social services. However greatly the taxation potential is mobilized, the budgetary deficit will still be considerable.

The situation showed little, if any, improvement by the end of 1971. The 1970/1 budget anticipated a deficit of £12 million. The estimated income of £21 million was allocated in its entirety to the public service sector, and no provision was made for development. The 1971/2 budget reduced the estimated deficiency to £9 million by further stringent economies. In practice, the country kept its financial head above water by not spending a great part of the budgeted expenditure, with the result that the country was running steadily down hill, for no country could be found, even in the friendly Eastern bloc to meet current currency needs as Britain had done earlier.

Commerce and Trade

Aden was a free port and there were no customs dues except on liquor, drugs, tobacco, motor spirit, and salt, but as the result of an economic study by foreign experts the Government ended this system

G

in 1969. It is important mainly as a port of trans-shipment, as an
entrepôt for neighbouring territories, and as an oil bunkering port, but
its prosperity depends largely on the Suez Canal which was closed at
the time of Democratic Yemen's independence. The BP refinery at
Little Aden is the second major commercial asset of the Aden area,
which otherwise has little to offer except salt produced by solar
evaporation, worth about SYD140,000 dinars a year, and a small but
steady income from inshore fishing, and from the cleaning, sorting, and
packing of coffee, hides, oyster shells, gums, and incense for export and
re-export. There are a number of small factories producing soap, pots
and pans, cigarettes, matches, aluminium, dyed and printed cotton,
and soft drinks, mainly to meet the needs of the local population.

The area outside Aden relies on agriculture and fishing. Cotton is the
only cash crop of importance. It is grown with success in the Abyan
Delta 50 miles east of Aden, in Lahej, 16 miles north of Aden, and in
Ahwar, in Aulaqi territory, 150 miles east. The Abyan area covering
120,000 acres is the most important; it also yields fruit and vegetables.
In the eastern region, grain and fodder are grown in the Hadhramaut
and in recent years have been greatly increased by the extension of
pumping schemes in the former Qaiti and Kathiri States. Citrus and
hard fruits are successfully grown on the plateaux.

A report published in 1967[1] gave the following break-down of the
Gross Domestic Product of the former federation in 1965:

Gross Domestic Product by Industry, 1965

	£ million
Agriculture & fishing	6
Manufacturing:	
Oil refinery	7
Other (including electricity generating)	3
Construction:	
Services contracts	3
Other	2
Transport & communications:	
Port (including bunkering)	6·5[1]
Other	1
Wholesale and retail trade	13
Tourism	0·5
Financial services	1·5
Government	10
UK Services	4·5
Ownership of dwellings	4
Personal services	7
Gross Domestic Product	69·0

Note: [1] Including petroleum distribution.

[1] *Economic Development and Policy in the Federation of South Arabia,* 1967. (Referred to
elsewhere as EDPF Report.) The experts who prepared this report noted the inadequacy of statistical information.

There are no accurate figures for the three eastern States which were not part of the federation but the Gross Domestic Product was estimated at £7 million, giving £76 million as the GDP for the area constituting the republic. It made a *per capita* income of about £50 a year (although this is misleading because of the uneven distribution over the region). The GDP of the republic is, however, considerably less, because in 1965 the British presence and aid was generating directly about 37 per cent and indirectly 15 per cent, so that by late 1968 the GDP had declined by approximately 50 per cent as residual British aid ran out. Foreign aid had improved the situation by 1971 but only slightly and Aden bore all the marks of a greatly impoverished town.

Agriculture only contributes 8 per cent of the GDP although it engages 75 per cent of the population. The Government is therefore looking to industrial development and diversification to improve the economy.

The following figures from the EPDF report give some idea of the

Trade and UK Government Expenditure in South Arabia, 1960–5

Year	Imports (cif)	Exports (fob)	Deficit	£ million UK aid and military expenditure
1960	76·6[1]	60·0[1]	16·6[1]	11
1961	82·9[1]	64·9[1]	18·0[1]	17
1962	85·8[1]	66·6[1]	19·2[1]	18
1963	97·0	69·6	27·4	22
1964	106·1	74·3	31·8	28
1965	108·3	66·7	41·6	33

Note: [1] Aden only.

Raw Cotton Exports: 1965

Country	Value 1965 £000
India	57
United Kingdom	980
Netherlands	59
	1,097

Aden Fruit and Vegetable Sales: Payment to Producers

	1964/5 £000
Lahej & Bir Ahmad	154
Abyan	195
Dathina	4·2
Lodar	36
Mukeiras	95
Other	0·1
	484

normal dimensions of trade but they do not include the three eastern
States and at the end of 1968 they did not reflect the republic's position
because of the continuing closure of the Suez Canal and other factors.

Little Aden Refinery

The refinery was commissioned in 1954 on a site comprising 470
acres, having been built in two years at a cost of £45 million for an
annual throughput of 7 million tons of crude oil. Its jetties can accommodate four tankers at once and the harbour is dredged to 40 feet depth
to accommodate ships of 42,000 gross tons. The refinery re-exports
60 per cent of its output and produces 60 per cent of the country's
export earnings. It provides 10 per cent of the GDP.

Aden Port

The harbour is the hub of the urban economy. In normal times (i.e.
when the Suez Canal is open) it is one of the four great bunkering ports
in the world and used by more than 500 ships a month. It keeps the
refinery busy and about 250,000 people, passengers and crews, spend
their money in the Aden shops.

The port is run by a Port Trust Authority, which was formed in
1888[1] when the invention of the steamship gave Aden major maritime
importance. Since 1954 the port has been greatly enlarged and improved by dredging and land reclamation. The two-mile-long entrance
and inner harbour of 291 acres have a depth of 36 feet, giving 18 berths
for ships up to 36 feet draught and four for ships of 16 feet draught.
There is ample anchorage for ships of up to 18 feet draught in another
area. The port revenue in 1966/7 was £SA1,850,504.

Communications

The country's communications are primitive. There are less than 100
miles of macadamized roads and the construction of roads in the highlands is extremely costly. The Tirah Pass road between Lodar and
Mukeiras is an example; at one stage it required cutting six miles of
road into a near-vertical cliff, rising through 45 hairpin bends. There
are, however, tracks fit for trucks and heavy cars, such as the motor
road and track connecting Aden with Lahej and passing through Wadi
Tiban to Taez in Yemen. Another motorable route goes from Aden
through the Abyan area, the Fadhli, Dathina, and Aulaqi territories to
Beihan—a roundabout way. The People's Republic of China undertook in 1970 to build a coastal road from Aden to Mukalla (see page 179).
There are no railways and connection with the eastern States is usually
now maintained by plane.

Aden Airways, which was in association with BOAC, maintained a

---

[1] In February 1968, the Board of Trustees was abolished and a committee responsible
to the President was appointed to take over its functions.

network of services throughout the federal area but closed down after independence. Its landing strips are still used by the Government for its own air force which is used as an official transport service.

Health

A free Government health service started in the former Aden Colony in 1960 is still operating and is available in some of the more advanced towns outside. There is a civil hospital of 350 beds in Crater and another in Khormaksar. The older Church of England Mission Hospital in Shaikh Othman is still in use. When possible, emergency or grave cases from the tribal areas are brought to these hospitals for treatment, but throughout the country as a whole hospitals and dispensaries are few and far between and totally inadequate. For every 1,500 people there is only one bed and for every 30,500 people there is only one doctor.

Improved health provisions in the former colony did, however, make headway against the high mortality rate resulting from tuberculosis. The birth rate (so far as known in the Aden area) is twice as high as the death rate but both are growing. The infant mortality rate is also growing, owing to overcrowding in Aden.

Education

The educational system is founded on that of the former Aden Colony, where the Government maintained 18 schools and subsidized 24 others and provided free education for children born in the Colony. It also maintained Aden College for academic secondary education, a technical institute, and two teachers' training colleges. The colony provided education for girls and a Girl's College was opened at Khormaksar in 1956. The level of education varied in the States outside the Colony, depending on their wealth, degree of development, and the enlightenment of their rulers but those children who did qualify from the former protectorate and federal areas could continue their higher education in Aden.

This remains true of the republic which as a whole has 227 primary schools, 37 intermediate, and 11 secondary. Nearly all the children in the towns get at least primary education but in isolated areas of the country no schooling exists. About 50 per cent of the children finishing primary education proceed to intermediate schools but only 20 per cent are able to follow a secondary course.

4. KUWAIT

The Amirate of Kuwait is set in the desert country which lies in the north-western corner of the Gulf around the Bay of Kuwait. Kuwait city occupies one of the rare firm coastal features lying between extensive areas of shoal, mudflat and coral reef although the city is rapidly expanding south eastwards towards Mina al-Ahmadi, the oil port on the Gulf proper. Inland a few small oases lie in the waterless undulating desert which rises in altitude to the west. Medium depth aquefers of slightly brackish as well as sweet water have allowed small-scale traditional oasis agriculture but the economy of Kuwait is almost entirely dependent on the exploitation of vast onshore and offshore oil deposits, export of which commenced in 1946 and which has overwhelmed the traditionally dominant marine trade. To the south lies the Partitioned Zone, jointly administered with Saudi Arabia and completely negative save for oil. To the north and east lie scattered islands of the marshland complex of extreme south Iraq.

In the 7,400 square miles of territory lives a population of 734,000, almost ten times larger than that of 1934 and most of which is concentrated in the city of Kuwait and in the industrial zone to the south which contains the centres of Ahmadi, Fahaheel, and Shuaiba. According to the 1970 census about 47 per cent of the population had Kuwaiti nationality.

RECENT HISTORY

Early in the eighteenth century members of the Anaiza tribe occupied the site of the present town and developed marine and trading interests which dominated the life of Kuwait until recently. By 1760 a fleet of more than 800 dhows was based on the port which grew even faster after the East India Company established its head of Gulf base at Kuwait following the Iranian occupation of Basra in 1776. Even so the population remained at between 10,000 and 12,000 until the end of the nineteenth century.

In 1756 a member of one of the leading Anaiza families, the Sabah, was chosen as first Amir of Kuwait and his line has ruled continuously ever since. Shaikh Mubarak the Great, 1896–1915, was first to assert the independence of the Amirate, at a time when Britain was concerned about German negotiations with Turkey for the southern part of the Berlin–Baghdad railway and its extension to the south, and when Russian attempts to secure a naval supply station at the head of the Gulf were also giving some anxiety to Britain. In 1899 Britain acceded to Shaikh Mubarak's request for support and protection, and the treaty was further extended to include recognition as an independent State under British protection. Turco-British negotiations over the status of Kuwait started in 1909 and the establishment of a British Political Agency in 1914 were landmarks in the history of the new State. In accordance with the 1899 treaty, Kuwait's foreign relations were conducted by Britain through its Political Agent. By 1910, as a result of the increased trade which was associated with growing world interest in the region the population had increased to about 35,000, the first stage in a rapid period of growth.

In the period of post-1919 settlements the most crucial was the 1922/3 conference to settle the Kuwaiti–Saudi Arabian frontiers in which the interests of the newly established State of Iraq, under British mandate, were also concerned. Two neutral zones were established, one to the west between Iraq and Saudi Arabia and one to the south, adjoining the coast, which thenceforward has been jointly administered by Kuwait and Saudi Arabia. During the 1920s and 1930s Shaikh Salim and Shaikh Ahmad ensured that economic growth in Mesopotamia and the oilfields of Iraq and Iran subscribed to the mercantile wealth of Kuwait whose population increased to about 75,000 by 1934. During the same period oil exploration commenced. Politically, relations with Saudi Arabia improved from the nadir of the Saudi blockade of Kuwait in 1919 although the land frontier remained closed for almost twenty years afterwards. Fears of Iraqi expansionism, however, have never been completely eliminated and the growth of dependence on the supply of fresh water from the Shatt al-Arab near Basra, a traffic which lasted from 1925 to 1951, made Kuwait conscious of vulnerability.

The first oil concession was granted in 1934 for a period of 74 years to the Kuwait Oil Company, representing the Gulf Oil Corporation and the D'Arcy Exploration Company (a subsidiary then of Anglo-Iranian, now of British Petroleum). The first well was drilled north of the city of Kuwait at Bahra in 1936 but not until 1938 was oil found at Burgan, 25 miles south of the city. The Second World War prevented the full exploitation of what appeared a rich field and the wells were plugged until 1946 when production effectively started. Shaikh Ahmad, then Amir of Kuwait, officiated at a ceremony for the first tanker loading and gave his name to the KOC oil township of Ahmadi and the port of Mina al-Ahmadi. Between 1946 and 1961 KOC drilled an average of 26 wells a year and KOC production rose in 1961 to over 81 million tons.

Throughout the 1950s the town of Kuwait was being dramatically transformed with the aid of its steadily increasing oil income from a small and somnolent mud-walled trading and fishing port into a modern city. Shaikh Abdullah, who succeeded Shaikh Ahmad as Ruler in 1950, was a social and religious conservative but he favoured the spread of education (for girls as well as boys) and rapid economic development. Under his rule Kuwait became a comprehensive welfare State not only for the native Kuwaitis but also for the immigrant Arabs, Iranians, and Indians who exceeded them in numbers. Political power remained in the hands of the ruling family but it was divided both traditionally between the Jabir and Salim branches of the Sabah family and on a basis of personality. The Deputy Ruler Abdullah

Mubarak, who favoured an old-fashioned type of shaikhly rule, was contrasted with the younger Shaikh Jabir al-Ahmad who was regarded as a 'progressive'.

In June 1961 Kuwait and Britain terminated the 1899 agreement and Kuwait became an independent State. In July it joined the Arab League and in 1963, after the USSR had withdrawn its objection, the United Nations. In June 1961 General Kassem, the ruler of Iraq, renewed Iraq's claim to Kuwait in strong terms. British troops landed at the request of the Ruler but these were replaced in September by an Arab League force of UAR, Jordanian, Saudi, and Sudanese troops. It was doubtful whether General Kassem seriously contemplated an outright military invasion of Kuwait; its survival as an independent State in any case depended more on the fact that this was the desire of all the other Arab states (except Iraq) than on British military support.

In December 1961 Kuwait took a major step away from traditional forms of government with the selection of 20 members of a Constituent Assembly who joined with the ministers in drafting a permanent Constitution. This was published in November 1962. In January 1963 a 50-member National Assembly was elected and Crown Prince Salim became Prime Minister at the head of a new Government.

In the new Assembly a small group of radical nationalist deputies succeeded in acquiring influence out of all proportion to their numbers and as a result Kuwait never openly sided with the camp of the conservative Arab kings in opposition to the revolutionary republics. Kuwait's influence and importance in the Arab world were greatly strengthened by the creation at the end of 1961 of the Kuwait Fund for Arab Development which provided loans on easy terms for viable development projects in the Arab states. By 1971 loans totalling KD80 million had been committed to schemes in thirteen Arab countries ranging from agricultural projects in Morocco and Tunisia to hydroelectric schemes in Iraq and Lebanon and aluminium smelting in Bahrain. Kuwait also made several special loans (which were, in fact, gifts) to the general reserves of several Arab countries.

The fall of Kassem in February 1963 made possible a rapprochement between the Kuwait and Iraq governments and in October Iraq recognized Kuwait as an independent Arab State. In February 1964 an agreement was signed for the supply of fresh water to Kuwait from the Shatt al-Arab but the scheme was not implemented and Kuwait increased its own sea-water distillation capacity. The Kuwaitis remained wary of making themselves dependent on good relations with Iraq. In December 1964 a new Government was formed which showed that the ruling family was prepared to relinquish some of its executive power to the merchant class and to the elected members of the National Assembly.

Kuwait's great wealth and consequent independence has enabled it at times to adopt a radical Arab nationalist stand on certain foreign policy issues. It was one of the first Arab states to break relations with West Germany in May 1965 after Bonn had established diplomatic relations with Israel. But the national interest remained paramount for both the Government and the majority of the National Assembly and Kuwait carefully maintained its neutrality between the conservative and radical camps in the Arab world while adopting firm measures at home to prevent non-Kuwaiti Arab immigrants from acquiring undue influence in the State. These measures, which included the expulsion of a group of 'subversive' non-Kuwaitis, were unsuccessfully opposed by the Arab nationalist deputies in the National Assembly. In 1966 the Government tried, though unsuccessfully, to mediate between Saudi Arabia and Egypt on the Yemen question.

In November 1965 the much respected Shaikh Abdullah died and was succeeded by the 51-year-old Shaikh Sabah Salim. Shaikh Jabir, the Minister of Finance, became Prime Minister and Crown Prince. At Kuwait's second National Assembly elections, held in January 1967, pro-Cairo Arab Nationalist Movement candidates did rather less well than expected. Only four were successful and their leader Dr. Ahmad al-Khatib was defeated. After the elections 32 unsuccessful candidates signed a protest accusing the Government of gross interference in the elections. Other protests were made by two outgoing ministers, the Kuwaiti Newspaper Owners Association, and various student and professional associations.

In the June 1967 war Kuwait expressed its support for the other Arab states and sent a small contingent of troops to Egypt; it also cut off the supply of oil to the US and Britain. It did not, however, withdraw all its funds deposited in Britain as many Arabs expected. There were some withdrawals by individual Kuwaitis but these later returned. In Khartoum in August 1967 the Ruler agreed to make the largest single contribution of £55 million a year to aid Jordan and Egypt.

Following Britain's announcement of the withdrawal of all its forces from the Gulf area by 1971, the Anglo-Kuwaiti defence agreement concluded after Kuwait's independence was cancelled in May 1968 by mutual agreement. Kuwait took a leading part in negotiations concerning the Iranian claim to Bahrain, the clarification of sovereignty rights over various Gulf islands, and, together with Saudi Arabia, in promoting the development of a viable federation of Arab States in the Trucial States region.

In 1968 Kuwait became a founder member, together with Libya and Saudi Arabia, of the Organization of Arab Petroleum Exporting Countries, OAPEC, expressing the need of states whose economies are dominated by the export of oil, particularly to the West, to be free from political pressures. It was, however, in association with other OPEC oil producers using the Gulf export route that Kuwait negotiated higher revenues (in Kuwait's case about KD150 million) from the oil companies in 1971.

In 1969 the Kuwait Government became seriously alarmed at the sharp increase in the non-Kuwaiti population, estimated at 200,000 since the 1967 war, many of them unemployed. As a consequence new restrictions were imposed in March. The National Assembly elections held in January 1971 were widely regarded as having been entirely free. The composition of the Assembly remained basically conservative but the radicals considerably increased their representation. Out of 50 members 12 university graduates were elected as opposed to two in the previous Assembly.

THE ECONOMY

Kuwait's GNP *per capita* ranks with that of the USA and Abu Dhabi as among the highest in the world in spite of its having virtually no commercially viable agriculture, of being dependent on desalination plant for freshwater, and of having limited manufacturing activity. Oil is the dominant factor in the country's economy, and revenue from its production and sale—some £350 million—accounts for about 95 per cent of total budget revenue. Of the GNP approximately one-third is directly derived from exports, another one-third from private consumption, about 20 per cent from Government expenditure, about 20 per cent from fixed investment and less than 4 per cent from local manufacturing. Approximately 93 per cent of the oil production (which totals about 6 per cent of world production) comes from the Kuwait Oil Company (50 per cent each BP and Gulf Oil). The Arabian Oil Company, a Japanese concern, and Aminoil, an American independent, have achieved production in the partitioned zone but problems of oil quality have prevented much expansion. Hispanoil is associated with KNPC in exploration work. Kuwaiti private foreign investment is estimated at over £350 million. The major channel to the private sector of oil revenue has been through major expenditure on urban renewal and development, in particular through land acquisition by the Senate. Oil revenue rose relatively slowly at first after 1966 as a result of the closure of the Suez Canal but increased sharply in 1971/2. Major industrial developments have been based on domestic oil and natural gas, the main features being the opening of a five million ton crude capacity oil refinery and a fertilizer plant producing ammonia and sulphuric acid (with their products) at Shuaiba, the Kuwait industrial area. Kuwait National Petroleum Company, with 60 per cent state shareholding, handles all internal sales and distribution of petroleum products, and, in addition, runs the Shuaiba refinery. The intention is to develop KNPC's activities in all oil and petrochemical fields. Other manufacturing activity is confined to the production of basic consumer goods such as bread, soft beverages, bricks, and tiles, almost all other products being imported. Further developments in petro-chemical based manufactures have been considered but the small size of the domestic market, high labour costs, and other limitations of resource tend to outweigh the advantages of ample domestic capital availability.

Kuwait's imports in 1970 totalled some KD280 million, the highest *per capita* rate in the world—almost \$1,000. Her chief suppliers are the USA (20 per cent), Japan (14 per cent) and Britain (13 per cent). Kuwait has a permanently favourable balance of payments but her considerable aid commitments to other Arab countries has resulted in a slowing down between 1968 and 1970 of the internal rate of growth to some 7 per cent per annum. Since this latter is mainly determined by the budgetary circulation of oil revenue, the deflection from reserves and budgetary funds produced a tightening in capital supply. The continued influx of Palestinians which has led to a preponderance of non-Kuwaiti citizens among the State's inhabitants has also increased domestic welfare demands.

SOCIAL DEVELOPMENTS

The rapid and continued growth of oil wealth has had vast direct and indirect effects on the whole of Kuwait's life. This wealth has made possible—and the Ruler and his Council have turned the possibilities into reality—the social and physical transformation of the city-state. Vast education programmes have virtually eliminated illiteracy and created a full range of educational facilities. Education is free from kindergarten to university and in addition students are provided with free transport, books, meals, and uniforms. A comprehensive and free health service is paralleled by other wide-ranging welfare and social services. Public utilities are free or heavily subsidized and consumption levels of all kinds are very high. The physical replanning and building of Kuwait has been extremely rapid as a result of lavish expenditure on land acquisition by the Government (which amounted to KD200 million in 1966).

All this, together with the establishment of a full range of political and economic organizations, has resulted in a great demand for expatriate skills, a demand which has only recently diminished as trained indigenous expertise has become available. The granting of citizenship has been increasingly restricted in an attempt to maintain a reasonable balance between various social and economic sectors. The effect has been over a long period to encourage immigration both of unskilled labourers and of highly skilled specialists. In 1965 77 per cent of the occupied population was non-Kuwaiti. Palestinian and Jordanian immigrants have greatly increased in numbers since 1967, during a period when the employment of expatriates was already being discouraged.

In 1971 Kuwait was in a position of having to choose the future course of its development. The problem had been shelved for some time and a First Five-Year Plan submitted by the Planning Board in 1967 had never been implemented. In 1971 the British firm of Colin Buchanan & Partners submitted a new plan which included three possible models of future population growth. Since the possibilities of granting Kuwaiti citizenship to local bedouin had been exhausted Kuwait was faced with the choice of extending it to some of the Arab immigrants (e.g. those born in Kuwait and perhaps also their parents) or becoming a continuously decreasing minority in their own country, as the rising demand for services of the Kuwaitis made it impractical to consider reducing the numbers of the non-Kuwaitis who provided them.

5. BAHRAIN

The Shaikhdom of Bahrain comprises a small group of low-lying limestone islands located in generally shallow waters some twenty miles off-shore from Saudi Arabia and from the Qatar peninsula. From over 500 drilled wells and natural springs sweet water is obtained in quantities which have always seemed inexhaustible and which, utilized for irrigation, has provided the basis for sedentary settlement for five millennia and encouraged the growth of the port of Manama on the main island of Bahrain and of the second most important island of Muharraq.

Of the 1971 population of approximately 216,000, over 80,000 is resident in Manama, some 35,000 in Muharraq, and almost 18,000 in Isa Town, a new town designed to accommodate about 35,000 by 1975. Both Sunni and Shii sects are represented in the population.

All executive and legislative power rests with the Ruler of Bahrain, Shaikh Isa ibn Sulman al-Khalifa, who is assisted by a Council of Administration composed of other members of the Ruling Family and the appointed heads of certain government departments. By various treaties, dating in the first instance from 1820, Great Britain had special responsibilities for defence and foreign affairs which were relinquished when Bahrain declared its independence in 1971.

RECENT HISTORY

In 1783 the chief family of the Utub tribe, the al-Khalifa, was instrumental in expelling the Iranians from Bahrain and became hereditary rulers. Iranian claims to sovereignty were based on their control of this region of the Gulf prior to that date. Until 1935 the history of Bahrain was closely associated with entrepôt trade and pearling and it is as a mercantile centre victualled by spring-watered agriculture that Bahrain developed. During the nineteenth century this fundamental charac-teristic involved Bahrain in the changing geopolitical scene in a new way. The British desire to maintain a free and fluid position in the Gulf ran counter to Ottoman and Iranian political claims and to German politico-economic ambitions; in 1861 Britain supported the indepen-dent sovereignty of Bahrain in return for anti-piracy and anti-slavery agreements. Further treaties in 1880 and 1892 resulted in the British Government assuming all responsibility for external affairs. Bahrain be-came the seat of the British Resident in the Gulf and of the Chief and Full Courts for the Gulf. Following the discovery of oil Bahrain became the first of the Gulf States to experience the difficulties of socio-economic change, particularly since 1948. In 1956 the first non-traditional ad-ministrative councils were established and in 1957 the powers of the Bahrain judiciary were extended to their present limits. Education and welfare services date from the 1920s, the earliest in the Gulf. These did not prevent Bahrain from being the scene of socio-political trouble, notably in 1956 when anti-British sentiment inflamed by the Suez affair exacerbated internal (but externally-encouraged) unrest, the outward manifestations usually taking the form of strikes in the oil industry.

No organized political opposition was tolerated by the Ruling Family and there was no move during the 1960s towards a more democratic form of government. However, serious political unrest was largely stifled by the island's prosperity during this decade as the educated Bahrainis who were the potential source of opposition to the regime devoted themselves to commercial enterprise. Nevertheless, the with-drawal of British protection was a matter of serious concern to the Ruling Family. Baathist and other radical elements were active in parts of the Gulf area and the Marxist opposition elements in Oman were regarded as a threat by all the shaikhly rulers. Bahrain took part in the negotiations for a federation of Arab Gulf states between 1968 and 1971 but finally opted for full independence because the other Rulers would not agree to allow Bahrain the preponderant position which Bahrainis felt that their population and degree of development allowed them.

In contrast to the effect of the British withdrawal Bahrain's sense of security was greatly enhanced by Iran's abandonment of its long-standing claim to the island. Following the Shah of Iran's agreement that Iran's claim should be referred to the UN, the UN under-secretary general Vittorio Guiccardi went to Bahrain in March 1970 to seek the views of the inhabitants and in his report said that the Bahrainis were virtually unanimous in wanting Bahrain to be a fully sovereign State; the great majority added that it should be an Arab state. This verdict was accepted by Iran.

THE ECONOMY

Bahrain has been an oil-exporter for longer than any other Arab state. Since shipments started in 1934 and the refinery began processing local crude in 1936 oil revenue has increased to over £7 million a year. Production, entirely by the Bahrain Petroleum Company—Bapco—(Caltex Group), is in the main from onshore wells but since 1964 the offshore field of Abu Saafa, shared with Saudi Arabia, has been of increasing importance. The future for oil seems uncertain since reserves are now rapidly declining and no significant new discoveries have been made. Natural gas, however, exists in considerable quantity and is the resource base for the most important new industrial development— aluminium smelting. An Anglo-Swedish consortium with a $27\frac{1}{2}$ per cent Bahrain financial interest (ALBA) has established a £30 million smelter with a capacity of 85,500 tons a year, the alumina being shipped from Australia. By 1972 this together with ancillary industries was providing full-time employment for 400, these ancillary industries being based on recent technological advances in the use of aluminium in 'atomized' and in plate form as protective covering. The oil refinery which has a throughput of 90 million barrels a year increasingly relies on Saudi oil, in 1968 three-quarters of the crude handled. Other aspects of diversification include plastics, modern fish-processing plant, and above all trade. During 1969 customs dues contributed over £2,500,000 to State revenue. Bahrain is also an important regional airport and telecommunications centre. Agriculture has steadily declined in importance as other employment possibilities have appeared but a revival based on the more efficient use of groundwater resources is planned. The Bahrain Development Bureau has been set up to encourage industrial investment.

1969 imports were valued at BD56,904,000 ($ = BD 0·459) while exports and re-exports, excluding oil, amounted to BD19,874,000. Britain remains Bahrain's chief supplier but Japan, as everywhere in the Middle East, has increased her share and is slightly ahead of the USA. Saudi Arabia is the chief trade recipient taking over 50 per cent of Bahraini exports and re-exports (half of these are textiles). The other main destinations lie in the Gulf, including Iran.

Almost 50 per cent of the occupied population is non-Bahraini, this immigrant group being most heavily employed in general labouring work and in the construction industry. Bapco employees and farmers are almost totally Bahraini.

Bahrain has pioneered much in the fields of education and social

services and has one of the most diversified social and economic structures. Industrial and service activities over a wide spectrum are the
main growth areas.

6. QATAR

The Shaikhdom of Qatar comprises the peninsula of that name lying
midway along the western coast of the Gulf. It has an area of about
4,000 square miles, with a population (in 1971) of just over 100,000, of
whom more than half were foreigners, including foreign Arabs. From
a shallow coastline the land rises to a low monotonous plateau. The only
natural water supply is from wells. Its only land frontier, with Saudi
Arabia and Abu Dhabi, has never been demarcated.

Economic development is concentrated in the capital Doha where
nearly all the population lives. Executive and legislative power is in the
hands of the ruling al-Thani family. In February 1972 the Ruler
Shaikh Ahmad ibn Ali al-Thani was ousted in a bloodless coup by his
cousin Shaikh Khalifa ibn Hamad al-Thani the Deputy Ruler, heir to
the throne, and Prime Minister.

From 1868 Qatar was an independent shaikhdom in treaty relationship with Britain which undertook its military defence and the conduct
of its external affairs. With Britain's final withdrawal from the Gulf in
1971 and the breakdown of negotiations for the creation of a federation
with Bahrain and the Trucial Coast states, Qatar decided to opt for
complete independence.

RECENT HISTORY

An agreement with Britain of 3 November 1916 had provisions similar
to those with other Trucial shaikhs, and included a clause making the
grant of pearling concessions or other monopolies dependent on British
consent. Relations are close with Saudi Arabia, whose rulers are also
Wahhabis, and with Dubai, with which the al-Thani family is linked
by friendship and marriage, but relations with the neighbouring island
of Bahrain have not been good since Qatar seized in 1937 the ruined
village of Zubara, on the Qatar Peninsula, which is claimed to be the
ancestral home of the Ruling Family of Bahrain. Qatar's refusal to join
a federation of Arab Gulf Shaikhdoms which seemed likely to be
dominated by Bahrain was the principal reason for its opting for complete independence. The size of its population allows Qatar to attain
the normally accepted minimum qualifications for membership of the
United Nations.

Shaikh Ahmad ibn Ali al-Thani, who succeeded his father Shaikh Ali ibn Abdullah ibn Qasim al-Thani on his abdication in 1960, was ousted in a bloodless coup in February 1972 by his cousin Shaikh Khalifa ibn Hamad al-Thani who endeavoured to create a more dynamic and efficient administration.

THE ECONOMY

At one time pearl fishing and nomadic herding provided a primitive population with the bare means of subsistence, and the decline of the pearling industry from about 1930 reduced it to even greater poverty. The discovery of oil transformed the situation entirely. Doha has been rebuilt and social services provided for the entire population.

The first oil concession in the area was obtained in 1935 by Petroleum Development (Qatar), later renamed the Qatar Petroleum Company (QPC). Oil was struck in 1939 in the Dokhan structure but drilling was interrupted until 1948 by the war. Production began in 1950 with 1·6 million tons and then rose steadily to about 8 million tons. It reached a peak of 9·36 million tons in 1969 and declined to 8·88 million tons in 1970. According to present estimates, the field will be exhausted by 1975. A pipeline connects QPC's producing field with the terminal at Umm Said on the east coast.

The 'continental shelf' offshore area, east of Qatar and outside the three-mile limit, was conceded for development in 1952 to Shell Overseas Exploration Ltd. A storm in 1956 wrecked the offshore drilling platform. Drilling was resumed in 1959 and two fields were discovered. The operating company, Shell Company of Qatar, began production in 1966 at an initial rate of 5 million tons. The output of these fields is expected to replace that of the declining Dokhan field on land.

In August 1971 the Belgian Oil Corporation was granted a 30-year concession to explore for oil and natural gas in an area of 4,630 square miles covering the whole of Qatar and its territorial waters except for the Dokhan region. In 1961 Qatar joined the Organization of Petroleum Exporting Countries.

In 1971 QPC embarked on a £25 million scheme to liquefy and export natural gas from the Dokhan field. A plant capable of processing 800,000 tons of gas for export from the Umm Said terminal is due for completion in 1974. Dokhan natural gas is already used for the distillation of sea-water.

Local market gardening has been encouraged and Qatar is now self-sufficient in vegetables. A modern international airport has been built at Doha, and Doha Port has been deepened and modernized. But prospects for diversifying the economy are severely limited. A shrimp processing plant and a cement plant using local materials have been built.

Oil revenues have been used to provide schools and hospitals for the whole population and in 1972 plans were being made to open a university.

7. THE TRUCIAL STATES[1]

The Trucial States consist of seven sovereign states, Abu Dhabi, Ajman, Dubai, Fujaira, Ras al-Khaima, Sharja, and Umm al-Qaiwain. Their territories lie on the southern shores of the Gulf, extending eastwards to the Gulf of Oman. Following a series of treaties between individual rulers and Great Britain, dating from 1820, the UK Government has assumed responsibility for defence, for settling inter-state disputes and for external affairs.

In addition to the following, further information is given, individually, for Abu Dhabi and Dubai (pp. 203 and 202).

The Trucial Gulf coast, extending between Qatar and the rocky headlands of the Ras Musandum headland (in the State of Oman) is characterized by shallow seas, a fringe of sand bars, coral reefs and islands, and by stretches of *sabkha*, saline/alkaline mudflats. Wherever groundwater seepage has allowed human settlement on relatively firm sandspits, bars, and islands then small marine-based communities have become established. At Dubai, Ras al-Khaima and Sharja, the presence of creeks encouraged greater than average growth based on Gulf and long-distance trade. Inland lies a zone of inhospitable sand desert which grades into an arid gravel and silt outwash belt at the foot of the Omani mountains. Where this belt opens on to the coast at Ras al-Khaima settlement extends inland from the sea. Where water from the highlands percolates at shallow depths into this belt then oasis agriculture, on a large scale in the Buraimi complex, has been established. The spinal mountains themselves are inhospitably rugged except for small upland valleys and basins where surface water derived from higher rainfall supports grazing and crops. On the east coast rugged headlands alternate with small embayments in which communities subsist on fishing and garden-oases. Khawr Fakkan, the only true port, has grown around one of the few safe harbourages. Aridity is general, and on the coasts high summer temperatures and humidity make the climate very oppressive. Drier air and greater temperature ranges characterize the interior.

Approximately half the population may be described as urban and is concentrated on the Gulf coast. The 1968 census gave the following population totals for the states and the chief towns: Abu Dhabi 46,500 (township 22,000); Ajman 4,200; Dubai 59,000 (township 57,400);

[1] From 1972 known as the United Arab Emirates.

Fujaira 9,700; Ras al-Khaima 24,500 (township 5,240); Sharja 31,50
(township 20,600); Umm al-Qaiwain 3,700. The urban populations of
the four largest states have all grown significantly since 1968. In the
interior, apart from al-Ain in Abu Dhabi, the population lives in oasis
villages of up to about 1,000 inhabitants. Non-Arab immigrants are
numerous.

Each Ruler has absolute power over his own subjects, this power
being exercised through traditional institutions. Each State has full
sovereignty save for the limitations of British treaty responsibilities for
external affairs. From 1960 a Trucial States Council on which all
Rulers were represented met regularly to discuss problems of mutual
interest and to co-ordinate various activities. Its executive arm was the
Development Office financed principally by the Ruler of Abu Dhabi
and the UK Government.

Following the announcement by Britain in early 1968 that its forces
would be withdrawn from the area by late 1971 various discussions
concerning federation took place between the seven Trucial States,
Bahrain, and Qatar. Difficulties arose principally because of the disparities in size, wealth, sophistication and oil expectations between the
nine states which exacerbated the differences stemming from local
tribal loyalties.

At a meeting of the Rulers of the seven Trucial States held in Dubai
on 10–18 July 1971 it was announced that six of them—Abu Dhabi,
Ajman, Dubai, Fujaira, Sharja and Umm al-Qaiwain—had agreed to
form a federation. Membership of the federation was left open to Ras
al-Khaima, Bahrain, and Qatar. Ras al-Khaima, the only Trucial
State to reject the federation, did so because it was refused veto powers.
It changed its mind and accepted in 1972.

RECENT HISTORY

The British presence in the Trucial Region derives from the quasi
official status of East India Company agents in the Gulf during the
early eighteenth century. From 1770 onwards the Royal Navy became
increasingly active in the protection of maritime trade and expeditionary forces were landed in Ras al-Khaima, where Qasimi power was
strong, several times in the early nineteenth century. Treaties signed in
the 1820s binding the Rulers to refrain from piracy, developed into
annual truces negotiated through the Gulf Political Residency and the
Resident's Agency established at Sharja in 1823. Suppression of the
slave trade was the purpose of other British diplomatic interventions
while local and dynastic disputes, while not eliminated, became less
frequent. In 1892 various factors which included apprehension of
Turkish and Iranian infiltration, alarm at French activity, and concern
at the growing influence of Russia in Iran, caused the British Govern-

ment to conclude the so-called Exclusive Agreements with the Rulers of the Trucial States. In them the Rulers agreed never to cede any part of their territory except to the British Government, not to enter into agreements with any government other than the British and not to admit foreign representatives without British consent. A similar treaty was signed with Qatar in 1916 which carried a definite assurance of British protection (as had been done to Bahrain in 1861). No such assurance was ever given to the Trucial States although there was an implicit obligation on the British Government to protect them in return for the very considerable concessions the Rulers made and no British Government ever attempted to argue that there was not. Fujaira, which had formerly been part of Sharja, became independent in the early years of this century, and was admitted, at her Ruler's insistent request, to the Trucial system in 1952.

From 1892 onwards the Rulers conducted all their external affairs through the British Government, and local Political Officers were finally superseded by a Political Agent in 1953. Since the British Government's main aim was to maintain internal security, a central military force capable of intervening in inter-State disputes was established in 1953, the Trucial Oman Scouts. Active in 1953 and 1955 in the Buraimi area, in Oman at various periods since 1957, and the Fujaira–Ras al-Khaima frontiers in 1959 as well as on many more minor peace-keeping missions, the Scouts, with both Arab and British officers, were able to maintain stability effectively. The base for the British military forces was in Sharja. The expansion of Imperial Airways led to an airstrip being established in 1932 and in 1940 it became an RAF base. After 1945 Sharja became the main air-staging base for the Gulf and following the British withdrawal from Aden there was in addition an army build-up. This considerable base was abandoned as part of the British withdrawal from the Gulf in 1971.

In the 1970s Britain had maintained stability in the area for nearly a century but at the same time it had helped to create a political problem of the first magnitude. In recognizing and making treaties with these tiny states and defining their boundaries, Britain effectively froze them in their nineteenth-century condition. Without the British presence they would almost certainly have been swallowed by a neighbouring power such as Saudi Arabia. As it was, when the inevitable time came for the quasi-imperial British presence to be withdrawn, the Trucial States were clearly unsuited for independence while the very fact of the British presence had enabled the Rulers to postpone consideration of uniting to form a larger federation. At the same time, Britain's power to intervene in their internal affairs was limited. 'While the obligations Britain has incurred towards the littoral principalities are, in many cases, those of a colonial rather than a protecting power, she does not possess the legal attributes, particularly that of political

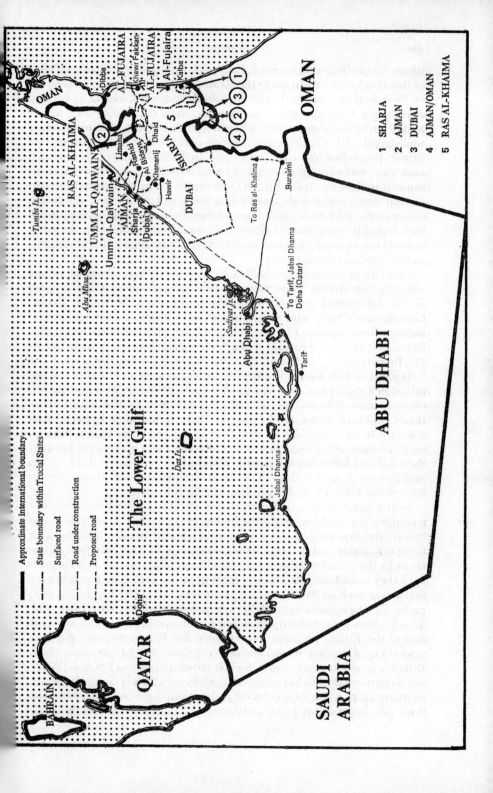

The Lower Gulf

QATAR

BAHRAIN

Doha

SAUDI ARABIA

ABU DHABI

Jabal Dhanna

Das Is.

Tarif

Abu Dhabi

Sadiyat Is.

To Tarif, Jabal Dhanna
Doha (Qatar)

To Ras al-Khaima

Hawir

DUBAI

Sharja
(Dubai)

AJMAN

Khananij

Al Bidaya

Dhaid

Rashid

Umm Al-Qaiwain

Umm Al-Qaiwain

Ummana

SHARJA

Buraimi

RAS AL-KHAIMA

Abu Musa

Tumbs Is.

OMAN

Dibba

AL-FUJAIRA

Khawr Fakkan

Al-Fujaira

Kalba

AL-FUJAIRA

OMAN

① SHARJA
② AJMAN
③ DUBAI
④ AJMAN/OMAN
⑤ RAS AL-KHAIMA

— Approximate international boundary
--- State boundary within Trucial States
——— Surfaced road
——— Road under construction
---- Proposed road

sovereignty, which would enable her to discharge those obligations effectively.'[1] Britain might have done more to urge the Rulers to form a federation but it is doubtful whether it would have been effective.

The British Labour Government's announcement in January 1968 of its decision to withdraw entirely from the Gulf by 1971 caused the Rulers at once to reconsider their position and an agreement in principle for a union of the seven Trucial States, Qatar, and Bahrain was signed in February 1968. But from this point little progress was made despite the strong encouragement of the British, Kuwaiti, and Saudi governments. Three provisional constitutions were proposed but none was ratified. There were external problems such as Saudi Arabia's claim to the Buraimi Oasis and a large slice of Abu Dhabi's territory, and Iran's claim to three islands in the Gulf, two of which, the Greater and Lesser Tumb, belong in the view of Arab and British governments to Ras al-Khaima and one (Abu Musa) to Sharja. Iranian forces occupied Abu Musa in November 1971 in accordance with an agreement with the Ruler of Sharja providing for Iranian troops to remain stationed in certain parts of the island while the rest remained under the Ruler's jurisdiction. Oil revenues will be shared by Iran and Sharja if oil is discovered. Iranian forces also occupied the two Tumbs but without the agreement of the Ruler of Ras al-Khaima. But it was the internal difficulties which were more serious. There was disagreement over the type of representation on the proposed Federal Council (such as whether it should be proportional to population), the site of the federal capital, the rights of individual states to maintain their own security forces, and on the size of the states' contributions to the federal budget. The basis of all these problems was the position of Bahrain. This has smaller oil revenues than Qatar, Abu Dhabi, or Dubai but it has a much larger population, a greater number of educated people, and more administrative experience than all the rest, hence their fear that Bahrain would dominate the federation. After three-and-a-half years of fruitless negotiations Bahrain and Qatar opted for complete independence and six of the Trucial States agreed to a federation between themselves. Ras al-Khaima, the only Trucial State with significant agricultural resources and with better oil prospects than the four without oil, decided to remain outside but changed its mind in 1972.

THE ECONOMY

The most important factors in the region as a whole have been the work of the Trucial States Council's Development Office and, in part through this Office, financial and technical assistance from Britain, Kuwait, and Saudi Arabia. After 1965 there was a rapid build-up of development expenditure through the Council. This was mainly

[1] J. B. Kelly, *St. Antony's Papers, 1958*.

concentrated on inter-State projects such as road building, technical education, health and agricultural advisory services, and on the five states without oil revenue. 1968 expenditure totalled about £2 million. After the creation of the United Arab Emirates in 1971 its Government took over the functions of the Development Office. Kuwaiti assistance has chiefly taken the form of setting up schools and medical centres while Saudi Arabia has financed major roadworks, housing, and agricultural projects. Excluding Dubai and Abu Dhabi the states' revenues are obtained from low ad valorem import taxes, traditional tribal contributions, and the sale of postage stamps.

DUBAI

The Amirate of Dubai is a compact territory almost entirely composed of sand desert and with a *sabkha* fringed coast broken by Dubai creek which provides safe anchorage for vessels of up to 10 feet draught. From the nucleus of old Dubai, situated on a spit head at the mouth of the creek, the town has now expanded along the sides of the creek and south along the coast. A new deep water port, constructed near old Dubai ensures that the present commercial supremacy in the southern Gulf will not be adversely affected by technical problems. The Ruler of Dubai exercises direct rule in the State. Because of the importance of Dubai Town, the most important administrative body in the state is the Dubai Municipal Council originally founded in 1957 and given a Charter and corporate existence in 1961. The Council of sixteen appointed members represents different sections of the community. Its decisions must be ratified by the Ruler but with his consent the Council makes Local Orders, has power to make contracts and own land, and administers this most important element in the State through specialized committees and paid officials. A Lands Committee has responsibility for land registration and transactions and is an entity independent of the Municipality.

Recent History

Dubai shaikhdom was established by the secession in the early nineteenth century of a section of the Al bu Falah branch of the Bani Yas from the Abu Dhabi tribal complex. This assertion of independence was essentially a statement of the trading orientation of the people inhabiting the shores of Dubai creek but remained disputed into the late 1950s and conflicts with Abu Dhabi and Sharja were not infrequent. Shaikh Rashi, Regent between 1939 and 1958 and now Ruler, has directed his State continuously along the path of commercial and trade development and Dubai has had a politically unexciting but rewarding thirty year history of consistent, single-minded progress which has made it, even without oil, the leading City State.

Economy

The economy of Dubai until very recently was almost entirely based on international trade and trade of such a type that normal economic mensuration at all levels becomes largely meaningless. During 1970, officially listed imports of £86 million were eight times larger than exports and re-exports. Customs dues levied on most imported goods at 4⅝ per cent produced a revenue to the State of almost £3 million, the single largest item, and the value of imports rising by an average of 100 per cent every two years between 1962 and 1969. Not included in the normal customs statistics is the trade in gold although trade in bullion is perfectly legal. Dubai merchants annually purchase between £50–£70 million of gold each year, most of which is smuggled into India (and Pakistan) at premiums of 10–30 per cent. The direct effect of this trade on Dubai income is significant but not quantifiable; indirectly it has contributed towards making Dubai the financial and trading centre of the southern Gulf.

Oil was first discovered in the Fatah offshore field in 1966 and production started in 1968 by the Dubai Petroleum Company. Oil revenue accruing to Dubai has now risen to an annual rate of £18 million and will rise rapidly following the completion of a revolutionary type of storage and tanker-loading installation sixty miles offshore.

Trade and oil, in the absence of virtually all other resources are likely to make Dubai the leading commercial centre in any Trucial Federation and even one of the great commercial cities of the southern Middle East.

In 1968 almost 500,000 tons of cargo were landed by ship and aircraft in spite of the necessity of offshore lightering all ships of over 800 tons burden; this amount of cargo was expected to double by late 1972 as the new deepwater port becomes fully operational. The main imported commodities are household and consumer goods, food and clothing, machinery and vehicles. Japan is the main supplier, with Britain a close second. Over 60 per cent of Japanese goods consist of clothing; approximately half of British and American goods are machinery; while Swiss commodities are almost entirely household goods. Trade with other Gulf regions consists mainly of re-exports of manufactures and imports of food and raw materials.

ABU DHABI

The Amirate of Abu Dhabi extends along the shoal southern coast of the Gulf between the states of Qatar and Dubai and into the mainly sand desert interior of the Empty Quarter. Until recently the only areas at all attractive to human settlement were some of the two hundred islands, including that of Abu Dhabi itself, on which small fishing and trading communities existed, the oasis complexes of Liwa, near the Saudi Arabian frontier, and Buraimi, on the edge of the Oman mountain ranges and the border of the State of Oman. Abu Dhabi is now connected by a causeway with the mainland. Das Island is the headquarters of the offshore oil extracting companies. Sir Bani Yas Island possessing deep waters is an oilport facing the Dhanna oil terminal of the inland Murban oilfield. Al-Ain is the centre of a developing agricultural area in the Buraimi region. There are no material resources other than limited groundwater, marine oyster-pearl-banks and oil, export of which started in 1963 and which is revolutionizing the Amirate.

Almost half the population is located in the seaport capital and this proportion is growing as inhabitants from parts of the interior, the Liwa oases in particular, move to the centre of economic growth. The population of the oil centres, Das Island, Dhanna, and Tarif is 2,500 and growing. Al-Ain, the official residence of the Ruler is being developed as a full urban centre whilst to the east the new town of Zayed is under construction. The indigenous population still sets store by tribal groupings which consist of the Bani Yas, the al-Manasir, al-Dhawahir and al-Awamer tribes. The Rulers of the Amirate are members of the al-Nihyan branch of the Bani Yas.

The Ruler of Abu Dhabi, Shaikh Zayed ibn Sultan al-Nihyan, possesses all executive and legislative power. Through Decrees dating from 1966 have been established a number of Government departments with specialized administrative responsibilities, and the Ruler appoints Chairman and Directors of these departments and through his Diwan exercises central authority. In 1968 a Planning Council was established with the Ruler as President, appointed members consisting of departmental Chairmen and Directors and seven others.

Recent History

By the end of the eighteenth century the land-based tribal group of the Bani Yas under Shaikh Isa ibn Nihyan had made the island of Abu Dhabi with its wells of potable water their main centre, while the al-Dhawahir tribe remained in the Buraimi region. The Amirate since then has remained in the al-Nihyan line during which time Shaikh Zayed ibn Khalifa (Zayed al-Kabir) during the latter half of the nineteenth century established sovereignty over what is approximately the present territory of the State, in particular establishing a *modus vivendi* with the State of Oman which left al-Buraimi proper in the Sultanate and brought al-Ain, Qattara, and Hili into the Amirate.

Between 1909 and 1928 the Amirate was ruled by Zayed the Great's sons on a provincial basis and for the period between 1928 and 1960, under Shaikh Shakbut ibn Sultan, the Amirate remained little changed. Abu Dhabi, a low-grade fishing port, was the residence of the Ruler, while al-Ain with its *falaj*-based traditional agriculture was administered and developed by the Ruler's brother Shaikh Zayed. Border disputes between Abu Dhabi, Dubai, Oman, and Saudi Arabia were not infrequent and British intervention was regularly necessary. In 1966 Shaikh Shakbut, overwhelmed by the problems of oil affluence, was deposed by family agreement (with British encouragement) and succeeded by Shaikh Zayed the present ruler. Since 1966 the history of Abu Dhabi has been marked by increasingly successful domestic policies of social and economic development, pacific and generous dealings with its Trucial neighbours, and a growing international stature in the Arab world and beyond.

Shaikh Zayed has established a well equipped defence force, independent of the Trucial and Oman Scouts. This includes armoured land units, naval patrol boats, and an embryo air force. The total armed force numbers approximately 4,000.

Economy

Before the discovery of oil in 1960 the economy of Abu Dhabi was extremely poor. The difficult coast prevented all but the most limited marine activity, including pearl fishing, while inland subsistence agriculture at al-Ain and Liwa was the only alternative to desert nomadism. Abu Dhabi is now the twelfth largest oil producer in the world and her proven oil reserves are approximately one-third of those of the North American continent.

Unlike Dubai, Abu Dhabi has neither the tradition of large-scale marine trade nor the physical suitability for it, but it does possess agricultural potential in the Buraimi region. The main elements in present economic development are therefore expenditure on urban modernization at Abu Dhabi town, al-Ain, and the new city of Zayed.

Oil revenue in 1970 totalled almost £90 million, approximately £1,800 per head of the population. Oil production is controlled by five main groups: (1) Abu Dhabi Petroleum Co. (IPC associate); (2) the ENI, Phillips, Aminoil Consortium onshore; (3) Abu Dhabi Maritime Areas (BP and CFP); (4) Mitsubishi; and (5) a Japanese consortium offshore. The main producing fields hitherto have been at Murban and near Das Island. In the last concession agreement (Mitsubishi 1968) a commitment to construct a refinery is included and the development of petro-chemical industries is planned for the future.

The Five-Year Plan for the period 1968–72 assumed a total allocation of over £250 millions with the following sectoral allocations:

(percentages)

Communications	24	Education	5
Municipalities (inc. utilities)	17	Public buildings	3
Electricity & desalination	14	Health	2
Industries	6	Tourism	2
Housing	5	Labour	1
Agriculture	5	Loans & investment	17

Abu Dhabi already has an international airport and is in the proce ss of constructing major harbour facilities. Exports, almost entirely of oil, are shipped from Jabal, Dhanna and Das Island; imports in 1970 were valued at approximately £25 million. A full radio and television service is in operation.

The high level of expenditure on development and the Abu Dhabi Defence Force created a serious budget deficit in 1969/70 but this was remedied by more prudent financial policies and an increase in oil revenues to about £135 million in 1971 as a consequence of the Tehran OPEC agreements with the oil companies.

8. OMAN

The State (or Sultanate) of Oman extends over a territory of some 82,000 square miles of south-east Arabia. Trucial Oman, separated from the main area of the Sultanate, occupies the rugged highlands of the Ras Musandum peninsula. The remainder of the Sultanate extends for some 200 miles along the south Arabian coast to the borders of South Yemen, and stretches inland to the Rub al-Khali, the Empty Quarter.

Until recently the economy of the Sultanate was based simply upon pastoral nomadism, agriculture, and traditional trading in the Gulf and the Indian Ocean. In this traditional economy was reflected the regional diversity of generally rather limited resources.

On the Batina littoral small coastal plains support a series of equally small settlements dependent both on irrigation agriculture (in which date production is dominant) and fishing. Muscat, the capital city, owes its eminence to its long history as a safe harbour on a difficult coast and to the participation of its inhabitants in the millennia-old coastal sea-traffic. South of Muscat the littoral becomes increasingly inhospitable, cliffs and small embayments giving way to desertic lagoon and *sabkha*-fringed coastlands. Only in the southern province of Dhufar around Salala does sedentary agriculture reappear in the coastal lowland. Here water from the surrounding ranges of Jabal Qara, which receive monsoon rains, provides the basis for the largest concentration of farming population in the whole of the Sultanate.

In the interior predominantly gravel desert capable of supporting only a very small population of bedouin tribesmen merges with the emptiness of the Rub al-Khali. West of Muscat however, between the desert and the sea, the land rises to the rugged Jabal Akhdhar ranges where precipitation is far higher than the otherwise normal annual total of some three or four inches. Still largely unknown outside of the State of Oman this highland region has immemorially supported village farming populations on seasonally good pasture, rain-fed cereals, and a great range of other crops. This region, even more than the Batina coast lowlands and Dhufar, is orientated towards local and tribal subsistence rather than to the outside world.

The predominantly hostile environment of the Sultanate has impressed itself on the life of the people. Nomadism, traditionally dominant over most of the territory, is not normally associated with socio-economic stability, and the areas which do have sedentary settlements have been cut off from each other by the negative nature of the intervening wastelands and by the absence of sufficient wealth to overcome the natural difficulties.

Until 1958 Government revenue was derived almost entirely from customs receipts. Since total exports then totalled some £900,000, half of which consisted of dates, and since imports were of the same order the income of the State was relatively limited. Between 1958 and 1967 British financial assistance was made available for a variety of development purposes and since 1956 expenditure by oil exploration companies has on an increasing scale contributed to the income of the state.

The recent history of Oman has been bedevilled not only by poverty and an inclement environment but also by political instability which was in part a consequence of the nature of society.

Muscat and Dhufar, as with the port-towns of the Gulf, traditionally existed in the two worlds of the sea and the desert. Maritime influences were foreign in the main until the eighteenth century. The mariners of the ancient world and of medieval Islam were succeeded by the Portuguese who established a naval and trading station at Muscat in 1508. In 1650 they were expelled by the local Arabs, whose regime grew in strength until by 1730 it had acquired the Portuguese possessions in East Africa, including Mombasa and Zanzibar. After a brief interlude of Iranian rule and a time of internal confusion, the Al Bu Said dynasty succeeded to these possessions and guided Muscat to the zenith of its power. The realm was divided (1861) among sons, Zanzibar and the East African possessions forming one sultanate, Muscat and Oman the other. The present Sultan, Qabus ibn Said, is the fourteenth of his dynasty.

The present Sultan's father Said ibn Taimur, inherited an empty treasury, an annual budget revenue of some £50,000 against which had to be set all State expenditure and large loan repayments, as well as a most uneasy political situation, the background to which is important to our present understanding of the situation.

The majority of the inhabitants of Oman are adherents of the Ibadhi sect of Islam whose leader has normally (though not necessarily) been an elected Imam. The present dynasty was founded in 1744 by Imam

Ahmad ibn Said who, himself an Ibadhi, expelled the Iranians from the territory. Two groups of tribes, the Ghafiris and the Hinawis, who inhabited an interior undemarcated by frontier lines, never completely accepted the authority of Imam Ahmad, an authority which became increasingly based on the maritime resources of the coast but which required for its full effectiveness the allegiance of the desert and mountain tribes.

Imam Ahmad was succeeded on his death in 1783 by his son Said who, a year later, as a result of tribal pressure was supplanted as temporal leader by his own son Hamad, but who retained the religious functions of the Imamate. This separation of the two functions, temporal and spiritual, was no novelty but on this occasion occurred at a critical time for the territory.

Imam Ahmad ibn Said, himself a merchant and shipowner, had been responsible for the resurgence of Arab power on the coast. His grandson Hamad as secular ruler established his capital at the port of Muscat and henceforth the interior tribal centres such as Rostaq and Nizwa became secondary centres of power. Hamad and his successors adopted the title of Sayyid or Lord to distinguish themselves from Imam Said who retained his office until his death in 1821. The title Sultan was added at a later date by visiting Europeans. During the nineteenth century the differences between the dynastic rulers and the tribal factions became more and more associated with differences between the ocean-orientated coast and the desert and mountain interior, a situation strikingly similar to that in thirteenth and fourteenth century Spanish Aragon. The struggle between the Sultanate and the Ghafiri and Hinawi was exacerbated by the intervention of the desert Wahhabis from what is now Saudi Arabia and the position was further complicated by dissension among the Ibadhis themselves. Wahhabi raids were to some extent controlled by British intervention from Egypt, intervention designed to minimize conflict in a region of growing importance to the Empire. Because the Pax Britannica involved the area in the problems of suppressing the slave trade and because it encouraged sea-trading it tended to emphasize the secular aspects of Muscat rule, and as a result the Sultanate became even more alien and suspect to conservative religious zealots and even more vulnerable to ambitious tribal leaders. In 1895 Muscat was attacked and sacked by a temporary coalition of hostile interests. The true climax of conflict however was not reached until 1913 when the Ghafiri and Hinawi sank their differences for long enough to elect Salim ibn Rashid to the Imamate which effectively had been vacant since 1821.

A series of confused conflicts led to varying swings of fortune but the Sultanate retained control at Muscat and gradually events moved towards negotiation. Through the good offices of the British Political Agent in Muscat a number of tribal shaikhs and the Sultan's representatives met at Sib and an Agreement was signed in September 1920. The general authority of the Sultan in the territory of Oman was recognized in a variety of ways, particularly in external matters and in dealings with foreign administrations concerning law and questions of status. However, the Imamate remained in the hands of the Hinawi and from that day to this the extent of the Imam's administrative power in the interior has become a matter in which internal dissentients and foreign interventionists have found opportunity for stirring up trouble. The Government of the Sultan of Oman has consistently maintained the view that the Agreement of Sib recognized the Imamate as autonomous only in the sphere of local and essentially socio-religious administration, and for some thirty years, during which the first oil concession was awarded, a reasonable *modus vivendi* existed between the Sultan and the shaikhs of the interior.

First in 1952 but more seriously between 1954 and 1957 problems of realpolitik reappeared in a more dangerous and less traditional form. In the Buraimi region there arose the classic problem of establishing formal frontier lines in relatively remote areas where tribal loyalties are dominant, and now sovereign states were involved as well as clan groupings—Saudi Arabia, Oman, and the Trucial States with their special relationship with Britain. The second factor was that of oil. Exploration during the early 1950s rapidly extended into the interior and by 1954 arrangements were being made with local tribes such as the Duru for geological operations. The area concerned lay one hundred and fifty miles west of Muscat and relatively near to Nizwa, the headquarters of Imam Ghalib ibn Ali elected in 1954 by a group of shaikhs mainly of the Hinawi. The combination of the lure of oil wealth, Saudi intrigues, and the traditional tribal struggles tempted Ghalib into military and political action in which the third factor, that of changing attitudes in the Arab world as a whole, appeared for the first time. Ghalib maintained that the Imam not the Sultan held sway in the interior region, challenged the validity of the oil concession grant, sent levies into Duru territory and applied for membership of and recognition by the Arab League.

This challenge was swiftly met and by the end of 1955 Ghalib's forces had been ejected from Ibri (the principal Duru town), and the Imam himself had been forced to flee from Nizwa. A separate operation, in conjunction with the ruler of Abu Dhabi, had led to the re-occupation of that part of the Buraimi oasis complex which had been seized by a Saudi Arabian raiding party. No action was taken by the Arab League and all the tribal leaders in Oman declared allegiance to the Sultan. The Imam was allowed to remain in his village, apparently shorn of authority. His brother Talib however fled to Saudi Arabia and other supporters including Isa ibn Salih, a Hinawi leader, found sanctuary in Egypt. From these bases propaganda campaigns of the anti-colonial and anti-British variety were mounted and in 1957 Talib entered central Oman with a motley band of followers which had been recruited and trained in Saudi Arabia and partly financed from Egypt. Imam Ghalib and Sulaiman ibn Himyar emerged to lead the insurrection.

The Sultan for the first time formally requested British treaty aid. The Trucial Oman Scouts and a few hundred British troops with air-support assisted the Sultan's forces in suppressing the rebellion. Internal support for the rebels did not materialize and within a few weeks they were reduced to small-scale guerrilla action from the more remote and intractable central regions of the Jabal Akhdhar massif from which they were not ejected until 1959. Guerrilla activity on the other hand con-tinued on a declining scale, with occasional attacks with explosives on road traffic and for a period on shipping also. In spite of the collapse of the rebellion, other Arab countries, with differing motivations, raised the matter with the United Nations in 1960 and 1961. The charge was made that Britain had carried out armed aggression against 'the inde-pendence, sovereignty, and territorial integrity of the Imamate of Oman', it being further argued that this constituted an independent State distinguishable from the Sultanate and that its inhabitants were fighting for that independence. A UN Commission of Inquiry did not support Arab charges of oppressive government and widespread oppo-sition against the Sultanate but in December 1965 the Arab states succeeded in having a resolution adopted by the UN General Assembly which among other things considered that the colonial presence of the UK prevented the people from exercising their rights of self-determination and called for the elimination of British domination in any form.

The situation of Oman was radically transformed by the discovery of oil in commercial quantities and the first exports in July 1967. Ex-ploration first started in 1956 in Fahud but it was not found in com-mercial quantities until 1962 when strikes were made at Yibal and later at Nitah and Fahud. Petroleum Development Oman (PDO) handles all on-shore drilling, with Shell holding 85 per cent, the Compagnie Française des Pétroles (CFP) 10 per cent and Partex (the Gulbenkian interests) 5 per cent. In 1960 BP, CFP, Esso, and Mobil withdrew from their parts of the original investment following a series of disappoint-ments and the apparent loss of over £12 million; CFP later bought its way back in after viability of exploitation and transportation seemed assured. Since 1967 PDO has invested over £60 million in exploration and development, much of which was expended on the 170 mile pipe-line from the three neighbouring fields to Mina al-Fahal, 50 miles to the north of Muscat where an offshore tanker terminal, capable of handling the largest ships now projected, has been built. Production is expected shortly to rise to some 300,000 barrels a day of low sulphur content crude oil from the present level of approximately 150,000 b.p.d.

The only offshore concession is held by a consortium of companies including Shell and CFP (20 per cent, and 12½ per cent respectively) but headed by the West German Wintershall group with 25 per cent. Exploratory drilling has commenced at Malaha, 124 miles north of Muscat.

In January 1968, as State revenues began to increase, the Sultan made a statement in which preliminary investment plans were announced publicly for the first time, and it was proposed to create a Development Council with budgetary, planning, and implementation responsibilities. But Sultan Said ibn Taimur was in favour of keeping social and economic change to a snail's pace. Three years after oil revenues began rising the Sultanate, with an estimated population of between 750,000 and a million still had only three primary schools with about 100 pupils. There was one hospital at Matrah (belonging to an American Protestant mission) and a score of dispensaries in various parts of the country in the charge of a handful of doctors dealing with a population ridden with a variety of endemic diseases such as malaria, leprosy, tuberculosis, and trachoma. Infant mortality was among the highest in the world (80 per cent according to one estimate).

The Sultan's rule was autocratic and authoritarian in the extreme. He personally issued all visas which were kept severely restricted. Government officials and all women were only allowed to leave the country with special permission. He forbade the inhabitants of the interior to visit the coastal areas and the reverse. The only surfaced road was the few miles between Muscat and Matrah. Dancing, smoking, and the playing of musical instruments were all forbidden. Three hours after dusk the gates of Muscat were closed and no one could leave or enter until dawn.

Said ibn Taimur was gifted, intelligent, and of considerable personal charm but the extreme reactionary nature of his rule stimulated opposition and alarmed his fellow rulers of Arabia who saw that it encouraged subversion. Apart from the continuing sporadic insurrection of the followers of the ex-Imam Ghalib, a Dhufar Liberation Movement started in 1965 in the southernmost province and became increasingly radical with active Chinese support. The Sultan, however, remained almost continuously in Salala on the coast of Dhufar, relying for protection on his army, the Sultan's Armed Forces (SAF) which was commanded by British officers on secondment with a number of Pakistani NCOs.

Said ibn Taimur was overthrown on 23 July 1970 in a palace coup led by his only son Qabus ibn Said who since his return from being educated in England had been kept virtually under house arrest by his father. Amid great public rejoicing Sultan Qabus undertook to introduce 'modern and forceful' government and announced the removal of his father's ban on smoking, dancing, and the wearing of Western dress. His uncle Tariq ibn Taimur returned from exile to head the new Government. The revolutionary opposition was divided in its attitude to the new Sultan. Some declared their loyalty but others described him as an imperialist puppet. Nearly all the British officers and Government officials remained in the service of Sultan Qabus. The war against the Dhufar Liberation Front was pursued and military expenditure absorbed about half the oil revenues of approximately £50 million.

III

Egypt

THE LAND AND THE PEOPLE

Egypt is about the same size as Spain and France with an area of 363,000 square miles. Of these, only 13,000 square miles, consisting mainly of the Nile valley, are cultivable and inhabitable; the rest is desert.

The Nile valley consists of:

(a) Lower Egypt, being the Nile Delta with its apex at Cairo and its base the Mediterranean coast between Alexandria and Port Said.

(b) Upper Egypt, being a strip of irrigated land in the Nile valley averaging about 20 miles wide, and stretching from Cairo to the Sudan frontier at Wadi Halfa.

The area of cultivation is divided about equally between Upper and Lower Egypt.

Apart from the Nile valley, there is the Canal Zone, consisting of a narrow strip of land some 100 miles long made cultivable and inhabitable by the Sweet Water Canal, by which drinking and irrigation water is brought across the desert from the Nile. There are also the five oases—Kharga, Dakhla, Faiyum, Farafra, and Siwa.

Egypt lies between latitude 32° N. on the Mediterranean coast, and 22° N. at Wadi Halfa. In Upper Egypt there is virtually no rainfall; in the Delta there is a slight winter rainfall which gradually increases towards the Mediterranean coast. Cultivation, and indeed the possibility of any life at all, in Egypt is entirely dependent on the Nile which rises in flood between July and October. Egypt has a hot summer from May to October when the average midday temperatures are about 105° F (40·6° C) in Upper Egypt and 94° F (34·4° C) in Lower Egypt. In early summer, a south wind (*khamsin*) is frequent, accompanied by sandstorms. At other times of the year the prevailing wind is northwest. In late summer, during the Nile floods, humidity is high. The winter climate, from November to April, is temperate in both Upper and Lower Egypt. In Alexandria and along the Mediterranean coast the rainfall is heavier and the climate generally is that of the eastern Mediterranean basin.

Population

The population at the time of the last official census in 1960 was 26,080,000 (compared with 22,924,000 in 1956 and 19,021,840 in 1947).

H

A sample census in mid-1966 gave an estimated population of 30·8 million and another sample census in mid-1968 an estimate of 31·8 million. This would give an annual net increase of 2·7 per cent as compared with the official estimate of 3 per cent. The combination of a very high birth rate and a fairly short life expectancy causes the population to be mainly youthful and nearly half are under twenty years of age. But the death rate is declining, according to published figures, from 22 per thousand in 1952 to 17 per thousand in 1957 and 14 per thousand in 1968. The official estimate is that the population will reach 53 million by 1985.

Of the total population in 1966, 39·8 per cent lived in towns with about 21·8 per cent living in the five largest cities and these proportions are rapidly increasing. In the 1960 census the population of Cairo was 3,346,000 and of Alexandria 1,513,000 and in 1966 the population of the Cairo Governorate (including Giza) was estimated at 4·2 million and of the Alexandria Governorate at 1·8 million. Since 1968 there has been a further increase as a result of the evacuation of most of the civil population of the Suez Canal towns of Port Said, Ismailia, and Suez. About 90 per cent of Egyptians are Sunni Moslems mostly of the Hanafi rite and Islam is the official religion of the State. Of the remainder the largest minority consists of about 2–3 million Copts who are racially the purest descendants of the ancient Egyptians. There are also about a quarter of a million Egyptians belonging to various other Christian communities.

HISTORY AND POLITICS

During the first 3,000 years of known Egyptian history, thirty Pharaonic dynasties followed one another, and Egyptian civilization and the colossal monuments which marked its evolution became widely known. At length disintegration and decay set in, and the Pharaohs of the last four dynasties occupied their thrones under Persian domination (525–332 BC).

In 332 BC Alexander the Great conquered the country from the Persians. He founded a Greek Empire in Egypt and for the next 300 years successive Ptolemaic kings, descended from his general Ptolemy Soter, held their Graeco-Egyptian courts in Alexandria. Their rule ended with the deaths of Cleopatra and Mark Antony in 30 BC, and Egypt became a province of the Roman Empire. When the Roman Empire was divided between East and West 400 years later, Egypt became part of the East Roman (Byzantine) Empire. In AD 640 the Arab conquest ended Byzantine domination and absorbed Egypt in the Umayyad Empire. Subsequently, after a period of semi-independence under the nominal rule of the Abbasids, Egypt became the centre of the Fatimite dynasty, which founded Cairo. Towards the end of the eleventh century A.D. Egypt was conquered by Salah al-Din al-Ayyubi (Saladin) and it was ruled for the next 400 years by a series of military oligarchies, known collectively as the Mamelukes. The period of Mameluke rule, which lasted until the Ottoman conquest in 1517, was notable both for military glory and for artistic achievement. (The Mamelukes finally expelled the Crusaders from Syria and it was under Mameluke rule that most of the remaining architectural glories of Cairo were created.) Under Ottoman rule the Mamelukes were reduced to the position of domestic tyrants who were, however, allowed to do much as they pleased in Egypt so long as they paid an annual tribute to Constantinople. Under the conditions of oppressive and inefficient government which prevailed Egypt was reduced to the lowest depths of economic and cultural decay.

Mohammed Ali and His Successors

The history of modern Egypt really began with the invasion of Egypt by Bonaparte in 1798. The French were driven out in 1801 by an alliance of British and Turkish forces and a short British occupation followed. An Albanian soldier named Mohammed Ali, who came to Egypt with the Turkish forces to help in expelling the French, remained after the British defeat and withdrawal to seize supreme power in Egypt, to smash the tyranny of the Mamelukes, and to be recognized by the Sultan as Viceroy of Egypt (1805). Under the nominal suzerainty of the Sultan, Mohammed Ali added the northern part of the Sudan to Egypt by conquest, subdued the Wahhabis in Arabia, and shared his suzerain's defeat in the Greek War of Independence, losing the Egyptian fleet at the Battle of Navarino. The vassal in due course rebelled against his suzerain and, after occupying Syria, provoked European intervention by marching on Constantinople, thus threatening the integrity of the Ottoman Empire. This European intervention, in which British participation was the decisive factor, resulted in the withdrawal of Mohammed Ali's forces from Asia Minor and Syria and in his formal submission to the Sultan, who, at British instigation, confirmed him and his successors in the viceroyalty of Egypt and the Sudan (1840).

The lasting results of Mohammed Ali's rule were seen not in his international adventures but in his administration of Egypt. Egypt's contacts with the West have been continuous since Bonaparte's invasion and the fruitful development of these contacts was initially due to Mohammed Ali. He used European technical experts but avoided the mistake his successors made, of becoming either subject to European political influences or indebted to European bankers. With their technical assistance and the proceeds of cotton exports, which he was the first to develop, he executed irrigation works, introduced railways and telegraph lines, organized the machinery of government in the form of state departments, created schools for engineering, medicine, and other purposes, started industries and reorganized Egypt's armed forces. Among Mohammed Ali's notable public works are the great Nile Barrage at the apex of the delta and its corollary canals of which the Mahmudia Canal between the Nile and Alexandria is one. Besides providing drinking-water for Alexandria, it enabled goods to and from the interior to pass through Alexandria, and this, together with the reconstruction of the port, revived some of Alexandria's former glories.

Mohammed Ali died in 1849. During his 45 years of rule the cultivated area of Egypt had increased from about 3 million to about 4 million feddans. The population had grown from about 2½ to about 4½ million, government revenue had increased from about £1 million to about £4 million per annum, and exports had risen from an average annual value of about £200,000 to over £2 million. Much of Mohammed Ali's modernization had been achieved through high taxation and a considerable use of forced labour, but when he died Egypt was still politically independent (except for the nominal suzerainty of the Sultan) and had no foreign debt. Mohammed Ali was succeeded for a few years by his grandson, Abbas, and then by Said, who gave de Lesseps the concession for the Suez Canal. (Mohammed Ali, although devoted to modernization, was opposed to the project for a Suez Canal, realizing perhaps that it would jeopardize Egypt's independence.) In 1863 Said was succeeded by Ismail, who confirmed the Suez Canal concession. As a result of wild personal extravagance and of an undiscriminating passion for modernization, Ismail within a few years pledged Egypt's credit, mostly to European bankers, to the extent of nearly £100 million. The growing realization of the commercial and strategic importance of the Suez Canal, the anxiety of the European bankers about the security of their loans, and the growth of the European population in Egypt, all tended to increase European interest in Egypt, and that led first to interference and finally to control.

Since Egypt was still a part of the Ottoman Empire, European communities in Egypt were living under the Ottoman Capitulations.[1] Increased European interests in Egypt, and particularly European ownership of immovable property, resulted in 1875 in the creation of the Mixed Courts for the settlement of disputes between foreigners and Egyptians, and between foreigners of different nationalities.

The British Occupation

Ismail's growing indebtedness led to forcible intervention by the European Powers, particularly Britain and France who, by 1879, had virtually assumed control of Egypt's finances and in that year prevailed on the Sultan to depose Ismail, in favour of his more amenable son, Tawfiq. In 1882 a military revolt, caused by dislike of foreign inter-

[1] See above, p. 7.

ference and particularly of a reduction of the army establishment as a measure of economy, resulted in a British occupation of Egypt in order to crush the revolt, reinstate Tawfiq, and retain European influence over Egypt's heavily pledged finances. For domestic political reasons the French abstained at the last moment from taking part in this occupation.

The army revolt in Egypt coincided with a revolt in the Sudan against Egyptian rule. After the occupation the British insisted on the temporary abandonment of the Sudan; Gordon's death in Khartoum in 1885 marked the end of this process.

The British, who were now *de facto* rulers of Egypt, were compelled by the suspicions of other European Powers, who considered Egypt as being under the joint trusteeship of the Great Powers, to act primarily on behalf not of the people of Egypt but of Egypt's European creditors. They had to retain the complicated apparatus of international control and to regard as their primary task the rehabilitation of Egypt's finances for the servicing of her foreign debts.

Sir Evelyn Baring (later Lord Cromer), the first British Agent and Consul-General, was in fact ruler of Egypt from 1883 to 1907. During these years irrigation works were actively developed, the army re-organized, the Sudan reconquered; and, in general, the country brought back from bankruptcy to solvency.

Egyptian nationalism, which had first appeared during the army rebellion of 1882[1] and had been temporarily crushed as a result of the British occupation, began to manifest itself again towards the end of Cromer's tenure of office. This nationalism was directed against both the throne and the British. (Since 1892, when Tawfiq died, the throne had been occupied by his son, Abbas Hilmi, who, unlike Tawfiq, was on bad terms with the British.)

Cromer was succeeded in 1907 by Sir Eldon Gorst, whose three years of office saw a move towards representative government, and also of nationalist terrorism in 1909 when Butrus Ghali, the Prime Minister, unpopular both for his Coptic religion and for co-operation with the British, was assassinated. In 1910 Gorst was succeeded by Lord Kitchener.

When war broke out between Britain and Turkey in November 1914, the anomalous situation of Egypt as a province of the Ottoman Empire was regularized by its being declared a British Protectorate. Abbas Hilmi, who was pro-Turkish, was deposed and succeeded by his uncle Hussein Kamil, who died in 1917 and was succeeded by his brother, Ahmad Fuad.

When the war ended in 1918, Egyptian nationalist feeling, which had been repressed by the restrictions and uncertainties of war, was now fired by Wilson's Fourteen Points and by the prospect of the liberation

[1] See above, p. 10.

of the Ottoman subject peoples and burst into active life. Saad Zaghlul came forward as the leader of Egyptian nationalism. He first came into prominence a few days after the Armistice when he headed a deputation, or *wafd*, to Sir Reginald Wingate, the British High Commissioner (the title of the British representative since the declaration of the Protectorate), demanding that he and his deputation should be allowed to go to London to present Egypt's demands. The demand was refused and there followed three years of demonstrations, riots, and assassinations, tempered by negotiations during the course of which Wingate was succeeded as High Commissioner by Lord Allenby. During this period Egypt's demands crystallized in the slogan 'Complete independence for Egypt and the Sudan'. The British Government, once convinced of the need to make some concession to Egyptian nationalism, envisaged a treaty of alliance which would reserve to Britain what were then regarded as the essentials of the British position in Egypt. In November 1922 the problem was temporarily resolved on their terms by a unilateral British Declaration which conferred sovereign independence on Egypt subject to the retention of full British responsibility for (*a*) the security of the communications of the British Empire in Egypt; (*b*) the defence of Egypt against all foreign aggression and interference, direct or indirect; (*c*) the protection of foreign interests in Egypt and the protection of minorities; (*d*) the Sudan.

Politics and Anglo-Egyptian Relations, 1923–47

On the basis of this Declaration an Egyptian Constitution was promulgated in 1923 and Ahmad Fuad, who had taken the title of Sultan, now became King Fuad I of Egypt. The first elections brought Zaghlul to power as Prime Minister, but his tenure of office was brief. His encouragement of nationalist agitation caused anti-British terrorism to flare up again, the most important victim being Sir Lee Stack, Governor-General of the Sudan and Commander-in-Chief of the Egyptian army, who was murdered in Cairo. The British Government demanded an indemnity and an apology and the withdrawal of all Egyptian forces from the Sudan, and laid down the right to increase at will the quantity of Nile water used for irrigation in the Sudan at the expense of Egypt (this clause was in fact never invoked). Zaghlul and his Government resigned.

The forces of nationalism in Egypt were now becoming diverted by a struggle for power between on the one side Zaghlul (and later his successor Nahas) and the Wafd, and on the other side the King, together with such supporters as he could detach from the Wafd. This rivalry enabled the precarious basis on which Anglo-Egyptian relations had been poised in 1922 to last until 1936.

In 1925 Allenby was succeeded as High Commissioner by Lord Lloyd; in 1927, on Zaghlul's death, Mustafa Nahas became leader of

the Wafd. Between 1927 and 1930 there was a series of abortive negotiations between the British Government and successive Egyptian
Governments for a treaty to place their relations on a firmer basis. In
1930 Fuad dismissed Nahas, who was then Prime Minister, and replaced
him by Ismail Sidqi, who abolished the 1923 Constitution and launched
Egypt on a term of autocratic government. Since this administration
was reasonably competent by Egyptian standards and considerably
better than the misgovernment of the Wafd, the attempt at autocracy
might well have succeeded but for the insensate greed of the King and
of his entourage, and for the growing international importance of Egypt
as a result of Mussolini's ambitions in East Africa. These factors brought
about a united front of Egyptian politicians, determined on the one
hand to check the royal power and on the other to use the international
situation to obtain a fuller measure of independence from Britain. A
coalition Government was formed, the 1923 Constitution was restored,
and negotiations were opened with Britain.

In view of Mussolini's ambitions and the growing menace of war, the
British Government urgently wished to establish such relations with
Egypt as to guarantee a friendly country as a base in the event of war.
The Egyptian Government for its part realized that it was a choice
between Britain and Italy; King Fuad's ardent Italophile sentiments
worked strongly in favour of Britain.

In the 1936 Anglo-Egyptian Treaty Britain abandoned one of the
four points reserved in the 1922 Declaration: the protection of foreign
interests in Egypt and the protection of minorities, but retained the
other three: imperial communications, defence of Egypt, and the future
of the Sudan. A convention signed at Montreux in 1937, on British
initiative, abolished the Capitulations and set a term to the existence
of the Mixed Courts.

The rights retained by Britain under the treaty were made more
palatable to Egypt by arrangements (*a*) to remove British forces from
Cairo and Alexandria to the Canal Zone; (*b*) to allow virtually unrestricted immigration into the Sudan; and (*c*) to sponsor Egypt for
membership of the League of Nations.

The treaty was concluded in August 1936. In April, immediately
after the death of Fuad, there had been elections which returned the
Wafd with a large majority. Farouk was a minor, and Nahas, at the
time of the treaty and for about two years thereafter, was both Prime
Minister and head of the Regency Council.

Farouk attained his majority in 1938 and the struggle between
Palace and Wafd was renewed. It was interrupted by the outbreak of
the Second World War: under the terms of the 1936 treaty Britain,
behind the façade of the Government of the day, was now in a position
to exercise almost supreme power in Egypt. It was, however, important
that the governmental façade should be co-operative, and the successive

Palace-inspired governments of the first two years of war became increasingly unsatisfactory in this respect by reason of the pro-Italian influence of the Palace and of the effect of the Axis victories. In February 1941 Lord Killearn, the British Ambassador (the title of the British representative after the 1936 treaty), presented an ultimatum to Farouk demanding the replacement of the Cabinet by Nahas and a Wafdist Government. This change was effected and Nahas worked in co-operation with the British until October 1944 when he was dismissed by the King. By then the tide of war had receded from the Middle East and the British Government no longer needed to interfere in Egyptian domestic politics. Moreover Nahas's increasing tendency to corruption deprived him of a claim to British support.

Elections were held in January 1945 as a result of which the new Prime Minister, Ahmad Maher, and the Saadist Party (whose leaders had split off from the Wafd in 1938) were confirmed in power. (In pre-revolutionary Egypt, the government in power almost invariably won a general election; because of this the Opposition, as on this occasion, usually boycotted the elections. The percentage of the electorate voting rarely exceeded about 15 per cent.) In April 1945 the new Government declared war on Germany—a step postponed until then on British advice. Probably as a result of this Ahmad Maher was assassinated. He was succeeded as Prime Minister and party leader by Mahmud Noqrashi.

Nationalist feeling soon began to demand a revision of the 1936 treaty, although it was not due for revision until 1956. The aim was the withdrawal of British forces from Egypt and the union of the Sudan with the Egyptian Crown. Under heavy pressure from the Wafd Opposition, from the press, and from the usual student demonstrators, the Egyptian Government, while maintaining a correct and even friendly attitude, endeavoured to induce the British Government to come some way towards meeting nationalist demands. The British Government was slow to respond and it was not until 1947 that British forces were withdrawn from Cairo and Alexandria to the Canal Zone area.

In February 1946 the Noqrashi Government fell, mainly through inability to deal with student demonstrations, and was replaced by a Government formed by Ismail Sidqi. He was able to reach a provisional agreement by which the British would evacuate the Canal Zone in return for a suspension of the Egyptian demand for union between Egypt and the Sudan, the future of the Sudan being left for future negotiations. Final agreement was not reached, mainly because of intrigues against Sidqi by the Palace and by his political rivals. Sidqi resigned and Noqrashi took his place.

In the summer of 1947 Noqrashi brought Egypt's case against Britain before the Security Council of the United Nations. His presentation of the case was designed rather to appease the mounting nationalist feeling in Egypt than to convince the Security Council of the rightness of his cause. As a result, Britain and Egypt were merely adjured by the Security Council to resume direct negotiations.

Meanwhile other matters were beginning to claim the attention of politicians and people in Egypt. Ever since the formation of the Arab League, adherence to which had been Nahas's last political act in October 1944, the problem of the future of Palestine had been dominating the minds of the Arab world, in which Egypt played an important and, at least in her own opinion, the leading part. During the winter of 1947-8, when Egypt's normal unreadiness for war was accentuated by a cholera epidemic and by rising economic discontent, it gradually became apparent that Britain would be relinquishing the Palestine mandate and in effect leaving the Arabs and Jews to fight it out. With effect from May 1948 Britain formally terminated the mandate; the State of Israel was proclaimed and was recognized by the United States, followed closely by the Soviet Union. Almost simultaneously the Egyptian and other Arab armies invaded Israel, Egypt's humiliating performance in the Palestine War, owing mainly to military unpreparedness and domestic corruption, was precariously terminated by an armistice.

The disasters of the Palestine War brought to a head domestic discontent resulting in the first place from post-war inflation, and in the second from governmental incompetence and corruption and particularly the growing corruption and profligacy of the Court, which for the first time exposed the King to widespread and barely-veiled criticism.

The principal outward expression of this discontent was the growing influence and numbers of the Moslem Brotherhood, which had started as a reactionary and obscurantist religious society in the early 1930s and had now become a fanatical, ultra-nationalist, and terrorist organization. The Brotherhood had probably been responsible for the assassination of Ahmad Maher and other statesmen and officials and certainly for the murder of Noqrashi in December 1948.

There was also a clandestine revolutionary movement within the army later known as the 'Free Officers', which had been patiently organized since the early 1940s by Captain Gamal Abdul Nasser, an instructor at the Military Academy in Cairo.

Noqrashi was succeeded by Ibrahim Abdul Hadi, who set himself ruthlessly to the task of crushing the Moslem Brotherhood as a serious threat to organized government. He succeeded in this for the moment, but he was unable even to alleviate the underlying causes of discontent. This discontent resulted in the return of the Wafd to power at elections held in January 1950. Hopes built on the Wafd's election propaganda about social reform were disappointed. It appeared that the Wafd and the Palace had ended their old feud by a 'gentleman's agreement' to live and let live, each conniving at the corruption and incompetence of the other.

This was the situation when the Korean War boom in cotton prices ended in 1951. Corrupt manipulation of the market during and after the boom by the Government and the big exporters, with the connivance of Farouk, helped to turn a natural decline of prices into a disaster causing unemployment, bankruptcies, and acute budget and balance-of-payments difficulties. The Government's attempt to keep prices up by intervening on the Cotton Exchange, and buying at a fixed minimum price, resulted in a virtual cessation of exports and the accumulation of large stocks financed by increasing the note issue. A subsequent reduction in the minimum price effected only a slight improvement.

The Wafd Government soon found it convenient to divert the growing discontent from itself to the British. The Anglo-Egyptian dispute had lain dormant since the appeal to the Security Council, but it was now revived and on 15 October 1951 the 1936 treaty, as well as the Condominium agreement about the Sudan,[1] was abrogated by the unanimous vote of the Egyptian Parliament. A proposal was made by the Western Powers to Egypt on 13 October 1951 that she should join a Middle East Defence Organization as an equal partner with Britain, France, the United States, and Turkey. This proposal was rejected by the Egyptian Government which insisted on the immediate and unconditional withdrawal of British forces from the Canal Zone and on the union of the Sudan with Egypt.

The Egyptian Government now promulgated, unilaterally, a 'Constitution' for the Sudan under which Egypt would retain control over the Sudan's armed forces, foreign relations, and currency. The Sudanese, who at that moment were discussing self-government and subsequent constitutional development, were not impressed by this Constitution, which was rejected by the Sudan Legislative Assembly with only one dissentient.

A state of virtual guerrilla warfare broke out in the Canal Zone and the Egyptian Government succeeded, by a mixture of propaganda and intimidation, in withdrawing the whole Egyptian labour force from the Zone. With anti-British propaganda at full blast in the press and on the radio, with government-encouraged recruitment of students and roughs in 'liberation units' to fight in the Canal Zone, and with tens of thousands of unemployed workmen from the Canal Zone roaming the streets of Cairo, an explosion could hardly be long delayed. The explosion, when it came, was touched off by forcible British action at Ismailia to disarm a battalion of auxiliary police which had been indulging in hostile acts against the British. A number of auxiliary policemen were killed, and the next morning, 26 January 1952, rioting broke out in Cairo. Although these riots started as anti-British and although

[1] See below, p. 425.

twelve Britons were murdered in Cairo, the violence soon turned to indiscriminate looting of the prosperous in the course of which much damage was done and many lives were lost. In the late afternoon order was restored by the army on instructions from the King after the Government had failed to cope with the situation. The following night the King dismissed the Nahas Government from power for inability to maintain order.

THE REVOLUTION AND AFTER

The interval of some five months between the January riots and the revolution in July 1952 calls for little comment. The situation calmed down considerably in the Canal Zone, and relations with the British improved. At the centre a series of conventional Governments succeeded each other with little effect on the public weal, and with little consciousness of the storm brewing over the heads of the Palace and the pashas. It was an open secret that there was grave discontent in the army against the Palace. At the beginning of July the Prime Minister attempted to appease the army by asking the King to approve the appointment of Brigadier Mohammed Neguib, a prominent critic of the regime who was brought in by the Free Officers to head their movement early in 1952, as Minister of War. Farouk refused and demanded the appointment of a relative of his instead. The Prime Minister resigned but his successor had barely taken office when, on 23 July 1952, Neguib, at the head of a few battalions of troops, marched on Cairo. He seized the city and the administration without resistance or bloodshed, and, within a few days, dismissed the Government, secured the abdication and departure from Egypt of Farouk, established a Regency Council for Farouk's infant son, and arranged for a new government under the premiership of Ali Maher.

The Free Officers' junta was virtually the same as their executive council of 1949 consisting of Gamal Abdul Nasser, Kamal al-Din Hussein, Abdul Hakim Amer, Hassan Ibrahim, Abdul Moneim Abdul Raouf, Salah and Gamal Salem, Abdul Latif al-Baghdadi, Khalid Mohieddin and Anwar al-Sadat. Zakariya Mohieddin and Hussein al-Shafei now joined to form what they decided to call the Revolutionary Command Council (RCC). Neguib was President although the fiction of a monarchical constitution was maintained for the time being by the appointment of a Regency Council.

The Free Officers knew what they wanted to destroy in Egypt—the monarchy, the power of the landlords, foreign influence, and the corruption of political life—and they had a vision of the kind of society that they wanted a truly independent Egypt to become. But they had never had time to acquire the political techniques to make the vision a reality. They had had contacts with the Moslem Brotherhood and a few of them were sympathizers; Khalid Mohieddin was a Marxist but the great majority had no political ideology or affiliation.

The Free Officers had the alternative of ruling themselves or leaving the task to the traditional political parties after eliminating the monarchy. It was soon apparent that only the first alternative would enable them to carry through the reforms they wanted. They struck out alternately at left and right. On 12 August the workers in one of Egypt's largest spinning mills seized control of the factory. Fearing this might lead to workers' uprisings throughout the country the Junta occupied the mill, arrested some 200 workers and hanged two of the leading agitators. In September the RCC introduced its first important radical measure—agrarian reform. Land holdings were reduced to 200 feddans (1 feddan = 1·038 acres) and agricultural rents were compulsorily reduced. The measure was far from revolutionary or Marxist and the redistribution only affected 10 per cent of the cultivated area, but it significantly reduced the political power of the large landowners which was its main purpose. When Ali Maher objected to the measure he was removed from the Premiership and replaced by Neguib.

The Wafd Party was a potential threat to the regime but it was easily outmanoeuvred by Nasser's tactical skill. In January 1953 all political parties were abolished and their funds confiscated. Neguib announced the formation of Egypt's new political organization, the 'National Liberation Rally' and on 10 February a Provisional Constitution was promulgated which placed supreme authority for three years in the hands of the RCC. On 18 June 1953 the Egyptian Republic was formally proclaimed and the monarchy abolished along with the titles of 'bey' and 'pasha'. The property of the ex-King and his family was confiscated and the proceeds, estimated at £70 million, were earmarked for social development. Neguib became President and Prime Minister, and Colonel Nasser Deputy Premier and Minister of the Interior. In September a Revolutionary Tribunal was set up to try prominent figures of the old regime.

A division between Neguib and the rest of the RCC soon appeared. Neguib was nearly twenty years older than their average age and conservative by temperament. He did not understand collective leadership and believed he had been chosen to lead. He clashed with the Junta on several matters of policy and tended towards the view that civilian political life should be restored.

Neguib was politically maladroit but his strength lay in his popularity with the masses who looked on him as a father figure. The RCC also needed Neguib, who was half-Sudanese, because of his popularity in the Sudan which was about to become independent as a result of the Anglo-Egyptian agreement reached in February 1954. When Neguib resigned on 23 February the RCC at first accepted his resignation but was obliged to reverse the decision because of pro-Neguib sympathies in the army which were stimulated for his own purposes by the Marxist Khalid Mohieddin. But although Neguib had apparently recovered his power, in the following months Nasser succeeded in consolidating his own position in the army, police, and trade unions. He also manoeuvred Neguib into a position of responsibility for a restoration of political parties which was highly unpopular with the army. On 17 April 1954 Neguib in effect capitulated. Nasser became Prime Minister and the RCC was given a new lease of life. Neguib's power was broken, he lingered on as President for six months until the revelation of his association with the Moslem Brotherhood which had attempted to assassinate Nasser enabled the RCC to remove him from the Presidency.

The power of the politicians had been broken with little difficulty in the first year of the Revolution but there remained two groups which caused the RCC concern—the Moslem Brotherhood and the Communists. The former, with its organization and terrorist wing, was the more formidable. The Brothers had at first believed that, having helped to make the Revolution possible, they would be given a share of power and their Islamic programme put into effect. When it was apparent that the RCC had no such intention, they turned against the regime. The attempt on Nasser's life on 26 October 1954 by a poor workman who accused the Brotherhood leaders of having instigated him gave Nasser the opportunity to suppress the Brotherhood's organization by closing its branches and confiscating its arms. It was more than a decade before the Brothers again threatened the regime inside Egypt.

While heavily involved in the struggle to consolidate his regime Nasser had never lost sight of his primary goal—the withdrawal of British forces from Egypt. The first obstacle was overcome with the Anglo-Egyptian agreement on the Sudan of February 1953—the RCC having previously reached agreement with all the Sudanese political parties on the principle of Sudanese self-determination. Although the pro-Egyptian party won the subsequent Sudanese elections the Egyptians' hopes that the Sudan would opt for union with Egypt on gaining full independence were not realized. But a Sudanese settlement left the way open for a final agreement with Britain.

During the negotiations which began early in 1954 Nasser made use of his control over the army and police to bring the maximum pressure on Britain to withdraw its forces from the Canal Zone. He restrained and encouraged the sabotage groups as the occasion demanded. On 27 July, after several weeks of hard bargaining, Heads of Agreement were initialled providing, (a) for the evacuation of all British forces from Egypt within twenty months; (b) for all British bases in the Canal Zone to remain activated and to be operated and maintained by British civilian contractors for a period of seven years; (c) for Britain to re-occupy the Canal Zone with Egypt's agreement in the event of an armed attack by any outside power on Egypt, or any other country which was a party to the Arab Treaty of Joint Defence, or Turkey. The agreement was signed on 19 October 1954.

Britain had agreed to withdraw militarily from the Suez Canal base because its usefulness had declined, but despite continued Anglo-Egyptian rivalry for influence in the Sudan the British Government looked to an improvement in relations between Britain and Egypt. Similar hopes were expressed by Nasser and the RCC who had to face sharp criticism at home (especially from the Moslem Brotherhood) for the provision in the Agreement allowing Britain to reoccupy the Base.

The Years 1955–1958

Two years after the Revolution, Nasser had achieved many of his aims: a British military withdrawal, the abolition of the monarchy and the former political system, land reform and the breaking up of the big estates. But this did not mean that henceforth he would concentrate on Egypt's internal problems of social and economic development. Partly through circumstances and partly inclination he was increasingly immersed in foreign affairs. Domestic problems were not entirely neglected. After the Revolution the regime began to build schools and rural health centres much faster than before but resources were limited—especially with the conservative financial policies pursued by the regime in its early years. The Government began to place its main hopes for rapid development on the building of a High Dam at Aswan.

Two things in particular diverted Nasser's attention from home affairs along lines which were to become established—the Israeli–Arab problem and Western efforts to set up an anti-Soviet Middle East defence organization.

At first Nasser paid little attention to the Arab–Israeli dispute in which he could rightly be described as a moderate. But in 1955 the situation at the Israeli–Egyptian armistice line became highly explosive. From the Gaza Strip under Egyptian protection Arabs were crossing singly or in small groups on raiding expeditions and the Israelis responded with their usual heavy 'punishment raids'. As the situation worsened the Egyptian army and civilians demanded retaliation. Nasser could not ignore these demands although he knew the Egyptian forces were quite unprepared for a 'second round' with Israel. His response was to allow *fedayeen* (commandos or saboteurs) to penetrate deep into Israel. This brought heavier retaliation but it achieved Nasser's main purpose of avoiding full-scale war. At the same time he began to consider the need for a full-scale rearmament of Egypt's forces.

The second main problem confronting Nasser in 1955 concerned the other most powerful independent Arab state—Iraq—and its strong-minded leader and elder statesman, Nuri Said. At this time Nasser still had little interest in ideas of Arab nationalism or Arab unity but he did feel tied to the other Arabic-speaking states by their common history (see his *The Philosophy of the Revolution*, 1954). It was therefore a disaster in Nasser's eyes that Nuri should be the chief friend and ally of the Western imperialist powers in the Middle East. Nasser himself was strongly anti-Communist at this period and his sympathies if anywhere lay with the United States which in November 1954 had signed an agreement to provide Egypt with $40 million in unconditional aid for development purposes. Despite some mutual suspicion, relations even with Britain had improved as Britain faithfully implemented the 1954 agreement and there was reasonable hope of Anglo-US financing of the Aswan High Dam.

There was rivalry between Egypt and Iraq, which had historical origins, for leadership of the Arab world. But in 1954 Nasser made several attempts to reach an understanding with Nuri. The Iraqi leader wanted Iraq and as many of the independent Arab states as possible to join a Middle East defence organization which had been initiated by the US Government but for which the Eden Government of Britain had now taken over the chief responsibility. Nasser was strongly opposed because he foresaw that this would tie all the Arabs to the West through the Arab Collective Security Pact (of which Iraq was a member). Nasser still believed that Nuri would wait for the Arab League Foreign Ministers' Conference to discuss the matter and was taken by surprise when a Turkish–Iraqi agreement was announced in January 1955.

This was the nucleus of the Baghdad Pact which was the principal subject of inter-Arab divisions in 1955–8. Cairo's press and radio at once launched an offensive against the Pact and relations with Britain sharply deteriorated.

The Baghdad Pact was not the only factor that helped to turn Nasser and the RCC away from the West to a neutralist position. Daniel Solod, the Soviet Middle East expert who was appointed Ambassador to Cairo in September 1953, skilfully encouraged the trend. As the traditional sales of Egyptian cotton to England steadily declined (although British purchases from the Sudan increased) Egypt looked to Eastern Europe and China for new markets. Also at about this time Nasser established close personal relations with the Indian Premier Mr. Nehru and President Tito of Yugoslavia who both influenced Nasser's outlook. His views on Arab neutralism were strengthened by his attendance at the Bandung Conference of Afro-Asian Powers in April 1955 where he made a favourable impression and was treated with respect by senior Asian statesmen such as Nehru and Chou en-Lai.

In February 1955 Israel launched a heavy and destructive retaliatory raid on Gaza. Nasser at once began secret negotiations with the Russians for the supply of arms and on 27 September he announced the conclusion of a deal with Czechoslovakia for the supply of very large

quantities of arms, including Soviet aircraft and tanks, in exchange for
rice and cotton. This action was denounced by the British and US
governments but applauded by the Arab masses. The Egyptian Government, supported by Saudi Arabia and Syria, pursued its campaign
against the Baghdad Pact and in December 1955 British efforts to include Jordan in the Pact were thwarted by hostile popular demonstrations. By the end of 1955 Nasser's breach with Britain was almost
complete, his prestige in the Arab world rapidly mounting, and his
dependence on the West diminishing at the price of increasing dependence on the Soviet bloc.

The trend continued in 1956. In May Nasser without warning
recognized the Peking regime. Egypt's trade with Communist China
was steadily increasing and Nasser had the additional motive of evading
a possible UN embargo on Middle East arms supplies (China not being
a UN member). The US reaction was strongly hostile. The Western
powers had not altogether given up hope of keeping Egypt within their
orbit. In 1955 the British and US governments had begun tentative
discussions with Egypt to finance the High Dam at Aswan and in
February 1956 a provisional agreement was announced under which
the IBRD would loan $200 million on condition that the US and
Britain would loan an additional $70 million to pay the hard currency
costs of material and technical services. Egypt was to provide the
equivalent of $900 million in the form of local services and materials.
The offer was primarily a political move in the Cold War, for the
Western powers were sceptical of Egypt's ability to provide its share.
There was strong domestic opposition to any large-scale US and British
aid to Egypt. Convinced that the USSR would not make good its hints
that it was prepared to finance the Dam, the US Government abruptly
withdrew its offer (on which the IBRD loan depended) in July 1956.

The US and Britain believed that even if he did not fall from power,
Nasser would become more pliable. Instead he retaliated by announcing
a week later (the fourth anniversary of the Revolution) the nationalization of the Suez Canal Company and the creation of an Egyptian Canal
Authority to manage the Canal.

The Third World as a whole was thrilled by this defiant gesture if
apprehensive about the consequences; the Western powers were predictably hostile. There followed three months of abortive negotiations
in London and New York in which Britain took the lead in trying to
enforce some international control of the Canal. They failed largely
because the US Government refused to consider the use of military
force to coerce Egypt. But the British and French governments were
determined to use force—the British because they regarded Nasser as
a threat to all British interests in the Middle East and the French because they believed Egyptian support to be the principal factor behind
the continuation of the Algerian Rebellion. The British, French, and

Israeli governments secretly agreed on joint action and on 29 October
Israel invaded Sinai. On 30 October Britain and France issued a joint
ultimatum calling on Egypt and Israel to cease fighting and withdraw
their forces ten miles from the Suez Canal. Israel, whose forces were not
within ten miles of the Canal, accepted the ultimatum but Nasser rejected it and ordered his troops that had been sent across the Canal into
Sinai and were suffering heavy losses to return. When the ultimatum
expired on 31 October British and French planes began to bomb
Egyptian airfields destroying almost the entire Egyptian air force except
for the planes that had been sent into Syria for safety. On 5 November
an Anglo-French force assembled in Cyprus landed in the Port Said
area and after capturing the city advanced southwards along the line
of the Canal.

World opinion was overwhelming hostile and on 4 November the
UN General Assembly decided to create a UN Emergency Force
(UNEF) to supervise a ceasefire. Britain and France agreed to a cease-
fire on 6 November. As soon as UNEF began to arrive the Anglo-
French forces started to withdraw and their evacuation was completed
by 23 December.

The British and French governments had miscalculated that the
Egyptians would be unable to run the Canal without British and
French pilots and that the Egyptian people would turn against Nasser.
Despite Egypt's military defeat and the loss of 2,000 to 3,000 men killed
or taken prisoner the final result was almost a complete victory for
Egypt. United Nations pressure, led by the US and the USSR (especially the former) forced the British and French to withdraw from the
Canal and later the Israelis from Sinai and Gaza leaving Egypt in full
control of the Canal and its immense quantities of British military
stores. With US assistance the Canal was cleared of the ships sunk to
block it by the Egyptians, and was reopened in April 1957. All British
and French property in Egypt was sequestered; about 3,000 British and
French nationals were expelled and many thousands more left because
of loss of livelihood.

Egypt's loss and Israel's only gain was the replacement by a UNEF
detachment of the Egyptian military post at Sharm al-Shaikh which controlled the entrance to the Gulf of Aqaba. The net result of the Suez War
was that Nasser's popularity among the Egyptians and the Arabs rose
to new heights. Egypt moved further away from the West; the Western
economic boycott which the United States chose to join, thereby
dissipating most of the credit it had gained through opposing the Suez
action, did not bring Egypt to its knees, because Soviet aid intervened.

Nasser had consolidated his position at home in June 1956 when a
new Republican Constitution (which declared Islam to be the religion
of the State, recognized Egypt as part of the Arab nation, and provided
for government by a President and Council of Ministers and a single

legislative chamber) was promulgated and approved by a 99 per cent affirmative vote in a referendum which also confirmed him as President for a six-year term. The Constitution also provided for a single political organization to replace all the political parties and the rather vague Liberation Rally which Nasser had founded after the Revolution. The National Union was formally established in May 1957 and played a leading role in the elections held to the National Assembly in July 1957.

The years 1956–9 marked the high tide of Nasserism in the Middle East as it seemed that he swept all before him. But although his appeal to the Arab masses was immensely powerful the rulers of most independent Arab states, in addition to Nuri Said of Iraq, were basically pro-Western and conservative and therefore hostile to Nasserism. In the spring of 1957 King Hussein successfully carried out a coup against his own pro-Nasser Government which had aimed to establish diplomatic relations with the Soviet Union. The US Government endeavoured to rally pro-Western elements in the Middle East with the 'Eisenhower Doctrine' which in January 1957 named 'international Communism' as the greatest threat to the Middle East and promised financial aid to any government which helped to resist it. Egypt attacked the Eisenhower Doctrine as a form of imperialist pressure but Iraq and the pro-Western Lebanese regime of President Chamoun accepted it and so did King Saud of Saudi Arabia (though somewhat ambiguously). In February 1958 President Nasser's 'neutralist' camp was immensely strengthened by the proclamation of a complete political union between Syria and Egypt, the United Arab Republic. The initiative came from the Syrians, led by the Baathists, and was primarily intended as an insurance that growing Soviet influence in the Middle East would not replace that of the West.

In March 1958 King Saud of Saudi Arabia was forced to relinquish his powers to his brother Prince Faisal after the Syrians accused the King of plotting to assassinate Nasser and prevent the Syrian–Egyptian union. Faisal was regarded as more pro-Egyptian and less pro-Western than his brother. In Lebanon the internal divisions between Lebanese nationalists and Arab nationalists which had first appeared at the Suez crisis developed into a muted civil war with Syria, now part of the UAR, assisting the rebellion against President Chamoun and his pro-Western Government.

The climax came with the Iraqi Revolution of 14 July which at one blow destroyed the basis of remaining Western, and especially British, power and influence in the Middle East. In reaction US marines were landed in Lebanon and British troops flown to Jordan to prevent the remaining pro-Western forces in the Arab world from being swept away by the nationalist tide. Eventually the Lebanese civil war was settled by a compromise which in fact ensured that Lebanon would revert to a more neutral foreign policy.

The United Arab Republic

To all appearances Nasser and Nasserism were triumphant. Egypt's chief rival had been destroyed while the union with Syria had established Egyptian power in the Arab heartland. Yet the seeds of immense difficulties had been sown. When the Syrian leaders came to Cairo to ask for a merger of the two countries Nasser had argued that Syria must first achieve its own internal unity and that another five years were needed. When he did consent to the union it was on his own conditions: not a federal union, as some of the Syrians wanted, but a heavily centralized one. He insisted that all political parties should be dissolved. The Baathists had expected Nasser to rule Syria through them but he soon revealed that he had no such intention. They were brushed aside and their leaders went either into self-exile or bitter opposition. Nasser's new six-year Presidency of the UAR was approved by a referendum in the two regions. The Egyptian National Assembly was dissolved in March 1958 to make way for a reorganized political structure to include the whole Republic. The National Union system was extended to Syria.

Nasser subsequently described the union with Syria as 'three and a half years of endless troubles' which absorbed three-quarters of his energies and attention. He appointed two Syrian Vice-Presidents of the UAR, several Syrian Ministers to the Central Government and an Executive Council for the Syrian region, but he kept most of the executive and legislative powers in his own hands. Inevitably, the Syrians regarded themselves as junior partners in the union. Some of the Egyptian officials who went to work in Syria were tactless and overbearing; some others were corrupt. The Syrian army suffered from wounded pride while the Syrian urban middle class and landowners were alarmed as Egypt began to apply socialist principles to Syria. The Government's popularity was not improved when Syria's chiefly agricultural economy suffered three consecutive years of disastrous drought. The mass of the Syrian people still regarded Nasser as their hero and leader but the middle class and intelligentsia were increasingly disaffected. In 1960 Nasser sent Field-Marshal Abdul Hakim Amer, his closest and most trusted friend, as a sort of pro-consular governor in Syria but he failed to remedy the situation.

Nor did Nasser's friendly relations with the new Iraqi regime last long. The Iraqi leader Abdul Karim Kassem purged his regime of pro-Egyptian elements and in February 1959 blamed an abortive revolt in Mosul on Nasser. As the Iraqi Communists strengthened their position *vis-à-vis* Arab nationalists, Nasser became convinced that Communism was now a mortal danger to the Arab nation. During 1959 several hundred Egyptian left-wing intellectuals were interned. His bitter attacks on Kassem and the Communists led to an open breach with the

Soviet Premier N. S. Khrushchev. Nasser was taking a severe risk because Egypt was heavily dependent on Soviet economic and military
aid and the Russians were about to decide whether to finance the
second stage of the High Dam. Eventually the crisis receded as the
Russians concluded that their relations with Nasser's Egypt were of
more importance than those with the unstable and politically incom-
petent Iraqi Communists.

1961–1963

On 28 September 1961 the disaffected elements in Syria combined
forces to secede from the union, to the expressed delight of the Iraqi,
Saudi, and Jordanian governments. Nasser at first considered resisting
the secession by force but desisted when he realized the secessionist
forces had full control in Syria. He declared that he would never
proclaim the dissolution of the United Arab Republic but he would not
oppose Syria's re-entry into the UN or the Arab League as a separate
State.

Many believed that this enormous setback would end Nasser's
political career. At the least it would compel him to abandon his claim
to Arab leadership and concentrate on Egypt's internal affairs. In the
long run this did not happen because despite the collapse of this first
experiment in Arab unity under Nasser's authority, Nasser and Egypt
remained the most substantial force in the Arab world. In the shorter
term, Syria's secession gave Nasser an opportunity for the first time
since the Revolution to examine his political and economic ideas in
depth. His first reaction to the secession was to conclude that the Syrian
property-owning classes had inspired it because of their fear of Egyptian
socialism and that they had been able to do this by infiltrating into the
National Union. He also feared that the equivalent Egyptian classes
might try to do the same. In a precautionary counter-offensive six
hundred of Egypt's wealthiest families had their property sequestered
by the State.

In November 1961 Nasser convened a Preparatory Committee of the
National Congress of Popular Powers whose task was to prepare a
Charter of National Action to be the basis of the country's political,
social, and economic policies. The National Congress had 1,750 members elected by labour unions, professional associations, and other
community groups and it met in May 1962 to debate President Nasser's
30,000 word draft National Charter. After a series of televised debates
presided over by Nasser the draft was approved without amendment by
the National Congress.

The National Charter

The Charter begins with a brief historical analysis of Egypt's problems.
It concludes that previous revolutionary movements failed because they

were weak in strategy, narrow in vision, and overlooked the need for social change. The essence of the Charter is contained in the words, 'Political democracy cannot be separated from social democracy. No citizen can be regarded as free to vote unless he is given the following three guarantees: (a) he should be free from exploitation in all its forms; (b) he should enjoy an equal opportunity with his fellow citizens to enjoy a fair share of the national wealth; (c) his mind should be free from all anxiety likely to undermine his future security.'

The Charter laid down the principles on which the majority of the economy should be publicly owned (see below, Economic Policy and Industrialization). Ownership of agricultural land was limited to 100 feddans per family but there was no question of land nationalization, and private ownership of buildings was maintained.

As regards the political organization of the State, the National Union was replaced by the Arab Socialist Union with its various branches at all levels from the roots in the villages, workshops, and factories up to the National Executive headed by the President. The parliamentary branch of the ASU is the National Assembly with its 350 members elected by adult suffrage in 175 constituencies. In all elected bodies of the ASU, including parliament, half the seats had to be filled by workers and farmers (defined as anyone owning less than 25 feddans). The ASU was to have the task of drafting a new permanent constitution.

In September 1962 Nasser restored Cabinet government by creating a Council of Ministers headed by Ali Sabry, the former head of his private office.

During 1961–2 Egypt was under heavy attack from the regimes in Jordan, Syria, Saudi Arabia, Iraq, and Yemen. Egyptian troops in Kuwait as part of the Arab League force replacing the British troops that had been invited in by Kuwait to protect its independence were withdrawn on the ground that they could no longer associate with the Syrians and Saudis. Nasser refused to recognize the Syrian secessionist regime and broke off relations with Jordan.

After a series of bitter exchanges with the Syrian secessionist Government, Egypt walked out of an Arab League meeting in Lebanon in the summer of 1962 and announced a boycott of the League. To Jordanian, Syrian, and Saudi accusations that he was destroying Arab unity, Nasser replied that their kind of unity only served the interests of imperialism. He was only interested in 'unity of purpose' and not 'unity of ranks'.

Between 1961 and 1963 Egypt became increasingly involved in African affairs through its association with Morocco, Mali, Ghana, and Guinea in the 'Casablanca' group of radical African states which in 1963 established on paper a joint military command and a common market. But by the time of the first OAU Conference at Addis Ababa

in May 1963 Nasser had concluded that there was nothing to be gained
and much to be lost through the polarization of the African continent
between radicals and moderates.

Henceforth Nasser was a moderating, almost conservative influence
in the OAU. He constantly affirmed that the African states should seek
the spirit of unity before adopting any constitutional form.

The Arab political scene was transformed in September 1962 by the
republican rebellion in Yemen led by Brigadier Abdullah Sallal, which
overthrew the Imam Badr who had just succeeded his father Imam
Ahmad. In answer to Sallal's call for help Nasser sent a substantial expeditionary force. The Yemeni coup had given Nasser the chance to
seize the initiative once again in the Middle East. The campaign was
a severe strain on the Egyptian economy and the Egyptian forces
suffered heavy losses at the hands of the Saudi-supported Yemeni
royalists. Egyptian aerial bombardment of tribesmen (including
the alleged use of poison gas) antagonized world opinion but the
immediate effect of the Yemeni rebellion and Egypt's intervention was
to place the Arab conservatives on the defensive. Because the Saudis
and Jordanians assisted the Yemeni royalists seven Saudi pilots and
three Jordanians (including the Air Force Commander) defected to
Cairo.

On 9 February 1963 Kassem was overthrown by Arab nationalists
led by Iraqi Baathists and a month later the secessionist regime in Syria
collapsed under joint pressure from Baghdad and Cairo. In both Iraq
and Syria the new regimes pledged themselves in support of 'the new
movement of Arab unity'. Iraq, Syria, and Egypt at once began
negotiations for a close federal union.

Obstacles very soon appeared. Nasser and the Baathists were still
mutually suspicious and the Iraqi and Syrian Baathists soon eliminated
their non-Baathist allies from power. In Syria pro-Nasser demonstrations were rigorously suppressed and although the differences were
papered over to allow a tripartite federal State to be proclaimed on
17 April this had no substance. Purges of non-Baathists in Iraq and
Syria continued and after an ill-planned pro-Nasser coup was ruthlessly
crushed in Syria in July Nasser openly denounced the Syrian regime as
'Secessionist, inhuman and immoral' and added 'To ensure unity, there
must be a single Arab nationalist movement'.

Egypt's relations with Syria and Iraq steadily worsened throughout
the summer but in November 1963 Abdul Salam Aref who had been
kept as a figurehead President by the Iraqi Baathists, seized power with
the help of the army and ousted the Baath who had split between
moderate and extreme wings. Relations between Cairo and Baghdad
improved again but although the idea of an Iraqi–Egyptian union
was revived again at President Aref's request, Nasser remained
cautious.

1963–1967

In the winter of 1963 Nasser reached the conclusion that a serious danger threatened the Arab world. The Israelis had completed the diversion of some of the waters of the River Jordan to the Negev Desert. The Arab states had often sworn to prevent this by force and although there was little hope of their taking effective joint action in their divided state there was a serious possibility that one of them—most probably Syria—would act on its own in launching a war for which Israel was unprepared. In a speech at Port Said on 23 December 1963 Nasser proposed that all thirteen Arab Heads of State should meet in Cairo to consider the situation. He knew it would be difficult for them to refuse and he made use of the occasion to repair his relations with President Bourguiba of Tunisia, King Hussein of Jordan, King Hassan of Morocco, and King Saud of Saudi Arabia. In effect Nasser was reverting to his earlier policy of 'unity of ranks' taking precedence over 'unity of aims'. The Arab Summit agreed to set up a Unified Arab Military Command under an Egyptian general. There was an agreement not to go to war with Israel but instead to build up the armies of Israel's neighbours and set about diverting the head waters of the River Jordan in Arab territory.

The Arab Heads of State decided to meet again in September 1964. On this occasion Prince Faisal (who had replaced the ailing King Saud as the real ruler of Saudi Arabia) agreed publicly with President Nasser on the need to settle the Yemeni problem but neither side was genuinely prepared for a compromise and the Yemeni royalists continued to struggle with Saudi support against the republican and Egyptian forces. The United Military Command had been set up but was handicapped by the continuing bad political relations between the Arab states.

In May 1964 the Soviet Premier Nikita Khrushchev visited Egypt to inaugurate the second stage of the High Dam project with the diversion of the Nile waters through the diversion canal. There were signs of friction when the Soviet leader referred to Arab nationalism as a stage on the road to Communism but the visit was generally successful. From 1956 onwards President Nasser paid frequent visits to the Soviet Union and relations were generally cordial. Although President Nasser always emphasized his independence of action there was no doubt that Egypt was placing increasing reliance on Soviet economic, military, and technical aid. In contrast, relations with the Western powers, especially the US, deteriorated fairly steadily. There had been a temporary improvement at the end of the Eisenhower Administration and under President Kennedy who was much admired in Egypt. The State Department had concluded that Egypt could still be a barrier to Communism in the Middle East and between 1958 and 1964 the US provided Egypt with over $1,000 million in aid—mostly in cheap long-term loans under the PL 480 arrangement for the sale of surplus foodstuffs. This continued even after a sharp deterioration in US–Egyptian relations as a result of Egyptian military assistance to the Congolese rebels. But although there was no complete diplomatic break until 1967 and President Nasser always made clear that he had not abandoned hope of a reconciliation with Washington, US influence on Egyptian policy was minimal. Nasser had reached the conclusion that it had been a mistake for Egypt to become so heavily dependent on US food supplies.

Except for a brief interlude after the conclusion of the Anglo-Egyptian agreement in 1954 relations between Britain and Egypt were almost uniformly bad between 1952 and 1967. From 1956 onwards the British Government regarded Nasserism as the principal threat to British interests in the Middle East (including the Persian Gulf and South Arabia). A half-hearted attempt by the Labour Government to establish a new relationship failed (chiefly because of Anglo-Egyptian differences over South Arabia) and in December 1965 diplomatic relations were broken by Egypt in accordance with an OAU resolution on Rhodesia. In contrast, relations with France steadily improved after the ending of the Algerian War in 1962, and after 1967 it became the most popular of the Western powers in Egypt.

In July 1964 Cairo was host to the second summit conference of the OAU and in October fifty-six Heads of non-aligned States or their representatives met there. The constant flow of foreign statesmen from West, East, and the Third World into Cairo gave it the status of a major world political centre. In February 1965 Nasser took the initiative among the Arab states in trying to prevent Western Germany from carrying through a big arms deal with Israel. He invited the East German President Herr Ulbricht to Egypt and when Bonn protested he publicized the secret German–Israeli deal. West Germany stopped sending arms to Israel but established diplomatic relations with Israel nevertheless. Egypt led nine other Arab states into breaking relations with Bonn.

Egypt's leadership of the Arab states was far from unchallenged. In July 1965 a coup in Algeria removed President Nasser's close friend Ahmad Ben Bella from power. In August Nasser paid a sudden and unexpected visit to Saudi Arabia to conclude an agreement with King Faisal on Yemen providing for a ceasefire and the formation of a republican-royalist provisional Government to be followed after one year by the withdrawal of Egyptian troops. Nasser's immediate purpose was to provide a breathing-space for the transfer of Egyptian troops from Northern Yemen to the less exposed areas around the main towns in the south but the public impression of his visit to Jedda was a grave admission of weakness.

In the summer of 1965 Nasser was also faced by serious trouble at home in a revived threat of the Moslem Brotherhood. Elections to a 350-member National Assembly had been held in March 1964 under the new Provisional Constitutional and Electoral Law and a start had been made in creating the pyramidal framework of the ASU as provided in the National Charter. At the inauguration of the new Assembly Nasser had emphasized that the Egyptian Revolution was entering an important new stage of development; the period of 'transformation' was over and the period of 'upsurge' had begun. A year later Nasser was elected for a further six-year term as President (having consistently refused to be elected for life). But the continued stagnation of Egypt's political life showed the difficulty of endowing the nation with a lively political organization within an authoritarian framework. Although the National Assembly and ASU basic unit elections aroused widespread interest and the Assembly debates were frequently animated and controversial, all real executive and legislative power remained in the hands of the President whose dominance over the Vice-Presidents and the Cabinet was absolute. Despite the affirmation of freedom of the spoken and written word contained in the National Charter, in practice there was little public criticism of the Government's domestic policies and none of foreign policy. It was partly as a reaction against this conformism that an illegal and extra-constitutional movement such as the Moslem Brotherhood gained support.

From Jedda Nasser went to Moscow to meet for the first time the Soviet leaders who had succeeded Khrushchev and while he was there he announced the discovery of the Brotherhood conspiracy in a speech to Arab students. The subsequent trials of about 400 Brothers revealed that many of them were of the new élite of engineers, scientists, and university lecturers.

The summer of 1965 was also a time of exceptionally acute economic difficulties. The first Five-Year Plan had achieved a high growth rate but some of it had been too ambitious, factories were lying idle for lack of spare parts or raw materials and Egypt was losing its international credit-worthiness as it failed to pay its debts.

In September 1965 Nasser moved Ali Sabri from the Premiership to be Secretary-General of the ASU and replaced him with Zakariya Mohieddin both to improve the internal security situation and to introduce a new policy of economic realism and retrenchment.

In 1966 the division between the 'radicals' in the Arab world (led by Egypt) and the 'conservatives' (led by Saudi Arabia) grew steadily wider. King Faisal's diplomatic efforts to create a new grouping of Islamic states was regarded by Egypt as an attempt to create an anti-Nasser front. The Jedda agreement on the Yemen collapsed with the failure to form a provisional Government. Egypt's position in Yemen was strengthened by Britain's announcement of a complete withdrawal from the Aden base by 1968 but Egypt completely failed to assist in the formation of a stable republican regime in Yemen and the drain of its resources continued.

Despite Zakariya Mohieddin's efforts the general economic situation had shown little improvement and in September 1966 when he was about to conclude an agreement with the IMF which would have involved accepting a form of devaluation Nasser dismissed him together with the veteran Finance Minister Abdul Moneim al-Kaissouni because he believed the US was using the IMF loan to influence Egypt's foreign policy. He replaced Mohieddin with Sidqi Sulaiman, a 'technician' who had shown high ability as Minister of the High Dam.

The Six Day War

In February 1966 a new coup in Damascus had brought to power in Syria a group of left-wing Baathists who cautiously began to improve their ties with Egypt. In November 1966, under strong Syrian pressure Nasser agreed to a highly comprehensive Egyptian–Syrian defence agreement. Shortly afterwards Israel launched a strong attack against three villages near Hebron in Jordan and after the ensuing disturbances among Palestinians on Jordan's West Bank King Hussein bitterly criticized both Nasser and the Syrians and taunted Nasser with hiding behind the protection of the UNEF in Sinai. Both friends and critics of Egypt in the Arab world were now asking why, if Egypt had the strongest forces in the Arab world as its leaders often claimed, it had not asked for the UNEF to be withdrawn so that the Straits of Tiran might again be closed to Israeli shipping.

Meanwhile, Nasser's relations with the Arab monarchies deteriorated (in the summer of 1966 he had caused the indefinite postponement of summit conferences on the grounds that Arab reactionaries were exploiting them for their own ends) and the United Arab Military Command had virtually ceased to exist.

Although Nasser had no affection for the Syrian regime he felt closer co-operation with Damascus was necessary. Tension with Israel rose sharply in April and May 1967 as Israeli leaders threatened Syria with retaliation if guerrilla attacks from Syrian territory continued. Nasser, who had been warned by the Russians of an impending Israeli attack on Syria, felt compelled to react and his response was an official request to the UN Secretary-General for the withdrawal of the UNEF from Sinai. When this was done and Egyptian troops were once again at Sharm al-Shaikh at the mouth of the Gulf of Aqaba Nasser announced the closure of the Straits of Tiran to Israeli shipping, as the whole Arab world expected him to do.

On 30 May King Hussein flew to Cairo for a last-minute reconciliation and the signing of a Jordanian–Egyptian defence agreement. Egypt now had agreements with both Syria and Jordan but there was no co-operation between these two and no semblance of a joint Arab Command.

On 5 June Israel attacked all seventeen of Egypt's military air-fields, destroying most of its air force on the ground and on 6 June Israeli forces advanced rapidly into Sinai. The seven Egyptian divisions in Sinai were defeated and put to flight and an estimated 10,000 Egyptian soldiers were killed or died of thirst in the struggle to return across the Suez Canal which Israeli forces reached in the early hours of 9 June. Acting on the basis of information from King Hussein on the morning of 6 June that Jordanian radar stations had detected approaching from the sea a large flight of aircraft which could only come from British and US carriers, Egypt broke relations with the US and expelled all US and British citizens.

The Egyptian public who had been roused to a high pitch of optimism in the days preceding the war understood that the worst had happened when Egypt followed Jordan in accepting a ceasefire on 8 June. On the next afternoon President Nasser spoke on Cairo Radio accepting full personal responsibility for the grave national setback and announced his decision to resign and hand over the Presidency to Vice-President Zakariya Mohieddin. It was understood that the First Vice-President and Deputy Commander-in-Chief of the Armed Forces Field Marshal Abdul Hakim Amer had resigned also.

Whether or not Nasser had expected it, the reaction was an overwhelming emotional demand from the Egyptian masses that he should remain in office. There was some official encouragement of the popular demonstrations but they had their own impulse. On 10 June Nasser announced his agreement to the unanimous demand of the National Assembly that he should stay on.

1967 and After

Egypt was in a desperately serious situation in June 1967. Most of its air force and much of its armour and artillery had been lost. The Suez Canal was closed and with the Israeli occupation of Sinai half of its oil production (about 9·5 million tons a year) was lost. Above all the authority of the President, the nation's trusted leader and father-figure had been irreparably damaged.

After withdrawing his resignation Nasser at once took over the Premiership and the ASU and formed a 'government of reconstruction'. The Russians at once showed their readiness to replace most of Egypt's lost arms and equipment and these began pouring into the country during the summer but most of the senior officers had been dismissed and the armed forces had to be reorganized. Nasser was well aware that Egypt was in no position for a counter-offensive against Israel. When he broke several weeks silence to make a public speech on 23 July 1967 he declared that there was no question of surrender but he emphasized his belief that Israel's real aim had been the overthrow of the Egyptian Revolution and this had not been achieved.

Army discontent came to a head in August with a plot by dissident officers to reinstate Abdul Hakim Amer at the head of the armed forces. With the help of loyal and anti-Amer elements in the army Nasser crushed the plot without much difficulty and Amer shortly afterwards committed suicide in mysterious circumstances. The former War Minister Shams Badran and Salah Nasser, the head of military intelligence, had been associated with Amer; they and numerous other officers and a few civilians were arrested and put on trial. In a separate trial the air force commanders in June 1967 were charged with criminal negligence of duty. Although Nasser had taken the *political* responsibility for the defeat he did not accept the military responsibility; he said that he had repeatedly warned the army commanders to expect an Israeli attack and that it would take place on 5 June.

At the end of August the Sudanese Government succeeded in arranging an Arab summit meeting in Khartoum which only the Syrians refused to attend. Nasser made use of the meeting in two important respects: first he reached a kind of bargain with the conservative Arab oil states—Kuwait, Saudi Arabia, and Libya—whereby all pressure on them to continue their boycott of Britain and the US would be removed in return for a large financial payment to Egypt and Jordan 'until the traces of aggression are removed'. This was fixed at £135 million a year of which Egypt would have £95 million and Jordan £40 million. At the same time Nasser reached a final agreement on the Yemen with King Faisal which meant that all Egypt's 40,000 troops were withdrawn by the end of 1967.

In October the Egyptian navy scored an important success by sinking the Israeli flagship, the destroyer *Eilat*, with a missile from a Soviet-made Komar-class patrol boat in Port Said. The Israelis responded with heavy shelling of Suez and other Canal cities and during 1968 the Egyptians were forced to evacuate most of the civilian population from the Canal Zone and move the rest of the oil refinery installations from Suez.

Although President Nasser's public speeches in Egypt were defiant and even bellicose in tone he made it clear that he would prefer what came to be known as a 'political solution' to a 'military solution' of the Middle East problem when he announced Egypt's acceptance of the 22 November 1967 British-sponsored UN Security Council resolution calling for an Israeli withdrawal from the occupied territories in return for Arab *de facto* recognition of Israel.

On 20 February 1968 a military court passed sentences of fifteen and twenty years' imprisonment on the senior air force officers on trial for their conduct during the Six Day War. During the following days there was serious rioting by workers at Helwan and students in Cairo and

Alexandria. Initially the rioters were protesting against the leniency of the sentences but some of the demonstrators began to call for freedom of the press and the dissolution of the ASU. The riots reflected wide-spread dissatisfaction with the failure to make the fundamental changes that had been expected following the June War. Nasser responded by forming a new Government on 20 March still under his premiership but with several new civilian ministers drawn from universities and the professions. Ten days later he announced what came to be known as the 30 March programme to revitalize the revolution. Its basis was the holding of democratic elections to complete the structure of the ASU. In April Nasser held a meeting with university students and faculty representatives to discuss their grievances and agreed that students should be allowed to form their own union and be free from political supervision. On 2 May the 30 March programme was approved by a national plebiscite with 99·99 per cent of the votes in the affirmative and on 25 June the first round of the ASU elections was held with 180,000 candidates contesting 75,000 seats in 7,584 basic units. The ASU National Congress met on 23 July and, on Nasser's advice, drafted an agenda for it to follow. The 1,701 members of the Congress met again in September to elect a 150-member Central Committee with a core of 25 nominated by the President and in October the Central Committee empowered Nasser to nominate twenty of its members for the Supreme Executive Committee of whom ten would be selected by the Central Committee. In November the President dissolved the National Assembly and announced that fresh elections would be held early in 1969. These took place on 8 January. On 24 November he ordered the closing of all Egyptian universities and higher education institutes after further student riots and demonstrations in favour of more democratic government.

In early July Nasser visited Moscow where he agreed with the Soviet leaders on the need for a political settlement in the Middle East. After his return he announced that he would be going back to the USSR for medical treatment. This caused widespread concern about his health but the official version that he was suffering from defective circulation in his leg as a side-effect of diabetes was generally accepted and he returned from the USSR in improved health.

Sporadic fighting with Israel on the Suez Canal front took place throughout 1969 and the first half of 1970. In July 1969 Nasser said that the best strategy for the Arabs was to conduct a 'war of attrition' against Israel. The Israelis launched several commando raids deep into Egyptian territory and Egyptian forces also crossed the Canal into Sinai on several occasions. The Israeli Air Force bombarded Egyptian positions in the Canal Zone with increasing severity and claimed to have destroyed all the missile sites in the area.

President Nasser's planned visit to Moscow in September 1969 was cancelled for health reasons but he paid a secret visit in January 1970 when he was promised increased Soviet aid for Egyptian air and ground defences. The number of Soviet military advisers in Egypt was increased from 3,000 to 8,000–10,000; Egyptian defences improved their performance and succeeded in shooting down at least six Israeli planes in the summer of 1970. Nasser had still not abandoned hope that a political solution to the Middle East problem could be achieved through US pressure on Israel to withdraw from occupied Arab territories. On 1 May he made what he called a 'final appeal' to President Nixon to withhold support for Israel as long as it occupied Arab lands and on 23 July he announced Egypt's acceptance of the Rogers Plan for peace in the Middle East which led to the ceasefire in the Suez Canal area on 7 August. After the ceasefire, Israeli accusations that Egypt had violated the military standstill agreement by installing scores of new missile sites in the Canal Zone were supported by the US.

The much delayed Arab summit meeting held in Rabat in December 1969 was generally regarded as a failure from Egypt's point of view but Egypt's general position in the Arab world was greatly strengthened by the support of the new revolutionary regimes in Sudan and Libya. Plans for a political federation of the three states were under discussion during 1970.

President Nasser was criticized by the Palestinian resistance organizations for his acceptance of the US peace plan but in September he took a leading part in efforts to settle the Jordanian civil war. It was at the conclusion of these negotiations that he died suddenly of a heart attack on 28 September.

Egypt after Nasser

The disappearance of the man who had dominated the country and taken all the major policy decisions for over fifteen years inevitably left a political vacuum. In appointing Anwar Sadat as the only Vice-President in late 1969, Nasser had clearly indicated him as his successor. Under the constitution Sadat became acting President and after the unanimous approval of his candidature by the Arab Socialist Union Higher Executive and the National Assembly his election was confirmed by a national referendum on 15 October in which 90·04 per cent of the votes cast were affirmative. On 20 October Sadat appointed the former foreign minister and presidential affairs adviser Mahmud Fawzi to be Egypt's first civilian prime minister since 1952.

Collective leadership appeared to work well for a time as President Sadat broadly continued Nasser's policies, although in his own style. The removal of Nasser's dominating presence resulted in a perceptible relaxation in the atmosphere of public life. For the first time in many years 'Egypt First' as opposed to Arab nationalist policies were openly advocated in some quarters. It was announced that all the sequestered property of Egyptian nationals would be restored. Through a vigorous diplomatic campaign Egypt succeeded in repairing or improving its relations with Turkey and Iran and several European states. Plans for a tripartite Arab federation (Sudan having dropped out but been replaced by Syria) were pursued and on 17 April 1971 the three heads of state of Libya, Syria, and Egypt announced in Benghazi that it would come into existence on 1 September. This decision was the immediate cause of an open rift in the Egyptian regime. President Sadat dismissed Vice-President Ali Sabry who had led criticism of the federation plans in the ASU and two weeks later several senior ministers and officials (including the Defence and Interior Ministers) resigned en bloc in a clear challenge to President Sadat's authority. President Sadat, who was widely popular and also had the support of most of the army, responded vigorously. He replaced with his own supporters all the resigning officials who in many cases were arrested and charged with planning a coup. In direct appeals to the nation the President promised that all the police state apparatus would be destroyed, that the rule of law would be rigorously applied and that genuinely free elections for the National Assembly and ASU would be held.

Although the upheaval in Egypt was basically a struggle for power, the fact that Ali Sabry and his associates were known for their pro-Soviet sympathies indicated a possible shift to the right. Obviously concerned with the trend of events in a country in which they hold such an important investment, the Russians sent a high-powered delegation led by President Podgorny to Cairo in June. The result was the signing of a fifteen-year Egyptian–Soviet treaty of friendship and co-operation. In fact in the absence of any general Middle East settlement there was little question that Egypt would remain closely associated with the Soviet Union whoever was in power.

SOCIAL SURVEY

Social Welfare

At the time of the coup d'état national income per head of population (after rent had been deducted) was £25, one-seventh of the average for Western Europe.[1] Moreover it was estimated to be no more than three-fifths of what it had been in 1913,[2] and there was every reason to expect that it would fall ever more rapidly as the population increased. Perennial irrigation had had evil as well as good effects, by providing a breeding-ground for water-borne and mosquito-borne diseases in the canals which were often the only water-supply for the villages. Malaria, which had formerly affected more than half the villagers, had been very greatly reduced by the special measures taken since the Second World

[1] Doreen Warriner, *Land Reform and Development in the Middle East* (London, 1957), p. 20.
[2] RIIA, *Middle East*, 2nd ed., p. 245.

War, but three-quarters of the villagers still suffered from bilharzia, and two-fifths from hookworm, with disastrous effects on their vitality. Tuberculosis claimed many victims in the country and still more in the towns, there was much preventable blindness, and the poor in the towns were subject to pellagra. Addiction to hashish was widespread. The Egyptian labourer of 1950 was generally admitted to be a much weaker man, physically, than his father had been.[1] Government medical services, including free treatment in hospitals, mass radiography, and other preventive services already existed, and the sickness, death, and infant mortality rates were falling, but the magnitude of the problem needed action on a corresponding scale.

Since 1952 the regime has made concentrated efforts to improve health standards. The achievements have been considerable although much remains to be done. Bilharzia, which still affects two thirds of the *fellahin*, remains the greatest scourge but there has been encouraging progress in controlling other diseases. Tuberculosis is much reduced and there is good hope of eliminating malaria entirely in the near future. Eye diseases in Egyptian children have also been much reduced and free midday meals for four million schoolchildren have done much to build up their health and resistance to disease.

Although some rural health centres had been established before the Revolution, the programme has since been enormously expanded and speeded up. Experience having shown that villagers will not go more than three miles for treatment, the aim is to establish 2,500 new rural health units each serving 5,000 people within a radius of two miles. By 1964 about 800 of these had been opened, in addition to 168 comprehensive treatment units for endemic disease and 275 combined units which all include health sections. By 1967 there were about 1,680 rural health units with 8,009 beds.

The National Charter states: 'The right of each citizen to medical care, whether treatment or medicine, should not be a commodity for sale or purchase. Medical care should be within the reach of every citizen, in every part of the country and under easy conditions. Health insurance must be extended to cover all citizens'. A comprehensive national health service together with old age pensions, sickness and unemployment benefits for all citizens are inevitably distant goals for a country at Egypt's stage of development. A start has been made with Government employees and by the end of 1964 three million of them were included in a comprehensive insurance scheme.

The provision of free medical care is only part of the problem; the attitude of the people themselves towards disease and infection has to be changed. Ignorance is mainly responsible for the infant mortality rate which has been reduced but remains high. Officially it was 105 per 1,000 in 1962 but because many births and infant deaths are never

[1] Issawi, *Egypt at Mid-Century*, p. 65.

recorded it is probably higher. One of the outstanding achievements of the regime has been the provision of clean drinking water to almost the entire rural population—to 18 million (compared with only two million at the time of the Revolution). Yet this alone does not solve the problem because many *fellahin* still prefer to use Nile or canal water.

The Egyptian Public Health budget has risen from £E10·1 million in 1951–2 to £E31·2 million in 1963–4 and £E44·3 million in 1964–5. In 1951 there were 5,200 doctors or one for every 4,000 inhabitants; in 1964 there were 13,000 or one for every 2,000 inhabitants. In 1962 there were over 57,000 beds in all the treatment establishments in the country or one to every 482 inhabitants compared with one to every 600 inhabitants in 1952. Inevitably the rapid increase in the number of doctors has meant some decline in standards but no very high level of skill is required to deal with the basic needs of the mass of the population; and the Government's decision to make two years' service in the countryside compulsory for all qualified doctors after internship has been a major contribution towards tackling these needs.

Family Planning

Egypt, with its very limited cultivable area, faces a population explosion as dangerous as any in the Third World. Since there is no solution to Egypt's problem within the agricultural sector, rapid industrialization is essential but cannot provide a complete answer. It was not until ten years after the Revolution that President Nasser publicly advocated family planning. This was partly the natural reluctance of the ambitious leader of a developing nation to advocate restricting its manpower and partly acknowledgement of the strength of conservative forces in Egyptain society. But the National Charter states clearly: 'This [population] increase constitutes the most dangerous obstacle that faces the Egyptian people in their drive towards raising the levels of income and production in an effective and efficient way.'

Some experimental birth-control clinics were established and in 1964 the Ministry of Social Affairs decided to establish clinics in all parts of the country. In 1966 415 new family-planning centres were established. Both the loop and the pill were used and all the common difficulties of reluctance and hostility were encountered. As expected, the response was much better in the towns than in the countryside. In 1968 it was estimated that about 350,000 women were using either loops or pills and about 80,000 using loops (excluding those—mainly in the towns—employing birth-control methods privately). In 1967 a three-year programme was launched with the aim of reaching 2,800,000 women by 1970 and reducing the present annual net increase in the population of 2·7 per cent to 2·1 per cent. Nevertheless, many Egyptians feel that the problem is so urgent that it should be tackled still more vigorously and with larger funds.

I

The Status of Women

The success of family planning and the effort to raise social and educational standards is intimately bound up with the status of women. This has been slowly but steadily improving in Egypt since the First World War and there has been some acceleration since the Revolution. President Nasser favoured a far more gradualist approach than Kemalist Turkey out of respect to conservative and religious opinion but the principle is clearly stated in the National Charter that 'Woman must be regarded as equal to man and she must therefore shed the remaining shackles that impede her free movement so that she may play a constructive and profoundly important part in shaping the life of the country.'

The change has been much more apparent in the towns than in the country. There is now a substantial number of women doctors, university teachers, and lawyers. Egypt's first woman Minister, Dr. Hikmat Abu Zeid, was appointed in 1962 and there are always a handful of elected women members of the National Assembly. The strongest single factor behind the emancipation of women has been the growing acceptance of their right to equal educational opportunities with men. The proportion of girls in primary and secondary schools rose to 37 per cent in 1966 compared with 10 per cent in 1913. In 1961–2 26 per cent of Egypt's university students were girls. Social segregation of the sexes remains the rule even among university students but is gradually breaking down.

Easy divorce in Islam and early marriage are both obstacles to family planning and female progress in Egypt. Reforms advocated by the Egyptian intelligentsia have made little headway both because of the strength of conservatism and because of the difficulty of enforcing any change in the law (such as the raising of the legal age of marriage for girls from sixteen to eighteen).

Education

Elementary education has been free and compulsory since 1923, the year after Egypt became independent, and all branches of education have expanded since that time. The British authorities had not, however, left much foundation for the Egyptians to build upon and much still remains to be done. The total school population increased from 324,000 in 1913 to 924,000 in 1933 and 1,900,000 in 1951 although in 1953–4 only 41·8 per cent of the children aged between six and twelve were registered as attending school.[1] The revolutionary regime increased its efforts until an average of two new schools was being opened every three days. By 1961 the total school population was 3·5 million and by 1970 it was approaching 4 million. Vocational schools for

[1] Permanent Council for Public Welfare Services *The Atlas of Services*, 1955, p. 42.

industry, commerce, and agriculture were greatly increased in size and number. From 15,000 students in 1953 these had over 100,000 in 1965.

The number of university students rose from 38,000 in 1951 to 144,981 in 1967. A new university was opened at Assiut in 1957 and the ancient Islamic University of al-Azhar was partially transformed into a modern university in 1961 by the addition of science, medical, and engineering faculties. The number of foreign students studying in Egypt rose from 3,200 in 1952 to 18,845 in 1962, a demand on facilities only in part offset by an increase in the number of foreign students studying abroad from 1,984 to 5,575 in the same period. The Ministry of Education's budget rose from £E40·2 million in 1951 to £E96·5 million in 1964.

By 1965 there were school vacancies for about 80 per cent of the population attaining the age of six and the declared aim of providing primary education for the entire population was within sight. However, the figures for school enrolment do not give the whole picture. In the towns attendance at primary schools is normally about 85 per cent of the enrolment but in the country it drops to 60 per cent or lower in the summer when the children are needed to work in the cotton fields.

It has been the declared intention of the regime to end the socially harmful domination of the country's educational system by the 300 foreign schools. Since 1956 these have all either been nationalized or put under close state control and forced to adapt their curricula to conform with the state system. This and the extremely rapid expansion of the entire system has caused some decline in standards. Classes are far too large at all levels while many teachers are unqualified for their jobs. The shortage of teachers is accentuated by the export of many to other Arab countries (about 5,000 in 1964). The result is that although the illiteracy rate has undoubtedly fallen from its pre-Revolutionary level of 80 per cent it has not fallen as fast as had been hoped.

Trade Unions

Trade unions were first given legal status in 1942 but until the Revolution effective unionism was largely confined to those facing modern foreign companies such as Shell, and confederation was forbidden. In 1952 the organization of agricultural workers—the great body of impoverished Egyptian workers—was legalized. The automatic deduction of union dues from wages, given a certain minimum enrolment, was shortly afterwards instituted, a union could now only be dissolved by decree of a court of law and in 1957 a Trade Union Confederation was established. However, by 1959 there were still over 1,300 separate unions in Egypt of which 120 were in the textile industry alone and average membership was about 100. With Government encouragement, these were amalgamated until by 1964 there were 27 unions covering the whole of industry, mining, transport, agriculture, the civil service, etc.

The socialization of the economy since 1956 has greatly assisted the growth and strengthening of trade unions. Because of the degree of Government sponsorship unions are to some extent part of the state system. Strikes are illegal as in the Communist countries. But the unions are also an independent force of considerable power and some economists consider that they have succeeded in acquiring for industrial workers an undue share of the national wealth.

Some important labour legislation for the protection of industrial workers was enacted before the Revolution. This has been extended since 1952 with the special aim of providing security of employment. A socialist decree of 1961 fixed the maximum working day in industry at seven hours with the declared object of increasing employment rapidly. Other legislation makes it extremely difficult for an industrial worker to be dismissed. There can be little doubt that this has arrested the increase in productivity.

Apart from almost complete security in their jobs, workers have been given two seats on company boards of directors (out of a maximum of seven) and 25 per cent of the profits (10 per cent in cash and 15 per cent in social security benefits).

THE ECONOMY

Agriculture

Despite recent strides in industrialization, agriculture remains the largest single section of the economy absorbing over half the labour force and contributing over 25 per cent of the national product. Egyptian agriculture itself is based almost entirely on the River Nile. The original form of irrigation was to confine the river between high mud banks and to break them in time of flood to cover the fields with water and silt. When the water drained off the crop was sown in the autumn and reaped in the spring, the land being left fallow until after the next Nile flood. This age-old 'basin' irrigation was supplemented from about the middle of the nineteenth century by the development of 'perennial' irrigation which involves the damming and storage of the flood water and its subsequent release during the period of low Nile so as to provide irrigation water all the year round and in particular to permit the growing of summer crops. This was developed considerably during the British occupation; the Delta Barrage was repaired and in the ten years from 1898 a dam at Aswan and various subsidiary barrages were completed until virtually the whole of the Delta and parts of Upper Egypt were converted to perennial irrigation. By 1950 the cultivated area was about 6 million feddans and the cropped area about 10 million feddans.

The building of the High Dam (see p. 256 below) marks a new stage in providing permanent water storage in the gigantic Lake Nasser reservoir to even the supply of irrigation water between years of low and high flood. This has enabled the rest of Upper Egypt to be converted to perennial irrigation and eventually will increase the cultivated area by about 25 per cent.

It is officially estimated that 825,900 feddans of uncultivated land had been reclaimed between 1952 and mid-1968, including 84,700 using subsoil water through tube wells. The current target is a total reclaimed area of 1,299,000 feddans by mid-1975. Priority is now being given to the area with greatest potential which is within the Nile Delta (to the west of Mansoura), to the east in land south of Port Said, and to the west of the Delta near Alexandria where some 300,000 feddans are to be reclaimed with Soviet assistance. Other important reclamation schemes include the Kom Ombo Valley in Upper Egypt where the 50,000 Nubians displaced by the rising waters of Lake Nasser have been resettled and the so-called New Valley project to tap the underground water resources of the Western Desert near the five oases of Kharga, Dakhla, Farafra, Bahriyah, and Siwa.

Although Egypt's cultivated land is very limited the soil is rich and yields are among the highest in the world. The large-scale development of cotton which is still the principal feature of the Egyptian economy was made possible by perennial irrigation in the nineteenth century.

In 1967/8 1·6 million feddans were devoted to cotton cultivation out of a total crop area of rather less than 10·5 million feddans. A total of 1·07 millions feddans were planted with rice of which Egypt is a substantial exporter (650,000 tons in 1967/8) and 1·24 million feddans with wheat of which the country is a big importer (1·5 million tons in 1967/8). Maize accounted for 1·48 million feddans, millet for 0·52 million, barley for 0·10 million, bersim (Egyptian clover planted for fodder and nitrogen-fixing) 2·71 million, beans for 0·33 million, onions for 0·04 million, lentils for 0·06 million, and vegetables for 0·72 million.

Cotton remains the country's biggest cash crop and export item although its proportion is declining. In 1966 it accounted for nearly 60 per cent of the country's foreign currency export earnings.

Yields per acre of cotton, wheat, rice, and sugar can be increased very little because they are so high already. Some economists have therefore advocated that a substantial increase in profit per acre could be achieved by switching to fruit, vegetables, meat, and dairy production. Egypt already grows most Mediterranean types of vegetables and fruits and some tropical ones (such as mangoes) as well as roses, gladioli, and other flowers. It is argued that by concentrating on these Egypt could build up an export trade to Europe and other Arab states in winter and early spring. At the same time mechanization and reduction of the areas under cereals and rice could dispense with many of the draft animals and eliminate the large area used for growing fodder. This intensification of Egyptian agriculture would however require heavy investment.

Agrarian Reform

With the rapid expansion in the cultivated area during the nineteenth century, agricultural production outpaced the increase in population for a time. But this did not last and between 1897 and 1947 while the cultivated area increased by 14 per cent and the cropped area by 37 per cent the population doubled. Yields per acre also increased fairly steadily and it is thought that total agricultural production approximately kept pace with the increase in population.

In 1947 the *per capita* real income of Egypt's rural population was roughly what it had been fifty years before but the distribution of income had become still more uneven.[1] The situation was worse than this might suggest since two feddans is estimated as the absolute minimum from which a *fellah* family can make a living and in 1952 there were 2,018,000 (or 72 per cent of all proprietors) who owned less than one feddan. In addition there were about 1·5 million families (about 8 million people) who owned no land at all and lived by share-cropping or casual labour. More and more were forced to eke out a living by renting or share-cropping an additional small area and between 1939 and 1949 the proportion of land that was rented increased from 17 to 60 per cent. Net income per head of the active agricultural population was estimated at £E34 in 1953. Because of his poverty and the cheapness of labour the *fellah* had neither the ability nor incentive to use modern techniques.

The principal aim of the first land reform of 1956 was the political one of reducing the power of the large landowners. Maximum holdings per family were reduced to 200 feddans then to 100 feddans in the second land reform of 1961 and finally to 50 feddans according to a decree of July 1969. In the redistribution of expropriated land preference has been given to former tenants owning less than five feddans and to permanent labourers. This means that the very large estates have disappeared. Middle-sized estates have been untouched and there has been a small increase in the number of holdings of five feddans or less. The general pattern of Egyptian land ownership, with the vast majority consisting of very small properties, has not changed. When redistribution under the first and second land reforms has been completed it will have affected about one million feddans (out of 6 million) and benefited about 8 per cent of the *fellahin*.

Article 3 of the 1952 law which decreed the compulsory reduction of all agricultural rents, benefited many more—perhaps four million of the farming population—through an average net increase in income of about 50 per cent.

Some, although not all, of this benefit was lost as the pressure of population on land made it easier for the landlords to evade the rent controls, often with the connivance of the tenants.

[1] See Peter Mansfield, *Nasser's Egypt* (London, 1969), table on p. 199.

The Egyptian agrarian reform is regarded as one of the more success-ful of such attempts. There was no drastic fall of output. In the land reform areas where land had been redistributed special supervised co-operatives were established with a large measure of control over the farmers' cultivation and marketing. Output per acre in these areas has generally been well above the national average.

The Nawag Experiment

Improvement of farming methods is much more difficult to achieve outside the reform areas but at the village of Nawag in the Delta an experiment was tried at persuading the villagers, while they retained ownership of their highly fragmented holdings, to group them for the purpose of cultivation into several large fields each under a single crop, as in the supervised co-operatives. The experiment was a success and in 1960 the Government took the decision to extend the supervised co-operatives gradually throughout the country. A start was made with the Governorates of Kafr al-Shaikh in the Delta and Beni-Suef in Upper Egypt. The emphasis is on persuasion rather than compulsion and the response is varied. One limiting factor is the supply of trained super-visors for the co-operatives.

Economic Policy and Industrialization

The economy inherited by the Free Officers in 1952 could only be described as stagnant. Owing to the pressure of population, real in-comes per head were scarcely rising while inequalities of wealth (accentuated by the Korean War cotton boom) were increasing. Hope-less poverty, malnutrition, and disease were Egypt's hallmarks.

While agricultural productivity and rural conditions clearly needed to be improved, industrialization was the obvious priority for develop-ment. Between 1920 and 1950 industrial expansion based on the re-placement of imported consumer goods by domestically-produced substitutes, had been fairly rapid but between 1950 and 1952 the rate of growth had slowed down. Highly protected Egyptian industry showed no signs of becoming internationally competitive and three decades of government-encouraged industrialization had failed to produce more than a handful of efficient industrial entrepreneurs and managers.

Initially neither Abdul Nasser nor the great majority of the Free Officers subscribed to any economic doctrine. If anything they were rightwards inclined and in the years 1952–6 economic policies were liberal and orthodox. Some of the pre-Revolutionary protectionist legis-lation was repealed in an effort to attract foreign investors. Deflation and austerity produced both budget and balance of payments surpluses.

By the end of 1954 it became apparent that economic expansion was essential to prevent a fall in *per capita* income and provide for increased expenditure on social services. A separate Development Budget was

created and public expenditure increased from £E233 million in
1953–4 to £E358·1 million in 1956–7. But there was no attempt to
adopt socialism or centralized planning. The regime's real hopes lay in
the building of a High Dam (with Western assistance).

The Suez War in 1956 had several important effects on the economic
scene. Domestic prices rose sharply and there was a drastic fall in the
price of the Egyptian pound abroad, an economic boycott by the West
and the consequent loss of exports caused a severe strain on the balance
of payments. Net holdings of foreign assets were reduced from £E214
million in 1954 to £E110·6 million in 1957. The economy was only
saved from disaster by the Communist bloc.

The response to the Anglo-French invasion was the sequestration of
all British and French property. In January 1957 all foreign banks and
insurance companies were ordered to Egyptianize themselves and
British and French banks were sold to Egyptian banks. Together with
the nationalization of the Suez Canal Company this meant that the
greater part of the foreign share in the Egyptian economy had been
liquidated. Much of this share was transferred to the Egyptian economy
and between 1957 and 1960 several public economic organizations
were created while others already in existence were expanded to look
after the Government's interests and to fill the vacuum left by Egyptian
private capital.

The State's share in the economy was growing and the trend was
certain to continue. A State National Planning Committee was established, and in 1958 a Five-Year Plan for Industry was launched and in
1959 the Iron and Steel Works built by the West-German Demag was
opened. By 1959–60 74 per cent of total investment compared with only
31 per cent in 1932–58. By the end of 1957 President Nasser was speaking of a 'socialist, democratic, co-operative system' as Egypt's goal. Yet the
regime had not abandoned hope that 'national capital' would undertake an important share of industrialization in addition to the State.

In 1959 the Bank Misr and the National Bank of Egypt were
nationalized. The significance of this step was that for the first time it
concerned Egyptian firms rather than foreign-owned companies. In
June and July 1961 in a series of socialist decrees the Government took
over the entire import trade and a large part of the export trade including cotton. All banks and insurance companies were nationalized
and about 300 industrial and trading establishments were taken over
either wholly or partly by the State.

In July 1960 a comprehensive Five-Year Plan for 1960–5 was
launched to be followed by a Second Five-Year Plan with the ambitious
target of doubling national income by 1970. Eighty per cent of the
investment would be undertaken by the public sector.

One of the factors behind Syria's secession from the UAR in September 1961 was reaction against the application of the Socialist

Decrees to Syria. President Nasser for the first time formulated his economic ideas in the National Charter of May 1962. In this he laid down that the entire economic infrastructure, the majority of heavy, medium, and mining industries should be publicly owned. All the import trade, most of the export trade, banks, and insurance companies must be within the public sector.

The economic framework of the National Charter was fairly closely adhered to. Most of the remaining companies still in private hands were taken over by the State. In August 1963 a further series of nationalization affected some 300 concerns which were either private companies or had already been partly nationalized. All contracts for quarrying and mining issued to private concerns were ended. In April 1964 Shell-BP interests in Egypt were nationalized.

In March 1964 119 contracting companies—already 50 per cent nationalized by the 1961 decrees—were fully nationalized and merged into 35 larger companies.

Since 1964 there have been no major nationalization measures. In theory the private sector was still to play an important though minor role in the economy but not surprisingly private entrepreneurs were nervous and reluctant to invest. Since 1967 the Government has made a special effort with some results to revive the private sector—especially in export industries and construction.

Domestic trade has remained largely in private hands although Government co-operative retail shops have played an important role. The Government has used various techniques to hold down the cost of living including rationing, subsidies, and price and rent controls. These measures combined with industrialization, increased industrial wages and the distribution of profits have substantially increased the incomes of the urban working class. In 1965–6 prices began to rise more steeply but despite the disaster of 1967 the Government was able to check the rise in 1968–9. Increased urban incomes have to be set against the flow of underemployed agricultural workers from the countryside into the towns where industrialization is quite unable to provide them all with employment.

Development Plans

The targets for the first Five-Year Plan were ambitious but most of them were either attained or nearly attained. The annual increase in GNP between 1960 and 1965 was between six and seven per cent[1] despite a drastic fall in cotton output in 1961/2 due to pest attacks. However, this rate of expansion could not be maintained because the sources of foreign exchange were drying up. In 1966 it was decided to deflate and rename 1965–7 the 'years of consolidation'. Drastic cuts

[1] See Hansen and Marzouk, *Development and Economic Policy in the UAR (Egypt)* (Amsterdam, 1965).

were made in imports of raw materials and capital goods and investment plans were scaled down. The result was a marked improvement in the balance of payments. In early 1967 Egypt was ready to begin a new period of expansion from a stronger base as the benefits of the High Dam (see p. 256 below) were beginning to be felt, Suez Canal revenues were steadily increasing and the outlook for the oil industry was highly promising.

The Effects of the Six Day War

The 1967 war caused the loss of £90 million a year in Canal revenues, about half of Egypt's oil output of approximately 9·5 million tons a year and most of Egypt's tourist income.

In addition it imposed a huge new armaments bill. Disaster was avoided because of the aid from Arab and East European states which after the Khartoum Conference in August 1967 was put on a regular basis of £95 million a year. Also discoveries of crude oil made by US independent companies, Pan-American in the Red Sea and Phillips in the Western Desert in 1966 soon more than made up for the loss of the Sinai fields. Total output in 1969 was about 15 million tons a year or 290,000 barrels a day and had risen to 400,000 barrels a day by the end of the year with a target of 500,000 b.p.d. by the end of 1970.

In addition the international agricultural terms of trade turned in Egypt's favour in 1967–8 and finally the High Dam was unaffected by the 1967 War.

In 1968 Egypt recorded its first trade surplus for many years as a result of continued import restrictions and strenuous efforts to increase exports. In the same year the Government decided to resume industrial expansion although with a determination to avoid the recurrence of unmanageable debts. The biggest project in the next phase of development will be the expansion with Soviet aid of Helwan Iron and Steel Works from its present capacity of 300,000 tons a year to 1·5 million tons. The Soviet Union has pledged £E70 million for equipment and machinery for the first stage estimated to cost £E277 million.

Foreign Aid and Indebtedness

From 1956 onwards Egypt's foreign indebtedness has increased at an alarming rate. It is estimated that between 1957 and 1965 Egypt received a total of £1,321 million in foreign loans and credit facilities (excluding military credits). In addition there were compensation payments for British, French, Belgian, Swiss, Lebanese, and other nationalized and sequestrated property.

Egypt's credit-worthiness reached its lowest point in 1966 when it actually stopped its $3·5 million monthly principal and interest payment to the IMF. After 1967 the Government made a determined effort to improve its reputation for paying its debts. It restored relations with the IMF and successfully rephased most of its commercial debts. But Western creditors remain extremely wary as Egypt's total indebtedness is estimated to have reached $1,500 million.

Manufacturing Industry

Egyptian industrialization really started between the two world wars and production rose by 138 per cent between 1938 and 1951. But the pace has been greatly increased since the Revolution and especially from 1957–8. The 1960/5 Five-Year Plan provided for an investment of £E519 million in manufacturing industry and the 1965–70 Plan for £E960 million although this was later scaled down. According to the Egyptian Ministry of Industry total investment in industry between 1952 and 1967 amounted to £E1,029 million and the value of production rose in value from £E313·8 million to £E1,256·40 million. The manufacturing sector now accounts for over 20 per cent of GNP. Textiles are the most important branch of industry contributing over a third of the total value of output.

Egyptian industry produces a wide range of production and fills local demand for most manufactured products. Fiat buses and cars, Yugoslav tractors and US RCA television sets are assembled in Egypt with more of the manufacturing process carried out in the country each year. One of the problems has been that the rapidly growing home market has reduced the surplus for export. However, in the second half of 1969 industrial exports (including crude oil) were worth £E58·2 million as against £E75·5 million agricultural exports in the same period. Apart from textiles, exports include tyres, cement, oil products, fertilizers, bicycles, and refrigerators.

Communications

The compactness of Egypt's inhabited area means that it is not seriously handicapped by a shortage of transport facilities. Today it has about 4,400 miles of standard gauge and 870 miles of light railways or about 15·5 miles of railway for every 100 sq. miles of inhabited area. In 1964/5 the railways carried 2·05 billion ton miles of freight and 3·8 billion passenger-miles.

Since 1952 the Government has concentrated more heavily on roads and in 1966 there were 15,160 miles of which 35 per cent had improved surfaces. The Cairo–Alexandria dual carriageway Delta road was completed in 1960 and the Cairo–Ismailia desert road in 1965. About half the country's freight goes by road.

Egypt has a total of about 1,930 miles of navigable waterways divided equally between the Nile and the canals. The bulk of passengers and goods entering and leaving Egypt go via the port of Alexandria which ranks third among Mediterranean ports after Genoa and Marseilles.

Egyptair is now operating regular services between Cairo, Alexandria,

Port Said, and seven other centres as well as the various international routes.

The Suez Canal

The Canal Company was nationalized in 1956 and in 1958 the new Suez Canal Authority began implementing a major £E40 million scheme, known as the Nasser project, for widening and deepening the Canal to permit the passage of ships of 55,000 tons instead of 30,000 tons. In 1966 the Authority outlined further plans to deepen the water-way further to enable 100,000-ton tankers to use the Canal fully loaded. However, with the oil companies building 250,000-ton tankers designed to sail around the Cape of Good Hope it seems that some of the Canal traffic would have been lost even without the closure of the Canal in June 1967.

In 1968 the Egyptian Government decided to build a 200-mile 42-inch oil pipeline with an initial capacity of 50 million tons a year from Suez to Alexandria which would enable super-tankers to unload at Suez the oil which would then be trans-shipped to smaller vessels at Alexandria. Arrangements for the financing of this scheme by a con-sortium of French, Italian, and Spanish companies were completed in the summer of 1972.

The High Dam

The Aswan High Dam has been the core and mainstay of Egypt's eco-nomic development over the past decade although its effects have only begun to be felt. Ultimately it will increase the cultivated area by about 25 per cent but the cheap power that it will provide for industry is of almost equal importance. The official estimate of the increase in the national income that it will produce is as follows:

		£E (millions)
1.	Increasing the present cultivated area by about one million feddans and converting 700,000 feddans in Upper Egypt from basin to perennial irrigation	63
2.	Guaranteeing water requirements for crops even in years of low flood, improving drainage, and guaran-teeing the cultivation of one million feddans of rice annually	56
3.	Protecting the country against the dangers of high flood, preventing seepage and the inundation of small islands and river banks	10
4.	Improving navigation conditions on the Nile	5
5.	Producing electric power annually of about 10 thousand million kwh.	100
	Total	234

The total cost of the Dam including turbines, canals, drains, roads, etc., is estimated at £404 million. The main body of the Dam was completed on schedule in 1969 and the hydro-electric station (which will triple Egypt's electric energy production) was completed in July 1970. The 300-mile-long Lake Nasser above the Dam will have reached full storage capacity by 1972–3.

The High Dam has certain drawbacks which were mostly foreseen before its construction began. The fertilizing silt which was held back by the Dam has to be replaced by artificial fertilizers. The fact that Nile waters no longer reach the Mediterranean destroys the important sardine fisheries at the mouth of the Delta by depriving the fish of their food supplies. The change from basin to perennial irrigation means the spread of bilharzia which is already endemic in Lower Egypt. Erosion of the river and canal banks owing to the increased water supply has turned out to be more serious than expected. However, there is no question that the advantages greatly outweigh the drawbacks. In particular the plan launched in 1971 with Soviet aid to bring electricity to all the 85 per cent of Egyptian villages which are at present without it amounts to a revolution in Egyptian rural life.

IV
Iran

Iran, comprising some 628,000 square miles in the western half of the Iranian plateau, is bounded on the north by the Caspian Sea and the Soviet Union, on the south by the Persian Gulf and the Gulf of Oman, on the east by the Soviet Union, Afghanistan, and Baluchistan, and on the west by Iraq and Turkey. The greatest extent of the country from north-west to south-east is some 1,400 miles, and from north to south some 875 miles. It can be broadly divided into the following regions:

The Caspian littoral is a narrow strip of land between the Caspian sea and the Elburz mountains, containing the provinces of Gilan and Mazandaran. The rainfall, well distributed throughout the year has a maximum in early autumn, and varies from 50 to 60 inches in the west to 20 inches in the east, and rises to over 100 inches on the northern slopes of the Elburz. The natural vegetation is dense deciduous forest, but where this has been cleared fruit, rice, cotton, and other crops thrive. Summer temperatures seldom exceed 90° F (32·2° C), but from June to mid-September there is excessive humidity. Winter frosts are unusual. The prevailing wind is north.

The Persian Gulf and its hinterland. The climate is hot and humid; temperatures of 125° F (51·8° C) have been recorded. The eastern end of the coastal region comes under the influence of the south-west monsoon. In the coastal district of Baluchistan the average annual rainfall is 3–4 inches. Bushire has an average annual rainfall of about 10 inches. The hottest month is August when the temperature rises to 115° F (46·1° C), and from towards the end of July to mid-September the humidity is excessive. The prevailing wind is north-west, with short intermittent periods of south-eastern to south-western winds accompanying periods of winter rainfall. In Khuzistan the hottest month is July, when the temperature rises to 120° F (49·0° C). The average annual rainfall is 12–15 inches, with a maximum in December. The hinterland includes some of the poorest parts of Iran.

The plateau. The plateau is ringed by mountain ranges, the general trend of which is from north-west to south-east. Its elevation varies between 3,000–5,000 feet; numerous peaks rise to over 12,000 feet; vegetation on the plateau is generally limited, but some forest is found in Kurdistan and Luristan, and a narrow belt of oak forest in Fars. Considerable areas, notably in Azarbaijan, Kurdistan, and northern

Fars, consist of hill country and mountain pastures. Considerable variations of climate are found. The seasons are regular; the atmosphere is dry and clear, and the sun powerful at all altitudes. There is a great range of temperature, the mean daily maximum in Tehran being 44° F (6·7° C) in January and 99° F (37·2° C) in July, with a relative humidity of 76 and 47 respectively. In Yazd the summer temperature ranges from 90° to 115° F (32·2° to 46·1° C); in winter there are several degrees of frost; dust storms occur in spring and summer due to local winds between mountain and plain. Temperatures in Khurasan range from 10° F (− 12·2° C) in winter to 110° F (43·3° C) in summer. The only source of rain or snow is a series of depressions swinging eastwards along the Mediterranean, which are to some extent concentrated across north Iran, giving Mashad (9 in.) higher rainfall than, for example, Kerman (5 in.). They are, however, mostly interrupted by the Armenian massif and the Caucasus in the north and the Zagros in the west, so that much of the available water is lost and the plateau within the mountains is in a rain shadow. In general the 10-inch rainfall line follows the inner foothills of the Zagros–Elburz–Kopet Dagh ring of mountains, and also marks the boundary between areas where cereals can be cultivated extensively without irrigation and areas dependent on irrigation. The summer grazing areas of the nomadic tribes also lies in or near the 10-inch line. Rain begins in November and continues intermittently to the end of March, and in the south and north-east to the end of April. Heavy snowfalls are common in winter. Most of the plateau drains into inland lakes and swamps. The only navigable river is the Karun, which flows into the Persian Gulf.

Hot and relatively low land, comprising primarily the two great salt deserts south-east of Tehran, the Dasht-i Kavir and the Dasht-i Lut, and Sistan. The climate of Sistan is one of extremes: May and June are hot, but in winter blizzards occur. The average annual rainfall is 2½ inches.

The People

Many peoples, both in ancient and modern times, have passed through or settled in Iran. Those known to history as the Medes and Persians probably came originally from the Eurasian steppe. Later migrations, notably of Semitic tribes and, from Central Asia, of Turkish tribes, changed the ethnological structure of the country. The most important of these migrations in modern times was that of the Oghuz Turks in the eleventh and twelfth centuries AD; the large Turkish admixture in the Iranian population is mainly attributable to them. Turki-speaking elements are found today among the settled and semi-settled population, especially in Azarbaijan, Gurgan, eastern Mazandaran, and the districts of Qazvin, Hamadan, and Saveh, and also in Varamin and Khwar, near Tehran.

The 1956 census put the total population at 18,944,821, that of Tehran (*c.* 300,000 in 1939) at 1½ million. A 1969 estimate gave the total population as 28,165,837 and that of the metropolitan area of Tehran as 2,980,041. Approximately 60 per cent of the total population are dependent on agriculture and 20 per cent are semi-nomadic tribes. Density over the whole country, even if the desert areas are excluded, is extremely low; it is highest in north-west Azarbaijan, the coastal regions of Gilan and Mazandaran, Khuzistan, and the Tehran area. There are no vital statistics, but infant mortality is known to be very high.

Among the more important tribes are: the Turki-speaking Qashqai of Fars, who start to migrate in March from their winter quarters in southern Fars to their summer quarters near the northern boundaries of Fars, west of Shahriza and Yazd-i-Khast, extending to the eastern slopes of Mt. Dinar, whence they return in September; the Kurds, found chiefly in western Azarbaijan, Kurdistan, and the Kermanshah region;[1] the Bakhtiaris, who range from north-east Khuzistan to west of Esfahan, and are divided into two main divisions, the Haft Lang and Chahar Lang; the Lurs of Luristan; the Shahsavan, a Turkish tribe ranging from the Mughan steppes to Qum and Saveh; the Guklan and Yamut Turkomans in the north-east frontier districts; and the Baluch of Iranian Baluchistan. Other tribal groups in Fars include the Khamseh, of mixed, partly Arab origin, the Mamasani, the Boir Ahmadi, and the Dushmanziari. In Khuzistan are a number of sedentary and pastoral Arab tribes speaking Arabic; in Khurasan the Hazara are supposed to be descended from colonists left by Jenghiz Khan in the Oxus valley.

Language

The Persian language is a member of the Iranian group of Indo-European languages. Old Persian was the language of the Achaemenian emperors, known through cuneiform inscriptions and Avestan texts; Middle Persian belongs to the Sasanian period, the chief sources for which are Zoroastrian literature and secular texts in Pahlavi; modern Persian is the most widely known branch of New Persian. Kurdish, Luri (spoken by the Lurs and the Bakhtiaris), Mazandarani, and Gilaki (spoken in the Caspian provinces) also belong to this group. Modern Persian is the language of the administration and is spoken by the educated classes throughout the country. It is written in the Arabic script and contains a large number of Arabic loan words. It has an extensive literature going back to the tenth century.

Religion

The Iranians are predominantly Moslem. The Ithna Ashari or Jafari

[1] Small settlements also exist in western Mazandaran and Khurasan.

rite of the Shii sect,[1] which recognizes twelve hereditary Imams, is the official religion of the country. The cities of Najaf and Karbala in Iraq, being the burial places of Ali, the first Imam, and of his son Hussein, the third Imam, respectively, are important centres of Shii pilgrimage; Mashad, the burial place of the eighth Imam, Reza, and Qum, the burial place of his daughter Fatima, are also pilgrimage centres. The Kurds, Turkomans, and Baluch are mainly Sunni. Christianity, Judaism, and Zoroastrianism are also officially recognized. The largest Christian group is formed by the Armenians, numbering some 80,000, mainly concentrated in the large towns, especially Tabriz, Tehran, and Esfahan. There are some 40,000 Jews, mainly in the large towns. About 7,000 Zoroastrians are concentrated chiefly in Yazd, Kerman, and Tehran. There are also a number of Bahais, whose religion is not officially recognized and against whom there have been sporadic outbreaks of violence in recent years, the most serious in 1955.

HISTORY AND POLITICS

Iran's existence as a national state in the modern sense goes back to the sixteenth century. The area over which successive Iranian governments ruled has varied; the frontiers of present-day Iran, compared, for example, with those of the reign of Shah Abbas (1587–1629) or at the beginning of Fath Ali Shah Qajar's reign (1797–1834), have contracted considerably. The main losses have been to Russia in the north-west and north-east and to Afghanistan in the east. During the Middle Ages Iran did not exist as a political entity and was merely a geographical term.

The first great Iranian empire was the sixth-century BC Achaemenian Empire, which, at its height, extended from Transoxiana to North Africa, and was overthrown by Alexander in 334–330 BC. The Seleucids, the Arsacids, and the Greek principalities of Bactria then arose as succession states.

In the first half of the third century AD, with the rise of the Sasanians, there was a reaction against Hellenism. Sasanian rule was mainly notable for centralization, the re-establishment of Zoroastrianism as the state religion, and a hierarchical society of priests, warriors, the bureaucracy, and peasants and artisans. The main external problem was to hold the north-eastern frontier against pressure from the Eurasian steppe, while in the west the Sasanians were occupied in a struggle for power with the Byzantine Empire. The Sasanian Empire reached its height under Anushiravan (AD 531–79), but after his death it rapidly declined until its extinction by the Arabs in the seventh century.

Arabs, Turks, and Mongols

It was largely the incorporation of the Sasanian domains into the

---

[1] See above, p. 34.

Arab empire of the Umayyad Caliphs (661–750), with its capital at
Damascus, that eventually led to the transfer of power to Baghdad, the
capital of the Abbasid Caliphs (750–1248). The majority of the
Iranians became converted to Islam, until recent times the strongest
single influence in Iranian cultural development. Under the Abbasid
Caliphs Iranians played an increasingly important part in the life of the
empire. After the reign of Harun al-Rashid (786–809) the effective
authority of the Caliphs began to decline, and from the ninth to the
eleventh centuries a series of semi-independent Iranian dynasties
reigned in the eastern part of the empire. Pressure from the nomads of
Central Asia was meanwhile renewed, and in 1040 Masud ibn Mahmud, the Ghaznavid, was defeated at the battle of Dendenqan by the
Oghuz Turks, who subsequently overran the whole of the eastern
Caliphate. The most prominent group among them was the Seljuqs,
who established an empire extending, in its heyday, from Transoxiana
to the shores of the Mediterranean. Under the Seljuqs the Iranians
again played an outstanding part in administration and culture.
Finally, in 1153, Sanjar, the last of the Great Seljuqs, was defeated by
fresh bodies of Oghuz from Central Asia, and the Great Seljuq Empire
broke up into a number of succession states, including that of the Shahs
of Khwarazm.

During the period from the ninth to the twelfth centuries considerable
changes took place in the social and economic structure of the country.
Whereas in the early period of Arab domination the economy was predominantly a gold economy, the administration bureaucratic, and the
civilization predominantly urban, by the tenth century the financial
economy had broken down and the administration was becoming
largely militarized. In Seljuq times these changes took firmer shape.
The new structure, which, in broad outline, lasted until the nineteenth
century, was not feudal in the European sense of the term. It was rather
a bureaucracy of the Asiatic type. With the breakdown of the power of
the central Government, the military leaders, as provincial governors,
diverted the revenue from the state treasury into their own pockets, and
arrogated to themselves such privileges as the former ruling class had
enjoyed.

The next wave of invasion from Central Asia was that of the Mongols. The Shah of Khwarazm was defeated during the lifetime of
Jenghiz Khan (d. AD 1227) and the way to Iran was opened. Its final
conquest was brought about by his grandson, Hulagu, who founded
the Ilkhan dynasty, which lasted for something under 100 years,
breaking up into warring factions about AD 1335. Towards the end
of the fourteenth century Iran was incorporated in the immense
empire of Timur (d. 1405), which stretched from the Oxus–Jaxartes
basin in the east to Iran and Iraq in the west, and whose capital was
Samarkand. It did not outlive its founder in western Iran and Iraq,

and the eastern portion disintegrated on the death of Shahrukh in AD 1447.

The Safavids

The political vacuum thus created was eventually filled by the Safavids, originally the heads of a religious order centred on Ardabil in north-west Iran. By 1508 the dominions of Ismail, the founder of the dynasty, extended from Herat to Baghdad and Diyarbekr. In the west the ulti-mate result of a long-drawn-out struggle with the Ottoman Empire was the establishment of a frontier running from the Caucasus southwards to the Persian Gulf. Using Shiism as a political instrument in this struggle with the Sunni Ottomans, Ismail imposed this form of Islam upon his subjects, most of whom had till then remained Sunnis; from this time onwards the Islamic world was split into two groups, Sunni and Shii.

During the rule of the Safavid dynasty, which reached its height under Shah Abbas (1587–1629), an Iranian political and commercial revival took place. Contact with Europe increased; a variety of missions was sent by European countries to the Safavid courts, and European trading stations were established on the Persian Gulf.

The Safavid dynasty virtually came to an end with the revolt of the Afghans (1721–30), who were in turn overthrown by Nadir Shah Afshar (1735–47), under whom the Iranian Empire extended, for a fleeting period, from the Indus to the Caucasus. The Afsharid dynasty was succeeded first by the Zands and then by the Qajars, the first of whom was Aqa Mohammed (1779–97). The Qajar dynasty lasted until 1925.

The Qajars

The emphasis in Iran's relations with Western countries during the eighteenth century began to change from commerce, where it had lain during the Safavid period, to strategy. By 1914 the main emphasis had been transferred to oil. The dominant feature of nineteenth-century Iranian politics was the rivalry of the Great Powers. During the Napoleonic period both France and Britain sent missions to enlist the support of the Iranian Government. Russian pressure upon Iran, which had been felt in the first half of the eighteenth century, when Gilan had for a while passed into Russian hands, meanwhile increased. Two Russo-Iranian wars ended disastrously for Iran: by the treaties of Gulistan and Turkmanchai she lost to Russia all her territory west of the river Aras. By the latter, Iran granted extra-territorial privileges to Russian nationals, and fixed at 5 per cent ad valorem (though this was reciprocal) the customs duty on all Russian goods entering Iran. This became the basis for commercial agreements concluded with other European Powers and the grant to them of extra-territorial privileges.

Subsequently there were losses of Iranian territory to Russia in the north-east. During the nineteenth century Anglo-Russian rivalry in Asia increased and there was a tendency on the part of the British Government to regard a Russian threat to Iran as tantamount to a Russian threat to India. This situation almost inevitably created a cleavage in Iranian internal affairs between those who looked to Russia and those who looked to Britain.

During the latter half of the nineteenth century maladministration reduced Iran to critical straits. Largely in order to replenish the exchequer rather than to modernize the country, concessions were granted by the Shah to foreign governments and foreign nationals for commercial and industrial enterprises, banks, road-building, and the like, and large sums were borrowed from abroad. Meanwhile, misgovernment, the extravagance of the Court, the grant of wide economic privileges to foreigners, and the restrictions put upon the political freedom of the country by the terms of certain of the foreign loans, aroused more and more discontent. This feeling, coupled with the stirrings of a desire for progress among the educated classes, culminated in the constitutional revolution of 1905–6, and the grant of the Constitution by Muzaffar al-Din Shah in 1906. The new regime, however, soon met with difficulties. On 31 August 1907 came the Anglo-Russian Agreement, which divided Iran into Russian and British spheres of influence and a neutral zone. Neither party was to seek political or commercial concessions in the sphere of the other. This agreement was a profound shock to Iranian opinion, which could not realize that with a war with Germany on the horizon Britain was compelled to compromise with Russia. It was also a prelude to more flagrant intervention by Russia, who seemed determined to prevent the successful working of the Constitution. Mohammed Ali Shah attempted with Russian support to overthrow the Constitution, one of his principal instruments being the Iranian Cossack Brigade, which had been formed in 1879 by Nasir al-Din Shah, and was led by Russian officers who remained on the active list of the Russian army. The Russians occupied Tabriz in April 1909 and remained there for over a year. In 1909 Mohammed Ali Shah was forced by the constitutionalists to leave the country. He returned, with Russian connivance, but was again driven out; and his son Ahmad Shah was placed on the throne. In 1911 north Iran was again occupied by Russia, who issued an ultimatum to the Iranian Government demanding the dismissal of Morgan Shuster, an American who had been engaged as Treasurer-General some nine months before. The result was a coup d'état, the closure of the Majlis, and Shuster's dismissal. Thereafter Russian ascendancy continued to increase until the outbreak of the First World War, when Iran became a battleground for Turkish, Russian, and British forces.[1]

[1] Sir P. M. Sykes, *History of Persia* (London, 1930), vol. 2.

Iran emerged from the war in a state of chaos, with three armed forces and an empty treasury. In 1919 the Government signed with Britain the abortive 1919 agreement, which provided for the supply of British advisers for the administration, some military officers and equipment for a single armed force, a loan, and co-operation in the development of transport. By the early 1920s Russian pressure began to relax, and on 26 February 1921 the Soviet–Iranian treaty[1] was signed, by which the Soviet Government renounced 'the tyrannical policy' of Tsarist Russia, remitted all Iranian debts to the Tsarist Government, and abandoned extra-territorial privileges for Russian nationals. The treaty also gave up all concessions then held by the Russian Government or Russian nationals, but they secured under pressure the most valuable concession, the Caspian fisheries, which had formerly been held by Russian nationals but had lapsed. All previous treaties and conventions concluded by the Tsarist Government were declared null and void. This treaty was ratified by the Majlis, which however refused to ratify the Anglo-Iranian agreement of 1919. The latter had been much criticized, especially in the United States, as aiming at a disguised protectorate over Iran, whereas the Russo-Iranian treaty received little study, and few even noticed the clause authorizing Russia to send troops into Iran in circumstances of which Russia would be the sole judge.

Reza Shah and Modern Iran

It was at this juncture that Reza Shah, a colonel in the Cossack Brigade, came into prominence. He led troops on Tehran and brought about the coup d'état of 1921, making himself first Minister of War and Commander-in-Chief, and later Prime Minister. In October 1925 the Majlis voted for the deposition of Ahmad Shah Qajar. A Constituent Assembly was then convened, and in December it voted that the throne be entrusted to Reza Khan, who took the name 'Pahlavi' for his dynasty, and to his male descendants. The early years of Reza Shah's reign were largely occupied in the establishment of law and order by a series of successful campaigns against the tribes. Some of the migratory tribes were 'settled' by him, in the sense that they were forbidden to move between summer and winter pastures, whereby they and the economy of Iran were impoverished. Compulsory military service was introduced, and the army was more than doubled in size. Communications were improved, legal reform was carried out, and the Capitulations were abolished. The finances of the country, which had been entrusted to an American economist, Dr. Millspaugh, as Administrator-General, were reorganized; but in 1927 a dispute between the Shah and Millspaugh as to expenditure on the army led to the dismissal of the American financial mission. Education was reorganized on Western

[1] *British and Foreign State Papers*, cxiv. 901.

lines, though with greater attention to numbers of schools and pupils than to quality; in 1936 women were compelled to discard the veil, and European costume was made obligatory for both sexes. Industrialization was encouraged. Gradually, however, the regime became increasingly totalitarian; the façade of parliament was preserved, but the people were deprived of political responsibility and had little opportunity for effective action. Meanwhile the Shah became the owner of large areas of good land, by confiscation on political charges or by methods of purchase which, however disguised, amounted in fact to expropriation.

It is still too soon to make a fair estimate of the reign of Reza Shah. In that he restored order, abolished the privileges of foreigners, and raised the status of Iran in international affairs, he deserved well of his country. On the other hand by doing everything himself he deprived a generation of Iranians of training in the art of government. He encouraged industry but neglected the main occupation: agriculture; he built the Trans-Iranian Railway without recourse to foreign loans but crushed the poorer classes by indirect taxation to pay for it. Through failure to take advice or from other causes his efforts were often misdirected, so that at the end of his reign his country had grain elevators with no grain in them, a steel works under construction in a spot economically impossible for a country without assured supplies of local iron ore, and a string of palaces in a capital lacking a proper water-supply. The latter part of his reign made his people forget the real services he had performed in the earlier years, and his abdication in 1941 was received in Iran with almost universal acclaim. Attempts which are sometimes made in Iran to represent him as a beloved monarch torn by the Allies from his sorrowing people have no support from contemporary Iranian records.

Reza Shah took up strongly the Iranian claim to Bahrain,[1] from which the Iranians were driven by the Arabs in 1783. The claim was maintained by successive Iranian governments but dropped in 1970.

The Second World War

On the outbreak of war Iran declared her neutrality. The country was in feeling pro-German, and in 1941 a vehement correspondence took place between the British and Soviet governments and the Shah about the removal of the Germans resident in Iran, the Allies regarding them as a great danger and the Shah denying this. On 26 August 1941 British and Russian forces entered the country, and Iranian resistance ceased after two or three days. The United States Government, appealed to by Reza Shah both before and after the invasion, emphasized in reply 'the global nature of the conflict with the Axis', advised Iran to avoid assisting the Axis and to aid the Allies, and placed the invasion

[1] See above, p. 193.

'in its true light as one small element in the vast effort to stop Hitler's ambition of world conquest'.[1]

The immediate problem confronting the Allies, in addition to the danger which the Axis missions and nationals constituted, was to guard against the threat to British oil supplies and Allied security in general if the Germans should continue their successes in Russia and enter Iran. It was also essential to secure for the dispatch of aid to Russia a way less exposed to German attacks than the route to Murmansk and Archangel. On 16 September Reza Shah, believing, wrongly, that an advance on the capital by Russian troops was directed against him personally, abdicated in favour of his son, Mohammed Reza, then aged 23. The Iranian Government broke off relations with the German and Italian Governments and later with the Japanese Government. In September 1943 the Government declared war on Germany and thereby qualified for membership of the United Nations.

On 29 January 1942 a tripartite treaty of alliance was concluded with Britain and the Soviet Union,[2] who undertook 'to respect the territorial integrity, sovereignty, and political independence of Iran' and 'to defend Iran by all means at their command from all aggression'. The Iranian Government for its part undertook to render specified non-military assistance to its allies. These were permitted to maintain armed forces on Iranian soil, but their presence was not to constitute a military occupation, and they were to be withdrawn not later than six months after the termination of hostilities between the Allied Powers and Germany and her associates. The Allied Powers undertook not to interfere in the internal affairs of Iran, and jointly 'to use their best endeavours to safeguard the economic existence of the Iranian people against the privations and difficulties' resulting from the war.

After the German attack on the Soviet Union in June 1941 but before the Japanese attack on Pearl Harbour made the United States a belligerent, the Lend-Lease Act of 1941 'made the United States an auxiliary of Great Britain in the task of delivering supplies to the USSR through the Persian Corridor'.[3] In the end there were some 30,000 American troops in Iran, but they were non-combatants: they were employed in dispatching aid to Russia, and in particular in running the Trans-Iranian Railway from the Persian Gulf to Tehran instead of the British, who had handed over in May 1943. The Soviet authorities administered the railway section north of Tehran. The American troops operated throughout as part of the British forces, who were responsible for law and order, and in the execution of that task often incurred the sole odium for acts undertaken in the interests of the

---

[1] *Memoirs of Cordell Hull* (New York, 1948), ii. 1501–2.
[2] Cmd. 6335.
[3] T. H. Vail Motter, *The Persian Corridor and Aid to Russia* (Washington, Dept of the Army, 1952), p. 4.

Allies in general. Some Americans held that United States interests required the regularization of the position of her troops by an agreement with the Iranian Government, but negotiations to that end dragged on for a long time and were never completed. However, on 1 December 1943 Roosevelt, as well as Stalin and Churchill, signed the Tehran Declaration, undertaking to continue to make available to Iran such economic assistance as might be possible, and expressing the desire for the maintenance of the independence, sovereignty, and territorial integrity of Iran.[1]

Except in the matter of aid to Russia the Allies were far from being united in Iran. In Millspaugh's opinion,[2] 'the Soviets acted strongly, with self-confidence, a consciousness of power, and a clear conception of their postwar national requirements, while the British and Americans acted timidly, without clarity of purpose, postponing issues, and compromising principles'. The country became divided in practice into two zones, roughly north and south of the latitude of Tehran. In spite of the treaty of 1942 the Soviet authorities interfered with the movement of goods and the passage of Iranian officials, police, and troops between the Soviet zone and other parts of Iran. Iran's internal economy broke down. Transport was dislocated; the food situation worsened; security deteriorated; inflation became serious. In these circumstances the Iranian Government again had recourse to American advisers. A food adviser was appointed in 1942, a military mission under General Ridley in July of the same year, and advisers to the gendarmerie, headed by Colonel Schwartzkopf, shortly afterwards. Finally in November 1942 Millspaugh was invited to return to Iran, with a financial mission. He took up his duties as Administrator-General of Finances in February 1943, and in May was granted additional powers to control imports and exports, prices and distribution, to fix rents, and to control wages in all public works and services. He met with opposition from various internal quarters, and he was regarded with suspicion by the Soviet authorities, who withheld their co-operation. For these and other reasons he attained only a limited success, and in February 1945 he resigned.

The Iranian–Soviet Dispute and the Separatist Movements

In 1943 the Royal Dutch Shell Company applied for an oil concession in south-east Iran, and in the spring of 1944 the Socony-Vacuum and Sinclair Oil Companies also submitted proposals. The applications were still awaiting a decision when early in September a Soviet official arrived in Tehran, and, after a tour in the north, asked for an oil concession. The Iranian Government then announced that applications for

---

[1] Texts of this Declaration and of the 1942 treaty are given by Arthur C. Millspaugh, *Americans in Persia* (Washington, D.C., 1946), App.
[2] Ibid. p. 157.

oil concessions must wait until the end of the war, but on 2 December 1944 the Majlis adopted a law forbidding ministers and officials even to discuss oil concessions with anyone. Fierce attacks by all the means of Soviet propaganda brought about the fall of the Iranian Prime Minister. Meanwhile the Soviet authorities prevented Iranian security forces from entering Azarbaijan and the Caspian provinces; in Azarbaijan the Tudeh party, which had changed its name to the Democrat party, with the support if not at the instigation of the Soviet authorities set up an autonomous government in December 1945.

In January 1946 the Iranian Government referred the matter to the Security Council, which decided to leave the parties to negotiate directly with each other, but to retain the question on the agenda. No agreement had been reached by 2 March 1946, the date after which, under the treaty of 1942, no Allied troops were to remain in Iran. The last British troops left on that date (the Americans had all been withdrawn by the end of 1945); but the Soviet Government announced that it would retain troops in north Iran until the situation should be clarified. It was not until 9 May that the Iranian Prime Minister could announce that the Soviet troops had left the country. On 5 April an Iranian spokesman had announced the conclusion of an oil agreement with the Soviet Government, subject to ratification by the Majlis. The agreement provided for the formation of a Soviet–Iranian Oil Company, in which the Soviet Government would hold 51 per cent of the shares for the first 25 years and 50 per cent for the next 25, the Iranian Government in each case holding the remainder. In June there were negotiations between the Democrat party in Azarbaijan and the Iranian Government.

In July 1946 a general strike occurred at Abadan, with violent rioting and bloodshed. Genuine grievances were exploited by the Tudeh Party, which used various non-economic cries, including the incitement of Iranians against their (Iranian) Arab fellow workers. The Prime Minister took some members of the Tudeh party into his Cabinet, and one of them 'discovered' a plot among the Bakhtiari and caused several leaders of the tribe to be arrested. A serious tribal revolt broke out in the south and the Prime Minister dismissed the Tudeh ministers and then sent troops into Azarbaijan, where the 'autonomy' movement collapsed, as did a linked movement in Kurdistan.

The oil company bill was not presented to the Majlis within the seven-month period prescribed by the Iranian–Soviet agreement. Electoral and other delays prevented its submission until 22 October 1947, and then it was rejected by 102 votes to two. The Majlis also passed a resolution forbidding the grant of any oil concession to any foreign Government or the acceptance of any foreign Government as partner. It decided that Iran should embark on a five-year prospecting programme out of her own resources and that, if oil was found, the

Government might negotiate for the sale of the product to the Soviet Union. The Soviet Government accused Iran of treacherously violating her commitments and of hostile actions 'incompatible with normal relations between two states'. Soviet propaganda became increasingly menacing.

On 10 December the Prime Minister, Qavam al-Saltaneh, was defeated on a vote of confidence—a sacrifice probably to Soviet anger. His policy, reinforced no doubt by the watchfulness of the United Nations, had secured the departure of the Soviet troops without payment of the price in oil that the Soviet Government had obviously counted on securing. In the same month a significant speech was made in the Assembly by Dr. Musaddiq. In its propaganda the Soviet Government had argued that the Iranian rejection of the oil agreement constituted unfair discrimination against the Soviet Union since the British held an oil concession in the south of Iran. Musaddiq maintained that Iranian interests demanded a policy of 'negative balance'. 'Positive balance', he said, would involve giving Russia an oil concession in the north because the British had one in the south—a suicidal policy. 'Negative balance' meant, by implication, the elimination of the British concession. From that moment the AIOC concession was doomed.

The American–Iranian Military Agreement

The American policy enunciated in 1947 which came to be called the Truman Doctrine[1] was soon extended from Greece and Turkey to Iran. On 22 December the United States submitted to the United Nations an American–Iranian agreement,[2] signed on 6 October 1947, which provided for the establishment of a United States military mission in Iran to co-operate with the Iranian Minister of War in 'enhancing the efficiency of the Iranian Army'. The agreement was to remain in force until 20 March 1949. It included a clause providing that Iranian army affairs might not be entrusted to military experts of other Powers without American consent. A Soviet note of 31 January 1948 accused the Iranian Government of lending itself to American plans for converting Iran into a military-strategic base, and demanded that it should take immediate steps 'to eliminate the existing abnormal situation', which it considered incompatible with the state of good-neighbourly relations proclaimed in the Soviet–Iranian Treaty of 1921.[3] An Iranian reply of 5 February contained counter-allegations. The exchange of notes continued against a background of bitter Soviet radio propaganda. It was a year later, but perhaps not without relation to that propaganda, that

---

[1] See above, pp. 25–6.
[2] US Treaties and Other International Acts, series no. 1666 (1948). The agreement has been extended annually for one year.
[3] Full version of note in *Soviet News*, 3 February 1948; see also 'Persia and the USSR', *World Today*, March 1948.

the Shah was shot at and wounded by a member of the Tudeh party. The party was proscribed and a number of its leaders were arrested.

Nationalization of the Oil Industry

In 1948 negotiations with the AIOC had been opened for the conclusion of a Supplemental Agreement for a revision of the royalty terms. An agreement was initialled in July 1949, but although the revenue receivable by Iran with effect from 1948 would have been increased considerably thereby, the Oil Committee of the Majlis reported against the agreement in November 1950 and the Government withdrew it. The opposition to the agreement was led by Musaddiq and supported by the extreme nationalists and the religious elements. Long dissatisfied with the Iranian share of the oil proceeds, the opponents of the AIOC were easily able, in a country where since the Anglo-Russian Agreement of 1907 Britain had been the scapegoat, to persuade the public that the AIOC was responsible for the grievous state of the country and moreover guilty of political interference in the internal affairs of Iran. In March 1951 the Prime Minister, General Razmara, was assassinated; this murder, and the assassination of the Minister of Education a few days later, hastened the passage of bills for the nationalization of the oil industry through both houses of parliament in April 1951. In May Musaddiq became Prime Minister. He was now in a position to establish that 'negative balance' which he had recommended in 1947. He rejected the request of the AIOC to submit the dispute to arbitration in accordance with the terms of the 1933 agreement, and by October 1951 the company found its position impossible and withdrew the last of its employees from Iran. The British Government and the company severally filed petitions with the International Court, the former asking the Court to declare Iran bound by the 1933 agreement to accept the company's request for arbitration, the latter asking the Court to nominate an arbitrator. The Iranian Government declined to recognize the Court's jurisdiction. Britain meanwhile referred the dispute to the Security Council, which decided on 19 October 1951 to defer consideration of the Iranian case pending the pronouncement of the International Court. The judgement was not delivered until 22 July 1952, when the Court held that it had no jurisdiction owing to the limitations imposed by the Iranian Government when it accepted the compulsory jurisdiction of the Court; it also held that the 1933 agreement, although concluded under the auspices of the League of Nations, was not a treaty, and that the British Government was not a party to the contract. The majority of seven to four in Iran's favour included the British judge.

From August 1951 to February 1953 repeated efforts were made to provide a solution. Proposals were put forward by the AIOC, by British and Americans jointly (on one occasion with a personal appeal from

Truman and Churchill), and by the International Bank, but Musaddiq would listen to none of them. The oil industry which he had undertaken to make more profitable to Iran brought in virtually nothing. To maintain his position he was compelled to rely more and more upon the Tudeh, and there were frequent clashes between supporters and opponents, often with fatal casualties.

In August 1952 Musaddiq was given full powers for six months, in economic, banking, judicial, administrative, military, and financial matters, and this period was subsequently extended for a second six months. He was thus free to try to effect a social revolution if he wished. One possible change, viz. the breaking up of large estates in favour of peasant proprietorship, he opposed strongly, and he stopped the Shah's land-distribution scheme. He did issue decrees reducing the landlord's share of agricultural produce for the benefit of the peasant and abolishing certain dues and services, but as the reforms were to be carried out by newly created bodies whose members in most cases would be the nominees of the landlords, and as the decrees were extremely complicated in other ways, the good effects were insignificant.

Musaddiq pursued the disagreement with the British Government to the extent of closing down all British Consulates in Iran and finally of breaking off diplomatic relations. In home affairs he quarrelled with all the other elements of government: the Senate, the Majlis, and finally the Shah. He forced through a law (abrogated after his fall) reducing the period of office of senators from six years to two and thereby brought about the dissolution of the Senate. He then arranged a plebiscite, not provided for in the Constitution, declared that the vote was in favour of the dissolution of the Majlis, and dissolved it forthwith. On 13 August 1953 the Shah, in the exercise of his constitutional powers, appointed General Zahedi Prime Minister; Musaddiq, who was unable to oppose this constitutionally by trying to prevent the new Prime Minister from getting a vote of confidence from the Majlis (since it no longer existed), refused to recognize the Shah's order. Zahedi's attempt to establish himself as Prime Minister at first failed, and the Shah and the Queen left the country and went to Rome. On 19 August, however, Musaddiq's supporters were defeated and he was arrested and the Shah returned. Musaddiq was sentenced to three years' solitary confinement for trying to overthrow the regime and illegally dissolving the Assembly. His Minister for Foreign Affairs, Hussein Fatemi, was sentenced to death for treason and executed (November 1955).

The Post-Nationalization Era

In the reaction that followed the overthrow of Musaddiq, opposition activity and political parties of all shades were suppressed and the press subjected to strict controls. With Musaddiq under arrest, its leaders and members in prison or otherwise harassed, and its ranks in disarray, the

National Front ceased to function as an organized political force and had to resort to covert activity. The Tudeh party was again proscribed and disappeared underground, but in January 1954 fifty of its members were arrested on charges of conspiring to murder the Shah. In the autumn the Government published details of a conspiracy in the armed services designed, it was stated, to establish a Soviet republic in Iran. Many officers were arrested and over fifty were condemned to death, but in the end only six of these were executed and some thirty had their sentences commuted to life imprisonment; the majority of those arrested received a royal pardon in the autumn of 1956. A member of the Central Committee of the Tudeh was also executed. The *Fadayan-i Islam* came into notice again when one of its members in November 1955 made an unsuccessful attempt on the life of the Prime Minister, Hussein Ala. This led to the execution of the assailant, of two other members of the society, and of the assassin of Razmara, who had been released from prison by Mussadiq. The latter was himself released from prison in August 1956 on the expiry of his sentence and confined to his estate at Ahmadabad, where he remained under house arrest until his death in 1967.

Power, especially after the retirement of Premier Zahedi in 1955 and the appointment of Ala, a staunch upholder of royal prerogatives, as his successor, tended increasingly to be concentrated in the hands of the Shah, a trend that continued under Premiers Manuchehr Eqbal (1957–60) and Jafar Sharif-Emami (1960–1). In the elections to the eighteenth Majlis in 1954 and the nineteenth Majlis in 1956 (when the term of the Majlis was extended from two to four years), care was exercised to ensure that only those with acceptable political views secured seats to the two Houses.

These measures of political control were tempered by efforts at economic development, through which it was hoped to secure a higher standard of living for the middle and lower classes. The budgetary position of the country, in spite of the resumption of oil revenues, was still serious, and in February 1955 the Majlis approved a Loans Bill authorizing the borrowing of $150 million from the United States and £10 million from Britain for public works and for meeting the budget deficit. However, the steady growth of oil revenues continued, American aid permitted more ambitious economic planning, and in February 1956 the Second Seven-Year Plan Law was approved.

In foreign policy, the Government was induced by both political and economic considerations to identify itself closely with the Western camp. Diplomatic relations with Britain were resumed, and Ambassadors appointed, in January 1954. On 3 November 1955, Iran joined the Baghdad Pact, an act reflecting a desire for increased Western arms assistance and also for security against Communist subversion. These steps further strained relations with the Soviet Union. Nevertheless, the two countries concluded a trade agreement in June 1954; on 2 December they signed an agreement for settlement of Iran's financial claims against the Soviet Union arising out of the Second World War and a second agreement settling frontier claims. Iran's participation in the Baghdad Pact, however, elicited violent verbal attacks from Moscow, to which Iran replied in kind. The campaign died down shortly before the Shah's visit to the Soviet Union in 1956; but the goodwill generated by that visit did not last long. When negotiations on a non-aggression pact between the two countries broke down in 1959, probably because Soviet terms proved unacceptable to Iran and also because the Government had its eyes fixed on securing increased military assistance from the United States, Moscow resumed its vehement propaganda campaign.

The internal political atmosphere remained strained, however. Nationalist passions released during the oil nationalization struggle were not quelled by the post-Musaddiq settlement. The anti-Western feelings generated during the period rendered the Government's pro-Western orientation, symbolized by adherence to the Baghdad Pact, even more unpopular. Reformist aspirations could find no outlet in the restrictive political atmosphere. Large-scale Second Seven-Year Plan Development Projects, though necessary to build up Iran's infrastructure, could not yield results quickly. Besides, the sudden inflow of oil revenues and aid money led to widespread corruption. Political unrest was also fed by galloping inflation. The cost of living rose by almost 40 per cent in the 1955–60 period and at about one per cent per month in 1960–1. By the late 1950s unemployment was widespread, and imports of luxury goods had sapped the country of its foreign exchange reserves. By May 1961 there was sufficient foreign exchange for only two weeks of operations. At the instance of the International Monetary Fund and as a condition for the provision of foreign exchange, the Government in 1960 agreed to an economic stabilization programme severely restricting credits, imports, and foreign exchange spending. But initially at least this only added to economic pressures on the middle and lower classes.

The corrective measures adopted proved to be chiefly gestures rather than genuine attempts at reform. Anti-corruption legislation, known as the 'Where did you get it from?' law, passed in 1958, was never seriously implemented. A second bill, for land reform, was submitted to parliament in 1960 but it was shorn of its teeth before it was approved by the two Houses and was in any case not vigorously applied. In 1959, at the Shah's initiative, two of his loyal supporters formed two political parties: the first, Melliyun, to serve as the majority party and the second, Mardom, to serve as the loyal opposition. But this conferred the trappings of democracy without the substance, and won no support.

These various political and economic dissatisfactions came to a head in the summer of 1960 during the elections to the twentieth Majlis, when it was expected that the Mardom and Melliyun parties and other acceptable candidates should divide the seats among themselves. Extra-parliamentary criticism could not be suppressed, however, and the National Front, Mozaffar Baqai's Toilers' Party and a group of independents led by Ali Amini spearheaded a campaign attacking election rigging, corruption, the lack of civil liberties, and the economic situation. Election irregularities were so widespread and blatant that in August the Shah expressed dissatisfaction with the conduct of the vote and asked the deputies so far elected to resign, thus in effect annulling the election. Eqbal resigned as Prime Minister and Sharif-Emami, a member of the out-going Cabinet, was appointed to replace him.

The Sharif-Emami Government lasted a brief eight months. The period witnessed the beginning of economic stringency, a call for reform and revision of the electoral law, and the replacement of a number of high-ranking military officers, including the unpopular and publicly-feared chief of the Security Organization, General Teymour Bakhtiar. But all activities were over-shadowed by the necessity of legalizing Government operations by convening parliament. Elections were held and Majlis convened by February 1961. But widespread irregularities and arrests of opposition leaders and of students fed public unrest. In Majlis men like the National Front leader, Allahyar Saleh, who had been given seats as a gesture to opposition pressures, found a public forum from which to attack the Government. The final blow came on 2 May when a teachers' strike for higher pay led to the shooting of one of the strikers. The Sharif-Emami Government fell on 6 May.

The Amini Reforms

Ali Amini, whom the Shah appointed as Prime Minister at this critical juncture, was a wealthy aristocrat who had held a string of important government appointments. He also was believed to be a liberal and a reformer, a reputation he had enhanced as a critic of the Eqbal Government during the abortive 1960 elections, and initially at least was moderately acceptable to both the Establishment and its left-wing opposition. The new Premier moved with great energy during his first few weeks in office. Several high-ranking civil servants and retired military officers, including five generals, were arrested on charges of corruption. Among these were General Alavi-Moqaddam, the former Chief of Police and Interior Minister, General Ali Zargham, a former Minister of Finance, and General Hajj Ali Kia, a former chief of army intelligence. Amini also loosened controls on the press and permitted a far greater measure of freedom to the National Front and other left-wing groups, allowing them to reopen their clubs, to hold public meetings, and to issue statements. He brought into the Cabinet as Agriculture Minister Hassan Arsanjani, a left-wing politician committed to land reform and the break-up of the large estates. And he announced further programmes for economic retrenchment and civil service reorganization.

These measures, considered radical in the prevailing atmosphere of caution and conservatism, bespoke a degree of autonomy and independence that the Shah had not granted to any Prime Minister since Musaddiq. The Shah also acceded to a demand by Amini for the dissolution of Majlis, a body which the new Premier believed an obstruction to reform, and issued a decree to this effect on 9 May. On 14 November, the Shah conferred even greater authority on Amini by issuing a *farman* (royal decree) empowering the Prime Minister to rule by Cabinet decree until such time as Majlis was reconvened. The *farman*, while instructing the Prime Minister to carry out a programme of reforms, stated that Cabinet decrees would have the force of law once they received the royal assent. It thus had the effect of bypassing the constitutional provisions requiring Majlis approval of all statutes and of making the Shah party to the Premier's conviction that elections could be held only after far-reaching reforms had been implemented.

The measures undertaken by the new Government met with some degree of success. Amini was able to curb several years' runaway inflation and to introduce greater rationality in Government planning, to end nearly a decade of political paralysis by opening up a dialogue with the opposition, and to begin the great task of administrative reform which was to bear fruit five years later. A High Administrative Council (transformed in 1966 into a Civil Service Commission) was established to undertake the task of civil service reorganization. The ambitious Third Development Plan Law was approved. A revised land reform bill, perhaps the most important single step taken in Iran in the decade of the 1960s, was passed by the Cabinet on 9 January 1962. The work of breaking up the big estates was begun, and Arsanjani pursued the task with great vigour.

Amini's programmes were, however, frustrated by deep institutional problems, the difficult economic situation he had inherited from his predecessors, and opposition from both the right and the left. Several privileged and powerful factions reacted unfavourably to the Prime Minister's reform measures. The great landowners opposed the break-up of their estates and received support from their allies among the Moslem authorities. High-ranking civilian and military officials feared the extension of the anti-corruption drive. Politicians who had been prominent in former governments resented the closure of parliament and their exclusion from the higher circles of government by Amini's younger technocrats. The army was restrained by the arrest of some of its retired officers and by a well-founded belief that the Prime Minister intended to cut their budget in favour of other sectors of the economy. Amini's excessive reliance on US support also left him open to charges of permitting foreign interference in Iran's internal affairs and caused serious deterioration of relations with the Soviet Union. The Prime Minister's tendency to blame internal riots on Soviet machinations (leading, on one occasion, to a formal Government protest to the Soviet embassy in Tehran) further exacerbated this trend.

Much more crucial was the fact that the Prime Minister's relative independence of the Court and his energetic assertion of prime ministerial prerogatives strained relations between Amini and the Shah. Finally, many of the more sympathetic members of the public, though aware of extenuating circumstances, were genuinely disturbed by the continued suspension of parliamentary rule and contravention of the Constitution, while economic restrictions and the Premier's own excessively gloomy prognostications led to a flight of capital and further economic stagnation. The National Front, although enjoying greater freedom than at any time since Musaddiq, also failed to support the Government, insisting that parliamentary elections be held. This Amini refused to do, arguing that elections could not be free nor the incoming Majlis liberal unless reforms had first taken effect. A meeting between the Premier and National Front leaders on 7 June failed to resolve the deadlock. Under increasing pressure from its own following, and against the Government's wishes, the National Front leadership called for demonstrations on 30 Tir (21 July) to mark Musaddiq's return to power a decade earlier. The demonstrations were suppressed, National Front leaders arrested, and party headquarters closed. The next day in a public speech, Amini for the first time attacked the Front, practically equating it with the Tudeh. These events marked the end of the honeymoon between the left and the Government.

Another major confrontation between the Government and the opposition took place on 21 January 1962. University students clashed with police, the National Front called for a nation-wide strike, and hired thugs, in the pay of right-wing groups, took to the streets to incite violence. The Government moved ruthlessly against both the right and the left. Between 22 January and 26 January the Government arrested eight Front leaders, closed down three right-wing newspapers, and put one editor and two right-wing politicians, Assadollah Rashidian and Fathollah Forud, behind bars. On 26 January, Teymour Bakhtiar, the once powerful chief of the Security Organization (SAVAK) left the country on the Shah's orders, the monarch acceding to a request by the Prime Minister for his expulsion. The National Front later hotly denied charges that it had collaborated and conspired with right-wing groups. But the fact was that both the Front and Amini's reactionary opponents had been party to the violence in an effort to unseat the Government.

While Amini thus appeared to emerge victorious against his

K

opponents, from January on the Government's attention and energies were increasingly sapped by the need to fight its political opposition. Besides, Amini was clearly not in full control of the Government administration and even of many members of his Cabinet, while the growing estrangement between the Shah and Amini was paralysing Government activity in most spheres. Amini also failed to resolve a budget deadlock which in 1962 further widened divisions within the Cabinet and between the army and the Prime Minister. The budget, due before the beginning of the New Year on 21 March, was delayed as the Cabinet wrestled with a deficit ranging anywhere between $60 and $160 million. The deficit itself was due to unrestrained spending by the ministries and to the fact that US budgetary support which had totalled $39 million (of which $24 went to the army) had been cut off, a step of which the Prime Minister had been forewarned but for which he failed to prepare. Amini hoped to keep his development budget intact and to cut the deficit from the allocations for non-development spending, chiefly the army. The military failed to accept this decision and Amini, refusing to reduce development allocations, handed in his resignation in mid-July.

Reassertion of Royal Authority

The appointment of Asadollah Alam, a close personal friend of the Shah's, as Amini's successor marked the resumption by the Shah of direct control over governmental activities. Alam enjoyed a number of advantages over his predecessor. He was a more acceptable figure to the conservatives. His special relationship with the Shah precluded the tensions characteristic of the Amini period. Success in the foreign policy field relieved Alam from pressure from the Soviet Union at a time when domestic problems required all the Government's attention. These problems were not in essence different from those confronted by Amini or, later, by Alam's successors. There were several elements in the Government's aims: steering a middle course between its left-wing critics, who were demanding a wider distribution of wealth and power, and the conservatives on the right who opposed all change; reviving a stagnant economy; turning the inefficient and often corrupt civil service into a powerful administrative instrument; and securing mass support among an apathetic and (newly-landed farmers aside) largely dissatisfied populace. At all times, the Government was exercised to retain control in its own hands, to introduce change but to prevent the pace of change from spinning out of control.

The Alam premiership thus presaged no radical departures. In fact Alam retained seven members of the Amini Cabinet, and based his programme on the Shah's 14 November *farman* issued to the Amini Cabinet. The retention of Arsanjani as Agriculture Minister was particularly significant, indicating a commitment to a continuation of the land distribution programme. Alam wasted little time agonizing over the unresolved budget issue left over from the Amini administration. He dealt with a deficit of between $70–80 million simply by cutting back the Third Development Plan allocation by 25 per cent. The administrative budget was kept practically intact and allocations to the army were substantially increased over the previous year. On the vexed question of elections, the new Premier initially promised an early vote for the Majlis. But he later said elections for local town councils would have to come first. The Shah confirmed this view in an address on 5 August 1962 in which he outlined a plan for multi-tiered elections, beginning with village councils and working up through town and provincial councils to culminate in elections for the National Assembly. A law embodying these concepts was approved by the Cabinet in October.

The local councils law, however, met with strong opposition from the religious authorities. Although it did not specifically grant women the vote, it did not bar them from exercising the privilege either. Religious leaders argued that female suffrage conflicted with Islamic precepts and demanded that the Prime Minister revoke the new measure. Seeking to outflank the mullahs, Alam announced on 11 November that the Government would hold elections for Majlis in the spring and that these would precede local council elections. This failed to satisfy the mullahs however. On 1 December, Alam yielded and, describing the local councils law as 'unenforceable' at the present time, declared it 'postponed' but not 'cancelled'. However, the Government's retreat on this issue was only temporary, stemming from a decision to avoid confronting the mullahs on two fronts at the same time and to give precedence to land reform—to which the mullahs were also opposed—rather than to female suffrage.

Land reform itself moved ahead with determination under the energetic direction of Hassan Arsanjani. Government counsels were divided, however, as to the necessary speed and scope of land distribution. Arsanjani made no secret of his conviction that land reform, up to then limited to the large estates, should be extended to cover middle-sized estates and the *waqf* (religious endowment) properties as well. Other Cabinet ministers urged a more cautious policy. A remark by Arsanjani on 2 November that landholdings were to be further limited caused sufficient concern among landowners for Arsanjani to be forced to retract his statement and for Alam on 5 November to assure landowners that no further extension of land reform was contemplated. Peasant land hunger, on the other hand, exerted its own momentum, while land distribution was a measure popular both on the farms and among the urban middle and working classes. On 11 December, the Shah announced a scheme under which religious endowment (*waqf*) properties would be brought under the purview of land reform as well. Under the plan, the Government was to lease the *waqf* properties attached to the Shrine of Imam Reza in Mashad and to parcel them out on long-term sub-leases to the peasants.

To commemorate the first anniversary of land reform the Government convened a Farmers' Congress in Tehran in January 1963. It used this dramatic gathering of 4,000 peasants to mobilize public support behind land reform and other Government programmes and to still the voice of critics who charged that rule by Cabinet decree in the absence of parliament was unconstitutional. Inaugurating the Congress on 9 January, the Shah announced he was submitting land reform and five other bills approved by the Amini and Alam Cabinets to a national referendum. He justified this unprecedented step by citing powers vested in the monarch by the Constitution and Article 27 of the Fundamental Laws which stipulated that 'all power stems from the people'. The five measures in addition to land reform submitted to public vote were a bill for the sale of State-owned factories to help finance land reform; nationalization of the nation's forests; a law which required up to 20 per cent of factory profits to be distributed among its workers; a revision of electoral laws to give more weight on the powerful supervisory councils to workers and farmers; and the Literacy Corps, a scheme under which young high-school graduates would be recruited into the army but would fulfil their military service requirements by teaching in village schools.

Shortly before the referendum, the land reform law was revised and given wider application. Its provisions were extended officially to cover the *waqf* properties, and the upper limit on landholding, previously set at one village per landlord, was drastically reduced. The practice of sharecropping was declared abolished.

Opposition to the referendum quickly materialized among a number of groups. Smaller landlords were discomfited by the extension of land reform to the middle-sized estates, while businessmen feared the consequences of the workers' profit-sharing law. But these two groups were anxious rather than actively obstructionist. More serious opposition came from the mullahs and the National Front. The mullahs, who had from the beginning opposed land reform because of its effect on their traditional allies among the great landlords, were further roused by its extension to *waqf* properties. In mid-January, Ayatollah Behbahani, a notable religious leader, asked the Prime Minister to except the *waqf*, but Alam refused to make such a commitment. The National Front declared themselves in favour of the reforms but opposed to the 'unconstitutional' method of carrying them out. This distinction, however, was lost on the mass of farmers and workers who favoured the reforms, while the Government managed through intelligent publicity to lump the Front with the mullahs and to brand both as reactionaries. Denied the right to assemble in public or openly to voice their views, the mullahs and the Front resorted to extra-legal means and once again on 22 January 1963 took to the streets. The demonstration was suppressed on 25 January and almost all 35 members of the National Front Central Committee as well as numerous religious leaders and theological students were put behind bars. Most of the Front leaders were later released. But Mehdi Bazargan and Mahmud Taleqani, the leaders of the Iran Freedom Movement, the most radical faction within the Front, were kept in prison and eventually brought to trial. A military court in January 1964 sentenced Bazargan and Taleqani to ten years each and seven other members of the movement to prison terms ranging between one and six years. These sentences were confirmed by an appeals court in March. The referendum itself was held on 26 January 1963 and, according to official returns, 5,598,391 (or 99·9 per cent) voted 'yes' against 4,115 voting 'no'.

An incidental by-product of the referendum was that it paved the way for female suffrage. Largely at the instance of Arsanjani, women were permitted to set up their own ballot boxes and to vote separately and unofficially during the referendum. The experiment was successful enough for the Shah to announce in February that women would no longer be barred from voting in future elections, and a measure to this effect was approved by the Majlis the following year, in February 1964. The extension of land reform did not solve intra-Cabinet differences about the speed with which land distribution should be carried out, the funds which should be allocated to this end, and the ultimate authority in the villages. These differences led to Arsanjani's resignation early in March. Although initially the pace of land distribution slowed down after his departure (the 'second phase' was not carried out until much later), the reform, once begun, could not be contained and was widely extended in subsequent years. The referendum had, however, greatly strengthened the Government's hand and had largely discredited those who had opposed it. While little more was heard of the National Front after January 1963, religious opposition to the Government, led by Ayatollah Khomeini, the most prominent of the Iranian Ulema, continued. Khomeini, speaking from his pulpit in Qum, sharply intensified his attacks against the Government, whose measures he branded 'unconstitutional' and 'un-Islamic' during the mourning month of Moharram in May–June 1963. His arrest and that of 28 other religious leaders led on 4–5 June to riots in Tehran, which spread to Mashad, Tabriz, Qum, Shiraz, and Esfahan. The riots were quelled only after troops were sent into the streets with 'shoot-to-kill' orders and after many demonstrators had lost their lives. A national strike, called by the Ulema for 11 June, failed to materialize.

The Government later charged that the riots, instigated by Khomeini, were financed by foreign money and implied that funds for this purpose had been provided by President Nasser. This charge was not subsequently developed. On 6 July, however, the Government formally charged Hajji Tayyeb Rezai, the reputed 'baron' of Tehran's fruit market, and seventeen others with instigating the riots. On 4 August, a military court sentenced Tayyeb and four others to death, one of the accused to life imprisonment, eleven others to prison terms of varying length, and acquitted one man. An appellate court later commuted the death sentence for three of the condemned, and Tayyeb and a colleague were shot by firing squad on 2 November.

The Alam Government emerged victorious and the mullahs discredited from the June riots, and it was significant that the National Front had on this occasion not joined hands with the mullahs in seeking to unseat the Government. However, the cost of the collision was fearful, a lesson that was lost neither on the mullahs nor on the Government. Besides, it was clear that there were economic causes for working class and middle class unrest. The Alam Government's attempts to revive the economy had not borne fruit. Third Development Plan projects remained far behind schedule, unemployment soared, and investment by the private sector remained low. Businessmen's confidence had been sapped by land reform, by the workers' profit-sharing law, and the general atmosphere of uncertainty and disorder. The Government's own tendency towards budgetary indiscipline and unproductive spending aggravated the financial crisis. There was a continued clamour for an end to rule by Cabinet decree and a return to parliamentary government. Tribal disorder in Fars was not quelled until mid-1963.

On 17 September 1963, Alam finally held his long-promised general elections, this time under a revised set of procedures. For the first time, women were allowed to vote, the balloting itself, which used to drag on for weeks, held on the same day throughout the country, and voters required to use official, standardized balloting papers. Alam announced that the elections would be free, and that all would be permitted to participate. In fact, the candidates were carefully screened, participation limited and the choice largely confined to the Government slate. A year earlier, when the opposition appeared stronger, Alam had opened direct but secret talks with the National Front leader, Allahyar Saleh; these contacts were continued through intermediaries in the spring of 1963 when several National Front leaders were in prison. However, the two sides could not agree on basic issues such as freedom of activity for the Front and its participation in any future Government. The contacts were subsequently broken off. Thus in the September elections the major and practically only slate of candidates offered the electorate was the officially-blessed 'Union of National Forces', an organization of leading civil servants and officials, and including representatives of workers and farmers, put together with Government support. Official returns gave the bulk of seats to the Union and the new Majlis was inaugurated by the Shah on 6 October.

The largest group in the new parliament was the Progressive Centre, an elite club of high-ranking civil servants formed by Hassan Ali Mansur in 1961 with the stated purpose of carrying out scientific, economic, and social research. In June 1963 the Shah appointed the Centre his personal research bureau and a month later Mansur officially announced that his Centre would contest the forthcoming elections. The Centre, and Mansur himself, had played a leading role in the Union of National Forces and had won forty seats in the new Majlis. As soon as the Majlis met, 100 other deputies joined Mansur under the Progressive Centre banner. In December Mansur redesigned the Centre as an exclusive, 500-man political party known as the Iran Novin (New Iran) party. These careful preparations bore fruit in March 1964 when Alam resigned and the Shah appointed Mansur to head the Government.

An account of the Alam premiership would be incomplete without reference to developments in the foreign field. In September 1962 the Government gave the Soviet Union written and verbal assurances that it would not permit foreign missile bases on Iranian soil nor allow Iran to become a base for aggression against the Soviet Union. The assurance ended an extended period of hostile feelings and laid the foundation for numerous bilateral agreements. Most immediately, a series of accords, negotiated in earlier years but never ratified, were brought to conclusion. These included a transit agreement in October 1962 and a frontier delineation agreement in December. In July 1963 the two countries concluded an agreement under which the Soviet Union extended to Iran a loan of $36 million to help finance a joint hydro-electric dam across the Aras River on the Iran–Soviet frontier, a string of silos in Iran, and the development, with Soviet assistance, of Iran's fisheries. In November 1963 Leonid Brezhnev became the first Soviet President to make a State visit to Iran. In the wake of improvement of relations with the Soviet Union, trade was also expanded with Hungary, Poland, Yugoslavia, and other Eastern European countries.

Experiment in Party Government: 1964–

Mansur's premiership marked the beginning of a long period in which the Government was free from serious opposition pressure, either in parliament or out of it. In the Majlis, Mansur's Iran Novin party enjoyed a comfortable majority, and the Mardom party, nominally in the opposition, voted along with the Government on all bills. The only measure that created difficulty was one permitting American military personnel stationed in Iran and facing trial to be tried by American rather than Iranian courts, but even this bill was eventually approved. Outside Majlis, systematic arrests, prison sentences, and general controls weakened the ranks of organized political groups, while the Government's land distribution programme and other reforms undermined their appeal. Denied redress through normal channels, those opposed to the regime after 1964 tended increasingly to resort to underground activity and violence, although this was not of a scale to undermine governments. Ayatollah Khomeini, who had been released from house arrest in March 1964 and permitted to return to his base in Qum, once again took up the cudgels against the Government and intensified his activities over the US army immunity bill. He was arrested in November for 'instigations against the country's interests, security, independence, and territorial integrity' and sent into exile outside Iran. His arrest, unlike the previous year, did not on this occasion spark any unrest, an indication both of the Government's growing control and of the opposition's weakened position. On 6 October, six of the most powerful tribal leaders in Fars went before a firing squad after a military court found them guilty of fomenting and leading the 1962–3 tribal uprising in that province. Other Fars tribesmen were tried and imprisoned or executed in 1965–6.

These incidents aside, the Mansur Government was able to concentrate its full attention over the next few years on the twin pillars of its programme: administrative reform and economic development. On the administrative side, Mansur created four new ministries. He withdrew authority for drawing up the budget from the Ministry of Finance and established a separate Budget Bureau in the Plan Organization directly responsible to himself, a move which resulted in greater rationality in planning and budgeting. He appointed younger technocrats to Cabinet and high Government posts, a trend which continued under his successor with beneficial results for the country. But no action was taken on the proposed bill for civil service reform, under which the hopelessly inefficient and expensive civil service was to be reorganized; the bill was allowed to lie month after month in parliamentary committee, partly because of the resistance of civil servants to change and partly because the Mansur Government seemed uncertain whether to proceed with such a major undertaking. Yet the need for administrative reorganization was pressing. For example, Finance Ministry officials estimated in 1964 that there was a back-log of 185,000 unsettled tax dossiers left over from previous years which it would require thirteen years to clear at the then prevailing rate of progress.

The Government's legislative record was also limited in scope. A bill to create a Health Corps along the lines of the Literacy Corps was approved, as was a slightly revised bill for the second stage of land reform. Break-up of the middle-sized estates did not, however, get very far in 1964, as the Government's financial and administrative resources were already over-stretched. Some progress was made in collecting taxes from larger firms, but a projected new tax bill did not materialize.

On the economic side, the Mansur Government shortly after assuming office increased the size of the Third Development Plan from 145 to 200 billion rials, a step already contemplated by the outgoing Alam Government and made possible by anticipated revenues from a number of new oil concessions about to be granted. Although there was a slight upturn in the economy in 1964, the constant diversion of development funds to non-development purposes, the expansion of the civil service, the reluctance of the private sector to invest, and drought all militated against full recovery. When a preliminary estimate indicated that without corrective measures the deficit in the coming year's budget would come to $300 million, Mansur in November secured the Majlis's approval for heavy new taxes on kerosene, petrol, and on exit permits for Iranians leaving the country. The petrol price increase led to a taxicab strike which was broken only when a fleet of army vehicles was sent into the streets to transport passengers and the taxicab drivers were threatened with revocation of their licenses if they did not return to work. The tax was so unpopular, however, that Mansur was forced to rescind it in January, six weeks after it had been imposed. By then the Government had received about $200 million in welcome new revenues, $185 million of which constituted a cash bonus for five new oil concessions granted offshore in the Persian Gulf and the rest the result of a supplementary oil agreement concluded with the Consortium.

Political violence once again became the order of the day when on 21 January 1965, a twenty-two year old youth shot Mansur. The Prime Minister died five days later from bullet wounds. The Government later charged thirteen men, some of whom had been members of the *Fadayan-i Islam*, with participation in the assassination plot. After a military appeals court confirmed and in some cases increased sentences passed on all thirteen by a lower court, six of the men were executed, four were sentenced to life and the three others were given prison terms of five to fifteen years. On 10 April there was an unsuccessful attempt on the life of the Shah by a conscript soldier of the Imperial Guards. The would-be assassin was killed by the Shah's bodyguards. But the Government subsequently brought to trial fourteen young men, most of whom had studied at British universities. The accused denied any part in, and in some cases even knowledge of, the assassination plot. But the court, acquitting two, found twelve others guilty. Two were sentenced to death, one to life, and the others to various prison terms. An appeals court reduced the life sentence to ten years and confirmed the death sentences. But the Shah later commuted the two death sentences to life imprisonment.

Periodic trials of persons accused of plotting against the regime took place after this. The following examples constitute a partial list. In

1965, Darius Foruhar, a leader of the extreme wing of the pan-Iranists, was arrested and imprisoned for anti-Government activities. In January 1966, Ahmad Aramesh, who led the right-wing 'Progressive Group' (not to be confused with the Progressive Centre), and two of his associates, were taken into custody for publishing anti-Government leaflets and allegedly trying to foment rebellion. In March, a military court found several members of a group calling itself the Islamic Peoples' Party (which had been uncovered a year earlier) guilty of planning to incite an uprising. The leader was sentenced to death and many members to various prison terms. The Shah later commuted the death sentence. That same month, Khalil Maleki, leader of the Socialist League, at one time part of the National Front, and two colleagues were sentenced to prison terms of eighteen months to three years, but they were pardoned by the Shah before serving their full terms. Early in 1969, a group of eleven youths were sentenced to prison terms ranging from three to ten years for the possession of weapons (pistols were produced in evidence), for membership in a party that was 'collectivist' (i.e. Communist) in nature, and for intent to launch guerrilla activity.

With the death of Mansur, the Shah appointed as Prime Minister Amir Abbas Hoveyda, a man who was Mansur's Minister of Finance and his deputy in the Iran Novin party. Under Hoveyda, the country experienced a remarkable economic boom. This was due to a number of factors. Hoveyda finally succeeded in winning the confidence of the business community, and private investment, after a long lull, began once again in earnest. Against the advice of some members of his Government, Hoveyda pursued an expansionist policy with good results. Industrialization was further spurred by the Ministry of Economy's policy of encouraging home industry and by an extensive programme of trade exchanges with the East European bloc, as well as with Western Europe and the United States. Timely oil revenues provided the funds with which to finance this ambitious programme.

Under an agreement concluded with the Consortium in 1966, the members of the group agreed to relinquish within three months 25,000 square miles or one-fourth of their concession area and also to provide Iran, between 1967–71, with 20 million tons of crude oil to market on its own. The relinquished area was subsequently exploited through new concessions while the crude that Iran acquired was by 1968 being marketed in East Europe. The June 1967 war, which interrupted Arab oil exports, permitted Iran considerably to boost its own production. Relations with the Consortium were, however, strained owing to Iran's conviction that the Consortium was lifting less oil from Iran than the Government had a right to expect. The protracted and sometimes acrimonious negotiations of 1967, during which Iran pressed for a guaranteed annual increase of 16·8 per cent in production in the

1968–73 period in order to finance the Fourth Development Plan, led early in 1968 to an understanding under which the Consortium agreed to increase production sufficiently to allow Iran to meet her financial requirements for the first year of the Fourth Plan. But Iran's targets were not fully met and, with the balance of payments position under increasing pressure, the Government early in 1969 again opened talks with the Consortium with a view to securing production guarantees for future years.

In September 1967 elections for the twenty-second Majlis and the Senate were held. Once again, participation was limited to the approved parties and candidates. Some 80 per cent of the deputies to the twenty-first Majlis were returned, with the Iran Novin party taking 179 of 217 seats in Majlis, the Mardom party taking 31 seats, and the pan-Iranists taking five seats. In 1968 the Iran Novin party was able further to consolidate its position during the elections for municipal councils held in 136 towns throughout the country. Official returns gave the Iran Novin party control of a large majority of the councils and every single seat in 115 of them. But public apathy towards the elections was seen in the fact that only ten per cent of the entire eligible population in Tehran registered to vote, a ratio that was by no means untypical.

On the legislative side, the new Civil Service Code was finally approved in 1966, and its implementation begun on a piecemeal basis. Although many administrative difficulties were encountered, the Hoveyda period witnessed a distinct improvement in the calibre and efficiency of the Government administration. This process was helped along by a new tax law and an overhaul of the tax machinery. However, the need for even more comprehensive administrative reforms induced the Government to call an administrative congress early in 1968, during which the shortcomings of the bureaucracy were publicly aired; later in the year the Shah formed an Imperial Inspectorate to investigate public grievances against civil servants and to investigate corruption in Government. In 1967 Hoveyda created four new ministries. One of these, the Ministry of Science and Higher Education, reflected Government concern with the neglected state of university education. In mid-1968 the Government introduced a major programme to reform and improve the quality of teaching at Iran's institutions of higher learning.

The Hoveyda period also witnessed measures to settle the issue of the succession. According to the procedure laid down in the Fundamental Laws, if the Shah were to die while the Crown Prince was still a minor, Majlis was to meet to appoint the Regent. This meant there might be a delay of several days or even weeks (if, for example, parliament was not in session). After the attempt on his life in 1965, the Shah felt it essential that preparations be made for such an eventuality. A

Constituent Assembly convened in September 1967 amended the laws and provided that the Queen shall automatically be considered Regent unless the Shah in his lifetime designated someone else. In October 1967, in the twenty-sixth year of his reign, the Shah, along with the Queen, were crowned.

Foreign Policy: 1964–

In the field of foreign policy, major developments were centred on the expansion of ties with the Soviet Union and the East European bloc, on Iran's growing role in Persian Gulf affairs, and on the overall effect of these trends on relations with the United States and Britain. The rapprochement with the Soviet Union was initiated in 1962 and a trade and technical aid agreement was concluded in 1963. This was followed in 1965 by an accord under which the Russians agreed to extend to Iran a loan of about $300 million and to provide machinery and technical assistance for the construction of Iran's first steel mill. Iran agreed to repay the loan by exports of natural gas. A pipeline, running from the southern gas fields to the Iran–Soviet frontier at Astara, under construction for this purpose, was due for completion in 1971. The expansion of Iran–Soviet trade has in these years been matched by considerable increase in trade with countries of the East European bloc, primarily with Czechoslovakia and Rumania and to a lesser degree with Bulgaria, Hungary, and Yugoslavia.

These deals marked a significant shift in Iranian foreign policy, reflecting partly the freedom of manoeuvre provided by the general thaw in East–West relations, partly the desire to secure capital goods through barter deals not entailing expenditure of precious foreign exchange, partly a disenchantment with Western arms policy towards Iran. Thus, in 1964, the Heads of State of Iran, Turkey, and Pakistan met in Istanbul to create 'outside the framework of the Central Treaty Organization' a body named Regional Co-operation for Development (RCD) to promote economic, social, and cultural co-operation amongst their three countries. Although RCD did not subsequently fulfil all that was expected of it, its creation was an early and concrete sign of the decline in the importance of CENTO. British and American failure to come to Pakistan's aid during the 1965 Indo-Pakistan war further convinced the Shah that CENTO was not a viable military alliance. Although the Government made no move to withdraw Iran from CENTO, Iranian officials after 1966 were inclined to describe it as a 'paper alliance'. In 1966, American refusal to provide Iran with the arms it wanted and at the prices and terms it felt acceptable led to a flurry of reports that the Government would negotiate purchase of ground-to-air missiles from the Soviet Union. Eventually, however, the US Government was able to satisfy Iran's demands. In 1967 Iran did purchase $110 million worth of arms from the Soviet Union, but the deal was confined to light vehicles, half-tracks, and light weapons.

The desire to re-equip and strengthen the army arose from the Shah's concern over developments in the Persian Gulf. Iran–Egyptian diplomatic relations were broken in 1960 and the Government did not welcome Nasser's ambitions on the Arab side of the Gulf, his involvement in the Yemen war, or Arab nationalist claims to Khuzistan as an integral part of the Arab 'homeland'. These concerns were heightened by the fact that Iran's oil fields were concentrated in Khuzistan; the Gulf itself was the outlet for oil exports and the bulk of the country's import–export trade passed through the waterway. Iran also claimed the Bahrain archipelago and other Persian Gulf islands.

Against this background, the Government in 1965 secured Majlis approval to borrow $200 million abroad for arms purchases. Authorization for further military loans, of $200 million in 1965, $266 million in 1967, and another $266 million in 1969, were later also secured, and arms purchased in England and America. Relations with Egypt and Syria remained strained. Relations with Iraq were not much better where disputes over navigation rights in the Persian Gulf, the status of Iranians resident in Iraq, and frontier demarcation remained unsettled. The Government devoted its attention to building up relations with states whose policies were closer to its own. The friendship of Persian Gulf shaikhs was cultivated and special efforts were made in the direction of Kuwait and Saudi Arabia.

King Faisal visited Iran in 1965, when an agreement delineating the continental shelf in the Persian Gulf between the two countries was signed and the two monarchs issued a call for a conference of Islamic Heads of State. The conference did not materialize, and the continental shelf agreement was not ratified by the Iranian parliament when it was discovered that a large oil field in the Gulf lay almost entirely on the Saudi side of the agreed line. Although the two countries increasingly felt the need to co-operate on joint defence of the Gulf following Britain's decision to withdraw from the area after 1971, complications arose as King Faisal felt he could not support Iran's claim to Bahrain. When, early in 1968, Faisal received the Shaikh of Bahrain as a guest in Saudi Arabia, the Shah cancelled a planned visit to Riyadh. The quarrel was patched up and the planned visit took place before the end of the year. Relations improved sufficiently for the two countries finally to sign their continental shelf agreement once Saudi Arabia had made modifications in the median line in Iran's favour. The Shah considerably clarified Iran's position on Bahrain early in 1969 when he announced that Iran would not use force to make good its claim to the island and that it would abide by any decision the Bahraini people themselves made as to their future status.

In March 1970, on Iran's initiative, Britain and Iran submitted the question of Bahrain to the UN Secretary-General and agreed to abide by his findings. In April his representative reported that an overwhelming majority of Bahrainis wanted their island to be recognized as a sovereign State free to determine its own future. The UN Security Council accepted this verdict and the Majlis then formally renounced the Iranian claim to sovereignty.

The Bahraini settlement removed a major obstacle to improved relations with Iran's Arab neighbours but this was overshadowed by a fierce dispute with Iraq over navigation rights in the Shatt al-Arab. Iran, asserting that Iraq had consistently violated the treaty of 1937 which partitioned those rights, denounced it in April 1969 and claimed that the boundary with Iraq should follow a median line on the stream. Iraq then expelled large numbers of Iranians living in Iraqi territory and the two countries seemed on the brink of war. The situation further deteriorated in January 1970 when the Iraqi Government announced the discovery of a right-wing plot, accused Iran of financing and arming the conspirators and expelled the Iranian Ambassador in Baghdad and four of his staff. Iran massed troops near the frontier and announced a large increase in defence estimates. However, tension gradually fell and the general situation improved in March when Iraq reached agreement with leaders of its Kurdish minority whose nationalist insurrection the Iraqis had long accused Iran of aiding and abetting. In 1970 there was a marked improvement in Iran's relations with Egypt, and diplomatic relations were restored.

GOVERNMENT AND ADMINISTRATION

Iran is a constitutional monarchy, a Constitution having been granted in 1906. The reigning monarch is Mohammed Reza, who came to the throne in 1941. In 1939 he married Princess Fawzia, sister of Egypt's former King Farouk, divorced her in 1948, and married Soraya Esfandiari in 1951. The Shah had a daughter by his first wife, but Queen Soraya bore him no children. Moreover, Ali Reza, the only one of the Shah's brothers entitled to succeed him under the Constitution as amended in 1925 (which excluded from the succession anyone of Qajar blood) was killed in an aeroplane accident in 1954. There was thus no heir apparent.

In 1958, on the advice of the Imperial Council and as he was himself convinced that considerations of State required the country to have a Crown Prince, the Shah divorced Soraya and in 1959 married Farah Diba, the daughter of an army officer. She has since given birth to two sons (Reza in 1960 and Ali Reza in 1966) and one daughter (Farahnaz in 1963). The eldest, Reza, was designated Crown Prince by the Shah in November 1960. The Shah was crowned in October 1967, on his forty-eighth birthday, and on the same occasion placed a crown on the head of Queen Farah, making her the first Queen in Iranian history who is known to have been crowned.

A month earlier, in September, a 217-man Constituent Assembly amended three articles of the Fundamental Laws (nos. 38, 41, and 42) regulating the appointment of a Regent in the event of the Shah's death during the minority of the Crown Prince. The effect of the amendments was to permit the appointment of the Regent during the lifetime of the ruling monarch, instead of after his death as in earlier provisions, and to transfer effective power for naming the Regent from the Majlis to the Shah.

According to the new provisions, the Queen is automatically the Regent unless the Shah chooses to name someone else. When the Regent rules, he or she is to be assisted by a Regency Council comprising the Prime Minister, the Speaker of the Majlis, the President of the State, the Chief Justice of the Supreme Court, and four other persons to be named by the Regent. In the event that the Queen is incapacitated (by marriage, death, resignation, or otherwise), election of the Regent reverts to Majlis.

The Shah is Commander-in-Chief of the armed forces, and has the power to declare peace and war, to confer military rank, and to appoint and dismiss ministers. In practice his *farman* is also required in confirmation of appointments to all the major posts in the country. Government is by Cabinet; ministers are not members of the National Assembly or the Senate but are jointly and severally responsible to both Houses. The Prime Minister is appointed by the Shah, but requires a vote of confidence from Majlis. The Prime Minister and his ministers constitute the Council of Ministers which has general executive powers. The Cabinet today, with the Prime Minister, twenty ministers, and five ministers without portfolio, is the largest in the country's history. If the Government is defeated on a vote of confidence in Majlis it resigns.

The country is today divided into fourteen provinces, or *ostans* (Tehran, Gilan, Mazanderan, East Azarbaijan, West Azarbaijan, Kermanshah, Khuzistan, Fars, Kerman, Khorasan, Esfahan, Baluchistan and Sistan, Kurdistan, and the Persian Gulf and Sea of Oman Ports and Islands); and six independent governorates, or *farmandari-ye kol* (Bakhtiari and Chaharmahal, Boyr Ahmadi and Kohgiluye, Semnan, Hamadan, Luristan, and Ilam). These are further subdivided into governorates (*shahrestans*), which are in turn sub-divided into districts (*bakhsh*). The *bakhsh* normally comprises villages and small towns. The Governors-General (*ostandars*) of the provinces and the Governors (*farmandars*) of the independent governorates are nominated by the Ministry of Interior, approved by the Cabinet, and appointed by royal *farman*.

A law passed in 1949 and revised in 1967 provides for elected municipal councils in all major towns. In the past, however, few towns have had municipal assemblies on a continuous basis, and many have never had an assembly at all. In 1968, for the first time, elections for municipal councils for all towns with a population exceeding 10,000 were held on one day throughout the country. The councils, elected in some 136 towns of this size, are now functioning. The municipal councils elect the local mayors, but the mayor's appointment requires the confirmation of the Ministry of Interior and, in the case of the largest towns, of the Shah himself. The Ministry is also empowered under certain circumstances to dissolve the councils and to order new elections.

A study aimed at a major reorganization of the civil service was launched in 1962 and a new Civil Service Code, approved by parliament in 1966, replaced the earlier law of 1922. The new code is characterized chiefly by an attempt to impose greater central control over employment of civil servants and more uniform regulations on wage scales and qualifications for civil servants in different Government ministries and departments. The new law is currently being implemented gradually, on a step-by-step basis.

The Majlis

The Majlis, or Lower House (the term, *Majlis*, is also used to refer collectively to both Houses) is elected by universal adult suffrage, women having voted for the first time in the 1963 elections. The number of deputies was increased from 136 to 200 following the 1956 census and from 200 to 217 following the 1966 census. These numbers include one deputy elected by the Jewish community, one by the Zoroastrians, one by the Assyrians, and two by the Armenians. The term of each Majlis was extended from two to four years in 1957. By the Constitution, Majlis alone has the power to impose, reduce, or abolish taxes, make appropriations, approve loans, and grant concessions. All other bills have to be passed by both Houses. The groupings in Majlis are not normally along party lines. Since 1963, however, the officially sponsored Iran Novin party has controlled the majority of seats in parliament and its members have also led the Government. Not all ministers are party members, however, and since members of non-Government parties in Majlis also owe their seats more to official approval than to their prowess at the polls, Government bills are rarely challenged and there is no clear division between a pro-Government party and an Opposition.

Provision was made in the Fundamental Laws of 30 December 1906 for the formation of the Senate, consisting of 60 members, 30 to be nominated by the Shah and 30 to be elected, in each case 15 for Tehran and 15 for the provinces. The Senate was convened for the first time in 1950 and its legislative term fixed at six years. This was reduced to four years in 1963, so that the terms of Senate and Majlis would run consecutively.

Article 48 of the Fundamental Laws was amended by a Constituent Assembly convened in April 1949. As amended it enables the Shah to dissolve the two chambers separately or together, subject to his stating the reason and simultaneously ordering new elections so that the new chamber or chambers may convene within a period of three months; dissolution may not be ordered twice for the same reason.

Justice

The main civil courts are: the district (*bakhsh*) courts, the courts of the first instance, the provincial courts of appeal, and the Court of Cassation (Supreme Court) in Tehran. The criminal courts are organized in a similar way, and at the lower levels a court may have both civil and criminal jurisdiction. The civil code, the various parts of which were promulgated between 1925 and 1935, is based mainly on the *sharia* (the religious law), but the rules of procedure are largely modelled on French practice. The penal code is based mainly on French law but is also influenced by Swiss and Belgian law. The commercial code was first promulgated in 1932. A new commercial code was approved by parliament in 1969.

In 1967, the family law was revised chiefly to give women more liberal ground on which to sue for divorce, to prevent a man from taking a second wife without the consent of his existing one (marrying a second wife without the consent of the first constitutes grounds for divorce), and to give women stronger rights of custody over children in the case of divorce.

Two new types of court have also been created by recent legislation. In 1963, legislation was approved to permit establishment of elected 'equity houses' at the village level to deal with local disputes of a minor nature. By 1968 over 1,500 of these equity houses had been set up. The experience was successful enough for Majlis to approve legislation for similar courts, called 'arbitration councils' to be established in the towns as well. A number of these are now functioning and are by law permitted to deal with disputes where conviction carries a sentence of no more than two months and fines not exceeding £100.

Security

The regular armed forces, of which the Shah is the Commander-in-Chief, are the army, navy, and air force. Compulsory military service is for two and a half years. In 1962, the Government established the first of its many service corps (the Literacy, Health, and Development Corps now exist) under which young men of draft age are conscripted into the army, given several weeks of military training and then sent out into villages to complete their military service as grade schoolteachers, doctors, dentists, doctors' aides, and agricultural extension agents.

Defence expenditures account annually for about 20 per cent of the total budget. Since 1964 the Government has also borrowed abroad to make arms purchases (loans of $200 million each in 1964 and 1965 and of $266 million each in 1967 and 1969). These funds have been used largely to equip the air-force with supersonic jet bombers, to build up a naval force in the Persian Gulf and to purchase ground-to-air and sea-to-air missiles. Weapons purchases have been made chiefly in the United States and Britain. In 1967 the Government also concluded an agreement for the purchase of equipment worth $110 million from the Soviet Union although the deal was limited to armoured cars, trucks, and light weapons. Direct arms purchases have been made partly to offset a drop in recent years of American military grant aid. American military assistance programmes, however, remain in force.

A military mission agreement for training was signed with the United States on 6 October 1947. There is also a Military Assistance Advisory Group under the Mutual Assistance Programme, an agreement for which was signed in May 1950. A gendarmerie agreement for training and supply was signed on 27 November 1943. All these agreements have been periodically extended since that date. The original gendarmerie agreement was amended on 11–13 September 1948 to make the functions of the head of the mission purely advisory.

Political Parties

In the early period of the Constitution there were a number of political parties. Under Reza Shah all parties ceased effective existence. After his abdication, various parties were formed. These represented personal groupings rather than political parties, their membership was never large, and their life was usually short. A notable exception was the Tudeh party, formed in 1941, which had a Communist nucleus but enjoyed the support of many non-Communists. It was proscribed in 1949, and again after the fall of Musaddiq in 1953. Since then it has enjoyed a tenuous existence and in the 1960s split into pro-Peking and pro-Moscow factions. The National Front, actually a conglomeration of smaller parties which came together over the oil nationalization issue, went into demise after the fall of Musaddiq, enjoyed a brief revival in the 1960–3 period, but has since then declined in strength. The Melliyun and Mardom parties were formed with official support in 1957 to constitute a majority party and an official opposition. The Melliyun party disappeared from the scene after the abortive 1960 elections. The Mardom party continued to retain a few seats in parliament in subsequent elections. Since 1963, parliamentary politics have been dominated by the Iran Novin party, another officially sponsored organization. The pro-Government wing of the pan-Iranist party, an extreme nationalist grouping that was part of the National Front, was permitted to resume activities in 1964 and also has been able to send a few deputies to Majlis.

SOCIAL SURVEY

Education[1]

During the period 1956–66 the rate of illiteracy declined from around 85 per cent to nearer 70 per cent for all Iranians over ten years of age. In 1966 illiteracy among the female population was over 80 per cent, and it reached 85 per cent for males and females in the rural areas. The situation was, of course, much better in the larger towns where over 75 per cent of children between the ages of seven and fourteen could read and write. This compared with a figure of 35 per cent in the villages. But in spite of Adult Literacy Classes and the activities of the Education Corps—high-school graduates conscripted into the army to teach—the backlog of 7 million illiterate adults was still growing in 1968. At all levels of education there was a serious shortage of teachers and classes. 51 per cent of children between the ages of seven and twelve, who should have been receiving primary education in 1966, were not in fact receiving it. In that year there were 21,700 primary schools in the country, 1,700 high schools, 181 vocational and training schools, and 93 faculties or colleges for higher education. These figures were, however, a vast improvement over 1956 when there were 6,700 primary schools, 700 high schools, and 53 vocational and training schools. But in spite of significantly increased budget allocations for the Ministry of Education from 1956, the standard of education was not substantially raised; even at undergraduate level parrot-fashion learning was common. English gradually took over from French as the second language in the 1950s and 1960s, and a large number of private English-language schools sprang up following the pattern of those provided by the British Council and the Iran–America Society. Attempts were made by the planners to introduce an elementary form of manpower planning, although experience with existing vocational schools suggested that they were never fully utilized by either workers or industrialists. Two further problems facing Iran's educationalists in 1968 were the continuing brain drain of skilled and educated manpower to Europe and North America, as well as a growing army of educated unemployed. The solution to the first problem was being approached by the Government's offering of huge incentives to foreign-based doctors and engineers; the latter by trying to persuade graduates to change their attitudes to industrial working or administrative positions outside the major cities.

[1] Sources: Plan Organization, *1966 Census of Population*; Ministry of Education, *Statistics on Education* (Tehran, annually from 1962).

Health[1]

Substantial improvements in health and nutrition standards were achieved during the 1950s and 1960s. Life expectancy rose from 35 years to nearer 50 years; malaria and smallpox were eradicated in many parts of the country by spraying or vaccination schemes; and the import or domestic production of pharmaceutical products expanded rapidly. Nevertheless, most of the health and hygiene improvements were directly related to higher real income levels throughout the country. Many endemic diseases, such as trachoma, dysentery, typhoid, and the venereal diseases remained untreated. In 1968 the commonest contagious diseases, per thousand of population, were dysentery 26, influenza 22, and conjunctivitis (including trachoma) 14. Mortality from children's diseases such as measles, mumps, and whooping cough was high, as was the incidence of tuberculosis. The main causes of death through the country in the mid-1960s were diseases of infants, diseases of the digestive system, diseases of the respiratory system, and infectious or parasitic diseases. In 1965 there were 382 hospitals in Iran, almost exclusively in the urban areas, of which 361 were general hospitals. The number of hospital beds was 26,000—roughly 10 beds per 10,000 population, which compares with over 100 beds per 10,000 population in most developed countries. There were also 1,000 rural clinics, and 400 clinics run by the Health Corps (medical conscripts) to cover the entire village population. The main obstacle to the introduction of more treatment facilities was a lack of trained personnel. In 1968, Iran possessed under 8,000 doctors (although a further 8,000 were estimated to be working abroad), 1,400 dentists, 2,000 pharmacists, and 2,800 qualified nurses, and the majority of these insisted on working in Tehran.

The main nutrition problems in Iran in the 1960s were not those of calorific deficiency, as in many developing countries. They derived mainly from a low intake of animal protein and insufficient consumption of Vitamins A and B. The situation was most serious in low-income urban households. The average height of males in the country was about 5 ft. 5 ins., and the average weight about 9½ stone.

Living Conditions and Social Welfare[2]

In 1966, 42 per cent of households in the population were living in one room, and the average number of rooms per household was 2·1, with a slightly higher figure for the urban areas. Only 25 per cent of housing

[1] Sources: Ministry of Health, *General Picture of Health Statistics in Iran* (Tehran, 1965); Plan Organization, *Fourth Plan*; Food and Nutrition Institute, *Report on Activities* (Tehran, 1965).
[2] Sources: Plan Organization, *1966 Census of Population*; Plan Organization, *Fourth Plan*.

units in the country had electricity, the proportion being 69 per cent in urban areas and 4 per cent in the villages. 86 per cent of housing units were without access to a piped water system either inside or outside the unit (59 per cent in the towns) and washing and sewage facilities were primitive except in modern town houses.

Before the Fourth Plan the large number of small social welfare institutions were generally unco-ordinated in their work. For example, social insurance schemes were run by the Social Insurance Organization (500,000 members in 1968), the Civil Servants' Pension Fund and Insurance Organization (175,000), and the Bimeh Iran Rural Co-operatives Scheme (3,000). Family welfare, orphans' welfare, and youth welfare were also covered by numerous societies, workers' welfare by the National Iranian Oil Company and the Workers' Welfare Bank, and rural welfare by the Education, Health, and Development Corps programmes which started in 1963.

ECONOMIC SURVEY

National Accounts[1]

The economy of Iran started its upward climb in the 1930s. It was stymied by the onset of the Second World War but resumed an expansionary path in the late 1940s. The oil nationalization of 1951 brought the economy to a halt again, but a new turning point was achieved in 1955. Basic statistics on the national income of Iran and its components were built up in the late 1950s so that from 1959 onwards fairly consistent series are available. Although these individual figures may be subject to a wide margin of error, the trend of these statistics shows that, with the exception of a slackening in the period 1961–3, the process of economic development which recommenced in 1955 continued unabated until 1968. Expenditure on Gross National Product at constant (1959) prices increased from 280 billion rials in 1959 to 531 billion rials in 1968, an average annual growth rate of 8 per cent for the nine years. *Per capita* real GNP increased by 55 per cent in the same period to about 21,000 rials (about £115), and although the benefits of this increase were not evenly distributed throughout the population there is some evidence that Iranians at all levels of society were better off in economic terms in 1968 than they were in 1959.

The proportion of expenditure on Gross National Product taken by Private Consumption Expenditure declined from 75 per cent in 1959 to 66 per cent in 1968. This was due to increasing emphasis on Gross Domestic Fixed Capital Formation, which, though fluctuating, rose

[1] Sources: Bank Markazi Iran, *National Income of Iran, 1959–65* (Tehran, 1968); Bank Markazi Iran, *Annual Report and Balance Sheet* (Tehran, 1962 continuing, Annual Reports).

from 17 per cent to 20 per cent, and Government Consumption Expenditure, which rose from 11 per cent to 15 per cent. Net exports of goods and services took about 5 per cent, and were offset approximately by net factor income payments to the rest of the world. These trends imply that the Government was becoming associated to a greater extent with the development of the economy, and that the development effort was itself increasing.

In 1959, 52 per cent of Private Consumption Expenditure was accounted for by the 33 per cent of total population living in urban areas. From that date the rate of growth of Private Consumption Expenditure in the urban areas approximated to the rate of growth of urban population. Surveys completed in 1964–6 showed that in the urban areas 51 per cent of consumer expenditure was on food, 13 per cent on housing, and 9 per cent on clothing. Comparative figures for the rural regions were 68 per cent for food, 2 per cent for housing and 10 per cent for clothing. The proportions of total expenditure made in money were 85 per cent in the towns but only 66 per cent in the villages, where payment in kind was more common.

During the period 1959–68 wages and salaries of Government employees averaged about 80 per cent of total Government Consumption Expenditure. The major fields in which this category of expenditure increased were defence (particularly after the British decision to withdraw from the Persian Gulf) and the social services.

The Government also played a larger role in expenditure on capital formation. Whereas in 1959 it accounted for 35 per cent of Gross Domestic Fixed Capital Formation, the proportion had increased to 50 per cent by 1968. Most Government expenditure of this type was through the Plan Organization on large-scale infrastructure projects— roads, railways, ports, telecommunications, irrigation, and power networks. Capital formation by the private sector was, however, mainly in small and medium scale industry and in residential building. Expenditure on plant, machinery, and equipment declined relatively to Gross Domestic Fixed Capital Formation from 45 per cent in 1959 to 31 per cent in 1968, and the private sector's share of these types of capital goods also declined. Roughly 50 per cent of construction expenditure was on residential buildings during the same period although there was a distinctly falling trend.

The share of agriculture in Gross National Product declined gradually from 33 per cent in 1959 to 24 per cent in 1968. With the share of services (including transport and communications, finance, distribution) remaining fairly constant, the place of agriculture was taken by industry (including oil) which increased from 25 per cent to 38 per cent over the same period. The oil sector itself (excluding income earned by foreign residents in Iran) comprised 11 per cent of Gross National Product in 1959 and 17 per cent nine years later. These figures show that the planned moves towards an industrial economy were proving successful.

Detailed evidence on interpersonal distribution of the National Income is not available, but it is believed that the enlarged allocation of Government expenditure on social services combined with land reform had begun to change the highly skewed pattern known to have existed until the early 1960s. It is certainly clear to those who travelled around the country during the 1960s that economic welfare was increasing in absolute terms at all levels of society.

Balance of Payments[1]

During the nine years 1960–8 the Basic Balance of Payments was in deficit six times, and the foreign exchange reserves of the country were protected only by the receipt of substantial bonus payments from the expatriate oil companies. Moreover, the trade balance (including exports of oil) was favourable only twice. Since total receipts from the oil sector were expanding at about 14 per cent annually the causes of the generally adverse trade balance were the failure of non-oil exports to keep pace with the general expansion of the economy as well as an inability to stem the growing flow of imports owing mainly to the requirements of the development plans. On capital account the increased utilization of foreign long-term loans and credits more than offset the repayments of similar debts incurred in the past, and there was a net inflow of foreign private loans and capital.

The oil revenues played an increasingly important part in receipts on current account, representing 68 per cent of these receipts in 1960 and 75 per cent in 1968. In the latter year all but 6 per cent of the oil revenues derived from the activities of the Iranian Oil Operating Companies, 90 per cent of these being royalty payments, and the remainder resulting from IOOC's local purchases. Visible non-oil exports, accounting for 15 per cent of current receipts, and exports of services, accounting for 10 per cent, retained a depressing similarity for the planners, whose attempts to encourage industrial exports did not prove successful. 50 per cent of merchandise exports comprised carpets and cotton, 12 per cent dried and fresh fruit, and 25 per cent other primary products. A substantial proportion of invisible earnings stemmed from spending by tourists, who numbered nearly 300,000 in 1968.

On the side of expenditures there were significant changes in the pattern of imports. With growth of visible imports averaging about 14 per cent each year there was a trend towards an increased share of capital goods and raw materials in merchandise purchased from abroad. In 1968, 27 per cent of visible imports were capital goods, 60 per cent were raw materials and only 13 per cent consumer goods.

[1] Source: Bank Markazi Iran, *Annual Reports*.

However, the leading items continued to be vehicles, textiles, and metal building materials, each of which accounted for about 10 per cent in 1968. Purchases of foreign services during the 1960s were mainly for travel abroad and international freight.

The geographical distribution of foreign trade also registered changes between 1962 and 1968. Whereas 19 per cent of imports originated in the United Kingdom in 1962, this proportion fell to 12 per cent during the following six years. At the same time purchases from EEC member countries, mainly Germany, increased from 36 per cent to 40 per cent, and relatively larger amounts were bought from Japan and the East European countries. Exports to the United Kingdom also declined, from 12 per cent to 5 per cent of total non-oil exports, although sales to the United States increased. The balance of trade became more unfavourable with respect to Japan and the EEC countries during the period 1963–8 but less unfavourable with respect to the United States and the United Kingdom.

Following the Stabilization Programme of the early 1960s, during which stringent controls were introduced, there was a general relaxation of foreign exchange restrictions. The most visible result of this action was the decline of the traditional black market for hard currency in Tehran and the provincial capitals. The major reason for the easing of controls was the ability of the authorities to prevent the cost of living from rising more than about 1 per cent each year, combined with the success in channelling imports into productive enterprises.

The National Budget[1]

The National Budget comprises two parts—the General Budget and the Development Budget. In 1968 the National Budget was equivalent to 25 per cent of the Gross National Product. 45 per cent of funds were being used to finance the development plans and 55 per cent were being used for the general administration of the Government. 29 per cent of the Government's financial resources in 1967 were obtained from taxation, of which 26 per cent was from direct taxes, 45 per cent from customs duties and 28 per cent from indirect taxes. Oil revenues amounted to 39 per cent of total revenues; funds from other State monopolies 6 per cent; foreign loans 7 per cent; domestic loans 15 per cent and other resources 4 per cent. Compared with figures for the previous years the most significant trends were an increase in domestic and foreign loans and a decline in revenue from State monopolies. (And see Table 5, p. 542.) There was also a significant movement towards using an increased proportion of revenue for development purposes (28 per cent in 1963 compared with 45 per cent in 1968).

From the General Budget for 1968 approximately one third of total expenditure was for national defence, one third for the social services,

[1] Source: Bank Markazi Iran, *Annual Reports*.

20 per cent for general administration and 13 per cent for economic services, repayments of debts, and miscellaneous expenditure. In 1963 roughly 25 per cent of ordinary Government expenditure was on national defence, showing that this type of spending was increasing considerably faster than the General Budget.

The Development Plans[1]

During the period following the Second World War the notion of national planning which originated in the 1930s with State control over the economy gained general support. A preliminary report was drawn up in 1947 by International Engineering Company Inc., an American organization, and after further studies and the publication of a plan document the First Seven-Year Plan began in 1949. Both in its original form and in a revised version the plan intended to spread the development effort fairly evenly throughout the economy. However, political instability and the cessation of oil revenues following nationalization meant that only about 15 per cent of the revised allocations was actually spent. For the most part these were directed towards the renovation of State-owned industrial projects and the transport network of the country.

A new start was made with the Second Seven-Year Plan which began in 1955. The transport sector was to receive the lion's share of funds, and in the event accounted for 40 per cent of total expenditure as the road, rail, and port facilities of the country were substantially extended. A number of large-scale hydro-electric schemes were also started and these accounted for most of the expenditure in the agriculture sector. Neither of the first two plans was comprehensive as the planners did not even possess the basic statistics to estimate population or Gross National Product. Nevertheless within the Plan Organization itself the Economic Bureau completed a series of valuable studies as well as a critical appraisal of the progress of the Second Plan.

With the aid of an American advisory team a move towards comprehensiveness was made. Because of the stabilization programme imposed by the International Monetary Fund the first two years of the Third (Five-Year) Plan were shrouded in a mist of confused estimates about the extent of foreign assistance and the absorptive capacity of the economy. In addition the land reform programme, which had not been considered by the planners, was pushed through its first stages, and various other social reforms were implemented. Then, suddenly, the economy started growing at 9–10 per cent each year, the price level was held stable, and private industry gained an impelling position as production increased at an annual 15 per cent. By the end of the plan

[1] Sources: Baldwin, G. B., *Planning and Development in Iran* (Baltimore, 1967); Plan Organization, *Review of the Second Seven Year Plan Program* (Tehran, 1960); Plan Organization, *Fourth National Development Plan, 1968–72* (Tehran, 1968).

(which in fact was extended to cover 5½ years), actual disbursements closely matched the revised estimates and the overall growth target of the plan, an increase in GNP by 6 per cent each year, had been achieved. The Government had continued its massive investment in infrastructure projects throughout the plan period and had produced an aura of stability and confidence which was complemented by the vigorous enterprise of private investors together with the solid support of an emancipated farming community.

The GNP growth rate between 1964 and 1967 was taken as the datum for the Fourth (Five-Year) Plan which began in 1968. In this plan increased emphasis was laid on social affairs, particularly education, health, and living standards, as well as on heavy industry (steel mill, petrochemical complexes, machine tools, etc.). Total disbursements of 480 billion rials were expected to maintain the 9 per cent growth rate, although again there was considerable uncertainty about the scale of foreign investment and loans. A summary of the original and revised allocations in Iran's four development plans is given in Table 9 (p. 543), together with the actual disbursements for the first three plans.

Agriculture, Forestry, and Fishing[1]

The importance of agriculture in the economy declined during the 1960s. The proportion of GNP contributed by this sector had fallen from 30 per cent in 1963 to 24 per cent by 1968 and the ratio of agricultural workers to the total workforce had dropped from 55 per cent to 48 per cent. Growth of total agricultural output was on a par with the growth of population in the 1960s—around 3 per cent annually. Thus the necessity of importing extra food-stuffs was avoided but at the same time the growth of the export surplus was slowed down. Efficiency in the agricultural sector is fairly high if calculated on a cultivated hectare basis for individual crops, but productivity increases could certainly be achieved by use of crop rotation systems rather than the single-crop/fallow-field method presently in general use. Roughly 15 million acres are cultivated each year, but it is estimated that the margin of cultivation could be extended by up to 100 million acres if necessary. Traditional methods of cultivation using simple spades, ploughs, hoes, forks, and draught animals are still widespread, but since 1957 considerable quantities of tractors and agricultural machinery have been imported. Application of chemical fertilizers has also expanded at a slow rate, with only about 47,000 tons being used in 1967. Irrigation by deep well pumps is gradually superseding the

[1] Sources: Lambton, A. K. S., 'Land Reform and Rural Co-operative Societies in Persia' (*Royal Central Asian Journal*, 1969); Plan Organization, *Fourth Plan*; Bank Markazi Iran, *Annual Reports*; Agricultural Bank of Iran, *Annual Reports* (Tehran, 1962, continuing).

ancient system of underground water channels, and the construction of dams is enabling river water to be conserved and regulated.

Whereas the land tenure system had been decidedly feudal up to 1960, the land reform law, implemented in three stages beginning in 1962, brought about a complete transformation in the agricultural scene. By 1968 large landowners had almost completely disappeared from the rural areas (transferring their attentions to urban land or to industry instead) and the general welfare of the peasants in land reform villages had improved. Although the inception of the reform had had little effect on crop production, livestock holdings declined substantially as farmers were forced to find their own means of credit. Even in 1968 the animal population was seriously depleted and its growth was only about 1·3 per cent annually. Gradually, however, rural co-operatives were established (over 8,000 in 1968) and with the support of the Agricultural Bank these took over the credit-raising operations of the former landlords and also helped to introduce new types of seeds, fertilizers, and implements to the traditionally conservative peasants.

Of the leading crops wheat showed a 60 per cent increase in production between 1961 and 1967, output in the latter year being 4·6 million tons. Sugar-beet output increased from 0·8 million tons to 2·9 million tons in the same period owing to the reintroduction of this crop in the newly-irrigated Khuzistan plain. Rice increased from 0·4 million tons to 0·9 million tons; green tea from 11,000 tons to 63,000 tons and cotton from 105,000 tons to 338,000 tons.

Value added in forestry and fishing amounted to about 1 per cent of value added in the agricultural sector in 1967 and therefore had little economic significance. The total forest area is about 18 million hectares, but only about 1 million hectares in the Caspian area are suitable for economic working on a long-term basis with a sustained yield. Overcutting and overgrazing were gradually curtailed following the revision of the Forest Law in 1959 and the implementation of the Forest Nationalization Law in 1963. Experimental reafforestation schemes, albeit on a small scale, were introduced and the Forestry Department expanded its complement of forest rangers. Nevertheless in 1968 economic forestry was still in its infancy.

The fisheries industry exists in the two major regions—the Caspian Sea, where the famed sturgeon breed, and the Persian Gulf. The organized working of the Caspian fisheries dates from 1876 when a Russian industrialist obtained a concession from the Iranian Government. The concession became a joint Iranian–Russian venture from 1928 and in 1953 it was taken over by the Iranian Fisheries Company. The major product is, of course, caviare, although output was not increasing in the 1960s. In the Gulf area little progress was made after the installation of a 400 ton capacity fish canning plant in 1941 and between 1962 and 1965 annual production did not rise above 60 tons.

Mining and Quarrying[1]

Non-oil mining contributed roughly 0·3 per cent of GNP during 1959–68, and was thus of little economic significance. In this period coal production increased from 237,000 tons to 285,000 tons; chromite from 44,000 tons to 129,000 tons and zinc from 15,000 tons to 88,000 tons. Production from lead mines decreased from 172,000 tons to 82,000 tons and iron output decreased from 58,000 tons to 2,000 tons. Production of red oxide, copper, and manganese increased rapidly but remained relatively low in comparison with other metals. Extraction of rock salt grew from 132,000 tons to 155,000 tons while output of various types of stones and soils also expanded rapidly. The only semi-precious stone mined was turquoise, the output of which showed an increase from 6 tons to 8 tons. A substantial proportion of these minerals was exported, with zinc, lead, and chromite being the major foreign exchange earners.

The oil industry is, of course, the financial mainstay of the economy in terms of Government revenue and foreign exchange. It contributed about 17 per cent of GNP in 1968 and the trend from 1959 was for this proportion to grow. Net crude oil production maintained a rapid rate of expansion throughout the period and reached an average of 2·84 million barrels/day in 1968 making Iran the second largest oil producer in the Middle East. 95 per cent of production resulted from the development activities of the Iranian Oil Operating Companies (the Consortium), and the remainder from Iran-Pan American Oil Company and other concession-holders. As a whole the oil industry employed 41,000 workers in 1968, a cutback of 20,000 compared with the figure for 1959.

Although internal consumption of kerosene, fuel oil, gas oil, and petrol rose considerably during the 1960s owing to an improved distribution network, about 95 per cent of the crude oil produced was either exported directly (80 per cent) or refined at the Abadan refinery (15 per cent) before export. From the middle of the decade the pattern of foreign sales changes substantially with Japan taking a much higher share (40 per cent in 1968 compared with 15 per cent five years earlier). Sales to other Asian countries and to North America declined, although Western Europe continued to purchase about 42 per cent.

[1] Sources: Iranian Oil Operating Companies, *Annual Report* (Tehran, 1956, continuing); National Iranian Oil Company, *Iran Oil Journal*, monthly journal; Bank Markazi Iran, *Annual Reports*; Ministry of Economy, *Time Series of Mining Statistics in Iran* (Tehran, 1969).

Manufacturing[1]

The growth of manufacturing industry proceeded at a very high and rapidly increasing rate between 1959 and 1968, and was almost exclusively due to private enterprise. By 1967 nearly 300 different types of manufacturing establishment had obtained permission to start operation. This compares with under 100 in 1959. Following the completion of the first industrial census in 1963 a useful series of industrial statistics was produced by the Ministry of Economy. These indicate that from 1963 the major fields of investment were in the metal and electrical industries and in chemicals. Textiles and food processing, the two industries which traditionally signify the start of an industrialization programme, declined in importance relatively to more sophisticated industry. By 1968 heavy industry was still in the process of establishment although automobile assembly plants were producing 35,000 vehicles a year. The construction of a steel mill in Esfahan, a tractor factory in Tabriz, an aluminium smelting plant in Arak and three large petrochemical complexes at the head of the Persian Gulf were in hand and proposals to set up industrial estates in Ahvaz, Qazvin, and Tabriz were being considered.

Although production was increasing rapidly there was no evidence that productivity was rising. Plant owners in all sizes of factory still had not discovered the advantages of proper management on either a financial or a physical level. The most serious problems were an extravagant under-utilization of capital equipment and an almost complete ignorance of the need for long-term or even medium-term planning. Marketing procedures were practically unknown and little use was made of vocational training courses to increase the skill of workers.

In 1968 there were approximately 580,000 industrial establishments in Iran (including cottage industry) employing 1·4 million workers. These contributed about 15 per cent of GNP. Of total gross value added in the industrial sector, roughly 85 per cent was from urban establishments, where the average number of workers was five. 68 per cent of employed workers were wage and salary earners, the rest being unpaid family workers.

Banking and Finance[2]

The Central Bank of Iran, founded in 1960, controls the activities of

[1] Sources: Ministry of Economy, *Annual Industrial Survey* (Tehran, 1963, continuing); Min. of Economy, *Trends in Industrial and Commercial Statistics* (Tehran, 1965, continuing); Min. of Economy, *Report on Commencement and Operation Permits* (Tehran, 1964, continuing).
[2] Sources: Bharier, J., 'Banking and Economic Development in Iran' (*Bankers' Magazine*, 1967); Benedick, R. E., *Industrial Finance in Iran* (Boston, 1964); Reports of mentioned banks.

25 other banks in the country, most of which were introduced after the closing of the ubiquitous Imperial Bank of Iran in 1951. Four of the banks are specialized banks, three others have adopted specific functions in addition to normal banking transactions, and a number of others direct foreign business towards specific countries. The oldest specialized bank is the Agricultural Bank of Iran, with a history extending back to the 1920s. However, it was not until the 1960s that this bank became a significant influence on the rural development of the country by helping to finance the land reform programme and the rural co-operative movement. The Mortgage Bank of Iran has a parallel history. Only after becoming a member of the International Building Societies Association did development loans become available. These amounted to about 2 billion rials in 1968. Two industrial development banks also extended their spheres of influence during the 1960s. The Industrial and Mining Development Bank of Iran—a private joint-stock company of which the shares are quoted in the Tehran Stock Exchange—disbursed 229 loans totalling 8·3 billion rials in the period 1959–68, with loans of 1·8 billion rials granted in the year to March 1968. 80 per cent of the loans were for periods longer than five years and they were given to metal products industry (15 per cent), transport equipment plants (10 per cent), and about twenty other types of industrial enterprise. The Industrial Credit Bank—State-owned and financed by Plan Organization funds—was involved in 269 industrial projects during the Third Plan period (1963–8), granting loans amounting to a total of 1·8 billion rials.

Bank Omran (Development Bank) and Bank Refah Kargaran (Workers' Welfare Bank) have been the most successful of the semi-specialized banks. The former, financed by the Pahlavi Charitable Foundation, directs its activities to farmers and co-operatives on distributed Crown Estates and also to alleviation of credit difficulties in the tribal areas. The latter, financed by the State Social Insurance Organization, has provided loans, especially for housing and new-year expenditures, to workers through industrial workers' co-operatives. A third bank, the Distributors' Co-operative Credit Bank was established to eliminate 'profiteering' in food supplies, although by 1968 little progress had been made.

Of Iran's commercial banks, nine have mixed foreign and domestic capital. Business is confined mainly to foreign transactions, particularly import finance, and branches are generally confined to the commercial areas of Tehran and a few other cities. The remaining banks are wholly Iranian and are dominated by one State Bank and one private bank. The State-owned Bank Melli Iran (National Bank of Iran) was founded in 1927. In 1968 it comprised over 500 branches at which it handled most Government transactions as well as payment of water, electricity, and telephone accounts in all areas. The private bank is Bank Saderat, which by the end of 1968 had more than 2,000 branches throughout the country and which had taken the lead in introducing modern banking to even the most underdeveloped regions of Iran. The bazaar money merchants, who traditionally took on a large section of credit business are still influential in some fields, although their activities have gradually been confined to re-lending to second, third, and fourth class signatures.

The Central Bank's monetary policy retained a slightly deflationary flavour after 1963 in order to offset the expansionary spending of the general and development budgets. The domestic value of the rial was consequently held relatively stable:

Wholesale Price Index (1959 = 100)

Year	*1959*	*1960*	*1961*	*1962*	*1963*	*1964*	*1965*	*1966*	*1967*	*1968*
Index	100	102	102	104	104	110	111	110	110	111

Apart from its overall policies and the production of generally reliable statistics on all financial matters, the Central Bank also influenced the economic development of Iran through its Centre for the Attraction and Protection of Foreign Investment. By the end of 1968, 90 foreign firms had invested funds in the country (mainly in tyre, chemical, and pharmaceutical plants).

Transport and Communications[1]

By March 1968 Iran possessed 19,000 miles of all-weather roads, of which 5,000 miles were asphalted and 14,000 were gravelled. But the length of road per 100 square miles of land area (excluding the salt desert) was only 4·3 miles—one of the lowest figures in the world. During 1963–8, 2,400 miles of asphalted roads were built, using a variety of imported road-construction machinery. The main emphasis was on trunk routes, and an excellent network of highways in the western half of the country was completed. However, roads in the east were generally of poor quality and only a slow start had been made in improving the grading of feeder roads. (About 3,400 miles out of a surveyed total of 9,200 had been constructed.) As trunk roads improved so did the proportion of freight carried by road. Whereas 43 per cent of imported goods at the Persian Gulf ports were carried inland by road in 1959, the proportion had risen to over 60 per cent by 1965.

The main trunk of the Iranian Railway network was completed by 1938. Following improvements during and after the Second World War the major extensions in the 1950s were to the east and west of Tehran. By 1968 most of the Tehran–Tabriz–Turkey route was complete as were the extensions south of Kashan to Esfahan and Yazd in preparation for an ultimate link with the Pakistan system. Railway freight

[1] Source: Plan Organization, *Fourth Plan.*

rates were held artificially low during the 1960s, but in spite of this a considerable proportion of freight and passenger business was lost to competing road and air services.

The capacity of Iranian ports on both the Persian Gulf and the Caspian Sea was doubled between 1963 and 1968 to 4 million tons per year. This was mainly due to the creation of a huge new port at Bandar Abbas, which had become the country's biggest port by 1968. Airports, too, were enlarged or constructed during the Third Plan although in both the sea and air ports little improvement in operational efficiency or maintenance was noted.

In 1968 there were automatic telephone exchanges in 24 towns and magnetic telephones in 172 towns; there were 202,000 automatic telephones and 35,000 magnetic ones. Comparison with similar figures for 1963 shows that although a small number of additions had been made (in eight towns) to the magnetic system, the number of lines on automatic exchanges practically doubled. In 1967, 8·2 million calls were made compared with 1·4 million five years earlier. The number of telegrams showed a slower increase during the same period, rising from 5·3 million to 7·0 million. The expansion of postal services in the Third Plan was confined to 510 new post offices and 41,000 new post boxes. However, these enabled the number of domestic letters to increase from 165,000 in 1962 to 239,000 in 1967. Radio and television services also saw considerable expansion, so that by 1968 there were three television transmitting stations in Tehran alone and a radio network covering most of the country.

Electricity, Gas, and Water[1]

Towards the end of the 1950s moves were being made to reorganize the fragmented and inefficient power system which had been built up in disorderly fashion from the 1940s. An excellent survey of the electricity industry by an American organization was influential with the Plan Organization and although in 1968 industrial plants still tended to rely on their own power supplies, generating stations had been established in over 180 towns, and substantially expanded and rationalized in the major cities. Total generating capacity was about 1·5 million kilowatts of which roughly 0·8 million kilowatts had been installed in the period 1963–8. This included five hydro-electric plants. A long-term electricity programme was set up with the aim of providing one major grid system covering the entire western half of the country, together with two smaller grids in the north-east and south-east regions.

In addition a start was made to utilize the enormous natural gas resources of the southern oil fields. For this reason the National

[1] Sources: Sanderson and Porter, *Power Survey of Iran for Plan Organization* (New York, 1957); Plan Organization, *Fourth Plan*.

Iranian Gas Company was established in 1965. Plans were completed for the Gas Trunkline which will take gas to Russia for export and will also provide cities en route with industrial supplies.

A serious factor limiting the expansion of the agriculture sector has been the shortage of adequate, controlled sources of water. Average annual rainfall in Iran is only about 10 inches, while a large proportion of river water is lost through evaporation. Traditional methods of conserving water (by underground water channels—*qanats*) are inefficient and costly to maintain. Consequently the planners have laid great emphasis on irrigation schemes. At one end of the scale hydro-electric schemes for all major rivers were planned or started during the Second Plan period; at the other end credits were extended to farmers to dig deep and semi-deep wells. The programme met with two initial difficulties however. In the first place it was found that the utilization of wells had the effect of lowering the underground water table and thus rendering many existing *qanats* obsolete; secondly, farmers tended to use excessive amounts of water in the hope of obtaining higher yielding crops. Moreover, much of the new dam-conserved water has been required to meet the needs of urban consumers rather than agriculture.

Construction[1]

Investment in both private and public construction increased rapidly in the period 1963–8. Over 60,000 privately-financed buildings were completed annually—86 per cent of these being residential. 17,000 houses were built by the State in addition to nearly 500 urban development projects. From the end of the Second World War most new construction in the urban areas utilized modern building materials such as steel beams, cement, glass, and kiln-fired brick. In the rural regions, however, 97 per cent of constructions were still made of traditional mud, mud-brick, straw, stone, or unprocessed wood in 1966. The general construction boom since the late 1940s led to a rise both in the prices of building materials and in the wages of the generally unskilled building workers.

Distribution and Other Services[2]

Little was known about the pattern of wholesale and retail distribution in Iran until the first partial census of distribution in 1965. Of 5,200 wholesale establishments in 21 cities, 68 per cent sold non-durable consumer goods, 9 per cent durable consumer goods, 5 per cent capital

[1] Sources: Bank Markazi Iran, *Bulletin* (Tehran, bi-monthly, continuing); Plan Organization, Iranian Statistical Center, *National Census of Population and Housing*, vol. 168 (Tehran, 1968, *1966 Census of Population*).

[2] Sources: Plan Organization, *1966 Census of Population*; Min. of Economy, *Internal Trade Statistics, 1965* (Tehran, 1968).

L

goods, and 18 per cent intermediate goods. And for 71,300 retail establishments the respective proportions were 76 per cent, 14 per cent, 3 per cent, and 7 per cent. 75 per cent of the retail outlets were managed by a single individual. The remainder were corporations or companies. 97 per cent acted independently (i.e. were not agencies or branches), and under 10 per cent had means of transport. Almost all people employed in distribution were male. They worked, on average, 10·8 hours each day and 6·5 days each week. It was estimated that about 70 per cent of gross value added in the distribution sector was accounted for by wholesale and retail establishments in cities. A further 20 per cent was contributed by approximately 1 million pedlars in the cities while the remainder resulted from sales in villages. The proportion of working population engaged in the service trades increased by 8 per cent in the period 1956–66. Professional services expanded still more rapidly in the same period as the possibilities for educational attainment improved. Hotels and restaurants, as well as sports, entertainment, and recreation facilities improved substantially from the 1950s although supply constantly lagged behind demand.

V
Iraq

The area of Iraq within its present frontiers is approximately 175,000 square miles. It is most conveniently divided into three distinct geographical sections: the Mesopotamian plain, the Uplands, and the Folded Mountain Belt. The first of these is historically the most important for it was the plain which nursed great civilizations in the past, and its two great rivers which nourished them.

The plain. To the north-east the southern alluvial plain follows the foothills of the Iranian mountains up from the sea, turns south-east across the old river estuaries at Samarra and Hit, and returns parallel to and west of the Euphrates. Within these limits the soil is stoneless alluvium. The two rivers flow in channels somewhat above the rest of the plain, which is consequently liable to be flooded during the high-water period in the spring when the snows melt in Kurdistan; local rain has comparatively little effect on the rivers. The Tigris rises in late March or early April; the Euphrates rises two or three weeks later; both rivers are at their lowest in September–October. At no point is the plain higher than 150 feet above sea-level.

The annual rainfall in the plain averages about 6 inches only; this occurs usually between mid-November and mid-March, the wettest month being February; but it is impossible to generalize, as the whole season's rainfall may occur in a space of three weeks. Cultivation in the plain depends almost entirely on irrigation, the rainfall often being insufficient to mature a winter crop.

The rivers, which have frequently changed their courses throughout history, unite about sixty miles above the city of Basra in a single great channel, the Shatt al-Arab. Also above Basra is the marshland of the Muntafiq and Amara provinces, where a distinctive group of Arabs—the 'marsh Arabs'—live on fish and the produce of their mud-banks and swampy islands, or tend their buffaloes from shallow-draft canoes.

The uplands. This region, which corresponds approximately to ancient Assyria, is undulating gravel steppe and rich plough-land, with some stone. Here, in an average year, the rainfall of 13 inches is sufficient to yield a winter crop without irrigation. In the districts of Kirkuk and Arbil, however, the rainfall is supplemented by the *kahriz* system of underground water channels, which is widespread in Iran.

Mosul, Arbil, and Kirkuk are respectively 703, 1,250, and 1,087 feet above sea-level.

Between the two rivers in this area and south of latitude 36°N. is a wedge of uncultivable gypsum desert called al-Jazira (the Island).

The mountain belt. The crescent of mountain country included in the north-east frontier comprises the basins of the rivers Diyala, Lesser Zab, Greater Zab, and Khabur. It is peopled by Kurds, a hardy mountain race, living a life differing widely from that of the Arabs of the plain and uplands. Villages are stone-built and shelved into the sides of the hills, with tall silver poplars and terraced cultivation, including vineyards and tobacco. Large areas of mountainside are covered with scrub oak; the summits provide summer pastures.

Between the Euphrates valley and the western frontiers is a large section of al Badia, the Syrian Desert, populated only by nomad tribes with their flocks and camels.

Climate. The climate of Iraq is extreme. In the plains the January mean temperature is 42–52° F. (5·5–11° C.); in July, 86–96° F. (30–35·5° C.). In the mountains altitude decreases temperature in both seasons and increases the rainfall to as much as 40 inches.

The People

Between the censuses of 1957 and 1965 the population was recorded as increasing from 6·3 million to 8·3 million. But civil war was raging in the north and the count in 1965 was incomplete. In the same period the population of the Baghdad *liwa* increased from about 1·3 million to about 2·1 million. Vital statistics must be accepted with reserve: registration is still incomplete in some areas and the figures given for birth and death rates in the UN Statistical Yearbook for Iraq (as for the majority of Middle East countries) are unreliable. Iraq, however, has certainly shared in the widespread decline in the death rate of the past few decades, particularly among the younger age groups. Although statistics of causes of deaths are defective there can be no doubt that infant mortality and epidemic diseases have markedly declined. There has been a wide increase in the use of antibiotics. Their unrestricted sale without prescription has led to abuses but in view of the inadequate supply of doctors it is generally believed that the restriction of the sale of antibiotics to authorized prescription would have had even more adverse results. Extensive chemical spraying has been practised to reduce malaria; there was some retrogression in Basra in 1963 and in the north in some later years owing to the Kurdish War, but the eradication programme has been resumed. Bilharzia still presents special difficulties.

Religions

Islam. The Sunnis and Shiis are mutually distinguishing and to some extent mutually suspicious sections of the Moslem majority, as are also the Arab and Kurdish sections of the Sunni group. Statistics are lacking, but the Shiis outnumber the Sunni Arabs. The Sunnis were closer to the Ottoman ruling group and since Ottoman times have continued to occupy more leading positions than the Shiis in official and professional circles. But the advance of education has brought the latter into greater prominence than before.

The Sunnis live mainly in the north of Iraq and in the *liwas* of Baghdad, Diyala, and Dulaim. There is one notable Sunni shrine in the country, that of Shaikh Abdul Qadir al-Gailani, whose mosque and tomb in Baghdad are a centre of pilgrimage from regions as remote as Indonesia.

The Shiis form a majority in the central *liwas* of Kut, Diwaniya, Karbala, and Hilla and in the southern *liwas* of Basra, Amara, and Muntafiq. Their religious life has as its background the four Holy Cities of Karbala, Najaf, Kadhimain, and Samarra. Najaf is the burial place of Ali, the first Imam; Karbala of Hussein, the third Imam. Thousands of Shiis from Iran, Afghanistan, and India take part in the traditional pilgrimages to the Holy Cities, where, during the first ten days of the month of Muharram, is enacted the famous Passion Play commemorating the death of Hussein ibn Ali at the battle of Karbala in AD 680. The Shii Mujtahids exercise not only religious but at times also political influence, as was demonstrated in the insurrection of 1920 and on subsequent occasions.

Christian Churches. Christianity in Iraq dates from the second century AD. The main Christian sects are now the Nestorian, which seceded from the main body of Christendom at the Council of Ephesus (431), the Syrian 'Orthodox' (or Jacobite), and Armenian 'Orthodox' (or Gregorian), which seceded at the Council of Chalcedon (451), and minority sections of these three churches which from the seventeenth century onwards have acknowledged Papal supremacy and are known respectively as the Chaldean, Syrian Catholic, and Armenian Catholic Churches. At the end of the First World War some 25,000 members of the Nestorian Church, which had survived mainly in the mountains of Iran and Turkey, were settled by the British authorities in Iraq; these were the so-called 'Assyrians' who suffered in the events of 1933. Today the ancient theological differences which had distinguished the churches are almost forgotten by their ordinary members, among whom the difference is rather one of liturgy, ecclesiastical discipline, and hierarchy; this is, however, sufficient to constitute minute nations rather than congregations, recognized by the Government as possessing competence in matters of personal status.

Jews. Until the war in Palestine in 1948–9 Iraq contained a large community of Jews whose families had been settled in the country for hundreds or even thousands of years. A law of 1931 gave Jewish communities self-government in their own affairs, and there was a highly organized communal life, with schools, hospitals, and charitable institutions. In consequence of ill-feeling arising from events in Palestine the majority of Jews left Iraq in 1950–2, mostly for Israel.

Yazidis.[1] These are vulgarly known as 'devil-worshippers'. They are divided between Jabal Sinjar and the Shaikhan district north of Mosul and speak a Kurdish dialect; their sacred books, however, are written in Arabic.

Sabaeans. Most of them are craftsmen—especially silversmiths—in the large riverain towns.

Shabak. Of Kurdish origin, who live in the area of the Yazidis and are not clearly distinguished from them; their religion contains Yazidi and extreme Shii elements.

HISTORY AND POLITICS

Written history began in Iraq at the end of the fourth millennium BC, but archaeological remains from much earlier periods, first in the north and later also in the south, give evidence of palaeolithic man, of agricultural neolithic man and, from the sixth and fifth millennia, of increasing human progress expressed successively in extensive agriculture, copper and bronze work, wheeled vehicles, the potter's wheel, the sailing ship, bricks, temples, writing, seals, and sculpture of considerable maturity. Fully evolved urban life and written records appear before 3000 BC, with the emergence in southern Iraqi city-states of the magnificent Sumerian civilization, the first highly developed culture in the world. It was absorbed and transformed by the first historical Semitic immigration, that of the Akkadians (*c.* 2400 BC), who united the country into a single kingdom and extended it by foreign conquest. The unity, destroyed by tribal incursions from the east, was reestablished for two centuries under the hegemony of Ur of the Chaldees, to be disrupted again, at the beginning of the second millennium, by a further invasion, of Elamites and Semitic Amorites, from which, in the eighteenth century BC, arose the Babylon of Hammurabi. Babylon, under various dynasties, absorbed and was itself modified by incursions of Hittites and Hurrians from the north and west and Kassites from the east, and in 745 BC fell to the Semitic Power of Assyria, which, expanding during the ninth and eighth centuries from a local city-state in the north, came to dominate the whole riverland and for a time controlled most of the Middle East. Assyria itself fell in 612 BC to the combination of a revived Babylon and the new Power of Media; and the neo-Babylonian Empire—that of Nebuchadnezzar and 'Balthazar' —was overcome in 539 BC by Cyrus, the founder of the first of the three great Iranian dynasties, which, during the next thousand years,

[1] See above, p. 35.

extended westward over Iraq. The first, the Achaemenian, was over-thrown by Alexander the Great, whose Seleucid successors continued to dispute Iraq with the second great dynasty, the Parthian, after it·had evicted them; these fell in turn to the Sasanians, who, like their predecessors, warred with Imperial Rome from their capital at Ctesiphon.

In the seventh century AD the campaigns of the newly established Moslem community overthrew the Sasanian Empire, whose territories were thereupon governed successively from Medina and Damascus. In AD 750 the Abbasid family, which drew its support from Iraq and farther east, supplanted the related dynasty of Damascus; and in 762 it founded a new capital at Baghdad. During the 500 years of their Caliphate the area of Arab conquest became a religious and cultural unity in which Baghdad held an eminent, at times pre-eminent position; the material authority of the Abbasids, however, despite increased centralization and standardization of government, rapidly dwindled, as province after province fell to invaders, adventurers, or local princes and the central power was sapped in dynastic quarrels and the disputes of the powerful palace guard. From the tenth century AD the Caliph was little more than a religious figurehead under the temporal protection of successive Turkish dynasties, holding insecurely only part of an economically declining Iraq. In 1258 Baghdad was destroyed in a Mongol invasion and the Abbasid dynasty, long shorn of imperial power, was overthrown. The Mongol ravages intensified the ruinous aftermath of centuries of invasion and internal strife, and the country was subsequently despoiled and fought over by Turkomans and Tatars, then disputed by the Iranian and Ottoman Empires, each exploiting the internal religious division between Sunni and Shii Moslems and the opportunism of frontier Kurds. In 1638 Iraq, although still open to Iranian invasion, fell finally to the Turks and re-mained a province, or provinces, of the Ottoman Empire until the First World War.

The Period 1914–45

In November 1914 the Allied Powers, provoked by a Turkish attack on Russian sea ports, declared war on Turkey, and an Indian Army Brigade landed in Iraq. By the end of 1918 virtually the whole of what is now Iraq was in British hands.

British official opinion was divided in its policy towards Iraq and the civil administration which succeeded the military occupation was for long embarrassed by uncertainty about the future. Delay in making a definite pronouncement of policy had brought nationalist emotions in Iraq to the boiling point. The assignment of the mandate—highly unwelcome to nationalist sentiment—in April 1920 was followed by disturbances which developed in July into an insurrection; this, while it left large areas of the country unaffected, required considerable forces to suppress it. Pacification was completed early in 1921; and already, by October 1920, Sir Percy Cox, the first High Commissioner, had terminated military rule and established an Arab Council of State advised by British officials. The British Government decided to support for the headship of the new Iraq state the Amir Faisal, son of King Hussein, who had led the Arab revolt of 1916–18 and in 1920 had been expelled from Damascus by the French. Faisal's nomination as king was approved by the Council of State and confirmed in a referendum, and he was enthroned on 23 August 1921. The Anglo-Iraqi Treaty, in which the mandatory Power had decided to embody its obligations towards the League of Nations, was ratified by the Iraq Government on 10 October 1922 against the determined opposition of nationalist elements, who insisted that the treaty should terminate the mandate and British influence, whereas it in fact incorporated the provisions of the mandate, gave guarantees on judicial matters to make up for the abolition of the Capitulations, and guaranteed Britain's special interests in Iraq. Its period of validity, twenty years, was reduced the following year to four years from the ratification of peace with Turkey, which followed in July 1923.

In December 1925 the Council of the League of Nations awarded the Mosul *vilayet* to Iraq. In July 1926 a treaty between Turkey, Britain, and Iraq accepted the new frontiers as definitive and inviolable, while Iraq agreed to pay to Turkey 10 per cent of oil royalties for twenty-five years. In September 1929 the British Government undertook to support Iraq's candidature for League membership in 1932, and in 1930 yet another treaty was signed, which provided for a close Anglo-Iraqi alliance, to last for twenty-five years from the admission of Iraq to the League. There was to be consultation between the parties in matters of foreign policy which might affect their common interest; mutual assistance in the event of war, including provision by Iraq of communications and all other facilities and assistance and the right of passage to British troops; and lease of sites for air bases near Basra and west of the Euphrates. The treaty was badly received by the nationalists, but was ratified by the Assembly in November 1931. On 3 October 1932, on the strong recommendation of the British Government, Iraq was admitted to the League of Nations as an independent state.

From Independence to the Iraqi Revolution

The independent governments faced serious difficulties from the start. During the period of the mandate there had been much material progress and an administrative structure far ahead of the previous one had been created. But a sense of unity was still lacking. The division between a larger Shii and a smaller but more influential Sunni population was a constant source of political disunity and weakness, and of regional as well as sectarian antagonism. In the north a part of Kurdistan, where communications were poor and a different language was spoken, had been included in Iraq. In addition to these formal divisions the population lacked social cohesion. A small, comparatively rich class lived among a majority of extremely poor workers on the land and in the towns. In between lay increasing numbers of students, members of the professions, the more well-to-do shopkeepers and middlemen, and technicians. Representative institutions were in their infancy and it was difficult to establish political parties transcending the divisions within the population. The monarchy was new and the sense of legitimacy around it was not yet firmly established. Tribal divisions remained: not only did the tribes inherit turbulent traditions from the distant past, but their poverty was a temptation to urban political factions to make use of them in their rivalries. To complicate these divisions, an Assyrian minority which had been rescued by British troops after their flight from Iran and had been settled in Iraq in the First World War, when they supplied many of the troops used by Britain to keep order among the tribes, were demanding full settlement but were dissatisfied with the proposed arrangements. They attempted to cross into Syria but were sent back by the French authorities. An unjustifiable scare led to the cold-blooded massacre of some hundreds of them by the Iraqi army under Bakr Sidqi.

Tribal revolts were suppressed by the army and a temporary alliance was made between a civilian group of liberal reformers, a young officer group and Hikmat Sulaiman, who was inspired by the achievements of the Turkish nationalists under Atatürk. This alliance seized power by a coup d'état in 1936. The liberal social democrats soon found that the young officers were determined to keep control, and a disastrous precedent was set for military domination in Iraqi politics. King Faisal I had died in 1933 and his son Ghazi was too immature to control the military influence in politics. Early in 1939 he met a premature death in a car accident. He was succeeded by his son Faisal II, then an infant, with the Amir Abdul Ilah, his uncle, as Regent. In the following twenty years the Regent played an important part in Iraqi politics. The Hikmat regime disintegrated. The reforming social democrat ministers, opposed both by the army and the extreme conservative civilians, resigned. General Bakr Sidqi was assassinated, and the ministry gave way to another under Jamil al-Midfai. The new ministry attempted to curb the army's dangerous role in politics, with only temporary and limited success, and as the Second World War was approaching increasing differences over foreign policy began to develop.

Since independence popular feeling against Britain remained, but governments in practice kept on fairly friendly terms with British ambassadors in Baghdad. The Royal Air Force retained a base at

Habbaniya and Russia refused to recognize Iraq as an independent country on the ground that it was still under British control. A group of army officers shared increasing sympathies with the German Nazi regime. Developments in Palestine had further alienated public opinion from Britain. The White Paper on Palestine (Cmd. 6019 of 1939) issued about three months before the war had created a position more favourable to the Arabs which the Iraqi Prime Minister, Nuri al-Said, in 1940 endeavoured to use as the basis for a settlement. But Winston Churchill, by this time in power was not willing to negotiate on this basis.

When the Second World War began General Nuri al-Said was Prime Minister. His Government promptly broke off diplomatic relations with Germany. Nuri decided to go further and declare war on Germany but was held back by the army. Increasing dissension in the Cabinet and the murder of his Finance Minister led, after an unsuccessful attempt to reconstruct his Cabinet, to his resignation in favour of Rashid Ali al-Gailani. The new Government declared at first that it would continue to follow the Anglo-Iraqi Alliance. But the Arab nationalist inclination towards Germany was increasing, partly owing to an agitation organized in Iraq by the former Mufti of Jerusalem. The fall of France encouraged anti-British sentiment in these circles. When Britain asked for approval to land forces in Basra to cross to Haifa, disputes arose over the interpretation of the Treaty, and Iraqi opinion was divided. London was poorly informed on local conditions, and on ill-judged advice from the British Embassy prematurely issued a blunt demand for the removal of Rashid Ali from the premiership. The effects of the ultimatum were to create closer relations between Rashid Ali and the military group which favoured Germany and was plotting with Von Papen. Hostilities eventually resulted from a confused situation in which miscalculations were made on all sides. More skilful diplomacy, based on a better understanding in London of the local situation, might well have avoided armed conflict. After another military coup d'état the Regent, followed by Nuri al-Said, left for Transjordan. They were subsequently restored by British military action, and the four colonels who had instigated the coup d'état were executed. Though the British military operation was skilfully conducted the indirect effects of the episode on the Iraqi regime in the post-war period were unfortunate, both for the regime and for long-term British interests. The whole conflict requires reappraisal in the light of the evidence from the German, Italian, and Arabic sources which have become available since the war.[1]

During the rest of the war the Iraqi governments that were reconstituted under the Regent were formed mainly from moderate

---

[1] A first step in this direction has been taken by Majid al-Khadduri, *Independent Iraq*, 2nd ed. (London, 1960), chs. 8–10.

nationalists and co-operated with Britain in military matters. Iraq and Iran formed a main route for the supplies passing from the Western allies to Russia. In 1943 Iraq made a formal declaration of war against Germany and her allies. In 1945 diplomatic relations were established with Russia and the United Nations Charter was signed. But in nationalist circles reservations against close identification with British and allied policies remained, even though the extremist groups in the army and among those influenced by the Mufti of Jerusalem were discredited by the decline of Germany and Italy.

Difficulties developed after the middle of 1943 in Iraqi Kurdistan. Nuri al-Said toured the area in May 1944 and endeavoured to meet Kurdish grievances by special social and economic measures and by proposing the creation of a new *liwa* of Dohuk. But the Regent blocked the proposal, and other measures were sabotaged by narrow-minded army officers as well as by a number of civilian ministers. This sequence of events was to be repeated several times in the post-war years by different groups of ministers and army officers, and it was not surprising that Kurdish leaders lost hope that governments in Baghdad would deal with them in good faith.

Following the war martial law was ended, the censorship of the press was abolished, and political parties could be legally formed again, except the Communist party. The latter, however, carried on underground activities. The parties ranged from the right-wing Independence Party, through the mildly reformist Liberal Party to the National Democratic Party which modelled itself on European social-democratic policies and included some leading educated middle-class personalities. But ministries remained transient and subject to frequent reshuffling and intense personal rivalries. The parties remained poorly organized and attracted no mass representation: their members comprised only a small proportion of the population. So far as organization was concerned the Communist party was an exception, but in the period 1948–52 it was handicapped locally by the instructions which, along with other Asian parties, it received from the Comintern, led by Zhdanov, and by the indirect effects of Stalin's attempts, just after the war, to delay the Russian evacuation of Iran and to use the Tudeh party there for his own purposes. This pushed most of the moderate Iraqi leaders, especially Nuri al-Said, further towards the Western powers than they might otherwise have gone. The hanging of four Communist leaders in 1949 was resented even by the non-Communist left, and it created martyrs for the movement. A militant student group, aided by the Communist and Baathist organizations, organized political demonstrations against the regime from time to time.

But the growth of revenues derived from the operations of the oil companies in the 1950s enabled the short-lived oligarchic governments to lay the foundations for considerable economic and social advances.

Nuri al-Said, who headed a number of ministries in this period, took the lead in measures to use some 70 per cent of the oil revenues in economic development. His Government established a Development Board which was to allocate the revenues among different projects. The Board included several foreign experts. Nuri consciously based his policies on the theory that ten or more years of economic advance would reduce social and political discontent and remove the danger of revolution. He had no wish to be a dictator but from 1954 his suppression of political parties and manipulation of elections alienated important sections of the middle classes and his and Abdul Ilah's policies of close links with the 'Western' powers alienated not only the middle classes but also the growing student class, the 'intellectuals', and even conservative and traditional Islamic circles. He failed also to grasp the declining comparative importance of the tribal chiefs. In the hope of maintaining their political support he refrained from adopting the proposals for land reform that were drawn up by some of his ministers. The difficulties of reform without loss of productivity were serious, but the arbitrary actions of some of the large landlords, who were almost a law to themselves in some areas, aroused much popular resentment and stimulated the growth of a revolutionary spirit.

None the less the country was comparatively quiet for most of the 1950s preceding the revolution of 1958. Good order was maintained and both Iraqis and foreigners could travel freely and safely in all parts of the country. There was much outspoken criticism in which sections of the press sometimes joined. The regime could not be described as a dictatorship but was in practice an oligarchy. A number of ministers were men of capacity and experience. The customary accusations of corruption were levelled against the regime but there is little evidence that it existed on a large scale and the period seems to compare very favourably in this respect with what went before and what came after.

The Revolution of 1958

Rumours of a coming attempt to overthrow the regime had been circulating in Baghdad for some weeks before the blow came on 14 July 1958. The sudden creation of the United Arab Republic in February had been followed by the declaration of a formal union between Iraq and Jordan. In these moves and counter-moves the public had not been consulted in any of the countries concerned. In Iraq and Jordan the majority of people appeared indifferent and some sections of it disapproving. The conflict in the Lebanon had widened the gap between the Government and public opinion. The Prime Minister, sharply at odds with President Nasser, hoped for 'Western' intervention in Lebanon, and seems to have been prepared to use Iraqi troops if it came. This would have run sharply counter to sentiment throughout the country. Violent radio propaganda was launched from Cairo against the Iraqi Government and particularly against the Prime Minister.

For some time groups of 'Free Officers' had been meeting in secret to devise means of overturning the regime. A central organization was formed with Brigadier Abdul Karim Kassem as its chairman. An order to a brigade situated north-east of Baghdad to move to Jordan on 14 July gave them their opportunity. The second in command of this brigade, Colonel Abdul Salam Aref, a fellow-conspirator with Brigadier Kassem, agreed to direct the brigade into instead of around Baghdad, and to take over the capital, Kassem following close behind with another brigade from a neighbouring camp. The plan was successful. The police made no effort to repel the vanguard of Colonel Aref's forces. Security measures proved to be wholly inadequate. A contributory factor was the widespread lack of support for the regime. In the take-over the King, the Crown Prince, and all but one member of the Royal Family were shot dead. Though there has been some dispute over whether this had been planned or was done on the initiative of subordinate soldiers, the conclusion that it was planned seems to be more generally accepted.

The military officers had formed no agreed programme on the policy to be followed after power had been seized. In the first few days they suppressed mob disorders and obtained a firm hold on the country. The establishment of a Republic was announced. A 'Council of Sovereignty' was to exercise the functions of the President until a president was appointed. Two of its three members were army officers. A Cabinet was set up in which Brigadier Kassem was both Prime Minister and Acting Minister of Defence. Army officers were appointed to the ministries of the Interior and Social Affairs. Other ministries were headed by civilians who included, at the Ministry of Finance, Mohammed Hadid, a leading figure in the National Democratic Party which represented a non-Communist left-wing following, and produced a daily journal *Al-Ahali*. Although parties had been banned in 1954 they had continued underground and, although still without legal recognition, they began to appear above the surface again after the Revolution. The Communist party was the best organized though its membership was not large.

The leaders of the re-emerging parties and a large part of the middle class had expected that the Revolution would be followed by a return to a freer political life and more widely representative government. Mr. Chaderji, at the head of the National Democratic Party, called for the legalization of parties, free elections, and a genuinely democratic constitution. The opponents of the fallen regime had directed their main criticisms against its repressive political measures which had set back the development of democratic government and imprisoned a number of opposition leaders. It was widely expected that greater political freedom would follow their triumph.

From an early stage, however, the new regime was faced with serious dangers within and from without. The various groups which rejoiced at the passing of the old regime held widely different views over the nature of the regime that should follow it, ranging from the Moslem Brotherhood and the most conservative Islamic groups at one extreme to the Communists at the other. A large majority held intermediate, but still diverse, views, and the extent of political freedom which some of the most active among them desired fell far short of that advocated by the National Democratic Party. Among them were the Baathists, whose inspiration came from Syria, and the Arab Nationalist Movement, based largely on Beirut. The term 'Arab nationalist', however, was often given a wider and looser significance, at times almost synonymous with the term 'Nasserite'. The formation of the United Arab Republic only a few months earlier had created an expectation in some quarters that, following the Revolution, Iraq would be added to it. Radio and press in Cairo and Damascus had maintained a long and violent attack on the former Iraqi regime. Opposition groups in Iraq had applauded this campaign for their own ends, but their willingness to accept Egyptian intervention and leadership was greatly over-estimated. Brigadier Kassem and the majority of his associates soon showed that the new regime would pursue its own way and maintain the independence of Iraq. Colonel Abdul Salam Aref, Kassem's associate in the 'take-over', soon broke with Premier Kassem, partly over the issue of relations with Egypt. The Cabinet did not long operate as a unit. Differences were intensified in the autumn by intrigues between certain Iraqi groups and their supporters in Syria and Egypt, and a plot was uncovered to overturn the new regime and replace it by one allied with Egypt and led by Rashid Ali al-Gailani, the early wartime Premier who had been deposed by British pressure. At the same time relations with the United Arab Republic deteriorated.

Faced with verbal attacks from Cairo and Damascus which encouraged dissident groups at home to seek the overthrow of his regime, Kassem pursued a policy aiming at a balance of power among the contending groups in the country. Throughout the autumn and early winter his greatest danger came from the extreme groups on the right, together with the Baathists, who were not yet disillusioned with the UAR. In March 1959, a plot organized by Colonel Shawaf, a former 'Free Officer' stationed in Mosul, with the aid of Colonel Sarraj, the UAR Chief of Security in Damascus, led to an uprising in Mosul which was suppressed by military force aided by left-wing groups in Mosul. In the course of the affray excesses were committed by Mosul Communists retaliating after the murder of two of their leaders by extremists on the right. Numerous arrests were made and political tension heightened. Relations with the UAR, which had aided the plotters, deteriorated further.

The succession of plots in some of which UAR agents gave indirect help to Baathists; extreme Arab nationalists and dissident army officers had impelled Premier Kassem to give more scope to Communists than he wished to do, in order to maintain a balance of political forces. But when the outrages committed by them in Mosul in March were followed in July by the Kirkuk affray in which they played a part, Kassem acted quietly and swiftly to remove them from positions of power and arrest many of their members. This was scarcely done, however, when a group of Baathist extremists, aided by Syrians, attempted to assassinate him in August. Kassem survived, however, and continued his personal rule until February 1963.

The disappointment of the hopes in moderate circles that representative government would be set up may be explained partly by the constant threats and agitation, fanned from outside, to overthrow and replace the new regime by others inspired by Baathists or Nasserites; partly by the character of Kassem himself; and still more by the military domination of the Revolution.

These political preoccupations hindered economic reforms. Land reform was the most urgent need and the greatest failure, not only for the Kassem regime but for those which followed. For political reasons the power of the landlords had to be and was reduced, but at the expense of productivity, which fell disastrously, with unfortunate results for other economic sectors. The Development Board, with its foreign advisors, was abolished and a Ministry of Planning set up. In practice the new industrial programme was little more than a continuation of the old.

Political and economic relations were widened by the establishment of diplomatic relations with the Eastern European countries and China. This was followed by the conclusion of a variety of trade agreements and cultural exchanges with them as well as arrangements for loans and aid in economic development. Among the schemes which were eventually carried through was the conversion of the railway between Baghdad and Basra from narrow to standard gauge.

Notwithstanding the use at times of left-wing phraseology, the general economic policies of the new regime differed less than had been expected from those of its predecessor and the way was left open for private enterprise in industry. In 1961–2, however, Kassem took two steps which encountered much opposition abroad. The first, which is discussed elsewhere,[1] concerned the oil companies operating in Iraq; the second was to lay claim to Kuwait as part of Iraq. This was not a new Iraqi claim but it was made in April 1961 on the eve of Kuwait independence when rumours had circulated that she might join the

See p. 334.

Commonwealth. It alarmed the Ruler of Kuwait—who called for British military assistance—and other Arab states, which denied Iraq's claim. British troops were succeeded by Arab League troops. It does not appear that Kassem intended to use force, but the incident was a blow to his prestige.

In the later part of his period of rule Kassem lost much of his earlier popularity, except among the economically poorer classes. At the same time, however, the country became more settled and greater freedom prevailed. There was little or no sign of any widespread desire for further political upheaval. But the Premier's failure to mobilize political support and to share power with others among the politically active classes gave an opportunity for Baathist plotters in the army to organize a rising in February 1963. Fighting raged for several days and the issue was in doubt for a time. No public enthusiasm was shown when the Baathist military prevailed after considerable popular resistance. The new regime dealt ruthlessly with its opponents. Soldiers who had obeyed orders to resist them, and Communists who had been imprisoned by Kassem, were shot in considerable numbers.

From an early stage the new regime was torn by internal dissensions that became more and more acute as time went on. Its leaders established a 'National Guard' which became a paramilitary organization in the hands of its extremists on the 'left'. The Prime Minister, General Bakr, was unable to control the contending groups within the Government. Baathist ranks were unable to provide all the skills and experience required in government and the moderate group wished to fill positions from non-Baathists where it seemed desirable on grounds of efficiency. But the extremist groups were opposed to this and, led by a Deputy Prime Minister, Ali Saleh al-Saadi, obtained control of the National Guard which engaged in terrorist activities against political opponents. The police were powerless to protect the public against political acts of violence, including torture and murder.

In external affairs the career of the regime was almost equally stormy. The coup in Iraq was followed in March by a similar coup in Syria which overthrew the parliamentary regime that had followed the collapse of the UAR in 1961. The Baathist regimes in Syria and Iraq joined forces in demanding a new Arab union between the two countries and Egypt. The initiative was embarrassing to Egypt. It was obvious that the Iraqi and Syrian conception of union was one in which President Nasser would have had to share power with them, and the negotiations were foredoomed from the start. As a result the relations of Iraq with Egypt again deteriorated and Arab nationalists in Iraq, within the army as well as the public, were alienated further.

In November the crisis came to a head. The challenge to the army and police by the National Guard forced a showdown. On 11 November the moderate Baath leaders appeared to gain the upper hand with the expulsion of the Deputy Premier who led the extremists. On the 13th the Baathist leaders in Syria came to Baghdad. But a joint meeting failed to compose the issues and the moderate Baathist leaders were obliged to draw in non-Baathist officers as well as to co-operate with the President Abdul Salam Aref to suppress the National Guard in an armed clash on a large scale in Baghdad on 18 November.

The widespread relief felt at the downfall of the Baathist regime created a favourable atmosphere for the new Government which at first was composed of a mixture of moderate Baathist and of Arab nationalist officers, together with some civilian ministers chosen on technical grounds. It was not long before the Arab nationalist elements in the Government succeeded in eliminating, one by one, the Baathist ministers, with the exception of Tahir Yahya, who proved to be an opportunist ready to accommodate his views to the changed conditions. He became Prime Minister in what was now a non-Baathist Government.

Policy now seemed to be oriented externally towards friendship with Egypt—with unfavourable results for relations with Syria—and internally towards greater support for free enterprise and away from socialism. But this was to overlook competition in ideology. Egypt had turned to 'Arab socialism' in 1961–2 and began to apply it in Syria during the union. This was largely undone by the parliamentary regime which succeeded after the collapse of the union. But 're-nationalization' of the banks followed the Baathist seizure of power in 1963. These examples, among other influences, led to the introduction of sweeping nationalization measures in the middle of 1964 by the Aref–Yahya Government in direct contradiction to its previous declarations of policy. Business opinion was alienated and private enterprise has not regained confidence since. Difficulties quickly arose over the administration of such a wide range of public industries. While the Government could hardly be as unpopular as that of 1963, it soon lost its early favour. Outwardly it moved towards closer relations with Egypt, and an agreement was reached to establish a 'Joint Presidential Council' with subsidiary committees to meet once a quarter to prepare for the establishment of a union between the two countries. This was followed by agreement to set up a 'unified Political Command' which was to aim at 'constitutional unity' within two years. A third step was taken by the establishment of an 'Arab Socialist Union' on the model of Egypt, which was to constitute the sole political party in the country.

These moves were ineffective. The conditions for a real union did not exist. President Nasser was never ready to share power and President Aref, even if he had wished to do so, could not have overcome the opposition in Iraq, especially among the Shii and the Kurds, to Egyptian domination or any other form of autocratic outside rule in the name of unity. As it was, the two Presidents were not, in reality, on good terms. The various public declarations on unity gave lip-service to policies and aims proclaimed so often in the past that they could not openly be discarded.

Premier Yahya remained in office until September 1965 in face of growing discontent at the failure to achieve promised economic advances, and to create the confidence needed to stimulate investment. The middle classes in particular were weary of military governments. Towards the end of 1964, in a reorganization of the ministries, a programme was announced that would lead towards the restoration of constitutional government but no agreement was reached on the form to be adopted. Meantime the conflict in the north continued. The ministry collapsed in September 1965 and was succeeded briefly by one headed by Brigadier Aref Abdul Razzaq, with a civilian, Dr. Abdul Rahman al-Bazzaz as Deputy Premier. But the new premier, in the absence of the President, tried to seize complete personal power. His effort collapsed ignominiously and Dr. Bazzaz was installed as the first civilian premier since the Revolution.

A programme of reforms was promptly adopted. Nationalizations were to be limited in the future and private enterprise encouraged. Dr. Bazzaz boldly declared that the time had come to return to normal civilian life and steps were to be taken to adopt an electoral law. He aimed at ending the Kurdish war but was at first obstructed by his Minister of Defence, General Uqualy. By personal visits and judicious diplomacy he markedly improved Iraq's relations with neighbouring countries, including Turkey, Iran, and Saudi Arabia.

In April 1966 President Abdul Salam Aref was killed in a helicopter crash. He was succeeded by his brother, Abdul Rahman Aref, another army officer. Groups of officers led by retired generals began from an early stage to plot for the removal of Dr. Bazzaz. But the Premier held on to office long enough to bring the Kurdish war to an end on the basis of a well-conceived twelve-point plan which recognized Kurdish nationalism and provided for autonomy in a wide range of domestic affairs. Before these measures could be carried through, Dr. Bazzaz was removed—immediately after a successful visit to Moscow. His plans for a return to representative government were thus frustrated. He had achieved widespread popularity with the public and had demonstrated that the Iraqi people desired a return to constitutional civilian government. The succeeding military Government failed to gain public confidence. It was dominated by army officers who, though giving some lip-service to the Twelve Points, were in reality opposed to them and did nothing to carry them out. Meanwhile the Kurdish leader had firmly established his position in the north.

The new Government faced an early loss of revenue as a result of a Syrian conflict with the Iraq Petroleum Company which blocked the outlet for Iraqi oil. This led to the fall of the ministry on the eve of the war with Israel which started on 5 June 1967. Iraqi troops were sent to Jordan and remained there after the war had ended. Although Iraq's role was negligible in practice, the Government supported the position of Egypt and Jordan. Yahya returned as Prime Minister, and as long as the Aref–Yahya regime lasted it followed broadly the policy of co-operation with Cairo. It severed relations with Britain, West Germany, and the United States but later resumed normal diplomatic relations with the first two of these powers.

At home discontent with the Government increased: widespread accusations of corruption were directed against some of its members and their followers. There was renewed discussion of a return to more representative government. Since the authors of the nationalization decrees had returned to power, business remained unwilling to invest widely. The nationalized industries encountered difficulties in organization and management.

Meantime the displaced military Baathist leaders were plotting to regain the power which they had lost in November 1963. Their general unpopularity made it unlikely that they would have succeeded but for the unwitting aid given by two army officers, one of them Head of Security and the other Head of the Presidential Guard, Col. Abdul Razzaq al-Naif and Lt.-Gen. Ibrahim Abdul Rahman al-Daoud, who determined to oust the President and Premier. They represented the widespread middle-class discontent and were not among the left-wing opponents of the regime. The Baathist plotters seized the opportunity to join them.

In the first fortnight after the coup al-Naif and al-Daoud formed a moderate ministry which included Dr. Hani, a professional diplomat of the highest standing, as Foreign Minister. But Generals al-Bakr, Hardan Takriti, and Ammash staged a second internal coup and eliminated the two authors of the downfall of President Aref and his regime. Thus a military Baath regime returned five years after it had, to general public relief, been displaced. Its primary aim was to maintain itself in power at all costs and to eliminate possible rivals.

The change marked not only a more ruthless domestic policy which led to a number of executions and brought back memories of the murders perpetrated by the Baathist regime of 1963, but also an external policy no longer in harmony with Egypt. The Government rejected the Security Council Resolution of November 1967 and proclaimed it would not recognize the existence of Israel under any circumstances. At the same time it contributed nothing in practical terms to the conflict. In the clashes between the Palestinian organizations and the Jordan Government it professed to support the rebels but confined its support to radio broadcasts.

The most constructive achievement of President al-Bakr's regime was to reach a settlement with the Kurds. In March 1969 a 15-point agreement, based on Dr. Bazzaz's programme of 1966, ended the fighting, declared a general amnesty for all insurgents, gave the Kurdish language equal status with Arabic in Kurdish majority areas (which were to have Kurdish administrators), and stipulated the appointment of a Kurdish Vice-President in the Baghdad Government. However, obstacles remained to a final settlement—notably in the assessment of Kurdish majority areas. Kurdish leaders accused the Government of encouraging non-Kurds to move into existing Kurdish areas to alter the balance of population.

Relations between the Iraqi Government and the radical Baathist regime in Syria were far from cordial and in the summer of 1970 it reached the point of rupture with President Nasser's Egypt. Iraq's pretensions to Arab leadership lost credibility when its 12,000 troops stationed in Jordan failed to come to the assistance of the Palestinian guerrillas in the September civil war. The troops were shortly afterwards withdrawn.

Relations with Iran were also severely strained after the announcement in January 1970 of an attempted right-wing coup with alleged Iranian and US support. The ending of the Kurdish war and the withdrawal of Iraqi troops from Jordan were of some help to Iraq in the pursuit of a more active and ambitious policy in the Persian Gulf following the British withdrawal in 1971.

GOVERNMENT AND CONSTITUTION

Before the Iraqi Revolution of 1958 legislative power was vested with the King in parliament which consisted of the Senate and Chamber of Deputies. Senators, who were appointed by the King, were not to exceed in number one fourth of the Chamber of Deputies. The deputies were elected on the basis of one to every 20,000 male Iraqi subjects. Every bill had to be submitted to each Assembly in turn and then approved by the King.

The Cabinet consisted of at least seven ministers, including the Prime Minister and any ministers without portfolio. The Prime Minister was chosen by the King, who also appointed other ministers on the recommendation of the Prime Minister.

In the revolution led by the military in 1958 the existing regime was eliminated and a new provisional constitution was announced. But the history of the 1960s was marked by frequent military coups d'état, after each of which the previous constitutions (mostly 'provisional') were abolished and announcements made of the intention to draft new and 'permanent' constitutions. The only serious attempt to return to legality and genuine constitutional rule was made in 1965–6 by Premier Bazzaz, who was himself a distinguished lawyer, but this was terminated by the resumption of military rule in the late summer of 1966.

Education

Since 1957 the number of students at all levels of education has continued to increase much more rapidly than the population. Pupils in primary schools rose from about 430,000 in 1957–8 to about 977,000 in 1966–7. The numbers in secondary schools increased even more rapidly. By 1966–7 there were nearly a quarter of a million students in intermediate and secondary education combined. In higher education in the same year there were some 35,000 students. The University of Baghdad expanded greatly; another university expanded alongside it in Baghdad and additional colleges were established in the provinces. The Jesuit college of al-Hikma was taken over by the military-dominated Government and Baathist and military political influences on higher education have generally been strong. Educational administrators have confronted great difficulties. Medicine and some of the natural sciences have been subject to less interference.

The expansion of education has been achieved at the expense of quality. The position varies among different subjects and institutions but there is little doubt that standards of teaching and examination have actually deteriorated in some fields while in many others old-fashioned methods, such as the 'dictated lecture' continue unchanged. Students read little beyond a textbook and their knowledge of foreign languages is inadequate for extensive reading, while in many subjects the literature in Arabic is inadequate to keep abreast of contemporary developments. At the same time, women's role in higher education has expanded with fewer obstacles than in many Arab countries.

Agriculture

In spite of a movement of population from rural to urban areas over some years, agriculture still occupies more people than any other sector. Apart from oil, agricultural exports comprise about three-quarters of the total and recent difficulties in the agricultural sector have been one of the chief handicaps to economic development. Agricultural natural resources and possibilities for development differ widely throughout the country owing to variations in climate, soil, and transport conditions.

The cultivable area has two main divisions: first the region to the north and east of a line running south of Mosul and Kirkuk to Khanaqin, where the rainfall is sufficient to permit the cultivation of winter crops without irrigation; and second, the alluvial plain of the centre and south, where agriculture depends on the water of the Tigris and Euphrates for irrigation (by pump, flow, or natural irrigation). In the first region rainfed winter cereals predominate, and millet, maize, sesame and other summer crops are grown as subsidiaries where irrigation is possible. In the mountain regions of Kurdistan tobacco, timber, and fruit are produced.

In the central canal zone (Falluja–Baghdad–Diyala) wheat and barley are the principal winter crops: summer crops include millet, maize, sesame, and the produce of market gardens near Baghdad. Baquba, east of Baghdad, is an important centre for oranges and other fruit. From here southwards barley and rice predominate with a great concentration of date palms in all the riverain land especially around Basra on the Shatt al-Arab.

Rice growing has not been extended into all areas where it could be grown successfully because of the rival demands for water for other crops and uses.

Iraqi dates constitute about three-quarters of world production and it is estimated that there are altogether some 20 million date-palms of fruit-bearing age. Some 350 varieties of date are said to be grown in Iraq, of which only four (Zahdi, Sayer, Hillawi, and Khadrawi) are usually exported in quantity. Total average production in normal times averages about 400,000 tons of which between 200,000 and 250,000 tons are exported and the rest consumed in Iraq both as food— dates are a staple item of diet—in natural form or as date syrup, and as a raw material for the spirit industry.

Livestock

Raising livestock is of major importance both in the internal economy of the country, by providing food, transport, and raw materials for essential manufactures, and also in foreign trade. Livestock and their products—wool, hides, and intestines (casings) account for about one sixth of Iraq's exports excluding oil. The quality of much of the stock is poor, the selection of breeding animals is based on defective criteria, and veterinary services are inadequate and insufficiently supplied with materials to combat disease. Over-grazing has led to erosion in many of the pasture lands.

Forestry

The forests of Iraq are situated mainly in the mountainous regions of the extreme north and north-east of the country. Oaks predominate, but on the thin soil of the mountain slopes they rarely reach timber size. Walnut, oriental plane, mulberry, and poplar are found in the valleys—the last providing a valuable source of poles and small timber both for local use and for the treeless regions of the plains. The total area of indigenous forests, including patches of riverine scrub scattered along the banks of the twin rivers, has been estimated at 7,000 square miles, most of it state property.

Irrigation and Flood Control

The control of floods accompanied by the storage of water has been a major concern in Iraq since early in the century when Sir William Willcocks pointed out that the Tharthar depression, which lay between the Euphrates and the Tigris, and Lake Habbaniya were excellently situated for the diversion and storage of excess water. The project, after interruptions during the World Wars, was completed in 1956 and Iraq has benefited greatly from the elimination of the chronic recurrence of floods. The storage capacity of Wadi Tharthar was estimated at the time as adequate for ten to fifteen years. Since then consultants have made a number of proposals for the enlargement of storage reservoirs at alternative sites. Plans have been prepared for the construction of three new dams—the Mosul Dam on the Tigris, the Haditha Dam on the Euphrates, and the Himmin Dam on the Diyala. At the time of the Revolution, however, it was widely believed that the increase in irrigation water supplies had gone too far in advance of drainage, leading to increased salinity. The problem of drainage is one of the most serious handicaps in Iraqi agriculture. Its solution depends largely on the education of the cultivator, particularly in keeping his drains clear. It was aggravated by the Land Reform which was hastily enacted after 1958.

Agrarian Reform

Before the Revolution governments had refused to undertake comprehensive land reform measures, mainly from a desire to maintain the political support of the landlords. Opposition groups had committed themselves to reform and their propaganda tended to minimize the practical difficulties and to exaggerate the capacity of the agricultural labourers to dispense with the services rendered by the landlords. It was not realized that the removal of the landlord would require four or five well-staffed agricultural agencies to take his place.

The Land Reform Act of 1958 fixed maximum holdings of 750 hectares of rain-fed land and 500 hectares of irrigated land. Lands in excess were to be taken over and redistributed within five years. Compensation was to be paid to displaced landlords and the new landowners were to pay for their holdings over a period of twenty years. They were all required to join co-operative societies.

The Act was essentially a political measure designed to remove the power which many landlords exercised in their localities, where a number of them were a law to themselves. In this the Act was successful; but on the economic side its consequences were disastrous. The ministry established to administer the Act was crippled by political struggles over its interpretation and the manner of its administration. Long delays followed expropriation before redistribution was carried out and in the intervening period none of the cultivators had any incentive to produce. A large area went out of cultivation and salinity increased. The elimination of the landlord meant the elimination of the managerial class and in most areas the peasants were unable to take over the functions the latter had performed. Many of them abandoned cultivation as they were unable to cope with the problem of salination, or to obtain credit, or undertake the marketing of their produce.

The administration of the Act was subject to sharp fluctuations. Unstable military governments succeeded one another during the 1960s. Each new group of army officers had different aims and ideas and there was no continuity of administration. In 1961 the peasants were exempted from paying for their new lands and in some cases loans to them were converted into grants. The Baathist officers who overthrew Kassem in 1963 made further attempts to secure the support of the peasants. In the short-lived Bazzaz ministry of 1965–6 a competent and well-qualified Minister of Land Reform was appointed, only to be immediately displaced by the military regime that followed.

The provision that recipients of distributed lands must belong to a co-operative society, an imitation of the Egyptian agrarian reform, could not be applied overnight, only after a long process of education and experiment. It was difficult to educate the peasant in the meaning of co-operation and the functions of co-operatives. Similarly, the peasant tended to confuse agricultural credit and relief grants and often expected the Agricultural Bank to reduce loan repayments as a form of relief.

In 1965, after long delay, procedures were introduced for the first time to give reasonably accurate estimates of the production of agricultural crops. An Indian expert from the FAO staff spent some time in Iraq to initiate the Iraqi Ministry of Agriculture in internationally recognized methods of measuring the cultivated area and of cutting sections of crops in fields selected at random to estimate yields. Previously, the estimates of production had been almost worthless and, in view of the importance of the agricultural sector, estimates of national income had been subject to considerable errors. Statistics of crop production have become of value only since the change was effected.

The Oil Industry

Oil concessions covering most of Iraq and lasting for 75 years were secured by the Iraq Petroleum Company (IPC) in 1925 and the associated Mosul and Basra Petroleum Companies (MPC and BPC) in 1932 and 1938 respectively. They initially provided for royalties at the rate of 4s. gold per ton of crude oil exported. A new agreement, of

3 February 1952, made retroactive to 1 January 1951, provided that the Government should receive 50 per cent of the companies' profits from their operations in Iraq before deduction for foreign taxes, part of the half share consisting of oil in kind ($12\frac{1}{2}$ per cent of the net production of each of the companies).

As a result of this agreement and the increase in crude oil production, Iraq's oil revenues rose from £13·9 million in 1951 to £32·6 million in 1952 and £73·7 million in 1955.

Oil was struck for the first time in the IPC concession in 1927, near Kirkuk, and by the end of 1934 the company exported crude oil through two 12-inch pipelines, each of 2 million tons annual capacity, to Tripoli and Haifa on the Mediterranean coast. In 1949 a 16-inch pipeline of 4 million tons capacity was opened to Tripoli. In consequence of the first Arab–Israeli war work westwards on a similar pipeline stopped short at the Palestine frontier and for the same reason the Iraqi Government closed the 12-inch Haifa line which has since remained disconnected at the frontier. A 30–32-inch pipeline was opened to Banias in Syria in 1952.

In the MPC concessionary area exploration and drilling were carried out before 1931, and in 1939 oil of some commercial value was discovered at Ain Zalah, north-west of Mosul, though production had to wait until after the war. In 1952 the field was linked by a 12-inch pipeline to the IPC pipeline system, to permit the export of its crude oil to the Mediterranean coast.

In the BPC concession area two fields were developed after the war at Zubair and Rumaila, west of Basra. A new terminal was opened in 1951 at Fao on the Persian Gulf.

The Government refinery at Daura near Baghdad, which is administered by GORA (Government Oil Refineries Administration) came into production in June 1955. A lubricating oil plant and a bitumen plant have also been built at Daura. A small refinery (with a bitumen plant) at Muftiya near Basra and a bitumen plant, administered by GORA, has been built at Qaiyara, south of Mosul. A Government-owned sulphur recovery plant was opened in Kirkuk in 1968.

The oil agreement which had been in effect from 1 January 1951 between the Iraqi Government and the Iraq Petroleum Company, including its two associated companies in Mosul and Basra (hereafter referred to jointly as the IPC) were abruptly terminated in 1961. This was a profit-sharing agreement of the kind negotiated in Saudi Arabia earlier and prevalent throughout the Middle East. (See section on oil.) Under it Iraqi oil was developed with moderate speed, exports rising from around 18 million tons in 1952 to over 47 million in 1960 with payments to the government exceeding £95 millions. For some time, however, the Iraqi Government had been pressing for a variety of modifications in the agreement, and one of the first acts of Abdul Karim Kassem was to open new negotiations with the IPC.

In the beginning no drastic action was expected and the companies entered negotiations with some confidence, for Kassem had assured them that he did not intend to give in to the popular demands for 'nationalization'. The negotiations did not go well. The Government complained of the 'intransigence' of the IPC and the company complained of the unreasonable and changing demands of Kassem. The events in Algeria further raised public feeling against the 'imperialist' companies and demands for strong action against the IPC became more strident. Kassem himself took an active part in the negotiations, which centred on Iraqi demands for free natural gas, relinquishment by the IPC of the greater part of its non-exploited concession area, revision of the profit-sharing arrangements, and 20 per cent of the equity of the IPC. This last had been promised Iraq under the San Remo agreement of 1920 but had been given up in the 1924 concession negotiations in return for a royalty and 20 per cent of any shares that might be issued to the public. Since the IPC was a wholly-owned subsidiary of international oil companies, the issue of public shares had never been contemplated.

In 1960 cargo duties on oil were increased at the Port of Basra. The oil company declared that the increase made exports unprofitable and stopped production at its Rumaila field. The Iraqis were much incensed and the negotiations became increasingly difficult. Talks broke down completely in 1961 and Kassem promulgated 'Law 80' in December of that year which expropriated without compensation over 99·5 per cent of the IPC concession, confining the company to the areas from which it was actually producing. In particular, the Government obtained the rich North Rumaila field which the IPC had discovered and partially developed and which was known to contain very large reserves. Clause 3 of Law 80 did, however, envisage the possibility of a settlement and made it possible for some of the expropriated oil-bearing lands to be returned to the company if a settlement were reached.

The company did not accept Law 80 and demanded international arbitration. Intermittent negotiations continued, but the two sides remained deadlocked for several years and the rate of increase of Iraq's oil exports fell. In February 1964 Iraq established its own national oil company (INOC) with the intention of taking an active part in the exploitation of the country's resources. In the meantime there had been political changes in Iraq and changes in concession terms in other countries in the Middle East. Both the Government and the IPC had been manoeuvring in the hope of reaching some kind of agreement, for both were losing.

Oil exports were stagnating relative to those of other countries and the Government was unable to benefit under the royalty expensing and marketing allowance agreements which other OPEC countries were obtaining. The companies were particularly concerned about the future of the North Rumaila field. In consequence, negotiations proceeded under the guidance of Abdul Aziz Wattari, the then Minister of Oil. Eventually an agreement was reached—the 'Draft Agreement of 1965'. It was intended to provide a comprehensive settlement of all back issues and to lay the basis for future co-operation between the companies and the Government. The companies accepted Law 80 and agreed to relinquish all their territory except known fields, including North Rumaila, to raise exports substantially, to pay $56 million in settlement of all claims back to 1961, and—most important—to enter into joint ventures with the INOC in developing oil. All the major owners of the IPC, except Standard Oil Company (New Jersey), accepted the principle of joint ventures with the Government. This in itself was a significant innovation.

But it was not to materialize. The political winds changed and the agreement died. The 1967 war with Israel made further attempts impossible, and in August 1967 the Government passed a law which assigned to the INOC most of the territory of Iraq for exploration and development. This was virtually a 'no concessions' law, but it did provide for joint ventures between the INOC and foreign companies. The owners of the IPC, however, had threatened legal action against any company undertaking to operate in territory to which they still considered they had legal rights. This deterrent was ignored by ERAP, a French state-owned company, with whom the Iraqi Government made a contract to explore and develop part of the expropriated areas, but excluding North Rumaila. The financial terms of this agreement were less favourable than those that had been offered by the IPC, but the Government preferred the more novel agreement (which was similar to an earlier ERAP/Iran agreement) with a newcomer to oil in Iraq.

The INOC turned its own attention to the development of the rich plum—North Rumaila. For help it turned to the USSR, negotiating the first of a series of loans at $2\frac{1}{2}$ per cent interest, repayable in crude oil valued at international prices. The Russians were to develop North Rumaila, as well as some minor fields, build a pipeline, and reactivate the Fao port for export. The flow of oil from North Rumaila began in April 1972. The Russians supply equipment and technical assistance, selling the equipment outright to Iraq. It has been announced that seven million tons of North Rumaila oil will be exported to the Soviet Union over the next four years. Loan agreements have also been made with other Eastern European countries to be repaid in crude oil, although if the oil cannot be delivered Iraq is required to pay in dollars. For example, the Czechs are to build a refinery at Basra to be paid for partly in crude oil. The Western oil companies still produce and export Iraq's crude oil, but all of the new development is now dominated by the Russians.

In June 1971 Iraq and the IPC group finally came to an agreement on the issue of taxes and prices in line with the Tripoli agreement of the previous April between the Libyan Government and the companies (see pp. 120–1 in the section on oil). They also reached an agreement on a variety of other financial issues some of which had been hanging fire since 1955. The IPC agreed to raise exports substantially and to pay £20·2 million as a lump sum in settlement of all past claims, to grant a four-year interest free loan, and to change some of its accounting procedures in favour of the Government. In consequence the payments to Iraq by the IPC group are expected to rise from the 1970 figure of $512 millions to over $924 million in 1971, well exceeding a thousand million dollars a year in the following five years. Production of the IPC in 1970 was estimated at 75·2 million tons and was expected to rise another 10 million over five years.

Although relations between the Government and the company were much improved, the issue of 'equity participation' for the Government in the IPC group still remained. The Iraqi Oil Minister announced immediately on the signing of the new agreements that Iraq would continue to press for participation. In June 1972, after repeated accusations that IPC was holding back production to weaken Iraq, the Government nationalized IPC but offered to negotiate with the French 23·75 per cent share in the company.

Other Industries

Apart from oil, Iraq has no industries of any size despite the encouragement of industrialization in the 1960s. Factory industry is mainly directed to the processing of agricultural products and to the manufacturing of building materials and consumer goods for the local market. It includes the manufacture of soap, vegetable oil, cigarettes, textiles (cotton, wool, and rayon), footwear, beer, cement, bricks, and tiles. During the 1960s a number of factories were built under the terms of the Iraqi–Soviet Technical and Economic Co-operation Agreement of 1959.

Development

In the earlier years of statehood it was necessary above all to lay the foundations of economic advance by creating a network of transport and communications, a pure water supply, and various public services including an educational system, the beginnings of a health service, as well as, later, a number of welfare services. The Government took the initiative over a wide field but its financial resources were very limited until the great increase in oil revenues began in 1952.

A Development Board was established in 1950 in the hope of ensuring that oil revenues would not be dissipated by unstable governments but would be used for economic advance. However, the initial autonomy was removed three years later when it was brought under a new Ministry of Development although a considerable proportion of its members remained non-political and, until the 1958 Revolution, some were foreigners.

Before 1958 the Development Board drew up three investment programmes. Seventy per cent of the oil revenues were placed under the Board's control. Expenditures generally fell short of estimates owing to the difficulties in giving practical effect to development plans but from 1956 the machinery was working more effectively. The Board achieved its best results in the early stages in irrigation and flood controls which involved the building of dams and other construction activities and the improvement of communications.

A number of reports and recommendations were made by outside bodies and individuals—notably Lord Salter in 1955. His report pointed out the need to bring demonstrable direct benefits to a wide public rather than to concentrate on schemes the benefit of which would be obviously only in the long term. Housing, pure water, and direct help to farmers were given as examples. Most of his recommendations were adopted but in 1958 the Revolution interrupted the machinery and organization of development programmes. The Development Board was replaced by a Planning Board composed mainly of ministers. The allocation of oil revenues was reduced from 70 per cent to 50 per cent. A new Ministry of Industry was created in 1959 but the Ministry of Finance was placed in a position of control over the departments concerned with carrying out the plans. The plans and projects of the Development Board's final plan were largely continued in the 1960s but for most of the decade the emphasis was shifted from agriculture to industry. It was not until the new plan starting in 1971 was drawn up that renewed emphasis was placed on the need for recovery and progress in the agricultural sector.

In recent years there has been little correlation between the targets of the plans and actual achievement. Practical difficulties arising out of a lack of organizing capacity, bureaucracy, and the chronic political uncertainty obstructed any steady advance. In addition the sweeping nationalization measures which were adopted under the Industrialization Act of 1964 and imposed at a time when the civil service was already overburdened both aggravated the difficulties of industrial organization and alienated private entrepreneurs. Iraq, like Syria, was following Egyptian economic policies adopted in 1961–2 with little regard for differences in local conditions or for the difficulties these policies had created in Egypt itself. The gap between planning and execution was very wide. The elaborate system of agencies which had been set up to deal with various aspects of industrialization failed at essential points. One of these concerned the relation between finance and development. The Central Bank did not meet the needs of industry; the commercial banks did not supply adequate short-term loans to industry, with the result that the Industrial Bank, whose most appropriate function is to supply long-term capital for industry, was obliged to divert its attention to short-term needs.

Fluctuations in prevailing ideas on economic aims and priorities have stood in the way of steady advance. The controversy over the relative attention to be given to agriculture and industry was long influenced by prevailing sentiment among the student and urban professional classes who regarded the emphasis on agriculture as 'colonialist'. Their opponents, on the other hand, while correctly emphasizing the interdependence of industry and agriculture, sometimes exaggerated the ultimate scope for agricultural development by underestimating the fundamental limiting factors of water supply and salination. In the 1970s a much more realistic view of the necessity for a radical improvement in the skills and knowledge of the agrarian population is likely to go hand in hand with the realization that a faster rate of industrial and commercial development will be essential to provide improved living standards for the rapidly growing population. It is not likely to be achieved until the present cumbersome bureaucratic structure is reformed and a relationship worked out between the public and private sectors which will give adequate incentive to the latter to expand.

Foreign Trade

By far the most important export is oil which makes a very large contribution to the credit side of the balance of payments. Trade in oil and oil products is commonly listed separately in tables which exclude other exports. After oil, dates are the most valuable export. Barley was formerly exported in appreciable quantities in good years but it declined sharply in the 1960s. The uncertainties of rainfall in the north and the aftermath of land reform have retarded the development of agricultural exports.

The emphasis given to industrialization after the Revolution of 1958 led to the exemption of machinery and some types of materials from customs duty but small enterprises and handicrafts were not brought within the scope of the measure. In the same period restrictions were increased on imports competing with domestic products.

The sharpest break with the trade practices of the previous regime was made by the re-establishment of both diplomatic and trading relations with the Soviet Union and the Eastern bloc countries and the establishment of relations with China. Adopting a policy of non-alignment, the Kassem regime and its successors entered into valuable trading relations with these countries through a series of trade agreements providing for exchanges of goods in agreed proportions of exports to imports.

Transport and Communications

Railways. The railways built by the British forces in the First World War formed the basis of the Iraq State Railways, which became the property of the Iraqi Government in 1936. There were two gauges. A metre-gauge line ran from the Port of Basra to Kirkuk and Erbil via Baghdad, with branches to Zubair, Nasiriya, and Khanaqin. A standard-gauge line connected Baghdad to Tel Kochek on the Syrian frontier. A through service from Baghdad to Mosul and Istanbul connecting with the Orient Express to Europe was established.

In the 1960s the metre-gauge line between Baghdad and Basra was converted to standard gauge with the aid of a Soviet loan and Soviet technicians. Thus a through line has been established from the Gulf to the northern borders of Iraq and beyond.

Roads and Bridges. After the Second World War Iraq had some 5,000 miles of roads of which one third were surfaced and the remainder were earth roads. Since then oil revenues have been used for an extensive road-building programme. Two new bridges have been built over the Tigris in Baghdad and a new highway links Baghdad and Basra via Kut and Amara.

Basra Port, which lies 80 miles up the Shatt al-Arab from the Gulf, is the only general commercial port of Iraq. It has been directed in some periods by a progressive Port Authority which has greatly improved social conditions in the vicinity. The oil port at Fao came into operation in 1951. It later went out of use but its revival is provided for in the agreement with the Soviet Union on the development of the North Rumaila oil field.

VI

Israel

THE LAND AND THE PEOPLE

Israel today comprises an area of approximately 7,900 sq. miles or
roughly 77 per cent of the territory of British mandated Palestine. The
boundaries up to the June 1967 war were fixed in 1949 in accordance
with the armistice agreements signed with Lebanon, Syria, Egypt, and
Jordan and, as such, are provisional.

In the north and west these boundaries were similar to those of
mandated Palestine; to the north with Lebanon, to the north-east with
Syria and to the west with the natural frontier of the Mediterranean.
In the south, apart from the Gaza coastal strip, the frontier followed
the old international boundary from the north-west corner of Egypt's
Sinai Peninsula south-eastwards to Eilat on the Gulf of Aqaba. In the
east the frontier is with Jordan which was created by Transjordan's
annexation in 1949 of the West Bank—the 23 per cent of Palestine
which remained in Arab hands. Until 1967 Jerusalem was divided into
two cities: the old city within the walls and the suburbs in the east and
north-east which were in Jordan, while the greater part of the new city
was controlled by Israel. The Jordan river and the Dead Sea were
under the part control of both Israel and Jordan. Only the northern
section of the Jordan and the south-western part of the Dead Sea were
within Israel's 1949 frontiers.

As a result of the 1967 war Israel's military frontiers have been
extended to include the West Bank of the Jordan, the Gaza Strip and
the Sinai Peninsula, and the Golan Heights of Syria. All these territories were under Israeli military occupation in 1972 but only the old
city of Jerusalem had been formally annexed by Israel.

The country is divided into strikingly varied geographical regions.
The altitude varies from 3,963 ft. above sea-level—the height of Mt.
Azmon near Safad—to 1,286 ft. below sea-level where the south-east
boundary lies on the shore of the Dead Sea. Going inland from the
Mediterranean the first region is the coastal plain, which varies in
width from about four miles at Acre to about twenty miles at Ascalon.
The northern section of this plain is known as the Plain of Sharon; and
an extension of it running inland south-east from Acre is the Vale of
Esdraelon (the ancient Armageddon or valley of Jezreel), a former
swamp-land which, with the Huleh valley, is now one of the most
fertile parts of the country and one of the main agricultural centres of

Israel. Farther inland are the hill regions of Galilee in the north dipping down to the sub-tropical valley of Beisan south of Lake Tiberias and the hills of Samaria and Judea. To the south lies the arid Negev, which forms 60 per cent of the total land area, stretching from the southern edge of the Judean plateau to the Gulf of Aqaba at Eilat. Although in Byzantine times it supported a considerable population, the Negev was until the foundation of the State of Israel largely desert, small parts being intermittently cultivated. Within the last twenty years, however, the northern part has been extensively settled and put under the plough. The central part remains desert but contains mineral deposits which are being worked. In the far south of the Negev lies Eilat, Israel's outlet to the Red Sea,[1] which is also of considerable strategic importance.

The climate is as varied as the topography. The coastal plain has a Mediterranean climate; the winters are warm and wet and the summers hot and dry. The amount of rainfall increases towards the north, being greatest in the Carmel range above Haifa. Inland both summer and winter are cooler, snow being not uncommon in Jerusalem during the winter. In the Negev, desert or semi-desert conditions prevail. Rainfall is scarce and irregular and the summers are hotter than on the coast.

The chief river is the Jordan. The Yarkan (Auja) which flowed into the Mediterranean north of Tel Aviv, has been completely diverted to the Negev. The mouth of the Kishon which flows into the bay north of Haifa has been widened to enable ships arriving at Haifa to unload near warehouses which are built on the river banks.

Population

The population has trebled during the twenty years since the State was founded. At the end of 1948 the estimated total population was 879,000, of whom 758,702 were Jewish and 120,000 non-Jewish.[2] By January 1967 the estimated total had risen to 2,657,400, of whom 2,344,900 were Jews. Of approximately 1,200,000 non-Jews who lived in Palestine in 1947, only about 100,000 remained when the census was held in the winter of 1948 for the election of the Constituent Assembly. Although there has been no general return of those who were driven out or fled during the Palestine War, a steady infiltration took place, both officially and unofficially, until by July 1956 the number of non-Jews reached over 202,000. As they also have one of the highest birth rates in the world (3 per cent) their number in 1967 reached over 390,000. The rest of the former Arab population of Israel are living in the neighbouring Arab countries, for the most part in refugee camps, in the Gaza Strip and in the occupied Western bank.

[1] See below, p. 374.
[2] Central Bureau of Statistics, *Statistical Bulletin* (English Summary), February 1957.
M

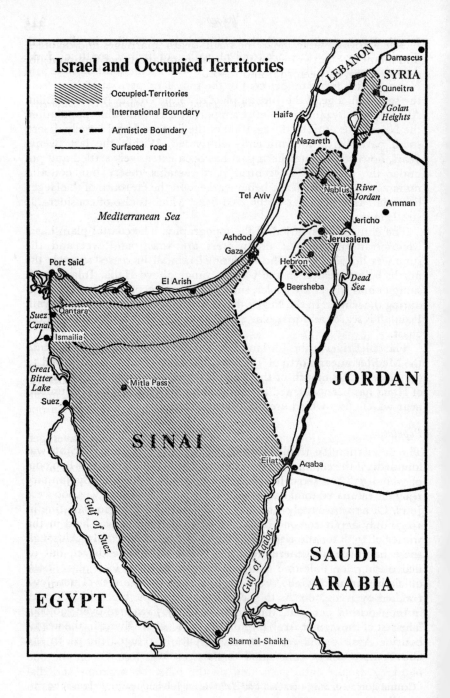

Israel and Occupied Territories

Occupied-Territories

International Boundary

Armistice Boundary

Surfaced road

LEBANON

SYRIA

Damascus

Quneitra

Golan Heights

Haifa

Nazareth

Tel Aviv

River Jordan

Nablus

Amman

Jericho

Mediterranean Sea

Ashdod

Gaza

Jerusalem

Port Said

Hebron

El Arish

Beersheba

Dead Sea

Suez Canal

Qantara

Ismailia

Great Bitter Lake

Mitla Pass

Suez

JORDAN

S I N A I

Eilat

Aqaba

SAUDI ARABIA

Gulf of Suez

Gulf of Aqaba

EGYPT

Sharm al-Shaikh

The following table shows the birth, death, marriages and divorces, and infant mortality rates for the Jewish population (per thousand) for selected years between 1951 and 1966.

Year	Births	Deaths	Infant deaths	Marriages	Divorces
1951	33·8	6·6	40·8	11·4	1·7
1953	32·1	6·7	39·6	9·4	1·5
1955	29·2	6·1	37·3	8·5	1·2
1957	28·1	6·5	39·0	8·3	1·2
1959	26·7	5·9	30·7	7·8	1·0
1961	25·1	5·8	29·1	7·2	0·9
1963	25·0	6·1	27·5	7·7	0·9
1964	25·7	6·3	28·2	7·8	0·9
1965	25·8	6·3	27·4	7·9	0·9
1966	25·5	6·3	25·3	7·9	0·8

Note: Infant death-rate per thousand live births; other figures, per thousand, mean population.

Immigration

During the years of British administration, 1919–48, about 452,000 entered, bringing the total, with natural increase, to some 650,000.

When the State of Israel was established, it immediately opened its gates wide, and up to the end of 1951 684,000 Jews came in. These included displaced persons and other refugees from Eastern and Central Europe, refugees from Arab countries like the Yemen and Iraq, immigrants from North Africa, and smaller numbers from Western Europe and the Americas.

Since then the tide has ebbed and flowed. Until 1960 it averaged 32,000 a year. During the next four years there was a large increase, almost 230,000 coming in, followed by a drop to about 81,000 in the period 1965–8. From that date immigration increased again and reached almost 33,000 in 1969 and about 45,000 in 1970.

This vast influx has raised serious problems, both economic and social. But the Government and people of Israel, at whatever cost, have stood by the 'Law of the Return', under which any Jew has the right to emigrate to Israel and settle there, unless he has been proved guilty of a criminal offence. The 'Ingathering of the Exiles' is a primary factor in Government policy and is embodied in the Declaration of Independence.

Immigration into mandated Palestine and into Israel has been largely determined by the conditions prevailing in the dispersion. The early settlers were largely from Eastern Europe, in particular Russia and Poland, where emigration to Palestine was fostered on the one hand by Zionist enthusiasm and on the other by pogroms and discrimination against Jews. Hitler's anti-Jewish policy brought to

Population[1] *and Jewish Immigration*[2] *1948–69*

		Population at End of Period		
Period	Immigration	Jews	Non-Jews	Total
1948	101,828[3]	758,702	120,000[4]	879,000[4]
1949	239,576	1,013,871	160,000	1,173,871
1950	170,249	1,202,992	167,101	1,370,094
1951	175,095	1,404,392	173,433	1,577,825
1952	24,369	1,450,217	179,302	1,629,519
1953	11,326	1,483,641	185,776	1,669,417
1954	18,370	1,526,009	191,805	1,717,814
1955	37,478	1,590,519	189,556	1,789,075
1956	56,234	1,667,455	204,935	1,872,390
1957	71,224	1,762,741	213,213	1,975,954
1958	27,082	1,810,148	221,524	2,031,072
1959	23,895	1,858,841	229,344	2,088,685
1960	24,510	1,911,200	239,200	2,150,400
1961	47,638	1,981,700	252,500	2,234,200
1962	61,328	2,068,900	262,900	2,331,800
1963	64,364	2,155,500	274,600	2,430,100
1964	54,716	2,239,000	286,400	2,525,600
1965	30,736	2,299,100	299,300	2,598,400
1966	15,730	2,344,900	312,500	2,657,400
1967	14,327	2,383,600	390,300	2,773,900
1968	20,544	2,434,800	406,300	2,841,100
1969	32,679	2,496,400	422,800	2,919,200
1970	36,928	2,561,400	440,000	3,001,400

[1] Until 1960: *de facto* population; 1961–69: permanent population to nearest thousand, excluding administered areas.
[2] Including tourists who became permanent residents.
[3] 15 May to 31 December.
[4] Estimated.

Jewish Immigration by Continent of Birth

	America, Europe and Oceania		Asia and Africa		Not stated	Total
		%		%		
1919–14.5.48	385,006	89·6	44,809	10·4	53,042	482,857
15.5.48–1951	334,971	50·3	330,456	49·7	18,774	684,201
1952–4	11,187	21·9	39,978	78·1	28	51,193
1955–7	49,630	30·0	110,714	69·1	617	160,961
1958–60	46,460	64·8	25,926	35·8	7	72,393
1961–4	86,748	39·4	133,561	60·6	14	220,323
1965–9	48,609	46·5	56,035	53·5	311	104,955
1948–69	577,605	45·3	696,670	54·7	19,751	1,294,026

Palestine a rising proportion of emigrants from Germany, Austria, and Czechoslovakia. After 1948 the majority of the immigrants to Israel came, to begin with, from Eastern and Central Europe, consisting partly of survivors of Nazi concentration camps and displaced persons and partly of Jews from the Iron Curtain countries, Hungary, Rumania, and Bulgaria; the 1950 immigrants were taken to reception camps until arrangements could be made for their permanent settlement. It was found that long periods of idleness in hard conditions not only were very costly but also tended to lower morale, especially for immigrants who had spent many years in concentration or displaced-persons camps. A new system was introduced whereby immigrants, after a short time in a clearance camp, were transferred either to permanent settlements or to Maabaroth, i.e. transit settlements, which were placed near opportunities for work so that immigrants could become self-supporting in a much shorter time. Maabaroth were of two kinds: temporary settlements set up near the sites of planned permanent villages, and those which were eventually to be converted into permanent settlements. Since 1954, when the stream of immigrants declined, the Government abandoned the policy of transit camps and transported the immigrants straight to new settlements in development areas, sending with them experts on agriculture, education, and hygiene.

The Government recognizes the difficulty of absorbing a large and varied mass of people, in particular Oriental Jews unversed in Western ways and often economically backward. The Messianic hope and the sense of brotherhood are, however, great factors in integrating the new population. At present the pattern of Israel is set by those who arrived before the creation of the State, and the proportion of Oriental Jews in high office is small; but the Government and the early-comers spare no effort to weld the diverse elements into a single conscious nation.

The Arabs in Israel

The Declaration of Independence offers complete equality to all Arabs, and Government policy, as outlined in October 1951, stated that 'the Arab minority . . . will be guaranteed full and complete equality of rights and obligations in the civic, political, economic, social, cultural, and every other sphere'. In practice, however, Israeli policy towards the Arabs is ambivalent. There is a sincere desire to make the Arab population a contented and prosperous section of the community; at the same time there are fears of the threat to security which it represents as long as a peace settlement with the neighbouring Arab countries remains unattainable.

At the beginning of 1971 the Arab population was 440,000, of whom half were living in 102 villages, the rest in towns; some 38,000 were nomads or semi-nomads. They included 76,000 Christian Arabs and also 36,000 Druzes who lived in 18 villages on the Carmel and in

Galilee. The Government has regularly granted loans to Arab farmers to assist them in cultivating their land more intensively, and since 1949 the output of Arab agriculture has been increased sixfold. The establishment of Arab co-operatives, as well as of joint Jewish–Arab enterprises, has been encouraged. Arab workers are members of the Histadrut (General Federation of Jewish Labour in Israel), entitled to the same pay and social benefits as the Jewish workers. Their participation in the state administration is not yet proportional to their number but is increasing steadily. The average Arab family income in 1967 was £I7,000 in Nazareth or $2,250. Arabs are served by 79 village clinics and 64 mother-and-child units. The infant mortality rate dropped from 20·8 per cent in 1948 to 5·9 per cent in 1966. In 1971 there were 597 schools in Arab areas, of which 225 were kindergartens, 277 primary schools and 95 post-primary schools, with 117,000 pupils, missionary and private schools excluded. Arabic is the language of instruction, but Hebrew is taught in the higher classes. 350 Arabs were studying at the Hebrew university and at the Haifa technicon. Special courses for training Arab teachers have been established.

Two Arabic daily papers, several weeklies, and other periodicals are published in Israel. Arabic books are widely available. There is an Arabic broadcasting station and an Arabic television programme. An increasing number of Arabs join regular Jewish schools; in Haifa a Jewish Arab school is operated by the municipality as well as a sports and cultural centre.

At the 1969 elections to the Knesset 85 per cent of the Arab population voted, including women. Six Arabs and one Druze were elected. Arabic is an official language of the Knesset in Government offices and in courts, and the official *Gazette* appears also in Arabic. Stamps, coins, banknotes bear Arabic inscriptions. There are two Arab municipalities, Nazareth and Shefaram, both in the north; and 47 Arab villages have local councils. 200 Moslem religious leaders are paid by the State, regular services being held in 90 mosques. About 76,000 of the Arabs are Christians, of 30 denominations. There were 200 churches, 1,200 clergy (including 160 monks and 600 nuns) in Israel in 1967. Moslems and Druzes have their own religious courts. The military administration which affected the vast majority of the Arab population living along the border was abolished on 1 December 1966. The provisions of the law of 1950, concerning the property of absentee owners deprived of their property many Arabs who are now resident in Israel but who were not in the country when the law was passed.

Integration of Immigrants

A primary aim of the State is to transform the heterogeneous mass of immigrants into a conscious national society, to substitute modern Hebrew for the babel of tongues which they bring from their native lands, and to raise the economic and educational level. Three instruments have specially served that policy. The first is the school: free compulsory elementary education was introduced in 1950 for all inhabitants, male and female, Jew and Arab, the importance of which is stressed by the following table showing the distribution of the population by age-groups:

Distribution of Population by Age-groups on 1 January 1967
(percentages)

Age	Druzes	Christians	Moslems	Non-Jews	Jews	Total
0–14	49·3	40·2	53·1	50·4	31·7	33·4
15–29	23·2	25·1	23·4	23·8	24·4	24·0
30–44	14·2	17·4	12·3	13·4	17·8	17·4
45–64	9·0	12·1	7·4	8·4	19·7	18·3
65 and over	4·3	5·2	3·8	4·0	6·4	6·0

The second instrument of integration—applicable only to the Jewish population, since the Arabs of Israel are liable but not called for military service—is the national service of three years for men between the ages of 18 and 35, and two years for women between the ages of 18 and 30. Only a part of the time is devoted to military training, the rest of the service being educational. The third instrument is the residential college for intellectuals, known as the Ulpan. There men and women who were engaged in the professions have intensive training in Hebrew for a period of half a year to a year to enable them to carry on their profession in Israel. About 30,000 attend these colleges at any one time. Adult education is intensively pursued. Specially trained lecturers, Hebrew teachers, and advisers on agriculture and sanitation travel to the remote settlements. It is a less welcome result that the younger generation tend to regard themselves as the true Israelis, superior to the immigrants of the older generation.

HISTORY AND POLITICS

While the conception of an independent Jewish state and the struggle to realize it, which culminated in the creation of Israel in 1948, emerged only with the foundation of the Zionist movement in the late nineteenth century, the events of the last fifty years can be fully understood only against the background of Jewish history from the time of the dispersion.

The subjection of the ancient kingdom of the Jews to the Roman Empire in 63 BC was followed by a period marked by a series of bloody nationalist uprisings. Attempts to regain Jewish independence continued until AD 135 when the revolt of Bar Kochba in Palestine was suppressed with great violence and the Roman religion was established in the Temple area in Jerusalem. Inside and outside Palestine Jewish political influence was in eclipse.

From that time until the beginning of the Zionist movement the Jews were scattered throughout the world, experiencing in varying degrees persecution and prosperity, discrimination and tolerance, but from the eighteenth century they shared in the general emancipation of Western Europe and in its economic expansion. During the nineteenth century liberalism and assimilation appeared to be steadily gaining ground in Western Europe, but persecutions continued in Eastern Europe, particularly in Russia and Russian Poland where the concentration of Jewish population was greatest. Just as anti-Jewish movements, influenced by the nationalist temper of the nineteenth century, began to emphasize race rather than religion, so the Jews themselves began, under the influence of their environment and pressure of persecution, to think in terms of a new Jewish nationalism. It was Theodor Herzl, an Austrian Jewish man of letters, who in 1897 founded Zionism as a political movement. Meanwhile there had been during the latter half of the nineteenth century a steady movement of Jews from Eastern Europe to settle in Palestine, many of them working on the land. As a result of this colonization movement, which was largely non-political and philanthropic, there were 80,000 Jews in Palestine by 1914. In 1903, when settlement by Jews in Palestine was difficult, the British Government offered the Zionist Congress a territory in East Africa for Jewish settlement, but the offer was rejected because the majority of the Zionists would not consider any other home than Zion. The aims of Zionism were given great encouragement when, on 2 November 1917, the British Government declared its 'sympathy with Jewish Zionist aspirations' in the Balfour Declaration.[1]

The Mandate

For nearly two years after the armistice with Turkey Palestine was under British military authority, which was superseded by a civil administration in July 1920, after the Supreme Allied Council (sitting at San Remo) had allocated the mandate for Palestine to Britain on 24 April 1920. The mandate came into force on 29 September 1923. Under Article 2 Britain was made responsible for: 'the establishment of the Jewish National Home . . . and the development of self-governing institutions, and also for safeguarding the civil and religious rights of all the inhabitants of Palestine, irrespective of race and religion.'

While the Balfour Declaration and the terms of the mandate pledged help in founding a Jewish National Home, Britain as the mandatory Power found herself in an equivocal position, for in both cases the promise was not unqualified. Fulfilment was almost from the start rendered difficult by the promise of independence made to the

[1] See above, pp. 13–14.

Arabs during the war and by the provision in the mandate that the administration of Palestine should facilitate Jewish emancipation 'while ensuring that the rights and position of other sections of the population are not prejudiced'.

Britain's task became increasingly complicated in the decade before the Second World War. Arab hostility to a Jewish National Home in Palestine was aggravated, on the one hand by the rising nationalist aspirations and achievements of other Arab States, and on the other by the increasing pressure to find a refuge in Palestine for the Jews of Central Europe who were the victims of Nazi persecution from 1933.

Although during the Second World War Jews everywhere rallied to the Allied cause, anti-British feeling remained among the Jews in Palestine. In May 1939 the British Government had issued in a White Paper a fresh statement of policy, restricting Jewish immigration in the next five years to 75,000, after which period it would be subject to Arab approval, and limiting narrowly the right of Jews to purchase land from Arabs. The strict implementation of the White Paper policy, especially of the immigration provisions, seemed inhuman to the Jews in Palestine, who were deeply concerned about the Jews in Hitler's power. Still more, the rejection during the war of several boatloads of refugees who had contrived to escape from Europe and reach the borders of Palestine, their transfer to Mauritius, and the total loss in the Black Sea of a ship with nearly 1,000 refugees after it had been refused permission to land its passengers in Palestine, inflamed and embittered Jewish opinion.

By the end of the war anti-British feeling among the Jews of Palestine and elsewhere, strengthened by ill-informed and sometimes irresponsible support in the United States, had finally convinced Britain that compromise between Jews and Arabs was impossible. Outbreaks of terrorism in Palestine became frequent, and there was increasing Zionist pressure on the United States Government to use its influence with Britain to secure free entry of Jews into Palestine. After a series of unsuccessful attempts to find a solution to the Palestine problem acceptable to both Jews and Arabs, and after an Anglo-American commission had recommended measures which the British Government was unwilling to consider unless the United States was prepared to share the financial and military consequences, the British Government decided in February 1947 to refer the question to the United Nations. On 29 November 1947 a modified scheme of partition was adopted by the General Assembly; Britain abstained from voting, making it clear that she would accept no solution which would have to be imposed by force. At the same time she maintained her intention to withdraw from Palestine and end the mandate by 15 May 1948. The General Assembly had neglected to provide any means of enforcing its recommendations, while the mandatory Power would do nothing that could be construed as implementing the United Nations resolution. The decisions of the United Nations brought to a head the barely concealed civil war in Palestine, and as the mandate drew to a chaotic close, guerrilla fighting between Jews and Arabs increased in bitterness until it reached a state of open warfare.

The State of Israel and the Palestine War

The mandate ended at midnight 14 May 1948, and the State of Israel was officially proclaimed that evening. The next day regular forces of Egypt, Jordan, and Iraq began moving into Palestine. By that time there was a well-defined area of Jewish control, which included the most important parts of the area assigned to the Jewish state by the partition resolution. The Arab armies succeeded in occupying those Arab areas which were not yet under Jewish control, but in spite of their initial superiority in heavier armaments and the almost indefensible location of many Jewish settlements, their only other military success was the occupation of the Old City and part of northern Jerusalem and the reduction of the fanatically defended Jewish quarter of the Old City. The Arab armies, although vastly superior in numbers, were fighting in a strange environment, without a united High Command and with long lines of communication from Egypt and Iraq, whereas the Jews were fighting not only for their Promised Land but for their very existence. The success of their efforts roused Messianic hopes and enabled them to endure years of hardship in the period of armistices.

The Palestine War left Israel in possession of a share of the former mandated territory larger by more than a quarter than that recommended by the United Nations; it also left four cardinal problems: how to attain a peace settlement, an impracticable zigzag frontier, the Arab refugees, and the controversy as to the status of the Holy City.

The efforts of the Conciliation Commission, set up by the Security Council in December 1948, to negotiate a permanent peace treaty, have so far proved unsuccessful. The Arab States have refused to consider a peace treaty unless the Israel Government agrees to accept all Arab refugees who wish to return to Israel, in accordance with the resolution of the General Assembly of December 1948, while the Israel Government maintains that the future of the refugees can be discussed only as part of a general peace settlement. Israel, however, offered at one time to accept on certain conditions up to 100,000 Arab refugees (including 25,000 already in Israel) and affirmed to the United Nations her willingness to help resettlement by paying compensation for the immovable Arab property which she had taken over. In July 1957 Ben-Gurion said that the Arab refugees could not return as their lands had been settled by Jewish survivors of Nazi persecution.

Direct peace negotiations between Israel and the Arab States have proved impossible, and the attempt made by the tripartite Declaration of 1950[1] to prevent an arms race between the Arab States and Israel was shattered by the arms deal of 1955 between Egypt and Czechoslovakia.

The United Nations plan for the internationalization of Jerusalem has not been carried into effect. Prior to the 1967 war, Israel claimed the Jewish part of Jerusalem as an integral part of the State, although she was willing to accept an international authority to safeguard the Holy Places and the rights of the religious communities. A proposal for the establishment of such a body was made within the United Nations but not carried out. King Abdullah of Jordan proclaimed his intention of resisting any attempt at internationalization and Jewish opposition was equally firm. In 1950 Jerusalem was declared the capital of Israel and the seat of Parliament, and most Government departments were transferred there. In 1967 the Jordan sector of Jerusalem was officially incorporated into Israel, and negotiations with various envoys as well as with the representatives of other churches, were started in order to achieve a solution, guaranteed by international law, for the safeguard of the Holy Places.

The Arab–Israeli Conflict

From 1953 Arab–Israeli tension grew more and more acute. Incidents resulting in loss of life multiplied on the Jordan frontier. The most serious occurred in October 1953, when Israeli forces, in a reprisal raid on the village of Qibya, killed some fifty persons. Strenuous efforts on both sides to prevent incidents, and to settle on the spot such incidents as did occur before they could be exaggerated by press and politicians, maintained something like tranquillity for a considerable time. In 1955 frontier trouble broke out in the south, the Gaza strip, and a demilitarized area along the Sinai Peninsula, and in the north in the demilitarized area of the Huleh region and along the shores of Lake Galilee. In that area the Syrians resisted Israeli attempts to carry out works for diverting the waters of the Jordan for a comprehensive irrigation project. At the same time they and the other Arab States rejected the project of American engineers (the Johnston plan) for the use of the waters of the Jordan and the Yarmuk for the benefit of Jordan as well as Israel.

The news of the large-scale purchase of modern Czechoslovak heavy armament and aircraft by Egypt and perhaps by other Arab States caused the greatest apprehension in Israel. Britain and the United States were unwilling to sell equivalent modern arms to Israel, but France supplied her with jet aircraft and other weapons.

An aggravation of the trouble was that Egypt maintained a strict

[1] See above, p. 24.

blockade, both in the Suez Canal and in the Gulf of Aqaba, not only against Israeli vessels but against those of any state which were carrying cargo to or from any Israeli port. She claimed this as a belligerent right, on the ground that she was still at war with Israel, though the Security Council in 1951 had resolved that her action was contrary to the terms of the armistice agreement.

The Sinai Campaign

The elections for the Jordan Parliament in October 1956 resulted in a victory for the pan-Arab parties. A unified command was established for Egypt, Syria, and Jordan, and the Arab States united in abuse of Israel and in announcements of an impending attack on her. Suddenly, on 29 October, Israeli forces began the invasion of Sinai. Within five days they were masters of Gaza, Rafa, and El Arish, and had also occupied the greater part of the Sinai Peninsula east of the Suez Canal, taken prisoner the Egyptian garrison of Sharm al-Shaikh, at the south-eastern tip, and occupied the island of Tiran which commands the eastern entrance to the Gulf of Aqaba. The declared objectives of the Sinai campaign were to wipe out the Egyptian outposts and *fedayeen*[1] bases in the Sinai Desert; to open sea communications with Eilat through the Gulf of Aqaba; to eliminate the Egyptian salient known as the Gaza strip; and, lastly, to put pressure on Egypt to negotiate a peace treaty.

On 7 November David Ben-Gurion declared that Israel would hold on to her conquests until Egypt made a settlement. The next day, however, after strong representations from Eisenhower and a severe warning from Bulganin, he announced that Israel would withdraw from Egyptian territory when satisfactory arrangements had been made in connection with the international force which the General Assembly had decided to send to Egypt. Israel took immediate steps to establish her hold in the Gulf of Aqaba and sent two frigates to Eilat. The evacuation of most of the Sinai Desert was carried out in December and January, but on 23 January the Knesset decided to maintain Israeli administration of the Gaza strip and forces at Sharm al-Shaikh. On 2 February the United Nations called on Israel to withdraw behind the armistice demarcation lines. After intensive negotiations and a further appeal by the President of the United States, backed by Britain and France, on 1 March the Israel Foreign Minister explained to the General Assembly that Israel was prepared to withdraw on the assumption that UNEF would take over exclusive responsibility for the Gaza strip and that Israel would be entitled to exercise the right of self-defence in the case of interference with her ships in the Gulf of Aqaba. The United States delegate did not support the Gaza strip assumption, but certain American assurances about freedom of

[1] 'Devotees' (of Islam).

navigation in the Gulf of Aqaba were given. The withdrawal was completed by 8 March and UNEF moved into both areas, but the Egyptian administration also returned to Gaza.

The Sinai campaign had produced some radical changes in Israel and in its relations with the outer world. Combined with the growing involvement of the Arab States, and especially of Egypt in inter-Arab and Arab internal affairs, these changes gave rise to many hopes for a more peaceful coexistence between the Jewish State and its neighbours.

The three main consequences of the campaign had been, for Israel, the opening of a direct sea connection with East Africa and South-east Asia through the straits of Aqaba; the new close collaboration with France and the end of Arab infiltrations from Sinai and Gaza. The new security and freedom of movement for the State spurred Israeli diplomacy to work for the creation of a new network of relations with both Europe and the Afro-Asian world.

Although on 3 June 1957 the Knesset approved the Eisenhower Doctrine—in spite of strong opposition from Mapam and Achdut Avoda—the following years saw a strong reorientation of Israeli foreign policy from the USA towards Europe. Such a trend was mainly inspired by the new close military, scientific, and cultural relations with France, which neither the arrival to power of General de Gaulle in 1958 nor the end of the Algerian war altered significantly. An important cultural agreement was signed with France on 30 November 1959; the official visit of Ben-Gurion to Paris in May 1960 established the basis for hope of Israeli–French co-operation in Africa, and in May 1961 President de Gaulle formally defined Israel as 'a friend and an ally' on the occasion of a second visit by Ben-Gurion to France. Although no fundamental change was visible in the French attitude, in June 1964, when Premier Levi Eshkol visited Paris, a reappraisal of mutual positions was progressively taking place, with French diplomacy increasingly returning to a more pro-Arab line and Israel once more seeking military equipment outside France, mainly in the USA. Quite independently of France Israel continued to work for its association with the European Common Market and for closer relations with European countries. Ben-Gurion visited the Scandinavian countries in August 1962. But it was with Germany that the most radical change of relations took place. After a long period of tension, lengthened by the Israeli demand to Bonn to restrict the services of German scientists in the Egyptian military industries and by Bonn's suspension of the supply of military equipment to Israel, diplomatic relations between Jerusalem and Bonn were established in May 1965 on the basis of a 1961 secret agreement. These were followed by an economic agreement in May 1966 on the conclusion of German Reparations. Pope Paul VI's visit to the Holy Places in 1964, the subsequent ratification by the Oecumenical Council of the 'Document on the Jews' helped to strengthen the position of the Jewish State in the Catholic world. At the same time the new Israeli Foreign Minister Abba Eban tried consistently, from 1966 onwards, to reach a better understanding with the Communist world, where he hoped to achieve a measure of support for a 'Tashkent' type of solution for the Arab–Jewish conflict. His efforts brought tangible results only with Rumania which considerably improved its political and economic relations with Israel.

Greater results were achieved by Israel in Africa and Asia as well as in Latin America. All the new African states, with the exception of Somaliland and Mauretania, recognized Israel. An important system of economic, political, and technical aid relationships developed between Israel and the Third World which were strengthened by the official visits to Israel of almost every African Head of State and many Asian and Latin American Government representatives and by the visits of President Shazar, David Ben-Gurion, and Levi Eshkol to Asia, South America, and Africa. In spite of substantial African and Latin American support, Israel was unable to muster the necessary majority for a United Nations resolution calling for direct talks with the Arabs.

The hostility of the Arabs gained strength once more after 1964, following Syria's demand that Israel be deprived of the use of the waters of Lake Tiberias for irrigation purposes. Tension began to rise along the Syrian–Israeli Armistice Line and was heightened by the renewed infiltration of Arab commandos who received uneven backing from the Arab states. Serious fighting took place in July 1966 along the Syrian–Israel border during which Israel destroyed most of the Syrians' diversion operations on the sources of the River Jordan. By the end of 1966 the Palestinian commandos also became active along the Jordan border and the Israeli raid on the village of Samua in October 1966 created considerable internal unrest in Jordan. Following a serious clash with the Syrians in April 1967 and Russian warnings to Egypt of an impending Israeli attack on Syria, Egypt mobilized its army in the Sinai Desert in May 1967, expelled the UN Force from the Gaza area and Sharm al-Shaikh and closed the Tiran Straits. Conflict once more became inevitable and the Six Day War brought the Israelis along the Suez Canal, the River Jordan, and the Golan Heights.

During this period, Israel's political life underwent considerable strain. Most of this was the direct result of the social and economic adjustment of a State rapidly moving from the agricultural era to an industrial, or even post industrial, era. But the new conditions of peace and economic prosperity made the country and the Government more attentive to the internal problems of the State and even to the fundamental question of the role of a Jewish State in modern times. The 1959 general election was fought against a background of growing social unrest owing to the demands of immigrants from oriental countries and some of the Arab minority for greater social and economic equality and better educational opportunities. Religious controversy increased sharply. The question of defining 'Who is a Jew?' caused a Government crisis in 1961 and anticipated a general election. It was followed by considerable tension between religious and secular Jews over such matters as work and travel on the Sabbath, the use of non-kosher food on national shipping lines, and medical autopsy. There was dissension among religious Jews over such questions as the rights of the Beni Israel from India to be recognized as full Jews by the Israeli Rabbinate, and also among Jewish and Christian missions mainly over the education of Jewish children in missionary schools. These very particular types of Israeli controversies took place in a society which was quickly changing through immigration and industrialization. In July 1960 Israel celebrated the arrival of its one millionth immigrant. Between 1961 and 1965 about 250,000 new immigrants entered the country—many of them from Eastern Europe. The problem of the integration of these generally highly skilled and educated immigrants deeply influenced the debates of the 25th and 26th Zionist Congresses which took place in Jerusalem in 1960 and 1964. The definition of 'Zionist', the ways of attracting Jewish immigrants from developed countries, and the relations between Israel and the Diaspora became the central themes of discussions on the work and future of the Zionist organizations. In this context it is worth noting the tremendous psychological impact, both on the Diaspora and on Israel, of the trial of Adolph Eichmann, captured in May 1960 in the Argentine and executed in May 1962.

Of no less importance was the 'Lavon Affair'—a clash between Ben-Gurion and Pinhas Lavon which originated in a security 'mishap' in 1954. At the time Israeli agents were arrested, tried, and some of them executed for allegedly attempting to blow up American installations so as to prevent a rapprochement between Washington and Cairo. Lavon, who was then Minister of Defence, was forced to hand in his resignation but in 1958 he made a partial political recovery when he became Secretary General of the Histadrut.

New evidence came to light in 1960 and induced Lavon to ask for a full rehabilitation which he obtained through a Cabinet Committee against the will of Ben-Gurion who pressed for a judicial enquiry. Ben-Gurion failed to have the affair discussed in court but he succeeded in obtaining Lavon's dismissal from his post in the Histadrut. In doing so Ben-Gurion provoked considerable public and party animosity against himself which resulted in reduced votes for his party in the 1962 elections and his consequent decision to withdraw from the Government in June 1963, and to create a new party, Rafi.

1967 and After

After the June 1967 war Israel soon abandoned any hope of an early peace settlement with the Arab states. At the same time, although the strongly anti-Israel resolutions in the UN General Assembly failed to secure a majority, Israel feared that the UN Security Council might take mandatory action against it. The Government did not oppose the passing of the British-sponsored compromise Resolution 242 on 22 November 1967 which the Foreign Minister, Mr. Eban, interpreted as meaning that Israel should not move from the 1967 ceasefire lines except as a result of properly negotiated peace treaties with its neighbours. However, it soon became apparent that this interpretation was not shared by many countries including the Soviet Union, France, and many Afro-Asian countries which believed that Israel should first withdraw from all the occupied territories.

Israel continued to insist on direct negotiations with the Arabs although, as time went on, it placed more emphasis on the need for secure and recognized frontiers. Meanwhile the Defence Minister, Moshe Dayan, who exercised virtually complete control over the occupied territories, adopted a policy of consolidating Israel's economic and political hold over them while awaiting a time when the Arabs would be ready to make peace on something closer to Israel's terms. His method was to deal firmly with opposition and unrest while making the occupation as inconspicuous as possible. The 'open bridges' policy which allowed Arabs of the occupied territories to travel in Jordan and other Arab states, was maintained. Palestinian guerrilla activity did not cause Israel any serious security concern; casualties were heavier on the Suez Canal front. Some prominent Israelis (but not members of the Government) were in favour of negotiating with leading Palestinians for the establishment of an autonomous Palestinian state on the West Bank.

Tension increased after the attack on an Israeli El Al plane at Athens Airport by members of the Popular Front for the Liberation of Palestine (PFLP) in December 1968, Israel's retaliation against Beirut Airport, and the second PFLP attack on an Israeli plane at Zürich Airport on 18 February 1969. Mrs. Golda Meir's assumption of the premiership following the death of Levi Eshkol on 26 February was reflected in the sharper tone of Israel's policy declarations. On 17 March she rejected the concept of Great Power mediation embodied in the four-power (UK, USA, USSR, and France) discussions on the Middle East which had been launched on French initiative. She also dismissed the six-point peace proposal of King Hussein of Jordan on the ground that it was not genuine.

At the end of June 1972 Israeli official figures for all military and civilian casualties caused by all types of action by Arab regular forces and guerrillas since the end of June 1967 were: 817 killed and 3,119 wounded compared with 778 killed and 2,558 wounded in the June war itself. The majority of casualties were on the Suez Canal although there was continued sporadic action by Palestinian guerrillas of al-Fatah and other organizations. The PFLP claimed responsibility for most of the bomb explosions in Israeli cities, and the sabotage of Haifa and Tel Aviv ports indicated that the *fedayeen* were receiving some support from Israeli Arabs. Strikes and demonstrations on the West Bank—especially by schoolchildren—were frequent during 1969 but they did not present any serious security problem for Israel. The most serious trouble and the most bitter opposition to Israeli occupation were in Gaza, where guerrilla activities were not contained until 1971.

Israel pursued its policy of saturation bombing of Egyptian positions in the Canal Zone and of occasional deep penetration raids into Egyptian territory but it stopped the latter after April, almost certainly because of the danger of a direct clash with the Russians who were stepping up their aid to Egypt. Israel succeeded in reducing its rate of casualties in the Canal Zone but in June and July the installation of new Soviet SAM-3 missiles caused the loss of five Israeli Phantom planes. The Israeli Government was constantly aware of the possibility of an erosion of its relationship with the US on which it now depended almost exclusively for supplies of arms and financial aid. In March 1970 Secretary of State Rogers said that Israel's request for more Phantoms and Skyhawks would 'remain in abeyance' for a time. Meanwhile Israel's defence costs were rising rapidly to nearly 50 per cent of an increased budget. At this time it was apparent that the US did not fully accept the Israeli Government's estimate of the threat to Israel's security caused by the increased Soviet presence in Egypt.

When, in June 1970, the US Secretary of State formally launched his peace initiative based on the UN Security Council Resolution 242 Israel followed Egypt and Jordan in accepting his proposals, and a ninety-day ceasefire came into effect on 7 August. After some initial doubts the US accepted the Israeli charge that Egypt and the Russians had used the military standstill agreement to install new missile sites in the Canal Zone. The US then agreed to fulfil Israel's request for Phantoms and financial aid.

GOVERNMENT AND CONSTITUTION

The provisional Government of Israel was established on 14 May 1948 and was authorized to act for the State until duly elected bodies should be appointed. The first elections were held in January 1949 for a Constituent Assembly and resulted in the formation of a coalition dominated by the Labour Party (Mapai). At the date of the opening of the Constituent Assembly (14 February 1949) the State of Israel had been recognized *de jure* or *de facto* by thirty-five other states. Israel was admitted as a member of the United Nations on 11 May 1949.

Israel is a republic headed by a President who is elected by the single-chamber Parliament, the Knesset, by simple majority. Israel has no written Constitution. The functions of the President, the powers of Government, and the legislative authority are contained in the Transition Law which was passed on 16 February 1949. The Constituent Assembly became a legislative chamber. The President of the Republic is elected for a term of five years, and has limited powers and ceremonial attributes. Israel's first President was the late Dr. Chaim Weizmann, formerly President of the World Zionist Organization, who died on 9 November 1952. Izhak Ben-Zvi was elected on 8 December 1952. Upon his death, Shneor Zalman Shazar was elected in 1963 and re-elected in 1968.

The powers of the legislative body are partly defined by law and partly by the customs of democratic parliamentary procedure. It consists of a single chamber of 120 members elected by adult suffrage under a system of proportional representation for a period which, although not laid down by law, is accepted as four years. Women have equal political rights with men.

Israel has maintained the municipalities and local councils established under the mandatory regime, and has created rural district councils. Local authorities are elected under the same system of proportional representation as that governing the election of the central authority and provide such social services as education and culture, health, sanitation, social welfare, road maintenance and public parks. In 1967 there were 26 municipalities (2 of them Arab), 115 local councils (41 Arab and Druze) and 47 regional councils comprising 670 villages, as against a total of 34 in 1948.

Israel has kept much of the judicial system inherited from the mandatory regime. The apex of the system is a Supreme Court of ten judges who are appointed for life, unless found guilty of misconduct, and who are completely independent of the executive. There are district courts and many magistrates' courts.

The rabbinical courts have maintained the jurisdiction which they had under the mandate in matters of personal status of Jews, and that jurisdiction has been enlarged in matters of marriage and divorce to be exclusive for all Jewish residents. In the mandate period the rabbinical judges were paid by the Jewish community, and the judges of the Moslem religious courts were paid by the Government. Now the courts of all communities are maintained by the Government, and the judges are paid by the State. An institution of growing importance is that of the State Comptroller. Appointed for five years by the President on the recommendation of the Knesset House Committee he is responsible to Parliament alone. His annual report on the legality, regularity, efficiency, economy, and ethical integrity of the public service, although deprived of any executive power, carries an almost unchallenged authority and a powerful disciplinary effect on the public administration. In 1971 he was given the duties of an Ombudsman.

Political Parties
Although the electoral system favours the multiplication of parties, the general tendency has been towards the regrouping of political formations. In the first general election in 1949 no fewer than twenty-one parties put forward candidates. The number was reduced in the two subsequent elections of 1951 and 1955 and by 1968 less than half these parties were significantly represented in parliament. This evolution has taken place because, in spite of the multiplicity of political organizations, the Israeli electorate has remained very stable in its fundamental political groupings: labour, religious, and national-capitalist.

Labour. In January 1968, after very long negotiations a new party, the Israel Labour Party, was created out of Mapai (Israel Workers' Party founded in 1930), Achdut Avoda–Poalei Zion (a group which split off from Mapai in 1954), and Rafi (another Mapai splinter group created in 1965). Most of the important political personalities in Israel belong to it with the exception of David Ben-Gurion who, after breaking with Mapai in 1965 and founding Rafi, refused to follow the rest of his new party back into reunion with Mapai in 1968. The Labour Party is the majority party and, ideologically, the centre party of Israel which has held power without interruption since the creation of the State.

Mapam (United Workers' Party). Founded in 1948, this is a left-wing Zionist Socialist Party which, while opposing Communists in Israel, advocated Israel's orientation towards the Soviet Union—at least until the 1967 war. It stands for progressive social legislation and Jewish–Arab working-class solidarity; its foreign policy is neutralist. It is above all the party of the Kibbutzim (collective settlements). Soviet-bloc anti-Zionism shook the foundations of the party. A few extremists split off from the party and joined the Communists in 1953. Today there is a strong trend calling for unity with the Israel Labour Party, with which it has been linked by an electoral alignment since the 1969 elections. The alignment controls, with some affiliated Arab groups, 60 out of 120 seats in the Knesset.

Gahal (The Herut-Liberal Bloc). Was established in 1965 by agreement between the Herut (Nationalist) Movement and the Israel Liberal Party formed by the Union of the General Zionist Party and the Progressive Party in 1961. Opposed to socialism, strongly orientated towards the West, it demands that Israel shall comprise the whole of the former mandated territory. It controls 26 seats in the Knesset. After joining the Government of National Unity on the eve of the 1967 war it returned to the opposition in August 1970 when the

Government accepted the USA peace initiative which they regarded as portending Israel's withdrawal from the ceasefire lines.

National Religious Party. Founded in 1956 through the union of two other religious parties, the aims of this party are the establishment of a society based on the ethical and social principles of the Torah (law of Moses) with a national economy founded on justice and equality for every citizen and class. It won twelve seats in the 1969 elections.

Agudat Israel (Religious League). This party, founded in 1912, stands for the strictest observance of the Torah, with jurisdiction entrusted to rabbinical authorities, the opening up of the country to private investment, and State control of the labour exchanges and sick funds. It differs from the National Religious Party in being unwilling to compromise on certain issues such as the conscription of women for national service. It won two seats in the 1969 elections.

The Independent Liberal Party, formerly the Progressive Party. The Progressives broke away in 1948 from the General Zionists because they were closer to Labour ideas. Their supporters come largely from the intellectuals and middle-class immigrants from Germany and Central Europe. They are a non-socialist party with progressive liberal tendencies. They won four seats in the 1969 elections.

Poalei Agudat Israel. Founded in 1924, it is a religious workers' movement closely associated with Agudat Israel but more leftist in its social outlook. It obtained two seats in the 1969 elections.

The Free Centre Movement. This party split off from Herut (1967).

The Israel Communist Party. Founded in 1919, it has one seat in the Knesset.

The New Communist List (Rakach). Pro-Arab, founded in 1965, has three seats in the Knesset.

The National List (Reshiha Hamlachtit). Founded in 1969 by former members of Rafi (the Ben-Gurion party) it has four seats in the Knesset.

Haolam Haze New Force. This is a non-party reform movement created in 1965 by the *Haolam Haze* weekly. It has one seat in the Knesset.

Arab Parties. Affiliated to the Labour Party are: Co-operation and Fraternity (Druze), and Progress and Development (Moslem and Christian Arab).

Political Developments and Foreign Policy

The main domestic issues in Israel's politics have centred on the controversy over education, religion, and economic policy. Although in all general elections Mapai was returned to power as the principal party, it had no clear majority and in each case had to form a Coalition Government. In 1949 and 1951 it had the support of the religious parties, and in 1952 it brought into the Government the second largest party, the General Zionists. The uneasy alliance between the moderate socialists and the religious groups on the one hand, and the bourgeois General Zionists on the other has led to frequent rifts and complicated the issues, involving the basic questions of church and state in Israel, a unified system of state education, conscription of women, and the formulation of a written Constitution. The inclusion of the General Zionists in 1952 enabled the Government to carry out the measures for a unified system of education. The formulation of an organic law setting out the rights of men and of a written Constitution was contemplated when the first Knesset was elected in 1949 to a Constituent Assembly. The plan, however, has been indefinitely postponed, partly because of the fundamental divergences on the religious issues. In the autumn of 1954 Ben-Gurion, who had been Prime Minister and Minister of Defence since 1948, announced that he would retire to a collective settlement in the Negev, and the Foreign Minister, Moshe Sharett, became Premier and maintained the existing coalition. Ben-Gurion was out of office, but not out of politics, for fourteen months. His retirement was part of an active campaign to inspire young Israelis to pioneer in the Negev and on the frontiers. In February 1955 he was recalled as Minister of Defence, and at once made it clear that he was prepared to be Prime Minister again if Mapai were successful in the general election. The results of the election disappointed Mapai, who lost 5 of the 45 seats they had held and 5 per cent of the votes. The General Zionists lost 8 of their 15 seats, and the extreme right-wing Herut won 15 and became the second largest party. The extreme left-wing Mapam, divided into two sections, increased their representation from 15 to 19 seats.

Ben-Gurion, unable to form a coalition of the centre parties and implacably opposed to Herut, turned to the three Left parties and the religious socialists and the small Progressive group. His new coalition commanded 80 out of the 120 seats and relied less than its predecessors on the religious middle-class sections. Its inner consistency was more substantial than that of the previous coalition, though less substantial than appeared on the surface.

In October 1958 the members of the National Religious Party withdrew from the coalition over the question of the administrative definition of 'who is a Jew' in the State of Israel. The question was not solved by the time of the general elections of November 1959 which were fought against the background of social unrest among immigrants from Oriental countries. The Mapai Party strengthened its position in the Knesset but its unity was shaken by the Lavon affair and Premier

Ben-Gurion's refusal to accept a ministerial enquiry to exonerate him. Ben-Gurion's resignation on 31 January 1960 was followed by long and unsuccessful negotiations to create a new Coalition Government which ended with a decision to hold fresh general elections in August 1961. The result was a disappointment for Mapai not only because it lost 5 seats (from 47 to 42) but because the new Liberal Party increased its representation to 17 seats which was equal to that of the Herut Party. The tenth and last Government to be led by Ben-Gurion took office in November 1961. It was a weak coalition of Mapai, Achdut Avoda, Poalei Agudat Israel, and the small Arab parties affiliated to Mapai and commanding 69 seats in the Knesset. It came to an end in June 1963 following Ben-Gurion's final resignation.

The succeeding Government headed by the former Finance Minister Levi Eshkol had the same composition as its predecessor and was officially described as a 'Government of continuation'. It soon faced internal difficulties because of the Lavon affair and the division of opinion among its members as to whether or not to reopen the enquiry and transfer it to the judicial commission Ben-Gurion was demanding. Another serious subject of controversy was the planned electoral union between Mapai and Achdut Avoda which many Ben-Gurion followers regarded as a move by the 'old guard' to block the access to power of the younger generation by a show of personal authority. Premier Eshkol resigned on 15 December 1964 but was asked by the President to reform his Government a week later. The rift with Ben-Gurion continued and a month later his leading supporters in the Government—Moshe Dayan, Joseph Almogi, and Shimon Peres all resigned. These formed a new party named Rafi under Ben-Gurion's leadership, fought the next elections in November 1965, and won 10 seats. Eshkol formed a new coalition of Mapai, Mapam, the Independent Liberals, plus some smaller parties and controlled 75 seats in the Knesset until the crisis preceding the June 1967 war when the opposition Rafi and Gahal parties joined the Cabinet of National Unity controlling 107 of the 120 parliamentary seats.

Rafi decided to rejoin Mapai and was shortly followed by Achdut Avoda. The new powerful Labour Party thus created found itself with an absolute majority for the first time in the history of the State and Mapam decided to align itself with it in preparation for the 1969 elections.

In these elections the Labour Party won 56 seats, the conservative Gahal Party 26 and the religious bloc 18. Eight other small parties held the remaining 20 seats. The results indicated a slight shift to the right in the national elections, and there was a greater emphasis on independents in the municipal voting.

Following the death of Levi Eshkol from a heart attack on 26 February 1969, Mrs. Meir had quickly emerged as his natural successor and had been sworn in on 17 March. The coalition government which she formed after the 1969 elections included six ministers of the Gahal Party but these withdrew from the Government in August 1970 in protest against Israel's acceptance of the Rogers peace initiative which they said would require Israel to hand back almost all the Arab territory occupied in 1967.

The new territorial position brought about by the 1967 conflict and the changed power relationship between Israel and its Arab neighbours, now directly supported by the military might of the Soviet Union, have changed the traditional basis of Israel's political life. The ideological issue is no longer between the various forms of social and religious life within the Jewish State but whether Israel should exist as a Jewish national entity or as a mixed Arab–Jewish State. The political struggle is now not so much between parties as between personalities and groups within the new Labour Party which is likely to dominate Israel's political life for a long time. The economic conflict is not so much between socialism and private enterprise as between efficiency and inefficiency and between Jewish labour and imported Arab labour in a rapidly developing society in which socialism and capitalism, both indigenous and imported, seem to have evolved a remarkable system of effective co-operation in management and investment. The new economic interest of the Diaspora in the State, as manifested by the regular meetings of the joint Israeli–Jewish Conference on Economic Development, reflects to some extent the dwindling of Jewish interest in the Zionist Organization. The Jews have recently undergone a considerable soul-searching process of readaptation to the new relations between the Diaspora and the State. One of the direct consequences has been the creation of a new Ministry for Integration and Immigrants to perform the functions previously carried out by the Jewish Agency in this field.

SOCIAL SURVEY

The influx of vast numbers of immigrants into Israel has brought with it profound changes in the social structure of the pre-state Jewish community. As has been noted, the fusing of the numerous strands of culture, language, and customs into a single nation is one of the most vital tasks facing Israel. The European ideal of economic aid and social progress on which Israeli life is based is strange to the Oriental Jews. Many immigrants have spent years in concentration and displaced persons' camps and must be trained to enter normal productive life, while others uprooted from their old professions and traditions must be helped to find new skills and attitudes of mind. Israel's immigration policy has, in addition, brought an increased, if willingly accepted, burden of old people, the sick, and parentless children, who must be cared for.

Education

Under the compulsory education law passed in 1949, free compulsory education is provided for all children between five and fourteen, Arabs as well as Jews. Secondary education, for which fees varying from £11,225 to £11,435 per year are payable, is provided for children over thirteen. Half of the pupils, including all those who have passed examinations in development areas, are exempt from payment. Children in the 14–18 age-group who have not completed elementary education must attend classes (free) till they reach the required standard. Primary education was complicated by the system of four 'trends' which was carried over from the mandatory period. Until 1953 there were within the state system four parallel types of school: general, Labour, Mizrahi (orthodox), and Agudat Israel (ultra-orthodox), corresponding in the main to shades of social, religious, and political opinion. By the state education law of 1953 all the administrative powers hitherto enjoyed by the bodies representing the trends were abolished, and the supervision and organization of all state schools was vested in the Ministry of Education. Private schools may be established provided the curriculum, teaching, and buildings meet the standards of the Ministry of Education. They are mainly religious schools.

The Hebrew University of Jerusalem has played a cardinal role in the training of the country's intellectual and academic leadership. Opened in 1925 on Mount Scopus (where the original buildings have been reopened since the 1967 war) it had 12,000 students including 250 Arabs and 1,400 from abroad (150 Afro-Asians) and 1,560 teaching staff in 1967/8. The University is responsible for the Beersheba Institute of Higher Education (500 students).

The Technicon or Israel Institute of Technology in Haifa had 6,900 students and 800 teaching staff in 1966/7. It also provided extension courses for 7,600 students. It financed £19 million worth of research projects in Israel (1965/6) and £13·7 million abroad (1966/7).

The Tel Aviv University had a teaching staff of 1,100 and a student body of 8,000 in 1967/8.

The University of Haifa is the new university of northern Israel. It has over 5,000 students, 1,510 Arab and Druze, and an academic body of 460.

The Bar-Ilan University is a religious institution with a teaching staff of 680 and a student body of 6,000 in Arts and Science Faculties.

The most prestigious scientific institute in the country is the Weizmann Institute of Science devoted to fundamental research in the natural sciences. With a staff of 1,100 including 300 full-time students it was engaged in 1967 in 400 research projects. A non-profit-making subsidiary — Yeda Research and Development Company—deals with the commercial promotion of the Institute's industrial research.

The Volcani Institute of Agricultural Research, founded in 1921, has been largely responsible for expansion and modernization of the country's agriculture. It has a staff of 1,300, including 290 scientists, engaged in 1967 in 600 research projects.

The annual expenditure on scientific research of the Academic Institutes had reached £1450 million in 1970/1 of which 60 per cent was provided by the Government. The research work is promoted and co-ordinated by: (1) the Israel Academy of Science and Humanities; (2) the National Council for Research and Development in the Prime Minister's Office which is responsible in particular for the National Physics Laboratory and the Negev Institute for Arid Zone Research at Beersheba; and (3) the Atomic Energy Commission supervising the work of the Sorek Nuclear Research Centre and the Negev Nuclear Research Centre.

Cultural Development

It is a remarkable achievement that within so short a time Hebrew has become the living language of a nation composed of so many linguistic elements. Thirteen Hebrew and ten non-Hebrew newspapers are published daily; the two foremost morning papers have a circulation of about 40,000 and the evening papers between 130,000 and 160,000. There are 400 other periodicals including 50 weeklies and 150 fortnightlies or monthlies. The *per capita* theatre attendance is the highest in the world (3 million tickets sold in 1966/7 for the five repertory theatres). Habimah, the Israel National Theatre, was founded in Russia in 1917. Of equal intensity is the musical life centred on the Israel Philharmonic Orchestra which was founded in 1936, and on the 29 Conservatoires.

Kol Israel, the Voice of Israel, broadcasts 55 hours daily in Hebrew and nine other languages including 14 hours in Arabic. Television began operating in 1969. There are 270 cinemas in the country but the cinema industry is still in its infancy.

European traditions dominate the plastic arts in Israel but this is not the case with music and folklore which have developed a distinctive local character. However, it is probably in the field of literature, crowned by the Nobel Prize awarded in 1966 to S. J. Agnon and Nelly Sachs of Sweden, that Israel has found its most original national expression.

Health Services

In spite of mass immigration which brought to Israel a million immigrants of whom about 13 per cent suffered from chronic diseases, health standards compare well with those of Europe. In 1969 life expectancy was 69·5 years for males and 73·2 for females; infant mortality was 19·2 per thousand among Jews and 39·4 per thousand among non-Jews. In 1970 there was a total of 23,758 beds in 161 hospitals of all types of which the Government was responsible for 34 hospitals and 8,000 beds. Apart from the missions and private hospitals most of the health services of the country were provided by the Trade Union Health Organization and the Hadassah Medical Organization sponsored by Zionist sources in the USA.

Kupat Holim, the health insurance fund of the Histadrut, has a membership of 2,090,000 (68 per cent of the population). In 1967 its budget was £I299 million and it maintained 1,021 clinics, 9 general hospitals, 5 specialized hospitals, 15 convalescent homes, 147 laboratories, and 233 pharmacies. The Hadassah is responsible for the University Medical Centre with 1,700 medical students in all branches. The Hagem David Adom, Israel's equivalent of the Red Cross, runs 63 first-aid stations, 8 blood banks, 300 ambulances, and has 6,000 volunteers.

The National Insurance scheme, started in 1954, covers 900,000 persons. This provides for pensions for men over 65 and women over 60, maternity benefits, and family allowances for children under 18 after the first child. The Ministry of Social Welfare provides most of the social workers, with special attention to youth. In 1967 there were 11 homes for delinquent children, 2 for the deaf, one for homeless Moslem boys, 26 residential homes for the handicapped, and 21 rehabilitation centres. Malben, financed by the American Joint Distribution Committee, has cared for more than 250,000 disabled immigrants. Ort, an international organization for vocational skills, had 60 institutions with 29,000 pupils in 1966. Various women's organizations provide additional social services. The Woman Workers' Council runs 400 kindergartens and day nurseries and the Women's Zionist Organization has 346 social work institutions of all types.

Labour and Trade Unions

The economic and industrial organization of Israel is dominated, and complicated, by the peculiar position of the Histadrut, which is a confederation of most of the trade unions in the country and of the growing numbers of co-operatives and collective societies engaged in agriculture and industry, and conducts medical and welfare services for its members. Its membership grew to 1,124,000 in the spring of 1971 and includes half of all adults, including 62,000 Arabs and Druzes.

The Histadrut is the owner or part-owner on a co-operative basis of a number of large industrial concerns and financial institutions. The most important of these are Hamashbir Hamerkazi (Co-operative Wholesale Society), which acts as supplier for the agricultural settlements and urban consumers' co-operatives, which in turn control a series of industrial enterprises including soap, flour, chemical, shoe-making, and rubber factories; Tnuva (Central Agricultural Marketing Co-operative), which markets the greater proportion of Israel's agricultural produce; Solel Boneh, which is the largest contracting enterprise, carries out public works both in Israel and abroad, and directly or indirectly exercises control over a large variety of industrial firms. The main financial institutions controlled wholly or in part by the Histadrut are the Workers' Bank, Hassneh Insurance Company, and two credit institutions. It also has interests in the Mekorot Water-Supply Company, two shipping companies, and Ampal (the American Palestine Trading Company), which extends dollar loans to the Government and to Histadrut-controlled enterprises and makes direct investments in the national air and shipping companies. It has entered into partnership with many private investors in Israel and abroad. All economic activities are controlled by the General Co-operative Association (Hevrat Ovdim) whose membership is the same as that of the Histadrut.

Apart from the social services, the Histadrut is responsible for many cultural and sports organizations, including three daily newspapers and hundreds of popular art circles. The Histadrut is affiliated to the ICFTU and through its Afro-Asian Institute provides courses for thousands of foreign students from developing countries.

There are three other trade union organizations formed on party lines, but associated for some purposes with the Histadrut: (1) the Mizrahi Workers' Organization (Histadrut Hapoel Hamizrahi) which maintains communal and co-operative settlements and has central organizations for the absorption of new immigrants; (2) the Agudat Israel Workers' Organization (Histadrut Poalei Agudat Israel), which also maintains settlements; and (3) the National Labour Federation (Histadrut Haovdim Haleumit), which was founded by the Revisionist Organization and has its own sick fund.

The Israel Labour League, which was an Arab trade union organization, and the Arab Workers' Congress, which was a near-Communist body, were dissolved in 1953. The Arab workers are now members of bodies affiliated to the Histadrut.

ECONOMIC SURVEY

The economic development of Israel since 1948 has been largely determined by her special political and social conditions. Some of these are a legacy from the mandatory period and the troubled events which preceded and accompanied the foundations of the State; some result from the struggle to maintain Zionist social ideals; and some from the absence of settled and peaceful relations with neighbouring states.

The last has been the most important single factor and it has compelled Israel to support an extremely heavy defence burden. It has been estimated at $65 million in 1954, $270 million in 1963, $1,000 million in 1969, and about $1,500 million in 1971, i.e. 25 per cent of GNP.

These political difficulties have also had an indirect effect. The blockade of Israel by the Arab States and particularly by Egypt, with her hold over the Suez Canal, has handicapped foreign trade. It has shut Israel off from natural markets in the Middle East and from natural sources of grain in neighbouring countries; it has obliged her to import refined oil products which could otherwise have been produced by the IPC refinery from Iraqi crude oil; and it exposes commerce to constant interference.

Despite all these economic difficulties the Government has endeavoured to maintain a European standard of living and a high level in the social services in accordance with Zionist ideals of social justice. But all these factors have placed a great strain on Israel's balance of payments. Shortage of foreign currency has been a constant threat to essential investment on the one hand and to the level of consumption on the other, in spite of great capital transfers amounting to $6 billion from 1949 to 1965, 59 per cent of which were supplied by world Jewry, $1·73 billion by West Germany, and the rest mainly by the United States. In 1970 unilateral transfers grew to $676 million, US loans to $334 million.

Pattern of the Economy

The Israel economy has continued to expand, although not at the same rate as the population. Between 1950 and 1970 GNP grew by an average of 9 per cent a year. It stood at £18,456 million in 1970, the upward trend being particularly steep since 1967. The reverse of the coin is the increased balance of payments deficit. Exports increased by 47 per cent from 1967 to 1970 standing at $1,370 million, but imports rose by 73 per cent and stood at $2,630 million in 1970.

The structure of the economy is similar to that of industrialized countries of Western Europe. Agriculture accounts for 8·2 per cent of the domestic product; industry 25 per cent; private commerce and services 18·5 per cent; Government and public services 19·5 per cent. A more detailed breakdown of these figures would show that the active population engaged in services of all kinds nears 50 per cent—much higher than in Europe. This is one of the main negative trends which successive Israeli Governments have tried to change with relatively little success.

Currency

Israel's currency is the Israel pound (£I), which is divided into 1,000 *agorot* (plural of *agora*). It was at first linked with sterling but has been successively devalued to $=£I 4·189 in 1972.

Agriculture

Jewish settlement in Palestine from Herzl to the end of the mandate laid stress on agriculture as a means of reclaiming land and as a way of life demonstrating *Haluziut*, the pioneering spirit which was so important to Zionists. This remains as important as ever. The Government has consistently encouraged immigrants to go on the land and considers agricultural training in the frontier villages as equivalent to army service. Moreover, since the creation of the State the economic grounds for developing agriculture have become more pressing, namely, to provide food for a rapidly increasing population and to conserve foreign currency by making the country as self-sufficient as possible.

Before 1948 three-quarters of the Arabs were cultivators, and they produced most of the grain, meal, fodder, and vegetable oil (olives). The Jewish settlements concentrated on mixed farming and citrus fruits. After 1948 and the departure of three-quarters of the Arab population, Arab cultivation had to be supplemented by imports until such a time as Jewish agriculture could be expanded and diversified to meet domestic requirements. In this the Government has been highly successful. Israel is now self-supporting in dairy produce, vegetables, and fodder; meat and wheat are the main items imported. In 1966 $107 million of agricultural goods were exported of which $84·5 million was citrus fruit. This fully covered all food imports. Real production in agriculture increased sixfold between 1948 and 1970 to reach a value of £11,974 million. Exports of oranges increased from 80,000 tons in 1948 to 1,261,900 tons in 1970. New crops have been introduced. Cotton which was planted for the first time in 1953 now covers all local needs. Ground-nuts have become an important export item. Sugar-beet is grown on 18,000 acres and processed by local refineries. Meat production, mainly poultry, amounted to 136,000 tons in 1969/70. Dairy cows have increased from 14,000 to 74,000 with one of the highest average milk yields in the world. Sheep have increased from 20,000 in 1948 to 190,000 in 1964 and the total catch of fish has risen from 3,500 tons in 1949 to 24,500 tons in 1967. Among 700 Jewish agricultural settlements, 480 have been established since 1948. Ninety per cent of the land is owned by the State or the Jewish National Fund which have both contributed to the reclamation of large tracts of land. In 1970 1·1 million acres of land were under cultivation (as against 400,000 in 1949) of which 480,000 are irrigated (as against 75,000 in 1949).

Irrigation

The planning and design of all main water projects, distribution systems, and drainage are the responsibility of Tahal (Water Planning for Israel Ltd.) which also carries out many projects abroad. It has a turnover of $12 million a year and employs 600 engineers and technicians.

The most ambitious hydraulic scheme which was completed in 1964 is the Lake Tiberias–Negev Project with an annual capacity of 320 million cubic metres. Two other important schemes are the Western Galilee–Kishon and Yarkan–Negev projects. Tahal is 52 per cent owned by the Government which has invested $1000 million in major water schemes and provides an annual budget of $65 million for irrigation investment.

Forestry

For centuries Palestine was gradually despoiled of its woods and forests which were famous in Biblical and Roman times. The conservation and reclamation of the soil, which has consequently been eroded, is one of the most important tasks facing the Government. During the mandate about 12,000 acres were planted with forest trees. By 1967 116,000 acres had been freshly planted and in addition 150,000 acres of natural forest have been protected. Some 60 million trees have been planted— 6 million to commemorate the Jews destroyed by Nazism in Europe.

Regional Development

Five areas have been planned for development as complete units consisting of groups of four to five villages with their own administrative centres around one semi-industrial town. These are the Lachis area, started in 1955 with 56 villages around the town of Kiriat Gat, the Taanach area, started in 1956, with 650 families in ten villages, the Adulam area, started in 1957, with 700 families in ten villages, the Korazih area on Lake Tiberias, started in 1962 and the Besor area south of Beersheba.

Agricultural Settlements

The settlements are of various types, distinctive in their social structure and organization. The principle of the collective settlement or Kibbutz is that the village is a unit commonly owned; all property is held in common, and no person has any private possessions. Members pool their labour in accordance with the needs of the settlement and receive their requirements within the means of the community. Each Kibbutz usually has a communal dining-room and kitchen, kindergarten and children's quarters, social and cultural centre, library, and central stores. In most Kibbutzim there has been a tendency in recent years to provide living quarters for married couples and for their infant children. The Kibbutzim are mainly agricultural, but many are developing industrial workshops such as canneries, foundries, and plywood factories. Some specialize in lake fishing or breeding carp in artificial ponds. The products are sold through a co-operative marketing organization.

The co-operative settlements can be subdivided into three types, each based on co-operative principles but with distinctive features. The Moshav Ovdim, or workers' smallholding settlement, is founded on the principle of mutual aid between members. Each farm is worked by a family individually but all the produce is sold through a co-operative and all purchases for the settlement are undertaken on the same basis. Hired labour is prohibited. The Moshav is similar in type but is worked on less rigid principles. The Moshav Shitufi is a compromise between a collective and a co-operative settlement. It is based on private small-holdings combined with communal farming but each family has its own house. In all cases the land belongs to the community. It is acquired by the Keren Keyemet le-Israel (Jewish National Fund) which receives contributions from the Jews of the world, and it is leased to the collective or co-operative society. The Moshava is a rural village based on private ownership, and was the principal form of Jewish agricultural settlement in the period before the mandate. The land and house are owned by the individual.

Industry

Since the establishment of the State, increasing quantities of exportable minerals have been discovered including phosphates, kaolin, marble, gypsum, oil, and natural gas. The Dead Sea Works, the main mining enterprise in the country, produced 909,300 tons of potash and 8,000 tons of bromine in 1971. In Arada a large chemicals complex is under construction. Copper reserves at the site of King Solomon's mines 15 miles north of Eilat are 20 million tons and the output of copper cement in 1970 was 10,000 tons. Oil was struck in 1955 at Helez near Ashkelon and natural gas in 1958 near the Dead Sea. Production of both equals 200,000 tons of oil. Production of oil in Sinai has reached 6 million tons. Most of the mining industries are financed by the State. The total value of investments in the industry amounted to £12,035 million in 1970.

The growth of industry in general has been very rapid, especially after 1962 with the new liberalization policy adopted by the Government after the devaluation of the Israeli pound. Both foreign and Israeli private investment increased. In 1967 71 per cent of wage-earners were employed in privately owned firms, 12 per cent in State undertakings and 17 per cent in Labour-owned factories. However, the Labour sector controls most of the heavy industry while the State runs the most advanced industries such as aviation, electronics etc. As a result, the industrial output of Israel's mixed economy has increased five-fold since 1950 to reach a total value of £112,785 million in 1970. The number of employees has risen from 89,000 to 261,000 and the output per head by 60 per cent. In the same period industrial exports have risen from $18 million to $606 million.

Because of the lack of water resources, the development of

thermoelectric energy and of oil production have been vital to the country's economy. The capacity of power stations has increased eighteen times since 1948 to reach 1·2 million kilowatts in 1971. Israel's major industrial exports are diamonds ($230 million in 1970); textiles and clothing ($95 million in 1970); chemicals and refined oil products ($53 million). The military industries are also an important foreign currency earner.

The building industry has been of special importance, owing to the rapid growth of population. Private investment in this sector has surpassed that of the Government and other public bodies. In 1971 £1804 million were invested in building.

Government Finance

Until 1966 unlimited expansion and inflation had been the main features of the Israeli economy as a direct consequence of the New Economic Policy introduced in 1962 and the constant increase in the amount of capital flowing into the country from private, public, and foreign government sources. In 1966 a recession set in owing partly to the reduction of immigration, which caused a decline in building activity, partly to the ending of German reparations payments, and partly to the Government's determination to limit consumption and redistribute the available manpower resources into more productive fields. The country passed from a situation of overemployment to one of partial unemployment (100,000 Israelis were idle by the beginning of 1967) while the growth of GNP was cut from an average of 9 per cent between 1950 and 1966 to less than 5 per cent in 1966/7. The 1967 war, however, reversed this trend again and caused some changes in the Israeli economy although it is too soon to say if these changes will be permanent. There were four outstanding effects of the June war on the Israeli economy: first the considerable increase in tourism (36 per cent) which was mainly due to the massive arrival of Jewish pilgrims wishing to visit the Wailing Wall in Jerusalem; secondly, the increase in Government expenditure on defence, military industries, and infrastructure development, on the construction of an oil pipeline from Eilat to the Mediterranean, as a permanent land alternative to the Suez Canal and on the development of land communications and industries in the Negev, especially in the Eilat area; thirdly, the expansion of the domestic market because the occupied territories absorb a growing proportion of Israeli industrial production while continuing to supply most of their agricultural produce to Jordan; and finally the much closer co-operation between Israel and Jewish businessmen abroad, formalized at the Economic Advisory Conference which took place in Jerusalem in April 1968. The idea of a Jewish–Israeli Common Market has been put forward, possibly as an alternative to Israel's unsuccessful attempts to acquire associate status with the EEC.

The Balance of Payments

The balance of trade has consistently been adverse since the creation of the State owing to the need for large-scale imports to supply the rapidly increasing population and to military requirements which are growing equally fast. The visible trade gap was reduced from $410 million in 1965 to $335 million in 1966 as a result of the Government's deflationary policies but it increased again following the 1967 war. However, in that year 70 per cent of imports were covered by exports as compared with 11 per cent in 1949, 28 per cent in 1956, and 50 per cent in 1966. By 1967 net imports had dropped from $811 million to $710 million while exports had increased by 5 per cent to $500 million.

The enormous increase in defence costs and in particular the crash programme to develop a self-sufficient aircraft and electronics industry following the French arms embargo were the chief causes for the sharp deterioration in the balance of payments position after 1967. In 1969 there was a balance of payments deficit of $800 million and foreign currency reserves fell from $1 billion in August 1967 to $500 million in October 1969. In 1969 the defence budget increased by 25 per cent on 1968 and amounted to 16 per cent of GNP; in 1971 25 per cent of GNP.

The gap in Israel's balance of payments has consistently been covered by a very big import of capital. Some sources of foreign capital have dried up over the years. US Government aid, which amounted to $249 million from 1951 to 1956, has ceased and been replaced by IBRD and US loans. West German Reparations ceased in 1965 and have been replaced by loans. German restitution payments to private individuals have been continued.

The Israeli Government continues to benefit from donations from Jewish communities abroad—donations which have considerably increased since the 1967 war, from the import of private capital, and the sale of Israeli State Bonds which provide for about 30 per cent of national development expenditure.

Since 1951 when the first series was issued, over one billion dollars of Bonds have been sold in the USA, Canada, Europe, and Latin America.

Communications

The rapid increase in the population and the accelerated economic development of the country have caused a vast increase in the volume of traffic, and the diversification and expansion of the economy have to a large extent depended upon an efficient transport system. In consequence the extension of the road and rail network has been made a high priority.

On 1 January 1971 Israel had 5,800 miles of roads with a highway from Eilat to Haifa providing the skeleton for the envisaged Israeli land alternative to the Suez Canal.

N

The railways are State owned and cover a total of 454 miles in operation. In 1971 there were 147,000 private cars and 3,700 buses.

Ports. The main port is Haifa which has become one of the principal ports of the eastern Mediterranean. Together with the Kishon River mouth in Haifa Bay it handled 80 per cent of the country's cargoes or 3·8 million tons. The Jaffa/Tel Aviv Port was closed in 1968 when Ashdot, a new deep-water harbour 12 miles south of Tel Aviv came into operation. The country's third port, Eilat, on the Gulf of Aqaba, is of great importance to Israel's economy, as the principal mines are in the south and the chief markets for potash, phosphates, and salt are in Asia; a drive is being made to capture markets in Africa; and it is through this port that Israel receives most of its fuel oil for its own consumption. In 1969 Eilat handled 413,000 tons of freight excluding oil.

Israel's merchant marine has grown steadily since the creation of the State. In January 1971 it consisted of 119 vessels with a total capacity of 3·3 million tons.

Air Transport. The main airport is at Lydda (Lod), which serves thirteen regular international airlines. Minor airports at Jerusalem, Mahanaya (Galilee), Herzlya, Beersheba, Masada, and Eilat are used by several internal companies. Israel's national airline, El Al, conducts regular flights to London, Paris, Rome, Johannesburg, Nairobi, Zürich, Athens, Vienna, Istanbul, New York, Nicosia, and Tehran. In 1967 it carried 52 per cent of all air passengers to and from Israel. A subsidiary company, Arkia, runs daily internal services.

Israel Aircraft Industries Ltd., at Lydda Airport, is the country's largest industrial organization. It manufactures the Arava cargo/passenger plane, the Fuga Magister jet trainer, and a twin executive aircraft. It repairs and maintains a wide range of aircraft and engines and has subsidiary integrated plants for electronics, fibre-glass, precision instruments etc.

VII

The Hashimite Kingdom of Jordan

THE LAND AND THE PEOPLE

The Hashimite Kingdom of Jordan lies on either side of the river Jordan. To the east is the whole of what was formerly the Amirate of Transjordan. To the west is the region of central Palestine that was taken over after the Palestine War (1948-9). Commonly known as the East Bank and the West Bank, the combined territories are about 36,715 square miles in area, 2,165 square miles constituting the West Bank and 30,700 the wide desert that encloses from the east the settled areas of the East Bank. The country is bounded on the north by the river Yarmuk and Syria, on the east by Iraq, on the south by Saudi Arabia, and on the west by Israel and the upper reaches of the river Jordan.

Passing from east to west the desert gives place to the Transjordanian Highlands extending from north to south. Within their broad northern and central slopes is a fertile strip, thirty miles wide on the Syrian frontier and tapering into arid steppe near Maan and Petra. Westwards the hills rise sharply to a maximum of over 5,000 feet, forming a great escarpment above the Jordan–Araba gorge. The gorge cleaves the land from end to end and, within Jordanian territory, consists of: (1) the middle and lower reaches of the river Jordan twisting through its valley (10 miles broad on the south) to pass its waters into the Dead Sea (1,290 ft. below sea-level); (2) the northern end and eastern side of the Dead Sea and surrounding wilderness; (3) the wide sandy trench of the Wadi Araba running from the southern end of the Dead Sea to Aqaba on the Red Sea Gulf, which is Jordan's only port.

West of the Jordan valley the land rises again to the Palestinian Hills. This West Bank block contains the towns of Hebron, Bethlehem, East Jerusalem, Ramallah, Nablus, Tulkarm, and Jenin. Until the Six Day War of June 1967 Bethlehem and East Jerusalem remained Jordanian in spite of the UN Partition Resolution which had designated Jerusalem as a *corpus separatum* and the General Assembly's restatement at the Fourth Session of its intention that Jerusalem and the surrounding villages and towns would be placed under a permanent international regime. At the time of writing the whole of the West Bank is under Israeli military occupation and Israel has unilaterally incorporated the whole of Jerusalem into Israel.

In the hill country the climate follows a Mediterranean pattern except that the summers are fresher and the winters cooler. There is less rainfall on the East Bank than on the West. Snow often occurs in winter. In the Jordan valley rainfall is slight, summer intensively hot, and winter mild and pleasant.

At the census of 1961 Jordan's population numbered 1,706,226. It is growing at about 3 per cent per annum and was estimated to have reached 2,016,618 by the end of 1965. In 1961 the settled population was divided almost equally between East and West Jordan, 820,289 living on the East and 790,503 on the West Bank. About two thirds of all Jordanians were originally Palestinians. In addition to the inhabitants of the West Bank which was incorporated into Jordan in 1950, many Jordanians lived until 1948 in what is now Israel. Some 800,000 left their homes during the Palestine War and more than half of these came to Jordan.

The East Jordanians were a homogeneous people largely descended from Arabian bedouin tribes of desert origin. The Palestinians derive from all the races that invaded or settled in Palestine before the Arab conquest and have been blended together by thirteen centuries of Islamic influence. Most of the Jordanian people are Sunni Moslems, but there is an important Christian minority. There are still a few nomads and semi-nomads. Tent dwellers made up a little more than 5 per cent of the population in 1961. The settled population live in towns and villages, more than one in three live in towns of over 10,000 inhabitants, and more than one in four live in Amman where the population has increased in 20 years from about 30,000 to about a quarter of a million.

The social pattern was distorted by the refugee influx from Israeli held Palestine in 1948. It is not yet possible to measure the further distortion resulting from the war of 1967 but that this must be considerable is indicated by the statement in the Annual Report of UNRWA for 1966–7 that 200,000 people fled across the Jordan in June and July 1967 and that only about 14,000 had returned. Jordan holds over half the total number of refugees registered with UNWRA. In May 1967 they numbered 722,687; more than 50,000 of these were self-supporting and some 3,000 more only received health and educational services from the Agency. The remainder all received rations, but since the standard ration (costing $1·20 per month) is insufficient to keep body and soul together, they cannot be regarded as living in idleness on international charity, but rather, in the words of the Agency's 1965–6 Report, as receiving a modest subvention from the international community in their struggle to support themselves. Some 60,000 Jordanians were living abroad in 1961. Most of these were originally Palestine refugees. Many of them have made good in other Arab countries. The oil producing countries in particular have been able to make use of their abilities, and their remittances have made a substantial contribution to Jordan's balance of payments.

Religious and Racial Minorities

There were 108,838 Jordanian Christians in 1961. Most of them live in Jerusalem and Amman, though other towns like Madeba and Salt on the East Bank and Bethlehem and Ramallah on the West Bank have substantial Christian populations. They are mostly Arabs of the Orthodox Church but there are many Catholics (both of the Latin and Byzantine rites) and Armenians, and a small community of Arab Anglicans.

A valuable element in the community is the Caucasian minority of some 10,000 persons. The greater proportion are Cherkasis (Circassians) and Sunni Moslems. The remainder (about 1,000) are known as Chechens and Shiis. These are all descended from Moslem immigrants from the Caucasus, who fled before the Russian advance in the nineteenth century.

HISTORY AND POLITICS

Southern Jordan was the scene of the wanderings of the Children of Israel before they crossed the river into Canaan. The histories of the riverside people overlap. The northern part of the cultivated strip on the East Bank was known as Gilead and attached to Solomon's kingdom, much of which is in contemporary Jordan. Ancient Ammon was situated on the East Bank, and Moab and Edom in the southern part of Jordan. In the Hellenistic period the Nabataeans, an Arabian tribe, established themselves in the south and gained control of the west Arabian caravan routes from their fortress capital at the 'rose-red city' of Petra: still one of the country's finest ancient monuments. To the north the country was Hellenized by the Seleucids, and the Greek cities of Philadelphia (now Amman) and Gerasa (now Jerash) came into being. Philadelphia and Gerasa were among the ten cities (the Dekapolis) which formed themselves into a defensive league against the nomad Arabs and Jews. The Nabataeans made formal submission to Rome and retained their autonomy, but then the kingdom was annexed by Trajan in AD 105 and became part of the Roman province of Arabia Petraea. Under Roman rule the country for five centuries enjoyed a high level of prosperity; many towns sprang up and Christianity spread. In the sixth century the control of the eastern areas passed to the Ghassanid Arabs, a tribal confederation which received an imperial subsidy, but just before the coming of the Moslems, the Ghassanids were overwhelmed by the Iranians, who sacked Jerusalem. A brief renaissance followed the Arab conquest when, under the Umayyad Caliphs, Islamic discipline was welded with Byzantine culture. Later, with the shift of the Moslem centre of gravity to Iraq and Egypt, the East Bank largely reverted to nomadism and during the Crusades was disputed for a time between Crusaders and Moslems. This period saw the last of the northward caravan trade, which thereafter passed either from the Euphrates to northern Syria or by the Red Sea to Alexandria, and Jordan's prosperity gradually crumbled away.

The Mandate

In Ottoman times the Damascus *vilayet*, with its western boundary on the Jordan, extended from Hama to Aqaba, while the country west of the Jordan—Palestine—was divided between the independent *sanjaq* of Jerusalem in the south and the *vilayet* of Beirut in the north. After the defeat of Turkey in 1918, in place of the large, independent Syria desired by Arab nationalists a French mandate was imposed upon Syria and Lebanon and a British mandate over Palestine, including Transjordan.[1] After Faisal had been driven out of Syria by the French, the British High Commissioner called a meeting of East Bank shaikhs and notables at al-Salt in August 1920 and declared that the British Government favoured self-government for them with the assistance of a few British officers; local administrations in Amman, Ajlun, and Kerak were then set up. Three months later Faisal's elder brother, the Amir Abdullah, appeared on the southern frontier with a small force from the Hejaz and was credited with the intention of raising the tribes against the French. On entering the country he was asked by the local administrations to form a national Government. This he proceeded to do and in March his position was acknowledged by the British Government, with whom he subsequently agreed to abandon anti-French activities and to accept the Amirate of Transjordan under a British mandate with a grant-in-aid. Under Article 25 of the mandate for Palestine the Mandatory was able, with the consent of the Council of the League of Nations, to exempt Transjordan from the operation of the Balfour Declaration. Jews were never allowed to acquire land or to settle in Transjordan.

On 25 May 1923 Transjordan was proclaimed an independent state, subject to British obligations under the mandate, and on 20 February 1928 an agreement was concluded under which the Amir Abdullah was to be guided by British advice (through a British Resident appointed by the High Commissioner for Palestine, who was also High Commissioner for Transjordan) in such matters as foreign relations, finance and fiscal policy, jurisdiction over foreigners, and freedom of conscience. The 1928 treaty was supplemented on 2 June 1934 by an agreement enabling the Amir to appoint consular representatives in other Arab States. In 1939 the British Government agreed to the formation (in place of the existing Legislative Council) of a Council of Ministers (or

[1] See above, pp. 13–16.

Cabinet), each member of which was in charge of a department of the Government and responsible to the Amir. Finally, by treaties and agreements with Britain between 1939 and 1948, Transjordan attained independence (1946), and in 1948 the Amir was proclaimed King of the 'Hashimite Kingdom of Jordan', though it was not until 1949, after the Palestine War had left Transjordan in control of parts of 'Cis-Jordan', that the title was internationally recognized. The kingdom was recognized by the United States on 31 January 1949.

The Treaties with Britain

By an agreement concluded on 19 July 1941 the Amir allowed Britain to maintain armed forces in Jordan, and to raise, organize, and control sufficient armed forces in the country for its defence and for the preservation of peace and order. A treaty more in keeping with existing conditions in the country was signed in London on 22 March 1946, but it too was soon felt to be too vulnerable to Arab nationalist criticisms of King Abdullah's dependence on Britain. It was therefore replaced by another, signed in Amman on 15 March 1948. This treaty was for twenty years with provision for revision after fifteen, and provided that either party would come to the aid of the other if engaged in war. The Annex provided *inter alia* for the maintenance of RAF units at Amman and Mafraq until the parties agreed that 'the state of world security renders such measures unnecessary'. An accompanying Exchange of Letters provided for British help in economic and social development as well as for financial assistance. The Treaty was ended by an Exchange of Notes on 13 March 1957 and the last British troops stationed in Jordan under this Treaty left Aqaba on 6 July of that year.

The Palestine War and its Aftermath

On 15 May 1948, the date of the expiry of the mandate, Jordan's army (the Arab Legion) took part, with Egyptian and other forces of the Arab League, in the occupation of the Arab areas of Palestine.[1] The Legion did not intervene in Jerusalem until it became apparent that no steps were being taken by the United Nations to install an international regime in the city, which was in danger of being overrun by the Jews. With its Iraqi allies it held the central sector of Palestine and maintained the siege of the Jewish population in Jerusalem until both sides accepted the first United Nations truce in the summer of 1948. Desultory fighting continued until an armistice agreement between Transjordan and Israel was signed in Rhodes on 3 April 1949. By this agreement Transjordan was left in control of the part of Palestine that was not in the possession of Israel. The act of union took place on 24 April

[1] i.e. those areas not already occupied by the Zionist forces before the end of the mandate. The aim of the intervention was, however, stated more ambitiously to be the elimination of the Zionist state.

1950, after general elections had been held on both sides of the river. Four leading Palestinians had already joined the Jordan Cabinet and, with the extension of the franchise to the West Bank, membership of the House of Representatives was doubled in order to give equal representation to Palestinians. The first act of its duly elected members was to vote for union.

The Palestine War had changed Transjordan into Jordan. With the accession of what remained of Palestinian territory allotted to the Arabs by the General Assembly Resolution of November 1947 Jordan acquired a Palestinian population more than twice as numerous as King Abdullah's former Transjordanian subjects. Nearly half a million of this new population were destitute refugees from the area allotted to the Jewish State and its extensions won by the Jews in the fighting. The new frontiers were mere Armistice lines which often separated villages from their lands or from their water supplies, divided Jerusalem into two unequal sectors, and cut off Jordan from any access to the Mediterranean Sea. The newly proclaimed Hashimite Kingdom of Jordan had to be built from the ground up under almost impossible economic and extremely adverse political conditions. It had been proclaimed without the prior agreement of the other Arab Governments whose war aims had not included the enlargement of Transjordan. The Palestinians were consulted and by majority welcomed this solution, but some were irreconcilably opposed to it and almost all harboured reservations about rule from Transjordan whose inhabitants they thought of as less advanced than themselves.

King Abdullah correctly perceived that peace with Israel presented the main hope for a viable Jordan. His realism however did not extend to a recognition of the state of mind produced in growing numbers of Arabs by years of impotence against European domination ending in humiliating defeat at the hands of a people they had been accustomed mildly to despise. This would in all likelihood have prevented a successful outcome of his discussions at Shuneh in 1949 and 1950 with Ben-Gurion's special envoy Moshe Dayan. In the event these failed because of Israeli intransigence but they could not be kept completely secret and their main effect was to strengthen distrust of King Abdullah which other Arab Governments did little to dispel and too often allowed themselves to encourage.

On 20 July 1951, when the King was entering the mosque al-Aqsa in Jerusalem, he was shot and killed by a Palestinian youth. At the trial a former Arab Legion officer who was nursing a grievance and had gone to live in Cairo was named as the instigator. Of the five others found guilty, the most prominent was Musa Husseini, a member of the Jerusalem clan whose leader, Hajj Amin Husseini, had been the most determined and uncompromising opponent of Zionism and the Mandate between the wars. He had thrown in his lot with the Axis Powers during the Second World War, but had returned to the Middle East in June 1946 and had become the leading figure in the so-called 'All Palestine Government' set up in the small area of Palestine around Gaza which was occupied by Egypt under her Armistice with Israel. Though possibly not unwelcome to Hajj Amin there is no evidence to connect the crime with the 'Gaza Government'.

Abdullah's elder son, Tallal, was mentally ill when he came to the throne. He succeeded, nevertheless, in improving relations with the Arab States with which his father had differed, and encouraged domestic reforms. Abdullah's patriarchal rule had begun to be criticized in Jordan, especially by the Palestinians who had imbibed democratic ideals under the British mandate. King Tallal accepted at once a revised Constitution that gave more power to the politicians. His reign opened with popular ovations, but by 11 August 1952 he had become so ill that his Government felt obliged to declare him unfit to rule. The succession passed smoothly to his eldest son, Hussein, who was only seventeen years old and was at school in England. Until his coming of age at eighteen and his enthronement on 2 May 1953 the duties of the Crown were vested in a Regency Council consisting of three elder statesmen, two from the East Bank and one from the West.

The long slow revolution in the Arab world—hitherto mainly directed against British or French domination began to take on a more radical complexion after the Second World War. The shock of defeat in the Palestine War powerfully reinforced disenchantment with the regimes responsible for its conduct and political violence increased in most Arabic speaking countries. King Abdullah fell a victim to these emotions but his death was not immediately followed by further political upheaval in Jordan. His long tradition of paternal rule had prevented the emergence of strong political antagonisms, while the strength of the British-officered Arab Legion provided an effective restraint on popular agitation.

The move away from paternalism under King Tallal was continued in the new reign by a new Prime Minister Fawzi al-Mulki, but the strength of the nationalist attack on the British connection and the fears and suspicions aroused by the Israeli policy of punishing individual forays of frontier villages into their lost lands, by organized military operations against their villages, led King Hussein to replace al-Mulki by the more conservative Tawfiq Abul Huda in May 1954. His success in getting a more reliable parliament elected was dimmed by demonstrations of protest in the larger towns and this led him to seek popularity by demanding a revision of the Anglo-Jordan Treaty. The efforts of the Western Powers to organize the defence of the Middle East against a possible Soviet attack had had a partial success early in 1954 in the Baghdad Pact. This had enabled Great Britain to replace the Anglo-Iraqi Treaty of 1930 with an arrangement for reactivation of bases in time of war. The visit in December 1955 of the Chief of the Imperial General Staff, General Templer, to explore the possibility of a similar solution in Jordan caused the resignation of the four West Bank Ministers and serious rioting throughout the country.

The 1956–7 crisis

King Hussein bowed to the storm. His dismissal of General Glubb and most of the British officers in March was followed by an election in October 1956 which brought in a parliament of nationalists and a Prime Minister, Sulaiman Nabulsi, pledged to terminate the Anglo-Jordan Treaty. The Suez attack on Egypt by the forces of Britain, France, and Israel inflamed nationalist opinion further and the Anglo-Jordan Treaty was brought to an end by an Exchange of Notes in March 1957. The financial obligations it imposed on Britain were to be assumed by Saudi Arabia, Egypt, and Syria. In the same month the Jordan Government rejected American Aid under the Eisenhower Doctrine and moved towards diplomatic relations with the Soviet Union.

The King counterattacked in April; with the aid of the bedouin regiments he foiled an army 'coup' and strengthened by declarations of support from Washington and London, he imposed martial law, dissolved political parties, prorogued parliament, and purged the army and the civil service. The attempt to carry Jordan into the ranks of what were later called the 'progressive' Arab States had miscarried.

The only change brought about by the struggle between the King and the nationalists in 1957 was to transfer the main financial burden of keeping Jordan afloat from Great Britain to the United States of America; no more was heard of the Egyptian, Saudi Arabian, and Syrian commitments to replace the British subsidy. The basic predicament of Jordan's rulers remained unaltered. Jordan stayed in the front line facing Israel and was still the major target for Zionist punitive raids while her economy remained almost totally dependent on a major power committed to Israel's future. The ruler of Jordan still had every logical incentive to seek a settlement with Israel, as King Abdullah had tried to do seven years before. He could not do so because his subjects, two thirds of them Palestinians and a third of them destitute refugees from that part of Palestine now controlled by Israel, not only had strong emotional reasons for rejecting any settlement but presented an easy target to the radio propaganda of other Arab States whose distrust of the Hashimites for their traditional co-operation with the British Government had been sharply increased by King Abdullah's unilateral annexation of the West Bank.

The ten years following 1957 were therefore perilous for Jordan and her King who was alternately engaged in fierce propaganda polemic with his Arab allies or warily joined with them in expressions of Arab solidarity. Because Jordan still contained a traditionally minded minority unequivocally loyal to the throne, an exceptionally resolute monarch was able to maintain and until 1967 even to strengthen his position. The crucial factor was that although she no longer had treaty relations with any Western power Jordan was able to count on their support because her independent existence seemed to them to be a necessary condition for preserving the precarious *status quo* on the borders of Israel.

The Arab Union

In February 1958 the two Arab countries in which Great Britain still retained some influence, Jordan and Iraq, tried to offset the emotional appeal which the union of Egypt and Syria exercised on their citizens by proclaiming a counter union of their own. This was killed six months later when the fall of the Hashimite monarchy in Baghdad moved Iraq decisively into the radical Arab camp. In this crisis King Hussein appealed for British military help and the 16 Independent Parachute Brigade landed at Amman airfield on 17 July. The permanent stationing of Western troops in any Arab country north of a line from Bahrain to Aden was not, however, practical politics in 1958 and arrangements were made for a United Nations 'presence' which enabled them to leave before the end of the year. Although Jordan's diplomatic relations with the UAR, broken in July 1958, were restored in the autumn of 1959, they remained strained through most of the period of Egyptian/Syrian union and the threat to Jordan's internal security was formidable—in 1959 a Brigadier and ten others were arrested in March and a Major-General in May while the Syrian border was closed through June and July; in 1960 the Prime Minister, Hazza al-Majali, and eleven others were murdered by a bomb explosion; in 1961 an attempt to blow up the Amman radio station was foiled. In the spring of 1961 King Hussein tried to start a serious dialogue with President Nasser, but relations with the UAR were again broken when Jordan immediately recognized the Syrian Government which broke away from Egypt in September of that year.

Jordan's relations with Saudi Arabia had tended to improve as Saudi relations with Egypt had deteriorated, and in September 1962 Jordan joined with the Saudis in supporting the traditional side in the struggle in Yemen which began after the death of the Imam Ahmad. 1963 was a troubled year in Jordan. The overthrow of General Kassem by a Baathist coup in Iraq in February and the continuing struggle between Syrian factions over the kind of Arab unity they wanted led to tripartite unity conversations in Cairo in March and April. These talks raised exaggerated hopes among the Arab peoples and demonstrations in favour of unity and against the monarchy mainly by refugees and young people took place in all the larger towns in Jordan. Curfews were imposed in April on Irbid in East Jordan and on several West Bank towns; the Lower House was dissolved and six deputies arrested, while the army reported having killed 13 and wounded 106 in suppressing the disorders. The climax of this wave of emotion was the publication on 17 April of the Cairo Manifesto which provided for union between Egypt, Iraq, and Syria. The wave receded rapidly during the inaction which followed and collapsed after the abortive coup in Damascus in July which led President Nasser to declare that Egypt would not unite with the 'Fascist Government' in Damascus. Jordan's general election was held without disturbance on 6 July and the Jordan Government obtained an overwhelming vote of confidence in August. Jordan widened her international contacts in the second half of the year with visits by King Hussein to France and India and the announcement of the opening of diplomatic relations with the USSR. Arab fences were not neglected and in December King Hussein accepted an invitation to attend the first Arab Summit meeting in Cairo.

The Palestine Liberation Organization

For several years the Arab governments had been threatening war if Israel should carry out her plans to take water out of the Jordan Valley for irrigation in the Negev. When this event became imminent it was necessary to adopt some public attitude. President Nasser at least was aware that the Arab armies were in no state to challenge Israel, and he called the Arab Summit meeting in January 1964 to halt the drift to war resulting from the competition among the Arab States in the unreal bellicosity of their public statements about the problem of Israel. Among the issues which called forth this kind of competition was the question of the so-called Palestine entity.

The quarrel between those Arabs who accepted and those who rejected the Jordanian annexation of the rump of Palestine had never been settled. In 1958 it had risen again to the surface of inter-Arab politics when Hajj Amin Husseini demanded that the Arab Higher Committee, in its capacity as representing the Palestinians, should join the newly constituted United Arab Republic. President Nasser had no intention of allowing his Palestine policy to be dictated by the ex-Mufti, but could hardly reject the principle that Arab Palestine should one day form part of the UAR. He accordingly accepted the principle but postponed action until Palestine should be liberated. General Kassem saw his opportunity to outbid the Egyptians and from early 1960 onwards he gave full support to the Palestine entity including the training of a Palestinian Liberation force. In 1963, after the breakaway of Syria from the UAR and the consequent change of partners among the Arab States, Iraq and Syria jointly proposed in the Arab League that a Palestinian National Assembly should be elected and that its delegation should take the Palestine seat in the League. Although Jordan steadfastly asserted her sole right to speak for the Palestinians—in February 1960 she had offered Jordanian nationality to any Palestinian, wherever resident, who asked for it—she was unable to prevail. Egypt, although at one with Jordan in not wanting an immediate war with Israel, could not accept the total Jordan claim. In the event it was agreed that Ahmad Shuqairy, a Palestinian lawyer who had for years represented Saudi Arabia at the United Nations was commissioned to consult with his countrymen and draft a Palestinian National Charter for presentation to a conference in Jerusalem in May 1964. This conference duly endorsed Shuqairy's draft which established a Palestine Liberation Organization. The Charter stated *inter alia* that the PLO would not exercise any political sovereignty on the West Bank of the Jordan nor in the Gaza strip, but since it also asserted that the Arab Palestinian people alone had the right to Palestine territory, and that the organization would operate on the national level in the fields of liberation, organization, policy, and finance, it is perhaps remarkable that an overt clash with the Government of Jordan did not take place until September 1965 when Shuqairy made an attack on the Jordan Government from the Cairo-based Voice of Palestine radio station.

The Amman/Cairo rapprochement brought about by the Arab Summit meetings was never quite whole hearted, and although Jordan accepted the Egyptian whip in breaking relations with West Germany in May 1965 she had already begun to move back to relations with Saudi Arabia as was shown by a frontier adjustment in her favour near Aqaba in August. The second Arab Summit meeting in September 1964 had brought about a meeting between President Nasser and King Faisal from which an agreement 'to co-operate fully in solving existing difficulties between the various parties in Yemen' emerged, but practically no progress in this direction came to pass and King Faisal was beginning to appear as the main challenger to President Nasser's leadership of the Arab world.

The Moslem Summit Movement

In the course of a State visit to Iran in December 1965, King Faisal joined with the Shah in calling for a Moslem summit. This was taken as a challenge to Egypt and was fiercely denounced in Cairo and Damascus. It received varying degrees of welcome from Tunisia, Jordan, Sudan, and Kuwait. Both sides were obliged by Arab public opinion to justify their policies in terms of Arab defence against Zionism and imperialism and to claim to be better Moslems than the other side. In this situation Shuqairy was able to make the maximum mischief. His Voice of Palestine had already started broadcasting from Cairo in March 1965 and although considerable effort was expended to bring about a *modus vivendi* between his PLO and the Jordan

Government—in March 1966 an agreement between them was announced after talks with Shuqairy in Cairo—their objectives were fundamentally irreconcilable. As King Hussein put it in a letter to President Nasser dated 14 July 1966—'these saboteurs [the PLO] are seeking to push the Arabs into a war for which they are not yet ready.' In the same letter King Hussein defended his attitude to King Faisal's Moslem Front and this may have contributed to Nasser's decision announced a week later, not to attend a fourth Arab Summit meeting. The Summit agreement to refrain from inter-Arab attacks had finally broken down.

The Way to War

King Hussein's complaints about PLO activities were amply justified—Israeli reprisal raids for guerrilla actions mainly mounted from Syria, fell mainly on Jordan. There was a heavy raid on Qalqilya in September 1965, others on Irbid and Hebron districts in April 1966 and one on Samua supported by tanks and aircraft in November 1966 led to sustained disorders in a number of West Bank towns. By the end of 1966 King Hussein had joined King Faisal and President Bourguiba as a target for the scurrility of broadcasts from Cairo, Damascus, and Baghdad and in the spring of 1967 was hitting back with suggestions that Egyptian troops should leave the Yemen for the Egyptian–Israeli border instead of leaving its defence to the UNEF. Taunts of this kind were one of the pressures which brought about the Six Day War.

Since the breakdown of the attempts at Arab unity in 1963 Syria had been governed by the Baath. The revolutionary Marxist wing of this party took control in a coup d'état in February 1966. In response to Israeli threats of reprisals for guerrilla raids the Syrian leaders made a joint defence agreement with Egypt in November. Tension on the Israel/Syria border increased in the early months of 1967 and the familiar pattern of Syrian shelling of Israel cultivation in the demilitarized zone recurred in April. This time however Israeli aircraft took a hand, penetrated deep into Syrian territory and shot down several Syrian fighters, two of which came down in Jordan. The Syrians believed Israeli menaces, and the pressure on Egypt to react grew heavy. Accused of sheltering behind the UNEF Nasser asked the Secretary-General for its withdrawal. Its departure entailed Egyptian occupation of Sharm al-Shaikh and two days later on 23 May he declared the Gulf of Aqaba closed to Israeli shipping.

Up to this point the Arab world had remained divided. Egyptian and Syrian broadcasts were still demanding the overthrow of King Hussein and the Jordan radio was saying out loud what the Syrians were saying more quietly, that Egypt was a paper tiger. The state of Jordan/Syrian relations was shown on 23 May when explosives intended for sabotage in Amman exploded prematurely in a Syrian car at the Jordan frontier post of Remtha and killed fifteen Jordanians. However, once Nasser had risked war by closing the Straits of Tiran, the Arab States fell in behind him. King Hussein, who had been assured that Israel would not attack if he remained passive, hesitated for a week longer. Then on 30 May he flew to Cairo and signed a defence pact with Egypt which was immediately joined by Iraq. Hussein's position had become impossible as the war parties on either side gained the ascendancy. If war came, he was lost if the Israelis won, and equally lost if the Arabs won without Jordan. Six more days of tension were ended when the Israeli airforce attacked Egyptian airfields on 5 June.

For Jordan the result of the Six Day War was disastrous. It ended with the whole of the West Bank under Israeli occupation, the refugee population of the East Bank increased by about 200,000 and the economy practically non-existent. The basic contradiction of a State without much internal cohesion, threatened by a powerful neighbour, and distrusted by her natural allies because her economy is in pawn to the great powers who protect that neighbour, remained unaltered except in one respect. Jordanians and Israelis have been forced into contact and trade, and visitors as well as bullets and raiders now crossed the Jordan.

Throughout 1968 there were almost daily artillery duels with Israel across the cease-fire lines in the Jordan Valley and on several occasions Israel launched heavy air and rocket attacks on Jordanian territory in reprisal for Palestinian commando raids. Jordan's internal stability was increasingly threatened by the rising power and prestige of the Palestinian guerrilla organizations. The Jordanian civilian and military authorities were divided in their attitude towards these organizations. Some were in favour of compromise while others wished to restrict and control their actions severely. In February 1968 King Hussein strongly denounced the commandos for provoking a heavy Israeli reprisal attack but his Government afterwards compromised by taking the line that Jordan could not be held responsible for attacks on Israelis inside occupied Arab territory. In March the Jordanian Army and Palestinian commandos co-operated in a major engagement against an Israeli raiding force at Kerameh which inflicted heavier losses on the Israelis than on any previous occasion.

Relations between King Hussein and the commandos depended heavily on the King's views of the prospect of a Middle East peace settlement. In March 1969, when he was fairly optimistic, he replaced the pro-Palestinian Prime Minister Bahjat al-Talhouni with his uncle Sharif Nasser Ibn Jamil, a known opponent of the guerrillas. After a commando attack on the Israeli port of Eilat in April he announced that those responsible had been arrested. As before the King conducted his own vigorous diplomatic campaign by visiting Washington, London, and Paris but during the summer his hopes for a settlement faded. In

August he brought back al-Talhouni as Prime Minister and the Jordanian Army began increasingly to co-operate with the guerrillas.

It was part of King Hussein's foreign policy to press continuously for the holding of a new Arab summit but for a long time he was unsuccessful, mainly owing to the opposition of King Faisal. When the summit was finally held in December 1969 Jordan derived little satisfaction as it only served to accentuate Arab divisions. Jordan was anxious to establish a co-ordinated Arab military policy but although the Iraqis had some 12,000 troops stationed in north Jordan, some Syrian units were moved into the same area in August 1969 and the Saudis maintained about 5,000 men near Kerak, no semblance of a cohesive Arab front against Israel was created.

Relations between the Jordanian authorities and the Palestinian guerrillas rapidly deteriorated during 1970. After each serious clash, which became increasingly frequent, an arrangement intended to avoid further clashes was made but it consistently broke down. The King still wavered between a policy of compromise with the Palestinians and accepting at least some of their demands, and listening to the advice of his 'hard-line' officers and advisers. The Palestinians were also divided in their attitude towards the Jordanian regime although the leading organization al-Fatah still aimed to avoid a direct confrontation with the authorities. The guerrillas as a whole were acting more and more like a 'state within a state' in Jordan and this increased the resentment of loyalist Jordanian Army elements and especially those of bedouin origin.

The situation deteriorated further after the King's endorsement on 26 July of the US Middle East peace initiative (or Rogers plan) which the Palestinians regarded as a betrayal of their cause. The hijacking on 6–9 September of three Western airliners to a deserted air strip in east Jordan by the left-wing extremist Popular Front for the Liberation of Palestine led almost inevitably to the civil war which followed. The King appointed General Habis al-Majali as military Governor-General with sweeping powers and the Palestinians responded by calling a general strike.

By 17 September the fighting was general. It was heaviest in Amman and north Jordan—where the guerrillas, reinforced by Syrian armoured units that crossed the border on 19 September, held the towns of Irbid and Ramtha. Formal hostilities ended on 25 September when an inter-Arab mission representing Arab Heads of State who had hastily met in Cairo, arranged a cease-fire. This left the guerrillas in control of their two northern strongholds and some districts of Amman. Total casualties were variously estimated at 1,500 to 5,000 killed and up to 10,000 injured. A high proportion were civilians.

Meeting in Cairo on 27 September, King Hussein and al-Fatah leader Yasir Arafat signed a 14-point truce agreement calling for the restoration of civilian rule and a series of further agreements were negotiated during the autumn. Both sides had over-estimated the strength of their positions before the civil war. The guerrillas had counted on more outside Arab help (notably from the Iraqis) and the Jordanian Army had expected to reduce the guerrilla strongholds in the towns more easily. But the guerrillas were gravely weakened by the war and in the ensuing months they found themselves gradually expelled from the towns and confined to a few strongholds in the north. On 28 October King Hussein brought back one of his closest advisers Wasfi al-Tel as Prime Minister who adopted an uncompromising attitude towards the guerrillas. The inter-Arab civilian and military commission which was set up after the civil war under the chairmanship of the Tunisian Premier Bahi Ladgham to mediate between the Palestinians and Jordanians withdrew in April 1971. Various Arab Heads of State expressed concern with the internal situation in Jordan but they were unable to exert much influence. In July 1971 the guerrilla military bases in Jordan were finally liquidated.

GOVERNMENT AND CONSTITUTION

The agreement with Winston Churchill in 1921 had stipulated that the Amir should rule constitutionally; an Organic Law was adopted in 1928 and a Constitution for the new Kingdom was passed in 1946. In practice, however, King Abdullah's powers were pervasive and the main check upon them was advice from the British Resident. On 1 January 1952 King Tallal signed Jordan's present Constitution. It vests the Legislative Authority in the King and the National Assembly, made up of an appointed Senate and an elected Chamber of Deputies. The Executive Authority is vested in the King acting through his Ministers. By Article 51 the Prime Minister and the Ministers are individually and collectively responsible to the Chamber of Deputies. The members of this body, elected by 'universal, secret, and direct suffrage' sit for four years and elections must take place within the four months preceding the end of the four year term. The King may dissolve the Chamber; in such a case elections must be held and the new Chamber must meet within four months of the dissolution; it cannot be dissolved again for the same reason. Amendments in 1954 and 1955 increased the powers of the Chamber as against the Council of Ministers, while an amendment in 1960, empowered the King to extend the duration of parliament by not less than one and not more than two years. An electoral Law of 1960 increased the number of deputies to sixty, half from either bank.

Jordan's parliamentary experience has not been entirely happy. The elections of 1954 generated demonstrations against alleged irregularities, and political parties have been banned since 1957. The episode of Arab union interrupted Jordanian constitutional life early in 1958 and after the Iraqi revolution in July Jordan remained under martial law until December. In October 1959 the Jordan Chamber met once more and its life was prolonged by Royal decree after the murder of the Prime Minister in August 1960. Elections in October 1961 produced a Chamber composed predominantly of right-wing independents some two-thirds of whom were elected unopposed. This Chamber was dissolved in September 1962 and the next one, elected in rather more liberal conditions, was dissolved in the following April after refusing a vote of confidence to Samir Rifai. Between a third and a half of the members of the next Chamber were returned unopposed and they gave the King's uncle a vote of confidence by 57 votes with one abstention and two absentees. This parliament ran its normal term; the new Chamber elected in April 1967 had not met when the Six Day War broke out in June.

The country is divided into seven administrative divisions (*liwas*) under a Governor, and a desert area. The *liwas* are subdivided into districts under Administrative Councils. Municipal Councils serve the towns and larger villages.

Armed Forces

The Jordanian Army, known as the Arab Legion until 1956, was raised for internal security purposes in 1921. Its first commander was Peake Pasha. In the 1930s under General Glubb it became an effective desert patrol which ended inter-tribal raiding among the Transjordan nomads. During the Second World War it played a distinguished part in operations in Iraq and Syria in 1941. Serving British officers were attached to the Legion from 1945 and a rapid expansion in the first half of the 1950s was financed by a British subsidy under the 1948 Treaty. The Jordanian Army preceded the independence of the State and played a major role in its construction under King Abdullah. Its cost still makes up the largest item in the budget; in 1951 and 1957 it exceeded the whole of the rest of Government expenditure. Until 1956 it was commanded and partly led by British officers and until about 1950 it mainly relied on British Middle East Forces for logistic support and technical services. The rank and file were generally recruited from tribesmen whose personal loyalties were given unreservedly to the King. Their basic education as well as their military training was provided by the Legion. The demand for more educated men as a result of the rapid growth of administrative and technical units in the early 1950s could not be met from the Legion's internal education system. Townsmen therefore came to be increasingly recruited and the army was no longer completely insulated from the radical nationalist political ideas current in the Arab world. Nevertheless the core of bedouin regiments personally loyal to the King has so far prevented Jordan's Army from playing the revolutionary role of many other Arab armies. Defence estimates for 1967 amounted to JD20·165 million out of total estimated expenditure of JD69·031 million.

SOCIAL AND ECONOMIC SURVEY

From its inception as the Amirate of Transjordan after the Cairo Conference of 1921 the main reason for the existence of the Jordan State has been the political convenience of other states. Its economy has always been precarious and for the last twenty years its political and social balance has been unstable. Until 1948 its population was overwhelmingly agricultural and pastoral, and standards of living and political awareness were low. The Turkish Government did little to administer the country which was part of the *vilayet* of Damascus and the main problems facing the Amir's Government in 1922 were public security and the control of nomadic lawlessness. These were solved by the Arab Legion, though there was naturally some backsliding during the anti-Zionist rebellion in Palestine which began in 1936. Land settlement was speedy and efficient and by 1939 political stability and a rather modest measure of prosperity had been achieved. The Second World War brought no fighting and no particular hardships to Jordan.

The 1948 war led to the incorporation of the poorer parts of Palestine into the newly proclaimed Hashimite Kingdom of Jordan and completely upset the balance which had been achieved. With the acquisition of the small part of Palestine successfully defended against the Zionists it brought to Jordan a new population twice as numerous as the East Jordanians, as King Abdullah's former Transjordanian subjects were now to be known. The elite section of this influx was better educated and socially more advanced than the corresponding class of East Jordanians and therefore posed a formidable threat to the balance of political power, while the destitute refugees from the areas of Palestine occupied by the Israeli State provided strong competition for jobs and homes to the ordinary East Jordanian townsman. Since 1948 the major internal problem for Jordan has been to integrate East and West Jordanians, politically, socially, and economically.

This problem has been aggravated by the fact that the refugees, of whom there were 722,687 in Jordan in May 1967, look to the United Nations Relief and Works Agency for some part of their needs, and since Agency ration scales in the words of the Agency's report for 1965–6 'provide about two thirds of the normal food intake of a poor Middle Easterner' are yet obliged to press heavily on Jordan's economy. The social distortions both among refugees themselves and caused by their presence can be judged by the fact that about 130,000 children of refugees have to be kept on the waiting list for rations because the

Jordan Government has allowed no systematic certification of ration rolls since 1953 when disturbances in the camps led the Government to stop verification by the Agency.

Without a settlement of the problem of peace in the Middle East Jordan's social and economic problems seem doomed to remain chronic and acute. In their report on the economic development of Jordan an International Bank Mission which visited the country in 1955 wrote as follows: '. . . even with foreign aid, Jordan's resources cannot be developed to the point where they will provide a living even for all the present population and their children, much less for the future population as it will grow over the years.' Since that was written Israel has occupied the West Bank which provided more than a third of Jordan's revenue and the ranks of the refugees on the East Bank have been reinforced by about 200,000 destitute unfortunates.

Education

In common with most newly independent countries Jordan's educational facilities were rapidly expanded after the end of the Mandate. Arab education had been one major success of the British Mandate in Palestine and the influx of Palestinians after 1948 both stimulated and assisted education in Jordan. Legislation bringing all schools under Government control bore hardly on some foreign, mainly Christian, schools but on the whole education has both expanded and improved. In 1965 there were 1844 schools; 174 of these were maintained and staffed by UNRWA. In these schools 383,362 pupils (an increase of more than 60 per cent over the previous decade) were taught by 11,507 teachers. 66,649 of the pupils and 1,814 of the teachers worked in UNRWA schools. The University of Jordan was founded in 1962 and in 1965 had a staff of 48 of whom 22 held Ph.D. degrees. The advance of education may be illustrated by the fact that although, in 1965, only 3·7 per cent of the population had five or more years of secondary schooling and 70 per cent had no schooling at all, only 43·6 per cent of the 15–19 age group was totally unschooled as compared with 94 per cent of the over fifties.

Economic Development

The IBRD mission of 1955 had recommended a ten-year economic development plan, and the Jordan Government brought out a Five-Year Plan to run from 1962 to 1967. It was superseded in 1965 by a Seven-Year Plan (1963–70) which was designed to raise the Gross National Product by about 50 per cent to JD149 million, and to reduce dependence on foreign assistance to JD14·9 million annually. Public investment planned over the seven years was to be JD145 million and more than JD50 million of this was required in foreign exchange. The breakdown published in 1967 was as follows:

	Public sector	Private sector	Total	Percentage of total
		(JD millions)		
Agriculture & water	57·940	16·270	74·210	27
Tourism	2·785	9·700	12·495	5
Mining	7·589	22·645	30·234	11
Industry & power	5·832	10·984	16·816	6
Transport & communications	40·742	12·300	53·042	19
Education, health, & social welfare	6·693	3·860	10·553	4
Housing & construction	16·494	31·720	48·214	17
Trade & services		7·070	7·070	3
Other	7·571	14·650	22·221	8
TOTAL	145·656	129·199	274·885	100

Source: Central Bank of Jordan, *Quarterly Bulletin*, quoted in EIU, *Annua Supplement*, 1967.

The main agricultural projects which will absorb some JD30 million are the irrigation of the Jordan Valley and the Yarmuk dam. Schemes for these areas have been bedevilled by political factors. The first big project had to be abandoned because it included the use of Lake Tiberias, which is under the control of Israel, as a storage reservoir. Another scheme involving damming the Yarmuk absorbed considerable sums in preliminary planning costs before being killed by Israel's complaint that use by Jordan (in agreement with Syria) of the whole of the Yarmuk waters might prejudice agreement on a wider scheme for developing the Jordan system as a whole. An attempt to achieve such a wider agreement, sponsored by the US Government, foundered, perhaps predictably, in 1955 and Jordan had to fall back on a less ambitious project using part of the Yarmuk waters to irrigate the East Ghor or eastern half of the Jordan Valley. Excavation of the East Ghor canal began in 1958 and the first 14 miles were completed in 1963. A scheme for damming the Yarmuk, to be financed by the Arab League, was taken on in 1966 by a Russian group, but there have been difficulties over finance.

Currency and Banking

The Palestine pound was replaced in 1950 by the Jordan dinar which is at parity with sterling and is divided into 1,000 fils: the conversion was completed in 1951. Jordan is a member of the sterling area; the circulation of the dinar is controlled by the Central Bank which took over the functions of the former Currency Board in October 1964. Jordan is a member of the International Bank and of the IMF. There are several commercial banks, an Agricultural Bank, and a Development Bank which was launched in 1951 with backing from UNRWA.

Agriculture

The importance of agricultural development to Jordan's prospects of self-sufficiency is shown by her considerable import of agricultural products and foodstuffs. Wheat and flour normally figure prominently among the imports in the trade tables of the Annual Statistical Year Book. However, the possibilities for increasing production are not unlimited. Much of Jordan's land is desert and although only some 10 per cent is cultivated, the cultivable land available for expansion is small. There is more scope in improvement of the primitive agricultural methods which are generally employed, though such improvement would increase the numbers of unemployed in the towns. Agricultural workers are already under-employed and a recent UN socio-economic survey of the Wadi Ziqlab area estimated that the farm workers were idle for 150 days in the year. Main crops are cereals, other crops include fruit and vegetables. Production over the last few years is given below (p. 550).

An estimate of livestock population in 1964 gave 802,600 sheep, 650,000 goats, 65,000 cattle, and 19,200 camels.

Mining and Industry

A basic law of 1964 vested all mineral resources in the State, but Jordan has little wealth of this kind and the deposits of phosphates at Roseifa, north of Amman, provide the bulk of her mineral resources. Originally exploited by a private company, the Jordan Government reorganized production in 1952. By 1961 exports of phosphates amounted to over 40 per cent of all Jordan's exports. After stagnating, during the next two years exports of phosphates recovered after talks with Jordan's principal competitors, Morocco and Algeria. An Arab Potash Company was planned in 1958 but efforts to exploit the rich potash deposits of the Dead Sea have been less successful. A pilot plant was inaugurated in November 1959, but difficulties over finance have prevented further progress. In 1956–7 the participants were to have been Egypt, Saudi Arabia, and Iraq. By 1966 the scent had changed and financial talks were reported between the Jordan Government and Kuwait and United States groups.

Oil exploration was undertaken by IPC before 1948, by Phillips Petroleum until 1961, by John Mecom until 1966, but without success. Jordan's dependence on supplies of oil products from abroad, which necessitated an American air lift in 1958, has however since been relieved by the construction of a refinery at Zerqa which came on stream at the end of 1960, produced 250,000 tons of products in 1961 and saved an estimated JD1·2 million of foreign exchange. Crude oil is supplied under an agreement made with Tapline in 1958.

Electricity generation reached 156 million kwh. in 1965.

Industrial establishments in Jordan, mainly in the Amman and Nablus areas, increased from 1,035 in 1957 to 6,887 in 1961, but most of these were very small. They only employed 24,000 workers and JD6·3 million of capital. The most important enterprise is a cement factory established in 1951 with Government participation. It produced 341,000 tons in 1965. Other industries include food processing, clothing, soap, vehicle body building, matches, cigarettes, olive oil refining, and alcoholic drinks.

Communications

Since the establishment of Israel Jordanians could only reach the Mediterranean through Syria and Lebanon, a roundabout and expensive route which was, moreover, quite often interrupted by political disagreements between Jordan and Syria. Jordan's only direct access to the sea is through Aqaba on the Red Sea. In 1948 this was merely a fishing harbour without any modern communications linking it with the centres of population. The port had been successfully developed first with British financial help and later with a loan from West Germany. Special phosphate and oil handling facilities have been installed and the tonnage of cargo handled by the port increased from 147,000 in 1957 to 829,870 in 1964. Access to Aqaba is difficult and formerly goods had the choice between the rough and rocky Kerak road which crosses two deep and precipitous gorges and the Hejaz Railway to Maan and thence fifty miles by lorry over a rough track. An all-weather road alongside the railway to Maan was continued to Aqaba and completed in November 1960. A new Amman–Jerusalem road completed in 1958 on a new alignment south of the earlier road via Salt has cut the time of transit down to less than two hours. Another new road via Jerash has made the journey from Damascus more interesting to tourists than the trunk road via Mafraq which crosses mainly desert country in Jordan. From Mafraq an all-weather road runs eastward to the Iraqi frontier. Jordan's only railway is the section of the Turkish-built Hejaz Railway which traverses Jordan from north to south. The Deraa (in Syria)–Amman–Maan section was put back into use after the First World War and in 1954 the Governments of Jordan and Saudi Arabia agreed to rehabilitate the section south of Maan. However, apart from surveys, work on this section did not get under way until the end of 1963 and although by 1966 some 2,000 bridges had been repaired and about £1·5 million spent, little track had been laid. 26,000 telephones were in use and 269,000 radios licensed at the end of 1965.

Foreign Trade

Vegetables and phosphates are Jordan's only steady exports; olive oil occasionally figures after a good year and there is generally a small export of cigarettes. Jordan's exports go mainly to other Arab countries, but both India and Yugoslavia have bought Jordan phosphates. Imports come from the industrial West and from Japan. The USA replaced the UK as Jordan's principal supplier in 1963. Jordan's adverse trade balance has grown fairly steadily since 1948; it varied between JD35·7 million and JD53·3 million between 1961 and 1966.

Jordan's earnings from tourism were rising steeply in the years before the 1967 war but her balance remained dependent on massive grants from the Western powers.

Public Finance

Transjordan depended on small British grants-in-aid throughout the mandatory period, but in 1946 it was hoped that self-sufficiency would soon follow political independence. The Palestine War dissolved these hopes and Jordan's political independence has ever since been qualified by a growing financial dependence.

Money Supply
(JD millions, end of year)

	1962	1963	1964	1965	1966
Currency in circulation	19·04	20·39	23·02	26·36	30·33
Demand deposits	14·43	16·45	19·99	23·20	25·34
	33·47	36·85	43·01	49·56	58·67

Source: IMF Financial Statistics, quoted in EIU, Annual Supplement, 1967.

The main subsidy from the British Treasury for the Arab Legion grew from £1 million in 1937 to over £10 million in 1956–7. In addition from 1953 onwards the British Government provided budgetary aid of about £1 million annually and between 1949 and 1957 a total of about £7·5 million in interest-free loans for development.

The termination of the Anglo-Jordan Treaty in 1957 changed the main source of Western aid. In the ten years 1958–67 the United States Government provided Jordan with a total of $560·7 million in grants and loans. In January 1958 Britain agreed to make interest-free loans totalling £1·13 million which represented the balance of the 1956–7 loan and in the next ten years they provided Jordan with £16·678 million in grants and £6·23 million in loans.

Other contributors to Jordan's balance of payments have been West Germany, with loans for port and railway development, the United Nations, through IDA and the Special Fund and of course the UNRWA, and the Kuwait Arab Development Fund which supplied a loan of KD7·5 million in 1962. In 1964 Jordan approached other Arab countries in the hope of lessening her dependence on the Western countries but results were disappointing. It was not until after the 1967 war that substantial aid to Jordan was forthcoming from other more fortunate Arab countries. A first instalment of £7·3 million from Saudi

Arabia, Kuwait, and Libya then joined Western subventions in maintaining the rising trend in Jordan's reserves. More help will be needed to keep Jordan afloat if the Israelis continue to occupy the West Bank from which some 43 per cent of national income and 90 per cent of tourist revenue was derived.

The Economy since 1967

The 1967 war dealt a shattering blow to the Jordanian economy. Although economic viability had been a distant goal before 1967 and the country was destined to remain heavily dependent on foreign aid, *per capita* income increased steadily in the 1960s and there had been substantial development of the economic infrastructure, agricultural and mineral exports, light manufacturing industry, and tourism. The consequences of the war affected all these sectors with varying degrees of severity but its most serious long-term effect was to wreck the 1964–70 Seven-Year Plan in which so many hopes had been placed. Since Jordan was far from resigned to the permanent loss of East Jerusalem or to the occupied West Bank it lacked the incentive to devise a new revised plan for the rest of the country. After some measure of recovery in 1968 and 1969 the situation deteriorated again as a result of the civil war in September 1970.

Lacking a Mediterranean outlet, Jordan suffered severely from the closure of the Suez Canal. Before 1967 Aqaba had been developed, with strong government encouragement, as an alternative to Beirut. Facilities for handling phosphates and oil products had been established. As a result of the Canal closure, merchandise handled at Aqaba fell from 1,004,700 tons in 1967 to 743,500 tons in 1969 and 381,900 tons in 1970. Jordan had again become vulnerable to Syria's actions and it was severely inconvenienced by Syria's closure of the frontier in August 1971.

Tourism was the sector which suffered most drastically since all the country's main tourist sites, except Petra and Jerash, had been occupied by the Israelis. The number of visitors fell from 617,000 in 1966 to 301,000 in 1970. Western visitors were particularly affected by the 1970 disturbances and their numbers fell from 153,000 in 1966 to 2,000 in 1970. Tourist receipts fell from JD12·27 million in 1966 to JD2·40 million in 1970.

About 45 per cent of the country's vegetable acreage and about 25 per cent of its cereals acreage are on the occupied West Bank. Irrigation and other agricultural development schemes in the Jordan Valley were held up by sporadic fighting with Israel in 1968 and 1969 and the vital East Ghor Canal was twice put out of action by the Israelis. However, a high proportion of foreign technical and financial aid went to the agricultural sector and in 1971 plans were revived for the use of the Yarmouk and Azrak waters for irrigation.

Despite the closure of the Suez Canal phosphate production rose from 796,400 tons in 1966 to 1,090,000 tons in 1969 and contributed 35 per cent of the country's export earnings. But the Seven-Year Plan's production target of 2 million tons still seemed remote and the 1970 civil war caused production to decline to 939,000 tons. In 1971 exports were again held up by the closure of the Syrian border and Jordan was forced to seek new export outlets in Asia.

Manufacturing industry was the sector least severely hit by the war because, apart from a few factories in the Nablus area, it was mainly sited on the East Bank. From 1967 to 1970 Jordan's budgetary difficulties were considerably relieved by the provision of aid by Kuwait, Libya, and Saudi Arabia under the terms of the Khartoum summit agreement of August 1967. This aid amounted to about JD35 million a year. But Libya and Kuwait suspended their aid in 1970 following the fighting between government and guerrillas and Saudi Arabia alone continued providing about £16 million. Jordan appealed to the West and the United States, which had much reduced its aid following the 1967 War, made treasury grants totalling $40 million in 1971. Britain, West Germany, and the World Bank also provided loans. There was still an urgent need for austerity. It was estimated that GNP fell from JD229 million in 1969 to JD197 million in 1970 and the damage caused by the civil war and its aftermath was conservatively estimated at JD20 million. With exports at JD12·2 million and imports remaining high at JD65·8 million there was a record trade deficit of JD53·6 million in 1970. The external public debt which had stood at JD31 million before the Six Day War rose to JD47·4 million by the summer of 1971. The Government was compelled to introduce several measures to reduce Government expenditure. These included the politically significant decision to suspend payment of salaries to officials in the Israeli-occupied West Bank who were also receiving salaries from the occupying authorities.

VIII
Lebanon[1]

The Lebanese are of very mixed ancestry with a great variety of racial types especially on the coastal lowlands. The great majority are Arabic speaking; about 5 per cent speak Armenian and in some middle-class Christian families French is spoken equally with Arabic. Both French and English are widely spoken in official and commercial circles.

From the end of the nineteenth century there has been considerable emigration from Lebanon although the rate has declined from about 15,000 a year to 4,000 a year in recent years with increasing prosperity at home and reduced opportunities abroad. Between half a million and a million Lebanese live abroad in North and South America, Australia, and West Africa.

There has been no census since 1932 but a mid-1968 estimate gave a population of 2·58 million compared with 1·41 million in 1953. There are about 360,000 resident foreigners in Lebanon of whom 50 per cent are registered as Palestinians and 35 per cent as Syrians. Immigration by other Arabs—often political or economic refugees—has been considerable. No statistics are available for the number who have acquired Lebanese nationality but the authorities have made it increasingly difficult. The natural annual increase is estimated at 3 per cent.

The population of the largest towns (1964 estimate) is Beirut 330,000; Tripoli 182,000; Zahle 116,000; and Sidon 90,000.

Religious divisions are of greater political importance in Lebanon than any other Arab state. The largest single community is the Maronite Catholics with about 30 per cent of the population. Among the Christians there are also substantial communities of Greek Orthodox, Greek Catholics, Armenian Orthodox, Armenian Catholics, and Protestants. Among the Moslems there is a small majority of Sunnis over Shiis while about 6 per cent of the population are Druzes. There are about 7,000 Jews.

As a political compromise governments have refrained from holding a census since 1932. The 1932 census showed the Christians to be in a small majority of six to five over non-Christians and political positions were allocated accordingly. It is quite possible that the Christians have

[1] For geographical description and history, see pp. 457–63, where Syria and Lebanon are treated as a single entity.

now lost their majority owing to the higher birth rate among Moslems and the greater tendency for Christians to emigrate. However, there is no prospect of a census being held to establish the true position.

POST-INDEPENDENCE HISTORY

During 1944 the French Government gradually handed over its mandatory prerogatives to Lebanon to give the country control over customs, concessionary companies, press censorship, and public security until by 1945 Lebanon possessed almost all the powers of a sovereign government. The French retained only the locally recruited *troupes spéciales*, which remained attached to their own local command. However, the French Government had not abandoned the idea of replacing the lost mandate with a special treaty and on 17 May 1945 landed a contingent of Senegalese troops in Beirut to reinforce the French army in Syria and Lebanon. The Lebanese assumed that the French were planning to force a treaty on Lebanon which would limit the country's sovereignty. The strong public reaction reinforced by support from France's Allies obliged the French to give way. On 1 August 1945 the *troupes spéciales* were handed over to Lebanon and Colonel Fuad Chehab was appointed commanding officer of the new Lebanese Army.

The 1943 elections had resulted in an overwhelming victory for the Constitutional Bloc led by the Maronite Bishara al-Khoury and his principal Moslem allies led by Riyadh al-Sulh. The new Chamber of Deputies elected Bishara al-Khoury President of the Republic and he called upon al-Sulh to form a Government. As the joint authors of the National Pact al-Khoury and al-Sulh were regarded as the founders of Lebanon's independence in the form that it was finally achieved two years later.

As soon as the last French troops had left Lebanon President al-Khoury took the initiative in restoring good relations with the former mandatory power. Lebanon was one of the five signatory states of the Protocol of Alexandria of September 1944 which led to the foundation of the League of Arab States in March 1945. Lebanon was also a founder member of the United Nations.

The task of creating a viable political system was not easy for the Lebanese Republic with the heterogeneous and often conflicting elements among its people. President al-Khoury achieved it through the creation of a machine consisting of political 'bosses' who could control the country through traditional affiliations. For a time he was remarkably successful and it may be said that his methods prevented Lebanon's disintegration and ensured its survival as an independent state. But they also encouraged factionalism and corruption which subsequently became the hallmarks of Lebanese political life. The increasing authoritarianism which was needed to maintain himself in power produced a counter-reaction which ultimately led to his downfall.

From 1943 onwards there were numerous defections by regional political leaders from President Khoury's coalition. However, he was still able to ensure an overwhelming victory for his allies in the 1947 elections and had no difficulty in persuading Parliament to amend the constitution in order to vote him a second term of office in 1949. The worst defect of his system was that each of the political bosses on whom he relied had their own following or clients who expected to be rewarded with places in Government service or other favours. This not only did great damage to the efficiency of the country's administrative services but led to the violent clashes between the followers of rival leaders.

In the 1951 elections President Khoury still succeeded in having some 60 of his supporters elected among the 77 members of the Chamber of Deputies. But the regime was increasingly unpopular in the country as a whole. Economic recession had followed the end of the wartime boom, the customs union with Syria had collapsed, the Arab defeat in Palestine had brought additional problems (including the arrival of over 100,000 refugees) and the example of Colonel Husni Zaim's military coup in Syria, the first of its kind in the Arab world, had encouraged Antoun Saadeh's Syrian Social National Party to attempt its own uprising in Lebanon. The attempt failed and the SSNP was suppressed and Antoun Saadeh shot; but this only added to President Khoury's enemies.

In the 1951 elections opposition crystallized around a group in the Chouf area of Mount Lebanon led by the Druze socialist Kamal Jumblat, head of one of the principal Druze clans, and the Maronite Camille Chamoun.

Opposition to President Khoury did not run on sectarian lines. His mildly Arab nationalist foreign policy was satisfactory to most Lebanese Moslems and although all the key posts in the state, such as the command of the army and security services, were still reserved for Christians the proportion of Moslems and Druzes in the Government service was significantly increased. Finally as long as Riyadh al-Sulh headed the Government (he was Prime Minister continuously from 1943 to 1951 except for January 1945 to December 1946) the Moslem community as a whole could feel that their interests were strongly represented.

In the summer of 1951 Riyadh al-Sulh was assassinated in Jordan by SSNP members in revenge for Antoun Saadeh's execution. This gravely weakened President Khoury's position and in 1952 the Jumblat-Chamoun group spearheaded the movement which forced him to resign on 18 September, two years before the end of his term. Five days later the Chamber of Deputies elected Camille Chamoun.

President Chamoun 1952–8

Camille Chamoun was elected with high hopes that he would institute a reformist and progressive regime. If these hopes were not realized it was largely because the influence of external events aroused sectarian differences which had lain dormant under President Khoury. However, in the initial stages of his presidential term Chamoun's problems were chiefly domestic. He had come to power at the head of a loose and temporary coalition of traditional political leaders, who had been excluded from power by President Khoury, and middle-class reformers outside the establishment. Inevitably this coalition soon fell apart and many of its leading members such as Kamal Jumblat himself, turned against him. However, Chamoun showed considerable skill in consolidating his position and in undermining the power of the traditional leaders. This was first revealed in the parliamentary elections which Chamoun called for on his election and took place in 1953. Chamoun succeeded in dividing and weakening his opponents but he failed to form a cohesive party of his own.

Under Chamoun the liberal and laissez-faire economic policies inaugurated by President Khoury were maintained. These were undoubtedly suited to the mercantile characteristics of the Lebanese. Moreover there was no Government machine capable of administering socialist or *dirigiste* policies. The lack of State controls in Lebanon, in contrast to the increasingly centralized economies of most of its neighbours, attracted a flow of Arab and foreign capital to Beirut which was largely responsible for the country's marked prosperity in the 1950s. Similarly the freedom of the written and spoken word in Lebanon contrasted with the growing authoritarianism in most other independent Arab states. Beirut became the one Arab capital where all types of political ideas found expression and where Arab political exiles of various shades found refuge.

Nevertheless a Swiss type of neutrality was not possible for Lebanon; it could not insulate itself from the emotional currents sweeping the Arab world even if it had tried. This became apparent from 1954 when the Arab world began to polarize between a radical 'neutralist' camp led by Abdul Nasser and Egypt and a pro-Western camp led by Nuri Said's Iraq and the Baghdad Pact. Although Chamoun accepted the impracticality of Lebanon joining the Baghdad Pact he made no secret of his pro-Western inclination. Lebanese Moslems, on the other hand, who had felt the weakness of their position in Lebanon since the death of Riyadh Sulh were strongly attracted to Abdul Nasser as the rising star of Arab nationalism. In effect this meant the breakdown of the 'National Pact' and the division of Lebanese opinion between Arab nationalists (mostly, but not exclusively, Moslems) and Lebanese nationalists (mostly, but not exclusively, Christians).

The crisis sharpened suddenly with the nationalization of the Suez Canal Company and the subsequent Suez crisis which raised Abdul Nasser to a new peak of popularity. As an Arab state, Lebanon officially sympathized with Egypt but President Chamoun refused to break off diplomatic relations with Britain and France as Abdullah Yafi the Prime Minister and Saib Salam, the two leading Moslems in the Government were urging. Yafi and Salam resigned and Chamoun formed a new Government led by the veteran Sami al-Sulh and with Dr. Charles Malik as Foreign Minister. This amounted to a declaration of war against neutralist and Nasserist influences in Lebanon. Sami al-Sulh had little following among Lebanese Moslems and Dr. Malik, who had for many years been Ambassador to the US and delegate to the UN, was known as strongly pro-Western.

In 1957 Lebanon, against strong Moslem opposition, accepted the Eisenhower Doctrine which purported to guarantee Middle Eastern states against foreign (i.e. Communist) subversion. Chamoun's opponents, Christian and Moslem, formed a united opposition which fought the parliamentary elections as a National Front. In the elections Chamoun exerted all his influence to see that an overwhelming majority of his supporters were elected and Salam, Yafi, and Jumblat were all defeated. The National Front was convinced that Chamoun's intention was to use his majority in Parliament to amend the constitution to enable him to have a second consecutive term of office. With its leaders excluded from the Chamber the Front was forced into unconstitutional opposition. Bomb incidents became increasingly frequent in Beirut and Jumblat's Chouf area of Mount Lebanon. Chamounists were alarmed and Arab nationalists aroused by the declaration of the Syrian–Egyptian union in February 1958 which brought Nasserism to Lebanon's borders.

The assassination on 8 May 1958 of an opposition (Christian) newspaper editor was the signal for the National Front to begin an armed insurrection. There was serious fighting in Tripoli and virtually all the Moslem and Druze majority areas in the country, including the Basta quarter of Beirut, turned themselves into rebel strongholds receiving arms and support from Syria. General Chehab, the army commander, rejected Chamoun's orders to suppress the rebellion and confined the role of the Lebanese Army to holding the ring for the disputants and preventing the rebellion from spreading. Although a large majority of army officers were Christians the proportion of Moslems was higher among NCOs and privates and General Chehab was uncertain of the loyalty of his troops if the situation should deteriorate into open civil war.

The Lebanese Government accused the UAR before the UN Security Council of aiding and instigating the rebellion. The UN sent observers to report on the situation but the results were inconclusive.

The situation worsened even if open civil war was avoided; Beirut was under dusk-to-dawn curfew for five months. Elation of the opposition when Nuri Said was overthrown in an apparently pro-Egyptian coup on 14 July 1958 turned to anger when the US Government, fearing that all pro-Western forces in the Arab world might be swept away, answered President Chamoun's urgent request for help by landing 10,000 US Marines in Lebanon who were deployed in and near the capital.

If Chamoun and his supporters had expected the US to help him suppress the rebellion and ensure his second term of office they were disappointed. US Secretary of State Robert Murphy arrived in Beirut on 16 July as President Eisenhower's special representative and at once set about mediating between the two sides to reach the compromise that was essential if the Lebanese Republic was to survive. The consensus soon settled on General Chehab as Chamoun's successor. Although Chehab had only grudging support from many Christians and was bitterly accused of treachery by the more extreme Chamounists he was the only prominent Maronite who enjoyed some measure of confidence from all communities. He was elected President by Parliament on 31 July. However, Chamoun refused to step down until the last day of his term, 22 September, and the emergency continued.

The country came closest to civil war when President Chehab took office. When he appointed a Government with a majority of National Front sympathizers and led by Rashid Karami the leader of the insurrection in Tripoli, the Christians reacted with a general strike supported by armed action of the paramilitary Katayib party. When the situation deteriorated Chehab formed a new emergency four-man cabinet headed by Karami but including also the leader Pierre Jemayel. Under the slogan 'no victor, no vanquished' the Karami Government succeeded in restoring normality.

President Chehab 1958–64

With his shrewd and relatively objective understanding of the problem of governing Lebanon, President Chehab set about restoring the National Pact and adapting it to new circumstances following the state of near civil war. In foreign relations he restored the neutrality of Lebanon's attitude between the radical non-aligned and conservative pro-Western camps in the Arab world. In essence he revived President Khoury's policy, in a form suitable for the 1960s, by supporting Arab nationalist causes while safeguarding Lebanon's sovereignty and abstaining from projects for Arab political union. That President Nasser had welcomed his election gained him Arab nationalist support in the initial stages. Later the collapse of the Syrian–Egyptian union in 1961 and the general decline of Nasserism from its high peak in 1958–9 assisted his task in reducing the attraction to Lebanese Moslems of an external movement.

Domestically Chehab's first task was to restore and strengthen national unity. His first instinct was to attempt to destroy the sectarian factionalism which was at the basis of Lebanese political life but he soon realized that this would only leave a vacuum. Instead he chose to bypass the traditional system while allowing it free play.

In the 1960 elections for a parliament expanded from 77 to 99 members, almost all the political leaders with army following, Chamounist, anti-Chamounist, or neutral, were elected. But increasingly Chehab relied upon his own cadre of loyal technocrats to govern the country. Since he retained the loyal support of the army this opened him to the charge of ignoring the democratically elected parliament to govern through a concealed military dictatorship. But Chehabism gained the support of most progressive and moderate reformers in the country. Chehab reduced his official contacts with politicians to a minimum and moved his personal office to his private residence outside Beirut where for the first time in the history of the Lebanese Republic it was properly staffed by competent civil servants.

In December 1961 a coup d'état was attempted by the Syrian Social Nationalist Party. There was general relief even among anti-Chehabists that the attempt failed. The leaders of the party and scores of suspected sympathizers were arrested and put on trial.

Aware that the key to unity and stability in Lebanon was that the Moslem and Druze communities should feel that the country belonged as much to them as to the Christians, President Chehab took steps to see that more Moslems and Druzes were appointed to Government posts. The fifty-fifty principle for the allocation of posts between the two communities was applied even at the expense, in certain cases, of a decline in standards. The educational level of the Christian community is still higher although the gap has narrowed in recent years.

Chehab not only favoured the principle of greater equality of treatment for the different communities but also for the various regions of Lebanon. Lebanon's undeniable prosperity of the 1950s had been unevenly distributed, with the capital receiving the lion's share. Yet the majority of the population consisted of mountain peasants and under-employed villagers who drifted to the towns to find work. The public works policy of the Chehab regime was to devote attention to the previously neglected (and principally Moslem) areas outside Beirut and Mount Lebanon. The declared aim which was on its way to being achieved by 1964 was to bring roads, running water, and electricity to every Lebanese village. Although there was no serious question of abandoning Lebanon's basically laissez-faire principles the need to introduce some degree of planning was obvious. President Chehab

o

called upon a French organization, the Institut de Recherches et de Formation en vue de Développement (IRFED), to prepare a comprehensive report on Lebanon's social and economic conditions which was published during his last term of office.

Corruption and inefficiency in the administration and factionalism in political life were not eliminated during President Chehab's term of office. Six years were too short for such fundamental changes. But Chehab's achievements were considerable. Taking office in a supreme crisis he restored national unity and went far towards assisting all the communities to feel they had a stake in the country. He initiated a reforming trend which could be continued by his successor. If his actions earned him the enmity of some of Lebanon's leading politicians and if his strongly non-sectarian approach never attracted the sympathy of much of the Christian community, he clearly regarded the price as worth paying. He left office with dignity after refusing repeated efforts to allow an amendment of the constitution to enable him to serve a second term.

President Helou 1964–70

Parliamentary elections held in June 1964 had resulted in the re-election of almost all the former deputies although the two leading Maronite critics of Chehabism, ex-President Chamoun (who had formed his own National Liberal Party) and Raymond Eddé, leader of the National Bloc, were defeated. In August the new parliament met to elect Charles Helou, a lawyer and former Minister, to succeed President Chehab. As President-elect Helou attended the second Arab summit meeting in Alexandria in September to discuss Israeli plans to divert the Jordan waters. Lebanon's position was crucial because on the one hand it felt its defences were inadequate to hold a possible Israeli attack if the River Hasbani, a tributary of the Jordan, was diverted inside its territory while on the other it was not prepared to have other Arab forces stationed on its soil for additional protection. Most of the Arab states showed understanding of Lebanon's position.

President Helou pledged himself to continue President Chehab's reform policies but he lacked Chehab's power and authority. The attempt to bypass parliament by appointing a Government in July 1965 under Rashid Karami with all its members from outside the Chamber of Deputies aroused strong opposition from Lebanese political leaders and had to be abandoned a year later. However, the Karami Government did institute a sweeping reform of the civil service which involved the enforced retirement of a number of senior judges and diplomats.

In October 1966 the country's mercantile economy was seriously shaken by the failure of Intra, the country's biggest bank. Foreign investors' and depositors' confidence was affected and the dangers of the total lack of Government supervision of Lebanon's economic system became apparent. The Government undertook the reform of the banking system and set up a special body to guarantee small deposits.

Except for a brief air engagement Lebanon was not directly involved in the June 1967 war but the whole country was aroused and there was a serious danger of Christian/Moslem differences being sharpened as in 1956. Anti-British and anti-US feeling reached a high pitch, especially among the Moslems, and there was serious rioting and damage to Anglo-US property on 10 June. The British and US ambassadors were asked to leave but they returned in September.

The war and its outcome did further damage to business confidence. Tourism, construction, and other important sectors all suffered. But the most serious consequence of the war for Lebanon was the growth in political and military power of the Palestinian guerrilla organizations. Unlike Syria and Egypt, Lebanon lacked the means to control their activities. In Beirut they had virtually complete freedom to publicize their cause which had strong emotional support from many sectors of the Lebanese public. While most Lebanese had some sympathy with the Palestinian struggle opinion ranged from those such as the Maronite political leaders Camille Chamoun, Raymond Eddé, and Pierre Jemayel who believed that the Palestinians should not infringe Lebanon's sovereignty and that their guerrillas should be excluded from Lebanese territory to those such as the Socialist Party leader Kamal Jumblat who felt that it was Lebanon's duty to lend them all possible support. All Lebanese were sharply aware of the danger of Israeli reprisals and of Lebanon's relative defencelessness. Some believed that the occupation of the Litani River basin in South Lebanon was a major Zionist objective for which Palestinian guerrilla attacks from Lebanon would provide Israel with an excuse.

Fears of Moslem/Christian conflict were raised by the attempted assassination on 31 May 1968 of Camille Chamoun by a young Moslem; however, the Government succeeded in surmounting the trouble. In parliament the allies and partisans of ex-President Chamoun continued to be set against supporters of ex-President Chehab, with the Chamounists insisting on a greater share in the Government. The premier, Abdullah Yafi, resigned on this issue on 9 October and when he failed for a week to form a new Government President Helou himself resigned. His move succeeded in uniting all the deputies who requested him to withdraw his resignation. Yafi then formed an emergency Government of two Christians and two Moslems but three weeks later he again resigned on the ground that he was unable to handle the disturbances which arose out of demonstrations by Arab nationalists in favour of the Palestinian guerrillas and counter-demonstrations led by right-wing Lebanese nationalists. After two days Yafi agreed to withdraw his resignation at the President's request but the situation remained tense.

In May and June there were two major incidents on the southern border when the Israelis shelled Lebanese villages which Israel said had been harbouring Arab commando raiders. However, Lebanon managed fairly well to stay apart from the Arab–Israeli conflict until 28 December when an Israeli helicopter-borne commando raid on Beirut destroyed thirteen civil aircraft. The raid was a reprisal for an earlier attack on an Israeli air-liner at Athens by two Palestinians who, the Israelis said, had come from Beirut. Lebanon at once appealed to the UN Security Council and disclaimed responsibility for commando activities on its territory.

The raid was followed by violent demonstrations led by students demanding that Lebanon improve its defences and adopt a more anti-Israeli line. On 8 January 1969 Yafi's resignation was finally accepted and Rashid Karami headed the new Government.

The Maronite Christian leaders Pierre Jemayel and Raymond Eddé at once resigned because their ally in the right-wing Triple Alliance, Camille Chamoun, had not been invited to join the Government.

The issue of the Palestinian guerrilla presence in Lebanon had become of the utmost seriousness for the country, threatening to provoke civil war. In April, after a clash between the Lebanese Army and al-Saiqa, the commando group supported by the Syrian Baathists, there was serious rioting in Beirut and other towns. Karami resigned saying that he would not take office again until a common policy concerning the Palestinian problem had been worked out. This proved impossible. The Fatah guerrilla leader Yasir Arafat came to Beirut for talks which were inconclusive despite Egyptian mediation. But since no other Sunni leader had a better chance of success President Helou asked Karami to stay on as head of a caretaker Government.

As Israel continued to launch reprisal raids against guerrilla bases in Lebanon there were frequent clashes between the guerrillas and the Lebanese army in which the Palestinians suffered severe losses. In late October negotiations to end the dispute began in Cairo and on 2 November a ceasefire was arranged followed by an agreement between the Lebanese army and the Palestinian leadership whereby Lebanon endorsed the presence of guerrillas on its territory in return for a pledge by the guerrillas to co-operate with the Lebanese army. The Palestinians were also given the right to administer their own refugee camps in Lebanon.

Civil war had been arrested, at least temporarily, by the Cairo agreement and the authorities were encouraged by the fact that sectarian passions were less aroused than many had feared. But the agreement had by no means decided Lebanon's attitude to the Arab–Israeli conflict nor had it removed the danger of Israeli reprisals.

On 25 November Karami finally succeeded in forming a Government which included both the socialist Kamal Jumblat, a supporter of the guerrillas, and Pierre Jemayel, a leader of the right-wing Triple Alliance. Although Jemayel expressed misgivings about the Cairo Agreement he rejected his allies' attempts to put him away from the Government. At the same time Jumblat as a member of the Government tried to restrain the guerrillas and remove the potential causes of trouble between them and the Lebanese army and civilians. To some extent both the Palestinians and the Israelis helped to increase the solidarity of the Lebanese towards the threat they presented to the country's integrity. Some left-wing Lebanese groups who demand a revolutionary change in Lebanon's socio-political system supported the guerrillas for their own purposes. But the sense of loyalty to Lebanon was undoubtedly stronger among the Lebanese Moslem community as a whole than in 1958.

At the end of March 1970 there was renewed threat of civil war after clashes between Palestinian guerrillas and the right-wing Christian Katayib in which forty Palestinians died. The crisis was surmounted with the help of Salah Buwaisir, the Libyan Foreign Minister, and the Cairo Agreement was again affirmed by both sides. In June the Government served notice that the guerrillas would be banned from firing rockets across the frontier and from carrying arms in the cities. The ban had little effect, but its announcement coincided with a particularly heavy flow of refugees from the southern border areas which provoked a threat by Imam Moussa al-Sadr, leader of the predominantly Shii southern Moslems, to paralyse the country's vital services failing adequate defence measures. The Government then voted £L30 million to help an estimated 22,000 southerners driven from their homes by Israeli incursions. On 17 August the National Assembly elected (on the third ballot and by a majority of one) Sulaiman Franjieh, the Economics Minister, to succeed President Helou in September. The result caused some surprise as it had been widely expected that General Chehab would be re-elected or, when he refused to accept nomination, a 'Chehabist' candidate. The Chehabist camp was weakened by the last minute defection of Kamal Jumblat, Interior Minister and Progressive Socialist leader.

President Franjieh 1970–

President Franjieh was the dark horse candidate of the anti-Chehabist Centre Bloc in parliament. He came late to politics and his views on foreign policy were not clearly defined but the majority of his supporters expected him to assert Lebanese independence and national interests and to act more firmly than his predecessors towards the Palestine guerrillas. But he soon showed his own independence of mind and toughness of character (a well-known feature of the North Lebanese).

He chose the veteran Moslem politician Saib Salam to head the new Government and gave him his full support when, after ten days of vain attempts to satisfy all the factional interests inside parliament, Salam formed a cabinet entirely from outside it consisting mainly of young and highly educated 'technocrats'. The Lebanese public who had become increasingly exasperated by the sterile activities of the elected politicians, generally welcomed the new Government.

In foreign policy President Franjieh and the Salam Government were helped by several factors. The Jordanian civil war and its aftermath had left the Palestinian resistance organizations in a weakened condition. This meant they were less of a threat to Lebanon's internal stability although the Lebanese–Israeli frontier continued to be the only one on which the guerrillas were still active and Israeli reprisal raids against south Lebanon continued to occur. Palestinian opposition to the US peace initiative in the Middle East at the end of 1970 mattered less than the fact that President Nasser and then his successor President Sadat, had accepted it. Finally, the assumption of power by General Assad in Syria resulted in an immediate improvement in Syrian–Lebanese relations. A number of outstanding economic and administrative disputes were settled and in March 1971 President Franjieh made the first visit of a Lebanese Head of State to Damascus since independence.

GOVERNMENT AND ADMINISTRATION

The Lebanese Constitution dates from 1926 with amendments in 1943 and 1947. Lebanon is a Republic with a President who is Head of State and of the Executive. It has a single Chamber of Deputies and a Council of Ministers. The President is elected by a two-thirds majority of the Chamber for a period of six years and may not immediately be re-elected. He appoints the Prime Minister and the members of the Cabinet. All Lebanese adults are electors; women were given the vote in 1952.

The normal term of the Chamber is four years. It has 99 members (increased from 77 in 1960) and the proportion of six Christians to five non-Christians is maintained in parliamentary seats. By a very strong tradition the President of the Republic is a Maronite, the Prime Minister a Sunni Moslem, and the President of the Chamber of Deputies a Shii Moslem. All the other principal religious communities are normally represented in the Chamber and the Cabinet. The Foreign Minister is always a Christian, the Interior Minister is usually a Sunni, and the Defence Minister usually a Druze. Positions in the Government service are also allocated on a sectarian base.

Political organizations range from cliques or caucuses centred on one political family or regional leader (such as Raymond Eddé's National

Bloc or Camille Chamoun's National Liberal Party) to proper political parties such as the Katayib (Christian), Najjadeh (Muslim), or Tashnaq (Armenian) although these are narrowly based and sectarian in outlook. Other parties such as Baath Socialists, the Communists, the SSNP, and the Arab Nationalists are also active although until 1970 they were illegal because of their connections outside Lebanon.

SOCIAL SURVEY

As a result of the great expansion and development of Lebanon's mercantile economy since the Second World War, commercial interests have supplanted the former political power of the semi-feudal landed families. Beirut now has a large, expanding, and socially mobile middle class.

In the Druze community, however, feudal loyalties to a few leading families remain. Because there has been no agrarian reform and no socialistic legislation the distribution of wealth and property is highly uneven. There are many small proprietors in the mountain regions but in the plain of Tripoli and the Beqaa large estates take up most of the cultivated area. Over half the cultivated land is owned by 200 landlords.

General health and living standards have risen substantially over the past two decades but the rise has been uneven. Successive governments have done little to assist or protect the poorer sections of the community. Popular housing and welfare services have depended on private or religious organizations. Labour unions have been too small and fragmented to exert any general influence towards social reform although there were signs of change in 1970 when the Government agreed to introduce a comprehensive national health insurance scheme under pressure from the General Confederation of Labour. The IRFED report of 1960–1 estimated that half the population with family incomes of below $830 could be classified as 'destitute' or 'poor' and accounted for only 18 per cent of GNP.

Education

Although the state education system has been developed since independence, private institutions are still the mainstay of the system, especially at the secondary and university levels. In 1966–7 there were 365,403 pupils in primary schools, 96,482 in secondary schools and 1,482 in vocational schools. There were about 1,000 state schools and 1,200 private schools in the country. There are four universities with 23,475 students in 1966–7 including the American University of Beirut (with teaching in English), the Jesuit University of St. Joseph (with teaching in French), and the Lebanese University founded by the Government in 1953.

Educational standards are the highest of any Arab state and literacy is estimated at 88 per cent for those over fourteen years of age.

ECONOMIC SURVEY

Since independence the Lebanese economy has been remarkably prosperous. Lebanon has acted as a link between the rapidly developing countries of the Middle East and the Western world. The 1948 Arab–Israeli war and the consequent Arab boycott of Israel helped to make Beirut the principal entrepôt, traffic and banking centre of the area by eliminating Palestine as a competitor. Transit trade benefited further from the closure of the Suez Canal in 1967. Foreign companies doing business in the Middle East had almost invariably established their regional offices in Beirut while the investment of funds from other Arab states (including some political flight capital) has helped to create an extraordinary real estate boom. Tourism and the entertainment industry have flourished. However, an economy so heavily based on services is inevitably sensitive to political developments in the area. Business confidence was severely shaken by the 1958 crisis and the 1967 war and its aftermath but the Lebanese have shown a remarkable adaptability. National income is estimated to be growing at between 4 and 5 per cent per annum. *Per capita* income is second only to those of the oil shaikhdoms in the Arab world and was estimated at $500 in 1966.

In 1948, following the Arab–Israeli war, President Khoury's Government established a free foreign exchange and trade system which has since become synonymous with Lebanon in a Middle East where controlled economies are the general rule. In 1952 the exchange system became completely free and with a gold coverage of between 85 per cent and 95 per cent, the Lebanese pound acquired a reputation for stability. The liberal laissez-faire system and lack of controls helped to encourage foreign investment. Few Lebanese economists and fewer politicians question the basic assumption that Lebanon should maintain a predominantly private enterprise system. However in recent years the opinion has been gaining ground among the younger intelligentsia that complete laissez-faire is incompatible with the modern world and that the Government should play a bigger role in planning overall development and ensuring a fairer distribution of wealth. Also the growing importance of manufacturing industry (which has been the fastest growing sector of the economy since 1967) has enabled Lebanese industrialists to challenge the formerly dominant political influence of the merchants and obtain some forms of protection for Lebanese industry.

Currency

In January 1965 the Government adopted as the official rate of exchange the prevailing free market rate of £L3·08 = $1.

Agriculture

About one quarter of Lebanon is uninhabited mountain country; only 11 per cent of the land is cultivable and much of this is marginal. However there are some highly productive areas on the coastal plain and in the Beqaa Valley. Farming is much more intensive than in Syria and about 25 per cent of the 270,000 hectares that are cultivated are irrigated.

About half the working population is engaged in agriculture but this sector accounts for only 15·8 per cent of GNP (IRFED Report 1960–1). In 1967 total agricultural production was estimated at £L354 million of which £L194 million was in fruit production, £L67·5 million in vegetables, and £L31·5 million in cereals. The annual wheat crop (grown on about 60,000 hectares) varies between 50,000 and 70,000 tons, and about 200,000 tons has to be imported to cover local needs.

Fruit and vegetables are Lebanon's principal visible export. Production of citrus fruit, apples, and bananas doubled between 1948 and 1958 mainly through investment in terracing and irrigation. Citrus exports were 145,828 tons in 1968 and 137,220 tons in 1969. The most rapid expansion has been in apple production which reached 9·25 million cases in 1967 and 8·75 million cases in 1968 and exports of 136,780 tons. Owing to weather conditions 1969 was a bad year; apple production fell to 4 million cases and exports to 86,578 tons.

In 1966 there were estimated to be 442,000 goats, 105,000 cattle, and 220,000 sheep in Lebanon. Poultry production has developed rapidly in recent years to become much more important than other forms of livestock. In 1967 poultry production was estimated at £L103 million.

Mining, Fuel, and Power

No mineral deposits of importance have been discovered. A little iron ore is smelted at Beirut and salt is produced from sea water. Attempts to find oil have been abandoned. The IPC oil refinery at Tripoli has a capacity of 1·2 million tons following expansion by 0·75 million tons to provide high octane fuels. The Sidon (Zahrani) refinery is owned by Medreco (Mobil Oil 50 per cent, California Standard 25 per cent, and Texaco 25 per cent). It obtains crude oil from Tapline and has a capacity of 0·825 million tons. Lebanese refineries formerly supplied much of Syria's and Jordan's needs but those countries have now built their own refineries. In 1970 the Lebanese Government was considering the alternatives of the expansion of the two refineries or the building of a third refinery. Strong Saudi pressure was exerted in favour of the third refinery in which the Saudi firm Petromin would have a 40 per cent interest.

Total electricity has increased from 147 million kwh. in 1952 to 1,035 million kwh. in 1968 of which 763·3 million kwh. were hydro-electric and 272·1 million kwh. thermal. The Litani River scheme of which the first part was completed in 1965, will eventually increase capacity by 600 million kwh. per year.

Manufacturing industry

Lebanon is relatively highly industrialized compared with other Middle Eastern countries. In 1954 all new industrial concerns with a capital of more than £L1 million were exempt from income tax for six years. The principal industries are textiles, food-processing, cement, beverages, leather, soap, cigarettes, furniture, metal items, paper, cosmetics, pharmaceuticals, detergents, and paint. In 1966 a total of £L987 million was estimated to be invested in industry.

The industrial sector now accounts for 12–15 per cent of national income. Although agricultural production remains much the most important export item, exports of manufactured goods have been increasing rapidly in recent years (from £L87·4 million in 1967 to £L128·5 million in 1968 and £L166·2 million in 1969). The most important customers are Saudi Arabia, Iraq, Kuwait, and Libya for Lebanese furniture and metal goods.

Transport and Communications

Beirut Port with its free port area and lack of currency or other restrictions remains the principal entrepôt centre for the Middle East. Transit traffic declined from 574,000 tons in 1954 to 317,000 tons in 1965 as Syria increasingly imported directly through Latakia, and Jordan through Aqaba, but it recovered after the 1967 war and the closure of the Suez Canal to reach 642,750 tons in 1967 and 832,000 tons in 1968. Beirut handled a total of 2·7 million tons of cargo in 1969 compared with 2·57 million in 1968. The port company was nationalized in April 1960.

Expansion and improvements for the port (including the construction of a third basin and a new quay) had cost £L4·5 million by the end of 1969, and it can now handle 27 ships at one time. New silos built with the help of a Kuwaiti loan were due for completion in August 1970.

Railways consist only of a standard gauge line from Beirut to Tripoli and thence inland to Homs in Syria, a section of standard gauge in the Beqaa, and the narrow gauge Beirut–Damascus line across the mountains. Freight traffic totalled 23 million ton/miles in 1968 and passenger traffic 41 million passenger/miles. There are about 3,700 miles of road of which 1,080 miles are surfaced. The Beirut–Tabarja coastal highway is to be extended to Tripoli. At the end of 1967, there were 116,450 cars, 2,170 buses, and 12,800 lorries and vans registered in Lebanon.

Beirut International Airport is one of the most important airports in the world and carries a large international traffic (38,405 in 1968).

Middle East Airlines and Air Liban, the two main Lebanese air transport companies, merged in September 1967. The airport handled 1·51 million passengers in 1968 of whom 270,861 were in transit. Under an agreement with the Paris Airport Authority work began in October 1969 on the extension of the runways to meet the needs of supersonic aircraft. A new terminal building was completed in 1971. But the work of expansion is virtually continuous.

Foreign Trade

The direction of Lebanese trade tends to fluctuate according to the state of political relations with the other Arab states. Normally about 30–40 per cent of Lebanese exports go to Arab countries. About 20 per cent go to members of the Arab Common Market (Syria, Iraq, Egypt, Jordan, and Kuwait) and in 1970 Lebanon was considering joining the Market as an alternative to an Arab Economic Union in which the country's liberal economic system could hardly be accommodated.

The Lebanese have come to accept a large visible trade deficit as a permanent feature of the economy. Although there was little cause for alarm as gold and currency reserves continue to rise the Government is constantly seeking measures to reduce it. In 1969 total imports were £L1,993·3 million and exports £L558·2 million. In the same year imports from the EEC were £L569·7 million and Lebanese exports to the Community £L38·7 million. In 1970 Lebanon was attempting to negotiate a preferential trade agreement with the EEC. The Government was also pressing the USSR and other East European countries to increase their purchases of Lebanese goods.

As the policy of licensing for certain listed imports proved highly unpopular with Lebanese merchants and caused the prices of protected Lebanese products to rise steeply on the home market the Government was considering replacing it with a system of export subsidies.

Development and Planning

Development planning hardly existed in Lebanon until 1962. A £L800 million five-year plan was prepared in 1958 but was held up by the political crisis of that year.

A new five-year plan came into effect early in 1962, under the influence of President Chehab, providing for a total expenditure of £L450 million of which £L124 million was for roads, £L76 million for drinking water and £L72 million for electrification schemes. Some progress has been achieved although the Government is constantly held up by political crises, shortage of finance, and most recently by the need to increase defence expenditure to meet the Israeli threat to south Lebanon.

Improvements have been carried out to Beirut Port and Airport, new motorways and roads have been built, and there has been a considerable extension of drinking water and electricity supplies to rural villages. In the capital there have been major improvements in roads and municipal services as part of the 'Greater Beirut' scheme which has been assisted by a £L45 million Kuwaiti loan.

The Government's 'Green Plan' aims to bring 100,000 hectares of arid land under cultivation at a total cost of £L27 million but progress has been slow. Similarly the Litani River project is aimed to increase the irrigated area from 60,000 hectares to 85,000 hectares but so far only the hydro-electric part of the scheme is being implemented.

Until 1968 there were constant budget surpluses despite a steady increase in expenditure as revenues increased correspondingly. Indirect taxes and customs duties were the principal source of revenue; income tax provided only 12 per cent in 1968. In 1969, however, there was a budget deficit of £L67 million as the Government was faced with need for heavily increased defence expenditure as well as pressing demands for salary increases from schoolteachers and civil servants. Hopes that other Arab states would jointly contribute towards the improvement of Lebanon's defences were disappointed at the Rabat summit meeting in December 1969 although there was a possibility that Libya might help.

In 1969 the Government increased customs duties and a number of existing indirect taxes but any attempt to impose new taxes raised a storm of political opposition. For development purposes the Government relied heavily on loans from Kuwait and the issue of £L155 million in Government bonds.

Banking

Beirut remains the key banking centre for the Middle East despite the severe shock suffered by the system as the result of the Intra Bank crash in November 1966 and the 1967 Six Day War. The fact that numbered accounts are legal in Lebanon has helped to attract deposits from all parts of the Middle East and beyond. A new banking law in 1967 was designed to encourage the merger of weaker banks. Since then ten of the country's 85 registered banks have been taken over by the State but only two have merged. The State has also established a National Organization for the Insurance of Deposits up to a limit of £L30,000. The Intra Bank's affairs were taken over by a new company formed with 45 per cent Lebanese capital (Government and private), 35 per cent Kuwaiti, 7 per cent Qatari, and 13 per cent from the US Commodity Credit Corporation.

Recovery was sufficient for total deposits to reach £L3,381 million at the end of January 1970 compared with £L2,725 million at the end of 1967 and £L3,453 million at the end of September 1966 (i.e. before the Intra crash). However while demand deposits had increased, time and notice deposits had declined as political insecurity has given the public a marked liquidity preference. Also it is primarily the non-Lebanese banks that have gained from the partial return of confidence to the banking sector. An estimated two-thirds of total deposits are held outside Lebanon and even these resources which were invested locally in 1968 were attracted to European financial markets by high interest rates. In 1970 there were seventeen foreign banks operating in Lebanon and the Government placed a five-year ban on the opening of new branches of foreign banks in the country.

A Central Bank was created in April 1964 and took over responsibility for the fiduciary issue from the Banque de Syrie et du Liban. There is also a semi-State Agricultural, Industrial, and Real Estate Credit Bank (BCAIF).

IX
The Sudan

Stretching across North Africa between parallels 22 and 4 of north latitude from the Red Sea coast to the borders of the Central African Republic, the Sudan has been for many centuries a corridor between West Africa and Arabia, and at the same time a 'vestibule' of swamp and desert between negroid Central Africa and the Mediterranean civilization of Egypt. The country is an immense plain covering 967,500 square miles with drainage entirely through the Nile, bounded on the east by the Red Sea hills and the Eritrean and Ethiopian foothills, and on the south by Kenya, Uganda, and the Congo.

The Climate

The determining factor of the climate is the rainfall which gradually increases from north to south, dividing the country into three fairly distinct zones. The northern zone is mainly arid desert inhabited by camel-grazing nomads and by the sedentary owners of the narrow strip of cultivation and date-palms on the fringes of the Nile; the centre has clay plains, which extend just north of Khartoum and as far east as Kassala, with 'goz' country of undulating sand to the west of them. The centre is the most thickly populated and most highly developed part of the country, with irrigation schemes, extensive rain cultivation, gum forests, and grazing for cattle. Towards the south of the clay plains are found steep-sided hills of which the largest group is the Nuba mountains in Kordofan Province, and at the western boundary of this great plain there is the Jabal Marra range of mountains in Darfur Province, rising to nearly 10,000 feet above sea-level and forming the Nile–Chad watershed.

South of the 12th parallel heavy tropical rains occur and the country consists partly of vast treeless plains and partly of savannah forests; much of it is the *sudd* or swamp area of the Upper Nile Province. Still farther south tropical forests are found along the banks of rivers, and to the east of the Bahr al-Jabal is a series of massive mountain ranges with peaks rising to 10,000 feet; to the west in the Bahr al-Ghazal Province the country is an elevated plateau which forms the catchment area of that province.

The People

The Sudan's first population census was held in 1955–6. Provisional results put the total population at 10,109,619. In mid-1970 it was estimated at 15·5 million with an annual growth rate of 2·8 per cent a year. Over half the population is under twenty years of age. Average density is 4·8 to the square km. but about half the people live in 14 per cent of the country.

At the time of the 1955–6 census the capital Khartoum had 93,000 inhabitants but together with the adjoining towns of Omdurman and Khartoum North the conurbation had a population of 246,000 (over 350,000 mid-1966 estimate). Other main towns include al-Obeid (52,000), Wad Medani (48,000) Port Sudan (48,000), and Atbara (36,000).

There is a substantial resident population of West Africans in the Sudan. Many of them are staying temporarily in the country to earn money for the next stage of their journey to Mecca while others settle permanently. In 1971 the Government estimated that their number exceeded one million.

The division of the Sudan into two distinct areas—North (including centre and west) and the South—springs from differences in historical origins, geographical factors, and the character of the population. The North, corresponding more or less to the Ethiopia of the ancients and to medieval Nubia, is largely arabized and Moslem in religion, and thus culturally belongs to the Middle East. It contains the two chief towns: Khartoum the capital, and Omdurman. The South, first penetrated by Arab slave-raiders and occupied by the Turco-Egyptian Government after 1860, is inhabited by a variety of negroid pagan tribes who speak Sudanic languages and whose material culture and social organization are African. Three of the nine provinces, Equatoria, Bahr al-Ghazal, and Upper Nile, are entirely southern in character; one of the northern provinces, Kordofan, includes a large area inhabited by Nubas of southern type. It may be assumed that nearly three-quarters of the total population are Moslem northerners, mostly Arabic-speaking.

The Northern Sudan

The vast majority of the northern Sudanese are Arabic-speaking. Arab infiltration began soon after the Arab conquest of Egypt, but the mass migration of Arab tribes dates from the thirteenth and fourteenth centuries, and the process of arabization and islamization was completed about AD 1500, when the last remnant of independent Christian Nubia disappeared. But the Sudan Arabs differ from the other members of the Arab family owing to the presence of negroid and Hamitic substrata which have modified their physical character, and because the centuries-long separation from the rest of the Arab-Moslem world enforced by the desert has produced a distinctive national type. The spoken Arabic of the Sudanese also occupies an independent position among the Arabic dialects. But the northern Sudanese have maintained their essential Arab character in social organization and customs, and, in the sociological and political sense, they must be classed as Arabs.

The northernmost inhabitants of the Nile valley are Nubians, and have close affinities with the people of Upper Egypt, speaking Nubian languages of Hamitic origin. Apart from this narrow fertile river strip which crosses its centre from south to north, the dry steppe lands between the 15th and 13th parallels are the home of cattle-breeding nomadic tribesmen, with the Beja and Beni Amer in the east, the Shukriya and Lahawiyin of Kassala, and, west of the Nile, the Kababish, Dar Hamid, and Hamar of Kordofan. The first two speak Hamitic languages, but all follow a way of life and observe tribal customs still having a strong affinity with those of the bedouin of Arabia.

South of them, in regions where a higher rainfall provides suitable pasture and until the tsetse-fly areas are reached about the 10th parallel, there are nomadic and semi-nomadic cattle-owning Arab tribes whose territories extend across the Sudan in a vast strip from Ethiopia in the east to Chad in the west. Here and there, especially west of the Nile in Kordofan and Darfur, are substantial non-Arab communities generally in the more mountainous parts where they, the earlier inhabitants of the area, were driven by the invading Arabs. Of these the most numerous are the now flourishing cotton-growing Nuba tribes in the hills of south and east Kordofan, and the more backward Fur people of the Jabal Marra range in western Darfur.

The Southern Sudan

A few miles south of Juba the whole character of the Sudan changes from the Middle East to Africa, with the Dinka on the east bank and the Shilluk on the west. Farther south are more Dinka, and then Nuer. All these are designated Nilotes, but their languages and customs differ, and a century of contact with the Moslem and Western world has effected little change in their beliefs or mode of life. Their weath consists in their cattle, which are also the medium through which they maintain relations with the spirits of their ancestors. The largest group is the Dinka, who number over half a million and are divided into several independent tribes which are, in the main, culturally homogeneous. The Nuer also have a homogeneous culture, but, like the Dinka, they are split up into a number of independent tribes.

The Nilo-Hamites of Equatoria Province differ greatly from the Nilotes in languages and cultures. They are shorter in stature and are now more agricultural than pastoral. They were greatly reduced in numbers by the slave-raids of the nineteenth century.

The most important of the tribes inhabiting the Ironstone Plateau to the west of the Bahr al-Jabal are the Zande, who are also found in greater numbers in the Congo. They differ widely from the Nilotes and Nilo-Hamites in physical appearance, temperament, and culture, and, possessing no cattle, cultivate extensively and show themselves readily adaptable to settlement and economic development. Under the Zande Scheme, based at Nzara, they are learning to grow cotton, sugar, and oil-palms.

HISTORY AND POLITICS

The present-day Sudan, as a political entity, is a creation of the Turco-Egyptian period (1820–85). Knowledge of the early history of the Sudan is restricted to the northern part of the country (Biblical Kush and classical Ethiopia), where the remains of a distinct civilization, ante-dating Egyptian penetration, represent the presumed origins of later Meroitic culture. Powerful Egyptian frontier fortresses dating to about 2000 BC have been excavated somewhat to the south of the present frontier. After a withdrawal from about 1700 BC, probably caused by the Hyksos invasions of Egypt itself, the Egyptian presence was renewed under the New Kingdom (1580–1100 BC) and an Egyptian administration penetrated as far as Jabal Barkal (near modern Merowe), perhaps only for a short period, but leaving behind a strong cultural influence, especially in certain religious centres, on the temple architecture, and on the cult itself. In return the local dynasty (the best known rulers were Piankhy and Taharqa) invaded Egypt in the eighth century BC, where it established its rule for a time. In 23 BC the Prefect of Egypt, Publius Petronius, provoked by a raid on Upper Egypt by the Queen Candace, or Queen Mother, in the previous year, retaliated in force, but it is now thought less effectively than Roman claims at the time made out. Two principal (but so far as our present knowledge goes, not necessarily separate) areas of civilization are known, in the north (modern Merowe) associated with the name of Napata, and further south (modern Shendi area) associated with the Isle of Meroe. The history and even the full geographical extent of the kingdom are still obscure; the kingdom was at its zenith at about the beginning of the Christian era, but little is known about the causes of its decline. It is uncertain what the situation was at the time of the Axumite invasion (from modern Ethiopia) of the fourth century AD. During the reign of Justinian, in the sixth century AD, the conversion of the Sudan to Monophysite Christianity began, and the Christian kingdoms of al-Maris, extending north to Aswan (capital Faras, where a remarkable series of frescoes was discovered), al-Muqurra (capital Dongola), and Alwa (capital Soba) were the successors to Napata and Merowe. Al-Maris and al-Muqurra, united perhaps in the early seventh century, formed the Kingdom of Nubia; Alwa extended southwards in the direction of Sinnar. The Mameluke defeat of the Nubian Christian King Dawud in 1276 is only one among many episodes that mark the gradual process of the arabization of al-Muqurra and its conversion to Islam by conquest, infiltration, and inter-marriage, especially by nomadic tribes who themselves were moving south under Mameluke pressure. The conversion of Dongola Cathedral into a mosque by the first Moslem king of the old royal house in 1317 marks the end of Christianity as the religion of the state, though it is now known that the Christian hierarchy lingered on much later than was formerly supposed. The kingdom disintegrated under Arab rule, the essential defect of which, according to Ibn Khaldun, was that it 'denied the subordination of one man to another'. In Alwa the Christian hierarchy suffered from its increasing isolation, but Christian rule of a kind survived until Soba fell to the attack of the Arab tribes towards the end of the fifteenth century. The Arabs in their turn were defeated by the rising kingdom of the Funj (a people of uncertain origin) in 1504 and Funj rule from Sinnar dominated this central area of the Sudan until the Egyptian invasion in 1820. It was during this period that the real conversion of the Sudan to Islam took place under the influence of a series of Ulema and Sufi leaders who came from all parts of the Arab world, but particularly from Egypt and from the Hejaz. The later years of the Funj kingdom were described for European readers by the Scottish traveller, James Bruce.

The Turco-Egyptian Period[1]

During the later Middle Ages Egypt shared in the outside cultural influences on the Sudan and there was a regular trade. Two caravans, from Sinnar and from Darfur, annually brought ivory, gum, ostrich feathers, gold dust, and slaves to Asiut in Upper Egypt, and returned with manufactured goods. About 1810 most of this trade was diverted to Red Sea ports, and at about the same time the survivors of the Mamelukes established themselves in Dongola. Political and economic reasons combined to motivate the invasion of the Sudan by the armies of Mohammed Ali Pasha (later Viceroy) of Egypt; the search for mineral wealth and for slaves to conscript as soldiers were prominent among them. The first few years of Turco-Egyptian rule in the Nile Valley were unhappy; heavy and unaccustomed taxation stimulated revolt, which the murder of Ismail (son of the Viceroy) by Nimr, *mak* of the Jaliyin of Shendi, sparked off, and which was brutally suppressed. The capital of Sinnar was transferred from the eponymous site near the present city to Wad Medani, and again in 1824 to Khartoum, then an insignificant village. The long rule of Ali Khurshid from 1826 to 1838 saw the introduction of the whole machinery of modern government; in 1833 he became Governor of the united Sudan, joining

[1] R. Hill, *Egypt in the Sudan, 1820–1881* (Oxford, 1958).

Kordofan to Sinnar. It is to the fifty-five years of Egyptian rule, gradually extending east, west, and south, that the Sudan owes its present boundaries, the basic organization of its government, and even a tradition of administrative method which shows continuity through Mahdist and British rule into modern times.

The Mahdiya

In 1881 occurred a widespread revolt led by Mohammed Ahmad al-Mahdi, which ended in the capture of Khartoum in 1885. The causes of this revolt have been much debated. A common opinion is that the Turco-Egyptian regime deteriorated, inflicting on the Sudan misgovernment, financial oppression, and the slave trade, and that the proclamations of the Viceroy Said abolishing slavery remained a dead letter; and the reports of the explorer Sir Samuel Baker, who returned to the southern Sudan as Governor of Equatoria in 1870, and of his successor General Gordon, can be cited in support of this point of view. Egyptian opinion, on the other hand,[1] holds that the Mahdiya was caused by European (and specifically British) interference to suppress slavery and the slave trade; by the Khedive Ismail's injudicious appointment of European (particularly British) officials to implement this policy; and by the paralysis, through British action, of Egyptian attempts to retain hold of the Sudan after the British occupation of Egypt.

After the destruction of the Egyptian force under Hicks Pasha in November 1883 the British Government advised that the Sudan should be evacuated. The major problem was the withdrawal of the Egyptian garrisons and their families, and General Gordon was sent to advise on this. The failure of his mission, and his tragic death in Khartoum in January 1885, stirred the imagination of the British people and contributed to the revulsion from the Mahdiya which coloured contemporary accounts.[2] These works, also written or greatly modified by Wingate, created a body of emotional opinion and can best be characterized as war propaganda. The Mahdi died in June 1885, by which time most of the former Egyptian Sudan had come under the control of his agents. In his last months he founded the city of Omdurman, across the junction of the two Niles from Khartoum. He had sought to restore the pristine purity of Islam and to supersede the tangle of Sufi sects. Unfortunately the unity he had begun to create did not survive the test of time, and ended by dividing the Sudanese people into two opposing camps. The Sufi sects, deeply implanted in Sudanese history, would

[1] M. F. Shukry, *The Khedive Ismail and Slavery in the Sudan* (Cairo, 1938).
[2] F. R. Wingate, *Mahdism and the Egyptian Sudan* (London, 1891) and R. C. Slatin, *Fire and Sword in the Sudan* (London, 1896). Cf. P. M. Holt, 'The Source-materials of the Sudanese Mahdia' in *St. Antony's Papers*, 4 (London, 1958), and N. Daniel, 'The Sudanese Mahdiya' in *Islam Europe and Empire* (Edinburgh, 1966).

always resent the attempt of the Mahdist revolution to obliterate their contribution to the national consciousness. His successor, the Khalifa Abdullahi, developed the rudimentary fiscal and administrative system into an elaborate bureaucracy which owed much to the traditions and personnel of the Egyptian regime. The governorships were increasingly confined to the Khalifa's own kinsmen, the Ta'aisha, who with other western tribes were brought to Omdurman. This great population movement, following on the anarchy of the revolutionary war, contributed to a severe famine, while epidemics were frequent. A diminution of agriculture and a decline of population ensued, but there is no statistical basis for the traditional estimate of a fall from 8 to 2 millions. The riverain tribes, who had been influential under the Mahdi, were hostile to the Khalifa personally, though they gave indispensable co-operation to his administration. At first he attempted to realize the Mahdi's policy of the *jihad* against neighbouring states. The invasion of Egypt was tacitly abandoned after the Mahdist defeat at Tushki (Toski) in 1889, but frontier raiding was subsequently resumed. Intermittent warfare against Abyssinia culminated in the Mahdist victory of Gallabat in 1889: later, however, diplomatic relations were established between Abdullahi and Menelik. In 1886 and 1891 Abdullahi was threatened by armed risings of the riverain element, whose head was the Mahdi's relative, the Khalif Mohammed Sharif. These however failed, as did a widespread revolt in western Darfur in 1888–9. Other and less serious disturbances resulted essentially from Abdullahi's attempt to establish a strong personal monarchy over tribal communities scattered over a vast territory where communications were difficult. When the reconquest began in 1896 the Khalifa's rule was firmly established in most parts of the northern Sudan, but it was virtually ineffective in the South.

The rule of Abdullahi had done much to strengthen the unity of the Sudanese state, and not least by bringing to Omdurman at once the supporters he trusted and the opponents he feared, and so creating a capital city which was more than an administrative centre. On the other hand he had profoundly alienated the tribes of the North, whose influence was destined to grow, and to intensify the division between the friends and enemies of the Mahdiya.

The reconquest of the Sudan in 1898 by British and Egyptian forces under Sir Herbert Kitchener was welcomed enthusiastically by the British people. The motives underlying the campaign, which was undertaken as soon as the rehabilitation of Egyptian finances permitted, have not yet been elucidated with certainty. A widely accepted opinion is that the object was to avert a threat to Egypt which the policy of the Mahdi was believed to constitute; on the other hand it is held that the aim was, by extending Anglo-Egyptian influence southwards, to forestall any French attempt to establish a footing on the Upper Nile.

The expansion of European colonization in Africa during the rule of the Khalifa had brought Italy, France, and Belgium to the borders of the Sudan. The Italians in their new colony of Eritrea were threatened by the Ansar[1] and asked for British support. The French occupied parts of former Egyptian territory in the Bahr al-Ghazal, and an expedition under Major Marchand was sent to the White Nile in 1896 to extend French influence to that region, or, possibly, to provoke an incident which would enable France to reopen the question of the British occupation of Egypt. After negotiations between the British and French governments the Marchand expedition was withdrawn. The victory over the Ansar at Omdurman established Anglo-Egyptian authority in their place, but at first over a relatively small area. It spread slowly, and many years were to pass before it was firmly established in the Southern Sudan. Darfur was added to the Sudan by conquest in 1916.

The Anglo-Egyptian Convention and the Condominium

On 4 September 1898, two days after the battle of Omdurman, the British and Turkish flags were hoisted on the ruins of Gordon's palace in Khartoum; and on 19 January 1899 there was concluded the Anglo-Egyptian Convention; a working compromise which recognized that the reconquest had been effected by the joint financial and military efforts of Britain and Egypt. The Sudan became a condominium which its author, Lord Cromer, described as a 'hybrid form of government hitherto unknown to international law'. Supreme military and civil command were vested in a Governor-General appointed by the Khedive of Egypt on the recommendation of the British Government; the Governor-General was invested with full legislative powers; the two flags were to fly throughout the Sudan. Two very important provisions, adopted in the interests of the Sudanese, were that future Egyptian laws, and the privileges enjoyed by foreigners in Egypt under the Capitulations, should not apply to the Sudan. No foreign consuls were to be allowed to reside in the Sudan without the consent of the British Government. Thus the new regime in the Sudan made a start unfettered by the disabilities suffered by Egypt and other parts of the Ottoman Empire at the hands of their foreign creditors.

The New Administration

In the early years of the Sudan administration the senior posts were filled by recruitment in Britain and by the secondment of British and Egyptian officers from the Egyptian army; the great bulk of the

[1] This word, meaning 'helpers', was originally applied to the supporters of the Prophet Mohammed at Medina. The Mahdi ordered it to be used for his followers, who at first had been generally known as Dervishes. During the Condominium the word came to be applied to the followers of Sayyid Abd al-Rahman, the Mahdi's posthumous son.

medical, technical, and clerical staff came from Egypt and Syria. The original administration, as was natural in a newly-occupied area, was direct. The District Commissioner and his assistant, the *mamur*, were judges, policemen, tax-collectors, builders, road engineers, and sometimes doctors and veterinary surgeons of a rough-and-ready description. This system, efficient enough from the purely administrative point of view, contained no germ of future development and was little more than a military occupation.

Political Developments under the Condominium

These developments can be conveniently studied under three broad themes: (*a*) the political differences between the co-domini over the administration and the future of the Sudan; (*b*) the development and expression of Sudanese national feeling; and (*c*) the liquidation of the Condominium regime and transfer of power to the Sudanese.

Anglo-Egyptian Differences over the Sudan[1]

The Condominium Convention presupposed that Egypt would continue to acquiesce in British predominance and that the Sudanese should continue to accept a status about which they had not been consulted. So long, however, as Britain held authority in Egypt the Sudan Government could continue to administer the Sudan without outside interference. This was in fact the case until after the First World War, when there was intense Egyptian agitation against the British Protectorate which had been declared in 1914, and for the restoration of the Sudan to Egypt. Egyptian demands were partially met by the Declaration of 1922, which recognized Egypt as an independent sovereign state but included the status of the Sudan in a list of four reserved points.

For over twenty years Egypt shared in the administration of the Sudan, the garrisons throughout the country consisting of Egyptian troops and the great majority of the junior officials in charge of districts (*mamurs*) being officers seconded from the Egyptian army. In 1924, however, Egyptian officials and military units were withdrawn. For twelve years after 1924 all that remained for Egypt in the Sudan was in fact the Egyptian flag.

Lengthy negotiations followed, and it was only in 1936 that Egypt and Britain signed their 'treaty of friendship and alliance'. This provided for the continuance of the Sudan administration in accordance with the Condominium Agreement of 1899, specifying the welfare of the Sudanese as the primary aim of the two governments, and leaving the question of sovereignty over the Sudan open.

The Egyptian case for the indivisibility of the Nile valley was

[1] Mekki Abbas, *The Sudan Question* (London, 1952); J. S. R. Duncan, *The Sudan: a Record of Achievement* (Edinburgh and London, 1952).

continually restated and was submitted to the Security Council in 1947 without result, except that the Council unanimously recognized the right of the Sudanese people to self-determination. Subsequent negotiations in Cairo led only to the abrogation of the 1936 treaty and the 1899 agreement by the Government of Nahas Pasha in October 1951. Neither the British nor the Sudan Government recognized this unilateral action and the administration continued as before.

The revolutionary Egyptian Government of 1952 adopted a new attitude towards the Sudan which resulted in direct talks in Cairo between the leaders of Sudanese political parties and Egyptian representatives. Under an agreement reached in February 1953 Egypt recognized the right of the Sudanese to self-government and to the exercise of self-determination within three years.[1]

The Early Development of the National Movement

British negotiations with Egypt provide only a background to Sudanese opinion, but Egyptian attitudes naturally affected the growth of political opposition in the Sudan. The first twenty years of the Condominium saw the establishment of a stable system of administration and justice based on an exiguous Political Service. (There were never more than 150 officers in the Sudan at one time.) The Sudan's budget rose from £E140,000 in 1900 to only £E932,000 in 1920. The 1920s and 1930s were a period of formation of Sudanese opinion and of the search by the British for a secure basis of rule under changing conditions. The support of the Ansar during the war very greatly modified British hostility to Mahdism and in 1919 the delegation of notables travelling to Britain to congratulate King George V on his recent victory included Sayyid Abd al-Rahman, the Mahdist Imam. Meanwhile, Sudanese educated opinion had been developing faster than their rulers realized. The Sudanese Union Society was formed early in 1920. The founders came of good family; they were mostly Gordon College graduates and were active in literary as well as political discussion. Their movement was based on the cell system; they distributed leaflet attacks on British imperialism and published articles supporting the unity of the Nile Valley in Egypt, but not in the Sudan. In 1922 a junior subaltern of Dinka origin, 2nd Lt. Ali Abd al-Latif, endeavoured to publish a paper demanding greater opportunities for Sudanese, and was imprisoned. On his release in 1927 he joined forces with Ubaid Hajj al-Amin and others of the Sudan Union Society to form the White Flag League. It is uncertain how far the League defined its pro-Egyptian objectives, or whether Egypt was rather a source of inspiration and tactics. Certainly the movement was closely linked with the Wafdist movement in Egypt, and with the organization of trade unions by Ali Ahmad Salih. It appears that there was an alliance with a Communist organization, the

[1] See below, pp. 432–3.

importance of which 'rested on its being not an ideology but a method and a technique in political agitation'.[1] From this perhaps derives a certain revolutionary phraseology common to Communism and nationalism. In 1924 public demonstrations had some success, reaching a climax in an Egyptian mutiny in Atbara. The murder of Sir Lee Stack in Egypt was followed by Allenby's demand for the withdrawal of Egyptian troops and officials from the Sudan. The Sudanese troops mutinied in loyalty to the Egyptian King but the mutiny was suppressed with considerable loss of life and the Egyptian withdrawal was completed. The White Flag League, now defeated by an effective show of force, had achieved considerable success among the educated people in the towns, but little in the country; British Intelligence estimated a hard core of 150 members, mostly junior clerical staff, young Government officials, students, some merchants, artisans and teachers.[2]

British Reaction and Indirect Rule

Already in the summer of 1924 Sayyid Abd al-Rahman al-Mahdi had organized the 'loyal petition' of the older and wealthier Sudanese, which asserted their traditional right to govern, and the independent nationality of the Sudanese. Ostensibly an attack on the Egyptian influence, it also seemed to the British at that date a dangerous claim to 'ultimate independence'. Nevertheless, during the later 1920s Sayyid Abd al-Rahman was allowed to build up both wealth and authority, becoming a major landlord in the new cotton schemes and also in the capital itself, and receiving Government contracts and loans. His agents collected *zakat* (alms) from his tribal followers, although his personal movements were still restricted. He was a man of remarkable personality, with a gift for leadership and, to the sons of his father's supporters, an undeniable charisma.

The style of Sayyid Ali al-Mirghani, leader of the Khatmiyya, was different; he preferred to remain always in the background, and throughout his long life he would never commit himself to a political party or solution as closely or as publicly as the descendants of the Mahdi came to do. At this time both the Sayyids encouraged the now

[1] Jaafar Muhammad Ali Bakheit, *Communist Activities in the Middle East between 1919 and 1927* (Khartoum, 1968).
[2] For this and succeeding sections see Muddathir Abd al-Rahim, *Imperialism and Nationalism in the Sudan, A Study in Constitutional and Political Development 1899–1956* (Oxford, 1969), and Jaafar Muhammad Ali Bakheit, *British Administration and Sudanese Nationalism, 1919–1939* (Khartoum, n.d., 1966?), restricted circulation. These two works are most important, not only in themselves, but also in that they quote and reprint classified political and intelligence documents. Two accounts of modern Sudanese history by British authors are P. M. Holt, *A Modern History of the Sudan from the Funj Sultanate to the Present Day* (London, 1961, 2nd ed., 1967), and K. D. D. Henderson, *Sudan Republic* (London, 1965). Both authors have a close personal knowledge of the Sudan.

rather subdued educated class in a moderate nationalism which was often more a sentiment than a policy. The British, though suspicious of the older leaders, were much more so of the small group that they themselves had educated. In the Sudan Defence Force (which had replaced the Anglo-Egyptian army) the former class of graduate officers was thinned out, and in their place was created a class of non-commissioned officers whose interests were professional. The Defence Force was recruited from tribes not too closely affiliated to the religious leaders. Tribal leaders and tribal customs were seen as the great force of conservatism. The British admired 'feudalistic training' and suspected the 'effendia class' to which, *mutatis mutandis*, they themselves belonged. Lugardism became a conscious doctrine among many of the administrators; Sudanese nationalists could only 'hate and wait'.

Sir John Maffey (Governor-General 1926–33, later 1st Baron Rugby) explicitly wished to build up the tribal leaders as a shield between the 'agitator' and the Government, to 'sterilize and localize the political germs'. Sir Harold MacMichael, his Civil Secretary, was sympathetic to this in principle, but he was also reluctant to trust the tribal leaders, either too far or too soon. In practice little was done because of shortage of funds. Devolution of powers was confined to petty courts, culminating in the Native Courts Ordinance of 1932. Opportunities for higher education, despite the foundation of the Kitchener School of Medicine, were severely restricted. A strike at Gordon College in 1931 was ended by the influence of the graduates and by the personal intervention of Sayyid Abd al-Rahman, for fear that the College would be closed entirely. V. L. Griffiths, a distinguished educationist with long service in the Sudan, describes how the District Commissioners would object to 'educating the children out of their environment': 'You saw that we had cut the legs off the desks so that the children could sit on the floor as their fathers do?' British attitudes in this period reveal a genuine antipathy modified only by paternalism; MacMichael speaks of 'the young modernist' who 'sees himself in a dream as a brilliant leader of a progressive and enlightened community. . . . In reality he is a minor employee on modest pay born into a primitive social group which he despises'. Yet Maffey had only achieved a passing alliance with the tribal leaders, without strengthening their powers; he did not change the institutions of the country or impose more than a check on its political development.

The approach of Sir Stewart Symes (Governor-General 1933–40) was radically different. A soldier and administrator with long experience in the Middle East (including the Sudan) and East Africa, he reversed his predecessor's policy, building up revenue for a modest development programme, encouraging the expansion of education and the health service, and trying to make friends with the intellectuals. To him were due the beginnings of an Anglo-Sudanese political service, better opportunities for promotion of Sudanese in the police, the development of professional agricultural and veterinary services, and fuller utilization of Sudanese who were qualified in medicine and the law. Even so, the progress of the Sudanese in the administration, whether in the capital or the provinces, was not fast enough to satisfy educated people, and in the end Symes was a disappointment to them. He had lacked the money to implement his own policy, a policy which could only tend to the termination of British rule. He diminished the bitterness of anti-imperialism, and set a course which, however much the British might drag their feet, successfully avoided the violent clash which might otherwise have preceded independence; his modernization was effective administratively, but politically it was in advance of his day, looking inevitably to the ultimate transfer of power.

One element in his thinking was a fear of the resurgence of the influence of the sects; Sayyid Abd al-Rahman was almost ostentatiously powerful, and Sayyid Ali al-Mirghani was pressing for equality of treatment. Some British administrators were for playing them off against each other, but Symes preferred to try to isolate the intellectuals from sectarian influences. In fact Mahdist influence was strong in the early days of the Graduates Congress, and it was the qualified Mahdist support of the Government during the war which allayed British suspicions, while arousing those of the nationalists. His reforms met opposition from British administrators of the old school, and perhaps the most lasting benefit he conferred on the country was the creation of a new school of professional service, of which Dr. (now Sir Eric) Pridie in the medical service, and Mr. (now Sir Christopher) Cox, a Fellow of New College, in education, are examples, and it is significant that both these are frequently invited to revisit the Sudan today. Symes also set up the de la Warr Commission, which recommended the foundation of more schools, the raising of standards, the establishment of higher schools as the first step towards the foundation of a university, and the education of more Sudanese at universities overseas. The pattern of future development was thereby established.

Nationalist Pressure and Self-determination

From 1939 to 1955 the political intentions of the British rulers limped painfully after Sudanese opinion, which exerted a not immoderate but a continuous pressure. Government tolerated rather than encouraged the formation in 1938 of the Graduates General Congress by more than a thousand school graduates, already organized in graduate clubs and literary societies in different parts of the country. ('Graduate' in this terminology does not involve a university degree, though of course university graduates were not excluded.) British acceptance was the last product of the Symes policy of co-operating with the intelligentsia, and

in 1939 both sides were already disenchanted. The nationalist movement, perceiving insufficient advantage from British liberalism, turned
again to Egypt for alliance and support; the British were increasingly
preoccupied by the war effort; the Italians invaded the Sudan and held
Kassala, and the threat did not disappear until the battle of Keren in
1941, in which Sudanese troops played an important part; the Sudan
remained an important link in African communications as long as the
fighting in North Africa continued. The Congress leadership supported
the war effort at least until 1942, but in return expected to be treated as
representative of the nation, and Sir Douglas Newbold (Civil Secretary
1939–44) maintained his predecessor's refusal to regard the Congress in
that light. He was suspicious of the Committee of Sixty, containing
many younger men, who forced the resignation of the older moderates
of the Executive Committee of Fifteen in 1940, and he specifically
withdrew the official support that had previously been conceded. The
members of Congress, in view of the Government's attitude, could most
easily find nation-wide support through an alliance with one or other
of the major sects. From this period dates the definitive translation of
sectarian rivalry into national politics, but also an increasing gap
between educated and tribal groups, and between urban and rural
interests.

In April 1942, Newbold rejected a Memorandum, presented by
Congress, which demanded self-determination after the war, nationalization of the Gezira Cotton Scheme and full Sudanization of the civil
service; he did so on the now familiar ground that Congress was
unrepresentative. Realizing that it was necessary to create some organ
for maintaining touch with public opinion, Government now devised
an Advisory Council to represent such opinion as it was itself willing
to listen to. Congress was offered slight representation on the Council
but refused it; the Council had no real powers and represented the most
conservative opinion.

The Ansar co-operated with reservations within the framework of
the Council, and in 1945 formed the Umma party to express the secular
policies of the sect, independence from both Egyptian and British
influence, and a dominant position in the country. This group remained
more or less constant in Sudanese politics, at least until 1969, while
the parties opposed to it changed and re-formed in different patterns.
The Ashigga ('full brothers'), formed in 1943 under the leadership of
Ismail al-Azhari, at first represented the Khatmiyya sect (with which
it and its successor groupings maintained changeable relations) and
also all those interests which opposed a neo-Mahdist hegemony. The
term *Unionist* applied to this group and to related groups up to 1969;
in the 1940s the term related to the Union of the Nile Valley. The
Ashigga worked indefatigably to build up political support, allowing no
occasion to pass which might be used to help create a wide personal

network of alliances in the capital and larger towns, and employing in addition all the usual devices of party propaganda. Government intelligence was good, but it is doubtful how far the growth of hostile opinion was realized in a situation where intimate personal relations between rulers and ruled were almost non-existent.

The Sudan Administration Conference of 1946 (boycotted by Congress) led to the creation in 1948 of a Legislative Assembly. It compared favourably with the Advisory Council in that it was mostly elected, was more representative, and had more powers, but it continued to lag behind the accelerating public demand. Congress also boycotted the Assembly and the boycott was largely effective, but in consequence the Umma party naturally gained most of the seats. The leadership of the Assembly and of the new Executive Council was held by Abdalla Khalil, Secretary-General of the Umma party, and effectively advisory Prime Minister during the whole life of the Assembly. He was dependent on rural support of a rather poor quality; the Civil Secretary later admitted that only twelve out of sixty-five elected members were 'sufficiently educated and intelligent to take a real share in committee work'. The British preferred the Umma party because it was anti-Egyptian but the Mahdists themselves had little confidence that the British would not surrender to Egyptian demands, and from 1950 pressed hard for an end to the Condominium. The Ashigga and related Unionist groups preached the union of the Nile Valley, but this seems to have represented recognition of a common cause with Egypt against Britain, and of a common cultural inheritance, rather than any planned constitutional policy, or consideration of what union might actually involve. The progressives now called, not for 'independence', like the Umma, but for self-determination; they seem to have argued that it would be time enough when the principle had been achieved to decide what to do. The Unionist parties passed through a period of division and disruption; the National Unionist Party was formed finally in 1952; a National Front, related to the Khatmiyya sect as the Umma to the Ansar, was formed and then dissolved; it was replaced after independence by the People's Democratic Party.

By 1952 a Draft Self-Government Statute had been prepared and had been criticized by all shades of Sudanese opinion for reserving too many powers to the Governor-General, for setting no date for self-determination and for making no proposal for the transfer of sovereignty. The constitutional crisis, however, was overtaken by international events. In 1951 Egypt (arguing that Britain, in establishing the Legislative Assembly, had acted unilaterally and not as one of two co-domini) had declared Farouk King of Egypt and the Sudan, and so brought about a deadlock of which it was difficult to see an easy solution; but it was in fact quickly resolved by the new revolutionary Government which came to power in Egypt in July 1952. The new regime was capable of more flexible action than the old, and it could take advantage of Sudanese sympathy for the best in the Egyptian revolutionary tradition, and personally for General Mohammed Neguib. The Umma party, more than ever suspicious of the British authorities since the formation of a political party by tribal leaders (quaintly known as Socialist Republican), signed an agreement with the Egyptian Government in October, and in January 1953 an Agreement, known as the Agreement of the Parties, was signed between the Egyptian Government and all the Sudanese political parties. It specified immediate full self-government, self-determination within three years, and elections to be held under an international commission. In addition it settled a number of outstanding questions. It was now Britain that had no room to manoeuvre, and an Anglo-Egyptian Agreement in February, incorporating the points included in the January Agreement of the Parties, was given effect in a Self-Government Statute of 31 March.

A general election, the first in the country's history in which all parties took part, was held in the same year, under international supervision. The result was an overwhelming victory for the National Unionist Party, which won 51 seats. If, as was generally believed, some British officials had hoped for the success of the Socialist Republicans, who gained three seats, they were disappointed, and the party disappeared. Although the Mahdists amount to about half the nation, the Umma party gained only 22 seats, and Ismail al-Azhari became the first Prime Minister of the Sudan, with a clear mandate. It was incontrovertibly demonstrated that he had correctly interpreted the wishes of the country, at least so far as the end of the colonial regime was concerned.

In two years of Unionist rule before independence, Sudanese opinion also turned decisively away from union with Egypt. The Governor-General and his staff dealt honestly and constitutionally with the new Government, and earned the confidence of men who after so many years of frustrated opposition had come to expect hostility. The programme of Sudanization proceeded quickly and efficiently, and a scheme of generous compensation hastened or facilitated both forced and voluntary retirements of British officials. It was now clear to all that the British were handing over power. Meanwhile, in a serious riot in March 1954, the Ansar demonstrated the strength of the threat underlying their objection to a formal link with Egypt; Sayyid Abd al-Rahman, moreover, went out of his way to renounce any monarchical ambition. Sudanese opinion, finally, tended to disapprove of a number of developments in Egypt itself. For all these reasons it became clear that self-determination would after all mean independence.

The work of Sudanization was complete by August 1955, and (apart from the British and Egyptian military, whose evacuation, demanded in

August, was effected by November) only Britons in the professions, including a large group of teachers, remained. It was proposed to hold a plebiscite on the question of independence, and on 3 December Britain and Egypt reached agreement about its conditions. On the same day the two Sayyids announced a common programme of general aims; a joint announcement was quite unprecedented. On 19 December, parliament, correctly interpreting the country's wishes and its impatience with complex voting procedures, declared the country independent from 1 January immediately following, without plebiscite. Sovereignty was vested in a Commission of Five, and a transitional constitution was completed and approved only on 31 December. The Governor-General, who had spent Christmas in Britain, never returned, and the Prime Minister was able to read to parliament the British and Egyptian ratifications of the unilateral Sudanese decision, and formally to declare the Sudan independent, on 1 January 1956.[1]

The First Parliamentary Regime

Economic and foreign policy and the constitutional issue were the main topics of political interest in the years 1956–8. Not only did the country need development; successive governments also needed to show that they had promoted it, despite their unsuccessful financial control. The beginning of the Manaqil extension of the Gezira scheme and the extension of the railway to Darfur were planning achievements of the period. A Foreign Ministry and diplomatic service were created, and the general lines of foreign policy, from which the Sudan has not yet seriously deviated, were given expression: neutralism, Arabism, and Africanism, all dictated by the country's geographical position. The maintenance of efficient government was in part the achievement of an able body of civil servants. Little progress was made towards agreement on a permanent constitution. The Unionists wanted an executive presidency, the Umma a Head of State with formal powers and elected by

[1] In addition to the works of Abd al-Rahim, Holt, and Henderson already cited, part of this period is covered by K. D. D. Henderson's *The Making of the Modern Sudan* (London, 1953), which includes the period of Newbold's Secretaryship (as well as his earlier career) and quotes extensively from his papers and other documents. Two contemporary studies of the later Condominium are Mekki Abbas, *The Sudan Question* (London, 1952), and J. S. R. Duncan, *The Sudan; A Record of Achievement* (Edinburgh and London, 1952); H. MacMichael's *The Sudan* (London, 1954), came out just twenty years after his earlier book, *The Anglo-Egyptian Sudan* (London, 1934), but an interesting contrast as to contents. Another British view of the handover of power is cogently put in J. S. R. Duncan's *The Sudan's Path to Independence* (London, 1957), though this is a view not altogether acceptable to modern Sudanese scholars. A Sudanese view of the country's development written shortly after independence is Mekki Shibeika's *The Independent Sudan* (New York, 1959). For a reflection of social conditions in the Northern Province in the first decade of independence, see Tayeb Salih, *The Wedding of Zein* and *Season of Migration* (trans. Johnson-Davies, London, 1969).

parliament; and those who were not Mahdists wanted a non-Mahdist Head of State.

During the period preceding independence, Azhari had quarrelled with and dismissed the most distinguished of his colleagues. Independence was not generally seen to be his personal achievement, and his Government carried the responsibility for the serious mutiny of Southern troops in August 1955, and was under pressure from Southern politicians to establish the federal State they believed they had been promised. Once independence, on which alone all were agreed, had been achieved, a number of dissensions were brought out of cold store. In February was formed a coalition which included the dismissed ministers, notably Mirghani Hamza and Mohammed Nur al-Din, and Umma party men, Abdalla Khalil and Ibrahim Ahmad (a former Congress leader). Mirghani Hamza was a founder of the new People's Democratic Party, which had just been founded explicitly to represent the Khatmiyya interest. In July, Abdalla Khalil was elected Prime Minister and a new coalition was formed, within the existing parliament which excluded Azhari from office; he now led the loyal NUP in opposition. This Government was considered to be the fruit of the agreement between the Sayyids, but the differences between the sects and the parties were unresolved, not only in respect of the Presidency, but also within the agreed foreign policy. The neutralism of the PDP leant towards Egypt, and that of the Umma party was biased to the West. However, the coalition was returned to power in a general election held early in 1958 on a revised electorate. The Umma (with 63 seats) and the PDP (26) had a majority that was a little less than safe; the NUP won 44 seats and the Southern Federal Party won 40. The Government was weakened by the causes of dissension outlined above, and a poor cotton crop brought financial weakness to crisis proportions. The NUP vote was significant in representing the loyalty of the progressive and urban vote to a secular policy based upon neither sect.

In July an American Aid Agreement was ratified only after difficulty, and parliament was adjourned till November. The autumn was a period of conflicting rumour in which the sense of instability increased. Sayyid Abd al-Rahman was mortally ill, his son al-Siddiq left the Sudan for Europe, the PDP Ministers went to Cairo; the Umma and the NUP were negotiating to form a new coalition. An agreement between them was announced on 16 November, but on the following morning the army was found to have seized power, and ministers were under house arrest. The Umma party was divided; the Prime Minister, Abdalla Khalil, was convinced that an Egyptian takeover was imminent, and he was generally believed to have been privy to the army coup; on the other hand, Sayyid al-Siddiq, who succeeded his father as Imam in 1959, always remained hostile to the new regime. The PDP and the Khatmiyya for a considerable period supported it.

The First Military Regime

The Commander-in-Chief, Major-General Ibrahim Abbud, now held power delegated to him by a Supreme Council of the Armed Forces; he was constitutionally President of the Council, not of the Republic, and also Prime Minister and Minister of Defence. A somewhat neutral and even gentle figure, he never seemed to dominate either the country or his own regime. This was not altogether a true impression; he worked closely with the Chief Justice, Mohammed Mustafa Abu Ranat, an internationally distinguished lawyer. Civilian ministers, notably Ahmad Khair (Foreign Minister) preserved a link with the revolutionary politics of the Condominium past. Among the officers, a struggle for power ended with the retirement of Maj.-Gen. Ahmad Abd al-Wahhab and the imprisonment of Brigadiers Muhyi al-Din Ahmad Abdalla and Abd al-Rahim Shannan in September 1959. The two most influential officers for the remaining duration of the regime were Generals Hassan Bashir Nasr and Mohammed Talat Farid.

The new regime concentrated on a restoration of the country's finances by orthodox measures which at least at first were successful. In many ways the greatest success of the regime (though one that brought many difficulties with it) was the Nile Waters Agreement with Egypt which the parliamentary regime had failed to negotiate and which had been increasingly urgent ever since the decision to erect the High Dam at Aswan. The new Government also left the matter in suspense for nearly a year but then came quickly to an agreement in Cairo in November 1959. The Sudan increased its share of the waters to 18,500,000 cubic metres, a quantity in excess of its immediate requirements, even taking into account the major irrigation works which could now be undertaken at Khashm al-Qirba and al-Rusayris. Egypt paid £E15 m. compensation to the inhabitants of Wadi Halfa, who were to be flooded. They were to be resettled at 'New Halfa' at Khashm al-Qirba; the amount of the compensation was far too little for the cost of resettlement. The irrigated Nubian strip can support only a limited population, and Nubians have a long emigrant tradition; the exiles hold influential offices and are united in a close bond of loyalty. Their relatives at home objected to a compulsory emigration of the whole people to a new and different climate; and their criticisms and hostility were given maximum publicity by Halfawis everywhere. Nevertheless, an intractable and inescapable problem had been solved, however imperfectly.

The regime lasted six years, in the course of which a number of its activities were acceptable to most shades of opinion, notably the exercise of a genuinely neutralist foreign policy (including the acceptance of aid from the USA and from the USSR and other countries in Eastern Europe, and a particularly friendly relationship with Yugoslavia), and a rapid expansion of the school system, especially while Talat Farid was Minister of Education (1962–4). The ten-year development plan was a careful and reasonable scheme for the period 1960–71.[1] It has been criticized chiefly for neglecting communications in a country of immense distances and often impassable roads. An expensive proposal to re-open the port of Suakin came to nothing, and the railway bottle-neck through which all goods must pass on their way to or from Port Sudan remained untouched.

There seemed to be little serious opposition to the regime at first. The Communist party, already illegal, was suppressed with greater severity than is usual in the Sudan. A protest by twelve leading politicians against the use of torture resulted in their internment in Juba (Equatoria Province), but after some seven months they were released. On the whole, the Government was only gently repressive, making the public aware of surveillance without making itself feared. A number of senior civil servants went voluntarily into private life rather than work for ministers they did not respect, but remained amicably linked with their colleagues who stayed in service. People of this high calibre and academics of the University of Khartoum were accustomed to voice their criticisms of the Government in public and with impunity. Teachers in the schools were largely left-wing in sympathy, and were very critical; the Gezira tenants were prosperous, but illustrated Tocqueville's thesis that revolutionary discontent flourishes most among those who wish to prosper faster. The university students in particular, divided more or less equally between the Communist party (and its sympathizers) and the Moslem Brothers, realized that they were less encumbered by personal and family obligations than any of their compatriots, and so felt it their duty to express the political opposition with particular force. A public protest made in doubtful taste before foreign visiting Vice-Chancellors from African universities at the graduation ceremony of 1963 resulted in the extension of the powers of the Minister of Education to control the university, hitherto independent. These powers were remote and ineffective, and the result was to make the Government more, rather than less, vulnerable to student attack, as would become clear a year later. In the meantime a form of 'pyramidal democracy' had been introduced, with local councils elected on a wide suffrage and a Central Council (or legislature) partly nominated and partly elected indirectly by Provincial Councils. This did nothing to meet the criticism; but before we can consider the revolution of 1964 it is necessary to review the Southern problem.

[1] See Abdel Rahim Mirghani, *The Sudan Ten Year Plan of Economic and Social Development 1960/1–1970/1* (Khartoum, n.d., lecture delivered 1962).

P

The Southern Sudan to 1964

It is convenient to deal separately with the earlier history of the Southern Sudan, although it is intricately and inextricably tied to the
history of the North.[1] The Anglo-Egyptian reconquest of the Sudan in
1898 had the strong support of the churches; the missionary bodies
most actively interested were the Church Missionary Society, which
had founded a Gordon Memorial Mission, and the Verona Fathers,
successors to Bishop Comboni, who hoped to resume their interrupted
Khartoum mission. The churches do not seem to have expected the ban
on proselytization in the North which both Kitchener and Wingate
imposed, and the Anglican Bishop Gwynne continued to hope that
'aggressive religious teaching' would be allowed. It was natural that
the Government should wish to divert Christian interest to the largely
pagan South, where, at that date, it still seemed to Gwynne that Islam
had 'overwhelming advantages'. As late as 1910 Wingate doubted the
wisdom of replacing Arabic by English as the Southern lingua franca,
or transferring the weekly holiday to Sunday in the area. The missionaries continued throughout their history to fear Islamic advance; the
Government, though the attitude of officials to the Missions varied,
tended to be unenthusiastic about conversion, even when it turned
decisively against Arab influence in the South. In any case, the
Southern provinces were divided between the missionary societies, of
which the two principal ones were the two already mentioned; the use
of English and the Sunday holiday were conceded; and their position
was strengthened by the failure to introduce a Government school
system; indeed, the Christian schools were given grants in aid from
1927 onwards. This has been a chief source of criticism by both Northern and Southern Sudanese; the former object that baptism was made
the price of education, and the latter that the ultimate consequence of
the policy was an educational system very much inferior to that which
obtained in the North. Many British administrators criticized the
quality of education provided.

A policy of excluding Arabs from the North, their trade as well as
their language and religion, began with the Passports and Permits

[1] A well-balanced case is put by a Northern Sudanese scholar who was Secretary-
General to the Round-Table Conference of 1965, Mohamed Omer Beshir, in his *The
Southern Sudan, Background to Conflict* (London, 1968), who also prints a number of useful
documents. See also Abd al-Rahim, op. cit. A more partisan presentation is *The Sudan
—Crossroads of Africa*, by Beshir Mohammed Said (London, 1965), but this also prints
interesting source material. The case as it stood at an earlier date is given by Mekki
Abbas, op. cit. The best presentation by a British author is Henderson's, op. cit.,
chapter 10; he also prints a number of documents. A Southern case was published in
Joseph Oduha's and William Deng's *The Problem of the Southern Sudan* (London, 1963),
but this is political rather than scholarly in intention and does not altogether do itself
justice.

Ordinance of 1922, and the rather scattered threads of policy were gathered together in 1930 by the Civil Secretary (Sir Harold Mac-Michael) and defined as being 'to build up self-contained racial or tribal units'; measures already adopted or to be adopted were: (*a*) provision of non-Arabic speaking administrators and clerical and technical staff; (*b*) control of immigrant traders from the North; (*c*) necessity for British staff to be familiar with 'the beliefs and customs and languages of the tribes'; (*d*) 'use of English where communication in the local vernacular was impossible'. This policy, which may be associated with the policy of indirect rule in the North, was effectively implemented in some respects only. Arab traders and Moslems generally, including non-Arabs of Nigerian origin, were prevented from entering, or were discouraged or expelled, and Greek and Syrian traders were encouraged to enter the region; the traditional areas of communication between Arab and Southern tribes in the West were closed, and a pass system prevented circulation in either direction. Other aims of the policy were not realized. Missionary funds were inadequate to improve the educational system, but in so far as it was successful, it necessarily militated against the intention of restoring a strong and traditional tribal pattern. The ultimate tendency of policy seemed to be to integrate the Southern provinces into East Africa, but, though this was often discussed, nothing was done to put it into effect.

Acknowledging the fact that it was 'the Sudanese, northern and southern, who will live . . . in this country', the Civil Secretary (Sir James Robertson) in 1946 reversed the previous policy. He rejected the idea of joining all or part of the Southern Sudan to East Africa as impracticable, and accepted the necessity of trade with the North, the need for Southerners to get a higher education in Khartoum, and the justice of abolishing the anomalous differences in rates of pay; he saw that an end to the isolation of the South was inevitable. It was at last recognized that, though the Southerners were a distinct people, 'geography and economics combine . . . to render them inextricably bound for future development to . . . the arabicized Northern Sudan'. He also realized that they must be 'equipped to stand up for themselves in the future as socially and economically the equals of their partners' in the North.[1]

The complaint of Southerners is that not nearly enough was done to equip them to deal as equal partners; to the Northern objection that the South was isolated they add that they feel that it was at the same time retarded. The Juba Conference on the Political Development of the Southern Sudan, held in 1947, included a number of Southern administrators and tribal leaders, very senior British officials, and some distinguished Northerners. The Conference agreed that there should be a unitary State; both Southerners and British expressed a belief in a

[1] Beshir, loc. cit.

need for some safeguards, but this had no practical result. Southerners have always regarded this Conference as unrepresentative, and in no way binding on them. As independence approached there was an increasing lack of confidence in the South; the Sudanization programme gave them far fewer posts than they had hoped for, and there was a series of conflicts and misunderstandings with some Northern administrators. On 18 August the Southern Corps at Torit mutinied, shot their officers, and massacred Northern civilians. During the rest of the month the 'disturbances' spread across Equatoria, affecting primarily the non-Nilotic peoples. Order was restored by the army during the first week of September; there were some conciliatory measures, some mutineers were executed and many were taken to prisons in the North; the Torit garrison, which had apparently for a time believed it would receive British support, retired into the bush, and formed the nucleus of a guerrilla force which was to continue its struggle with the North for sixteen years. The mutiny had a traumatic effect on both Northerners and Southerners. The problem of independence was an immediate one; no Southerner had taken part in the Cairo Agreement of the Parties, and the Southern members of parliament agreed to independence on condition that a federal constitution would be granted. The Southern case has been based in part upon this in later controversy.

In 1954 an International Commission on Secondary Education had recommended the re-adoption of Arabic in the South, as the medium of instruction in the schools; but it was only in 1957, when the effects of the mutiny seemed past, that policies previously determined were resumed. The Minister of Education now announced the immediate takeover of elementary schools, and an early takeover of other schools by the Government. The missionaries had never liked the new Southern policy of 1946, but the Protestant missions now accepted guarantees of freedom to teach religion, and a promise to put their existing teachers on the Government cadre. With the Catholic missionaries, however, a conflict soon developed out of a total lack of understanding on both sides. The Catholic missionaries saw the reversion to the Friday holiday, for example, as part of a plan to extirpate Christianity; the Northerners, accustomed to allow Christians time off to attend services on Sunday mornings, did not even begin to understand the objection. Mohamed Omer Beshir describes the Catholic demands in respect of the schools as 'trying to continue to control educational policy and practice'.[1] What he so describes is effectively the same intransigent attitude to education that the Catholic Church has adopted in Europe and elsewhere, and which does often arouse opposition. It was wholly outside Northern Sudanese experience, and mutual suspicion mounted.

The situation deteriorated rapidly during the military regime. In establishing a number of Moslem religious schools and institutes, the

[1] Beshir, op. cit., p. 77.

Government considered that it was only reversing the Condominium policy, and attaching education to religious conversion. Southern intellectuals, however, considering that this policy and that of taking over the Christian schools consorted unequally, decided that the policy was a device for retarding development. In 1961 religious meetings for prayer or catechism, other than in church, were forbidden, and in 1962 a Missionary Societies Act was passed which forbade proselytization except under licence. The Government saw its actions as an attack, not on the Christian religion, but on foreign interference in religious affairs. They resented the way that Southern MPs in the last regime had contributed to the moral collapse by switching their crucial votes, and believed that this had been done at the instigation of missionaries. The Government was increasingly reluctant to issue re-entry visas to missionaries on home leave. Early in 1964, believing that they had collected incontrovertible evidence of missionary interference in politics, all the foreign missionaries in the South (272 Catholics and 28 Protestants) were expelled. This was put into effect abruptly and arbitrarily, and lost the Sudan considerable European and American goodwill; yet it may not have been entirely to the disadvantage of the Churches that the future of Sudanese Christianity in the South, however great the difficulties, would henceforth be solely in the hands of Sudanese Christians.

The 1955 Commission of Enquiry had rightly judged that 'the real trouble in the south is political, not religious'.[1] That the military regime superimposed a religious problem over the political one was one of many errors; but its political repression was of itself sufficient to create large-scale emigration of villagers over the borders of Ethiopia, Kenya, Uganda, the Central African Republic, and the Congo from 1960 onwards. A number of active politicians fled, and were given political asylum in Uganda, where they were allowed to carry on political activities. With them was William Deng, an outstanding personality, and an able administrator whose defection caused the Government more concern than that of the politicians. The exiles, accusing the North of colonization, began to demand separation, instead of that federation which they believed they had been first promised and then refused.

In 1961 a large number of former mutineers were amnestied without being offered employment, and not unnaturally they joined their fellow-mutineers already in the bush. The earlier part of 1963 was quiet, but in the autumn the guerrillas reappeared under the name of Anya-Nya; they were now a highly organized group comparable to the Mau-Mau, independent of the exiled politicians in Uganda, and determined to wage war seriously, and under no leadership but their own. From this time forward unhappy villagers were punished by both sides for help

[1] *Report*, p. 6.

rendered to the other. Their attempt, early in 1964, to capture Wau, capital of Bahr al-Ghazal Province, showed them to be a genuine military danger, and in any case the climate and vegetation make the Southern Sudan at certain seasons ideal for guerrilla operations. The military Government began to pour men and money into an attempt to regain military control, for which the army had not sufficient experience. A commission was set up in September to study the problem more rationally—an indication of uncertainty on the part of the authorities. It had no chance to prove its value; and from this date onward it will be more convenient to discuss the history of North and South together.

The October Revolution of 1964

The failure of policies of repression in the South, and much more mildly against the students, combined to bring about a crisis of confidence. After students were shot by police in the course of suppressing a meeting at the university, which had been defiantly advertised to discuss the South, rioting by the crowd, and non-co-operation by officials, began to gain momentum. A National Front was formed, in which Babikr (Abu Bakr) Awadalla—who as Deputy Chief Justice had refused police the legal authority to disperse a crowd—was prominent. When on the seventh day a crowd was scattered by indiscriminate machine-gun fire, young army officers, in no way divided in opinion from their civilian relatives, insisted on returning to barracks. On 30 October a caretaker Government was announced, under the premiership of Sirr al-Khatem al-Khalifa, an educationist with long experience in the South. For the first time the Communist party and its sympathizers were included in a Government composed of all who considered themselves progressives. A 'Night of the Counter-Revolution' when it was erroneously believed, as the result of an unauthorized Communist broadcast, that the army was about to attempt a counter-coup, brought thousands of ordinary citizens into the streets to defend their freedom, and demonstrated the substantial unity of the nation at this date. It was after this that Abbud himself resigned, and that a five-man Council of Sovereignty was reinstated.

For the first time a sensitive ministry was given to a Southerner. Clement Mboro, then Deputy Governor of Darfur, became Minister of the Interior, and a leading member of the new Southern Front. On 6 December another traumatic day in the history of the South, a large crowd was waiting for his delayed flight back from a Southern tour, when a rumour circulated that he had been betrayed. The crowd ran amok in central Khartoum. The same night a large number, perhaps hundreds, of Southerners were murdered in North Khartoum, and the day after most of the Southern population was brought into the Omdurman football stadium and other centres for protection. Very many returned to the South, some joined the Anya-Nya and others took to robbery and murder on their own account. It was a classic case of an unhappy cycle of violence. In spite of these events it was obvious that for the first time there were men in authority who really wanted a solution to the problems of the South, and it was this that made it possible to convene the Round Table Conference which met in March after some complex negotiation.

The Southerners came to the Conference rather in the mood of Sinn Fein during the Black and Tan troubles. The Sudanese African National Union (SANU), the organization of the Uganda exiles, split on the question of attendance, and the section that came was headed by William Deng. Aggrey Jaden, himself an exile, and not strictly a member of the Khartoum Southern Front, nevertheless voiced the views of the Front. SANU demanded federation, and the Front demanded total independence; the Northern parties, which were well represented by their best known leaders, could agree to neither. Yet if the Conference achieved nothing else, it did achieve a good deal of plain speaking, and the strength of Southern points of view was now perhaps for the first time widely understood in Khartoum. Time given by Northerners to blaming imperialists, and by Southerners to blaming slave-raiders, was not altogether wasted, if it drew attention to the need for a new start on both sides. Some resentment was felt in the North that the Anya-Nya had not recognized the Conference, or agreed to a truce. The revolutionary impetus had in any case run down, and politicians were preparing for elections.

At the revolution the Government amnestied all political prisoners, except of course its own, and even these were not detained for long. Purge proposals were made, but amounted to very little, and four accused military ministers were acquitted in March. Revolution gave foreign policy a new orientation in favour of other revolutionary African movements, even to the extent of helping Congolese insurgents believed to be allied with the Anya-Nya. By February, the political parties, confident of their support in the country as a whole, were pressing very hard for elections. The manoeuvres of the factions were suspended for the visit of Queen Elizabeth II, but immediately resumed, and the Prime Minister formed a new Government with stronger representation of the old parties. The elections were held in April and May and gave the Umma party 74 seats against the NUP's 51, sufficient to enable a coalition of the two to have an overwhelming majority. Mohammed Ahmad Mahjub became Prime Minister as senior Umma politician, and lost no time in amending the provisional constitution to allow Ismail al-Azhari to become perpetual President of the Supreme Council. The PDP boycotted the election; of the old parties, they had been the most compromised by co-operation with the late regime, and in order to clean the record they now entered into a tactical alliance with the Communist party, demonstrated publicly, and forced the Government to arrest their leaders briefly. One argument against the election had been sound enough; conditions were far too unsettled in the South to allow elections there, and these seats were put into cold storage. Most progressives disliked the election because it brought the revolution to an end; indeed, the country now stood exactly where it had stood on the eve of the military coup, when an Umma/NUP coalition had just been announced.

The Second Parliamentary Regime

The fluctuations of political intrigue during a period of minimal achievement make dull reading. The leaders of the late regime were released in July; the Government resumed a foreign policy based on support for the Accra principle of African non-intervention, and, in reaction against the spirit of revolution, a period of mild repression set in in the North. This culminated in the banning of the Communist party (as the Courts subsequently ruled, unconstitutionally) in December, which engendered considerable communal heat at the time; it was not seriously enforced. In the South the situation deteriorated rapidly. The Anya-Nya had never suspended their operations, and these were stepped up in July and August; the Government, disillusioned about the prospect of conciliation, ordered the restoration of law and order; and the shooting of considerable numbers of civilians occurred in Juba and Wau. Accusations of genocide were unjustified, but there can be little doubt that at this date the morale of the army was low and discipline poor. A real Southern opposition now existed, however, in Khartoum: the section of SANU headed by William Deng and the Southern Front, which included most of the intellectuals. They had no seats in parliament, and the acceptance by the Courts of the claims of a number of persons, mostly Umma and NUP Northerners, to represent some of the Southern constituencies, was regarded by most Southerners as an act of bad faith.

The Imam al-Siddiq al-Mahdi had been succeeded by his brother al-Hadi, but the political charisma descended to his son al-Sadiq, who emerged after the Revolution, though then barely thirty, as the leader of the reconstituted Umma party. In two respects he was genuinely in accord with the aims of the late Revolution, now already in abeyance; he wanted to root out corruption, and he wanted a real settlement in the South. He had published a pamphlet on the South in 1964 in which he advocated the integration of an Arabic-speaking Moslem South into a united country on a basis of real equality; he believed that Islam would quickly succeed, if it were allowed to compete with Christianity on equal terms. Though this might seem unrealistic, he could offer a genuine assurance against pan-Arabism, and a sincere alliance was formed between him and William Deng. At this date a number of progressives observed al-Sadiq's political tendencies with sympathy; he on his side realized that his party depended wholly on a sectarian vote, and that this was inadequate support for national leadership. His uncle the Imam remained firmly sectarian and bitterly resented his nephew's political leadership. It was in an atmosphere of bitter party and family division that al-Sadiq was elected Prime Minister at the end of July 1966, and that the outgoing premier, Mohammed Ahmad Mahjub, led a section of the Umma party into opposition.

Many members of his Cabinet were imposed on him by the continuing requirements of the coalition, but he was able to bring in some of his own choice, notably Hamza Mirghani (son of Mirghani Hamza, the PDP founder), until then a senior official in the World Bank, as Minister of Finance. The new Government paid particular attention to the rural water problem, though the ultimate effect of some of the action now got under way was the creation of new areas of erosion. In the South, the Anya-Nya again stepped up activity in October and November during the Prime Minister's tour of the disturbed areas. Nevertheless pacification had had some success; by the end of the year the Upper Nile Province was largely quiet, and the 'peace villages' established at different points to encourage the return of refugees, achieved something, though less than was hoped. A greater emphasis on ordinary civil government was one factor in restoring stability. A twelve-man committee set up by the Round Table Conference to implement its decisions was now meeting.

Parliament was slow to fulfil its function as a Constituent Assembly, but constitutional preoccupations now came to the fore. In April 1967 al-Azhari announced that he supported an Islamic constitution ('a democratic socialist republic founded on the teachings of Islam'), like the Umma party and the Islamic Charter Front (a product of the late Revolution which included the Moslem Brothers). In March elections had been held in those Southern constituencies which were still vacant, to the benefit principally of SANU and the Southern Front; it was unlikely that any Southern party would accept an Islamic constitution. The constitutional committee came to agreement on a Presidency of executive type, and it was clear that the Umma and the National Unionists would have to compete for this single major office. The Imam announced his candidacy; relations between al-Sadiq and al-Azhari deteriorated, and even more between al-Sadiq and the Imam. Al-Sadiq was neatly eliminated in a parliamentary manoeuvre in May, and the former coalition under Mahjub was resumed. Shortly after the new Government took office the Israeli war occurred; the country necessarily rallied to the Government, which, by the time the crisis was past, was firmly established. (Diplomatic relations with the USA and the UK were broken, but consular, cultural, and commercial relations continued, in the case of the UK, unimpaired, and diplomatic relations with Britain were resumed in the January following.) For reasons generally attributed to the weakness of his position in the coalition and to his lack of experience, al-Sadiq had lost the confidence both of favourable observers outside his party and, of course, of those within it who supported the Imam. SANU was now divided between the ruling coalition and the Sadiqist opposition.

In December 1967 the NUP and the PDP merged as the Democratic Unionist Party, with al-Azhari (NUP) as Chairman, and Ali Abd al-Rahman (PDP) as his Deputy in the party. In February 1968 parliament was dissolved (according to the opposition unconstitutionally), barely in time to save the Government. At the general election in May the two factions of the Umma party put up rival candidates and feeling between them ran more bitterly than between either and the DUP. The whole influence of the Imam was concentrated against al-Sadiq and his chief followers, all of whom lost their seats. Al-Sadiq proposed that the opposition should be led by William Deng, who retained his seat, but who was found after the election murdered in an ambush near Rumbek (which occurred, it was publicly alleged, with the connivance of the Government). Of the two principal parties, the DUP won 101 seats, Umma al-Sadiq 36, and Umma al-Imam 30; the total number of votes cast for the two Umma factions together, however, exceeded those cast for the DUP. This meant that if an election for the executive Presidency were held on the basis of a simple majority, the Umma could be expected to win; this could only be avoided by requiring an absolute majority, and so a run-off between the two highest candidates, which al-Azhari would be likely to win with support from outside his party. The constitutional issue, both as regards the Presidency and as regards the position of Islamic law, became of increasing importance during the remainder of the life of this Government, with Southerners and progressives united at least in their resistance to the religious establishment.

The coalition (DUP and Umma al-Imam) remained in power for a further year. There was no real improvement in the South (and in April 1969 a provisional Government of 'The Nile' on Sudanese soil was announced by the rebels, apparently the result of the impatience of Anya-Nya fighting men with the politicians in exile; a similar provisional Government had been announced the year before and apparently 'elected' in 1967.) The Khartoum Government tended, at least formally, to follow the traditions of its immediate predecessors. Foreign policy was based on four points: neighbourliness, neutralism, Arab League membership, and OAU membership. Economic aid continued to be sought more widely, though US aid ended in June 1967; it was official policy to promote Sudanese control of commercial and financial interests. Corruption was generally said to be rife, and there was a general mood of disillusion. In November 1968 the reunion of the Umma party was announced, but al-Sadiq continued in active and outspoken opposition. As Imamist Prime Minister, the position of Mahjub, now very ill, was difficult. In April 1969 a full reunion of the Umma party was celebrated; al-Sadiq had agreed finally to take second place, but the Imam announced in effect that al-Sadiq would replace Mahjub. In May the Prime Minister did not attend a meeting between the two major parties, and said that he would resign or remain according to the results of the discussions. On the morning of 25 May Radio Omdurman announced that the army under Col. (later Maj.-Gen.) Jaafar Mohammed al-Nimairi had taken over the country and put all ministers and the Sovereignty Council under arrest.

The Second Military Regime

In the previous months the idea of a new military coup had been widely and sympathetically discussed, and doubtless considered, by most politicians, but the form that it took and the date that it happened were universally a surprise. The initial public reaction was favourable, but most members of the official class listened to the announcement of a new Cabinet with some dismay at the inclusion of members and friends of the Communist party. Most ministers had apparently been chosen (and without their knowledge) as much for their known abilities and talents as for their general progressive attitudes and non-sectarian commitments. The Prime Minister, Babikr Awadulla, the former Chief Justice who had been living in retirement for rather more than a year, announced a programme of Arab unity (subsequently endorsed by al-Nimairi's personal meetings with President Nasser), of support for liberation movements everywhere and of replacing foreign capital, if necessary by self-help. It now became known (what had been known to the IMF for some months) that the country was on the verge of bankruptcy, and the new Government met this situation with orthodox financial measures. In October 1969 al-Nimairi replaced Babikr Awadalla as Prime Minister, while Babikr remained Foreign Minister and became Deputy Chairman on the Revolutionary Council (which had replaced the Sovereignty Council). Other changes in the Government during 1969 were all designed to reassure a public suspicious of Communist influence. All political parties were dissolved in May 1969, and the effective continuation in being of the Communist party led to the events of July 1971. The new Government was conscious that it was renewing the revolution of 1964; al-Nimairi said (October 1969) that its allies were those who had fought for independence against British rule and those who had struggled for a new society against the reactionary military dictatorship; its enemies the leaders of the defunct reactionary political parties. These categories were not altogether mutually exclusive; al-Azhari, who undoubtedly belonged in the first as well as the third, had died (under arrest but in his own house) in August. Ali Abd al-Latif was posthumously promoted, nearly half a century after his revolt, to the rank of Lieutenant-Colonel.

General al-Nimairi is known to believe, and with reason, that no Government can finally remain in power that does not solve the problem of the South. In June 1969 the Government announced a programme of 'regional autonomy within a united Sudan' for the South, and of amnesty, development, and training for Southerners; this would have been wholly acceptable in 1956, but in February 1970 the attitude of the Anya-Nya was as intransigent as ever, and their position rather stronger than before. A Ministry for Southern Affairs was created, and the Minister appointed was Joseph Garang, a member of the Communist party, one of the ablest of Southern politicians, well-known in the North and familiar with Northern society, but relatively unknown (and as a Communist suspect by some) in the South. His Ministry was staffed by Southern civil servants confident of their own ability. Over the last few years an increase in self-confidence has been noticeable among Southerners in Khartoum whose leaders, in public life, in the university, and elsewhere, are now of a quality that need fear no comparison; because of inferior education this had not hitherto been the case. They are less committed to the old issues or to European interests. Garang probably represented educated opinion when he said in February 1970 that the problem is neither religious nor racial, but one of even development and equality of opportunity. How this can be given expression in an acceptable constitutional solution is not yet clear.

The other great problem over the years has been the sectarian division of the nation. The new Government early showed itself sensitive to counter-plots; the revolution in May 1969 was followed by immediate opposition from the Moslem Brothers, many of whom were arrested. Progressives were divided, and many at this time inclined to the centre, partly from fear of provoking an ultimate right-wing reaction. Sayyid Ali al-Mirghani, the leader of the Khatmiyya who had come to Sudan at the Reconquest, died in 1968 and was succeeded by a young son, Sayyid Uthman. The sect had no real quarrel with the new revolution, unless on the Communist issue, and Sayyid Uthman gave it his support. The real danger to the regime came from al-Sadiq, who could now offer the only alternative government, and from the Imam, who was totally irreconcilable. Al-Sadiq was early placed under arrest, while the Imam took refuge in Gezira Aba, an island in the White Nile which had once been a base of the Mahdi, and where Sayyid Abd al-Rahman had acquired extensive interests. In March 1970 General al-Nimairi judged that the attitude of the Mahdists constituted a threat to his Government, and landed troops on the island. Fighting inevitably resulted in the destruction of the Ansar as an organized force capable of bearing arms. On 31 March it was announced that the Imam al-Hadi had been shot dead while trying to cross the Ethiopian border. Al-Sadiq was transferred to the hospitality of the Egyptian Government. These events may mark the end of the reign of the sects over the Sudan, although they do not exclude the possibility of an ultimate Mahdist revival in a form adapted to changed conditions.

During the following year, the Government was seeking substantial and reliable support, without wholly satisfying any group. The military leaders did not seem united in their aims. On the whole they did not show themselves vindictive, and corruption trials were conducted with moderation; but a continuing sequence of arrests and releases suggested an uncertain hand, as did the long imprisonment without trial of the leaders of the Moslem Brothers. Significant opposition developed in the university, where a number of distinguished members of staff, including the previous Vice-Chancellor, were dismissed, and where dissatisfaction reached a peak in a narrowly-averted massacre of students by the armed forces and the closure of the university in the spring of 1971. This period was marked by constant rumours of impending political changes.

Second al-Nimairi Regime

The seizure of power by Major Hashim al-Atta on 19 July 1971, was quickly recognized as a bid for domination by the Communist party, and a military government was in course of formation when, three days later, the revolutionary process was reversed by the spontaneous action of army elements under junior leadership, who restored the authority of al-Nimairi. Within a week, and after trial in camera, a number of soldiers involved in the temporarily successful coup were shot; some civilians were hanged, and others associated with the Communist party received severe sentences of imprisonment. Among those executed were Abd al-Khaliq Mahjub, Secretary of the Communist party, but widely respected in more moderate circles, and Joseph Garang, who was succeeded in the Southern Ministry by Abel Alier, subsequently also third Vice-President of the Republic. Southerners were now appointed to the three Southern Governorates, without, however, solving the problems of the South. Al-Nimairi felt the need of more widely-based support, began to move in the direction of civilian rule, and showed a new sympathy with moderate and even conservative elements. The Revolutionary Command Council was dissolved in August, and from elections conducted in September al-Nimairi emerged the first President of the Sudan, and was sworn in on 12 October. The occasion was marked by the release of a very large number of political prisoners, and those who remained in prison were treated more leniently. The Sudan Socialist Union, which had been set up in May, was retained, and developed along lines comparable to those followed by the parallel organization in Egypt. Sudan retained its close links with Egypt, but did not join the Confederation of Arab Republics when it was formed in September 1971. In April 1972 an agreement to end the Southern rebellion and establish a Southern Regional Government was reached in Addis Ababa between the Khartoum Government and Southern leaders. Although immense rehabilitation problems remained the agreement offered the first real hope of restoring peace to the south after sixteen years of civil war.

GOVERNMENT AND ADMINISTRATION

From independence on 1 January 1956 until the first military coup in November 1958 Sudan was governed according to a Provisional Constitution. This was revived after General Abbud's overthrow in 1964 and amended, but in the following four and a half years of parlimentary government successive governments failed to push a permanent constitution through the Constituent Assembly. After the second military coup in May 1969 led by Colonel Nimairi real power lay in the hands of the Revolutionary Command Council. Political parties were banned although the Communist party, whose leadership at first co-operated with the new regime, continued to function. In 1971 it took steps to establish a political organization along the lines of Egypt's Arab Socialist Union and arranged public debates on the drafting of a Permanent Constitution.

The Sudan is divided into nine provinces which have powers of taxation and responsibilities in the spheres of health, education, and veterinary services. Provincial governors are responsible to the Minister of the Interior.

SOCIAL SURVEY

Education

The 1955–6 census showed that over 85 per cent of the population aged five years and above had never attended school of any kind. In mid-1967 there were 3,086 sub-grade and elementary schools, 554 intermediate schools, and 133 secondary schools (including one technical). These included about 200 non-Government schools run by the National Schools Boards, missionary societies, and foreign communities. The total number of pupils was about 600,000 of whom about one third were girls. In 1952 there were over 500 mission schools in the South but most of these have been taken over by the State.

There are three universities—the State Khartoum University (formerly the Gordon Memorial College) with faculties of agriculture, arts, science, economics, engineering, law, medicine, and veterinary science; the Khartoum Branch of Cairo University; and the Islamic University at Omdurman. English is the medium of instruction at Khartoum University and in the secondary schools but it is being replaced by Arabic in the secondary schools. In 1971 there was discussion as to whether Arabic or the principal Southern languages (Shilluk, Dinka etc.) should be used in elementary schools in the South.

Health

In the early years backwardness of communications and popular suspicion of Western medicine complicated the task of dealing with an ill-nourished and disease-ridden people. The Sudan had the reputation for being extremely unhealthy, and epidemics of sleeping sickness, meningitis, and yellow fever were frequent. Today there are about 70 Government hospitals and in mid-1967 the ratio of hospital beds to population was 0·79 per 100 (Sudan Almanac 1968). Rural areas are served by dispensaries, dressing stations, and health centres which numbered about 1,250 in 1965–6. The major task of preventive medicine in the Sudan is the control of malaria, meningitis, and bilharzia and other parasitic diseases.

Labour

During the Second World War, and especially after it, the rising cost of living and the enhanced political and social consciousness of the workers caused some unrest and minor strikes. The railway workers took the lead in forming an association and the Sudan Government responded by securing the services of a British trade union expert to advise both workers and Government on the most suitable lines of development. The result was a series of enactments in 1948 which constituted an advanced scheme for the improvement of working conditions, the development of trade unionism, and the regulation of industrial relations. At independence 130 trade unions were registered although some were very small and the general level of union administration was low owing to the lack of full-time unionists.

Under an amending ordinance of the 1948 law in 1960, provision was made for closer control by the labour commissioner and it was prescribed that labour disputes should be compulsorily arbitrated when negotiation and conciliation failed. Sudanese trade unions, which are generally highly political in character, remain among the most developed in the Arab world.

ECONOMIC SURVEY

The Sudan is a predominantly agricultural country dependent largely on cotton. Successive governments have attempted to diversify the economy and a number of pilot schemes for the cultivation of alternative crops have been carried out. Industrialization is still in its early stages and the lack of sources of fuel and power is a serious handicap. The rivers are generally unsuitable for generating hydro-electric power. The South is a particularly difficult region to develop because of its remoteness and the backwardness of its tribes on the one hand and the widespread unrest on the other.

At the time of the 1955–6 census there were 8·2 million persons aged five and over; of these, 4·9 million were described as economically-active adults but only 3·8 million of these were 'economically active as main occupation'. About 20 per cent of children in the eleven to fourteen age group were working, but by 1970 the proportion was estimated to have fallen to 12–13 per cent.

Total labour resources in 1955–6 were estimated at 7·54 million of whom 75,000 were in urban areas and 6·79 million in the countryside. By 1969–70 it was estimated that the total had risen to 8·62 million with 980,000 in the urban areas and 7·64 million in the countryside. It was estimated that about 75 per cent were employed in the various economic sectors and the rest engaged in household activities and receiving no wages.

Agriculture

In general it may be said that Sudan has a large unexploited agricultural potential. It is estimated that about one third of the country's land surface could be used but that only one eighth or 75 million feddans is in any way productive at present. Of this total, about 18·5 million feddans were being used for arable farming and the rest was grazing land.

During the 1960s there were big increases in output but these were achieved by bringing more areas under cultivation rather than by the introduction of improved methods. In 1970 the irrigated area totalled 3·54 million feddans of which 700,000 feddans had been added during the 1960–70 period, but the Sudan in 1970 was still using only about half the Nile water allocated to it under the 1959 agreement with Egypt. In 1970 work was started on the Rahad scheme designed to irrigate 1·4 million feddans. This uses the waters stored by the $100 million Roseires Dam which was completed in 1966 with Western financial aid, mainly from the IBRD.

Cotton

Cotton is much the most valuable cash crop and brings in about 50 per cent of total export earnings. The Sudan is a major producer of long-staple cotton which still accounts for 80–85 per cent of the total crop although weakened world demand for long staples since 1960 has prompted some increase in the production of medium- and short-staple (mainly American) varieties. As part of the 1970 nationalization measures a State Corporation for Cotton Marketing was established. Four state-owned companies, incorporating fourteen former private firms, operate as exporting agencies and so contribute an element of competition in both buying and selling within the nationalized system.

The Gezira Scheme

The Gezira Scheme was initiated with the completion of the Sinnar Dam in 1925 which made cotton the mainstay of the Sudanese economy. The area between the Blue and White Niles south of Khartoum was transformed into good arable land, especially suitable for cotton but also for grain and fodder. The original gross area of 300,000 acres has been steadily increased and in 1970 reached 1·8 million acres, including the Manaqil extension.

The scheme is worked as a three-cornered partnership between the Sudanese tenant-farmers, the Government, and the Sudan Gezira Board (which in 1950 replaced two private commercial companies— the Sudan Plantations Syndicate and Kassala Cotton Company). The net proceeds from cotton are divided 42 per cent to the Government, 42 per cent to the tenants, and 10 per cent to the Sudan Gezira Board; the remaining 6 per cent is distributed between social services, a tenants' reserve fund, and local government councils. The Government provides the land and is responsible for dam construction and maintenance; the Sudan Gezira Board is a public corporation which administers the scheme, makes loans to tenants, and markets the produce.

Besides constituting the backbone of the Sudan's economy, the Gezira Scheme has been widely acclaimed as a model of a pioneering effort on a partnership basis. About 80,000 tenants and their families now benefit from the scheme.

The cotton area of private estates rose from about 97,000 acres in 1953 to about 197,000 acres in 1958. Licences for further development were then suspended because of the fall in cotton prices but subsequently there was an increase in the planted area. Since 1969 it has been the policy of the revolutionary Government to break up the large private estates.

Other Crops and Livestock

In the west and south of Sudan both crops and livestock are produced mainly for subsistence and little is sold. In the north and east surpluses are available and are moved to the towns or exported. Sudan is virtually self-sufficient in basic foods, the only large imports being sugar, wheat flour, coffee, and tea. The chief food crops are the common millet (*durra*) and bulrush millet (*dukhn*), the cultivation of which has been steadily extended during the twentieth century to meet the needs of the growing population. Wheat and maize are also grown, and sugar

cane output has been increasing in recent years (938,000 tons in 1969–
70). Clover and alfalfa are grown on irrigated land. Dates are also
grown and exported and tobacco in Darfur where it is the only crop
which will justify the high cost of transport.

Experiments have been made with new crops in an effort to diversify
agriculture. Sesame and groundnuts are grown and the amount exported has increased over the past decade so that groundnuts now
compete with gum arabic as Sudan's second most important commodity
export after cotton. Gum arabic is tapped from hashab trees. The
Sudan produces 85–90 per cent of total world production.

In Southern Sudan tobacco, coffee, sugar, rice, and the oil palm are
all grown experimentally but commercial output has so far been negligible.

Pastoral farming extends throughout the country except in the desert
of the north and north-west and on the south-western plateau which is
infested with tsetse fly. In 1969–70 there were estimated to be 10·3
million sheep, 7·2 million goats, and 12·3 million cattle (which are
bred mainly in the central rain lands). There are about 2 million
camels owned by the nomadic tribes of the north and west. Both
camels and cattle are exported to Egypt and Saudi Arabia. Meat
production was 421,000 tons in 1969–70 of which 396,000 tons were
consumed in the country. About 5,000 tons of hides and skins are
exported annually.

Industry and Mining

Industry still accounts for only a small proportion of economic activity.
In 1969–70 the value of output of both mining and industry was estimated at 9 per cent of gross domestic product. Industry is engaged
almost entirely in the primary processing of raw materials for the local
market. Initially industrial development was left to the private sector
and the Approved Enterprises Concession Act was replaced in 1968
by the Industrial Development Act which gave generous incentives to
private enterprise. However, in recent years the public sector has
increasingly entered the industrial field and even before the series of
nationalizations in 1970 it comprised most of the large and modern
enterprises in the country—two sugar factories, a tannery, a cardboard
factory, a dozen cotton ginneries, a date-packing plant, saw mills, ship
and motor vehicle workshops, two fruit and canning factories, a dairy
products plant, and grain silos at Port Sudan. In 1970 several important
foreign-owned concerns were nationalized, including a cement company, a shoe factory, a brewery, and a truck assembly plant. Capacity
has in general been under-used in both the public and private sectors
but at the same time production has failed to meet local demand.
Textile output was satisfying barely half the country's needs in 1969–70
and a substantial quantity of yarn had to be imported. The country's

tanneries were processing only about 30 per cent of the hides available from within the Sudan.

No large mineral deposits have been discovered but iron, manganese, and chromites are exploited on a small scale. The most promising area for commercial production is in and around the Red Sea hills and a Government enterprise for mining iron ore is planned for 1970–5. No oil has been discovered and prospects are not considered good except perhaps offshore in the Red Sea.

Communications

Railways provide the chief means of communications in Northern Sudan. Sudan Railways operate 3,262 miles of railways. Goods traffic amounted to an estimated 1·5 billion ton/miles in 1969–70 compared with 0·99 billion ton/miles in 1960. The railways provide the means for bulk movement of cotton, oilseeds, hides, and gum arabic for export through Port Sudan. The Khartoum–Port Sudan line suffers severe strain during the cotton-exporting season and there is an urgent need for modernization and improvement. The situation is the more serious because Sudanese roads are inadequately developed. They are mostly merely cleared tracks which are impassable after rain. However, a Khartoum–Wad Medani highway has been built, partly with US aid and plans are now being considered for highways linking Khartoum with Port Sudan, and Wadi Halfa in Egypt with Omdurman. Both of these will be of vital importance to the economy. Port Sudan handles most goods and passenger traffic. The port and river transport are managed by Sudan Railways.

Foreign Trade

Sudan's foreign trade has increased very considerably since 1939. Imports in 1939 were £S5·93 million and exports and re-exports £S5·67 million. In 1970, according to the Government Department of Statistics, imports were £S108·34 million and exports and re-exports £S102·21 million. Before 1956 Sudanese foreign trade was principally with Western countries but in that year the Soviet Union began to buy Sudanese cotton in large quantities. By 1970 the Soviet Union had become the Sudan's most important trading partner, buying about 20 per cent of exports and providing about 7 per cent of its imports, although the UK remained the most important supplier (followed by India). The trend towards trade with Eastern European countries is likely to continue as they are playing an increasing role in Sudan's economic development.

Economic Policy and Development

The shift towards economic links with the Eastern bloc began after the 1967 Middle East war which led to a major arms deal with the USSR in 1968. The 1969 coup meant a further shift to the left and added a strong political element. The sweeping nationalization measures of May and June 1970 were promoted by the extreme left-wing members of the regime. However, some of these measures were hasty and ill-considered and led to serious economic consequences. In 1971 general economic policy was being reconsidered.

In 1962 a ten-year development plan was announced covering the period 1961/2–1970/1. In the first five years of the plan period gross fixed investments exceeded the plan target but in the next four years they fell well below and by 1967 the plan had in effect been abandoned. After the 1969 coup a new five-year plan for the 1970/1–1974/5 period was prepared by Soviet advisers to the revolutionary Government.

X

Syria

For purposes of geographical description and historical narrative it will be convenient to treat Syria and Lebanon together. They can be regarded as forming part of a single geographical and social entity, and until the most recent period it would be difficult wholly to separate the history of the one from that of the other.

THE LAND

The following rough geographical divisions may be made:

1. *The coastal strip.* A strip of low and fertile land runs along the Mediterranean coast of Syria and Lebanon. Near Latakia it is about twenty miles wide, and rather less north of Tripoli; but in some places it practically disappears, and the mountains meet the sea. Olives, vegetables, citrus, and bananas are cultivated, particularly round Beirut.

2. *The mountain ranges.* These stretch mostly from north to south. Just behind the coastal strip in the north is the Jabal Ansariya, which averages 4,000 feet; vines, olives, tobacco, and cotton are grown in places, and the population is comparatively large. South of it lies a gap of low land leading from Tripoli to Homs, and south of this again lie the ranges of Lebanon, with peaks of over 10,000 feet, which drop (to the south) into the hills of Galilee in Palestine. Here too water is plentiful, vines, olives, tobacco, and (in recent times) apples are cultivated on the seaward slopes, and the villages are prosperous—particularly those near Beirut which have become summer resorts for the city folk as well as for visitors from other Middle Eastern countries. Parallel to Lebanon, and east of it across the plain of the Beqaa, lie the ranges of Anti-Lebanon (over 7,000 ft.) and Hermon (9,200 ft.). Here water and cultivation are less plentiful, although they are found in patches. Farther inland still, lying east of Hermon across the plain of Hauran, is the Jabal Druze (5,000–6,000 ft.), where also patches of vines and olives lie around the springs and streams.

3. *Plains and plateaux.* East of the mountain ranges, the land consists of a plateau, high above sea-level, but sloping generally in a south-easterly direction. Those parts of it which lie nearer the south, and within the area of heavy rainfall, and also those through which rivers flow, are capable of rich agricultural development. The countryside of Aleppo,

Homs, and Hama; the valley of the Beqaa, with the Orontes and Litani flowing through it; the Ghab depression through which the Orontes flows farther north; the Jazira district lying south of the foothills of Asia Minor; the valleys of the Euphrates and its tributaries, the Balikh and Khabur—all these districts contain good land where cereals and cotton can be cultivated, and where possibilities of irrigation and hydro-electric power exist. The Jazira has seen particularly rapid development in the last few years. Around Damascus too there is a fertile region, the Ghouta, where an ancient system of canals makes use of every drop of water in the rivers which fall eastwards from Anti-Lebanon, and fruits of many kinds are grown. Elsewhere, however—in the plain from Homs to Damascus, and in Hauran south of Damascus—water is not sufficient to provide a good crop every year, although cereals are grown in parts, and livestock are pastured.

4. *The steppe and desert.* To the south and east of the fertile area stretches the Syrian Desert, the northern extension of the great deserts of Arabia. Covering more than one-third of the total area of Syria, it is rock and gravel steppe, not sandy desert, and has hills rising more than 3,000 feet both north and south of Palmyra.

Temperature and rainfall vary from one region to another. In the mountains about 40 inches of rain fall every year, in the desert almost none. In general, rain is heaviest in the west and north. On the coast winters are not severe, but in summer humidity is great and diurnal variation small. In the mountains snow lies on the topmost peaks for most of the year, and even main roads are sometimes blocked in winter; summer days are hot but the nights are cool. Farther inland, plateaux and steppes have low humidity and great extremes of heat and cold.

HISTORY

The history of Syria and Lebanon has been moulded by three processes: the movements of tribes and smaller groups from the Arabian Peninsula, and their mingling with peoples of earlier settlement to form a rural population whose languages and folk-ways have been Semitic for thousands of years; the movement of armies as well as goods along the great trade routes, and the establishment (at least in the towns and river valleys) of alien governments, and often of alien languages and cultures; and the resistance of the mountain communities to the incursions of governments, peoples, and ideas from outside.

Egyptians, Babylonians and Hittites, Greeks and Romans in turn established their rule and made Syria part of their empires. In AD 636 Damascus fell to the Moslem armies; from that time Syria formed part of the Caliphate, and gradually the Arabic language replaced the older Semitic speech, and the religion of Islam conquered the majority, although the Christian sects maintained themselves, and Moslem heterodoxies found refuge in the mountains. Under the Umayyads (661–750) Damascus was the capital of the Caliphate, but with the Abbasids the centre of gravity shifted to Iraq. As the unity of the Caliphate broke up, parts of Syria fell under other domination. The Crusaders held the coast for a time, and first the Ayyubids and then the Mamelukes incorporated Syria and Egypt in a single state. Then in 1516 the Ottoman Turks occupied the country, which remained part of their Empire until 1918.

Under the Ottomans, Syria was divided into a number of provinces administered by governors sent from Istanbul. In its great days Ottoman rule was reasonably just and efficient. Agriculture and trade were protected and regulated, and the great towns flourished: Aleppo, the centre of foreign trade, Sidon (Saida), a port much frequented by the French, and Damascus, the point of departure of the Pilgrimage and a home of Islamic culture. In the seventeenth and eighteenth centuries the strength of Ottoman rule decayed, security declined, the nomads began to penetrate the settled land, rural production diminished and many peasants left their villages. But the great cities still flourished, and the semi-autonomous life of the mountains went on. Even when Ottoman rule had been strong it had scarcely extended to Lebanon, whose local ruling families controlled the mountain community, subject to collection of taxes for the Ottoman Government, and to some control by the governors of Tripoli and Sidon.

No government of Egypt can be indifferent to what happens on its eastern frontier. The Mameluke Ali Bey, and later Bonaparte, tried to conquer Syria from Egypt, and thirty years after Bonaparte Mohammed Ali succeeded in doing so. The ten years of Egyptian rule under his son Ibrahim Pasha (1831–40) were important for Syria. The Egyptians centralized and improved administration, reformed the tax system, increased international trade, extended the area of cultivation, allowed missions to open schools, and established equality of Moslems and Christians. But they also brought heavy taxation, conscription, and disarmament, and when British and Ottoman forces drove Ibrahim out in 1840 they were supported by a popular rising. The Turks returned, but their rule was not so effective as that of the Egyptians, and in Lebanon they began a policy of destroying the traditional autonomy by undermining its basis, the entente of Druzes and Maronites. They were aided in this by the growth of social tension. For 100 years the Maronites had been growing in numbers and strength. Missions and closer contacts with Europe had revived their intellectual life, and their peasantry was moving southwards into lands controlled by Druze lords. Social tension gave rise, for the first time in the history of the mountain, to religious hostility, which led to the civil war of 1860; Druze victories in Lebanon touched off a massacre of Christians by Moslems in Damascus, and the Powers intervened. Napoleon III sent an army, and a conference of Powers resulted in the creation of an autonomous province of Lebanon, with a Christian majority and a Christian governor; it included the mountain range, but neither the Beqaa valley nor the coastal towns of Tripoli, Beirut, and Sidon with their mainly Moslem populations. For the next half-century autonomous Lebanon flourished, under the protection of France and the other Powers. Emigration and silk brought prosperity to her villages, and the mission schools produced an educated class. The rest of Syria prospered too. Turkish administration and rural security improved. Railways were built: the French network linking Beirut, Damascus, and Aleppo was constructed from 1895 onwards, and the Pilgrims' Railway linking Damascus and Medina was opened in 1908. Thanks to security and railways, the area of settled agriculture expanded, and at the same time economic links with the outside world grew stronger. Beirut became the main centre of foreign trade and influence: one of the largest ports in the eastern Mediterranean, the home of the Jesuit University of St. Joseph (1875) and the Syrian Protestant College (1866—later to become the American University of Beirut), and, largely through them, second only to Cairo as a centre of modern Arabic literature and thought. The Lebanese journalists and writers, alike in Cairo and in Beirut, played an essential part in the transformation of the Arab mind. Beirut, and Lebanon behind it, were centres of radiation of French influence; the French Government subsidized the missions, and French investments in public utilities were considerable. By 1914 Lebanon and the Syrian coast were generally regarded by the other Powers as being in the French sphere of influence.

As prosperity and culture grew, there grew also a more articulate sense of community, which was given form by the Western idea of nationalism, and impetus by the attempts of the Young Turks (1908–18) to impose Turkish domination on the multi-national Empire. There emerged both a Lebanese nationalism, mainly among the Maronites, and a more general Syrian or Arab nationalism, which organized itself in political societies, both open and secret. When war broke out in 1914 Lebanese sentiment was on the side of France, and some of the Arab nationalists were willing to make an agreement with Britain, and use her help to obtain their independence. When the Sharif Hussein revolted in 1916 after negotiations with Britain, he had behind him the Syrian nationalist societies. Syrian Arabs helped in the Arab revolt, many nationalists both in Syria and Lebanon were executed by the Turks, and Lebanon had her autonomy suppressed and was ravaged by famine.

The French Mandate

When the war ended in 1918, Syria and Lebanon were controlled by Allied troops, mainly British. Under British supreme control there was

a French military administration on the coast, and an Arab administration, under Hussein's son Faisal, in the interior with its centre at
Damascus. The views of French and Arabs on the future of the country
were opposed. The French wanted to control it, both for the sake of
their Christian protégés and for reasons of strategy; the Maronites and
some of the other Christians wanted an enlarged Lebanon under French
tutelage; most of the other groups wanted Syrian independence, and
would have preferred American or British to French tutelage. French
and Arabs alike looked for support to Britain, which possessed real
control and had made commitments to both sides.[1] The Peace Conference discussed the subject and made no decision, except the general
decision to apply the new idea of the mandate to the Arab provinces of
the Ottoman Empire. At the end of 1919 British troops were withdrawn, and matters moved rapidly to a crisis. In March 1920 a Congress at Damascus proclaimed Faisal King of a united Syria; in April
the inter-Allied conference at San Remo refused to accept this, and
allotted the mandate for the whole of Syria to France; in June France
sent an ultimatum to Faisal and occupied Damascus and the interior.
The text of the mandate was approved by the League of Nations in 1923,
but before that France had started organizing the territory. In 1920 the
state of Greater Lebanon was set up, including the Beqaa and the
coastal towns; in 1926 it became the Lebanese Republic. In the rest
of the mandated region, after some experiments, separate Governments of Jabal Druze and the Alawis (or Latakia) were set up, and the
remainder was formed into the State of Syria; within it the district of
Alexandretta was given a special administrative regime, in view of the
mixed nature of its population (Turkish, Arab, and Armenian). A
French High Commissariat exercised general supervision and control
over the Governments, through a network of 'advisers', and also
administered certain services, such as the customs, in which they had a
common interest.

During the twenty or so years in which France had the full exercise
of her mandate, there was much economic and social progress in both
countries. Trade and agriculture increased; the decay of the silk
industry in Lebanon was offset by the development of the Jazira;
modern textile factories were started; education was expanded, and
the amenities of urban life improved. Partly this was a natural process,
but partly it was due to the mandatory Government, which built roads,
improved internal security, began land survey and settlement, and
founded state schools (although more in Syria than in Lebanon, where
religious bodies still had almost a monopoly of education). But on the
other side, the standard of the French administration was not uniformly
high; economic life suffered from the fluctuations of the franc; little was
done to train the peoples in the exercise of authority; and the French

[1] See above, p. 13.

never established a harmonious relationship with those whom they were supposed, by the terms of the mandate, to prepare for self-government.

In Lebanon, the main political difficulty was that the state in its enlarged form included groups which did not want to belong to it—some non-Catholic Christians as well as most Sunnis and Shiis. An attempt was made to appease them by the system of distributing offices according to the relative strength of the sects, while effective power was kept in French and Maronite hands. But a large part of the population remained unwilling to accept the existence of Lebanon, the domination of Maronites in it, and French control; this, and the universal rule of sectarian considerations, made it difficult for Lebanon to develop unity or a stable national life.

In Syria the Sunni Arab majority was even more unwilling to accept French domination, because of the separation of Syria from the other Arab countries, its internal subdivisions, the denial of the promised independence, and the fear that France would wish to make it a permanent part of her Empire. In 1936 Franco-Syrian and Franco-Lebanese treaties were signed by the Popular Front Government. They provided for the transfer of power, the entry of the two states into the League of Nations, the incorporation of the Druze and Alawi districts into Syria, and the retention by France of two air bases in Syria, and of unlimited military rights in Lebanon. The treaties, however, were never ratified by the French Government. Their main results were to increase the resentment of the nationalists, and to lead to the loss of Alexandretta.[1]

The Syrian Constitution was suspended in 1939, just before the outbreak of war, the Lebanese just after. The collapse of France and the German advance through the Balkans brought both countries within the zone of war. In 1941 the use, contrary to the terms of the Franco-German Armistice Agreement, of air bases in Syria by German and Italian aircraft on their way to support Rashid Ali in Iraq, the use of the French-controlled railway for that purpose, and German infiltration and the danger of an attack across Turkey led Britain to occupy both countries, with Free French collaboration, after a short campaign. Before the entry of the British and French troops the Free French issued a proclamation of Syrian and Lebanese independence which was confirmed by the British Government, and in an exchange of letters between them and Britain the latter recognized that France should have a predominant position over other European Powers, once the promises of independence had been carried out. The Free French, however, hesitated to carry out their promises while the war was undecided; they did not wish to appear to France to be liberating French territories only to give them up, and they feared that Britain wanted Syria and Lebanon to be independent in order to draw them into her

[1] See above, p. 20.

own sphere of influence. If forced to carry out their promises they wished to secure a treaty in return. The Syrians were unwilling to sign a treaty, not only because of memories but also because there was no advantage to be gained in linking themselves with a France which could no longer help or protect them. They wished to bring matters to a crisis while Britain was still there. Their attitude was shared by a large proportion of the Lebanese; many Lebanese now felt strong enough to stand by themselves without French protection, and the mercantile interests of Beirut, which played an increasing part in the life of the Republic, wanted more scope for their activities than the mandate gave them. In 1943 a 'national pact' was reached between certain Moslem and Christian leaders, to the effect that Lebanon should remain independent within its existing frontiers, but should follow an Arab foreign policy. The British were insistent that the promises of independence should be carried out, for reasons of general Middle Eastern policy; they wished this to happen, if possible, without disorders which might affect other Arab countries, but equally without harm to Anglo-French relations.

Elections were held in 1943, and in both countries opponents of the mandate were in the majority. The new Lebanese Government proposed to remove from the Constitution those clauses which safeguarded French control; the French replied by arresting the President of the Republic and almost the whole Government. Faced with a popular rising, world-wide protests, and a British ultimatum, the French gave in. From that time they gradually transferred power to the two Governments. Syria and Lebanon were allowed to establish their own foreign representation, and they joined the United Nations. But the French still retained control of the local armed forces, and tried to use this as a bargaining counter to compel the Governments to make treaties. In May 1945 a new contingent of French Senegalese troops landed at Beirut. The Syrian Government and people took this as a first step in an attempt to do what had been done in 1920: to build up French strength and crush Syrian nationalism as soon as the British withdrew. Tension grew, local fighting broke out, and the French bombarded Damascus. The British Government now intervened and asked the Free French authorities to order their troops to cease fire and withdraw to their barracks. This was virtually the end of French rule, but French and British troops still remained. After some delay, the matter was brought before the Security Council of the United Nations in February 1946, and in March agreement was reached on the simultaneous withdrawal of British and French troops from Syria by the end of April, and from Lebanon by the end of December. From this time the history of the two States diverges, and it will be more convenient to deal with each of them separately.[1]

[1] For Lebanon see p. 399.

2. SYRIA

POST-WAR HISTORY AND POLITICS

When foreign troops withdrew in 1946, Syria had already been ruled for three years by a nationalist Government, whose adherents were soon to organize themselves in the National Party. Shukri Quwatli, one of the leaders of the party, had been President since 1943, and two others, Saadullah Jabri and Jamil Mardam, became Prime Minister in succession. Until 1949 the main struggle for power was between them and other politicians of the same type, although mainly of a slightly younger generation, organized in the People's Party (Shaab). But beneath the surface both of them were losing their hold on the country. The men who had led the struggle against the French did not prove adept at the task of ruling. They had to try to impose the authority of the Government in a country where local, tribal, and religious leaders were strong, and where the transfer of power had taken place suddenly, without the co-operation of those who had previously possessed it; to build up an administration; and to face the economic difficulties involved in the change from war to peace, and from dependence to independence. Something, it is true, was done. New elements were drawn into the administration; Syria left the franc bloc and became financially independent; agreement was reached with the American Tapline Company for the building of a pipeline from the Persian Gulf across Syria to Sidon (ratified in May 1949). The President obtained an extension of his term of office in April 1948, but his influence and that of the regime were waning. To the rising cost of living and the knowledge of corruption in high places was added public anger at the failure of the Arab governments in regard to Palestine. This anger first vented itself against the Communists in 1947, after the Soviet bloc had supported the partition of Palestine in the United Nations. The failure of the Arab armies to prevent the emergence of the State of Israel, and the signature of armistices by the Arab governments, turned public opinion against the regime. In December 1948 there were riots against the Government. Order was restored by the army, and a change of Government was made. The army had shown it was the only force which could maintain the authority of the Government, and from that it was only a short step to its taking upon itself to decide what government it was willing to maintain. On 30–31 March 1949 an army group under Colonel Husni Zaim carried out a bloodless coup d'état. The President and the Prime Minister resigned, and Zaim himself took the latter post, and later the Presidency. The Chamber was dissolved and all political parties abolished, and Zaim announced his intention of carrying out sweeping reforms. Among the measures planned or promulgated were the building up of the army, the political emancipation of women, the proclamation of a civil code, the reorganization of the Syrian University, and the building of an international port at Latakia. Some of these measures were later achieved; but Zaim himself soon lost what popularity he had at first possessed. In his foreign policy he alienated Iraq and Jordan, after at first inclining towards them, and leaned strongly towards Egypt and also towards France; he shocked a powerful group by first giving asylum to the Lebanese leader of the Syrian Popular Party, Antoun Saadeh, and then handing him over to the Lebanese Government to be executed. On 14 August 1949 another army coup took place under Colonel Sami Hinnawi; Zaim and his Prime Minister were executed, and Hashim Atassi became President; he was one of the most respected of the older nationalist leaders, and had already been President from 1936 to 1939. He took office with a Government drawn largely from the People's Party, and elections held in November (the first at which women had been allowed to vote) gave this party the largest number of seats. It had a leaning towards the Iraqi connection, and the question of union with Iraq under a Hashimite King was now raised. The National Party withdrew its objections, and union seemed near. Those who opposed it, inside and outside Syria, joined forces to prevent it, and on 19 December a third coup d'état took place, this time under Colonel Adib Shishakli, a former member of the Syrian Popular Party (Hizb al-Qawmi al-Suri), who had played some part in the Palestine War. A new Government was formed, under an independent Prime Minister but with representatives of the People's Party, and constitutional life proceeded apparently undisturbed; on 5 September 1950, the Constitution now in force was promulgated. But there was a shift in foreign policy, as the pro-Hashimi wing of the People's Party naturally lost ground after their failure; and, what was more important, there was a persistent and growing tension between the two seats of authority, parliament with the People's Party as its dominant group, and Shishakli and his collaborators in the army. Gradually the balance shifted in favour of the army, both because of splits among the politicians, on personal matters and on great issues of policy, and also because it was the holder of real power. In 1951 a political crisis was precipitated by the Four-Power proposals for a Middle East Defence Organization.[1] The struggle between Government and army came to a head, and on 29 November Shishakli carried out a further coup, and arrested almost all the members of the Government. President Atassi resigned, and Shishakli dissolved parliament. From that time power was in his hands. He became Chief of Staff and Deputy Prime Minister, and one of his associates, Fawzi Silo, became Head of the State and Prime Minister. In April 1952 all political parties were dissolved, and later an official party, the Arab Liberation Movement, was set up. In the summer of 1953 a further change took

[1] See above, p. 26.

place, when a new Constitution was issued, more on the American than the French model, and a referendum in July resulted in the Constitution being adopted and Shishakli elected as President and Prime Minister for five years; Silo withdrew from public life. In October 1953 elections were held; although the ban on parties had been lifted they boycotted the elections, and the official party secured the great majority of seats. But beneath the surface opposition to the dictator was growing. In February 1954 trouble broke out in Jabal Druze, and this gave the opportunity for an army rising, beginning in northern Syria. Shishakli resigned and left the country; part of the army still supported him, but after a confused period agreement was reached on the return of Atassi as President.

The four years during which Shishakli dominated Syria left their mark. However unpopular his rule, he imposed the authority of the Government on the whole country. He had leanings towards social reform, and for a time worked closely with Akram Hourani, who founded the Socialist Party in 1950; in October and November 1952 he issued two decrees limiting the amount of state domain[1] any individual could hold, and providing for its distribution in smallholdings. In economic matters he initiated the policy which subsequent governments have carried on. The young industries of Damascus and Aleppo were protected by tariffs. This involved the dissolution, in March 1950, of the customs union which Syria and Lebanon had inherited from the French mandate; Lebanon's interest was as much in free trade as Syria's in protection, and the two countries have not yet been able to reach a satisfactory permanent trade agreement. Some public works were started; work began on Latakia harbour in 1950, and preparations were made for land reclamation in the Ghab depression. But this raised the question where to find the capital. Syria refused aid from the United States; negotiations for a loan from the International Bank began, and a team of experts from the Bank was sent to survey the economic possibilities of the country, but in April 1956 Syria rejected the Bank's offer of a loan of $26 million partly because the Government was not prepared to accept the loan conditions. In 1953 negotiations began for an increase in pipeline dues. In general economic development was left to private enterprise, with some official control. After the failure of the cotton crop in 1951, a Cotton Office was established; and in 1953 a Money and Credit Board was set up. In foreign policy Shishakli's policy was pro-Egyptian and pro-Saudi in Arab affairs; he tended to lean towards France and away from the other Western powers, but he was also opposed to Communism, although it was at this time that certain leaders began to speak of Arab alignment with Russia.

After the fall of Shishakli the Constitution of 1950 was restored and

[1] i.e. property of which the title is vested in the state.

elections were held in September 1954. They resulted in the return of
about 28 members of the People's Party, 13 of the National Party, and
16 of the Baath (Socialist) Party; the rest of the Chamber of 142 were
Independents or belonged to smaller groups, and for the first time a
Communist was elected. This division of the Chamber has been the
dominant factor in Syrian politics since then. None of the organized
parties can form a Government without the support of some of the
Independents. In order to strengthen its own position inside the coalition, each group tries to make its own appeal to the Independents, and
still more to important sections of public opinion, and to one or other
group of army officers. Since the dominant political questions are
those of foreign policy—world politics, Arab politics, and Palestine—
each group tries to outbid the rest in its support of a foreign policy
which appeals to the masses.

The year 1955 was one of comparative quiet. A fairly stable coalition
governed the country, with only minor changes. In some ways it
continued the policy of the previous regime. It approved of the new
agreement on pipeline transit dues, and negotiated with the IPC. In
August the International Bank presented its report on economic
possibilities, and the Government decided to create a permanent
Economic Council and an Economic Development Board. In foreign
affairs it continued to align itself with Egypt and Saudi Arabia. In
March Syria joined with her two allies in announcing the formation of
a defence and economic organization, open also to other Arab countries, as a counter-balance to the Baghdad Pact. The election of
Shukri Quwatli as President in August, when Atassi's term came to an
end, was a sign of the movement of opinion in favour of the Egyptian
and Saudi connection, of which he had long been a supporter. The only
excitement of the year was provided by the assassination of Adnan
Malki, an army officer with Socialist connections, allegedly by members of the Syrian Popular Party; the party was dissolved and several of
its members brought to trial and convicted.

In 1956 the main line of Syrian policy continued. In March 1956
the heads of state of the three allies met in Cairo to co-ordinate action.
On 5 July Syria announced her intention of negotiating a federal union
with Egypt. In October a joint Syro-Jordanian-Egyptian military
command was agreed on. Next month, the Anglo-French armed intervention in Egypt led to the breaking off of relations with Britain and
France, and the blowing up of the IPC pipeline. At the same time
efforts were made to establish closer connections with Jordan, which was
now moving away from the British alliance. On 6 August a customs and
economic union was agreed on; in October, when it was feared that
Israel might attack Jordan, Iraqi troops at the request of the Jordan
Government were concentrated on the Iraq–Jordan frontier, while
Syrian troops with Jordanian agreement moved into Jordan. Under

the Arab Solidarity Pact of January 1957 Syria undertook to contribute £E2·5 million a year towards the £E12·5 million required to replace the British subsidy.

Throughout the year, however, there were signs of a change both in the balance of Syrian policy and in the composition of the Government. The Soviet offer to supply arms (through Czechoslovakia) first to Egypt and later to Syria, dependent hitherto on supplies doled out by the Western Powers under the 1950 Declaration, created a sharp pro-Soviet feeling in Syrian military circles. This was due less to Communist sympathies than to the perennial distrust of Western policy in regard to Israel and gratitude to the Soviet Union for general support of the Arab cause against Israel and in particular for the supply of arms. In July Syria recognized Communist China. In October a general strike in sympathy with Algeria, observed here as elsewhere in Arab countries, led to riots in Aleppo, in the course of which much damage was done to French-sponsored schools. In November, at the time of the attack on Egypt, Quwatli went to the Soviet Union on a state visit, and returned with news of an agreement to buy arms. The extent of this transaction was never disclosed. It is possible that jet aircraft and technicians took refuge in Syria from the Anglo-French attack on Egypt, and that this first gave rise to the tales about Soviet bases which the Syrian Government vigorously denied.

This new policy of friendship with the Soviet Union was closely connected with the growth in power of the Baath Party. On 15 June 1956 Sabri Assali, Secretary of the National Party, formed a new coalition Government in which the Baath Socialists were represented, and in the next months they gained strength. They succeeded, better than any other group, in canalizing popular nationalist feeling, pro-Egyptian, vaguely reformist, neutralist with an anti-Western inclination; and they were on close terms with a group of officers, led by Abdul Hamid Sarraj and strongly neutralist in feeling, which was dominant in the army.

There was, however, still opposition, both to the domination of the left wing and, perhaps rather less, to the pro-Egyptian and anti-Iraqi alignment of foreign policy. This opposition was led by certain members of the People's Party. In December 1956 the Government announced that they, as well as other opponents of the regime, had been discovered to be implicated in a plot, in agreement with Iraq and the Western Powers, to overturn the Government at the time of the attack on Egypt. Those of them who had not fled the country were arrested and brought to trial. A military court found many of the accused guilty. Twelve of them were condemned to death, but the four who were in custody had their sentences changed to life imprisonment—under pressure from other Moslem countries.

The beginning of 1957 was marked by the formation of a new parliamentary bloc with a neutralist and popular nationalist programme: it included a majority of the deputies, among them the Socialists, the only Communist member, members of the National Party, and some Independents. As a result the Government was reconstructed, with Assali still as Prime Minister. The new Government rejected the Eisenhower Plan on 10 January, calling it superfluous, and declaring that the United States had no right to send troops to any Arab country without the previous approval of the United Nations. Relations with Asian Powers were cultivated, and in January the Prime Minister visited Pakistan and India; but whereas he listened without comment to Pakistani explanations of the Baghdad Pact and scouted warnings of the dangers of Soviet friendship, he and Nehru seemed to talk the same language about neutralism, and when in June 1957 the visit was returned, Nehru was given the freedom of Damascus.

In March 1957, after a struggle which had lasted nearly a year, the contract for the construction of a government-owned oil refinery at Homs, at a cost of some £6 million (partly on a barter basis), was awarded on purely political grounds to Czech contractors, despite a very favourable American tender, and a wider economic agreement with Czechoslovakia was made. Delivery of Soviet arms ordered in 1956 continued and fresh arms contracts seem to have been passed.

Inside the Government there was a struggle between the influence of the Baath and that of Khalid al-Azm, an unsuccessful candidate for the Presidency of the Republic in 1955. It was perhaps with an eye to future elections and to outbid the Baath that he became the chief spokesman of the pro-Soviet group. On 6 August he secured in Moscow an agreement by which the Soviet Government undertook in principle to help Syria's economic development by providing financial and technical aid on apparently easy terms. On his return, the Chief of Staff and other right-wing officers were replaced by men reputed to have strong left-wing views.

The close relations with the Soviet Union as well as internal tension and instability complicated Syria's relations with the West and with her neighbours. It is true that in March the Government gave permission for the IPC to repair the damaged pumping stations, though not until the Israelis had been compelled to withdraw from Gaza and Sinai; that in May the export of wheat to France, prohibited since November, was once more allowed; and that there were even hints of better relations with Britain. But with America relations grew steadily worse. The United States Government made no secret of its anxiety about developments in Syria. On the other hand many Syrians suspected the United States of instigating the opposition in Syria, or her neighbours, to overturn the regime, while the neutralists fiercely opposed the Baghdad Pact, and then the Eisenhower Doctrine, as designed to draw Middle East states into the American sphere of

Q

influence. Above all the American attitude towards Israel, which remained unchanged, determined the attitude of the average Syrian towards the West, just as it was the main cause of any pro-Soviet feelings he might have. American financial and military aid was suspect as perhaps requiring in return some concession to Israel, while Soviet aid had no such conditions attached. In August the Government expelled three members of the United States Embassy in Damascus on the charge of plotting with the French, Turks, and Israelis, and with the Syrian opposition. The United States thereupon asked for the recall of the Syrian Ambassador in Washington.

The struggle between Right and Left continued. Sarraj remained in his post in spite of efforts to have him transferred abroad. During demonstrations in Aleppo bombs were thrown into government offices and into the houses of some supporters of the Baath. There was a brawl in parliament on 7 June when the Communist leader, Khalid Bikdash, described the People's Party (Shaab) as tools of the West. The Shaab deputies and other Opposition members resigned, to the number of 62 (the total membership of the House is 142). They were persuaded to withdraw their resignations, and in response to their demand martial law, imposed at the time of the Suez crisis, was abolished. Nevertheless the opposition felt growing pressure from the Government, and some of the most prominent left the country. A Shaabist, the President of the Chamber, was replaced by Akram Hourani, the most powerful of the leaders of the Baath.

The complicity of Syria in the troubles of the Nabulsi period in Jordan was shown on the occasion of the flight of Abu Nuwar and his successor as Chief of Staff to Syria. The intention of the Syrian Government to bring about the annexation of Jordan seemed sufficiently clear to Iraq and Saudi Arabia to prompt them to take military measures to forestall it. The Jordanian request for the withdrawal of Syrian troops, which were stated to have interfered in the internal affairs of Jordan, was complied with by Syria with an ill grace. The communiqué issued by Saud and Hussein when the former visited Amman in June 1947 was attacked fiercely by the Syrian Deputy Prime Minister, Khalid al-Azm, who described Saud and Hussein as co-operating with American foreign policy, and declared that the promised Syrian contribution to the subsidy required to replace that of Britain would not be paid. The charge against Saudi Arabia led to the temporary withdrawl of the Saudi Ambassador from Damascus, but the trouble was smoothed over

Only with Egypt did relations remain good. When opening the National Assembly in July Nasser gave fuller support than before to the idea of union with Syria, and in September a joint committee was set up to investigate the question of economic union. Nevertheless there were signs that Egypt feared lest Syria's policy should lead to a world conflict, and wished to bring her back to the path of strict neutrality.

After the visit of Loy Henderson, of the State Department, to Turkey and other neighbours of Syria in August 1957, Dulles declared that other Middle East states had been found to be deeply concerned about the growth of Soviet influence in Syria, and Eisenhower expressed apprehension lest international Communism should push Syria into acts of aggression. Thereupon the Soviet Government sent notes to Britain, France, and the United States, warning them against interference in Syria, while Iraq, Lebanon, and Jordan denied that they had expressed anxiety to Henderson, though Iraq and Jordan did admit anxiety about Syrian policy on other grounds. Such denials doubtless had local opinion in mind, but were probably due in part to the fear that to isolate Syria too much might rally the Syrians behind their Government and drive it even farther towards the Soviet Union than it wished to go. Similar reasons probably prompted the visits of Saud and the Iraqi Prime Minister to Damascus at the end of September, and the declarations by various Arab states that they would support Syria against aggression.

A threat of aggression against Syria was alleged both by Syria and by the Soviet Union, which in September charged Turkey with massing troops on the frontier with the intention of attacking Syria. Egypt sent a small body of troops to Syria and announced that it was to assist her against the Turkish threat, but the course of the proceedings in the Assembly of the United Nations suggested that other Arab states did not take the alleged danger very seriously. Syria refrained from pressing the charge and declared that the tension had relaxed, but the Government continued for some little time to maintain the state of alarm inside Syria.

Although the Syrian Parliament and political life were still apparently dominated by oligarchs of the old school such as the President Shukri Quwatli and the Prime Minister Sabri al-Assali, real power from 1954 onwards was shifting steadily into the hands of the Baathists, the Communists, and their respective sympathizers especially in the army. The right-wing Syrian National Social Party, the Moslem Brotherhood, and the People's Party were all discredited and losing supporters. In the summer of 1957 an officer with Communist affiliations, Colonel Afif al-Bizri, became Army Chief of Staff.

The Syrian–Egyptian Union 1958–61

The chief impulse behind the Syrian–Egyptian union was the Syrian Baath. Whether, as was later alleged, the Baathists were genuinely seeking Egyptian protection against a possible Communist takeover in Syria or whether the Baath merely wished to avoid sharing power with the Communists is uncertain.[1] President Nasser at first opposed the idea of union and when he agreed he insisted that it should not be heavily

[1] See Malcolm Kerr's *The Arab Cold War 1958–64* (New York 3rd ed., 1971).

centralized and not a federal union as the Syrians wanted and that political parties should be dissolved. The Syrian Prime Minister, Khalid al-Azm, the Deputy Premier, and the Communists all attempted to prevent the union but without success.

On 2 February 1958 Presidents Nasser and Quwatli jointly announced that a United Arab Republic of Egypt and Syria would be set up with legislative authority vested in an assembly in which Syria would have one quarter of the seats and Egypt three quarters. A plebiscite held in both countries on 21 February resulted in an almost unanimous vote in favour of the union and of Nasser as the first President. Shukri al-Quwatli retired with the honorific title of 'First Citizen of the UAR' and the Communists went underground.

The Syrian Baathists were given high office in the Union. Akram Hourani became a Vice-President and Chairman of the Executive Council for the Syrian province. Salah Bitar became a Minister of State and later Minister of Culture and National Guidance in the Central Government. But the Baathists, after nominally dissolving their organization together with the other political parties, had hoped to control Syrian political life through the National Union organization and to this President Nasser was strongly opposed. Colonel Sarraj, the powerful Interior Minister for the Syrian region, co-operated with Cairo against the Baath who were consequently unable to screen the candidates for the National Union elections held in July 1959. The Baath at first called on their candidates to withdraw from the elections and then relented. The result was that an estimated 250 Baathists were elected out of a total of 9,445 seats. In August President Nasser dismissed Riyadh al-Malki, the Baathist Minister of National Guidance and the remaining Baathists in leading positions resigned *en bloc* in December 1959 and went into retirement or self-exile in Lebanon.

Colonel Sarraj succeeded Akram Hourani as Chairman of the Syrian Executive Council and President Nasser increasingly relied upon him and his police methods for governing Syria. In 1960, however, Nasser sent his closest colleague, Field-Marshal Abdul Hakim Amer, as a quasi-proconsul to Syria with instructions to alleviate the causes of growing Syrian opposition to the union. These included army resentment against the appointment of senior Egyptian officers in the Syrian forces, middle-class antipathy for Egyptian socialist legislation, economic restrictions and bureaucratic methods, landowners' opposition to agrarian reform, and the intelligentsia's dislike of limitations to intellectual freedom. Since the departure of the Baath Syria appeared more than ever as the junior partner in the union. Finally, three years of consecutive drought in Syria's agrarian economy did nothing to increase the Government's popularity. President Nasser retained most of his personal popularity among the Syrian people and drew wildly enthusiastic crowds on his visits. But he had manifestly failed to discover a satisfactory method of governing Syria.

In August 1961 even Sarraj fell from favour and was moved to Cairo as Vice-President. A month later he resigned and returned to Damascus. But it was a group of other army officers who on 28 September arrested Field-Marshal Amer, put him on a plane to Cairo and announced Syria's secession from the UAR.

1961–1963

Jordan and Turkey immediately recognized the new Government formed of conservative Syrian politicians and led by Mamoun al-Kuzbari. President Nasser decided not to resist the secession by force but at once began denouncing the 'reactionary secessionist' regime in Syria. His strictures were apparently justified when the elections which were held under the pre-union electoral system in early 1962 resulted in a victory for the right-wing forces who watered down the UAR land reform and repealed most of the socialization measures. Although party labels were prohibited the elections marked a comeback for the People's Party. Dr. Nazim al-Qudsi became President and Maarouf al-Dawalibi Prime Minister.

The Syrians responded by strongly asserting their Arabism and continued devotion to the cause of Arab unity. They called their state the 'Syrian Arab Republic' and circulated Arab governments with a draft plan for federal union. In repealing the UAR socialist legislation they claimed to be replacing opportunist measures by 'constructive socialism'. But it was difficult for the Syrians to sustain a progressive socialist image and the Government was manifestly weak and unstable. Akram Hourani and Salah Bitar had signed together with other politicians the manifesto of 2 October 1961 supporting the secession but Bitar was soon to regret his action and in June 1962 Hourani was expelled by the Baath. The Syrian left-wing soon turned against the predominantly right-wing regime.

On 28 March 1962 the Syrian army high command moved against the civilian regime it had brought to power and arrested President Qudsi and most of his Government. But the army was divided in purpose; a pro-Nasser section in Aleppo which had declared for a new union with Egypt succumbed to a force sent from Damascus. Army officers of different tendencies either fled or were exiled and, after failing to find enough civilian politicians to form a new Government, the army command was obliged to release President Qudsi and his Cabinet. A Government was formed under Dr. Bashir al-Azma who had held office in the UAR and was more progressive in outlook than his predecessors.

The Azma Government partially restored some of the UAR socialization measures and took some steps towards improving relations with Cairo. Dr. Azma publicly declared that President Nasser had been 'stabbed in the back by Syria's secession'. But these gestures did not suffice to placate Cairo which regarded the Azma Government as only superficially different from its predecessors. The radio war was soon resumed and the deterioration in Syrian–Egyptian relations culminated in a violent clash at an Arab League meeting in Lebanon in August 1962. Egypt provocatively sent to the meeting a delegation led by three Nasserite Syrian exiles and the Syrians responded by circulating a 'Black Book' containing a detailed account of Egypt's authorities' alleged misdeeds during the union. When the Syrians accused the Egyptian Government of secretly working with the USA to freeze the Palestine question the Egyptians walked out. Syrian–Egyptian relations deteriorated even further in January 1963 when the Arab League Secretary-General dismissed the Syrian Commissioner of the League Office for the Boycott of Israel which is located in Damascus and replaced him with an Egyptian. With support from Jordan, Saudi Arabia, and Iraq the Syrians refused to recognize the new appointment.

In an effort to strengthen its fragile position the Syrian Government cultivated its relations with the Iraqi leader Abdul Karim Kassem. But this proved fatal as Kassem and his regime were overthrown by a Baathist coup on 8 February 1963. The new Iraqi regime's immediate restoration of relations with Cairo made the Syrian regime even more vulnerable. The Syrian Baathists, led by the Secretary-General Michel Aflaq and Silah Bitar had held aloof from the various governments since the secession but their political activities had not been restrained. Aflaq now made a triumphal visit to Baghdad where he was greeted as a hero by the Iraqi Baathists. Demoralized and weakened, the Syrian regime was easily swept away in a bloodless coup on 8 March.

1963–1966

As in Iraq, a National Revolutionary Command Council (NRCC) of anonymous officers and civilians assumed power and appointed a predominantly Baathist Cabinet headed by Silah Bitar.

The coup had not been led by the Baath but by Major-General Ziyad al-Hariri and other senior officers unaffiliated with any political group. But in the political vacuum created by the coup the Baathists were the only organized political group outside those associated with the deposed regime. The Nasserists may have been more numerous but they lacked cohesion. The NRCC chose as its president Colonel Louay al-Atassi a mild and moderate young army officer who, although not a Baathist, was known as a sympathizer. Brigadier Amin al-Hafez, a much stronger and more forceful character who was a Baathist became Minister of Interior in the new Government.

The Baathists held the key posts in the Government but it included members of other Arab unionist organizations such as Nihad al-

Kassem of the United Arab Front, who became Deputy Premier, Sami Sufan of the Socialist Unity Movement and Hani al-Hindi and Jihad Dahi of the Arab Nationalist Movement. At this stage these other parties assumed that the Baath would be prepared to share power with them. They believed that they would be indispensable to the Baathists in the tripartite unity negotiations between Syria, Iraq, and Egypt which began in a mood of pan-Arabist euphoria immediately after the Syrian coup. In return the Syrian Baathists showed readiness to co-operate but only as a tactical manoeuvre. They never doubted that they were destined to govern Syria and their morale was strengthened in the Cairo negotiations by the presence of their Iraqi Baathist allies.

The unity talks were held in three stages between 14 March and 14 April; some of the discussions included the Iraqis and some were bilateral Egyptian–Syrian negotiations. Most of the discussions concerned Syria and many of them related to events during the 1958–61 union. President Nasser did not conceal his dislike and suspicion of the Syrian Baathists whom he had not forgiven for their mass resignation from the UAR Government in 1959 and there were many sharp exchanges. There were also frequent clashes between the Baathists and non-Baathists in the Syrian delegation.

Friction between Damascus and Cairo had already become open with strong mutual press criticism before the end of March. Nevertheless the differences were papered over sufficiently to enable a final agreement on the form of a tripartite federal state to be published on 17 April. This favoured President Nasser's views in that it provided for a President with a Prime Minister responsible to a National Assembly or lower house which would be elected on a basis of population and would therefore be Egyptian-dominated. The agreement included a self-contradictory paragraph declaring that the federal leadership would 'gradually establish a unified political organization that will lead national political action inside and outside the Federation, and will work to mobilize popular forces. . . . But this does not mean the dissolution of existing unionist parties.'

In view of the mutual mistrust between the parties and their different interpretations of this agreement its collapse was inevitable. The fundamental flaw in the agreement was that the Syrian Baathists wanted President Nasser's approval and support for their government of Syria but not his interference; President Nasser rejected this arrangement. Nasser had reluctantly agreed that the actual proclamation of the union should be delayed five months with a further twenty months' transitional period before the new constitution came into force. Within two weeks of 17 April Syrian–Egyptian relations deteriorated sharply. The Syrian army expelled scores of Nasserist officers while the civilian Baathists foiled the efforts of the non-Baathist Arab unionist parties to obtain a larger share of power. The non-Baathist ministers resigned on 11 May but after efforts to form a new coalition had failed Silah Bitar headed a Government of Baathist and docile pro-Baathist independents. Pro-Nasser demonstrations during the visit to Damascus of the Algerian leader Colonel Boumedienne were firmly suppressed by General Hafez. On 8 July the Syrian Baathists succeeded in obtaining the dismissal and exile of the politically independent Army Chief of Staff General Ziyad Hariri.

Syrian–Egyptian relations had deteriorated to such a point that General Louay Atassi headed a delegation to Alexandria on 18 July to discuss them with President Nasser. A few hours after the Syrians left Damascus Airport an ill-organized pro-Nasser coup was attempted and ruthlessly crushed and on 22 July Nasser who had held his fire until then, made his long awaited speech attacking the Baath in Syria as a 'secessionist, inhuman and immoral regime'.

The Syrian Baathists were now on as bad terms with Egypt as the preceding regime had been. A tour of Egypt and Syria by President Abdul Salam Aref of Iraq at the end of August failed to improve matters. On the other hand, the Syrians drew closer to Iraq. On 8 October a Syrian–Iraqi military union was agreed upon and the Iraqi Defence Minister General Saleh Mahdi Ammash became Commander-in-Chief of the combined armies. A Syrian brigade was sent to Iraq to take part in operations against the Kurdish rebels in the north, and the Baath Party Congress in Damascus in October called for a federal union between the two countries.

Just when it seemed that the Baath Party might succeed in creating a Syrian–Iraqi union where so many earlier attempts had failed, the Iraqi Baathists, who had lost popularity and weakened themselves by a split into right and left wings, were swept from power by President Aref and other non-Baathist officers in a coup on 18 November. The Syrians bitterly condemned the coup.

At odds with both Iraq and Egypt, Syria was isolated within the Arab world. But General Hafez, who had quietly replaced General Louay Atassi as President of the Syrian NRCC, inaugurated a period of firm and authoritarian government. Syria's isolation was underlined at the meeting of Arab Kings and Presidents which convened in Cairo in January 1964 at President Nasser's invitation to discuss means of opposing Israel's plans to divert the waters of the River Jordan. Nasser made use of the meeting to repair his relations with other Arab Heads of State but this did not include Syria and he had no private conversations with General Hafez. Syria's demand for urgent military action against Israel was rejected by the other Arab states.

In February and March 1964 there was unrest in Banias, Homs, and Aleppo and in April there was serious rioting in Hama which the Syrian Army firmly suppressed. The Government blamed the demonstrations on 'reactionaries and feudalists' led by Aref supporters and

Nasserists but the Moslem Brotherhood, supported by merchants and landowners who were hard hit by the Baathist nationalization, were also undoubtedly involved. The Government used severe measures to end the strikes of merchants and shopkeepers.

On 25 April Hafez announced a provisional constitution under which Syria would become a 'socialist people's democratic republic'; on 9 May Salah Bitar formed his fourth cabinet since the Baathists took power in March 1963 and announced that there would be no class struggle in Syria and no more nationalization. On 14 May a Presidential Council was established with General Hafez as Head of State. On 3 October Bitar resigned and General Hafez himself formed a new coalition of thirteen Baathists and nine Independent Unionists.

Relations with the Aref regime in Iraq worsened and on 28 April the Iraqi–Syrian military union was abrogated. At the second Arab summit meeting in Alexandria in September 1964 the Syrians were again somewhat isolated but General Hafez, formerly one of Egypt's strongest critics, adopted a policy in favour of a rapprochement with Cairo. He was bitterly opposed by anti-Egyptian Baathist officers led by Colonel Silah Jedid.

Despite frequent reports that the Baathists intended to enlarge the Government to share real power with non-Baathist unionist elements this was not done. During 1965 the Baathists tightened their control of the country. A series of new nationalization measures provoked more anti-Government demonstrations and strikes to which the Government responded with harsh confiscatory measures. In January 1965 a special military court was established with sweeping powers to deal with all offences against the socialist revolution.

In August 1965 an all-Baathist National Revolutionary Council was established with the task of drafting a permanent constitution. However, there was a clear division within the party between the radical extremists and the more moderate elements who favoured conciliating the middle classes. In January 1966 the radical Cabinet led by Dr. Yusuf Zuayen was replaced by one more Government led by the moderate Silah Bitar. However, on 23 February 1966 the extremists seized power in a violent coup led by Colonel Jedid. General Hafez was imprisoned and Silah Bitar and Michel Aflaq went into exile. Dr. Zuayen formed the new Government and Dr. Nureddin Atassi became Head of State. The Cabinet included two Communist sympathizers and restrictions were lifted on the activities of the Syrian Communist party although the party was still officially banned.

The new regime moved closer to the Soviet Union which in April 1966 concluded, in place of West Germany, a deal for the construction of a Euphrates Dam. In September 1966 the Government announced that it had foiled a plot against the regime by the ousted Baathist elements in collusion with Jordan. Although the Government was

cool and mistrustful in its general attitude towards President Nasser
and Egypt, circumstances brought the two countries closer together.
The Syrians were anxious to end their isolation while Nasser hoped to
be able to exert some influence over the hot-headed young neo-
Marxists in power in Damascus. The previous regime of General Hafez
had been the most bellicose of all the Arab states towards Israel. It was
the only Arab Government to give open support and encouragement to
al-Fatah, the newly-formed Palestinian guerrilla organization. The new
Syrian regime was if possible even more anti-Israeli in its attitude. In
July 1966 the Israelis successfully bombarded Syrian diversion operations on the River Banias from the air and the Syrians abandoned
the work. Nasser declared that Egypt could not be expected to go to
Syria's aid whenever Israel destroyed a couple of tractors but he could
not ignore Syrian requests for a closer military alliance, especially
when Egyptian spokesmen had so often claimed that Egyptian forces
were the most formidable in the Arab world. In November 1966
Egypt signed a comprehensive defence pact with Syria providing for a
full merger and a joint command for the two armies in the event of war.
But the Syrians were still too distrustful of Egypt to accept the stationing
of Egyptian troops and planes on their territory which alone would
have made the pact effective.

The June War

The Syrians bear a measure of responsibility for the outbreak of the
1967 Six Day War. The Israelis had responded to Syria's open support
for the Palestinian guerrillas with military reprisals and threats of
heavier action. In January the UN Secretary-General U Thant was
successful in persuading Syria and Israel to hold a meeting of the
Syrian–Israeli mixed armistice commission but there was no positive
result. In the early months of 1967 there were frequent incidents on
Syria's armistice line with Israel and in April Syria lost six MiG
fighters in an air clash during which Israeli aircraft flew over Damascus.
On 12 May the Israeli Chief of Staff General Rabin declared that until
the revolutionary regime in Syria had been overthrown no Government
in the Middle East could feel safe.

Rumours were circulating in Syrian Government circles of an im-
pending major Israeli offensive. When these reports reached President
Nasser and were confirmed by his own intelligence services and Soviet
sources he felt compelled to take action and asked for the UN Emergency
Force in Sinai to be removed. Syrians and Jordanians had often
criticized Nasser for hiding his forces behind the protection of UNEF.
His subsequent closure of the Straits of Tiran led the Israelis to attack
Egypt on 5 June.

When war came the Syrians did not attempt to invade Israel although
they used their artillery from the Golan Heights against Israeli posi-

tions. After defeating Jordan, Israel turned against Syria, stormed the Golan Heights, and occupied the key town of Quneitra. The Syrians agreed to a ceasefire on 10 June, one day later than Egypt.

After the war the Syrians maintained the view that the Arabs should continue the struggle at all costs although they were widely criticized in the Arab world for having held back in the war. Relations with Jordan which had been at their worst just before the war because the Syrians believed King Hussein was planning to intervene in Syria with the help of some Syrian refugee officers, improved slightly after the war and President Atassi met King Hussein. There was a more real rapprochement with Iraq whose President Abdul Rahman Aref visited Damascus in August. But the Syrian regime continued to maintain that co-operation was only possible between 'progressive' Arab states. The Foreign Minister Ibrahim Makhous attended the Arab Foreign Ministers meeting at Khartoum in August but was not authorized by his Government to represent it at the summit conference that followed. Consequently Syria was excluded from the Arab oil states' aid to Egypt and Jordan to compensate them for their war losses.

Persistent rumours of splits within the ruling Baath Party were constantly denied. In September 1967 President Atassi was re-elected Secretary-General of the Baath but much of the real power remained in the hands of the army and especially of Colonel Silah Jedid. In August the Government dismissed Khalid al-Jundi who had acquired considerable power and commanded armed bands of workers. In September there was a minor Government reshuffle which brought in four pro-Nasser ministers although none in a position of importance.

Syria's total rejection of any political solution to the Arab–Israeli conflict was not backed up by any energetic military action and there were few incidents on the Golan Heights during 1968. Tension and uncertainty at home were increased by the July coup in Baghdad which brought to power in Iraq the orthodox Baathists of the kind that had been ousted in Syria in 1966. The widely expected anti-Government coup did not take place although a division appeared between Colonel Jedid, assistant Secretary-General of the Baath Party in Syria, who wished to pursue Syria's independent radical line, and the Defence Minister, General Hafez Assad, who favoured a rapprochement with the Iraqi Baathists and disliked Syria's increasing dependence on the USSR. A widely noted feature of the regime was that many of its leaders including Jedid and Assad were of the minority sub-Shii Alawite sect which had not traditionally held political power in Syria and are not generally attracted to pan-Arabist ideas. The Jedid–Assad rivalry remained indecisive although when President al-Atassi took the premiership from Dr. Yusuf Zuayen in September 1968 and the Foreign Minister Dr. Makhous also lost his post it was interpreted as a victory for al-Assad.

In May 1968 all the leading members of the regime went to Cairo to urge that Egypt associate itself more closely with Syria. President Nasser's reply was that for the strengthening of the Arab front the first essential was a rapprochement between Syria, Iraq, and Jordan.

In January 1969 the trial of 77 Syrian politicians associated with the right-wing Baathist regime ended with prison sentences of lengths ranging up to hard labour for life for 61 of them (including Salah Bitar who was tried *in absentia*). In March the struggle for power between Assad and Jedid reached a new crisis. It was not pressed to its conclusion although a compromise left General Assad in the ascendancy. The Jedid camp was weakened by the suicide on 2 March of the military intelligence chief, Colonel Abdul Karim al-Jundi.

General Assad was reported to favour a rapprochement with Iraq and at the end of March some Iraqi troops were stationed on Syrian territory at Syria's request. But there was no real reconciliation and the press and radio war between Baghdad and Damascus continued.

In the summer there was a serious crisis with Lebanon after the Lebanese Army clashed with al-Saiqa, the Palestinian guerrilla organization supported by the Syrian Baathists. Syria strongly supported the right of the Palestinians to operate from Lebanese bases. Syria's own border with Israel was relatively quiet but on 8 July the air forces of the two nations clashed over the occupied Golan Heights.

Despite Syria's cool relations with its Arab neighbours some attempt was made to co-ordinate its defences with theirs. On 30 July an Iraqi–Syrian defence agreement was signed and a few days later some Syrian troops were moved into Jordanian territory with Jordan's approval. In August, President Atassi and General Assad went to Cairo to revive the Syrian–Egyptian defence agreement.

Syria refused to attend the Islamic summit meeting in Rabat in September but it did take part in the Arab summit in December, despite its continued opposition to such meetings.

In May there were signs of a cooling off between Syria and the USSR, as the Syrians were dissatisfied with the slow delivery of Soviet arms supplies. President Atassi postponed his planned visit to the Soviet Union while the Syrian Chief of Staff, General Mustafa Tlass, visited Peking and it was reported that China would be building missile sites for Syria. However, in June, Syria pleased the USSR by recognizing East Germany and in July President Atassi paid his postponed visit to the USSR during which he signed a new agreement for Soviet technical and financial aid.

On 29 May the long-awaited new Cabinet with a broader base was formed under President Atassi. It included Arab nationalists, unionists, and independents as well as Baathists although the Baath kept all the key posts.

In the spring and early summer of 1970 the Syrians demonstrated their intention to reactivate their front with Israel which had been relatively dormant since the 1967 war. Their aim was to reduce the pressure on Egypt at the Suez Canal and to reassert their claim to the Golan Heights in the event of a Middle East settlement. In late March and early April Syrian forces made a series of raids on Israeli forces in the Golan Heights and there were more serious engagements in June. The Syrians admitted losing 45 dead and 75 wounded as well as two aircraft, but observers reported an improved spirit and standard of training in the Syrian forces.

As the Jordanian crisis deepened in August and September the Syrians expressed vigorous support for the Palestinian guerrillas. On 19 September, after the outbreak of the Jordanian civil war, Syrian armoured units entered northern Jordan; the Syrians claimed that they were elements of the Palestine Liberation Army. They withdrew a few days later, having suffered severe casualties and also, it was thought, because of Soviet pressure.

This action helped to bring to a head the submerged conflict between the civilian wing of the Baath led by Silah Jedid and the military wing led by General Assad. When the civilian Baathists criticized General Assad who had opposed the intervention in Jordan he took counter-measures to ensure his position and the loyalty of the armed forces. After failing in a final attempt to reach a compromise with President Atassi which would have excluded Silah Jedid from power but maintained the Baathist monopoly of Government, General Assad formed a new Syrian Regional Command of the Baath by his own supporters on 18 November. The relatively unknown Ahmad Khatib became Head of State, and General Assad himself as Prime Minister and Defence Minister headed a new Coalition Government of Baathists and Nasserists (with two Communists). He also took over control of al-Saiqa guerrilla organization. In early 1971 Assad became President.

THE PEOPLE

The September 1960 census gave a total population of 4,565,121 but this excluded an estimated 120,000 refugees and 140,000 bedouin nomads. A mid-1969 estimate put the population in 1967 at 6 million and the population of the capital, Damascus, at 636,000. The population of the other main towns (1964 estimates) were: Aleppo (547,000); Homs 182,000; Hama 132,000; Latakia 78,000; and Deir al-Zor 63,000.

The nomadic bedouin population has declined steadily since the war and the greatest population density is in the Hawran, Jabal Druze, and Hama regions. Arabic is the standard language, with English and French widely spoken. Most Syrians are of Semitic stock (primarily Arab); the principal minorities being Armenians (about 150,000) who live mainly in Aleppo and Damascus, and Kurds (about 50,000) who live mostly in the Turkish border areas and in Damascus. The Assyrians, estimated at 20,000, often speaking the Syriac language, live in villages along the Nahr al-Kabbur in the north-east and on the western slopes of the Anti-Lebanon Mountains.

Religious differences are of considerable although declining political importance. Christians, mainly Orthodox, form about 8 per cent of the population and are largely an urban middle-class community. The main Moslem sects are orthodox Sunni (the majority), Alawis, Shiis, Ismailis, and Druzes. The Druzes (about 160,000) and Alawis (about 500,000) both exert a disproportionate amount of political influence. There are about 5,000 Jews.

GOVERNMENT

Syria has a written Constitution dating from 1950 establishing it as a democratic parliamentary regime. After the Baath Socialist Party seized power in 1963 the country was ruled by the coalition of army officers and civilians who formed the National Revolutionary Council. Executive power was vested in the Presidential Council and the Cabinet; the former delegated the task of administration to growing cadres of technocrat civil servants headed by Cabinet ministers. On 25 April 1964 a Provisional Constitution was issued and on 23 August the Presidential Council, whose membership except for that of its chairman (President Amin al-Hafez) was secret, made policy decisions and administrative appointments. The left-wing Baathists, who seized power in February 1966 suspended the Provisional Constitution but a new one was introduced in 1969. In February 1971 the Provisional Constitution was amended to give the President wide powers similar to those of the Egyptian President and these were further extended in June 1972. In February a People's Council—Syria's first legislative assembly since 1966—was formed. It had 173 members of whom 87 were Baathists and the remainder representatives of various left-wing groups including Nasserists and Communists.

Administratively, the country is divided into 11 'Muhafazat' (provinces) which are subdivided into 37 *mantiqat* (districts) and 99 *nahiyat* (sub-districts). The Ministry of the Interior appoints the *Muhafiz* (Governor) of the province and other district officers.

Political Organizations

Political parties in Syria are banned except for the Baath but though dormant they are not extinct. The Communists remain a 'petit bourgeois' group drawn mainly from the professional classes and the religious minorities with little support from the peasantry although there are signs of Communist influence in the new industrial proletariat.

Relations between the Communists and the Baath fluctuate but the Baath does not accept a Communist challenge to its authority. Conservative forces in Syria were represented by the People's (Shaab) Party and the National (Watani) Party, twin heirs of the broadly based National Bloc which until the Second World War led the struggle against the French Mandate administration. The Moslem Brotherhood still has a following—especially in Damascus and Hama—but it was never a paramilitary terrorist organization as in Egypt.

SOCIAL SURVEY

The political power of the landowners who were formerly the most coherent social group in Syria has been steadily eroded during the 1950s and 1960s. The Shishakli Government's attempts at land reform achieved little result but the UAR agrarian reform which was only partially reversed by the first secessionist governments was completed by the Baathists after 1963. In the cities the older bourgeoisie of merchants (largely Christian and Jewish) had been replaced by a new middle class of lawyers, teachers, and Government officials.

Since 1958 various measures have aimed to improve conditions for industrial and agricultural workers. Decrees of March 1964 declared that farm labourers were to receive 40 per cent of the crop (10 per cent more than the traditional share) depending on the services supplied; they could also negotiate an agreement (usually 35 per cent) with the consent of both parties. The 1961 law passed under the UAR providing for 25 per cent of all industrial and business profits to be distributed to the workers remains in force.

There has been steady improvement in health standards in the 1950s and 1960s. Malaria is now almost eliminated and diseases such as trachoma, tuberculosis, and dysentery are on the decline because of improved water facilities and rural medical treatment through clinics built by the villagers and staffed by Government employees.

The Government's aim is to make primary education free and compulsory for a period of six years. Many new schools have been opened in recent years and by the mid-1960s there were more than 3,800 primary schools with 690,000 pupils and 16,000 teachers. There are about 600 secondary schools with 120,000 students and 4,500 teachers, 45 vocational schools and 9 teachers' training colleges. In 1965–6 there were 30,000 students at Damascus University and about 6,000 at Aleppo University.

ECONOMIC SURVEY

Syria has one of the greatest economic potentials of any of the Arab states. Largely owing to political instability this is still far from realized.

Agriculture remains much the most important sector employing about
60 per cent of the population and providing about one third of the
national income. However, its proportionate share is declining slowly
in relation to industry. The economic policies of the present regime are
broadly socialist and *dirigiste*. Much of the socialist legislation passed
during the union with Egypt remains in force. Syrian banks which
were denationalized after the secession have been re-nationalized by
the Baathists and amalgamated into five groups. Almost all imports
and exports are handled by the State-owned trading corporation
SIMEX.

The decade following independence at the end of the Second World
War was a period of fast growth, especially in the agricultural sector,
under a laissez-faire capitalist system. Reinvested war profits were used
to develop the dry farming areas of al-Jazira in the north-east and to
irrigate lands adjoining the Euphrates and Khabur rivers. Cotton and
grain production both expanded rapidly but capital investment in
agriculture began to fall off in the mid-1950s with the growth of
socialist influences on the Government. There was a further decline
during the Syrian–Egyptian union (1958–61) when land reform was
introduced and which coincided with three consecutive failures in
rainfall. However, the cultivated area (including fallow) increased
from 3·23 million hectares in 1951 to 6·097 million hectares in 1967.
It is estimated that a further 2·5 million hectares are cultivable but not
used. Dry farming in al-Jazira where production has been raised by
mechanized cultivation accounts for most of the increase but by 1967
the irrigated area covered 538,000 hectares (or about 9 per cent of the
cultivated area) compared with 284,000 hectares in 1946.

The chief Government irrigation schemes which are under way are
the drainage of al-Ghab Valley marshlands (begun by the French)
to reclaim and irrigate 30,000 hectares and of the Sind area of 10,000
hectares. The Italian firm Bonifica is reclaiming 13,500 hectares in
the Salhabiat and Hmeirat areas of the Euphrates Valley. The Syrian
Arab Irrigation Company is also irrigating 5,000 hectares at al-Fayd.
The Euphrates Dam will eventually make possible the irrigation of
600,000 hectares, thereby doubling the present irrigated area.

Syria's agricultural output depends heavily on the low but highly
variable rainfall. Bumper cereal harvests (wheat and barley) in the
mid-1950s were followed by the disastrous drought years of 1958–61
in which Syria was obliged to import large quantities of cereals. In
good years Syria can export up to 500,000 tons of wheat and 400,000
tons of barley. A bumper year followed in 1962 but 1963, 1964, and
1965, although good, were unremarkable. Poor harvests in 1966 and
1968 were followed by a good average one in 1969.

Cotton, which is less affected by rainfall, has become Syria's most
important cash crop accounting for over 60 per cent of Syria's exports.

Medium staple cotton had been grown in Syria for many years but high prices after the Second World War provided a big stimulus to the industry. The area under cotton rose from 135,200 hectares in 1953–4 to 293,000 hectares in 1965. Production rose from 35,000 tons in 1950 to 85,000 tons in 1955 and 180,000 tons in 1965 although it fell back to about 150,000 tons in subsequent years. The Ministry of Agriculture and Agrarian Reform has made vigorous efforts to improve and increase output through loans to cultivators, increased use of fertilizers, improved seeds, the import of tractors, and provision of technical advice to farmers.

Other important crops are maize, millet, pulses, vegetables, oilseeds, and tobacco. The tobacco industry receives special Government encouragement and both productivity and output (7·5 million kilos) reached records in 1969. Sugar-beet was introduced in the early 1950s and the area under this crop reached 8·5 million hectares in 1967. Olives and fruit are also important and there are estimated to be 89 million fruit and olive trees. In 1967 there were 467,600 cattle, 757,000 goats, and 5·6 million sheep.

Agrarian Reform

Agrarian reform was implemented in September 1969 by a decree which limited land holdings to 80 hectares of irrigated land or 300 hectares of rain-fed land per person. After Syria's secession from the UAR the Dawalibi Government amended some of the law's provisions in favour of the landlords but the amendments were rescinded by the Baathists.

Early in 1969 the Government announced the completion of the first stage of land reform in Syria whereby 708,000 hectares in 1,413 villages had been redistributed to 40,000 families. The sizes of lots distributed to new owners have been chiefly conditioned by the size of the family but limited to a maximum of 30 hectares of non-irrigated or 8 hectares of irrigated or tree-planted land. Confiscated but non-allocated land that would otherwise remain idle was rented to anyone who would farm it, and liberal credit was granted by the nationalized banks to finance the purchase of farm materials. The second stage of agrarian reform will be the development of agricultural co-operatives.

Mining, Fuel, and Power

Oil. Syria's oil production is estimated to reach about 12–15 million tons a year by 1975. The new fields are at Suweidiya, Rumailan, and Karachuk. Oil was first struck at Suweidiya by the West German firm Concordia, a subsidiary of Deutsche Erdol AG. The Syrian General Petroleum Authority, drilling on its own account with Russian rigs, struck at Rumailan in 1962. Karachuk was discovered in 1956 by the Menhall Company which later took Atlantic Refinery and Portsmouth

Steel (US) as partners and drilled four producing wells before its concession was cancelled by the Government in 1958. Since 1964 all oil and mineral concession rights have been restricted to Government agencies. Output in 1970 from the three fields was about 100,000 barrels per day.

The building of a 405-mile oil pipeline from the fields in north-eastern Syria to the Homs Refinery and the oil port of Tartous on the Mediterranean was carried out by the Italian firm SNAM Progetti, and completed in March 1968. Syria is the only Middle Eastern state which markets its own oil directly. Sales are made partly for convertible currencies and partly for barter payment for goods and services.

The oil refinery at Homs was completed by the Czech Techno-Export in 1959. The raising of the refinery's throughput capacity from 1·5 million to 2·7 million tons a year to meet Syria's rapidly increasing consumption of oil production was completed by the end of 1969. During 1970 Syria's oil industry for the first time replaced food processing as the country's second most important industry in terms of value of production. Spinning and weaving remains in first place.

Other Minerals. Apart from oil, only phosphates are of any importance. Natural gas, lignite, chromite, lead, manganese, and asbestos exist but are not of any commercial value. Production from the Kneifess phosphate mines started in 1971 at 300,000 tons a year which is to be increased to 1·3 million tons by 1973. The present capacity of Syrian phosphate factories is 1·2 million tons a year which is due to be increased to 3 million tons a year with Soviet assistance by 1975.

The nitrogenous fertilizer plant which was completed at Homs in 1969 after heavy delays has a capacity of 150,000 tons a year.

Total production of electric power rose from 116 million kwh. in 1950 to 420 million kwh. in 1968. The Euphrates Dam should provide extra capacity of 100,000 kwh. in its first stage and 800,000 kwh. in its final stage.

Manufacturing Industry

Light industry has expanded as a result of heavy protective tariffs and the availability of cotton and food products which require processing. Nationalization measures during the union with Egypt and again in 1964–5 caused a certain amount of stagnation but expansion has now been resumed with Government support. The most developed is the textile industry which includes spinning, weaving, knitting, dyeing, and finishing. In 1965 there were 153,000 cotton spindles and 5,000 looms. The output of yarn increased from 4,700 tons in 1950 to over 18,000 tons in 1966. There are cement plants at Damascus, Aleppo, and Homs, and cement production increased from 3,200 tons a month in 1951 to 56,800 tons a month in 1966. Other industries include sugar-refining (about 100,000 tons a year), tanning, vegetable oil extraction, canning, and the manufacture of soap, matches, glass, beer, plastic goods, washing-machines, and refrigerators. Whereas in 1958 only 13·7 per cent of the capital invested in industry was in the public sector, the proportion was about 60 per cent by the end of the 1960s.

Transport and Communications

The three railways (340 miles standard gauge and 190 miles narrow gauge) were built during the Ottoman Empire and so far increases in traffic have been absorbed by the roads. Of 8,586 miles of road in 1961, 3,294 miles were metalled. However a new Tartous–Akkari–Homs–Aleppo line is now under construction linking the coast with the north and east of the country, and the Hejaz railway from Damascus to Medina is under repair. A new trans-desert Damascus–Baghdad road is near completion.

The port of Latakia handled 152 million tons of cargo in 1969. The new port which was built at Tartous is the terminal for Syrian oil exports and is now handling a large part of Jordanian phosphate exports.

There are major airports at Damascus and Aleppo and others at Kamishli and Latakia. The new French-built Damascus International Airport which was opened in September 1969 supersedes the old one at Mezze. A substantial and rapid increase in traffic was recorded as many major international airlines began to make use of the new airport.

Foreign Trade

Syrian exports have increased considerably since the early 1950s although they fluctuate heavily according to climatic conditions. They rose from £S271 million in 1951 to £S415 million in 1958. After a sharp fall owing to the drought of the next three years they reached £S720 million in 1963, £S643 million in 1965 and £S743 million in 1971. Imports, on the other hand, have increased steadily from £S291 million in 1951 to £S898 million in 1964 and £S1,677 million in 1971. The character of imports has shifted to a heavier emphasis on machinery and capital goods. Restrictions on the import of luxury and semi-luxury goods were intensified in April 1970. The Government aims to reduce the 1971 visible trade deficit of £S934 million by at least 50 per cent.

Raw cotton is easily Syria's single most important export. France, Italy, and Belgium were the principal buyers in the early 1950s but they have since been superseded by the Soviet Union, Communist China, and more recently Japan. Lebanon remains Syria's single most important trading partner. Exports to Lebanon were £S144 million in 1968 and imports from Lebanon £S64 million. Syria is a member of the Arab Common Market (Jordan, Kuwait, Iraq, and Egypt) and its trade with the other members is increasing. Since the mid-1950s the trend in Syrian trade, apart from the Arab states, has been away from the Western countries and towards the Eastern bloc. In 1968 imports from the Communist states were £S414·1 million and exports to them £S147·7 million compared with £S369·7 million imports from the EEC countries and £S99·7 million exports to them.

Development and Foreign Aid

Since independence successive Syrian governments have recognized the need for foreign assistance in developing the country's economic potential. In 1955 an IBRD mission recommended a six-year plan costing £S1,000 million of which one third would be devoted to irrigation and agriculture and nearly 40 per cent to education, public health, and social welfare.

The Government adopted most of the IBRD's high-priority projects in its own Seven-Year Plan for 1955–61. In 1957 Syria accepted a £50 million 2½ per cent loan from the USSR for certain economic development schemes and since then Syria has relied increasingly on aid from the Communist countries. In September 1958, under the UAR, a ten-year plan (1958–67) was approved but this was superseded by a more specific five-year plan running from 1960/1 to 1964/5. This proved to be over-ambitious and by the end of 1964 only 60–70 per cent of public investments had been made and considerably less in the private sector. A second five-year plan 1965–70 went into operation early in 1965 with the aim of doubling the 1960 national income.

The Euphrates Dam is the biggest single development project. Ultimately it will irrigate 600,000 hectares of land and increase electric capacity by 800,000 kwh. The capacity of the reservoir will be about 40,000 million cubic metres (compared with the Nile High Dam's 130,000 million cubic metres) and the main dam will be 70 metres high. West Germany offered a DM350 million credit for this scheme but when the West German Government held back as a result of Syria's political instability and the 1964–5 wave of nationalization the Soviet Union stepped in. Its total contribution to the financing of the Dam is expected to be about £S500 million.

The Soviet Union is also providing financial and technical aid for the Syrian oil industry and for railway expansion. Czechoslovakia, Bulgaria, and Poland also give important economic assistance to Syria. Mainly for political reasons Syria now has only minimal economic relations with the US, the UK, and West Germany. France and Italy are the Western countries which have retained the closest economic ties with Syria.

XI
Turkey

The Ottoman Empire was for centuries a major power in Europe, in Asia, and in Africa. The Turkish Republic, from its inception, set its face resolutely westward, and it is now accepted as a European as well as a Middle Eastern power; witness its inclusion in OECD, the Council of Europe, and NATO, and its associate membership of EEC. It differs from many of its neighbours also in possessing great military strength and a high degree of political stability: only once since 1923 has a Turkish Government been violently overthrown, and that at the cost of just four lives.

THE LAND AND THE PEOPLE

Turkey forms a rough quadrilateral about 1,000 miles from east to west by 300 to 400 from north to south, with a total area of about 300,000 square miles, or three times the size of Britain. Her territory in Thrace, which constitutes 3 per cent of her total area, borders on Bulgaria and Greece, while on her eastern frontier lies, to the north, the Soviet Union, and to the south, the north-east corner of Iran. On the south she has a short common frontier with Iraq and a longer frontier with Syria.

Turkey has a wide diversity of climate and ecology. The Aegean seabord and the plains of Antalya and Adana have a Mediterranean climate, with mild rainy winters and hot dry summers. These areas are very fertile, producing cotton, tobacco, citrus and other fruits, and cereals. The narrow northern seaboard, where tobacco is the major crop, has a high and more constant rainfall: Rize has the greatest mean annual rainfall (over 70 inches) of the whole country. A geological fault runs parallel with the northern coast, from the head of the Gulf of Izmit through Bolu to Erzurum. Along this line earth-tremors are frequent; the population here is consequently smaller than the fertility of the region would lead one to expect. The Mediterranean and Black Sea climates overlap in the Marmara basin. Autumn and winter are rainy, and rain storms are frequent in spring.

The centre of Anatolia consists of a vast treeless plateau, broken up by marshes, which rises from about 2,000 feet in the west to 6,000 feet where it joins the great eastern highlands. Its climate is extreme, with temperatures ranging from −15° F (−27° C) to over 100° F (37·8° C). Over much of the plateau the rainfall is low and irregular (between 8 and 16 inches a year) and hot summers are followed by snow-bound winters. Production of cereals and sheep-raising are the main means of livelihood, usually practised together in varying proportions. The plateau is bounded on the north by a series of forested mountain ranges descending steeply to the sea along the whole length of the Black Sea coast; and on the south by the great Taurus range, which swings inland to merge with the eastern mountains. The highest point of all is Mount Ararat (16,945 ft.), close to the Iranian frontier.

The melting snows of Turkey's mountainous interior supply a large number of springs, streams, and rivers. Most of them vary from torrents in the spring to mere trickles, or even dry beds, by the end of the summer. Water is a scarce and precious commodity. The Euphrates rises in the east of Turkey and flows south into Syria, while the largest river completely within Turkey is the Kizil Irmak ('Red River', the ancient Halys), which rises some 60 miles east of Sivas and, flowing in the form of an inverted question mark, reaches the Black Sea at Bafra.

Except for the famous harbours of Istanbul, Izmir, and Iskenderun, and for the heavily indented Aegean coast, the Turkish coastline has few good natural harbours or safe anchorages. The Black Sea is renowned for its inhospitality.

The following figures were given for the use of land in 1965.

	Percentage
Cultivated	19·6
Fallow	10·9
Pasture	36·2
Vineyards	1·0
Market gardens	1·1
Olive groves	0·8
Forest	13·6
Unproductive	16·8
	100·0

Source: Press Counsellor, Turkish Embassy, London.

The Population

The Turkish language belongs to the Altaic group. At the present time people speaking dialects of Turkish extend across Central Asia, from north-west China through the Soviet Union to Iran. Turkish-speaking minorities have survived from the days of the Ottoman Empire in the Balkan countries, and there are a few Turks in the Arab States too. The population of the Republic exhibits a variety of physical types, including some with blue eyes and blonde colouring.

An anthropometric survey of 64,000 Turks in 1937 and 1938 showed that roughly 75 per cent of the sample were brachycephalic, and only 30 per cent had dark hair; 5 per cent had the slanting Mongol eyes.

Distribution of Population

	Total (000)	Village (%)	Town (%)	Density per sq. km.
1927	13,648	75·8	24·2	18
1955	24,121	71·5	28·5	31
1965	31,391	—	—	40

Principal Cities of Over 50,000 Inhabitants, 1965
(000)

Istanbul	1,743	Bursa	212	Kayseri	127
Ankara	906	Eskishehir	174	Sivas	108
Izmir	412	Gaziantep	160	Samsun	107
Adana	290	Konya	158	Erzurum	105

Source: as for Table on p. 490.

About 72 per cent of the working population is engaged in agriculture. Till recent years, the urban minority had almost a monopoly of post-primary education, of Western ideas, and of political and administrative authority. Although the gulf between urban and rural population is still profound, students from the villages are coming to the universities, and a growing proportion of them are recruited into the administration.

The census figures which serve as a basis for estimating minority groups are those based on mother tongue and religion.

The number of non-Moslems in 1965 was only 261,000 in a total population of 31,391,000. There is also a large minority, which may be 4 million or even more, of Shii Moslems, regarded by the majority of uneducated Sunni villagers as a distinct group, with whom there is no intermarriage. But the population is sufficiently homogeneous to form a united nation in the Western sense, without the problem of violent internal antagonisms which face so many of the states that have come into being since the First World War.

In the Ottoman Empire the Turks were in a minority. After the Treaty of Lausanne and the Iraq frontier arbitration, few Arabs remained in Turkey. The bulk of the Greek community in Turkey was exchanged for Turks in Greece during and after 1923. Their numbers have further shrunk in recent years because of the tension over Cyprus; at the 1945 census the Orthodox Christians numbered 104,000. Since 1945 too the size of the Jewish minority has been almost exactly halved, mainly because of emigration to Israel. The Armenians, on the other hand, have increased by over 3,000 since 1945. Some 11,000 of those who gave their mother tongue as Greek and just over 1,000 of those

Population by Mother Tongue,[1] *1965*
(000)

Turkish	28,317	Greek	49
Kurdish	2,181	Armenian	32
Arabic	369	Georgian	32
Zaza	148	Laz	28
Circassian	57	Jewish[2]	9

[1] Omitting small groups.
[2] i.e. Ladino.
See G. L. Lewis, *Turkey* (London, 1966), p. 177.

Population by Religion, 1965
(000)

Moslem		31,130
Christian:	Orthodox	76
	Catholic	29
	Gregorian	64
	Protestant	22
	Other	23
Jewish		38
Other & unknown		8

Source: State Institute of Statistics, *Population Census of Turkey 24 October 1965. 1% Sample Results*, 1966.

who gave it as Armenian live in localities with fewer than 10,000 inhabitants. The largest concentrations of Greeks, Armenians, and Jews are to be found in Istanbul, with lesser Greek and Jewish communities in Izmir.

The Kurds are the largest minority, and, although Moslems, the only one to have given serious trouble. They are traditionally a mountain people, largely pastoral, but considerable numbers of them have settled in permanent villages and in cities, notably Diyarbakir. There have been demands for an independent Kurdish state, or at least (with the encouragement of the Treaty of Sèvres) for autonomy, but it is doubtful whether the majority of Kurds in Turkey have any clear conception of such an organization. The revolts[1] which the young Turkish Republic had to face were attributed to religious reaction against the policy of Atatürk, but it is probably more reasonable to put them down to the objection to political control on the part of a tough, independent hill people, largely tribal in organization, and differing from the Turks ethnically and linguistically. In 1946 the 3,000 Kurdish families which had been deported to western Turkey after the 1936 troubles were allowed to return to their homes. Although the Government is still a little sensitive on the question, the main Kurdish areas are now peaceful and administered just as any other region in Turkey.

The minorities in general are gradually becoming integrated in the

[1] These occurred in 1925 (the most serious), in 1930, and in 1936.

citizen body. They suffer from no legal disabilities, but as yet very few non-Moslems have become civil servants, though they do obtain commissions in the armed forces.

Immigration

The spread of the idea of a nation as a culturally homogeneous territorial unit causes very serious problems in all areas of mixed population. Turkey sought to rid herself of her Greek Orthodox minority by arranging, through a convention signed at Lausanne on 30 January 1923, to exchange them for the Moslem minority in Greece. In the 1920s about 1½ million Orthodox Christians (many of them Turkish-speaking) left Turkey for Greece and about 700,000 Moslems came in from Greece.

Turkey has continued to encourage the immigration of Turks from other parts of the world, by far the majority of whom have come from Turkey's former Balkan possessions. During the 1930s there was a steady influx of about 10,000–30,000 a year, but from 1942 to 1949 it fell to a few thousands. In 1950 and 1951, however, the Bulgarian Government, probably to punish Turkey for her participation in the Korean War, sent over the frontier large numbers of refugees stripped of all their possessions, 55,000 in 1950 and 102,000 in 1951. At the end of 1952 and the beginning of 1953 some hundreds of Kazak tribesmen were settled in Turkey, refugees who had been living in Sinkiang until the Communist occupation in 1950, and thereafter in Kashmir. In the 1930s and 1940s a great many refugees from Nazi persecution were hospitably received, to the benefit of the Turkish universities. The same humane policy was seen at work in 1956, when 500 Hungarians were offered sanctuary in Turkey. At the end of January 1957 forty-three refugees from Turkmenistan reached Turkey via Tokyo. The Turkish Government and people have done their utmost to resettle all these refugees, with generous loans and with grants of land to families having farming experience.

HISTORY AND POLITICS

The Ottoman Empire

Turkish nomads from Central Asia, already converted to Islam, first established themselves in Asia Minor in the eleventh century AD. The Ottoman principality, one of a number of small Turkish states, was set up in the thirteenth century and rapidly became an empire,[1] though Constantinople did not fall until 1453. In the sixteenth and seventeenth centuries the Ottoman Empire was among the greatest Powers in the world, and at the end of this period its territories stretched

[1] See P. Wittek, *The Rise of the Ottoman Empire* (Royal Asiastic Society Monographs, vol. 23, 1938).

from the Persian Gulf to Algeria and from the Sudan to south Russia
and a point beyond Budapest. Europe was on the defensive. Largely
because of Europe's striking advances in administration and technology, the military balance began to turn against the Ottoman
Empire. By the beginning of the nineteenth century it was unable to
resist European pressure, and escaped final defeat only because no
European Power would permit its conquest by any other. Thus Britain
and France encouraged Turkey to resist the Tsar's demands, in 1853,
for a Russian protectorate over the Sultan's 12 million Christian
Orthodox subjects, and Britain and France fought on the Turkish side
in the ensuing Crimean War (1854–6). A further Russian aggression
occurred in April 1877, with the avowed purpose of winning freedom
for the Slav peoples of the Ottoman Empire, particularly the Bulgars.
Western support was too lukewarm and too late to be of any use until
Turkey had actually signed the humiliating Treaty of San Stefano
(March 1878). This was set aside by the Cyprus Convention of 4 June
1878,[1] which left Russia in possession of Kars, Batum, and Ardahan,
and stripped Turkey of much of her territory in Europe. On 4 June the
Sultan had reluctantly accepted a Convention of Defensive Alliance
with Britain, of which Article 1 reads as follows:

If Batoum, Ardahan, Kars, or any of them, shall be retained by Russia, and
if any attempt shall be made at any future time by Russia to take possession of
any further territories of H.I.M. the Sultan in Asia, as fixed by the Definitive
Treaty of Peace, England engages to join H.I.M. the Sultan in defending them
by force of arms.

In return, H.I.M. the Sultan promises to England to introduce necessary
reforms, to be agreed upon later between the two Powers, into the government,
and for the protection of the Christian and other subjects of the Porte in these
territories; and in order to enable England to make necessary provision for
executing her engagement, H.I.M. the Sultan further consents to assign the
Island of Cyprus to be occupied and administered by England.

The second paragraph is typical of the way in which the European
Powers had long been attempting to impose, in the name of reform,
political and social ideas totally inappropriate to the social structure
and the culture of the peoples of the Empire. Within Turkey itself there
was a ferment of new ideas—liberalism, constitutionalism, nationalism;
pan-Turanianism (the idea of uniting all the Turks of Asia in one
state); pan-Islamism (the idea of uniting all Moslems in one state);
pan-Ottomanism (the idea of forging a great single Turkish-speaking
nation out of the mixed peoples of the Empire). For as long as he could,
Abdul Hamid (1876–1909) maintained absolute power and resisted
the new ideas, but eventually he was compelled to grant a Constitution
by the revolution of 1908, led by a group of young intellectuals and

[1] Hurewitz, i, pp. 187–9.

army officers, the 'Young Turks', and he was deposed the following year. The new Government was hampered by the conflict of ideas and personalities, and the problems of rebellion and of the First World War, which Turkey entered in 1914 on the side of Germany. But after the war, in a situation simplified by the loss of the Empire, the experience gained in the previous abortive attempts at setting Turkey on the road to Westernization helped Mustafa Kemal to succeed where his predecessors had failed.

The armistice terms of 1918 were tantamount to unconditional surrender, but the defeated Turks, with remarkable resilience, completely upset the Allied plans by resort to force of arms. For not altogether creditable reasons,[1] the Allies allowed Greek troops to occupy Izmir on 15 May 1919. This action stimulated a popular and nationalist movement in Turkey, the more so as the Greeks openly attempted to annex a considerable area of western Anatolia. By 1922, under the able leadership of Mustafa Kemal, later to be known as Atatürk, the Turks defeated the Greeks, and the Allies were compelled to recognize the full sovereignty of Turkey by the Treaty of Lausanne (24 July 1923). Turkey had then been at war more or less continuously since 1911.

At this date Turkey had virtually no modern industries. Many of her peasants had died in the wars, and much land lay uncultivated because its owners had been away under arms. The extreme simplicity of technology and of economic organization were in one sense a strength. Land was plentiful, and subsistence farmers needed only draught animals to restore production rapidly. Atatürk however aimed not merely at restoration, but at the establishment of a modern Western state.

The Republic

Mustafa Kemal had abolished the Sultanate in 1922, and on 29 October 1923 Turkey was proclaimed a Republic, with supreme authority residing in the Grand National Assembly, through which he was governing. The Caliphate was abolished in March 1924, and on 20 April a Constitution was adopted which, with some amendments, remained in force until 1960. It guaranteed equality before the law and freedom of thought, speech, press, and association. Sovereignty lay with the people and was exercised in their name by a single chamber of deputies, the Grand National Assembly. It elected the President of the Republic, who chose a Prime Minister, and he in turn appointed the ministers, who were responsible to the Assembly for executive functions. Atatürk, however, overrode the Constitution when he chose. In 1924 he reorganized his supporters as the Republican People's Party, and this party came to dominate political life. All members of the Grand National Assembly belonged to it, and at both national and

[1] See A. J. Toynbee, *The Western Question in Greece and Turkey* (London, 1922).

local levels government officials were also party leaders, so that to a considerable extent the party hierarchy coincided with the government hierarchy. This party ruled Turkey for twenty-seven years.

The Reforms

Once firmly in power, the Republican People's Party proceeded to apply a programme of revolutionary legislation of startling thoroughness. The most important provisions were:

1924: Institutions of religious learning and religious courts abolished.
1925: The fez forbidden and replaced by European hats and caps. (The symbolic significance of this apparently superficial measure can hardly be exaggerated.)
Dervish orders suppressed.
1926: Use of Gregorian calendar (adopted on 1 March 1917) to be compulsory.
A completely new legal code replaced the existing mixture of Islamic law and statutes promulgated by the Sultans. The new code was an adapted translation of the Swiss civil, the Italian penal, and the German commercial codes. Thenceforth only civil marriage and divorce were recognized and polygamy became illegal.
1928: The state became officially secular.
A Latin-based alphabet was introduced and the public use of the Arabic letters made illegal.
1934: Women were given the right to vote and to be candidates in elections.
1935: Introduction of surnames on the European model. Mustafa Kemal took the name Atatürk, and his lieutenant, Ismet, that of Inönü.
Adoption of the Sunday holiday (since 1924 Friday had been the weekly holiday).

In addition, there were great advances in education. The financial and administrative machinery was completely overhauled. The adoption of Swiss civil law changed the legal position of women, and the change was supported by strong official encouragement of emancipation. For example, equal pay has been the rule from the first entry of women into the professions.

This revolutionary programme was imposed on the mass of the population by a small group of intellectuals with army backing. A pious, conservative, and in many cases isolated population does not easily adjust its behaviour to a new set of values ordained by a central authority. The reforms therefore had to contend not only with conscious opposition, both from a few liberal intellectuals and from religious and other conservatives, but also with the far stronger inertia of established customs and ways of thought.

Atatürk himself had tremendous prestige from his military successes, and the nation was loyal as a whole, but the new reforms were far from being generally popular. Realizing this, the party initiated in 1932 a far-reaching programme of adult education. In all parts of Turkey People's Houses and People's Rooms were set up (by February 1950 478 and 4,322 respectively). Their main use was for educational purposes but, being organs of the party, they became centres of party propaganda and were therefore closed by the Democrat Party Government in the autumn of 1951.

Atatürk's methods, though at times arbitrary, were designed to bring about a liberal and constitutional government. From the beginning the Assembly had real powers and Atatürk worked largely by persuasion. In 1930 he even made an attempt to establish an official opposition, but was obliged to abandon it.

Democracy in Action

On Atatürk's death in 1938 Ismet Inönü became President of the Republic and virtual dictator in his stead. As soon as the war was over, however, partially perhaps under the influence of the victors' political ideas, an opposition party, the Democrat Party, was allowed to form under Celâl Bayar, a former Prime Minister.

This party entered the 1946 elections, but the electoral law was hardly impartial and the results were patently rigged. Nevertheless, the Democrats won some 60 seats out of 465. Much more freedom of speech and press was allowed. The new party began to organize seriously and other parties were formed. Before the next election in May 1950 an admirably fair new electoral law was enacted. After the election the Democrat Party found itself in power with a majority of 408 to 79, having obtained 55 per cent of the votes cast in an 89 per cent poll. Celâl Bayar became President and Adnan Menderes Prime Minister, while Inönü gracefully retired to become the leader of the opposition.

For the first four years there was a large measure of popular satisfaction with the new regime. Some state industry was denationalized, some concessions were made to religious feeling, and a huge expansion of imports and of agricultural credits began. In the elections of May 1954 the Democrats polled 58·4 per cent of the votes cast, as against 55·2 per cent in 1950. But in that same year of 1954 the record run of abnormally good harvests, which had seemed like heaven's blessing on the new rulers, came to an end; this should have been the signal to retrench, but the Government chose to disregard it, confident that Turkey's allies would never allow her to suffer total economic collapse. Inflation set in: the rate of exchange, officially 9 liras to the US dollar, rose to 15 on the black market. The cost-of-living index for Istanbul, 100 in 1950, shot up to 129 in 1954 and 143 in 1955. But Menderes knew that most of his support came from the peasants, who did not mind the rise in food-prices and had not yet been schooled by advertising to want imported luxuries. The growing discontent was on the part of the urban middle class, the bureaucracy and the officers, not only because their standard of living was being depressed but because they considered Menderes a traitor to his class, who was wooing the ignorant peasantry at the expense of the Westernized section of the population. Though he was an intelligent man, of great personal charm, he was utterly intolerant of criticism. Legislation was passed empowering the Government to retire civil servants and judges and to prohibit political meetings and coalitions of political parties. Journalists who criticized members of the Government were jailed. But these measures did not silence the opposition. In April 1960 the Democrat majority in the Assembly voted into existence a fifteen-man Commission of Inquiry, with dictatorial powers of search, arrest, and detention, 'to investigate the opposition and a section of the press'. It was this contravention of the constitutional separation of powers which led to the overthrow of the regime (and in September 1961 brought Menderes and two of his ministers to the gallows). Protest meetings at the universities of Istanbul and Ankara were brutally suppressed by the police and on 27 May 1960, after a month of martial law and sporadic rioting, the army took over.

A National Unity Committee, consisting of thirty-eight officers under the chairmanship of General Kemal Gürsel, proclaimed itself as embodying the powers of the Grand National Assembly. A provisional Government was set up, with Gürsel as Head of State, Prime Minister, and Minister of Defence; two generals and fifteen civilians were the other ministers. The Committee had pledged itself to hand back power to an elected Government as soon as possible, and the pledge was honoured. In January 1961 a Constituent Assembly began work on a new constitution and electoral law, and the ban on political activity, imposed immediately after the coup, was ended. The Democrat Party had been liquidated by court order in September 1960 but its self-styled successor, the Justice Party, was among the eleven parties which emerged. At the general election of October 1961 it ran a close second (with 34·7 per cent of the votes) to the Republican People's Party (with 36·7). Pressure from the army persuaded it to join in a coalition Government under Ismet Inönü. But some officers resented the handing back of power to the politicians. In February 1962 the Commandant of the Ankara War College, Colonel Aydemir, led his cadets and some armoured units in a rising that was put down without loss of life. He was retired from the army but repeated the performance in May of the following year. This time eight people died, and Aydemir was executed in July 1964. The result was to convince those of Menderes's supporters who had been nervous about voting for the Justice Party that the army had shot its bolt; in the election of October 1965 the Justice Party won 52·73 per cent of the votes and formed a government under Süleyman Demirel, an engineer, the son of a peasant. In March 1966 General Gürsel, who had suffered a stroke, was succeeded as President by Cevdet Sunay, the Chief of the General Staff. Thanks to his humanity and common sense, qualities which were conspicuous in his predecessor too, the rift between the army and the politicians has been closing, although by no means all the junior officers are reconciled to being ruled by the Justice Party, which, like the Democrat Party before it, believes in giving the peasants what they want. There is obviously a point beyond which the senior officers too will not accept that the politicians know best. In May 1969 the Government, under pressure from the rank and file of its supporters, proposed to restore civil rights to members of the outlawed Democrat Party, which meant that, *inter alios*, the former President of the Republic, Celâl Bayar, would be once more eligible for public office. Ismet Inönü staged a reconciliation with his old rival, presumably to steal the Government's thunder, but just possibly because he genuinely felt that it was a bit silly for two octogenarians to go to their graves still at daggers drawn. The proposal was on the Senate's agenda for 21 May, but after some senators had received threatening messages from the military it was referred back 'for further consideration' to the committee that had drafted it.

At the beginning of March 1968, a new electoral law was passed. Previously, the number of seats each party obtained was proportional to its share of the national total of votes cast. The new law laid down that in each constituency the number of seats must be divided into the number of votes cast. No party polling fewer votes than that figure would obtain any seats in that constituency, and such votes as it did get would be divided proportionately among the other parties. This innovation was aimed against the Turkish Labour Party, which in 1965, with 2·97 per cent of the total votes, won 3·33 per cent of the seats; if the new law had been in force it would have won 0·66 per cent.

The 1961 Constitution

One great innovation of the new constitution was to reshape the Grand National Assembly as a bi-cameral legislature. The new Senate has 150 elected members (who must be over forty years old and have received a higher education) and fifteen nominated by the President of the Republic. The members of the National Unity Committee became Senators *ex officio* on condition that they did not join any political party. The term of office for elected and nominated Senators is six years, one-third being rotated every two years. Elections to the National Assembly, the lower house (450 members), are held every four years; candidates must be over thirty and have completed their military service. The lower house has the last word in legislation, except that if two-thirds of the Senate reject any measure it can be passed only by a two-thirds majority of the National Assembly. The President is elected by a plenary session of both houses from among those members who are over forty and have had a higher education.

He holds office for seven years and is not re-eligible. He appoints the Prime Minister from among the members of both houses; the Prime Minister nominates his ministers, who need not be members of either house. Ministers are jointly responsible for actions of the Government. The administration can be sued in the courts and is liable for damages resulting from its actions. Judges are totally independent and cannot be dismissed.

The elections held in October 1969 were fought largely on the issue of the political rehabilitation of the Democrats. The Justice Party won 47 per cent of the votes (compared with 53 per cent in 1965) and 257 out of 450 seats in the Assembly. The RPP which in 1965 had declared itself 'left of centre', thereby alienating its conservative wing without convincing its left wing, won 27 per cent of the poll (compared with 20 per cent in 1965) and 144 seats in the Assembly. The new Reliance Party, a breakaway from the RPP, won 7 per cent of the votes and 15 seats. The remaining five parties, including the right- and left-wing extremist parties, all won fewer than the 10 seats needed to form a parliamentary group.

On 12 November the electoral disqualifications of the old Democratic Party were finally removed.

In 1970 Demirel was under attack from the right wing of his own party whom he excluded from his new Cabinet and the opposition took the opportunity to step up their campaign against him in parliament. Demirel succeeded in reconstituting his administration and expelled the dissidents from the Justice Party. His regime also had to deal with severe unrest led by militant students and workers. Higher education was disrupted and there were widespread attacks on US property although the student movement was weakened by the dispute between right- and left-wing elements.

The militant workers were led by the minority Confederation of Reformist Workers' Unions (DISK). When the Assembly passed a bill restricting collective bargaining rights to unions representing at least one-third of the work force in a given industry, DISK organized a violent protest campaign which culminated in riots in Istanbul on 15–16 June. Martial law was imposed in the provinces of Istanbul and Kocaeli.

Following continued unrest, the army, represented by 100 officers of the National Security Council, sent a warning to President Sunay in December 1970 advising him to take a more active role in government and suggesting constitutional changes which would lead to the formation of a new Assembly 'of higher quality'. The opposition accused Premier Demirel of losing control of the country. As the situation failed to improve Mr. Demirel resigned on 12 March in the face of army threats to take power. At the same time a group of senior officers, including four generals and one admiral, who were allegedly planning a coup, were dismissed from the armed forces.

A new government was formed by Mr. Nihat Erim, a RPP deputy and former professor of law. He resigned from his party to form a cabinet 'above parties' which included only ten members of the Assembly and a number of young technocrats. Realizing that the alternative was an army takeover the Assembly voted overwhelmingly (321 to 46) in favour of Erim's programme which included agrarian, financial, and legal reforms as well as proposals for the nationalization of strategic mining interests.

In October five Justice Party members in the Cabinet resigned but two of them did not press their resignations and the Erim Government survived with army backing. In December 1971 Erim presented a new and less radical programme. Nationalization plans were abandoned and agrarian reforms postponed. Strong repressive measures were taken against the Turkish left—especially students and intellectuals.

In April 1972 Nihad Erim resigned after thirteen months as Prime Minister during which his efforts to restore stability were constantly frustrated by the activities of the left-wing Turkish People's Liberation Army. He was succeeded by the Defence Minister Ferit Melen who after some difficulties formed a 24-man Cabinet from members of the three main political parties and with nine from outside parliament. Melen promised to introduce tough measures to control extremism, and constitutional reforms to provide the necessary conditions for elections due to be held in October 1973. In July 1972 martial law was extended in eleven Turkish provinces.

Administration

Turkey is administered by a large and highly centralized bureaucracy in Ankara. There are twenty-three ministries, staffed by a permanent civil service, membership of which carries great prestige.

The country is divided into sixty-seven provinces (*vilayet* or *il*). Each has a Governor (*Vali*), who is under the Minister of the Interior. The Governor presides over the Provincial Council, which is elected for four years by popular vote. The Council has power, subject to the Governor's approval, to raise loans for education, health, and public works, to approve the provincial budget, and to make administrative decisions. Each province is divided into anything from 4 to 17 regions (*kaza* or *ilçe*), each under a centrally-appointed Lieutenant-Governor (*Kaymakam*), who is advised by a Regional Administrative Committee. Regions are subdivided into districts (*nahiye* or *bucak*) under a Director (*Müdür*), appointed by the Ministry of the Interior in consultation with the Governor. The Director is assisted by a District Council of *ex officio* and elected members. All provincial and regional capitals, whatever their populations, and all cities and towns with populations over 20,000 and 2,000 respectively, have municipalities with elected mayors and councils, who are also subject to the general supervision

R

of the appropriate centrally-appointed official. Each village has an elected headman and council. National Government agencies, such as State monopolies and banks, are outside the control of the provincial governors.[1]

Control of urban police is centralized in the security section of the Ministry of the Interior. The rural areas are policed by a military gendarmerie, 50,000 strong, under the same ministry. It is manned by selected army conscripts with regular officers and NCOs. Each village appoints and pays its own watchman. Authority is highly centralized, even minor decisions being constantly referred to Ankara. Initiative and responsible decisions at lower levels are not encouraged. The foreigner is commonly left with the impression that the average Turk regards any activity as forbidden unless it is specifically declared permissible.

Foreign Relations

By the Treaty of Lausanne, won from the unwilling Allies by Inönü in 1923 after months of patient negotiation, Turkey was recognized as fully sovereign and not required to pay reparations. Under the Treaty, a portion of the Ottoman debt was to be acknowledged but it was completely written off in 1947. The Straits were demilitarized and opened to ships of all nations unless Turkey was at war, when she might exclude enemy ships. Turkey was at first suspicious of the victorious Powers and officially friendly towards the Soviet Union, with whom, despite the ancient Russo-Turkish hostility, she had formed close ties during her War of Independence. These ties continued for a time, and during the 1920s she received economic aid and advice from Russia. During the 1930s Turkey found reason for apprehension in the expansionist policies of Bulgaria and of Italy. On 9 February 1934 she entered the Balkan Entente, a defensive alliance with Greece, Rumania, and Yugoslavia. On 11 April 1936 she asked the signatories of the Treaty of Lausanne for permission to remilitarize the Straits, and this was granted by the Montreux Convention, Italy abstaining. In October 1939 Turkey concluded a tripartite Treaty of Guarantee with Britain and France, but in 1941 she signed a ten-year pact of friendship with Germany. She was thereafter subjected to propaganda and pressure from both sides, but remained neutral, finally declaring war on Germany on 22 February 1945, with effect from 1 March, after the Allies had announced that only those states that had declared war by the latter date would be invited to the San Francisco Conference.

In March 1945 the Soviet Union denounced the Turco-Soviet Treaty

[1] *Mahallî idareler hakkında etüdler*, ed. by A. H. Hanson for the Institute of Public Administration for Turkey and the Middle East (Ankara, 1955); *T. C. Devlet teşkilâti rehberi* (Ankara, 1963).

of Friendship, signed in 1921 and due to expire in November 1945. In August 1946 the Soviet Union demanded revision, by the Black Sea Powers alone, of the Montreux Convention of 1936. Turkey refused, and her relations with the Soviet bloc have remained strained. Both the Soviet Union and Bulgaria protested in 1951 when Turkey joined NATO. On 8 November 1951, when Bulgaria had tried to pass off 1,000 gypsies as Turkish emigrants, Turkey closed the frontier and it was not reopened until 21 February 1953.

Britain supported Turkey in her resistance to Russian pressure at a time when the Republic felt nervous and isolated, by reaffirming loyalty to the 1939 treaty and sending a small military mission. Already in March 1947 President Truman had announced that the United States would give military aid to Greece and Turkey, and in July a United States Joint Services Mission arrived in the country and began work. From then onwards Turkey's relations with the United States and also with Europe became progressively closer. In 1949, at her own request, she was included as a founder member of the Council of Europe.

On 18 February 1952 Turkey became a full member of NATO and on 16 July NATO created a South-East Europe command with headquarters at Izmir. Turkey had at last the specific assurance that the Western Powers would go to war to defend her frontiers and she had the additional satisfaction of being recognized as a member of the Western family of nations. Her own formal request for admission to NATO had coincided with the beginning of the Korean War, and her claim was greatly strengthened by the prompt dispatch of over 5,000 Turkish troops to fight in the United Nations forces, where they formed the third largest contingent and greatly distinguished themselves in action.

Combined membership of NATO at first strengthened relations between Greece and Turkey. The two Powers also made joint approaches to Yugoslavia, with the result that on 28 February 1953 the three non-Cominform Balkan Powers signed a five-year treaty of friendship. On 9 August the signing of the Treaty of Bled turned the association into a formal military alliance.

But Turco-Greek relations began to deteriorate towards the end of 1954, with the intensification of the campaign for *enosis*. The Turkish attitude was that Greece was internally unstable and might conceivably go Communist; she must therefore not be allowed to control Cyprus which, lying just over forty miles from Turkey, could, in the wrong hands, render Turkey's southern ports useless. Reluctantly, when it became obvious that Britain would not try to maintain her sovereignty over the island, the Turkish Government agreed to Cypriot independence (after discussions at Zürich and London in February 1959). Cyprus became a republic in August 1963. But Ankara's resentment came to the boil after President Makarios proposed, in December 1963, to amend the constitution to the disadvantage of his Turkish minority.

In March 1964 Turkey gave notice that she was abrogating the 1930 agreement of establishment, commerce, and navigation, which governed the status of Greek nationals in Turkey. Out of some 15,000 of these, over 600 were deported. This move was not so uncivilized as it might seem. It acted as a safety-valve for popular emotion and thus saved the more than 70,000 Turkish citizens of Greek origin from possible mob-violence. In the same month the UN set up a peace-keeping force in Cyprus (UNFICYP). But communal strife continued, with the co-operation of the two mother-countries. In June 1964 the Turkish armed forces were on the point of invading the island, when Prime Minister Inönü received a letter from President Johnson, a well-meant letter with evil consequences. It was intended as a dispassionate statement of fact: if the Turks invaded Cyprus they would inevitably be censured by the UN and in that case the US Congress would certainly cut off military and possibly all other aid to Turkey. Unfortunately the urgency of the situation allowed no time for the message to be couched in tactful circumlocution. The invasion was called off, but to the Turkish press and public it seemed that their American ally had prevented them by threats from taking a fully justified action. Anti-Americanism as a serious political factor in Turkey dates from this incident. On 10 August, after 64 Turkish aircraft had strafed ground targets in Cyprus, Turkey and Greece accepted a resolution of the Security Council calling for a ceasefire. Thereafter the situation eased somewhat until November 1967, when, after 24 Turkish Cypriot villagers had been killed by Greek Cypriot troops, Turkey again prepared for war and Greece followed suit. Thanks largely to President Johnson's emissary, Cyrus R. Vance, the danger was averted and on 3 December 1967 an agreement was reached between the governments in Ankara and Athens. In January 1968 Greek and Turkish troops in excess of the numbers permitted by the Zürich and London agreements (950 Greek, 650 Turkish) were withdrawn and the Turkish invasion forces stood down. In December 1968 the mandate of UNFICYP was extended until 15 June 1969, 'in the expectation that by then sufficient progress towards a final solution will make possible a withdrawal or substantial reduction of the Force.'

After the fiasco of the proposed Middle East Defence Organization in October 1951, the concept of the 'northern tier' arose: a chain of allied states on Russia's southern borders. On 2 April 1954 Turkey concluded an agreement for friendly co-operation with Pakistan. On 24 February 1955 a treaty of co-operation was signed with Iraq. Out of this, with the subsequent accession of Britain, Pakistan, and Iran, grew the Baghdad Pact. The USA signed bilateral defence agreements with Turkey, Pakistan, and Iran on 5 March 1959, but on 24 March Iraq withdrew from the Pact. In August 1960 the name of the alliance was changed to the Central Treaty Organization (CENTO). It has proved particularly valuable to its Middle Eastern members in the field of technical co-operation and communications: a microwave system now links them, the harbours at Iskenderun and Trabzon have been enlarged and modernized, and a new road is under construction between south-east Turkey and Pakistan.

On 7 November 1956 Turkey associated herself with the other Middle Eastern members of the Baghdad Pact in condemning Israel's attack on Egypt, and in requesting Britain and France to end hostilities immediately, but Turkish opinion was very far from being pro-Egyptian.

Egypt had made no secret of her disapproval of Turkey's leading part in the new defence structure and of Turkey's recognition of Israel (28 March 1949). Turkey and India had signed a treaty of friendship on 14 December 1951, but during the Bandung Conference in April 1955 there was an obvious cleavage between the pro-Western party led by Turkey, and the neutralist and Communist party led by Egypt, India, and China. In April 1956 the Egyptian press violently attacked Adnan Menderes for criticizing Egypt's attitude towards the Baghdad Pact. On 26 November the Turkish Minister to Israel was recalled, but he seems to have taken his departure in the most amicable fashion, having assured the Israeli Foreign Ministry that the purpose of the move was to strengthen the Baghdad Pact, which was not aimed against Israel. The Turkish Legation in Tel Aviv would continue to work, with the Counsellor as chargé d'affaires. The Minister would probably have returned to Tel Aviv long before had the Turks not hoped for Arab support at the UN over the matter of Cyprus.

It might be thought that Turks would feel a natural sympathy for their Arab co-religionists. That they do not is due in part to the effects of Atatürk's policy of setting his country's face westward. But another reason, which applies even to the majority of the unWesternized, is that they think of the Arabs at large as having abandoned and betrayed the Islamic empire ruled over by the Sultan-Caliph when they threw in their lot with the infidel Allies in the First World War. This attitude may conceivably change as the older generation die out, if religious feeling waxes. But at the moment the number of Turks who regard themselves as Moslems first and Turks second is negligible. So although Turkish statesmen on visits to their Arab counterparts, and at the UN, may go through the motions of condemning Israel's retention of the areas taken in June 1967, relations between Turkey and Israel continue to be amicable.

Syrian talk of a retrocession of Hatay is a constant source of Turkish irritation. As recently as February 1967 the Syrian tourist organization was giving away maps which placed Iskenderun and Antakya well inside the Syrian border. Reports of increasing Russian and, latterly, Chinese Communist influence in Syria have gravely disquieted the Turks. There have been Turkish complaints also of large-scale

smuggling on the part of 'groups of foreign interests on the Syrian border', smuggling which is said to cost Turkey some $50 million a year.

President Johnson's letter to Inönü did more than trigger off vulgar anti-Americanism (which manifested itself in violent demonstrations whenever the Sixth Fleet visited Istanbul and in constant grumbling about the presence of American servicemen in Turkey, who in mid-1969 numbered about 10,000, plus dependents): it made the country's leaders question the value of an alliance which seemed to them to bind Turkey to fight America's battles but not vice versa. Not that any responsible Turk would think of ending that alliance, because, despite all changes of temperature in the cold war, in Turkish eyes the paramount duty of their armed forces is to defend the country against a possible Russian attack, and this, without American aid in money and material, they could not do. But the Government saw no harm in flirting with the Russians to make the Americans jealous. In March 1962, President Gürsel had said, 'Even if American aid were to be cut off we could never accept any aid from Soviet Russia.' But in October–November 1964 the Turkish Foreign Minister visited the USSR (the first such visit since 1939) and in the following January a delegation from the Supreme Soviet visited Turkey at the invitation of the Grand National Assembly, and Nikolai Podgorny addressed a joint session of both houses, though not without a certain amount of heckling. In May 1965 it was the Soviet Foreign Minister's turn to visit Turkey, and in August the Turkish Prime Minister Ürgüplü travelled the other way, returning with a Russian promise to finance the building of nine industrial plants in Turkey, including a steel plant, an oil refinery, a sheet glass factory, and a vodka distillery. And so it went on. Premier Kosygin visited Turkey in December 1966, Prime Minister Demirel visited Russia in September 1967. On his return to Ankara he announced that the total value of economic aid which Turkey would receive from the USSR would exceed $200 million, to be repaid in the form of exports. In July 1970 all US bases and facilities in Turkey except for the Incirlik air base near Adana, were handed back to the Turkish authorities.

The Armed Forces

Turkey probably possesses the most formidable land forces in continental, non-Soviet Europe. Military service is compulsory. The period is two years, except for university graduates, who receive commissions automatically if they pass a qualifying examination and who then serve for only eighteen months, the first six of which are spent on a special course. Conscript privates receive only nominal pay. There are no regular privates.

The army consists of 13 infantry divisions (one mechanized), one armoured division and 4 armoured brigades (equipped with M47 and M48 tanks), 2 armoured cavalry regiments, 2 mechanized infantry brigades, and 2 parachute battalions. The units are largely equipped with 10·5 cm., 15·5 cm. and 20·3 cm. howitzers. The total strength is 425,000, with 450,000 trained reservists.

The navy includes 10 submarines (all ex-US), 10 destroyers, 7 mine-layers, 18 escort minelayers, 6 coastal minelayers, 13 coastal and 13 inshore minesweepers, 6 patrol vessels, 8 motor torpedo-boats, 10 support ships, 6 boom vessels, and a submarine rescue ship. The naval bases are at Gölcük on the Gulf of Izmit, at Iskenderun, and at Izmir. Personnel strength in 1968 was 2,740 officers and 33,320 ratings.

The air force is organized in 3 tactical air forces. The 1st TAF has 6 squadrons (each of 20 to 25 aircraft) of F-100C Super Sabres, 2 squadrons of F-104G Starfighters, 2 squadrons of F-84F Thunder-streaks and one squadron of RF-84F Thunderflash reconnaissance aircraft. The 2nd TAF forms an air defence command, with 3 squadrons of F-86E Sabre day interceptors and 4 of Sabre all-weather interceptors, 2 of which are equipped with F-86Ds and 2 with F-86Ks. It also has Nike-Ajax and Nike-Hercules surface-to-air missile batteries. The 3rd TAF has 7 fighter-bomber squadrons, 4 of F-100Cs and 3 of supersonic F-5s. Personnel numbers 53,000, with 450 combat aircraft.

Apart from enormous American grants for war material, Turkey's own allocation for defence in 1969 was close on one sixth of the total budget.

SOCIAL SURVEY

General Structure

During the greater part of Ottoman history high administrative office and military rank was largely the prerogative of the Sultan's Christian-born slaves and consequently snobbishness is a vice seldom encountered among the Turks.[1] On the other hand, the attitude of many educated townsmen (though they will hotly deny this) towards the villagers is one of distaste, regarding them as a scruffy refutation of Turkey's claim to be part of Western civilization. Since 1945, however, the politicians have realized the power of the peasant vote, and the material prosperity of the villages is growing rapidly.

Traditionally, finance and commerce were beneath the dignity of the Ottoman Turks, who left them to Europeans or non-Turkish Ottoman citizens; but since the revolution Turks have been increasingly attracted to business and today the country's trade is almost entirely in Turkish hands. In the last ten years or so, business has begun to rival the civil service, the armed forces, and the professions, as a prestigious career.

[1] Geoffrey Lewis, 'Modern Turkish Attitudes to Europe' in Raghavan Iyer (ed.), *The Glass Curtain between Asia and Europe* (London, 1965).

A large section of the lowest urban stratum consists of villagers who have either migrated temporarily to the towns or who retain close ties with rural areas.

The village population has its own hierarchy. Some genuine villagers are wealthy men, though there may be little obvious display of wealth in the village. While village conditions vary considerably, the Anatolian village is perhaps the most typical. Composed of flat-roofed houses of mud or stone, it is a compact unit, set in its own land, part of which is communally-held pasture, part split up into small household plots. Many villages still remain isolated; even urban contacts and comparative prosperity have made little change in the traditional patterns of behaviour. Yet the beginnings of change are visible

Women and Family Life

There is no career that is not open to the Turkish girl if her family is willing. In Turkey, however, as elsewhere, the idea of equality of the sexes has not yet won general acceptance, particularly in small towns and villages. '. . . Turkey remains largely a masculine society which looks askance at unaccompanied and unattached women. . . . In Anatolia the absence of women from coffee houses and eating places is almost total. The equally marked absence of waitresses and manageresses contributes to a barrack-room atmosphere of rough-and-ready untidiness which has struck so many perceptive travellers.'[1] The conservative-minded young villager considers it his duty to murder his sister if she lets herself be seduced by a man the family do not approve of. To offset this bleak observation it should be said that love-matches are by no means uncommon in the villages. If the family withhold their consent, the form is for the girl to go off into the hills with the young man of her choice, for which crime of 'abduction' the courts impose a nominal sentence. The family then decide, more often than not, that the match is not so impossible as they had first thought. In perhaps two-thirds of village marriages, as with many conservative urban families, the bride goes to live in her father-in-law's house, which is why the same Turkish word does duty for 'bride' and 'daughter-in-law'. There are no strong feelings about marrying outside the village. It is perhaps a sign of the times that in January 1969 the Court of Appeal, quashing the verdict of a lower court, ruled that it was not criminal or indecent for a boy and girl to kiss in the street.

Housing and Clothing

The large towns of Turkey are full of modern blocks of flats and new houses, many in garden suburbs, but some are still built of wood, in the old style. There is nevertheless a housing shortage in the big towns, and rents are high. For the urban poor, housing conditions are often bad.

[1] Andrew Mango, *Turkey* (London, 1968), pp. 133-4.

Most large cities have a shanty-town, but slum-clearance and new housing are a major preoccupation of the authorities. The Workers' Insurance Administration makes 90 per cent advances for twenty years for house purchase, at low interest.

Low as rural housing standards often are, there is no rural housing problem. The villagers build their own houses at their own expense, often with their own hands, and renting is rare. Dwellings vary from caves, or single rooms shared with the animals, to large, well-built houses. Apart from storage chests, bedding, carpets for sitting on, divans built in against the walls, and large trays which are set on stools by way of dining tables, little furniture is used.

For men, Western-type clothes are general, but the traditional Turkish trousers are still seen. Villagers' clothing is often ragged, partly because of poverty and partly to avoid a display of wealth. Towns-women wear European-type clothes; the older and less sophisticated wear black, with head-shawls. Village women still wear the traditional voluminous trousers, skirts, and aprons, which vary in style and pattern from area to area. Large head-shawls are always worn, and Sunni Moslem women draw these across the mouth when in the presence of men.

Health

When the Republic was founded there was only one modern school of medicine in Turkey and few doctors, though a Ministry of Health and Social Welfare was set up in 1920. Since then much has been done to fill the gap. Istanbul, Ankara, and the Aegean University at Izmir have modern medical faculties, while the new Hacettepe University at Ankara is primarily a medical school. In 1966 there were over 10,000 qualified doctors and 60,000 hospital beds. The most serious deficiency is in trained nurses, though their numbers rose from some 700 in 1950 to 3,000 in 1966. The shortage is a reflection of the reluctance of many families to let their daughters out into the world; in Turkey as in most of the neighbouring countries it is customary for patients' families to nurse them, even if it means sleeping on the floor in the ward.

Doctors tend to concentrate in the cities: in 1966 there was roughly one to every 550 of the population in Istanbul, one to every 800 in Ankara, and one to 24,000 in Adiyaman. On the other hand, no town of any size is without its resident 'Government Doctor', and the free health service already operating in the eastern provinces was covering the entire country by the end of 1970. Vigorous and effective campaigns have been conducted against trachoma and malaria: the former is decreasing rapidly while the latter has been almost eradicated.

The Ministry of Health was allocated approximately 3·5 per cent of the 1969 budget.

Some voluntary social welfare bodies exist, including a few special schools and orphanages. The Red Crescent Association celebrated its centenary in 1968. There is also a great deal of totally unpublicized private philanthropy, much of it on the part of well-to-do ladies in the great cities; in this they are following long-established Turkish and Islamic practice.

Education

Until 1924 modern education, apart from a few schools for officials and army officers, had been confined largely to the non-Moslem minorities; for the rest, education meant religious education. When the *medreses* (religious schools) were closed, recourse was had to European examples. The introduction of the Latin script in 1928 greatly facilitated the acquisition of literacy and also diverted attention from Islamic to Western culture.

The percentage of illiterates among those aged seven and over has fallen from 79·6 in 1935 to 65·4 in 1950 and 52·3 in 1966. Close on two-thirds of the illiterates are female.

Primary education begins at seven and continues for five years. In 1966, however, there was only one teacher for every 430 children at primary school. Nevertheless the situation is improving; whereas in 1950 only 55 per cent of children of primary school age were attending school this percentage rose to 60 in 1950 and to 83 in 1966. In October 1968, 4·9 million children were at primary school.

From primary school the child may go to middle school, for three years, at the end of which he may either enter an unskilled occupation or go on to a vocational school or a high school. After three years in high school, if he passes the state 'maturity' examination he may enter a university; there are entrance examinations but the standard required is not very high, at least at Istanbul University. State education is mostly co-educational and is free to all.

In 1968 there were 682,000 pupils at the country's 1,296 middle schools and 169,000 at the 287 high schools. The 84 teacher training colleges had 61,000 students. Education's share of the 1969 budget was 10·4 per cent.

The educational system is highly centralized, curricula, text-books, and the posting of teachers being controlled from Ankara. Corporal punishment is forbidden, as are the assigning of positions in class and the giving of prizes.

A curious flaw in the system is that the methods of the primary schools are based on a blend of German and Austrian practice, latterly with an admixture of American ideas; the middle schools are run on French lines, the technical schools on Belgian. All this makes for difficulties when pupils pass from one stage to the next.

When Turks are discussing education one often hears the Village Institutes mentioned with regret. These seemed to be well on the way to providing an escape from a vicious circle: the standard of education of the average villager being so low that the young urban teacher found the village a forbiddingly uncongenial place in which to work. Village children who had completed primary school came to these institutes, the first of which was founded in 1940, for a five-year course. Half their time was spent on secondary education and half on practical work: for the boys, training in agricultural techniques, building, and carpentry; for the girls, housekeeping, first-aid, and child care. Between 1942 and 1952 they produced 20,000 teachers for village schools. But the Democrat Party did not like them—the stock reason given was that they were hotbeds of Communism—and in 1954 they were closed.

Istanbul has long been a seat of learning. It has had a university since 1865, but the university in its present form dates from 1932. It has also a technical university (1941). The University of Ankara was officially founded in 1946 but the name was applied to the Faculty of Language, History, and Geography, from 1941. Ankara also has the Hacettepe University mentioned above and the Middle East Technical University, where English is the medium of instruction. Other university cities are Izmir, Erzurum, and Trabzon. There is great pressure on the available university places, as there is in most other countries, but in Turkey the pressure is intensified by countless applicants who want a degree in order to avoid having to do their military service in the ranks.

There is an ambivalent feeling in the public mind about the 'private schools', a term which embraces both the one-room dressmaking academy in a side-street and the two beautiful campuses of the Istanbul American Colleges. The Government is loth to comply with the recurrent demands for their nationalization, because they are not hurting anybody and are indeed alleviating the pressure on the State educational system; moreover, it would cost too much to run them. Such demands come from a variety of quarters: the right-wing nationalists who think they inculcate too many foreign ideas, the left-wing socialists who see them as dens of privilege, and the would-be students who have failed to gain entry to them. The American Colleges, in particular, have higher entrance requirements than most Turkish universities; and it is not being unduly cynical to say that few Turkish critics of them would refuse to let their children attend them if they could.

Religion

The Republic has no official religion and the Constitution guarantees freedom of worship. There is, however, a Presidium for Religious Affairs attached to the Prime Minister's office, and this appoints and pays muftis, preachers, and urban imams, village imams being appointed and paid by their congregations. The administration of religious endowments is in the hands of the Directorate-General of Pious Foundations, and religious education is controlled by the Ministry of Education. But, just as in Ottoman times, the State does not concern itself at all with the religious affairs of those citizens who are not Sunni Moslems.

With the proclamation of the Republic, the schools for religious leaders attracted fewer and fewer students until 1932–3, when their work came to a standstill. Lest ignorant fanatics should fill the void thus created, the Ministry of Education in 1949 permitted religious education at the parents' option for children in the top two classes of primary schools. In many villages this measure was reported to have increased school attendance. In the same year, short courses for imams and preachers began in ten cities, open to graduates of middle schools, and a Faculty of Divinity was founded at Ankara University. From November 1950, children at primary schools were assumed to want religious education unless their parents opted out. In 1951, seven Imam and Preachers' Schools, at middle-school level, were opened, and by 1968 there were 68, with an enrolment of 41,000. In March 1952, religious instruction was added to the curriculum of the Village Institutes, and to that of the middle schools in September 1956. Although these measures won much popularity for the Democrats, they were based on decisions taken previously by the Republican People's Party. Every Turkish Government has been faced with the problem of the conflict between the principle of secularism and the wishes of the majority of the electorate.[1] The Democrat Party came to grief because it leaned too far in the latter direction; the Republican People's Party is probably doomed to be excluded in perpetuity from power, because it is linked in the popular mind with the policy of separating Church from State. The Justice Party Government, profiting by the lessons of its predecessors, seems to be moving more cautiously.

According to figures given by the Saudi Arabian Embassy in Ankara, 212,062 Turks went on pilgrimage to Mecca in 1967.

The Arts

The Ottomans played their part in shaping, as well as following, the traditions of Islamic civilization. Turkish poets and writers made their distinctive contribution, gaining inspiration from, sometimes using the languages of, their Iranian and Arabic co-religionists. The greatest contribution of Turkey to the arts during this period was in architecture.

The new generation of artists, writers, and musicians, who look to their own country for their subjects, look to Europe for their models. It is commonly said, particularly by visitors from abroad, who tend not to spend much time in Ankara, that Istanbul is still the cultural capital

[1] See Geoffrey Lewis, 'Turkey', in a symposium entitled 'Islam in Politics', *The Muslim World*, vol. LVI, no. 4, 1966, pp. 235–9.

of Turkey. But the cultural life of Ankara has progressed remarkably in recent years, and this is in part due precisely to Ankara's resentment at being regarded as provincial by the former capital. Ankara has a State conservatoire (founded in 1936), theatre, opera, ballet, and children's theatre, and the Presidential Philharmonic Orchestra, a continuation of the Imperial Court Orchestra founded in the 1850s. The State conservatoire includes the school of ballet opened in 1948 with the advice of Dame Ninette de Valois, who continued to be associated with it. The State ballet's development, however, is said by one perceptive critic, Metin And, to be stunted by its dependence on the State opera, which regards it as ancillary. Apropos of ballet, patriotic Turks will remind one that Nureyev is of Turkish ethnic origin.

Istanbul has a municipal conservatoire (founded in 1923) and theatre with comedy, drama, and children's sections, an academy of fine arts, a school of ballet and, since April 1969, the magnificent Istanbul Opera which was twenty-two years under construction. It includes an auditorium for 1,500 people, a concert hall for 750 and two small theatres each for 350. The gala opening featured performances of Verdi's *Aida* and of *Çeşmebaşi*, a ballet incorporating traditional Turkish dance motifs to the music of Ferit Tüzün's *Anatolian Suite*.

There are, in addition to what the State and local authorities provide, over a dozen private theatre companies in Istanbul and five or six in Ankara. Ankara University offers a four-year degree course in drama.

Many Turks have taken naturally to Western music, as composers and performers. The doyen of Turkish musicians, Ahmed Adnan Saygun, won the Sibelius Prize for his oratorio *Yunus Emre*, with words drawn from the poems of the thirteenth-century mystic and music based on native airs. Leyla Gencer, the soprano, has sung at most of the world's great opera houses. Idil Biret has an international reputation as a pianist. And many others could be instanced, thanks to Turkey's enlightened generosity towards gifted children, many of whom have been sent abroad with their parents to complete their training in music and the visual arts.

Painting and sculpture have begun to flourish in Turkey only under the Republic, having been inhibited in Ottoman times by the Islamic ban on the portrayal of living beings, although miniature painting did exist to adorn the libraries of the great, who on the whole took the ban less seriously than did the common people. Among the artists who have exhibited internationally are Bedri Rahmi, Aliye Berger Boronay, and Metin and Nazmiye Nigar. The ceramics of Füreya show an astonishing artistic inventiveness.

Only the cinema is disappointing. Apart from the exquisite short documentaries of Sabahattin Eyüboğlu there has been practically nothing worth exporting, although the Turkish industry turns out over

200 films a year, because it is deliberately working for a quick turnover from the domestic mass market and not for medals from the international festivals. The recent introduction of a television service is not likely to improve the situation.

As for literature, one can scarcely do more here than express regret at the paucity of English-speakers competent to translate from the Turkish. The novels and memoirs of Yakup Kadri, the short stories of Sait Faik, the essays of Sabahattin Eyüboğlu, the literary satire and surrealist short stories of Feyyaz Fergar; all these and many more deserve a wider readership.

The Press

The freedom of the press is guaranteed by the Constitution and manifestly exists. The Democrat Government's attempts to muzzle its critics between 1954 and 1960 did not save it from the coup d'état, and the lesson seems to have been learned. This is not to say that anybody can print whatever he likes, because some public prosecutors have their own ideas about what constitutes Communist propaganda, but happily the courts are usually more sensible.

The number of daily newspapers rose from 278 in 1955 to 402 in 1967. In the latter year there were also 541 newspapers other than dailies, and 592 magazines.

There is a constant output of books, amounting to some 5,000 titles a year, including many translations from European and American literature of all types, and transliterations and modernized editions of the Ottoman classics; it must be remembered that the change of alphabet has meant that the younger generation cannot read books printed before 1928.

ECONOMIC SURVEY

The Turkish population was estimated to be 33·2 million in 1968, some 5·4 million larger than the 1960 figure. In absolute terms the population of Turkey is now greater than that of any other Middle Eastern country and its rate of increase—2·5 per cent per annum—although declining, remains almost as high as that of Iran and Iraq. The relationship between this large and rapidly increasing population on the one hand and resources and wealth on the other has changed remarkably in recent years especially when one considers that Turkey unlike many of her neighbours has not benefited from the oil cornucopia or indeed from any sudden accession of riches.

In 1923, the date of the foundation of the modern Republic, the population numbered less than 13 million, of which approximately 10 per cent were literate. The new State, 40 per cent larger than France, inherited an abysmally poor infrastructure of communications and services, much of which had been destroyed, and a backward low-yield agricultural economy. Istanbul was the sole significant commercial and industrial region. Foreign trade ran at a level of 20 per cent of the national income, made up of exports almost entirely of non-processed agricultural commodities and imports of virtually all manufactures (other than craft goods) and fuels.

Today, agriculture still employs some 54 per cent of the population aged fifteen and over, and more than 65 per cent of the population was still officially classed in 1965 as dwelling in villages but the share of agriculture in the Gross National Product has declined from almost 70 per cent to approximately 30 per cent.

National income *per capita* has more than doubled and the national literacy rate risen to 48 per cent. Only about 35 per cent of Turkish exports in 1966–7 were of unprocessed agricultural commodities while manufactured goods had risen to about 50 per cent of the total.

This economic progress has been by no means easily achieved and the battle for self-sustaining growth has not yet decisively been won. Three distinct periods of economic change, each with their own characteristics, can be discerned and a brief examination of these helps to elucidate the contemporary situation.

The first period, extending from the establishment of the Republic in 1923 by Kemal Atatürk to 1938, the year of his death, is significant for actual economic achievement but even more so for the methods adopted and the structures created. During the 1920s the main effort was devoted to the creation of that minimal infrastructure, social and economic, necessary to the survival of the country. Communications, especially railways, received especial attention while in agriculture the main need was seen as being a simple improvement in dominantly subsistence life, particularly by removing the tithe imposts which made up such a large part of Ottoman revenue. The first steps towards economic diversification were marked by: the formation of the İş Bank to finance industrial and commercial ventures; the post-1927 laws which gave special tax exemptions and privileges to new undertakings; and the considerable efforts made, with Lenin-like fervour, to expand electricity generating capacity. The main difficulty remained the low rate of domestic capital formation which, coupled with the repayment of a large proportion of external debts, almost crippled industrial efforts. For this reason rather than because of any particular ideological belief, Turkey turned to '*étatisme*', State capitalism, in which budgetary funds were massively directed into industry, public utilities, and marketing. In the 1930s the dominance of the public sector was established in large areas of the economy, a dominance which did not destroy the concepts of individual property and enterprise but which produced a markedly skewed mixed economy which still survives. Nationalization of the coal mines, railways, water, and electricity supplies and many

other concerns was made easier by harnessing xenophobia to the dis-
possessing of foreign owners. State monopolies of production of tobacco,
salt, sugar, matches, potable alcohol, coal, and steel were merely
extensions of Ottoman practice and now vital for fiscal reasons. As a
result of these energetic measures total national income had almost
doubled by 1938 and *per capita* national income increased by 50 per
cent. There was also a legacy of direct State involvement in the economy,
through a complex of official banking institutions and producing organizations. The Sümer Bank, founded in 1933 with general development
implementation responsibilities, rapidly grew to own and control a
great number and variety of industries and also acquired many other
concerns such as the possession of a sales monopoly of all textiles however produced. The Eti Bank, dating from 1935, not only financed iron
and steel production and mining but through exploitation establishments dominated the whole field of mineral production. Through the
Deniz Bank a national merchant fleet was built up and shipping rights
safeguarded. Other state institutions such as the MTA, with sole rights
to mineral research and exploration, the TMO, the central purchasing
and storing agency for grain and other products of cultivation, and
the sugar factory organizations rapidly proliferated and gave precedent
to later developments of this kind.

The Second World War imposed immense strains on this highly
bureaucratized and financially extended system. Trade dislocation
resulted in shortages of consumer and capital goods while the markets
for export goods which remained predominantly agricultural were
largely closed. Heavy military expenditure further exacerbated an
inflationary situation while several bad harvests produced real distress.
Turkish national income slumped badly and did not rise again to 1938
levels for another decade while *per capita* income took two further years
to recover. Nevertheless this apparently inauspicious economic commencement to the second period, extending to 1960, was not wholly
negative, indirectly at least. Turkey for ten crucial years survived as an
independent State, where others in similar circumstances had not, and
had shown that an Atatürk was no longer indispensable. By 1950
convertible currency reserves were relatively large and all external
debts had been discharged. Even more important the post-war years
of world-wide reconstruction and shortages of capital goods saw
the beginning of the new era of multilateral and bilateral development aid. In the years between 1950 and 1960 external grants and
credits constituted between 15 and 25 per cent of Turkish gross
investments.

With the recovery from wartime difficulties Turkey entered a decade
of what has been called 'inflationist expansion'. At first the considerable
attention paid to agriculture, particularly in mechanization and the
improvement of storage and marketing facilities, proved very profitable.

The income accruing to the agricultural sector increased by 50 per cent between 1948 and 1960, the production of the staple cereals increased at first at a rate faster than that of the population and Turkey became a significant exporter of grain. In 1953 wheat production was almost double the 1948 volume and exports totalled 1,400,000 tons while domestic *per capita* consumption rose by over a quarter. Other commodities ranging from potatoes and sugar-beet to cotton, olive oil, and citrus fruit showed even higher rates of increase. Unfortunately almost all the additional field crop production during this second period resulted from an expansion in cultivated areas. By 1960 the trend towards extensive agriculture had reached, and from the ecological point of view had overpassed, all reasonable limits. The spread of the plough and the continued rise in the numbers of sheep and goats provided in the short term for a relatively high level of domestic consumption in bulk, calories, and animal protein, and for export commodity surpluses as well, but at the same time this had a disastrous effect on the capital assets of soil, water, and forest. Some 80 per cent of the economically active population was still engaged in agriculture, the absolute increase between 1950 and 1960 being of the order of 1·5 million—approximately three-and-a-half times the increment in the industrial labour force. Disguised unemployment in agriculture was estimated at one million in July 1962.

Other sectors of the economy grew even more rapidly, particularly in the years following 1950. Economic policy in general favoured all-round expansion of business activity at all levels. Increased revenue from agriculture, exports, taxation, and foreign aid produced a type of euphoria which resulted in a large and unplanned increase of investment. The Turkish Gross National Product (at constant 1948 market prices) rose from 10,067 million Turkish lira in 1948 to TL18,283 million in 1959. Gross investment accounted for about 9 per cent of GNP in 1948 increasing to 15·6 per cent by 1959 while investment as a proportion of public expenditure doubled to 30 per cent in the same period. Unfortunately an ever-increasing proportion of investment and public expenditure was actually met by deficit financing and reliance on foreign aid while defence expenditure remained at a high level, fluctuating between 25 per cent and 34 per cent of annual General and Annexed Budget expenditure.

The value of industrial production virtually doubled between 1948 and 1959 (constant 1961 factor prices) and consumption and production of basic goods increased remarkably. Electricity production rose from 789,600 kw. in 1950 to 2,815,000 kw. in 1960, cement production from 395,000 tons to 2,038,000 tons. Iron and steel consumption almost doubled, while the demand for fuel and energy approximately trebled during the same decade. As with agriculture, however, the boom in the manufacturing and service sectors was unstable. The annual trade deficit by the mid 1950s had risen to approximately half the value of Turkish exports, the supply of money was double that of 1950, and all price indices had risen by some 50 per cent. Inflation became hyper-inflation and a series of emergency controls of imports, currency supply, construction, and public expenditure only increased the pressure at various economic bottlenecks. In 1958 the administration was driven to devaluation and a stabilization policy which did nothing to ensure the survival of the regime which by its fall in 1960 marked the end of the second main period of economic change.

The revolution of 1960 marks in some ways the rise of contemporary technocratic Turkey and the very fact that this was a viable and vital revolution and not merely a negative or emotive discontent indicates that the years before had not been purely wasted. The new socio-economic élite commanded military support from the well-trained, patriotic leaders of the largest army in NATO because it too was trained, avid for responsibility, and fervidly believed in the future of planning a modern Turkey. This whole group, civilian and military, was after all the product of past efforts and while they inherited a variety of economic problems the legacy also included a sizeable infrastructure of communications, educational and welfare institutions, and basic industries.

One of the first actions of the new regime was to establish a State Planning Organization on 30 September 1960, and the First Five-Year Development Plan, covering the period from 1 January 1963 to 31 December 1967, was adopted by the Grand National Assembly during the summer of 1962. In the words of the Planning Organization, this plan 'was not born of an ideological necessity, as is the case for totalitarian countries, but of a realistic and pragmatic approach to economic and social development problems', designed 'to attain and sustain the highest possible rate of economic growth and to achieve social justice within the democratic system. . . .'

The strategy of the plan called for an annual increase of 7 per cent in GNP, a rate which would give an annual *per capita* increase of just on 4 per cent. The magnitude of the task may be measured against the 5 per cent gross rate of increase achieved during the 1950s by extensive, inflationary and deficit-financed policies. The first plan was itself set in a fifteen-year grand strategy during which the GNP was to be trebled, 7.5 million new jobs created, and a new equilibrium created between the different sectors, in particular an expansion in non-agri-cultural sectors sufficient to bring the agricultural contribution to GNP down from 43.8 per cent in 1962 to 29.4 per cent in 1977. High on the priority list of targets was the attainment of improved social welfare in the fields of health and education and the correcting of what were regarded as regional imbalances of wealth.

The hopes of the First Plan were not fully realized but in announcing the Second Five-Year Plan for the period 1968–72 various claims of success could properly be made for its precursor.

The most significant fact has been the rather faster than planned reduction in the dominance within the economy of the agricultural sector. As already noted, the contribution of agriculture to GNP has declined to 30·4 per cent as compared with planned expectation of 38·3 per cent. This change in sectoral balance came about in spite of short-falls in agricultural and industrial growth.

First Plan Annual Growth Rates, 1962–6
(value added at factor cost)

	Plan	Realization	(Second Plan)
		(percentages)	
Agriculture	4·2	3·3	(4·1)
Industry	12·3	8·9	(12·0)
Services	7·2	7·6	(6·8)
Net national product	6·8	6·4	(6·8)

In agriculture the disappointing level of performance (although in absolute terms it was one-third better than the average of the previous two decades), was in part a reflection of poor harvests during the first three years of the plan, a reminder that farming in Turkey as in all Middle Eastern countries is extremely vulnerable to climatic fluctuations from year to year. More important is the slowness with which changes in the structure in agriculture can be reflected in productivity. It has been estimated that in 1967 Turkish agriculture required 9·2 million workers during the busy periods of July and August but only 2·3 million during December, this immense seasonal variation resulting in particular from the great reliance on cereal production by predominantly small farmers. In 1967 82 per cent of the cultivated area was under cereals or fallow and the average holding size was only nineteen acres. Average yields of the basic cereals and pulses were only marginally higher than they were during the 1930s as the deterioration of marginal land neutralized the effects of improved husbandry in other areas. As long as Turkish farming is dominated by unirrigated and essentially non-commercially-orientated cereal growing and sheep and goat grazing, and as long as 70 per cent of the country's potential labour force lives in rural areas and is directly and indirectly affected by the requirements of this type of farming then the huge agricultural sector can make only a relatively small contribution to economic growth.

In cash-crop farming, limited in area but expanding, there have however, been important successes. The value of exports of cotton lint in 1967, TL1,183 million, was over ten times greater than the 1957 total, exports of tobacco were five times, and those of fruit six times larger. Acreage under cultivation and production of potatoes and sugar-beet have shown a steady increase. 45 per cent of the First Plan investment in agriculture was devoted to new irrigation and the effects of this policy are now beginning to come to fruition as are also the results of the introduction of improved crop strains, particularly of wheat.

Turkey is now self-sufficient, at a relatively high level of consumption, in agricultural products except for wheat; and the rise in agricultural exports has contributed more than was expected to balancing Turkey's overseas trade. Total exports in 1967 were valued at TL4,701 million, of which agricultural products and processed foodstuffs, beverages, tobacco, and textiles constituted 90 per cent.

The industrial sector has, however, grown at a more rapid rate than these figures would suggest, at an average annual rate of 8·9 per cent. The heaviest investment during the First Plan was in iron and steel. Expansion at Karabük and the new installation at Ereğli allowed production of steel to rise to 997,000 tons in 1967, over four times greater than in 1962, making Turkey self-sufficient over a great range of steel products. Further expansion of capacity is planned at both plants and also at a new complex at Edremit.

By 1967 other investment fields were beginning to yield returns, notably chemicals, petroleum, and vehicle tyres. The production of artificial fertilizers and cement has also risen markedly but the growth in textile and transport equipment industries has been disappointing. The main difference in performance has been between rapidly increasing output from new large-scale industrial plant, mainly in the public sector, and on the other hand less spectacular growth in the established areas dominated by small scale industry, mainly in the private sector, this in spite of the fact that public sector industrial investment during the First Plan ran at only 80 per cent of the projected total while in the private sector it exceeded expectation by 8 per cent.

The 1964 Census of Manufacturing and Business Establishments showed that large establishments (employing ten or more workers) only comprised 1·9 per cent of the total number but employed 69·4 per cent of the employees and handled 73·1 per cent of the purchased or transferred goods and services. In 1967 only 6·6 per cent of manufacturing enterprises employed more than 100 workers and of these very few were in private hands. The remaining establishments are still short of capital and of managerial expertise. Another important factor has been the greater emphasis on import savings which has led to a less than stringent control of marginal costs. Prices of domestic industrial products in 1967 were far higher than those in Western Europe, Ereğli plate and sheet steel being double the Federal German level, cement 33 per cent and vehicle tyres 128 per cent higher.

However, in spite of relative shortcomings, Turkish industry still dominated by State enterprises, has advanced considerably and the

Second Plan lays main emphasis in this area. Of total gross investment 22·4 per cent is allocated to manufacturing, a total of TL25,000 million, with over 20 per cent going to iron and steel production, 17 per cent to chemicals, 10 per cent to textiles, and approximately 5 per cent each to food, paper, petroleum, metal, machinery, and non-metallic mineral industries.

Fuel and energy production are now running at a high level. Annual coal production now runs at 7 million tons a year, almost entirely from the Zonguldak field and mainly consumed at the Karabük steel plant. Production of crude oil is now almost three million tons per annum and while this meets the major part of present domestic requirements, Turkish refining capacity of over 5 million tons a year, 3·2 million of which is located at Mersin, demands another 3 million tons import volume. Great emphasis is being laid on the need for further expansion of production, and various negotiations concerning the import of natural gas from Iran and Iraq have been taking place. Oil and gas are not only required for the increasing energy needs but also as feed-stock for petrochemical and plastics industries. The output of electricity is now running at almost 6,000 million kwh. a year, 80 per cent more than in 1962, and a growing proportion, now over 60 per cent, being supplied from hydro-electric plants. The Keban station now under construction on the Euphrates was planned to add over one million additional kw. by 1972 by which time total generating capacity would have doubled.

Mineral resource exploitation has not grown as much in recent years as during the 1950s but Turkey remains the third largest world producer of chromite and has important outputs of antimony, copper, and mercury. Copper and borate ore production and export are now rapidly rising while alumina exploitation (and eventually processing) is planned.

Turkish economic development is not as yet self-generating. During the First Plan period total foreign capital inflow, mostly in the form of aid and mainly from the OECD consortium and the USA, amounted to $1,638 million—equal approximately to half the total import bill. Merchandise imports and exports in 1967 were still showing a large deficit of $162 million whilst the net external debt was of the order of $1·3 billion. The cumulative deficit in current account has on the other hand shown encouraging trends. Receipts from tourism were extremely disappointing and between 1962 and 1967 net expenditures of $65 million were realized against an expected net earning of $20 million; this position is now showing some improvement. Export earnings, however, increased some 12 per cent higher than forecast and imports were some 3 per cent lower. Completely unforeseen was the windfall of about $270 million in invisible earnings, mainly derived from remittances by Turkish workers overseas who numbered over 180,000 by 1967. The expectation is that foreign currency earnings from this quarter should average over $150 million a year for the next decade.

Behind these facts and figures there are of course the human realities of the situation. The current rate of population increase, 2·6 per cent per annum, is lower than it has been in the past and the trend is downward; even so, in fields of employment, housing, and education Turkey has just managed to hold her own in qualitative and quantitative terms. The expectation is that, because the very heavy investments already made in these as well as the other sectors will begin to show returns in the near future, it becomes possible to talk of a viable Turkish economy at a self-sustaining and relatively high consumption level by 1975. If this expectation is fulfilled then almost within fifty years of the foundation of the modern State, Turkey will have emerged as one of the strongest, most populous and most economically diversified countries in the Middle East and the Mediterranean.

Statistical Appendices

APPENDIX I: GENERAL DATA

APPENDIX II: INDIVIDUAL COUNTRIES
ARABIA

APPENDIX III: OIL

Appendix I
General Data

1. Population Growth (estimates)
(thousands)

	1937	1950	1955	1960	1965	1970
Bahrain	82	110	128	147	185	198
Egypt	16,008	20,393	23,063	25,948	29,600	33,330
Iran[1]	16,200	16,276	18,325	20,182	23,428	29,260
Iraq	3,940	5,278	6,152	7,085	7,160	9,440
Israel	386[2]	1,258	1,748	2,114	2,563	2,910
Jordan	442[3]	1,269	1,437	1,695	1,976	2,320
Kuwait	n.a.	n.a.	n.a.	223	475	710
Lebanon	925	1,257	1,466	1,646	2,330	2,790
Oman	500	550	550	565	565	750
Qatar	16	20[6]	35	45	70	80
Saudi Arabia	6,130	n.a.	6,036	n.a.	6,750	7,740
Sudan	6,880	n.a.	10,263[4]	11,770	13,540	15,700
Syria	2,628	3,215	3,681	4,555	5,300	6,250
Turkey	16,923	20,947	24,065	27,818	31,086	35,230
United Arab Emirates ⎫ Ras al-Khaima ⎬	76	80	80	86	111	200
Yemen (Aden)	650	100[6]	139[6]	1,155	1,240	1,440
Yemen (Sanaa)	3,990	4,500	n.a.	5,000	5,000	5,700

[1] Excluding nomad population.
[2] Jewish population of Palestine only. Palestine 1,383,000.
[3] Excluding West Jordan.
[4] 1956.
[5] Aden Colony only.
[6] 1949.

Sources: United Nations (FAO, UNESCO); International Monetary Fund.

2. *Basic Economic Indicators*

	Land Area (sq. km.)	Pasturage & Cultivated Area (sq. km.)	Population 1969 (thousands)	Population Growth Rate 1960–9 (%)	Per capita GNP 1969 ($)	Growth Rate of Per Capita GNP 1960–9 (%)	Imports 1970 ($ millions)	Exports 1970 ($ millions)	Education Primary & Secondary (thousands of pupils)	
Bahrain	660	n.a.	212	3·9	420	4·7	168	49	1968/9	45·3
Egypt	1,001,450	35,580[1]	32,501	2·5	160	1·2	787	762	1968/9	4,807·5
Iran	1,636,000	183,340	28,475	3·0	350	4·9	1,658	2,354	1969/70	3,857·3
Iraq	434,920	117,600	9,350	3·5	310	3·0	509	1,099	1968/9	1,313·2
Israel	20,260	12,290	2,822	3·3	1,570	5·3	1,451	776	1969/70	683·6
Jordan	90,180	13,520	2,242	3·2	280	4·7	184	34	1966/7	441·8
Kuwait	16,000	3	657	10·0	3,320	−4·3	625	1,581	1969/70	154·3
Lebanon	10,000	3,260	2,645	2·5	580	2·1	559	184	1968/9	658·7
Oman	212,380	n.a.	730	2·9	210	12·2	64	136	n.a.	
Qatar	22,010	139	110	9·7	1,550	−0·9	64	172	1969/70	13·5
Saudi Arabia	2,149,960	854,620[2]	7,235	1·7	380	7·1	693	2,361	1968/9	311·1[5]
Sudan	2,376,000	311,000[3]	15,186	2·9	110	0·6	288	298	1967/8	622·6
Syria	185,100	113,090	5,866	2·8	260	4·7	360	203	1968/9	1,062·5
Turkey	770,760	527,360	34,450	2·5	350	3·4	904	578	1970/1	6,390·8
United Arab Emirates } Ras al-Khaima	83,600	n.a.	205	9·6	1,590	28·3	390	458	n.a.	
Yemen (Aden)	287,680	93,170[4]	1,220	2·2	120	−4·6	201	146	1967/8	74·7
Yemen (Sanaa)	195,000	21,000	5,556	2·1	n.a.	n.a.	52[e]	10[e]	1969/70	69·5

[1] Excluding rough grazing.
[2] Mostly rough grazing.
[3] Of which 24,000 ha. acacia + short grass scrub.
[4] Of which 90,650 sq. km. rough grazing only.
[5] Boys only.
[e] Estimate. The figures in Yemeni rials are: *for 1970* Imports YR 178,448,978 Exports YR 15,759,166.

Main sources: Food and Agriculture Organization Production Yearbook 1969; International Bank for Reconstruction and Development; UNESCO; International Monetary Fund; National Statistics; Middle East Economic Digest.

3. *Total Exports*

$ million fob	1955	1960	1963	1966	1967	1968	1969	1970
Bahrain	n.a.	23	22	26	31	39	43	49
Egypt	397·4	568	522	605	566	622	745	762
Iran	168·8	845	933	1,309	1,930	1,879	2,099	2,354
Iraq	506·6	654	781	939	828	1,043	1,045	1,099
Israel	88·2	217	352	503	555	640	729	776
Jordan	8·0	11	18	29	32	40	41	34
Kuwait	n.a.	960	1,110	1,304	1,313	1,397	1,476	1,580
Lebanon	33·3	42	61	103	119	165	161	184
Oman[1]	n.a.	n.a.	n.a.	n.a.	n.a.	84	110	136
Qatar[1]	n.a.	n.a.	n.a.	n.a.	n.a.	109	115	121
Saudi Arabia	558·8	820	1,120	1,650	1,786	1,945	2,001	2,361
Sudan	147·3	182	226	203	213	233	248	298
Syria	128·3	120	189	173	155	168	207	203
Turkey	313·3	321	368	490	523	496	537	578
UA Emirates and[1, 3] Ras al-Khaima	n.a.	n.a.	n.a.	n.a.	n.a.	375	372	458
Yemen (Aden)	176·5	168	195	190	137	110	144	146
Yemen (Sanaa)[2]	n.a.	n.a.	n.a.	n.a.	n.a.	n.a.	n.a.	10[e]

[1] The figures for these countries are derived from British sources and are not strictly comparable with the rest of the figures.
[2] Figures are available for some years but as there is no official exchange rate it is difficult to give a dollar figure.
[3] Abu Dhabi and Dubai only.   [e] Estimate

Main source: International Monetary Fund.

4. *Total Imports*

$ million cif	1955	1960	1963	1966	1967	1968	1969	1970
Bahrain	n.a.	27	69	88	95	108	121	167
Egypt	525·2	668	917	1,071	792	666	638	787
Iran	309.7	559	523	930	1,119	1,386	1,529	1,658
Iraq	272·2	389	319	493	423	404	440	508
Israel	325·6	503	672	838	778	1,121	1,331	1,451
Jordan	75·8	120	143	191	154	161	190	184
Kuwait	n.a.	242	324	463	593	611	646	625
Lebanon	259·0	311	354	493	445	498	527	559
Oman[1]	n.a.	n.a.	n.a.	19	n.a.	23	39	64
Qatar[1]	n.a.	28	28	30	29	42	52	64
Saudi Arabia	200·2	235	320	592	574	562	738	693
Sudan	140·1	183	285	222	214	258	257	288
Syria	179·2	239	235	289	264	312	370	360
Turkey	497·6	468	691	724	690	770	754	904
UA Emirates and[1, 3] Ras al-Khaima	n.a.	n.a.	n.a.	n.a.	n.a.	251	318	276
Yemen (Aden)	207·1	214	272	285	200	203	218	201
Yemen (Sanaa)[2]	n.a.	n.a.	n.a.	n.a.	n.a.	n.a.	n.a.	52[e]

[1] The figures for these countries are derived from British sources and are not strictly comparable with the rest of the figures.
[2] Figures are available for some years but as there is no official exchange rate it is difficult to give a dollar figure.
[3] Abu Dhabi and Dubai only.   [e] Estimate

Main source: International Monetary Fund.

Appendix II
Individual Countries

ARABIA
SAUDI ARABIA

1. Revenue Estimates
(rls mn)

	1967/8	1968/9	%	1969/70	%	1970/1	%
Oil	3,547	4,196	75·8	5,287·4	88·6	5,628·5	88·2
Others	518	703	12·7	678·5	11·4	596·5	9·3
General reserve	872	436	7·9	—	—	—	—
Development fund	—	200	3·6	—	—	—	—
Jihad tax	—	—	—	—	—	55·0	2·5
Total	4,937	5,535	100·0	5,965·9	100·0	6,380·0	100·0

Source: Saudi Arabian Monetary Agency.

2. Expenditure Estimates

	1968/9 rls mn	1969/70 rls mn	1970/1 rls mn	%
Expenditures (total)	5,535	5,966	6,380	100·0
Private treasury	173	173	173	2·7
Information	100	99	76	1·2
Defence	1,382	1,743	1,866	29·2
Interior	845	842	827	13·0
Education	487	484	546	8·6
Communications	795	701	633	9·9
Agriculture	487	382	312	4·9
Finance & national economy	258	232	251	3·9
Petroleum & minerals	75	76	59	0·9
Health	170	168	177	2·8
Commerce & industry	31	23	24	0·4
Others	732	1,043	1,274	20·0
Anticipated savings	—	—	162	2·5

Source: Saudi Arabian Monetary Agency.

3. Foreign Trade
(rls mn)

	1965/6	1966/7	1967/8	1968/9	1969/70
Total imports	2,058·4	2,288·2	2,212·4	2,804·0	3,212·9
Total exports	6,838·4	7,654·9	7,852·7	8,952·0	—

Source: Saudi Arabian Monetary Agency.

4. Main Commodities Imported
(rls mn)

	1965/6	1966/7	1967/8	1968/9	1969/70
Motor vehicles & parts	332	294	294	298	377
Machinery	181	252	199	213	199
Textiles & clothing	154	148	147	154	157
Chemical products	101	118	111	159	238
Live animals & meat	87	118	59	222	143
Rice	102	106	120	160	138
Milk & milk products	49	58	68	76	79
Fresh fruit & vegetables	58	63	77	77	82

5. Main Suppliers
(per cent of total imports by value)

	1965/6	1966/7	1967/8	1968/9	1969/70
USA	26·45	21·76	23·45	22·3	18·6
Japan	6·41	6·61	7·83	9·1	10·3
Lebanon	4·93	7·52	8·99	10·3	9·9
UK	7·25	8·02	6·59	7·4	8·9
West Germany	5·66	6·01	8·13	6·7	7·9
Italy	6·96	7·72	5·61	4·5	5·3
Netherlands	5·04	4·58	4·79	4·6	5·0

Source: Saudi Arabian Monetary Agency.

6. Industrial Origin of Gross Domestic Product at Current Factor Cost
(rls mn)

	1966/7	1967/8	1968/9
Agriculture, forestry, & fishing	862·4	895·7	974·4
Petroleum	6,052·2	6,772·9	7,360·6
Mining	35·4	39·8	41·7
Manufacturing	973·2	1,136·2	1,266·1
Construction	707·1	796·1	834·2
Electricity, gas, & water	166·9	181·3	195·6
Transport	976·4	1,060·1	1,172·1
Wholesale & retail trade	876·3	988·9	1,175·9
Banking, insurance, & real estate	81·9	93·0	102·7
Ownership of dwellings	494·0	545·0	601·0
Public admin. & defence	1,079·5	1,096·3	1,195·1
Services: education	379·8	413·1	426·0
health	136·0	135·4	140·2
other	257·5	304·3	324·6
Gross domestic product at factor cost	13,078·6	14,458·1	15,810·2
less net factor income paid abroad	2,961·0	3,204·0	3,492·0
Gross national product	10,117·6	11,254·1	12,318·2
less depreciation	1,011·8	1,125·4	1,231·8
National income	9,105·8	10,128·7	11,086·4

Source: Saudi Arabian Monetary Agency.

7. Development Budgets

	1967/8 Allocations rls mn	%	1968/9 Allocations rls mn	%	1969/70 Allocations rls mn	%
Transport & communications	709·2	28·0	794·4	30·7	705·6	26·2
Agriculture	380·3	15·0	398·8	15·4	300·0	11·1
Petroleum & minerals	49·1	1·9	56·2	2·2	57·7	2·1
Industry & commerce	11·6	0·5	14·4	0·6	8·7	0·3
Labour & social affairs	11·1	0·4	8·0	0·3	8·7	0·3
Education	91·2	3·6	60·6	2·3	42·2	1·6
Health	21·8	0·9	14·1	0·6	13·9	0·5
Municipalities	247·0	9·8	300·9	11·6	252·4	9·5
Others[1]	1,099·6	39·9	936·5	36·3	1,308·4	48·5
Less: expected shortfall	100·0					
Total	2,430·9	100·0	2,583·9	100·0	2,697·6	100·0

[1] Others include: defence, interior, information, royal household, religious affairs, etc.

Source: Saudi Arabian Monetary Agency.

YEMEN

1. Budgets 1967/8–1969/70
(rls mn)

	1967/8	1968/9	1969/70
Revenues	31·75	49·82	87·99
Tax revenues	26·36	35·87	57·56
Expenditure	88·73	109·06	165·12
Current	71·17	86·15	124·53
Development	17·56	22·90	40·53
Deficit	−56·98	−59·94	−77·14
Foreign loans	17·56	22·90	40·53
Domestic financing (Currency Board & YBRD)	28·94	69·31	48·96

2. Main Trading Partners
(per cent of total value)

Exports to:	1970	Imports from:	1970
Democratic Yemen	51·9	Democratic Yemen	23·4
USSR	31·7	Australia	12·5
Japan	11·8	USSR	12·0
		France	11·9
		UK	8·5
		Japan	5·7

3. Main Commodities Traded in 1970
(rls mn)

Imports		Exports	
Foodstuffs	97·36	Coffee	8·09
Manufactured goods	26·60	Qat	4·34
Beverages & tobacco	19·02	Rock salt	1·49
Machinery & appliances	8·57	Skins	1·20
Transport equipment	8·10	Potatoes	0·35
Raw materials	7·27		
Textiles & clothing	6·01		
Chemicals	5·55		

PEOPLE'S DEMOCRATIC REPUBLIC OF YEMEN

1. Three-Year Development Plan 1971–4—Allocations
(£ mn)

Transport & communications	13·18
Agriculture	10·50
Industry	9·87
Education	3·23
Geological surveys	2·30
Health	0·75
Culture	0·01
Unallocated reserve	0·86
Total	40·70

Plan Finance
(£ mn)

Foreign loans & aid	19·23
Treasury	17·66
Co-operatives & state corporations	3·81

2. Industrial Production

	1967 Quantity	1967 Value (£'000)	1968 Quantity	1968 Value (£'000)
Mineral water ('ooo bottles)	44·3	630·9	30·9	437·3
Dairy products (mn litres)	128·3	101·7	0·2	16·3
Salt ('ooo tons)	47·6	47·6	84·8	84·8
Soap ('ooo tons)	—	—	4·5	525·0
Aluminium utensils ('ooo tons)	527·0	32·9	700·0	47·8
Marble tiles ('ooo pieces)	1,032·0	21·9	863·0	19·6
Cement blocks ('ooo pieces)	228·0	8·17	337·0	11·8
Sesame juice (tons)	922·0	256·6	985·0	264·8
Shipbuilding & repair (tons)	—	538·0	—	—
Flour mills (tons)	415·0	25·1	448·0	27·1

Source: Ministry of Industry.

3. Activities at Aden Port

	1966	1967	1968	1969
Number of ships called	6,246	3,100	1,382	1,568
Fuel oil bunkers ('ooo tons)	3,486	1,400	388	576

	1966/7	1967/8	1968/9	1969/70
Revenues	1,851	962	925	948
Expenditures	1,500	1,455	1,011	720
Balance	351	−493	−86	228

Source: Central Statistical Office.

4. *Trend of Foreign Trade*
(mn dinars)

	1966	1967	1968	1969	1970
Exports	67·92	48·94	45·78	59·79	60·65
Imports	101·93	72·07	84·45	90·92	83·76
Balance	−34·01	−23·13	−38·67	−31·13	−23·11

5. *Main Commodities Traded in 1970*
(mn dinars)

Exports		Imports	
Distillate fuels	24·82	Crude oil	33·24
Lamp oil & white spirit	12·22	Clothing & footwear	3·26
Motor spirit	7·95	Synthetic fabrics	3·18
Bunker fuel	4·01	Rice	2·91
Ginned cotton	1·76	Wheat	1·99
Hides & skins	1·22	Wheat flour & meal	1·76
Cotton fabrics	1·11	Sugar	1·46
Fish	0·79	Livestock	1·42
Rice	0·50	Sesame seed	1·26
Coffee	0·48	Qat	1·26
		Spices	1·22
		Ghee	1·05
		Tea	1·01

6. *Main Trading Partners*
(per cent of total value)

Exports to:	1969	1970	Imports from:	1969	1970
UK	21·9	24·7	Arab states	27·5	25·8
Africa	20·1	21·3	of which: Kuwait	14·1	13·3
Japan	10·5	14·4	Iran	14·9	18·2
Arab states	10·3	7·1	Japan	13·1	10·5
Thailand	6·7	8·6	EEC	7·9	8·6
Ships' bunker fuel	6·3	6·6	Africa	4·8	6·0
			UK	5·6	5·5

KUWAIT

1. Budget Estimates
(KD mn)

	1969/70	*1970/1*	*1971/2*
Revenue			
Income tax	201·80	212·70	241·80
Oil royalties	77·70	80·50	91·30
Taxes & fees	7·30	7·70	7·90
Income from services	12·80	15·50	15·30
Other income & fees	1·10	1·30	1·70
Sale of land & property	1·80	1·70	1·60
Total	302·50	319·40	359·60
Allocations			
General reserve	3·07	1·70	4·75
Development projects & acquisition of property	67·45	75·76	90·01
Ordinary expenditure	232·02	241·92	264·83
of which: head of state	8·00	8·00	8·00
public works	10·79	10·68	11·33
information	5·14	5·19	5·41
telecommunications	3·10	3·23	3·87
posts	1·16	1·20	1·32
trade & industry	0·55	0·62	0·58
education	30·35	31·41	36·64
interior	20·16	20·94	22·14
defence	25·00	25·00	30·00
social affairs & labour	5·56	5·81	5·91
health	16·36	16·61	18·55
electricity & water	7·97	8·24	8·91
customs & ports	6·04	6·12	6·41
Total, including others	302·54	319·39	359·59

Source: Kuwait Planning Board.

2. Allocations for Development Projects and Acquisition of Property
(KD mn)

	1969/70	*1970/1*[1]	*1971/2*
Development projects:			
public works	26·60		24·18
Electricity & water	20·74		27·20
posts, telegraphs, & telephones	8·00		7·47
foreign affairs	1·35		1·00
information	0·29		0·14
Kuwait municipality	0·46		0·28
	57·44		60·28
Acquisition of property	10·00		29·74
Total	67·44	75·76	90·01

[1] Breakdown not published.

Source: Kuwait Planning Board.

S

3. Imports by Commodity Group
(KD mn)

	1966	1967	1968	1969	1970
Food & live animals	26·49	29·08	35·20	34·01	37·80
Beverages & tobacco	6·53	6·89	7·27	5·90	5·72
Crude materials (except fuels)	3·83	4·82	3·98	4·29	3·40
Mineral oils, lubricants, etc.	1·42	1·78	1·69	2·12	1·59
Animal & vegetable oils, etc.	0·40	0·70	0·79	0·76	0·61
Chemicals	6·74	8·33	9·77	11·13	10·35
Manufactured goods	61·68	78·25	83·39	86·59	83·34
Machinery & transport equipment	58·18	82·00	76·21	85·62	80·07
Unclassified	0·01	0·04	0·02	0·35	0·38
Total	165·28	211·89	218·32	230·78	223·27

Source: Central Statistical Office.

4. Principal Suppliers
(per cent of total trade)

	1967	1968	1969	1970
Japan	12·5	12·8	14·6	15·2
USA	21·7	17·1	14·9	13·1
UK	12·3	12·8	12·6	11·8
West Germany	9·4	9·5	10·7	8·4
Italy	4·7	5·1	4·9	4·8
France	2·8	2·2	3·1	4·8
Lebanon	3·1	3·7	3·5	4·4
India	3·1	4·0	4·8	3·8
China	3·1	3·8	3·9	3·2

Source: IMF Direction of Trade.

BAHRAIN

1. Budget Estimates for 1969 and 1971
(BD mn)

	1969	1971
Receipts	14·75	18·00
of which: oil	8·87	9·20
customs	2·50	3·00
rent on government property	0·75	5·00
Expenditure	14·75	24·00
of which: education	3·20	3·85
health	2·46	2·90
public protection	1·95	2·30
national guard	1·25	1·50
development	1·19	3·60
Deficit (from reserves)	—	−6·00

Source: Bahrain Government Finance Department.

2. *Main Trading Partners*
(per cent of total trade)

	Exports (non-oil)				Imports	
	1969	*1970*			*1969*	*1970*
Saudi Arabia	49·9	49·9	UK		24·6	31·0
Kuwait	8·7	11·9	Japan		14·3	12·2
Dubai	6·3	5·9	US		10·7	7·3
Qatar	11·6	5·2	China		6·6	5·1
Iran	3·3	3·9	India		4·9	4·2
Abu Dhabi	4·9	1·6	West Germany		4·1	3·4
			Pakistan		3·9	3·6
			Hong Kong		3·9	3·1
			Holland		2·9	4·7
			Italy		2·2	2·0

Source: Bahrain Statistical Bureau.

QATAR

1. *Main Imports*[1]
(QDR mn)

	1966	*1967*	*1969*
Building materials	10·5	14·1	17·2
Motor vehicles	10·5	10·2	36·5
Piece goods, cloth	7·5	4·6	15·4
Live animals	3·7	—	2·9
Foodstuffs	9·3	11·4	53·2
Radio & TV sets	2·7	3·5	2·4
Clothing	4·6	4·4	13·4
Electrical goods	3·3	4·3	7·8
Air-conditioners	5·9	3·6	5·5
Plant & machinery	3·2	5·1	8·6

[1] Figures for 1968 not available.

Source: Middle East Economic Digest.

2. *Main Suppliers*
(per cent of total trade)

	1966	*1969*
UK	17·1	22·6
US	12·9	12·5
Japan	4·4	7·7
West Germany	5·6	6·9
Lebanon	2·8	6·1

Source: Middle East Economic Digest.

ABU DHABI

1. Oil Production and Revenues

	Production (mn long tons)				Payments to government (£ mn)			
	1967	*1968*	*1969*	*1970*	*1967*	*1968*	*1969*[1]	*1970*[1]
ADPC	12·17	14·92	17·80	20·25	29·86	41·88	48·14	60·4
ADMA	5·70	8·71	12·20	14·45	9·63	21·97	29·59	37·9
Total	17·87	23·63	30·00	34·70	39·40	63·85	77·73	98·3

[1] Estimates.

Source: Middle East Economic Survey.

2. Five-Year Development Plan
(BD '000)

	Total cost	Annual allocations					Plan allocation
		1968	*1969*	*1970*	*1971*	*1972*	
Education	12,140	4,228	1,803	2,057	2,588	1,464	12,140
Health	6,510	830	2,465	2,040	845	330	6,510
Agriculture	13,696	880	1,769	2,560	4,130	4,050	13,389
Industries	63,100	11,270	14,460	9,970	8,220	15,420	59,340
Communications	82,870	17,260	16,990	17,370	11,060	8,350	71,030
Municipalities	54,260	8,725	12,925	11,650	9,520	7,490	50,310
Housing	16,700	2,750	4,700	3,150	2,400	2,800	15,800
Labour	2,785	260	930	640	550	375	2,755
Tourism	5,916	850	1,170	1,325	1,571	1,000	5,916
Public buildings	9,720	2,220	3,715	2,375	830	580	9,720
Loans & investments	49,000	3,000	4,250	11,750	14,500	15,500	49,000
Total	316,970	52,273	65,177	64,887	56,214	57,359	295,910

Source: Directorate of Planning and Co-ordination.

DUBAI

1. Main Commodities Traded
(QDR '000)

	Exports (re-exports)		Imports	
	1969	*1970*	*1969*	*1970*
Household goods	28,321	40,942	202,151	179,392
Foodstuffs	43,095	47,926	114,142	132,499
Clothing	11,276	11,123	163,910	145,278
Machinery	2,266	3,260	187,173	155,606
Building material	3,577	8,447	101,000	139,151
Electrical, radios, etc.	403	2,419	44,022	62,992
Oilfield materials	1,315	2,305	45,192	64,437

2. *Main Suppliers*
(QDR '000)

	1968	*1969*	*1970*
UK	125,055	161,227	196,991
Japan	130,321	179,102	162,668
US	71,658	75,595	88,305
Switzerland	89,523	105,722	82,679
India	36,003	42,008	56,048
Hong Kong	23,905	28,741	32,324
West Germany	26,288	39,360	31,514
Pakistan	53,647	34,603	20,720

Source: Annual Trade Review, 1970.

OMAN

Main Suppliers
(£ '000)

	1968	*1969*
India	527·3	841·1
UK	620·5	815·2
China	158·0	645·6
Australia	267·8	457·1
Burma	411·1	331·4
Pakistan	177·8	207·6
Japan	183·2	195·1
West Germany	118·1	117·1
Singapore	184·9	114·4
Total non-government non-oil company imports	4,044·8	5,619·2
Total UK supplies to government & oil companies	2,781·0	5,280·0

Source: Board of Trade, London.

EGYPT

1. Trend of Gross Domestic Product
(£E mn)

	1959/60	1965/6	1968/9
GDP at current prices	1,285·2	2,124·1	2,331·3
GDP at constant 1959/60 prices	1,285·2	2,063·3	2,167·5

Source: National Bank of Egypt after the Ministry of Planning.

2. Changing Industrial Structure of GDP 1959/60–1968/9
(current prices)

	1959/60 £E mn	1959/60 %	1965/6 £E mn	1965/6 %	1968/9 £E mn	1968/9 %
Agriculture	405·0	31·5	608·5	28·7	688·3	29·5
Industry & mining	256·3	20·0	461·1	21·7	495·8	21·3
Electricity	9·8	0·7	24·3	1·1	35·7	1·5
Construction	47·1	3·7	94·9	4·5	110·3	4·7
Transport & communications	92·9	7·2	196·6	9·3	116·3	5·0
Trade & finance	129·2	10·0	181·5	8·5	215·9	9·3
Housing	73·0	5·7	76·1	3·6	115·6	5·0
Public utilities	6·4	0·5	9·2	0·4	10·8	0·4
Other services	265·5	20·7	471·9	22·2	542·6	23·3
Total	1,285·2	100·0	2,124·1	100·0	2,331·3	100·0

Source: Ministry of Planning.

3. Agricultural Production (*excluding cotton*)
(mn metric tons)

	1965	1966	1967	1968	1969	1970
Wheat	1·27	1·47	1·29	1·51	1·27	—
Maize	2·14	2·38	2·16	2·30	2·37	—
Millet	0·80	0·86	0·88	0·96	0·81	—
Rice	1·79	1·68	2·28	2·59	2·56	2·60
Sugar-cane	4·74	5·19	5·26	6·08	4·91	5·15
Onions	0·67	0·71	0·58	0·44	0·57	—
Beans	0·34	0·38	0·19	0·28	0·30	—
Tomatoes	1·24	1·36	1·23	1·50	1·55	—
Potatoes	0·44	0·32	0·27	0·47	0·49	—
Oranges	0·34	0·48	0·53	—	—	—
Dates	0·38	0·31	0·31	0·32	0·36	0·36
Grapes	0·90	0·12	0·12	—	—	—

Source: Central Agency for Public Mobilisation and Statistics; FAO.

4. *Industrial Production*
('ooo metric tons unless otherwise stated)

	1965	1966	1967	1968	1969
Refined sugar	400	357	366	380	487
Cotton yarn	138	148	157	157	162
Cotton fabrics	80	97	93	102	106
Paper & board	106	110	92	116	122
Tyres & tubes ('ooo units)	1,201	1,136	1,301	1,832	1,465
Sulphuric acid	194	213	229	260	290
Fertilizers	1,000	1,055	999	1,076	805
Portland cement	1,778	1,764	1,929	2,309	2,455
Iron & ore products	373	406	453	474	—

Source: Federation of Egyptian Industries.

5. *Budget Outline*
(£E mn; year July–June)

Main heads of expenditure	1969/70	1970/1
Ordinary current	621·3	651·4
Public authorities	373·0	438·0
Economic organizations	366·2	483·0
Special funds	10·5	25·5
Emergency fund	170·0	264·0
Investment	350·0	300·0

Ordinary budget	1969/70	1970/1
Defence, security, & justice	245·0	293·8
Education, research, & youth	136·8	134·5
Finance (Treasury)	60·1	44·1
Health, social, & religious	55·4	54·2
Local administration	42·2	34·2
Agriculture & irrigation	41·5	52·3
Presidential services	18·3	18·2
Transport & communications	5·8	1·2
Housing & public utilities	4·4	7·9
Culture & national guidance	4·4	4·8
Trade, supply, & economic affairs	3·8	3·4
Industry, petroleum, & mining	2·6	1·9
Tourism	0·8	0·7
Electricity & the High Dam	0·2	0·2
Total	621·3	651·4

6. *Foreign Trade*
(£E mn)

	1965	1966	1967	1968	1969	1970
Exports fob	263·1	263·1	246·1	270·3	323·9	331·2
Imports cif	405·9	465·4	344·3	298·6	276·5	336·2
Balance	−142·8	−202·3	−98·2	−19·3	+47·4	−5·0

Source: IMF International Financial Statistics.

7. *Main Commodities Traded*
(£E mn)

Exports	1968	1969	Imports	1968	1969
Raw cotton	121·1	130·7	Cereals &		
Rice	49·9	55·3	milling products	62·8	39·8
Fuels & mineral oils	7·5	8·2	Mineral products	49·6	49·3
Cotton yarn	29·9	36·3	Machinery &		
Cotton fabrics	14·5	16·0	electrical equipment	42·2	40·9
Onions	6·1	7·8	Chemical products	29·6	37·5
Manganese & phosphates	2·0	1·7	Transport equipment	26·1	23·1
Potatoes	0·9	2·5	Wood, hides, & rubber	9·6	12·5
Cement	5·1	4·2	Edible oils	12·7	12·4
Fruit	2·1	6·8	Groceries	7·1	3·3
			Textiles	6·8	2·2
			Paper & paper products	7·0	6·4
			Tobacco	7·0	7·4

Source: Central Agency for Public Mobilisation and Statistics.

8. *Main Trading Partners*
(per cent of total)

Exports to	1968	1969	Imports from	1968	1969
USSR	28·1	33·1	USSR	15·5	14·1
India	7·5	5·2	France	11·1	10·4
Czechoslovakia	5·3	4·7	West Germany	6·4	7·1
West Germany	3·9	4·1	Rumania	6·2	2·0
Japan	3·7	3·8	USA	5·4	7·3
East Germany	3·6	4·5	Italy	4·9	6·0
Italy	3·4	3·9	East Germany	4·7	4·4
Poland	3·2	3·8	India	3·8	5·9
Rumania	2·8	1·9	Czechoslovakia	3·5	3·3
China	2·7	2·5	China	3·0	2·1

Source: Central Agency for Public Mobilisation and Statistics.

IRAN

1. *Land Use 1967/8*
('000 hectares)

	area	% of total
Total land under cultivation	19,000	11·5
Permanent pastures and meadows	10,000	6·1
Forests and woodland	19,000	11·5
Uncultivated land capable of reclamation	31,000	18·8
Uncultivated and non-agricultural land	86,000	52·1
	165,000	100·0

Source: Fourth National Development Plan.

2. *Sector Allocations of Fourth Plan*
(rls bn)

	Estimates 1968/73	Disbursements 1968/9	1969/70
Agriculture	65·0	7·3	7·3
Mines/industry	125·3[1]	13·8	20·1
Power & fuel	86·5[2]	25·6	25·7
Transport/communications	100·33[3]	12·7	13·8
Education	35·0	—	0·1
Health	13·7	3·5	4·5
Manpower/training	—	7·0	7·9
Urban development	7·0	1·6	1·1
Statistics	1·0	0·5	0·6
Housing	23·0	3·4	4·1
Others	23·2	—	—
Total	480·0	78·3[4]	92·1[4]

[1] Incl. rls26·33 bn for petroleum and natural gas.
[2] Incl. rls48·5 bn for water development.
[3] Incl. rls20·3 bn for telecommunications.
[4] Incl. others.

3. *Production of Principal Crops*
('ooo metric tons)

	1965/6	1966/7	1967/8	1968/9	1969/70
Wheat	3,648	4,381	3,800	4,400	4,200
Barley	935	1,080	1,035	1,204	1,100
Rice	681	788	930	1,354[1]	1,395[1]
Cotton	417	338	405	435	480
Sugar beet	1,411	1,900	2,857	3,403	3,500
Tea	50	59	63	79	75

[1] In the husk.

Sources: Central Bank of Iran Annual Report and FAO Monthly Bulletins.

4. *Estimates of livestock numbers—1967/8*
('ooo)

Sheep	33,000
Goats	14,500
Cattle	5,500
Pigs	40
Camels	230
Water buffalo	250

Source: FAO.

5. *Actual Treasury Receipts and Expenditure, General Budget*
(rls mn)

	Year beginning 21 March				
	1965/6	*1966/7*	*1967/8*	*1968/9*	*1969/70*
Receipts:					
Income tax	8,900	9,800	11,600	14,800	19,000
Indirect taxes	8,600	8,600	10,500	13,500	15,500
Customs duties	13,000	16,200	18,200	22,200	23,700
Oil revenues	12,000	13,000	13,000	15,000	14,700
Tobacco monopoly sales	3,000	3,200	3,600	4,600	4,700
Total including all other	54,000	62,300	66,400	70,200	87,200
Expenditure:					
General	53,000	58,700	68,300	83,200	99,700
Surplus or deficit	+1,000	+3,600	−1,900	−4,000	−12,500

Source: Central Bank of Iran, Annual Report.

6. *Foreign Trade* (*excluding petroleum except any sold by government*)
($ mn)

	1964/5	*1965/6*	*1966/7*	*1967/8*	*1968/9*	*1969/70*
Exports, fob	153·1	180·9	157·5	181·8	216·9	244·0
Imports, cif	742·3	898·4	963·7	1,190·3	1,389·2	1,410·0
Trade balance	−589·2	−717·5	−806·2	−1,010·5	−1,172·3	−1,166·0

Source: Central Bank of Iran, Annual Report.

7. *Main Imports* (*including duty-free imports*)
($ mn)

	1966/7	*1967/8*	*1968/9*
Machinery (excl. electrical)	218·3	286·0	328·4
Iron, steel & manufactures	144·0	224·4	252·7
Chemicals, pharmaceuticals	82·5	94·4	115·5
Electrical items	66·0	82·9	109·9
Road vehicles, parts	49·6	71·2	86·2
Tyres & tubes	15·5	10·9	27·8[1]
Sugar	17·3	12·6	8·0
Tea	11·1	8·9	10·7

[1] Including rubber and rubber products.
Source: Foreign Trade Statistics of Iran.

8. *Main Trading Partners*
(per cent of total value: Iranian years)

Imports from:	*1967/8*	*1968/9*	Exports to:	*1967/8*	*1968/9*
West Germany	22	21	USSR	2	2
USA	18	16	West Germany	5	4
UK	12	13	USA	11	10
Japan	7	9	UK	12	14
Italy	5	6	Japan	13	18
France	5	6			

Sources: Foreign Trade Statistics of Iran; IMF Direction of Trade Statistics.

9. *Expenditure Allocations in Iran's Plans*
(rls bn)

FIRST PLAN, 1949–55

	Original Plan		Revised Plan		Actual	
	Amount	%	*Amount*	%	*Amount*	%
Agriculture	5·3	25	7·3	28	1·0	25
Industry & mines	4·0	19	5·3	20	1·4	35
Transport & communications	5·7	27	7·7	29	1·5	38
Social affairs	6·0	29	6·0	23	0·2	2
Total	21·0	100	26·3	100	4·1	100

SECOND PLAN, 1955–62

Agriculture	18·2	26	18·9	22	17·4	25
Industry & mines	10·6	15	6·7	8	7·0	10
Transport & communications	22·8	33	30·4	35	27·3	40
Social affairs	18·4	26	11·7	13	9·3	13
Other	—	—	19·5	22	7·8	11
Total	70·0	100	87·2	100	68·8	100

THIRD PLAN, 1962–8

Agriculture	30·3	22	45·0	23	47·3	23
Industry & mines	16·6	12	21·9	11	17·1	8
Electricity & fuel	26·1	19	27·0	14	32·0	16
Transport & communications	30·0	21	50·0	25	53·8	26
Social affairs	37·0	27	56·1	28	54·4	27
Total	140·0	100	200·0	100	204·6	100

FOURTH PLAN, 1968–72

Agriculture	65·0	13	—	—	—	—
Industry & mines	99·0	21	—	—	—	—
Electricity & fuel	64·3	13	—	—	—	—
Transport & communications	100·3	21	—	—	—	—
Social affairs	151·5	32	—	—	—	—
Total	480·0	100				

10. *Production of Selected Industries*

		Level of production		
Industry	*Unit*	*1968/9*	*1969/70*	% *change*
Automobiles	unit	20,227	28,826	42·5
Buses	unit	1,842	1,540	−16·4
Trucks and vans	unit	1,879	2,789	48·4
Sheet glass	'000 sq m	2,183	3,812	74·6
Electricity	mn kwh	2,408	3,182	32·1
Vegetable oil	'000 tons	132	146	10·6
Beet sugar	'000 tons	478	498	4·2
Cement	'000 tons	1,972	2,289	16·1
Refrigerators	unit	140,895	177,454	25·9
Cigarettes	mn	11,621	11,386	−2·0
Paints	tons	11,639	13,461	15·7

Source: Central Bank of Iran, Annual Report.

IRAQ

1. Estimated Production of Principal Crops
('ooo metric tons)

	1946/50 aver.	1950	1960	1965	1970
Winter crops					
Barley	703	800	804	806	691
Wheat	375	520	592	1,005	1,059
Lentils	5	6	7[1]	12	4
Vetch	2	3	—	3	4
Summer crops					
Rice	273	242	118	198	204
Cotton	7	25	8	31	—
Sesame	10	10	26[1]	9	13
Tobacco	4	3	12	6	6
Dates	275	250	337	260	300

[1] UN data and assessed on different basis from others in same series.

Source: Ministry of Agriculture—Agricultural Economics Dept.

2. Actual Revenues and Expenditure of the Ordinary Budget
(ID mn; financial years 1 April–31 March)

	1963/4	1965/6	1966/7	1967/8	1968/9[1]
Revenues	126·8	179·1	158·6	210·4	212·9
Expenditures	149·0	187·5	192·4	205·6	191·4
Balance	−22·2	−8·4	−33·8	+4·8	+21·5

[1] Provisional.

Source: Central Bank of Iraq Quarterly Bulletin.

3. Foreign Trade
(ID mn)

	1961	1963	1965	1967	1968	1969
Exports fob (excluding oil)	7·87	16·73	18·12	20·66	23·03	22·00
Re-exports (excluding oil)	3·95	2·26	3·12	3·14	4·52	3·92
Imports	133·53	112·46	161·67	150·39	143·36	155·84
Trade balance	−121·71	−93·47	−140·43	−126·59	−115·81	−129·92
Transit trade	1·32	1·25	1·73	11·50	20·49	20·36

Source: Central Bank of Iraq Monthly Bulletin.

4. Main Commodities Traded
(ID mn)

Exports[1]	1968	1969	Imports	1968	1969
Dates	6·44	7·44	Boilers, mach.	22·45	31·07
Cement	4·36	2·14	Iron/steel	12·68	13·33
Wool (raw)	1·23	1·53	Vehicles	8·96	9·08
Raw cotton	0·88	1·02	Sugar	6·27	7·84
Hides/skins	1·48	1·70	Electrical mach.	6·55	6·78
Oilseeds	0·41	—	Piece-goods	4·94	5·94
Barley	0·68	1·28	Tea	6·10	6·49
Fodder	0·45	0·24	Fruit/vegetables	4·86	4·82
Other grains	0·11	0·62	Pharmaceuticals	3·09	5·79

[1] Excluding oil.

Source: Central Bank of Iraq Bulletin.

5. Main Trading Partners
(per cent of total)

Exports[1]	1968	1969	Imports[2]	1968	1969
Kuwait	14·0	14·6	USSR	8·7	9·9
Lebanon	12·3	24·5	UK	8·4	11·4
S. Arabia	11·2	2·9	W. Germany	7·3	3·7
China	8·4	11·7	France	5·1	5·1
Egypt	7·7	16·5	USA & Canada	4·4	4·2
USSR	6·4	9·2	China	4·3	4·5
Syria	6·0	7·1	Belgium	3·4	3·4
India	4·6	7·9	Ceylon	2·9	3·4
USA & Canada	4·5	6·7	Egypt	2·0	2·4
UK	1·3	1·7	Netherlands	1·3	1·6

[1] Excluding oil and re-exports.
[2] Excluding oil company imports and gold ingots.

Source: Central Bank of Iraq Quarterly Bulletin.

6. Balance of Payments
(ID mn)

Current Account	1966	1967	1968	1969
Exports fob less imports cif, oil sector	306·2	271·2	343·9	346·1
Exports fob less imports cif, other (commercial)	−148·6	−127·1	−116·3	−130·7
Net: interest and dividends (oil profits, etc.)	−137·7	−112·6	−156·8	−154·6
Other services (net)	−14·2	−1·2	−14·9	−8·2
Private remittances	1·1	0·3	1·9	2·1
Government remittances	−1·0	4·7	−0·3	0·4
Balance on current account	+5·8	+35·3	+57·8	+55·1
Capital Account				
Private	25·3	3·6	15·5	1·4
Government	1·4	3·2	−1·1	−4·6
Assets and liabilities of commercial banks	3·0	1·2	−3·2	0·4
Errors and omissions	−8·6	−23·3	−31·3	−57·9
Balance on capital account	+21·1	−15·3	−20·1	−60·7
Net change in reserves (− indicates increase)	−26·9	−20·0	−37·7	+5·6

Source: IMF International Financial Statistics.

ISRAEL

1. Trend of Foreign Trade
($ mn)

	1966	1967	1968	1969	1970
Exports fob	476·9	517·2	602·1	688·8	735·5
Imports cif	813·8	754·1	1,087·5	1,291·0	1,410·2
Balance of trade	−336·9	−236·9	−485·4	−602·2	−674·7
Terms of trade (1968 = 100)	—	99	100	100	98

Source: Monthly Bulletin of Statistics.

2. Main Commodities Traded
($ mn)

Exports	1969	1970	Imports	1969	1970
Polished diamonds	253·5	244·6	Transport equipment	81·0	112·9
Citrus fruit	91·5	88·6	Rough diamonds	210·4	174·7
Textiles & clothing	80·6	96·5	Machinery &		
Foodstuff industry	55·2	69·9	mechanical equipment	77·7	87·1
Chemicals	44·4	51·1	Electrical equipment	52·3	45·0
Mining products	35·9	40·8	Crude oil & products	69·9	68·0
Rubber & plastics	18·9	23·5	Chemicals	83·0	95·4
Fresh fruit & vegetables	9·5	14·4	Soya beans	30·9	25·6
Other agricultural			Iron & steel		
exports	17·1	28·7	plates & sheets	46·7	52·2

Sources: Monthly Foreign Trade Statistics.

3. Main Trading Partners
(percentage of total value)

Exports to	1968	1970	Imports from	1968	1970
UK	11·7	10·5	USA	23·1	22·4
USA	19·8	19·1	UK	20·3	15·5
W. Germany	9·6	8·5	W. Germany	10·8	12·0
Netherlands	5·3	5·9	Netherlands	4·8	4·9
Belgium/Lux.	6·7	5·1	France	5·0	4·2
Switzerland	4·9	4·2	Belgium/Lux.	4·1	4·3
Japan	4·0	4·1	Italy	5·2	5·3
EEC	28·1	26·3	EEC	29·8	30·8
EFTA	21·5	18·8	EFTA	29·6	24·7

Source: Monthly Bulletin of Statistics.

4. Structure of Industry in 1968/9[1]
(Establishments engaging 5 or more persons)

	Number of establishments	'000 persons engaged	Gross output £I mn	Percentage share of total revenue
Mining & quarrying	77	4·4	181·4	2·3
Food, beverages, & tobacco	805	30·6	1,724·3	21·7
Textiles	542	28·8	906·0	11·4
Clothing	558	9·6	227·5	2·9
Wood & furniture	552	10·6	342·5	4·3
Paper & products	114	3·7	202·4	2·6
Printing & publishing	394	8·0	214·3	2·7
Leather & products	229	3·7	89·8	1·1
Rubber & plastics	201	8·1	357·8	4·5
Chemicals	196	8·5	537·6	6·8
Non-metallic minerals	292	8·6	358·2	4·5
Diamond industry	375	10·0	613·9	7·7
Basic metals	97	4·4	264·5	3·3
Metal products	746	17·9	562·2	7·1
Machinery	355	11·4	365·5	4·6
Electric machinery & equipment	264	11·4	409·7	5·2
Transport equipment	485	18·5	480·7	6·1
Miscellaneous manufacturing	196	3·8	97·0	1·2
Total	6,478	202·6	7,935·3	100·0

[1] Provisional figures.

Source: Statistical Abstract of Israel No. 21, 1970.

5. Industrial Production: Selected Items
('000 metric tons unless otherwise stated)

	1967	1968	1969	1970
Cotton yarn	20·2	21·5	24·1	—
Cotton fabrics	8·2	9·6	10·3	—
Newsprint	14·8	13·2	11·3	9·3
Tyres ('000)	730·0	1,020·0	1,236·0	1,392·0
Cement	871·0	1,106·0	1,308·0	1,380·0
Sulphuric acid	166·0	187·0	185·0	203·0
Motor car assembly (number)	2,604·0	3,336·0	4,764·0	3,912·0

Source: Monthly Bulletin of Statistics.

6. Government finance: Trend of Income and Expenditure
(£I mn)

	1964/5	1965/6	1966/7	1967/8	1968/9
Income	3,655·0	4,386·1	4,471·5	6,359·3	7,427·1
Expenditure	3,676·0	4,397·8	4,855·5	6,516·1	7,862·4
Surplus/deficit	−21·0	−11·8	−384·0	−156·8	−435·3
Cumulative surplus/deficit[1]	+177·0	+165·2	−218·8	−375·6	−810·9

[1] Does not include the entire defence budget.

Source: Statistical Abstract of Israel No. 21, 1970.

7. *Cultivated Area*
('000 hectares)

	1966/7	1967/8	1968/9	1969/70
Field crops	272·5	270·4	267·4	275·0
Area in preparation	2·5	2·5	3·0	3·0
Vegetables, potatoes, & groundnuts	30·6	32·1	34·2	36·6
Fruit plantations	84·9	85·2	85·3	85·3
Fish ponds	5·9	5·7	5·5	5·4
Miscellaneous	17·4	17·7	17·8	17·8
Total	413·8	413·6	413·2	423·1
of which: irrigated	158·8	161·6	166·2	171·1

Source: Statistical Abstract of Israel No. 21, 1970.

8. *Agricultural Production*
('000 metric tons unless otherwise stated)

	1965/6	1966/7	1967/8	1968/9
Citrus fruit	907	1,082	1,265	1,178
Wheat	101	222	175	156
Barley	21	56	25	21
Maize & sorghum	15	24	21	16
Sugar beet	285	289	248	215
Cotton (lint)	25	29	33	39
Groundnuts	13	13	11	12
Vegetables & potatoes	448	436	491	558
Grapes	76	82	72	80
Olives	11	25	10	21
Melons & pumpkins	84	92	94	120
Cattle (meat)	28	31	35	34
Poultry (meat)	82	89	89	94
Fish	23	23	25	22
Eggs (mn)	1,233	1,402	1,224	1,219

Source: Statistical Abstract of Israel No. 21, 1970.

9. *Trend of Gross Domestic Product*

	1965	1966	1967	1968	1969
Total: £I mn					
At current prices	10,901·0	11,962·0	12·216·0	14·291·0	16,744·0
At constant (1964) prices	9,954·0	10,090·0	10,173·0	11,674·0	13,452·0
Real increase (%)	8·4	1·4	0·8	14·8	15·2
Per head: £I					
At current prices	4,253·0	4,550·0	4,577·0	5,206·0	5,938·0
At constant (1964) prices	3,884·0	3,838·0	3,812·0	4,253·0	4,770·0
Real increase (%)	4·8	−1·2	−0·7	11·6	12·2

Source: UN Monthly Bulletin of Statistics.

10. Structure of Output
(current prices)

	1967 £I mn	1968 £I mn	1969 £I mn	%
Agriculture, forestry, & fishing	849	919	990	7·6
Mining & manufacturing	2,265	2,851	3,412	26·3
Construction & utilities	799	1,015	1,342	10·4
Transport & communications	896	1,061	1,166	9·0
Commerce & other services	1,782	2,042	2,340	18·0
Finance	566	699	792	6·1
Ownership of dwellings	685	754	852	6·6
Government & private non-profit making institutions	2,212	2,372	2,587	20·0
Net domestic product at factor cost (adjusted)	9,699	11,245	12,966	100·0

Source: Statistical Abstract of Israel No. 21, 1970.

11. Structure of Expenditure at Market Prices
(current prices)

	1967 £I mn	1968 £I mn	1969 £I mn	%
Private consumption	8,113	9,244	10,707	65·2
Government consumption[1]	3,599	4,152	4,911	30·0
Gross fixed capital formation	1,987	2,880	3,710	22·6
Increase in stocks	52	284	122	0·7
Exports of goods & services[2]	2,693	3,894	4,269	26·0
Imports of goods & services[2]	−4,113	−5,912	−6,975	−42·5
Net factor payments abroad	−204	−249	−323	−2·0
Gross domestic product	12,331	14,542	16,744	102·0
Gross national product	12,127	14,293	16,421	100·0

[1] Including Jewish Agency, etc.

[2] Including transactions with Administered Areas.

Source: IMF International Financial Statistics.

JORDAN

1. Output of Main Industries

	1966	1967	1968[1]	1969[1]	1970[1]
Phosphates ('000 tons)	796·4	917·8	1,161·9	1,087·3	938·9
Cement ('000 tons)	375·3	289·2	375·6	480·4	377·6
Petroleum products ('000 tons)	430·4	392·6	392·9	464·1	445·8
Leather ('000 sq. ft.)	2,354·2	1,670·8	1,678·3	1,687·0	1,302·0
Liquid batteries ('000 units)	60·0	45·6	59·6	66·9	66·8
Cigarettes ('000 tons)[1]	1·5	1·8	1·6	1·8	1·6
Spirits & alcoholic drinks ('000 litres)[1]	2,321·0	1,911·0	2,188·6	2,192·0	2,162·0

[1] Excludes West Bank.

Source: Central Bank, Department of Research and Studies.

2. *Production of Main Crops*
('ooo tons)

	1965	1966	1967	1968	1969[1]	1970[1, 2]
Wheat	277·9	101·2	167·2	116·2	159·3	54·1
Barley	94·8	22·8	48·4	24·1	42·5	5·1
Tobacco	1·1	1·6	1·8	4·4	2·0	1·6
Tomatoes	188·9	179·0	167·5	152·5	150·1	107·0
Other vegetables	234·1	232·2	236·7	85·6	69·1	55·0
Olives	37·4	32·7	35·2	36·3	23·9	28·0
Grapes	79·2	61·9	47·3	19·3	14·2	19·0
Citrus fruits	47·0	48·9	45·3	37·3	24·3	18·0
Water melons	160·0	47·7	100·9	82·2	53·2	36·0
Other fruits	60·4	54·3	40·1	29·8	27·7	30·0

[1] Figures for 1969 and 1970 for East Bank only.   [2] Preliminary.

Source: Ministry of Agriculture, 1964–6; Department of Statistics, 1967–70.

3. *Foreign Trade*
(JD mn)

	1966	1967	1968	1969	1970[1]
Exports & re-exports, fob	10·40	11·33	14·18	14·7	12·2
Imports, cif	68·21	55·05	57·49	67·8	65·8
Balance	−57·81	−43·72	−40·31	−53·1	−53·6

[1] Preliminary.

Source: Department of Statistics.

4. *Main Commodities Traded*
(JD mn)

Exports	1968	1969	Imports	1968	1969
Phosphates	4·21	3·57	Machinery	7·27	7·83
Tomatoes	2·28	1·99	Fabrics & yarns	5·67	6·37
Fruits & nuts	1·32	1·45	Transport equipment	3·86	5·21
Cigarettes	0·54	0·56	Wheat & flour	3·46	1·78
Cement	0·42	0·48	Clothing & footwear	1·03	1·46
			Fruit, vegetables, nuts	2·52	2·52

Source: Department of Statistics.

5. *Main Trading Partners*
(per cent of total value)

Exports to	1968	1969
Arab countries	67·2	71·4
India	15·7	12·6
Yugoslavia	7·0	8·4

Imports from		
Arab countries	19·1	21·8
EEC	20·5	17·8
UK	12·5	14·5
Communist bloc	10·8	13·0
US	11·1	8·6
Japan	5·0	7·7

Source: Department of Statistics.

6. *Central Government Budgets*
(JD mn)

	1967	1968	1969	1970[1]	1971
		Actual			*Estimate*
Revenues	70·4	71·9	85·8	69·0	98·4
Local receipts	25·5	26·3	39·9	36·6	37·0
Foreign receipts	44·9	45·6	45·9	33·4	51·4[2]
Expenditures	68·2	80·5	87·3	84·8	106·6
Recurring	44·7	57·2	65·4	65·5	76·8
Development	23·5	23·3	21·9	21·3	29·8
Surplus or deficit	2·2	−8·6	−1·4	−15·8	−8·2

[1] Preliminary.

[2] Includes JD22·9 mn suspended aid from Libya and Kuwait.

Source: Ministry of Finance.

7. *Origins of Jordan's External Receipts in 1969 and 1970*
(JD '000)

	1969	1970[1]
Arab aid	37,553	33,070
Technical & economic assistance	824	279
of which: US	819	266
Ford Foundation	5	13
Development loans	4,837	1,042
of which: UK	1,253	262
West Germany	241	9
Kuwait	559	281
AID	977	165
IDA	195	143
Saudi Arabia	1,499	—
Denmark	113	186
Total	43,214	34,391

[1] Preliminary.

Source: Department of Statistics.

8. *Balance of Payments*
(JD mn)

	1967	1968	1969	1970[1]
Current account				
Trade balance	−42·90	−43·04	−52·79	−51·06
Travel	1·50	−2·40	−3·45	−5·12
Oil transit dues	1·08	1·35	1·07	0·98
Transportation	−0·08	−0·86	−0·69	−0·53
Investment income	3·61	4·92	6·04	6·12
Government n.i.e.	2·70	−7·47	−18·28	0·57
Receipts from abroad	6·55	4·10	6·92	5·54
Other services	−0·21	−0·96	−2·44	−1·31
Private transfers	2·35	1·41	1·55	0·94
Government transfers	51·58	53·07	45·79	37·87
Current account balance	26·18	10·12	−16·28	−6·00

Capital account

Private	0·04	−0·06	0·80	1·35
Local government	0·31	0·02	0·04	0·19
Central government	1·63	5·00	4·50	0·41
Net errors & omissions	5·03	1·25	0·02	4·27
Capital account balance	7·01	6·21	5·36	6·22
Change in reserves (− indicates increase)	−33·19	−16·33	10·92	−0·22

[1] Preliminary.

Source: Central Bank, *Monthly Statistical Bulletin.*

LEBANON

1. Trend of Gross Domestic Product at Current Market Prices

	1965	1966	1967	1968	1969
Total (£Leb mn)	3,523·0	3,867·0	3,820·0	4,274·0	4,565·0
% change	10·1	9·8	−1·2	11·9	6·8
Per head (£Leb)	1,468·0	1,572·0	1,516·0	1,657·0	1,729·0
% change	7·3	7·1	−3·6	9·3	4·3

Sources: IMF International Financial Statistics; UN Monthly Bulletin of Statistics.

2. Structure of Output
(£Leb mn, at current prices)

	1966	%	1969	%
Agriculture & fishing	441·7	11·4	431·5	9·5
Energy & water resources	87·5	2·2	104·2	2·3
Industry & handicraft	511·9	13·2	609·2	13·3
Construction	231·2	6·0	216·2	4·8
Transport & communications	309·5	8·0	382·9	8·4
Dwellings	286·0	7·4 ⎫		
Financial services	141·0	3·6 ⎬	992·7	21·7
Other services	357·3	9·2 ⎭		
Commerce	1,193·4	30·8	1,434·9	31·4
Administration	319·2	8·2	393·0	8·6
Gross domestic product	3,866·7	100·0	4,564·6	100·0

Source: Ministry of Planning.

3. Production of Main Crops in the Lebanon
('000 metric tons)

	1964	1965	1966	1967	1968	1969
Wheat	60	55	70	68	48	33
Oranges	145	149	164	153	161	148
Potatoes	85	54	79	81	78	87
Apples	120	115	102	157	163	67
Olives	60	30	29	68	32	46

Sources: L'Economie et le Marché Libanais; Le Commerce du Levant; FAO Bulletin of Agricultural Statistics; Recueil de Statistique Libanaise No. 5, 1969.

4. *Revenue and Expenditure*
(£Leb mn)

Calendar years	1966[1]	1967[1]	1968[1]	1969[1]
Expenditure	585·3	631·7	631·3	660·6
Receipts	504·0	561·2	570·0	587·0
Balance	−81·3	−70·5	−61·3	−73·6

[1] Estimates.

5. *Sources of Revenue 1971*[1]

	£Leb mn	%
Direct taxes	222·5	28·7
Indirect taxes	327·3	42·2
State & public services revenues	26·9	3·5
Other revenues	120·2	15·6
Extraordinary revenues	77·0	10·0
Total	774·0	100·0

[1] Planned.

Source: Lebanese Ministry of Planning.

6. *Ordinary Budget Expenditure*[1]
(£Leb mn)

	1968	1969
Presidency, Parliament, & President of Council	30·5	27·4
Justice	10·6	12·5
Foreign Affairs	26·8	25·1
Home Affairs	53·1	52·0
Treasury	22·4	23·5
Defence	135·9	160·0
Education & Health	125·0	133·1
Social & Works Ministries	13·9	12·9
Information	7·2	6·6
Public Works, Transport, & Communications	113·6	87·6
Agriculture	16·1	15·1
National Economy & Planning	5·0	4·8
Ministry of Power	21·3	17·7
Tourism	13·4	10·9
Others	53·7	70·4
Total	648·5	660·6

[1] Revised estimates.

Source: Le Commerce du Levant.

7. *Foreign Trade*
(£Leb mn)

	1966	1967	1968	1969	1970
Imports, cif	1,914	1,770	1,865	2,006	2,233
Exports, fob	369	453	510	554	643
Balance	−1,545	−1,317	−1,355	−1,452	−1,590

Sources: Recueil de Statistique Libanaise No. 5, 1969; Bulletin Statistique Mensuel, May 1971.

8. *Main Trading Partners*
(percentage of total value)

Exports to	1969	1970	Imports from	1969	1970
Saudi Arabia	21·1	20·0	EEC	28·6	28·6
Kuwait	11·0	12·2	USA	8·9	9·9
Syria	8·4	6·7	France	8·0	9·2
Iraq	6·0	5·7	West Germany	9·3	8·7
Libya	4·1	5·4	Italy	7·7	6·6
EEC	6·6	6·8	UK	12·7	11·5
USA	4·0	3·7	Syria	4·5	3·0

Sources: Recueil de Statistique Libanaise No. 5, 1969; Bulletin Statistique Mensuel, May 1971.

9. *Balance of Payments*
($ mn)

Current account (net)	1964	1965
Trade balance	−294·4	−349·0
Transportation	52·2	58·3
Travel	44·3	58·2
Other services	115·3	118·6
Private remittances	35·2	35·1
Government remittances	—	—
Balance on current account	−47·4	−78·8
Capital account		
Private	55·2	70·8
Government	6·7	1·6
Banks & other financial institutions net assets & liabilities	−38·4	−8·5
Errors & omissions	23·9	14·9
Balance on capital account	47·4	78·8

Source: IMF International Financial Statistics.

10. *Holdings of Gold and Foreign Exchange*
($ mn)

End of year:	1966	1967	1968	1969	1970
Gold	193·0	193·0	287·5	287·5	287·5
Foreign exchange	87·0	85·8	42·1	57·5	95·7

Source: IMF International Financial Statistics.

SUDAN

1. Cotton Production

Area '000 feddans[1]	1966/7	1967/8	1968/9	1969/70	1970/1
Long-staple type	775	783	778	720	827
American-type	383	365	384	398	435
Total	1,158	1,148	1,162	1,118	1,262

Production '000 cantars[2]					
Long-staple type:	3,258	3,110	3,482	3,877	4,031
of which: Gezira Board	2,487	2,312	2,618	2,974	2,896
American-type	534	614	708	753	830
Total	3,792	3,724	4,190	4,630	4,861
Average yield[3]	3·27	3·24	3·60	4·1	3·9

[1] 1 feddan = 1·038 acres.

[2] 1 cantar = 312 lb.

[3] Cantars per feddan.

Source: Ministry of Agriculture.

2. Output of Major Industrial Products

		1964/5 actual	1969/70 estimated
Iron ore	'000 tons	21·80	26·0
Manganese	'000 tons	1·00	3·0
Chromites	'000 tons	20·50	29·0
Cement	'000 tons	90·70	150·0
Petroleum products	'000 tons	83·80	890·0
Cotton lint	'000 tons	168·30	236·0
Cotton textiles	mn metres	36·40	91·0
Footwear	mn pairs	3·80	12·0
Knitwear	£S '000	365·00	960·0
Ready-made clothing	£S '000	426·00[1]	780·0
Sugar	'000 tons	16·60	80·0
Vegetable oil	'000 tons	40·00	93·0
Canned fruit & vegetables	mn standard cans	—	7·5
Macaroni & spaghetti	'000 tons	7·00	11·5
Confectionery	'000 tons	5·70	12·5
Soft box leather	'000 m²	114·00[1]	210·0
Hard leather	'000 tons	0·16	170·0

[1] Figures for 1965/6.

Source: Five-Year Plan 1970–5, Ministry of Planning.

3. Government Spending
(£S mn: year July–June)

Fiscal year	Central govt. revenue	Central govt. ordinary expendi-ture	Central budget surplus or deficit	Local govt. surplus or deficit	Statutory corpora-tions surplus or deficit	Develop-ment expendi-ture	External loans	Reliance on banking system
63/4	78·6	60·8	17·8	−5·5	2·7	42·1	15·8	19·0
64/5	73·7	63·0	10·7	−1·6	−5·3	30·6	13·8	21·3
65/6	75·1	72·8	2·3	−0·3	−10·0	29·3	17·5	16·4
66/7	81·8	82·4	−0·6	−1·2	−0·8	23·0	14·2	10·6
67/8	98·3	88·9	9·4	−1·0	3·2	29·7	16·0	5·1[1]

[1] On a net basis the reliance on the banking system in 1967/8 was £S3·1 mn.
Source: Bank of Sudan.

4. Foreign Trade
(£S mn)

	1965	1966	1967	1968	1969	1970
Exports & re-exports	68·78	71·68	74·70	81·15	86·20	103·91
Imports	72·29	77·46	81·18	89·71	92·48	100·12
Balance	−3·51	−5·78	−6·48	−8·56	−6·28	3·79

Source: IMF International Financial Statistics.

5. Main Commodities Traded
(£S mn)

Exports	1969	1970	Imports	1969	1970
Cotton	49·5	63·7	Textile yarn, cloth, & mnfrs.	16·6	12·5
Oilseeds, etc.	15·9	17·0	Foodstuff	11·3	20·9
Crude & vegetable materials	8·9	10·8	Transport equipment	11·2	13·8
Animal feeding stuff	4·2	4·6	Chemicals	9·9	9·9
Live animals	2·3	2·3	Petroleum & products	8·8	4·0
			Machinery, non-electric	8·6	11·4
			Iron & steel	4·6	3·8
			Electric machinery & apparatus	3·0	3·2

6. Main Trading Partners
(per cent of total value)

Exports to:	1969	1970	Imports from:	1969	1970
Italy	12·5	10·0	UK	18·9	16·5
West Germany	11·8	9·6	India	10·1	13·1
India	11·7	10·3	Japan	8·1	5·2
Japan	9·3	9·1	West Germany	6·5	7·2
China	7·4	5·9	China	5·4	3·7
UK	7·0	5·8	Italy	4·8	2·2
Egypt	4·5	4·9	USSR	5·4	7·7
USSR	3·9	16·9	Egypt	4·2	4·9
USA	3·4	3·9	France	3·8	1·6

Source: Sudan Trade Accounts.

SYRIA

1. Trend of National Income at 1956 Constant Prices

	1964	1965	1966	1967	1968
Total (£S mn)	3,792·0	3,709·0	4,037·0	4,295·0	4,585·0
Real change (%)	6·1	−2·2	8·8	6·4	6·8
Per head (£S)	742·0	709·0	750·0	775·0	804·0
Real change (%)	3·2	−4·4	5·8	3·3	3·7

2. Structure of Output at Constant 1963 Prices[1]

	1967		1969	
	£S mn	%	£S mn	%
Agriculture	1,039·3	27·8	1,181·7	24·0
Industry	442·7	11·9	701·7	14·2
Construction	132·1	3·5	191·5	3·9
Rents	359·8	9·6	377·2	7·6
Banking & finance	127·2	3·4	141·3	2·9
Government	480·4	12·9	705·6	14·3
Transport & communications	338·9	9·1	480·7	9·8
Commerce	489·3	13·1	782·7	15·9
Services	315·0	8·4	363·8	7·4
Foreign sector (net)	11·9	0·3	—	—
Total	3,736·6	100·0	4,926·2	100·0
Per capita income	670		834	

[1] Provisional estimates.

Source: Banque Centrale de Syrie, 1970.

3. Expenditure on the Gross National Product
(£S mn; at 1963 market prices)

	1963	1966	1967	1968
Private consumption	2,403	2,868	2,849	2,966
Government consumption	567	733	824	1,049
Gross investment	639	701	809	834
Exports	917	905	845	955
less: imports	969	1,187	1,044	1,229
Net factor income from abroad	17	17	12	10
GNP	3,574	4,037	4,295	4,585

Source: UN Yearbook of National Accounts Statistics, 1969.

4. *Land Utilization 1969* (*Excluding the Muhafazat of Kuneitra under Israeli Occupation*)
('ooo ha)

Irrigated	546
Non-irrigated	2,934
Cropped	3,480
Fallow	2,395
Cultivated	5,875
Uncultivated cultivable land	2,839
Cultivable land	8,714
Uncultivable land	3,748
Forest	440
Pasture	5,445
Total	18,347

Source: Syrie et Monde Arabe Publication
economique politique et statistique, May 1971.

5. *Production of Principal Crops*
('ooo metric tons)

	1965	1966	1967	1968	1969
Wheat	1,043·0	559·0	1,049·0	600·0	1,004·0
Barley	690·0	203·0	590·0	512·0	627·0
Pulses	66·0	22·0	83·6	73·9	90·0
Sugar beets	171·0	189·0	154·0	166·0	188·0
Cotton	473·0	375·0	329·0	400·0	382·0
Olives	66·0	117·0	113·0	117·0	129·0

Sources: Etude Mensuelle sur l'Economie et les Finances de la Syrie et
des Pays Arabes; Banque Centrale de Syrie.

6. *Output of Certain Industries*
('ooo tons except where stated)

	1965	1966	1967	1968	1969
Vegetable/olive oil	49·0	54·0	39·0	45·0	53·0
Cement	674·0	682·0	688·0	917·0	933·0
Sugar	94·0	92·0	71·0	83·0	114·0
Manufactured tobacco	4·0	4·1	4·1	4·0	3·9
Glass	15·0	11·0	13·0	16·0	14·0
Woollen fabrics ('ooo metres)	924·0	1,220·0	1,625·0	2,644·0	4,500·0
Cotton & silk textiles	36·0	36·0	38·0	39·0	28·0
Index of industrial production (1958 = 100)	174·0	180·0	191·0	238·0	348·0

Sources: Banque Centrale de Syrie, Bulletin Periodique; Etude Mensuelle sur
'Economie et les Finances de la Syrie et des Pays Arabes.

7. *Budget Expenditure Allocation and Revenue Origin*[1]
(£S mn)

Expenditure	1969	1970
Total	2,199·3	2,780·0
of which: administration	40·8	45·2
national & social security	728·8	738·6
social & cultural affairs	265·8	293·4
economic & finance	249·7	276·2
agriculture	318·2	554·5
industry & mining	301·0	443·6
transportation & public works	282·2	371·6
other	12·8	56·9

Total revenue		
Total	2,199·3	2,780·0
of which: tax & fee revenues	822·5	828·6
public revenues	17·6	20·1
special revenues	512·5	772·4
various revenues	358·9	70·9
extraordinary revenues	487·8	1,088·0

[1] Estimated.

Source: Banque Centrale de Syrie, 1970.

8. *Trend of Foreign Trade*

(£S mn)	1966	1967	1968	1969	1970
Exports, fob	645·6	591·3	673·0	789·9	775·3
Imports, cif	1,118·4	1,009·1	1,192·6	1,411·0	1,373·9
Balance of trade	−472·9	−417·8	−519·6	−621·6	−598·6

Sources: IMF International Financial Statistics; Etude Mensuelle sur l'Economie et les Finances de la Syrie et des Pays Arabes.

9. *Main Commodities Traded*
(£S mn)

Exports	1969	Imports	1969
Cotton	326	Machines & tools	226
Crude oil	83	Iron & ferrous metals	213
Oleaginous fruits	20	Fuel	145
Live animals	100	Transport equipment	111

Source: Etude Mensuelle sur l'Economie et les Finances des Pays Arabes.

10. *Direction of Trade*

(% of total)	Exports		Imports	
Group of countries	1968	1969	1968	1969
Arab Common Market	17·3	14·2	7·6	8·7
Other Arab states	25·9	16·9	5·3	5·4
Eastern bloc	23·0	36·7	32·8	29·6
EEC	15·5	17·9	29·3	26·4
Rest of world	18·3	14·3	25·0	29·9
Total	100·0	100·0	100·0	100·0

Source: L'Economie et les Finances des Pays Arabes; Banque Centrale de Syrie.

TURKEY

1. Trend of Gross National Product[1]

	1966	1967	1968	1969	1970[2]
Total: £T mn					
at current prices	93,578·0	103,996·0	114,752·0	127,989·0	147,517·0
at constant (1961) prices	74,382·0	78,888·0	84,159·0	89,439·0	94,544·0
real increase (%)	+7·1	+6·1	+6·7	+6·3	+5·7
Per head: £T					
at current prices	2,909·0	3,150·0	3,393·0	3,528·0	4,136·0[3]
at constant (1961) prices	2,330·0	2,411·0	2,509·0	2,602·0	2,651·0[3]
real increase (%)	+4·5	+3·5	+4·1	+3·7	+3·0

[1] At market prices.
[2] Provisional estimates as at 15 March 1971.
[3] Basic October 1970 census of population; population estimates for 1966/9 were slightly below actual average increase, which in 1965/70 was 2·7 per cent annually.

Sources: Ministry of Finance; Turkiye Is Bankasi, Economic Indicators; UN Monthly Bulletin of Statistics.

2. Agricultural Production
('000 tons)

	1966	1967	1968	1969	1970
Cereals					
Wheat	9,600	10,000	9,520	10,500	10,000
Barley	3,800	3,800	3,560	3,740	3,250
Rye	850	900	820	817	650
Maize	1,000	1,050	1,000	1,000	—
Rice	150	140	123	127	155
Industrial crops					
Tobacco	164	189	162	142	146
Potatoes	1,750	1,760	1,805	1,936	1,862
Sugar beet	4,422	5,253	4,714	3,356	4,240
Cotton	382	396	435	403	400[1]
Oilseeds					
Cotton seed	611	634	696	650	—
Sunflower seed	200	230	230	310	380
Sesame seed	32	40	50	41	—
Fruit & nuts					
Grapes	3,100	3,500	3,725	3,635	3,000
Oranges	310	380	476	414	—
Lemons	85	90	130	—	—
Olives	841	495	822	308	—
Sultanas	75	95	100	90	126
Dried figs	50	45	42	43	46
Hazelnut kernels[2]	95	35	68	85	120
Olive oil	155	80	150	54	115

[1] Provisional.
[2] 50 per cent of nut weight.

Source: Turkiye Is Bankasi, Economic Indicators and trade sources.

3. Mineral Production
('000 tons)

	1966	1967	1968	1969	1970
Copper (blister)	27	25	24	19	19
Chrome ore[1]	530	448	416	662[2]	696[2]
Iron ore[1]	1,618	1,498	1,936	2,506[2]	2,425[2]
Manganese[1]	24	42	25	14	9
Sulphur	23	25	24	25	27

[1] Saleable product.
[2] Pithead product.
Source: Turkiye Is Bankasi Review and Ministry of Finance Economic Indicators.

4. Industrial Production
('000 tons unless otherwise stated)

	1965	1966	1967	1968	1969	1970
Pig iron[1]	681·00	736·00	847·00	910·00	948·00	1,036·00
Ingots & steel for casting[1]	585·00	843·00	999·00	1,110·00	1,170·00	1,312·00
Coke[2]	1,188·00	1,440·00	1,368·00	1,428·00	1,595·00	1,540·00
Sugar[3]	522·00	645·00	729·00	650·00	588·00	669·00
Paper & board[2]	98·00	106·00	108·00	116·00	116·00	118·00
Cement	3,244·00	3,865·00	4,249·00	4,731·00	5,795·00	6,374·00
Bottles, glass, & glassware	70·00	72·00	92·00	109·00	137·00	159·00
Superphosphate & fertilizer	376·00	380·00	361·00	442·00	478·00	679·00
Ethyl alcohol[2] (mn litres)	2·23	2·08	2·63	2·60	2·06	2·00[4]
Cotton yarn[2]	32·00	33·00	34·00	37·00	37·00	35·00
Wool yarn[2]	3·10	3·50	3·70	3·40	3·20	3·10
Cotton cloth[2] (mn metres)	181·00	187·00	190·00	208·00	200·00	220·00
Woollen cloth[2] (mn metres)	4·40	4·50	5·50	5·90	5·30	4·70

[1] Karabuk and Eregli.
[2] Public sector only.
[3] Adjusted to campaign seasons.
[4] Estimate.
Source: State Institute of Statistics; Turkiye Is Bankasi, Economic Indicators.

5. Five-Year Plan: Investment Targets
(1970 prices: £T mn)

	1968–72 %	Public sector	1971 programme Private sector	Total	%
Agriculture	15·2	2,025	1,315	3,340	11·4
Mining	3·7	840	210	1,050	3·6
Manufacturing	22·4	4,150	4,000	8,150	27·7
Energy	8·0	2,347	175	2,522	8·6
Housing	17·9	373	5,450	5,823	19·8
Transport & communications	16·1	2,913	1,500	4,413	15·0
Education	6·7	1,422	20	1,442	4·9
Health	1·8	382	30	412	1·4
Tourism	2·3	206	400	606	2·1
Total (including other)	100·0	15,795	13,600	29,395	100·0

Source: 1971 Programme and Second Five-Year Plan.

6. *Foreign Trade*
($ mn)

	1966	1967	1968	1969	1970
Exports, fob	490·5	522·3	496·4	536·8	588·2
Imports, cif	718·3	684·7	763·7	801·2	947·7
Balance	−227·8	−162·4	−267·3	−264·4	−359·5
Terms of trade (1953 = 100)	70	69	74	—	—

Source: Turkiye Is Bankasi, Economic Indicators.

7. *Main Commodities Traded*
($ mn)

Exports	1969	1970	Imports	1969	1970
Cotton	113·6	173·2	Machinery & parts	224·0	274·1
Tobacco	81·5	78·4	Transport equipment		
Fruit, vegetables,			& parts	86·1	113·7
& nuts	161·5	137·7	Iron & steel	50·6	92·5
Livestock &			Chemical, dye-stuffs,		
animal produce	32·7	33·7	& pharmaceuticals	80·9	91·0
Copper (blister)	6·8	6·3	Petroleum & products	60·8	66·8
Minerals	34·8	45·4	Textiles, fibres,		
Cereals &			& yarns	38·4	37·1
leguminous seeds	6·8	9·8	Fertilizers	52·0	31·4

8. *Main Trading Partners*
(per cent of total value)

Exports to:	1969	1970	Imports from:	1969	1970
West Germany	21	20	USA & Canada	20	23
USA & Canada	12	10	West Germany	19	19[1]
Switzerland	5	8	UK	12	9[1]
Italy	8	7	Italy	10	8[1]
France	5	7	Switzerland	5	5[1]
UK	6	6	USSR	4	4
Lebanon	3	5	France	3	3[1]
Belgium–Luxemburg	3	4			
EEC	40	40	EEC	36	34
EFTA	15	18	EFTA	20	17

[1] Excludes 'free of foreign exchange payment' imports.

Sources: State Institute of Statistics; Turkiye Is Bankasi, Economic Indicators.

9. *Balance of Payments*
($ mn)

	1966	1967	1968	1969	1970
Current account:					
Total imports, cif	−718	−685	−764	−801	−948
Total exports, fob	490	523	496	537	588
Trade balance	−228	−162	−268	−264	−360
Interest payments[1]	−29	−34	−34	−44	−47
Workers' remittances	115	93	107	141	273
Profit transfers	−16	−25	−32	−32	−33
Tourism & travel (net)	−14	−14	−9	−5	−4
Other invisibles (net)	−9	13	2	−24	−44
All invisibles (net)	47	33	34	36	145
Infrastructure & offshore transactions	19	14	10	8	8
Capital account:					
Debt repayments[1]	−119	−99	−72	−108	−158
PL 480 & other £T payment produce imports	17	—	—	41	83
Private foreign capital	30	17	13	24	58
Use of project aid credits	56	83	127	174	179
Use of Aid Consortium credits[2]	175	162	145	106[3]	235[4]
Free of foreign exchange payment imports	11	12	22	20	34
Capital transactions (net)	170	175	235	257	431
Overall balance	8	60	11	37	224

[1] Excluding relief in form of debt servicing commitment postponements.
[2] Including drawings on IMF and EMA.
[3] Excluding drawings on IMF and EMA.
[4] Including $18 mn special drawing rights.

Source: Ministry of Finance publications.

Appendix III
Oil

1. World 'Published Proved' Oil Reserves at End 1970

Country/Area	Thousand Million Tons	Share of Total %	Thousand Million Barrels	Share of Total %
USA	6·1	7·2	46·7	7·5
Canada	1·3	1·6	10·4	1·7
Caribbean	2·3	2·8	16·3	2·6
Other Western Hemisphere	1·4	1·6	9·9	1·6
Total Western Hemisphere	11·1	13·2	83·3	13·4
Western Europe	0·6	0·7	4·4	0·7
Africa	9·8	11·7	74·7	12·1
Middle East	47·0	55·9	343·9	55·4
USSR, E. Europe, & China	13·7	16·2	100·0	16·1
Other Eastern Hemisphere	1·9	2·3	14·4	2·3
Total Eastern Hemisphere	73·0	86·8	537·4	86·6
World (excl. USSR, E. Europe, & China)	70·4	83·8	520·7	83·9
World	84·1	100·0	620·7	100·0

Notes

1. Proved reserves are generally taken to be the volume of oil remaining in the ground which geological and engineering information indicate with reasonable certainty to be recoverable in the future from known reservoirs under existing economic and operating conditions.
2. The recovery factor, i.e. the relationship between proved reserves and total oil in place, varies according to local conditions and can vary in time with economic and technological changes.
3. For the USA and Canada the data include oil which it is estimated can be recovered from proved natural gas reserves.
4. The data exclude the oil content of shales and tar sands.

Source: BP Statistical Review of the World Oil Industry, 1970.

2. *World Oil Consumption 1970 and 1969*
(mn tons)

Country/Area	1970	1969	1970 Share of Total %	Change 1970 over 1969 %	Change Annual Average 1965/70 %
USA	697	668	31	+4·0	+5·0
Canada	72	69	3	+4·5	+5·5
Mexico	23	22	1	+6·8	+7·0
Caribbean	50	47	2	+5·9	+5·8
South America	62	58	3	+5·3	+7·0
Total Western Hemisphere	904	864	40	+4·3	+5·3
Belgium & Luxembourg	27	25	1	+9·0	+10·0
Netherlands	37	33	2	+11·6	+7·8
France	95	83	4	+14·1	+12·0
W. Germany	131	117	6	+11·7	+10·5
Italy	87	77	4	+11·9	+10·8
UK	103	96	5	+7·1	+6·8
Scandinavia	57	51	2	+13·0	+10·8
Spain	23	21	1	+13·4	+15·5
Other Western Europe	68	61	3	+12·3	+10·8
Total Western Europe	628	564	28	+11·4	+10·0
Middle East	51	47	2	+8·2	+7·5
Africa	43	39	2	+9·2	+8·5
South Asia	29	27	1	+7·9	+10·3
South-East Asia	58	52	2	+10·9	+18·3
Japan	200	170	9	+17·7	+18·5
Australasia	29	27	1	+7·2	+7·3
USSR, E. Europe, & China	346	314	15	+10·2	+9·5
Total Eastern Hemisphere	1,384	1,240	60	+11·6	+11·0
World (excl. USSR, E. Europe, & China)	1,942	1,790	85	+8·5	+8·3
World	2,288	2,104	100	+8·7	+8·5

Differences between production and consumption are accounted for by stock changes and unknown military liftings.

Source: BP Statistical Review of the World Oil Industry, 1970.

T

3. Production of Crude Oil
(mn metric tons)

	First commercial production	1966	1967	1968	1969	1970
Iran	1912	105·1	129·3	141·5	168·1	190·7
Saudi Arabia	1938	119·4	129·2	141·1	148·6	176·2
Libya	1961	72·3	84·3	126·0	149·8	160·1
Kuwait	1946	114·4	115·2	122·1	129·5	137·5
Iraq	1934	68·0	60·1	74·0	74·9	76·9
Abu Dhabi	1962	17·3	18·1	24·0	28·9	33·3
Neutral Zone	1954	22·3	21·7	22·1	23·3	26·0
Egypt	1909	6·3	6·2[1]	11·3[1]	15·5[1]	21·7[1]
Qatar	1949	13·8	15·5	16·4	17·3	17·3
Oman	1967	—	2·8	11·8	16·4	16·6
Syria	1968	—	—	0·4	3·2	4·2
Dubai	1969	—	—	—	0·5	4·3
Bahrain	1934	3·0	3·4	3·6	3·8	3·8
Turkey	1949	2·0	2·7	3·1	3·6	3·5
Israel	1955	0·2	0·1	0·1	0·1	0·1
Total		544·1	588·6	697·5	783·5	872·2
% world total		32·0	32·3	35·2	36·7	37·0

[1] Including estimated production from Sinai fields held by Israel.

Sources: BP Statistical Review; companies' annual reports and production announcements; Petroleum Press Service.

4. Government Oil Revenues[1]
(equivalent in mn $)

	1965	1966	1967	1968	1969	1970	$ per caput
Saudi Arabia	655	777	852	966	1,008	1,200	270
Libya	371	476	631	952	1,132	1,295	720
Iran	522	593	737	817	938	1,076	40
Kuwait	671	707	718	766	812	897	1,660
Iraq	375	394	361	476	483	513	60
Abu Dhabi	34	100	106	153	191	231	4,600
Qatar	66	90	100	109	118	122	1,520
Oman	—	—	4	61	92	107	155

[1] Retroactive payments, including royalty expensing, have, where possible, been allocated to the years to which they are applicable.

Source: Petroleum Press Service, OPEC.

READING LIST

I. GENERAL

A. Historical

Arnold, Sir T. W., *The Caliphate, 632–1924* (London, 1924).

Bullard, Sir R., *Britain and the Middle East* (rev. ed., London, 1952).

Cambridge History of Islam (2 vols., Cambridge, 1971).

Coulson, N. J., *History of Islamic Law* (Edinburgh, 1964).

Faris, N. A., ed., *The Arab Heritage* (Princeton, 1944).

Gibb, H. A. R., *Modern Trends in Islam* (Chicago, 1947).

—— *Mohammedanism* (2nd rev. ed., London, 1969).

Goitein, S. D. F., *Jews and Arabs: Their Contacts through the Ages* (New York, 1955).

Hitti, P. K., *History of the Arabs* (London, 1940).

Hurewitz, J. C., *Diplomacy in the Near and Middle East: a Documentary Record*, vol. 1: *1535–1914*; vol. 2: *1914–56* (Princeton, 1956).

Kirk, G. E., *A Short History of the Middle East* (7th ed., London, 1964).

Levy, R., *The Social Structure of Islam* (Cambridge, 1957).

Lewis, B., *The Arabs in History* (4th ed., London, 1968).

Lloyd, Seton, *Foundations in the Dust: a Story of Mesopotamian Exploration* (London, 1947).

MacDonald, D. B., *Development of Muslim Theology, Jurisprudence and Constitutional Theory* (Lahore, 1960).

Mez, A., *The Renaissance of Islam*, tr. by S. K. Bakhsh and D. S. Margoliouth (London, 1937).

Shaban, M. A., *Islamic History A.D. 600–750: a New Interpretation* (Cambridge, 1971).

Toynbee, A. J., *A Study of History: Abridgement of vols. 1–6*, by D. C. Somervell (London, 1946).

Von Grunebaum, G. E., *Mediaeval Islam* (2nd ed., Chicago, 1953).

B. Modern Times

Atiyah, E., *An Arab Tells His Story* (London, 1946).

Antonius, G., *The Arab Awakening: the Story of the Arab National Movement* (Beirut, 1962).

Arberry, A. J., ed., *Religion in the Middle East* (2 vols., Cambridge, 1969).

Badeau, J. S., *The American Approach to the Arab World* (New York, 1968).

Baer, G., *Population and Society in the Arab East* (London, 1964).

Be'eri, E., *Army Officers in Arab Politics and Society* (London, 1970).

Blaisdell, D. C., *European Financial Control in the Ottoman Empire* (New York, 1966).

Berque, J., *The Arabs: their History and Future* (London, 1964).

Bonne, A., *State and Economics in the Middle East* (2nd ed., London, 1960).

Coon, C. S., *Caravan: the Story of the Middle East* (rev. ed., New York, 1962).

Davis, H. M., *Constitutions, Electoral Laws, Treaties of States in the Near and Middle East* (Cambridge, 1947).

Europa Publications, *The Middle East and North Africa* (London, annually 1948–).

FAO, *Problems of Food and Agriculture in the Near East* (Rome, 1955).

Fisher, S. N., ed., *Social Forces in the Middle East* (New York, 1968).

Fisher, W. B., *The Middle East: a Physical, Social and Regional Geography* (6th ed., London, 1971).

Haim, S. G., ed., *Arab Nationalism, an Anthology* (Berkeley, 1962).

Halpern, M., *The Politics of Social Change in the Middle East* (Princeton, 1963).

Hershlag, Z. Y., *Contemporary Economic Structure of the Middle East* (Leiden, 1971).

History of the Second World War: the Mediterranean and the Middle East (vol. 1, London, 1954).

Hoskins, H. L., *British Routes to India* (London, 1966).

Hourani, A. H., *Minorities in the Arab World* (London, 1947).

—— *Arabic Thought in the Liberal Age 1798–1939* (London, 1962).

Howard, H. N., *The Partition of Turkey: a Diplomatic History, 1913–23* (Oklahoma, 1931).

Kedourie, E., *England and the Middle East: the Destruction of the Ottoman Empire, 1914–21* (London, 1956).

Kerr, M. H., *The Arab Cold War* (3rd ed., New York, 1971).

Kirk, G. E., *The Middle East in the War, 1939–46* and *The Middle East, 1945–50* (London, 1953 and 1954) (*Survey of International Affairs, 1939–46*).

Kohn, H., *Nationalism and Imperialism in the Hither East* (London, 1932).

Laqueur, W. Z., *Communism and Nationalism in the Middle East* (London, 1956).

—— *The Road to War, 1967* (London, 1967).

—— *The Struggle for the Middle East: The Soviet Union and the Middle East, 1958–68* (London, 1969).

Lawrence, T. E., *The Seven Pillars of Wisdom* (London, 1935).

Lenczowski, G., *The Middle East in World Affairs* (2nd ed., Ithaca, NY, 1956).

Longrigg, S. H., *Oil in the Middle East* (3rd ed., London, 1968).

Monroe, E., *The Mediterranean in Politics* (London, 1938).

—— *Britain's Moment in the Middle East, 1914–56* (London, 1963).

Nuseibeh, H. Z., *The Ideas of Arab Nationalism* (New York, 1956).

Polk, W. R., *The United States and the Arab World* (Cambridge, Mass., 1965).

—— and Chambers, R. L., eds., *Beginnings of Modernization in the Middle East; the Nineteenth Century* (Chicago, 1968).

Rahman, F., *Islam* (London, 1966).

Rosenthal, E. I. J., *Islam in the National State* (Cambridge, 1965).

Smith, W. C., *Islam in Modern History* (Princeton, 1957).

Stocking, G. W., *Middle East Oil* (London, 1971).

Shwadran, B., *The Middle East, Oil and the Great Powers* (2nd rev. ed., New York, 1959).

Von Grunebaum, G. E., ed., *Unity and Variety in Muslim Civilization* (Chicago, 1956).

Warriner, D., *Land Reform and Development in the Middle East: a Study of Egypt, Syria and Iraq* (2nd ed., London, 1962).

—— *Land Reform in Principle and Practice* (Oxford, 1968).

Zeine, Z. N., *The Emergence of Arab Nationalism* (Beirut, 1966).

2. ARABIA

Belhaven, Master of, *see* Hamilton, R. A. B.

Busch, B. C., *Britain and the Persian Gulf, 1894–1914* (Berkeley, 1967).

De Gaury, G., *Rulers of Mecca* (London, 1951).

Dickson, H. R. P., *The Arab of the Desert: a Glimpse into Badawin Life in Kuwait and Sa'udi Arabia* (London, 1949).

—— *Kuwait and her Neighbours*, ed. by C. Witting (London, 1956).

Doughty, C. M., *Travels in Arabia Deserta* (2 vols., London, 1936).

Hamilton, R. A. B., 12th Baron Belhaven and Stanton, *The Kingdom of Melchior: Adventure in South-West Arabia* (London, 1949).

Hawley, D., *The Trucial States* (London, 1970).

Holden, D., *Farewell to Arabia* (London, 1966)

Hopwood, D., ed., *The Arabian Peninsula* (London, 1972).

Ingrams, D., *A Time in Arabia* (London, 1970).

Ingrams, H., *Arabia and the Isles* (3rd ed., London, 1966).

Little, T., *South Arabia: Area of Conflict* (London, 1968).

Marlowe, J., *The Persian Gulf in the Twentieth Century* (London, 1962).

Meulen, D. van der, *Aden to the Hadhramaut* (London, 1947).

Morris, J., *Sultan in Oman* (London, 1957).

Philby, H. St. J. B., *Arabian Jubilee* (London, 1952).

—— *Forty Years In the Wilderness* (London, 1957).

—— *Saudi Arabia* (London, 1968).

Sanger, R., *The Arabian Peninsula* (Ithaca, NY, 1971).

Scott, H., *In the High Yemen* (London, 1942).

Trevaskis, Sir K., *Shades of Amber* (London, 1968).

Twitchell, K. S., *Saudi Arabia* (3rd ed., Princeton, 1958).

Wenner, M. W., *Modern Yemen, 1918–66* (Baltimore, 1967).

3. EGYPT

Abdel-Malek, A., *Egypt: Military Society* (New York, 1968).

Baring, E., 1st Earl of Cromer, *Modern Egypt* (2 vols., London, 1908).

Berque, J., *Egypt, Imperialism and Revolution* (London, 1972).

Colombe, M., *L'Evolution de l'Egypte, 1923–50* (Paris, 1951).

Hansen, B. and Marzouk, G. A., *Development and Economic Policy in the UAR* (Amsterdam, 1968).

Hurst, H. E., *The Nile* (London, 1952).

Issawi, C., *Egypt at Mid-Century* (London, 1954).

—— *Egypt in Revolution* (London, 1963).

Lacouture, J. and S., *Egypt in Transition* (London, 1958).

Lloyd, Lord, *Egypt since Cromer* (2 vols., London, 1934).

Little, T., *Modern Egypt* (London, 1967).

Love, K., *Suez, the Twice-Fought War* (London, 1969).

Mansfield, P., *Nasser's Egypt* (2nd ed., London, 1969).

Marloe, J., *Anglo-Egyptian Relations, 1800–1953* (London, 1953).

Mitchell, R. P., *The Society of Muslim Brothers* (London, 1969).

Nasser, Gamal Abdul, *Egypt's Liberation: the Philosophy of the Revolution* (Buffalo, 1959).

O'Brien, P. K., *The Revolution in Egypt's Economic System: from Private Enterprise to Socialism, 1952–1965* (London, 1966).
Sadat, A., *Revolt on the Nile* (London, 1957).
Stephens, R., *Nasser* (London, 1971).
Vatikiotis, P. J., *The Modern History of Egypt* (London, 1969).

4. IRAN

Avery, P. W., *Modern Iran* (2nd ed., London, 1967).
Banani, A., *The Modernization of Iran, 1921–1941* (Stanford, 1961).
Bharier, J., *Economic Development in Iran, 1900–1970* (London, 1971).
Binder, L., *Iran: Political Development in a Changing Society* (Berkeley, 1962).
Cambridge History of Iran, vols. 1–5 (8 to be published) (Cambridge, 1968–   ).
Curzon, G. N., 1st Earl of Kedleston, *Persia and the Persian Question* (2 vols., London, 1891, repr. 1966).
Cottam, R. W., *Nationalism in Iran* (Pittsburgh, 1964).
Elwell-Sutton, L. P., *Persian Oil—a Study in Power Politics* (London, 1955).
Lambton, A. K. S., *Landlord and Peasant in Persia* (London, 1953).
—— *The Persian Land Reform, 1962–1966* (Oxford, 1969).
Lenczowski, G., *Russia and the West in Iran, 1914–48* (Ithaca, NY, 1949).
Millspaugh, A. C., *Americans in Persia* (Washington, 1946).
Pahlevi, M. R. Shah, *Mission for My Country* (London, 1960).
Sykes, Sir P. M., *History of Persia* (3rd ed., 2 vols., London, 1930).

5. IRAQ

Bell, G., *Letters* (2 vols., London, 1927).
Birdwood, Lord, *Nuri as-Said* (London, 1970).
Dann, U., *Iraq under Qassem, a Political History, 1958–1963* (London, 1969).
Edmonds, C. J., *Kurds, Turks and Arabs* (London, 1957).
Foster, H. A., *The Making of Modern Iraq* (London, 1936).
Haseeb, K., *The National Income of Iraq, 1953–1961* (Oxford, 1964).
IBRD, *The Economic Development of Iraq* (Baltimore, 1952).
Khadduri, M., *Independent Iraq, 1932–1958* (2nd ed., London, 1960).
—— *Republican Iraq; a Study in Iraqi Politics since the Revolution of 1958* (London, 1958).
Lloyd, S., *Twin Rivers: a Brief History of Iraq from the Earliest Times to the Present Day* (London, 1945).
Longrigg, S. H., *Iraq, 1900 to 1950* (London, 1953).
Main, E., *Iraq from Mandate to Independence* (London, 1935).
Salter, J. A., 1st Baron Salter of Kidlington and Payton, S.W., *The Development of Iraq* (London, 1955).
Wilson, Sir A. T., *Loyalties: Mesopotamia, 1914–17* (London, 1930).
—— *Mesopotamia 1917–30: a Clash of Loyalties* (London, 1931).

6. ISRAEL

Agress, E., *Golda Meir* (London, 1969).
Barbour, N., *Nisi Dominus, a Survey of the Palestine Controversy* (Beirut, 1969).
Bar-Zohar, M., *The Armed Prophet: a Biography of Ben-Gurion* (London, 1967).

Bentwich, N., *Israel: Two Fateful Years, 1967–69* (London, 1969).
Burns, E. L. M., *Between Arab and Israeli* (London, 1962).
Crossman, R. H. S., *Palestine Mission* (London, 1947).
Davis, J. H., *The Evasive Peace. A Study of the Zionist–Arab Problem* (London, 1968).
Eisenstadt, S. N., *Israeli Society* (London, 1969).
Halpern, B., *The Idea of the Jewish State* (Cambridge, Mass., 1961).
Horowitz, D., *The Economics of Israel* (Oxford, 1967).
McDonald, J. G., *My Mission in Israel, 1948–51* (New York, 1951).
O'Ballance, E., *The Arab–Israeli War, 1948* (London, 1956).
Perlmutter, A., *Military and Politics in Israel: Nation-building and Role Expansion* (London, 1969).
Stein, L., *The Balfour Declaration* (London, 1961).
Sykes, C., *Crossroads to Israel* (London, 1965).
Weizmann, C., *Trial and Error* (London, 1949).

7. JORDAN

Abdullah Ibn al-Hussein, *The Memoirs of King Abdullah of Transjordan*, ed. by P. P. Graves (London, 1950).
—— *My Memoirs Completed (al Takmilah)*, tr. by H. W. Glidden (Washington, 1954).
Dearden, A., *Jordan* (London, 1958).
Glubb, J. B., *The Story of the Arab Legion* (London, 1948).
—— *A Soldier with the Arabs* (London, 1957).
Harris, G. L., *Jordan: its People, its Society, its Culture* (New Haven, 1958).
Hussein, (King of Jordan), *Uneasy Lies the Head* (London, 1962).
IBRD, *The Economic Development of Jordan* (Baltimore, 1957).
Kirkbride, Sir A., *A Crackle of Thorns* (London, 1956).
Vatikiotis, P. J., *Politics and the Military in Jordan; a Study of the Arab Legion, 1921–1957* (London, 1967).

8. LEBANON (See 10. Syria and Lebanon)

9. SUDAN

Abbas, M., *The Sudan Question: the Dispute over the Anglo-Egyptian Condominium, 1884–1951* (London, 1952).
Abd al-Rahim, M., *Imperialism and Nationalism in the Sudan* (Oxford, 1969).
Albino, Oliver, *The Sudan, A Southern Viewpoint* (London, 1970).
Beshir, M. O., *The Southern Sudan* (London, 1968).
Gaitskell, A., *Gezira: a Story of Development in the Sudan* (London, 1959).
Henderson, K. D. D., *Survey of the Anglo-Egyptian Sudan, 1898–1944* (London, 1946).
—— *The Sudan Republic* (London, 1965).
Holt, P. M., *A Modern History of the Sudan* (2nd ed., Oxford, 1970).
MacMichael, Sir H. A., *History of the Arabs in the Sudan* (2 vols., London, 1967).
Trimingham, J. S., *Islam in the Sudan* (London, 1965).

10. SYRIA AND LEBANON

Binder, L., ed., *Politics in Lebanon* (New York, 1966).
Hitti, P. K., *History of Syria, including Lebanon and Palestine* (London, 1951).
Hourani, A. H., *Syria and Lebanon* (Beirut, 1968).
Hudson, M. C., *The Precarious Republic: Political Modernization in Lebanon* (New York, 1968).
IBRD, *The Economic Development of Syria* (Baltimore, 1955).
Lammens, H., *La Syrie* (2 vols., Beirut, 1921).
Longrigg, S. H., *Syria and Lebanon under French Mandate* (Beirut, 1968).
Salibi, K. S., *A Modern History of Lebanon* (London, 1965).
Seale, P., *The Struggle for Syria: a Study of Post-War Arab Politics, 1945–1958* (London, 1965).
Tibawi, A. L., *A Modern History of Syria including Lebanon and Palestine* (London, 1969).
Weuleresse, J., *Paysans de Syrie et du Proche Orient* (Paris, 1946).
Ziadeh, N. A., *Syria and Lebanon* (London, 1956).

11. TURKEY

Ahmad, F., *The Young Turks: the Committee of Union and Progress in Turkish Politics, 1908–1914* (Oxford, 1969).
Dewdney, J. C., *Turkey* (London, 1971).
Hershlag, Z. Y., *Turkey: the Challenge of Growth* (Leiden, 1968).
IBRD, *The Economy of Turkey* (Baltimore, 1951).
Kinross, Lord, *Ataturk: the Rebirth of a Nation* (London, 1964).
Lewis, B., *The Emergence of Modern Turkey* (2nd ed., London, 1968).
Lewis, G. L., *Turkey* (3rd ed., London, 1965).
Thomas, L. V. and Frye, R. N., *The United States and Turkey and Iran* (Cambridge, Mass., 1952).
Toynbee, A. J., *The Western Question in Greece and Turkey* (London, 1923).
Yalman, A. E., *Turkey in My Time* (Norman, Oklahoma, 1956).

JOURNALS WHICH DEAL WHOLLY OR PARTLY WITH THE MIDDLE EAST

Asian Affairs. London.
International Affairs (quarterly) and *The World Today* (monthly).
International Journal of Middle East Studies (quarterly). London, from 1970.
Journal of Palestine Studies (quarterly). Beirut, from 1971.
Middle East Journal (quarterly). Washington, from 1947.
Middle East Studies (three yearly). London, from 1964.
The New Middle East (monthly). London, from 1970.
L'Orient (quarterly). Paris, from 1957.
Oriente Moderno (quarterly). Rome, from 1921.
also
Palestine Monographs of the Palestine Research Centre, Beirut.

Index